FARM HOLIDAY
BUREAU

Stay on a farm

JARROLD
PUBLISHING

BWRDD CROESO CYMRU
WALES TOURIST BOARD

1/94
Published by Jarrold Publishing, Whitefriars, Norwich NR3 1TR
in association with the Farm Holiday Bureau (UK) Ltd, the English Tourist Board and the
National Tourist Boards of Scotland, Wales and Northern Ireland
© Farm Holiday Bureau UK 1995
National Agricultural Centre, Stoneleigh, Warwickshire CV8 2LZ

ISBN 0 7117 0804 5

The information contained in this Guide has been published in good faith on the basis of
the details submitted by the proprietors of the premises listed. These proprietors are
current members of the Farm Holiday Bureau and have paid for their entries in this
Guide. Whilst every effort has been made to ensure accuracy in this publication, neither
the publisher, the Farm Holiday Bureau nor the National Tourist Boards can guarantee
the accuracy of the information in this Guide and accept no responsibility for any error
or misrepresentation. All liability for loss, disappointment, negligence or other damage
caused by reliance on the information contained in this Guide, or in the event of
bankruptcy, or liquidation, or cessation of trade of any company, individual or firm
mentioned is hereby excluded.

The Farm Holiday Bureau of the United Kingdom gratefully acknowledges the
continuing assistance and advice offered by the National Tourist Boards, the Agricultural
Development Advisory Service of the Ministry of Agriculture, the Scottish Agricultural
Organisations Society Ltd, and all those who seek to maintain a balance in the rural
community.

Produced by The Pen and Ink Book Company Limited, Huntingdon, Cambridgeshire

Colour maps provided by Lovell Johns Ltd., Oxford

Printed and bound in Great Britain

Contents

Welcome to the Farm Holiday Bureau

The Farm Holiday Bureau is a national network of farming families offering affordable, quality accommodation, good food and a warm welcome for both self-catering and bed and breakfast breaks.

By choosing the Stay on a Farm guide, you have opened the door to over 1000 farmhouses, cottages and barn conversions, all of which are annually inspected by the Tourist Boards as well as by members of our 87 Farm Holiday Groups.

Staying on a farm is your perfect chance to discover the countryside. And what a variety there is to choose from.... our agricultural industry has helped create a whole range of countryside landscapes, from the undulating downlands of the south to the moors and rugged hill country more typical of the north.

Many farms have been handed down through families from generation to generation, and their houses often reflect many centuries of history. Whether you wish to stay in a medieval manorhouse, a thatched cottage, a stone croft or a converted oast house, the following pages will help you find the accommodation of your choice.

Staying on a farm offers every opportunity to

taste the glories of the countryside. You will be able to enjoy home-grown, home-cooked food – from the freshest of vegetables to eggs straight from the hen – you may even be able to collect your own! Many of our members have even won national catering awards such as the Taste of Wales.

Our members are keenly aware of the environment and will always be on hand to help you enjoy the countryside to the utmost. Indeed, many of them have created nature trails and conservation areas within their farmland to help preserve natural habitats and help our wildlife live alongside agriculture. And who else could tell you where the best countryside walks are or the best views? Who else would know which pub would have a roaring log fire on a damp autumn day or where to look for the first snowdrops?

There will be the chance to do as much or as little as you like. Riding and fishing are widely available on our farms, as well as miles of beautiful countryside to explore. But don't worry if you can't get around quite as much as you used to. Many farms are easily accessible for the less mobile and some have been commended by the Holiday Care Service or carry the reassurance of a Tourist Board accessibility symbol.

Children especially will enjoy the chance to experience a real working farm and even help to feed the animals.

Wherever you choose to go you will be assured of a warm welcome and a friendly atmosphere in a countryside setting which will be suitable for holidays and business. We're looking forward to meeting you!

Farm Holiday Bureau (UK) Ltd
National Agricultural Centre
Stoneleigh Park
Warwickshire CV8 2LZ
Tel: (01203) 696909
Fax: (01203) 696630

How to use the guide

Selecting your farm...

The guide lists all the members of the Farm Holiday Bureau (UK) Ltd in the countries of Scotland, England, Wales and Northern Ireland. Members belong to one of 87 Farm Holiday Bureau Groups: key maps in the section, Where to Go on pages 10–12 will tell you which counties and areas the individual FHB Groups cover. Arranged within countries, each Group has a numbered section in this guide which opens with a description of the area and an outline map showing the location of each farm. The Group contacts can help you find suitable accommodation if you wish.

Properties in each Group section are listed alphabetically under Bed and Breakfast, Self-Catering and Camping and Caravanning. All entries feature a brief description and a line illustration, along with an indication of prices for bed and breakfast and for evening meals where available. Clear symbols (see page 15) indicate what further facilities are provided.

An Index at the back of the guide (page 364) shows all members who offer facilities for camping and caravanning and those who welcome business travellers (with meeting room capacity where provided). The Index also lists those farms who welcome disabled guests (indicated in the entries by the wheelchair symbol). Facilities provided will vary so we recommend you check any special needs before booking. The Accessible Symbol (explained on page 14) identifies those farms who have invited the Tourist Board to check the facilities they offer to wheelchair users or those who have difficulty walking.

How to book...

All you have to do is telephone the farm of your choice. If the accommodation you want is not available, the owner will be happy to refer you to similar alternative FHB accommodation. **Alternatively, the Group Contact will be happy to help you find the right accommodation, and can usually provide you with a local group leaflet.**

Many members also offer a 'book a bed ahead' service to their guests. If you are touring, just tell your host where you wish to visit next, and he or she can make the booking for you.

PLEASE REMEMBER TO MENTION STAY ON A FARM WHEN MAKING A BOOKING

When making a booking...

• Mention the guide.

• Specify your planned arrival and departure dates.

• Specify accommodation needed and any particular requirements, eg. twin beds, family room, private bath, ground floor, cot.

• Specify terms required, eg. B&B, evening meal etc. Evening meal times vary and high tea may be available for children. Farms offering evening meals do not necessarily do so all year round so do check.

• Specify special requirements, eg. special diets, facilities for disabled people, arrangements for children, dogs.

• Check prices and any reductions that may be offered.

• Check whether a deposit is payable and, if so, what charges will apply if the booking is cancelled (see 'Cancellations' opposite).

• Check method and date of payment.

• Check whether B&B access is restricted through the day. Many farms are happy for visitors to stay in the house all day, but on some farms this is not practical and guests are asked to be out of the farmhouse between 10.30am and 4.30pm. Remember, it is essential that children are carefully supervised at all times on and around the farm.

• Check the best time to arrive and ask for directions to the farm. When you are near your destination, look out for the Farm Holiday Bureau member sign at the end of the drive. Your host will be glad to direct you by phone if you get lost.

• Give your name, address and telephone number

NB We recommend that, time permitting, all telephone bookings are confirmed in writing, specifying exactly what you have booked and the price you expect to pay.

Payment and deposits
For reservations made in advance a deposit is usually payable and this will be deducted from the total bill. When you book please check when and how payment should be made.

Cancellations
Once a booking has been agreed, on the telephone or by letter, a legally binding contract has been made with the host. If you cancel a reservation, fail to take up the accommodation or leave prematurely (regardless of the reasons), the host may be entitled to compensation if it cannot be relet for all or a good part of the booked period. If a deposit has been paid it is likely to be forfeited and an additional payment may be demanded.

Insurance
Travel and holiday insurance protection policies can be taken out to safeguard visitors in the event of cancellation or curtailment. Insurance of personal property can also be sought. Hosts cannot accept liability for any loss or damage to visitors' property, however caused. Do make sure that your valuables are covered by your household insurance before you take them away.

Compliments and complaints
Many visitors write to the Farm Holiday Bureau saying how much they have enjoyed their stay. If you feel that something or someone deserves acknowledgement, or if you have a suggestion on how to improve the guide, please write to the Farm Holiday Bureau (UK) Ltd, National Agricultural Centre, Stoneleigh, Warwickshire CV8 2LZ, or ring (01203) 696909.

If you are dissatisfied, please make your complaint to the host there and then. This gives an opportunity for rectifying action to be taken at once. It is usually difficult to deal with a complaint if it is reported at a later date. If the host fails to resolve the problem, please write to the Farm Holiday Bureau who will be happy to help.

Where to go

The Farm Holiday Bureau has 87 local Groups, each of which has a section in this guide. The maps show the location of each Group and their position in the countries. Page numbers are indicated in *italic*.

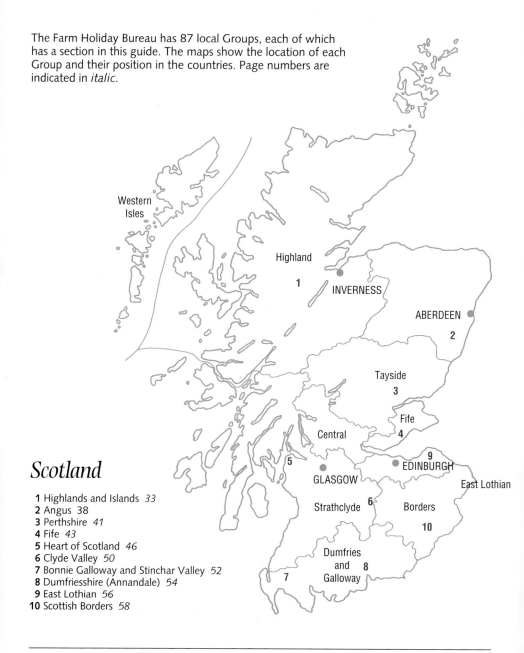

Scotland

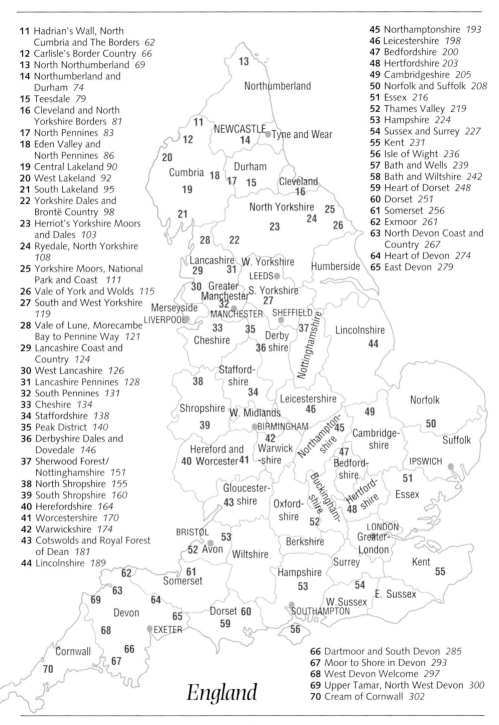

England

Wales

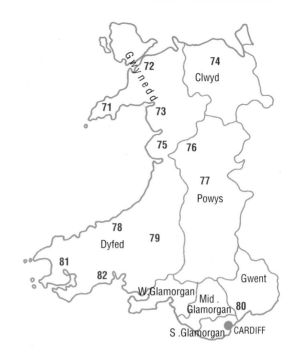

Northern Ireland

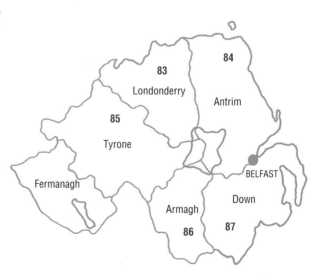

Accommodation classification and grading

Farm Holiday Bureau members are inspected by their Groups to ensure that a high standard of cleanliness, courtesy and service is maintained. All members must also be inspected by their National Tourist Board, agree to meet the Tourist Board's Minimum Standards and observe the Tourist Board's Code of Conduct.

Listed

Crown classification and grading scheme for serviced accommodation
The National Tourist Boards for England, Scotland and Wales operate a common classification and grading scheme for serviced accommodation including farmhouses. Each member has a thorough annual inspection by the Tourist Board and is classified, according to the range of facilities provided, within 6 bands from 'Listed' and then from 1–5 Crowns. The more Crowns, the more extensive the range of facilities.

Quality grading
Classified establishments can apply to be assessed for a separate quality commendation of 'Approved' ('Merit' in Wales), 'Commended', 'Highly Commended' or 'De Luxe'. When granted, the quality commendation appears alongside the classification. In Wales, members who offer superior standards and have completed a tourism training course also have the 'Award' sign indicating that they are in receipt of the Wales Tourist Board's Farmhouse Award.

Self-catering holiday homes
All Bureau members who offer self-catering accommodation must have been inspected by the Tourist Boards or have applied for an inspection.

England

Scotland

Wales

Those inspected in England and Scotland are classified according to the range of facilities they provide (1–5 Keys in England, 1–5 Crowns in Scotland). Holiday Homes with higher quality standards have the term 'Approved', 'Commended', 'Highly Commended'or 'De Luxe' alongside the classification. In Wales quality standards are indicated on a scale of 1–5 Dragons.

Northern Ireland
The Northern Ireland Tourist Board registers and grades all accommodation under a statutory system. All the farms listed offer a high standard and are inspected annually. Grades are 'Grade A', 'Grade B' and 'Approved'.

✓
✓ ✓
✓ ✓ ✓
✓ ✓ ✓ ✓
✓ ✓ ✓ ✓ ✓

British graded holiday parks scheme
The National Tourist Boards for England, Scotland and Wales operate a common quality grading scheme for holiday caravan, camping and chalet parks. The scheme grades parks according to the relative quality of what is offered, in a range of 1–5 ✓s. The more ✓s the higher the quality.

Wheelchair accessibility symbols

All the places that display one of the symbols shown here have been checked by a Tourist Board Inspector against standard criteria that reflect the practical needs of wheelchair users. There are three categories of accessibility:

 Category 1:
Accessible to all wheelchair users including those travelling independently.

 Category 2:
Accessible to a wheelchair user travelling with a helper.

 Category 3:
Accessible to a wheelchair user able to walk short distances and up three steps.

Please check at the time of booking if you have special needs.

Inspected accessible schemes have been developed throughout the UK as part of the nationwide Tourism for All campaign in conjunction with the Hotel and Holiday Consortium and are designed to provide disabled travellers with reliable information on standards and facilities. Additional help and guidance on finding suitable holiday accommodation for those with special needs can be obtained from: Holiday Care Service on (01293) 774535.

Welcome Host

The National Tourist Boards recently launched a Welcome Host scheme. Service and hospitality are as important as good accommodation and good food. The Welcome Host programme places the emphasis on warm hospitality and first-class service. Recipients of the Welcome Host certificate or badge are part of a fine tradition – a tradition for friendliness.

Look at the entries to find those farms participating in the Welcome Host scheme. Entries for Wales carry the Wales Welcome Host symbol.

Symbols

Symbol	Explanation	French	German
☼ (3)	Children welcome (minimum age)	Enfants bienvenus (âge minimum)	Kinder willkommen (Mindestalter)
🐕	Dogs by arrangement	Chiens autorisés sous réserve d'accord préalable	Hunde nach Vereinbarung
♿	Accommodation for disabled/less able people (check for full details)	Hébergement pour les handicappés (demandez les détails)	Unterkunft behindertengerecht (weitere Information auf akzeptiert)
🚭	No smoking	Non fumeurs de préférence	Nichtraucher bevorzugt
💳	Credit cards accepted	Cartes de crédit acceptées	Kreditkarten werden akzeptiert
💼	Business people welcome	Facilités pour hommes d'affaires	Geschäftsreisende willkommen
⚘	Waymarked walks on farm	Visite de fermes avec indication d'itinèncuies	Wanderwege gezeichnet
✿	Foreign language(s) spoken	Langues étrangères parlées	Hier werden Fremdsprachen gesprochen
🐎	Riding	Randonnée à poney ou équitation	Reiten auf Ponys oder Pferden
🎣	Fishing	La pêche à la ligne	Angeln
🏠	Country house, not a working farm	Manoir (pas une) exploitation agricole)	Landhaus, kein aktiver Bauernhof
⛺	Camping facilities	Camping	Camping – Einrichtungen
🚐	Caravanning facilities	Caravaning	Caravan – Einrichtungen
Prices		**Prix**	**Preise**
B&B	price per person per night for bed and breakfast	Prix par personne par nuit pour chambre + petit déjeuner	Preis pro Person pro Nacht für Bett und Frühstück
EM	price per person for evening meal	Prix par personne pour repas du soir	Preis pro Person für Abendessen
SC	price per unit per week self-catering	Prix par location par semaine	Preis pro Einheit pro Woche bei Selbstversorgung
Tents	price per tent pitch per night	Prix par tente par nuit	Preis pro Zeltaufstellung pro Nacht
Caravans	price per caravan pitch per night	Prix par caravane par nuit	Preis Pro Caravanaufstellung pro Nacht
	All prices include VAT and service charge if any.	Tous les prix tiennent compete de la TVA et du service, le cas échéant.	Alle Preise inklusive MWSt und Bedienungsgeld, wenn überhaupt

Further information

These official Tourist Boards will be happy to supply you with further general information on their areas.

National Tourist Boards

English Tourist Board
Thames Tower, Black's Road, Hammersmith, London W6 9EL
☎ (0181) 846 9000

Northern Ireland Tourist Board
59 North Street
Belfast
BT1 1ND
☎ (01232) 231221

Scottish Tourist Board
23 Ravelston Terrace, Edinburgh EH4 3EU
☎ (0131) 332 2433

Wales Tourist Board
Brunel House, 2 Fitzalan Road, Cardiff CF2 1UY
☎ (01222) 499909

Regional Tourist Boards

Cumbria Tourist Board
(covering the county of Cumbria)
Ashleigh, Holly Road, Windermere, Cumbria LA23 2AQ
☎ (015394) 44444

Northumbria Tourist Board
(covering the counties of Cleveland, Durham, Northumberland, Tyne & Wear)
Aykley Heads, Durham DH1 5UX
☎ (0191) 384 6905

North West Tourist Board
(covering the counties of Cheshire, Greater Manchester, Lancashire, Merseyside and the High Peak District of Derbyshire)
Swan House, Swan Meadow Road,
Wigan Pier, Wigan WN3 5BB
☎ (01942) 821222

Yorkshire and Humberside Tourist Board
(covering the counties of North Yorkshire, South Yorkshire, West Yorkshire and Humberside)
312 Tadcaster Road, York, North Yorkshire YO2 2HF
☎ (01904) 707961

Heart of England Tourist Board
(covering the counties of Gloucestershire, Hereford & Worcester, Shropshire, Staffordshire, Warwickshire and West Midlands)
Woodside, Larkhill, Worcester, Hereford & Worcester WR5 2EF
☎ (01905) 763436

East Midlands Tourist Board
(covering the counties of Derbyshire, Leicestershire, Lincolnshire, Northamptonshire and Nottinghamshire)
Exchequergate, Lincoln, Lincolnshire LN2 1PZ
☎ (01522) 531521

East Anglia Tourist Board
(covering the counties of Bedfordshire, Cambridgeshire, Essex, Hertfordshire, Norfolk and Suffolk)
Toppesfield Hall, Hadleigh, Suffolk IP7 5DN
☎ (01473) 822922

London Tourist Board
(covering the Greater London area)
26 Grosvenor Gardens, London SW1W 0DU
☎ (0171) 730 3450

West Country Tourist Board
(covering the counties of Avon, Cornwall, Devon, Dorset (parts of), Somerset, Wiltshire and Isles of Scilly)
60 St Davids Hill, Exeter EX4 4SY
☎ (01392) 76351

Southern Tourist Board
(covering the counties of Berkshire, Buckinghamshire, Eastern and Northern Dorset, Hampshire, Oxfordshire and Isle of Wight)
40 Chamberlayne Road, Eastleigh, Hampshire SO5 5JH
☎ (01703) 620006

South East England Tourist Board
(covering the counties of Kent, Surrey and East, West Sussex)
The Old Brew House, Warwick Park, Tunbridge Wells, Kent TN2 5TU
☎ (01892) 540766

Tourist Information Centres

There are over 800 Tourist Information Centres throughout the United Kingdom and they are there for you to use both before your holiday and during it. Look in your local telephone directory under 'Tourist Information' to find your nearest centre. TICs can give you details about local attractions, events and accommodation and many will even be able to book it for you. Look out for the information sign.

MAP OF GREAT BRITAIN

KEY TO MAP SECTIONS

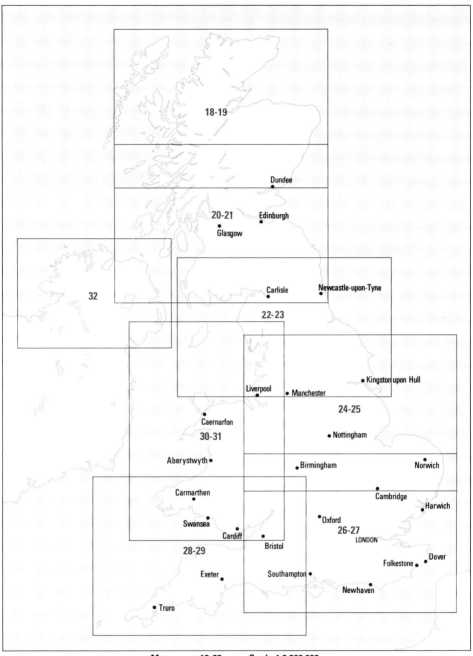

Map pages 18-32   **Scale 1:2 000 000**

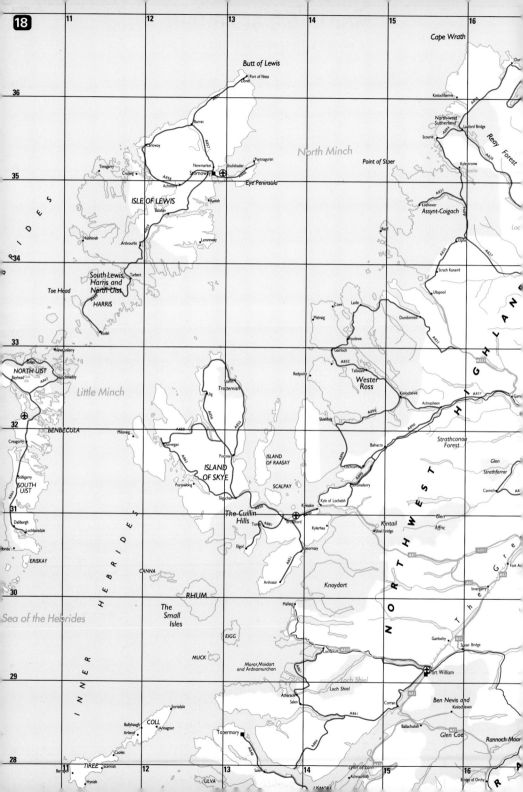

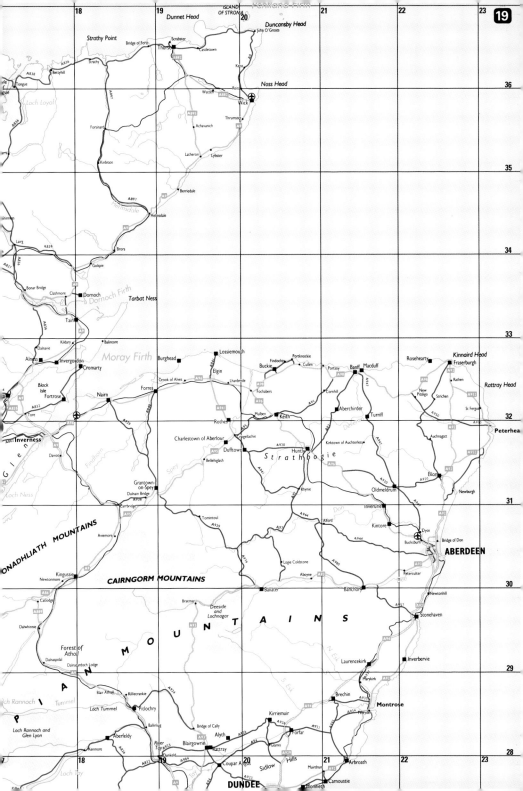

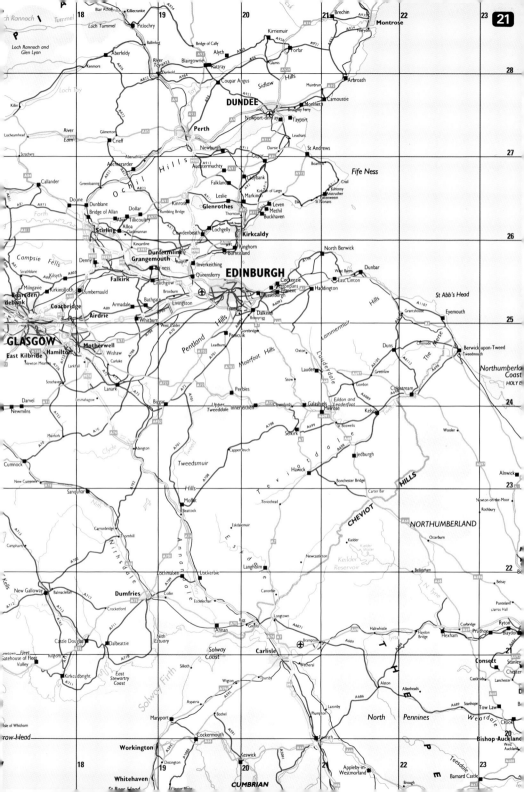

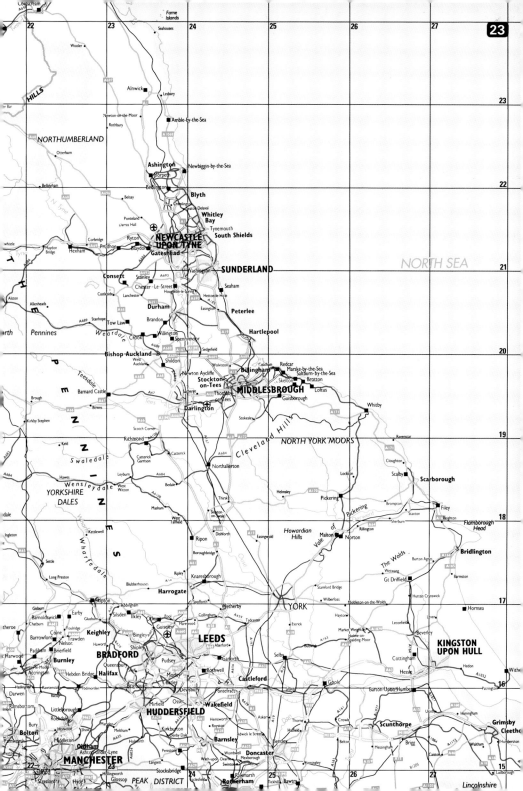

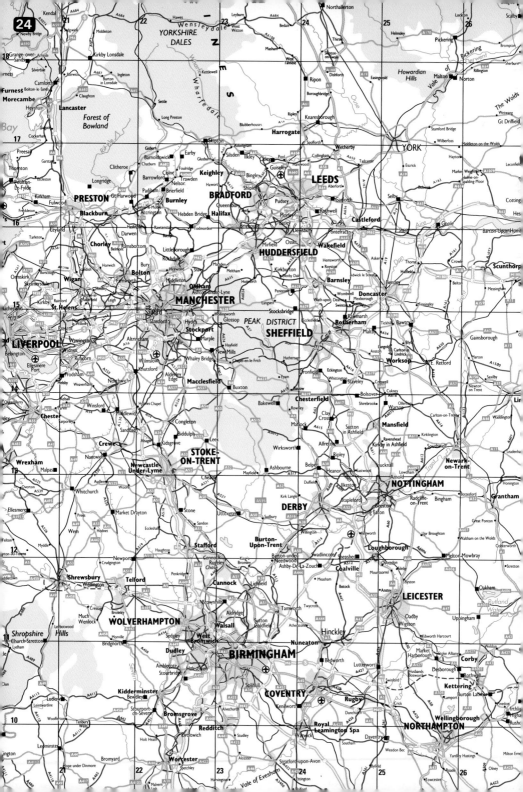

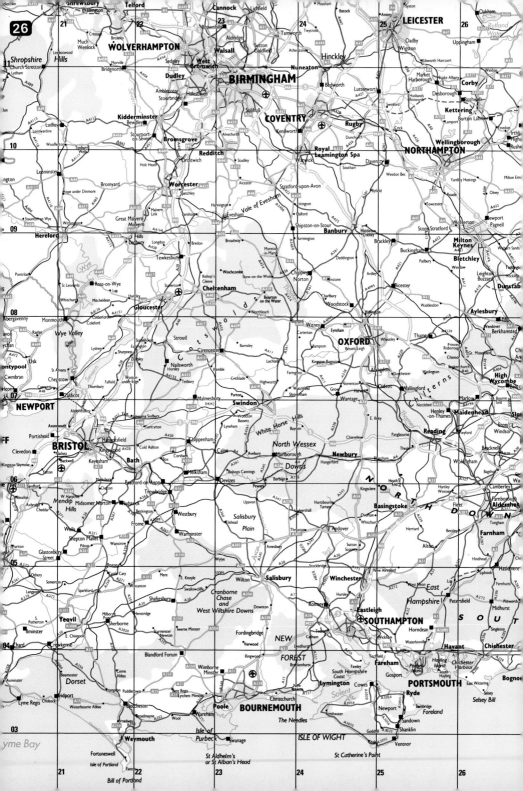

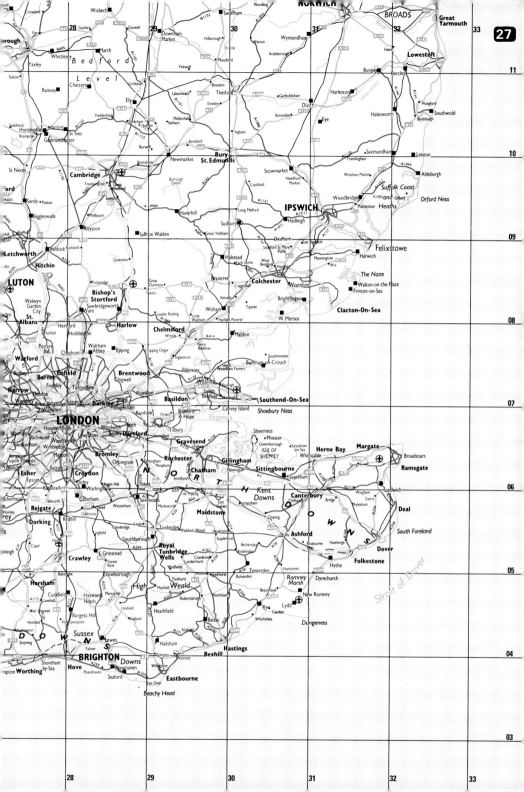

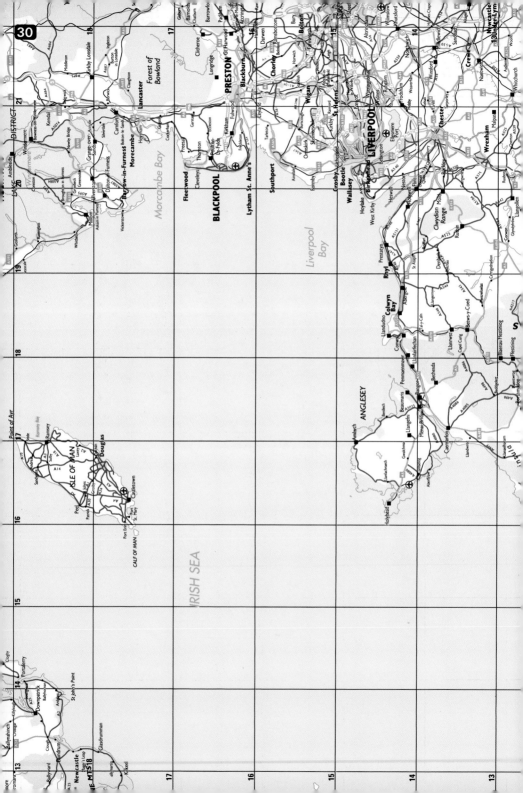

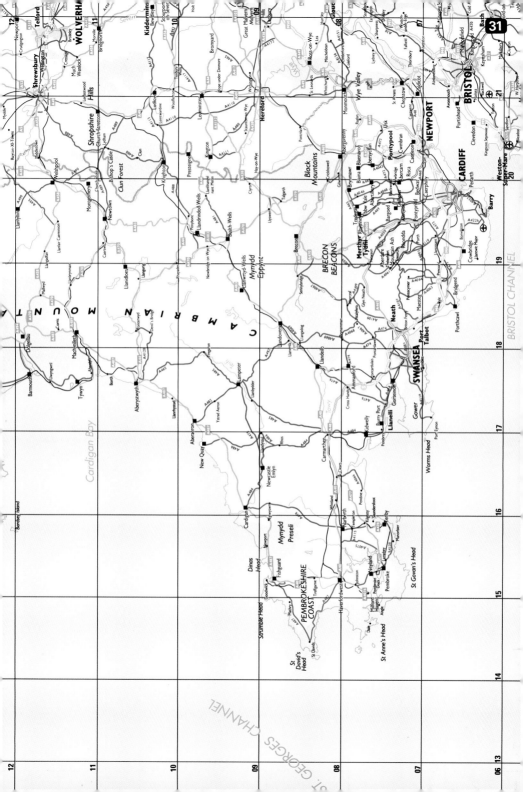

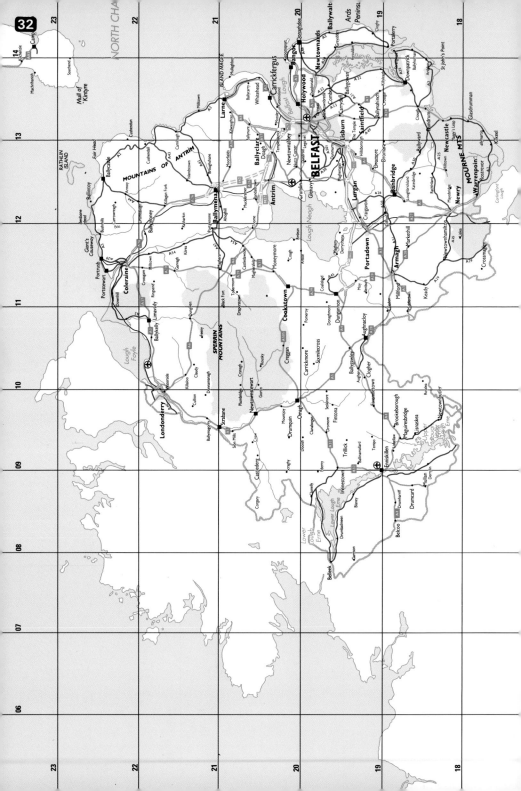

Scotland
Highlands & Islands

Group Contacts: 🅱🅱 *Margaret Pottie* ☎/Fax 01667 462213
🆂🅲 *Jessie Masheter* ☎ 01463 782423/782942

'Ceud mìle fàilte', – a hundred thousand welcomes – to the Highlands and Islands, the last great open space in Europe, a spectacular land mass and myriad islands covering nearly 15,000 square miles of unsurpassed scenic beauty. Mountains, glens, lochs, lonely sandy beaches and rugged unspoilt coastline.

Contrasting Highland landscapes provide an unrivalled backdrop for holiday activities. Enthusiasts of boating, fishing, golf, walking, birdwatching and geology are well catered for. In the land where deer and eagle roam free, wildlife lovers can also observe seals, ospreys and otters in their natural habitat. Old castles, battlefield monuments and folk museums testify to a past rich in history, culture and folklore. Land use ranges from small west coast crofts to larger hill sheep farms and to beef and grain producing units further east.

Easily accessible by road, rail and aeroplane from the south. You are assured of the clean air, peace and freedom and the traditional Highland welcome famed throughout the world. 'Haste ye back.'

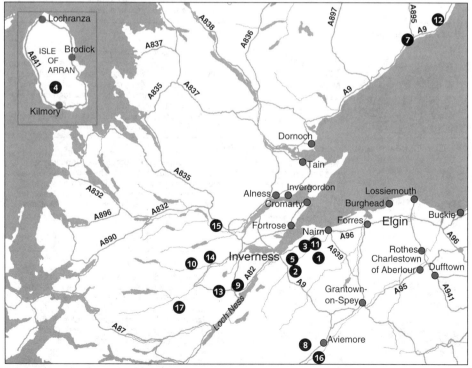

BED AND BREAKFAST

(and evening meal)

---

1 Balaggan Farm, Culloden Moor, By Inverness, Inverness-shire IV1 2EL

Mrs Phyllis Alexander
☎ 01463 790213
BB From £14
EM From £8
Sleeps 5
🛏 🐕 🐈
Listed *Commended*

A warm welcome awaits you on our small stock rearing farm set in peaceful surroundings. Good home cooking and baking is served whilst peat fires burn in living and dining rooms. 1 family and 1 twin bedroom, with tea/coffee-making facilities. An ideal centre for touring Highlands with Culloden battlefield and Candor Castle close by. Open Easter–Nov.

---

2 Daviot Mains Farm, Daviot, Nr Inverness, Inverness-shire IV1 2ER

Margaret & Alex Hutcheson
☎/Fax 01463 772215
BB From £15.50
EM From £10
Sleeps 8
🛏 ✗ 🐕 (3) ⊞ 🍴
🌸🌸
Highly Commended

Comfortable early 19th century listed farmhouse in quiet situation near Inverness. Relax in the warm atmosphere of this friendly home where delicious meals are thoughtfully prepared for you and where log fires burn in both sitting and dining rooms. En suite/private facilities available. The perfect base for exploring the Scottish Highlands. Selected by "Taste of Scotland" and recommended by Elizabeth Grundrey's S.O.T.B.T. Open all year.

---

3 Easter Dalziel Farm, Dalcross, Inverness, Inverness-shire IV1 2JL

Bob & Margaret Pottie
☎/Fax 01667 462213
BB From £15–£17
EM From £10
Sleeps 6
🛏 🐕 ⊞ 🍴 ⚘
🌸 *Highly Commended*

A friendly Highland welcome awaits the visitor to our 210-acre stock/arable farm. Delightful accommodation in early Victorian farmhouse, log fire, colour TV. Delicious home cooking and baking, choice of breakfasts offered. Lovely garden for guests' use. Ideal base for touring, golfing, birdwatching. Locally are Cawdor Castle, Culloden, Fort George, Loch Ness and nearby Castle Stuart. Brochure available. Open Mar–Nov.

---

4 Glen Cloy Farmhouse, Brodick, Isle of Arran KA27 8DA

Mr and Mrs Padfield
☎ 01770 302351
BB From £19–£25
EM From £10
Sleeps 9
🐕 (4) 🐈 🐓 ⚘ 🍴
🌸🌸 *Commended*

Glen Cloy farmhouse is a century-old farmhouse set in a quiet glen just outside Brodick. The house is surrounded by a mixed farm and offers warm, cosy rooms and excellent cooking using homegrown produce. A log fire burns cheerily in the drawing room. Taste of Scotland selected member. Open Mar–mid Nov.

---

5 "Taransay", Lower Muckovie Farm, Inverness, Inverness-shire IV1 2BB

Mrs Aileen Munro
☎ 01463 231880
BB From £15–£18
Sleeps 4
✗ 🐕 🛏
🌸🌸 *Commended*

A warm and friendly welcome awaits you at this comfortable, well-appointed bungalow on a quiet dairy farm. 2 miles south of Inverness, on the old A9, close to Drumossie Hotel. Magnificent views. 1 twin bedroom (en suite facilities) and 1 double bedroom. Close to Culloden battlefield, Cawdor Castle and golf courses. Good restaurants nearby. Open all year.

Thistle-Doo, Kilchrenan, by Taymuilth, Oban, Argyll PA35 1HF   **6**

K.Lambie
☎ 018663 339
🅱 From £16–£20
EM from £10
Sleeps 6
✂ 🐕 🧍 🛏 ⚕ ☞ 🎪 🛢
🐾 🐾 *Commended*

Awe-inspiring view of Loch Awe from our friendly family-run establishment. Ideal for all outdoor activities. Very peaceful and relaxing. 20 miles east of Oban, taking the B845 off the A85 at Taynuilt to the shore of Loch Awe. Open all year.

Upper Latheron Farm, Latheron, Caithness KW5 6DT   **7**

Mrs Camilla Sinclair
☎ 01593 741224
🅱 From £14–£16
Sleeps 6
🐕 🛏 🎪 🐎
Listed *Highly
Commended*

Idyllically situated with breathtaking views of coastline and mountains. Either relax in a peaceful atmosphere or use as an excellent base for touring northern highlands, visiting castles, gardens, nature trails. Also ideal for visits to John O'Groats, highland games or sheepdog trials, day trips to the Orkneys, or viewing puffins and seals at Duncansby. Riding/pony trekking available at our own STRA-approved stables. New-born foals offer an additional attraction. Open May–Sept.

Self-Catering

Alvie Holiday Cottages, Alvie Estate Office, Kincraig, Kingussie, Inverness-shire PH21 1NE   **8**

Marion Macadam
☎ 01540 651255/651249
Fax 01540 651380
🆂 From £250–£465
Sleeps 4–10
🐕 🛏 🗐 🎪 ☞ 🛢
🐾 🐾 🐾 – 🐾 🐾 🐾
*Commended to Highly
Commended*

Five traditional farm cottages and 2 flats in the estate shooting lodge, furnished to the most comfortable standard. Central heating, colour TV, washing machine, tumble dryer and microwave. Cattle, sheep, deer and fish plus opportunities for a wide variety of non-farming activities including skiing (4½ miles from Aviemore and 14 miles from Cairngorm). 6 golf courses within half an hour's drive. Open all year.

Borlum Farm Cottage, Borlum Farm, Drumnadrochit, Inverness, Inverness-shire IV3 6XN   **9**

Mrs Vanessa MacDonald-Haig
☎ 01456 450892
Fax 01456 450358
🆂 From £175–£440
♿ 🐕 (by arrangement)
🐕 🗐 🧍 🛏 🎪 ☞
🐾 🐾 🐾 *Commended*

Borlum Farm is a working hill farm with its own BHS-approved riding centre. The self-catering cottages are spacious, comfortable, and tastefully furnished, with splendid views overlooking Loch Ness. All are excellently equipped, including microwave cookers, hair dryers and even hot water bottles! Oil-fired central heating also available if required in colder periods. Open all year.

Culligran Cottages, Glen Strathfarrar, Struy, Nr Beauly, Inverness-shire IV4 7JX   **10**

Frank & Juliet Spencer-Nairn
☎/Fax 01463 761285
🆂 From £99–£359
Sleeps 5/7
🐕 🐎 ☞
🐾 🐾 🐾 – 🐾 🐾 🐾
*Commended to Highly
Commended*

A regular? You soon could be. So don't delay – send for a brochure! This is your opportunity to stay on a deer farm within the beautiful Strathfarrar Nature Reserve. Watch the wild deer from your window and feed the farm deer during a conducted tour. Choice of chalet or cottage. Bikes for hire. Salmon and trout fishing. Hotel and inn nearby. Open late Mar–mid Nov.

---

11   **Easter Dalziel Farm,** Dalcross, Inverness, Inverness-shire IV1 2JL

Bob & Margaret Pottie
☎/Fax 01667 462213
SC From £120–£340
Sleeps 4/6

Commended to Highly Commended

Enjoy a relaxing holiday in our cosy, traditional stonebuilt cottages. Between Inverness and Nairn on our stock/arable farm. A truly central location from which to explore the Highlands. The local area offers a wide range of activities to suit the sports-minded, tourer or walker alike. Look out for dolphins, badgers and buzzards, visit Cawdor, Culloden, Fort George and Loch Ness. Short breaks or Long Stays welcome all year. Brochure.

---

12   **Greenhill Farmhouse,** Mid-Clyth, Lybster, Caithness, Highland KW3 6BA

Mrs Camilla Sinclair
☎ 01593 741224
SC From £175–£375
Sleeps 6

Highly Commended

Farmhouse overlooking the sea (½ mile away), tastefully decorated, exceptionally well-equipped with all home comforts including dishwasher, washing machine, tumble dryer, fridge/freezer, payphone, microwave, hair dryer, all linen. Ideal for country walks/picnics. Archaeological cairn in farm. Golf, fishing, pony trekking nearby. Perfect centre for touring North of Scotland. Open all year.

---

13   **Lochletter Lodges,** Lochletter Farm, Balnain, Drumnadrochit, Inverness-shire IV3 6TJ

Miss M Brook/Mrs Bowden
☎ 01456 476313
SC From £140–£400
EM £10 max
Sleeps 4/6

Highly Commended

Four pine lodges situated on farm by Loch Meiklie, all equipped to a high standard, and all accessible to disabled people. Ideal for touring Highlands, hillwalking, golf, fishing. Indoor tennis, badminton riding on site. Home cooked bread and meals available daily. Open all year.

---

14   **Mains of Aigas,** By Beauly, Inverness-shire IV4 7AD

Mrs Jessie Masheter
☎/Fax 01463 782423/782942
SC From £180–£400
↩ ■ ⌂ **Guide dogs only**

Commended to Highly Commended

Situated in beautiful Strathglass, cottage nestling in hills overlooking Beauly valley and offering comfort with complete privacy. House and courtyard apartments attractively furnished and equipped to a high standard. Excellent touring base. Algas Golf Course, part of the farm, offers the leisure golfer easy terrain, good views and large greens in very pleasant surroundings. Open all year.

---

15   **Scatwell Farm,** Comrie, Contin, Strathpeffer, Ross-shire IV14 9EN

Margaret Cuthbert
☎ 019976 466234
SC From £100–£260

Approved to Commended

Three comfortable cottages in a quiet location in beautiful Strathconon. Ideal for fishing, hill walking, bird-watching and as a touring base yet only 25 miles north of Inverness. Come and see the Red deer, salmon, eagles and abundant wildlife. Electric heating, well equipped kitchens, TV's, cot available. Prices include linen, electricity on meter, laundry on site. Fishing arranged. Illustrated brochure on request. Open Apr–Oct.

---

16   **Strone Cottage,** c/o Lochbuie Croft, Newtonmore, Inverness-shire PH20 1BA

Mary Mackenzie
☎ 01540 673504
SC From £180–£370
Sleeps 6

Commended

Comfortable accommodation in quiet, picturesque situation on outskirts of village. Renovated stone-built crofthouse with open fire or new self-contained apartment at our family home. Both double glazed with central heating. Many local tourist attractions, also hill walking, bird watching, golf, fishing, skiing, water sports. Central for touring. Open all year.

Tomich Holidays, Tomich, by Beauly, Inverness-shire IV4 7LY   (17)

Mr & Mrs D J Fraser
☎ **01456 415332**
Fax 01456 415499
🅂🄲 **From £130–£395**
Sleeps 4–6
🏇 🐕 ↩ ⚘
⚘ ⚘ ⚘ *Commended*

Our magnificent farm steading now houses three luxury cottages and a heated indoor swimming pool. Other accommodation is in spacious chalets set in woodland and a Victorian dairy. All have central heating, hot water and electricity included in the price. Tomich, in the depths of the Highlands near Glen Affric, is an ideal base for walking, touring or just relaxing. Open all year.

FARM HOLIDAY
BUREAU

THOSE LITTLE EXTRAS

For advice on farms that can offer 'extras' such as four-poster beds, special diets, farm trails, fishing rights – even stabling and trekking arrangements if you are bringing your own horse – ring the Farm Holiday Bureau on (01203) 696909.

2

Scotland

Angus

Group Contact: *Mrs Deanna Lindsay* ☎ *01307 462887*

Whatever you seek in Scotland, you'll find in Angus, where the Braes of Angus meet the valley of Strathmore. From the glens with their gushing waterfalls to the numerous sandy beaches and bays along the east coast.

Visit Glamis Castle, former home of Queen Elizabeth the Queen Mother and birthplace of Princess Margaret, or Kirriemuir, birthplace of poet J.M. Barrie (Peter Pan). National Trust places of interest include the House of Dun (Adam), the Angus Folk Museum and many others.

Many sports are available, including hill-walking, birdwatching, riding, bowls, swimming, sailing and leisure centre sports. You can fish on the shores and banks of rivers and lochs, or hire a boat and fish the sea. Golf is Angus' most famous sport and can be enjoyed on a wide variety of courses: you can play a different course each day!

The Heritage Trail is a must for the visitor to our area, and Arbroath Abbey, Brechin Cathedral, Restenneth Priory and various Pictish standing stones and hill forts should be seen.

Angus is also an ideal touring base for a day visit to either Aberdeen, Dundee, Perth, St Andrews, Edinburgh or Balmoral. All Group hold Food Hygiene Certificates.

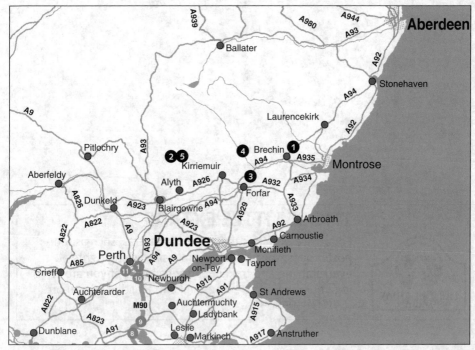

BED AND BREAKFAST

(and evening meal)

Blibberhill Farm, Blibberhill, Brechin, Angus, Tayside DD9 6TH

Margaret Stewart
☎ 01307 830225
[BB] From £14.50–£17.50
EM From £8.50
Sleeps 6
✌
🐾🐾🐾 *Highly Commended*

Situated in peaceful surroundings, between Angus Glens and coast, near Glamis Castle, 1 hour's drive from Royal Deeside and St Andrews and central to many golf courses, fishing and hill-walking. 1 twin/double room with bath en suite, 2 twin with shower en suite. All bedrooms tastefully decorated and furnished, with tea/coffee-making facilities. A warm welcome is extended to all guests, with home cooking, baking, marmalade and jams. Evening dinner optional. AA selected. Open all year.

Purgavie Farm, Lintrathen, Kirriemuir DD8 5HZ

Mrs Moira Clark
☎/Fax 01575 560213
[BB] From £14
EM From £7.50
Sleeps 6
🐕🐂🏕🐾
🐾🐾🐾 *Highly Commended*

A warm welcome in homely accommodation on our farm set in peaceful countryside and providing traditional Scottish fayre. All rooms have private bathroom, TV and tea-making facilities. Fishing on Lintrathen loch, pony trekking and hill-walking in Glen Isla. Glamis Castle 10 miles. Located 7 miles from Kirriemuir, follow the B951 to Glen Isla; farm signposted at roadside. Open all year.

Wemyss Farm, Montrose Road, Forfar, Angus DD8 2TB

Mrs Deanna Lindsay
☎ 01307 462887
[BB] From £13
EM From £8
Sleeps 6
🐂🐕🛍
Listed *Commended*

190-acre mixed farm situated on the B9113 with a wide variety of animals. Glamis Castle nearby. Shooting, fishing, golf, swimming, etc., all in the area. Bedrooms overlooking beautiful countryside. Children made welcome, reduced rates. Evening dinner, optional packed lunches. Ideal base for touring. Quiet and peaceful, yet within easy reach of all amenities. Food hygiene certificate held. Open all year.

Wood of Auldbar, Aberlemno, By Brechin, Angus, Tayside DD9 6SZ

Jean Stewart
☎ 01307 830218
[BB] From £14.50
EM From £8
Sleeps 6
🐕🐂✌
Listed *Commended*

Wood of Auldbar is a family farm of 187 acres with lovely farmhouse in first class condition. Very central for touring the Angus Glens, Royal Deeside, Balmoral, Glamis; many more castles within easy reach. Beaches, nature walks, birdwatching, fishing, golf, leisure facilities all near at hand. Standing stones and lovely churches. Excellent farmhouse cooking in award-winning farmhouse. Food hygiene certificate held. Tea facilities in all bedrooms. A warm welcome awaits you. Open all year.

LET THE TELEPHONE RING!

Some farmhouses are big places. Let the telephone ring long enough to give the owner time to answer it.

FARM HOLIDAY BUREAU

SELF-CATERING

 Purgavie Farm, Lintrathen, Kirriemuir DD8 5HZ

Mrs Moira Clark
☎/Fax 01575 560213
⛫ From £100–£350
Sleep 4/6
🐎 🐕 🛉 ⊠

🌼🌼🌼🌼 – 🌼🌼🌼🌼🌼
Commended to Highly Commended

Swedish log house also bungalow in lovely Angus glen. Wonderful views of the Valley of Strathmore. Pony trekking in Glen Isla and fishing in Lintrathen loch. Log house sleeps 6, bungalow 4. All linen supplied. Loghouse has 3 bedrooms, dishwasher and shower. Both properties have fridge freezer, washer, dryer, payphone and microwave. Located 7 miles from Kirriemuir, follow B951 signposted at roadside. Open all year.

THOSE LITTLE EXTRAS

For advice on farms that can offer 'extras' such as four-poster beds, special diets, farm trails, fishing rights – even stabling and trekking arrangements if you are bringing your own horse – ring the Farm Holiday Bureau on (01203) 696909.

DISABLED VISITORS

Many members offer a welcome to disabled/less able visitors. Please do check the extent of the facilities before booking.

Scotland

Perthshire

Group Contact: *Nigel Bruges* ☎ *01350 724208/724241*

Perthshire lies in the very centre of Scotland. For centuries the area has been the crossroads of the nation, and today's modern road, rail and coach service networks maintain that tradition, making it the ideal base for your Scottish holiday.

Here you'll find an area of outstanding beauty, the grandeur of mountains and glens, home of the native deer and other wild animals and flowers, the glimmer of lochs, hunting ground of the rare Osprey, and the River Tay, Scotland's greatest river – a true Angler's paradise.

See Perthshire at work producing top quality glass, pottery, hand-knitted woollens, leather goods, hornware and of course "the water of life". In Perthshire 4 malt whisky distilleries invite visitors to see (and taste) this unique product.

Perthshire is famed for its agriculture from quality cattle and sheep, barley for whisky and other arable crops to field vegetables and soft fruit.

There's something for everyone here – historic castles, houses and gardens, the world's highest beech hedge, Europe's oldest living tree, Perth's ultra modern leisure pool, 25 golf courses, Perth and Pitlochry theatres and of course numerous highland nights and ceilidhs.

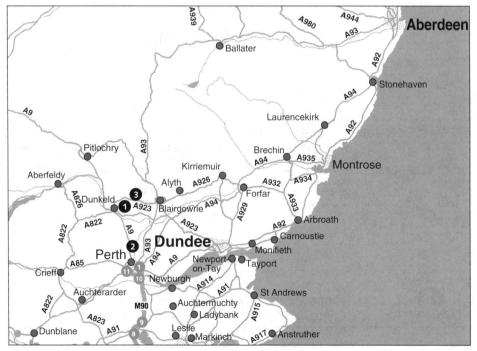

BED AND BREAKFAST

(and evening meal)

1 **Letter Farm,** Loch of Lowes, By Dunkeld, Perthshire PH8 0HH

Jo Andrew
☎ **01350 724254**
BB **From £18–£21**
Sleeps 6
🐕 🐎 ⚬
❀ ❀ *Commended*

This tastefully renovated farmhouse offers a warm, friendly welcome to all ages. En suite facilities, king size beds, log fires and good home baking. The farm is central to Perthshire's attractions, but exudes peace and tranquillity, nestled next to the Scottish Wildlife Trust's Loch of Lowes Reserve, home of the osprey. Open all year.

2 **Pitmurthly,** Redgorton, Nr. Luncarty, Perth PH1 3HY

Mrs Christine Smith
☎ **01738 828363**
BB **From £15–£18**
Sleeps 5
🐕 🐎 ⚬ ❀
Listed *Highly Commended*

Quiet, comfortable farmhouse in ideal touring location set amidst lovely countryside yet only 5 minutes from historic Perth with its unique shops and excellent restaurants. Log fires and full CH. Working farm with plenty to watch. Golf, fishing, riding and swimming can be arranged. Warm welcome assured. Open all year.

SELF-CATERING

3 **Wester Riechip,** Laighwood, Butterstone, Dunkeld, Perthshire PH8 0HB

W & WI Bruges
☎ **01350 724241**
SC **From £320–£500**
Sleeps 8
🐎 ❧
❀ ❀ ❀ ❀
Deluxe

Wester Riechip has been constructed from the west wing of a 19th century shooting lodge to create a luxurious detached holiday house with superb modern facilities. Comfortably accommodates 8. Spectacular views over surrounding hills and lochs. An ideal base for touring, golfing and birdwatching. Shooting and fishing available on our family-run hill farm. Open all year.

FARM HOLIDAY BUREAU

NO ANSWER?

Farmers are mostly out and about during the day.
Try to telephone before 9.30am or after 4pm.

Scotland

Fife

Group Contact: *Mrs Isobel Steven* ☎/*Fax 01337 828414*

The Kingdom of Fife, a unique corner of Scotland, has many attractions for visitors.

Visit Dunfermline Palace and Abbey, Falkland with its Royal Palace, St Andrews with its wonderful clean beaches and historic buildings.

Rural Fife is dominated by the Lomond Hills and the region's patchwork of fields, forests, well-kept farming communities and enchanting fishing villages.

There are many towns and places, catering for all interests – Auchtermuchty location of television's most recent 'Dr Finlay' drama series; the Scottish Centre for Falconry and Scottish Fisheries Museum; the Scottish Deer Centre near Cupar; Fife Folk Museum in Ceres; Kellie Castle near Pittenweem; St Andrews with its many golf courses including the famous Old Course, venue for the British Open Golf Championship in 1995.

North Fife is blessed with a mild, sunny climate, a coastline which complements its fertile hinterland and a great range of holiday activities including gliding, bird-watching, golf, sailing, cycling and sightseeing.

The farming families of Fife warmly welcome you to this enchanting corner of Scotland.

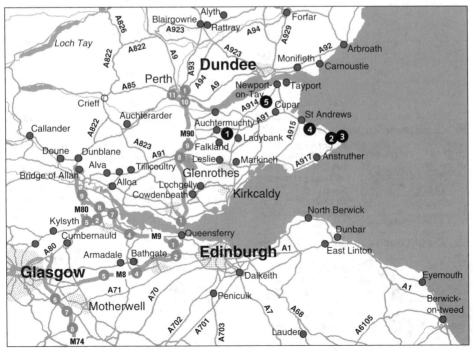

BED AND BREAKFAST

(and evening meal)

---

1 **Ardchoille Farmhouse,** Dunshalt, Nr Auchtermuchty, Fife KY14 7EY

Isobel Steven
☎/Fax 01337 828414
🛏 From £25–£35
EM £15
Sleeps 6
🐕 🛏 🐎 ⛺ ⚓
🌸🌸🌸 *Highly Commended*

Relax and enjoy the warm comfort, delicious 'Taste of Scotland' food and excellent hospitality. 3 en suite twin rooms, tastefully furnished with colour TV and tea/coffee trays with homemade butter shortbread. Large comfortable lounge, elegant dining room, 4 course dinners. Near Royal Palace of Falkland, 20 mins. St. Andrews, 1hr. Edinburgh. Ideal base for golfing & touring. Open all year. AA Premier selected 5Qs. RAC Highly acclaimed. Holder of REHIS diploma in advanced food hygiene.

---

2 **Cambo House,** Kingsbarns, St Andrews, Fife KY16 8QD

Peter Erskine
☎ 01333 450313
Fax 01333 450987
🛏 From £30–£50
EM From £18
Sleeps 6
🅲 🐕 ✂ 🖼 🐎 ⛺ ⚓ ⚒
🌸🌸🌸 *Commended*

Come and lose yourself in a glorious four-poster bed in our magnificent Victorian family home, set in parkland and woods that meander down to an unspoilt coastline with a fine sweeping beach. Only 10 minutes from St. Andrews. Open mid-Jan to mid-Dec.

SELF-CATERING

---

3 **Cambo House,** Kingsbarns, St Andrews, Fife KY16 8QD

Peter Erskine
☎ 01333 450313
Fax 01333 450987
🅂🄲 From £150–£500
Sleeps 30
🅲 🐕 🐎 🖼 🐎 ⛺ ⚓ ⚒
🌸🌸🌸 *Commended*

We offer the perfect family holiday in self contained self-catering apartments and cottages on a beautiful, traditional wooded coastal estate, only 10 minutes from St. Andrews. At the heart of the estate is a magnificent Victorian mansion with plenty of facilities for all the family from a tennis court to a sauna. Open June–September.

---

4 **Kingask Country Cottages,** Kingask, St Andrews, Fife KY16 5PN

Mrs Logan
☎ 01334 72011
Fax 01334 73264
🅂🄲 From £145–£428
Sleeps 30
🐕 🛏 🐎 ⛺ ⚓
🌸🌸🌸🌸 *Highly Commended*

The Kingsack cottages are situated 2 miles from St Andrews and the Kirkmar Cottages are ½ mile from Crail over-looking the May Isle and Forth estuary. All the cottages have been refurbished to a very high standard and provide an ideal base for experiencing St Andrews and the east coast of Fife. Open all year.

Mountquhanie Holiday Homes, Mountquhanie, Cupar by St Andrews, Fife KY15 4QJ   ⑤

Mrs Andrew Wedderburn
☎ 01382 330 252
Fax 01382 330 480
⒮ From £180–£695
Sleeps 6/12
🐕 🏕 🖾 🛆 ♿ ☂ 🏕 🛢 ♔
🥄🥄🥄 – 🥄🥄🥄🥄
Commended-Deluxe

Quality cottages and farmhouses in tranquil traditional countryside, or quality apartments in Georgian mansion, with all the ambience of country house living. Set in hundreds of acres of parkland with mature ancient trees. Experience harmonious integration of farming, forestry and conservation in action. Super for families, kids and pets. Magic for golfers – packages arranged. Open all year.

THOSE LITTLE EXTRAS

For advice on farms that can offer 'extras' such as four-poster beds, special diets, farm trails, fishing rights – even stabling and trekking arrangements if you are bringing your own horse – ring the Farm Holiday Bureau on (01203) 696909.

BUREAU ACCOMMODATION IS RELIABLE

This Guide lists **Farm Holiday Bureau** members only. They are all inspected by the National Tourist Board for standards (see introduction pages) and by fellow members to maintain a high quality.

5

Scotland

Heart of Scotland

Group Contact: *Mrs Elsie Hunter* ☎ *01236 830243*

Discover the Heart of Scotland, with its wealth of contrasting scenery and interesting places to visit – plus the friendliness of the people. The area lies between the main towns of Edinburgh, Glasgow and Stirling, with easy access from the motorways.

Visit Edinburgh Castle, Prince's Street Gardens, the Royal Mile and Palace of Holyrood House, the Scottish residence of the royal family; Glasgow's museums and art galleries, plus the world famous Burrell Collection and People's Palace.

The historic town of Stirling, 'the Gateway to the Highlands', with its magnificent castle is a must – also Doune Motor Museum and Castle nearby, Summerlee Industrial Museum, Coatbridge, and Bo'ness and Kinneil Steam Railway Museum.

Explore the beautiful hills and lochs of the 'Trossachs', sail on Loch Lomond, or visit Callendar House and park, Falkirk, Linlithgow Palace (birthplace of Mary, Queen of Scots), also Hopetoun House near the famous Forth Bridges. Outdoor and indoor sports enthusiasts are all well catered for in the area.

A warm welcome awaits you. Do come and enjoy good food, comfortable farmhouses and Scottish hospitality at its best.

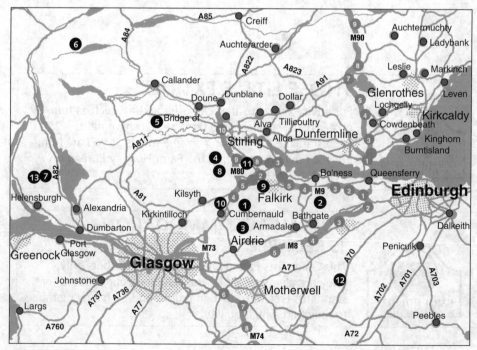

46

BED AND BREAKFAST

(and evening meal)

Bandominie Farm, Walton Road, Bonnybridge FK4 2HP   **①**

Jean Forrester
☎ **01324 840284**
🅱 **From £14.50–£15**
Sleeps 5
🐴 🐈
Listed *Commended*

A working farm located 2 miles from the A80 at Castlecary (B816). Easy access from Glasgow and Edinburgh. Lovely view with a homely atmosphere. Central heating, TV lounge. Ample parking. Open all year.

Belsyde Farm, Lanark Road, Linlithgow, West Lothian EH49 6QE   **②**

Mrs Nan Hay
☎/Fax **01506 842098**
Fax **01506 847611**
🅱 **From £17–£20**
Sleeps 6
🐴 🐕 ♞ 💼
🚶🚶 *Commended*

An 18th century farmhouse located in large, secluded gardens with panoramic views over the Forth estuary. Golfing and fishing available locally. All bedrooms have washbasin (hot & cold), tea/coffee-making facilities, colour TV, central heating, 1 bedroom en suite. AA listed. Located close to M8, M9 and M90 and to Edinburgh airport. Follow A706 south-west from Linlithgow (1½ miles); first entrance on left after crossing Union Canal. Open all year except Christmas.

Easter Glentore Farm, Greengairs, Airdrie, Lanarkshire ML6 7TJ   **③**

Elsie Hunter
☎ **01236 830243**
🅱 **From £18**
EM From **£9.50**
Sleeps 6
🐴 💼
🚶🚶 *Highly Commended*

Farm dates back to 1705, located in scenic setting on the B803, mid-way between the villages of Greengairs and Slamannan. Panoramic views. All bedrooms on ground floor, 1 en suite, all with washbasin, tea/coffee facilities and radio alarms. Central heating throughout. Lounge with colour TV. Warm friendly atmosphere with home baking and cooking. Best B&B award winner. Provides an excellent touring base, 25 minutes to Glasgow or Stirling. Open all year.

Lochend Farm, Carronbridge, Denny, Stirlingshire FK6 5JJ   **④**

Jean & Andrew Morton
☎ **01324 822778**
🅱 **From £16**
Sleeps 6
🐴 (3) 🐈
🚶 *Highly Commended*

Peace, panoramic view and good wholesome food – all may be enjoyed at Lochend. Delightfully situated over-looking Loch Coulter in unspoiled countryside, yet only 5 miles from M9/M80 (jct 9). A perfect base for exploring this beautiful part of Scotland. Farmhouse centrally-heated, traditionally furnished. 2 double bedrooms with washbasin, radio, tea-making facilities; also guests' own bathroom, dining room and lounge with colour TV. Open Easter till October or by arrangement.

Lower Tarr Farm, Ruskie, Port of Menteith, Stirling FK8 3LG   **⑤**

Mrs Effie Bain
☎ **01786 850202**
🅱 **From £16–£18**
EM From **£8**
Sleeps 6 + cot
🐴 🐈 💼 ⚘
🚶🚶🚶 *Commended*

A mixed arable farm with clear panoramic views, peaceful situation and pretty garden, with Ruskie burn running past. There are cattle, sheep and hens to be seen, plus lots of interesting wildlife. Good home cooking and baking using fresh local produce where possible. Central for touring the Trossachs, Loch Lomond, Stirling and Edinburgh. En suite rooms. Open Feb–Nov.

---

6 **Monachyle Mhor,** Balquhidder, Lochearnhead, Perthshire FK19 8PQ

Robert & Jean Lewis
☎ 01877 384622
Fax 01877 384305
BB From £23–£25
EM From £15
Sleeps 10
🛏(10) 🅿 🛇 🕭 ♿ 🏕 🍴 ☂
♨ ♨ ♨ *Commended*

Monachyle Mhor is an award winning 18th century farmhouse/hotel located in its own 2000 acre estate. All rooms are en suite and have magnificent views overlooking Lochs Voil and Doine. The hotel is delightfully furnished with family antiques and country fabrics. Fully licensed restaurant serving interesting dishes including game and herbs from our own estate. Taste of Scotland and AA listed private fishing and stalking to guests. Open all year.

---

7 **Shantron Farm Cottage,** Shantron Farm, Luss, Alexandria, Dumbartonshire G83 8RH

Anne M Lennox
☎ 01389 850231
Fax 01389 850231
BB From £14–£18
Sleeps 6
🛏 🐾 ☂
Listed *Commended*

Enjoy a relaxing break in a spacious bungalow with outstanding views of Loch Lomond. The farm is Morag's croft in 'Take the High Road' and other scenes. 3 miles south of Luss. Ideal for touring, hillwalking, fishing, watersports and golf on the new Loch Lomond Golf Course. Open Easter–Oct.

---

8 **The Topps,** Fintry Road, Denny, Stirlingshire FK6 5JF

Mrs Jennifer Steel
☎/Fax 01324 822471
BB From £18
EM From £13
Sleeps 14
🛏 🐾 ✗ 🅿 🕭 ♿ 🍴 ☂
♨ ♨ ♨ *Commended*

A chalet farmhouse in a beautiful hillside location with stunning, panoramic views. Family, double or twin-bedded rooms available, all en suite with tea-making facilities and TV. Food a speciality ("Taste of Scotland" listed). Easy access to all major tourist attractions, or spend your day on the farm with Alistair and Finlay (the dog). Your enjoyment is our aim and pleasure! Open all year.

---

9 **Wester Carmuirs Farm,** Larbert, By Falkirk, Stirlingshire FK5 3NW

Mrs Sheila Taylor
☎ 01324 812459
BB From £16
Sleeps 6
🛏 ☂
♨ *Commended*

A traditional Scottish farmhouse in a spacious garden on an arable/beef farm. Comfortable twin/double/family rooms, all with washbasins, tea/coffee-making facilities. Guests' own bathroom, shower room, dining room and TV lounge. An ideal centre to visit Loch Lomond, the Trossachs, Stirling, Glasgow and Edinburgh. Situated on the A803, near Falkirk (M9/A80). Open Jan–Nov.

---

10 **Wester Dullatur Farm,** Dullatur, Glasgow G68 0AA

Mrs Eleanor Duncan
☎ 01236 723218
BB From £15
EM From £10
Sleeps 4
🐾 🛏
Listed *Approved*

Easily accessible, in a peaceful setting, overlooking the Forth and Clyde canal to the Kilsyth hills, offering comfortable accommodation in a friendly atmosphere. 2 miles from motorway routes to Stirling, Glasgow and Edinburgh. An ideal base for scenic tours of surrounding villages or to see the 'city sights'. Open all year.

---

11 **West Plean,** Denny Road, Stirling FK7 8HA

Mrs Moira Johnston
☎ 01786 812208
BB From £18–£25
Sleeps 6
🐾 🛏 🏕 🍴 🌳
♨ ♨ *Commended*

Enjoy warm Scottish farming hospitality in an oasis of peace, with sweeping lawns, walled garden, extensive woodland walks, surrounded by our mixed farm. We offer quality food, spacious comfort, bedrooms en suite, hot drink facilities and attentive hosts. Riding and fishing can be arranged locally. Located on the A872 Denny road, 2 minutes from M9/M80 (jct 9). Open Feb–Nov.

SELF-CATERING

Crosswoodhill, By West Calder, West Lothian EH55 8LP

Mrs Geraldine Hamilton
☎ **01501 785205**
SC **From £140–£350**
Sleeps 4/6
🐾 🐕 ♿

🦪🦪🦪🦪 – 🦪🦪🦪🦪

Commended to Highly Commended

Choose between an attractively restored cottage on the Pentland Hills or a self-contained wing of our elegant 18th century farmhouse nearby. Both offer rural seclusion just ½ hour's drive from the heart of historic Edinburgh. Easy access from our 1700 acre beef and sheep farm to the Borders, Trossachs, Glasgow, New Lanark. Lots to see and do. Both properties very well equipped, CH, phone. Lovely atmosphere. Brochure. Open all year.

Shemore Cottage, Shantron Farm, Luss, Alexandria, Dumbartonshire G83 8RH

Mrs Anne M Lennox
☎/Fax **01389 850231**
SC **From £110–£260**
Sleeps 6
🐾 🎏

🦪🦪🦪

Commended

Regulars often return to this traditional stone cottage attractively situated on a hill sheep farm, 300 ft above Loch Lomond, over which the cottage has magnificent views. The farm has often been filmed for 'Take the High Road' TV series. 3 miles south of picturesque village of Luss. Edinburgh, Oban, Fort William, Ayr – 1½ hours. Ideal for hillwalking, fishing, watersports. Children love to feed lambs. Open all year.

FARM HOLIDAY BUREAU

FOLLOW THE COUNTRY CODE

Leave nothing but footprints,
Take nothing but photographs,
Kill nothing but time!

6

Scotland

Clyde Valley

Group Contact: *Mrs Margaret Kirby* ☎ *0189981 338*

The Romans were the first to cultivate 'Y Strad Cluyd' – the warm valley – where even today the Clyde Valley's many garden centres show the area to be one of Scotland's most fertile. In all, the valley boasts 23 golf courses, including Scotland's highest at 1,400ft in the Lowther Hills at Leadhills, and where gold and lead mines first worked by the Romans have been restored and serve as a unique museum to the industry.

Then 'Follow the Wallace' through Biggar, with its wide, sweeping main street, its four museums, and home to the internationally-famous Purves Puppets. It was here, in 1297, that Scottish patriot William Wallace, disguised as a beggar, hid from the English troops. Moving on to Lanark, pass Tinto Hill, Clyde Valley's highest point at 2320ft, and topped by a large Bronze Age cairn where Druids once held fertility rites. A most rewarding view for the very fit! Nestling in a gorge by the famous 'Falls of Clyde' is the cotton mill village of New Lanark, built in the 18th century, but now a living museum with working spinning looms, visitors' centre and magical history tour.

The Clyde Valley is steeped in history, from Blantre's David Livingstone Centre, which traces the explorer's journeys through Africa, to Chatelherault Country Park, a William Adam 18th century hunting lodge of the Dukes of Hamilton.

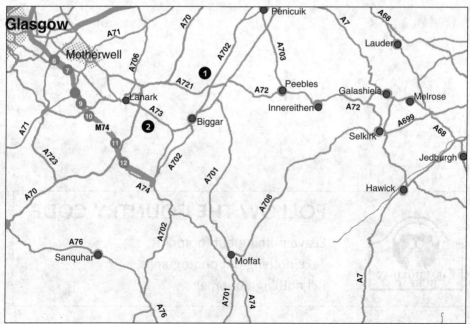

BED AND BREAKFAST

(and evening meal)

Walston Mansion Farmhouse, Walston, Carnwath, Lanark ML11 8NF

Mrs Margaret Kirby
☎ 0189 981 338
▨ From £12.50–£14.50
EM From £7
Sleeps 6
🐴 🐕 ♦
♛♛♛ *Commended*

A very pleasant family home situated 5 miles from Biggar. A friendly and relaxed atmosphere; children most welcome. Good home cooking with home-produced meat, eggs and organic vegetables. Guest lounge with log fire, TV/video and children's games. An ideal base for touring Strathclyde, Lothian and the Borders; Lanark, Edinburgh and Glasgow only a short drive away. Open all year.

SELF-CATERING

Carmichael Country Cottages, Estate Office, Westmains, Carmichael, Biggar, Lanarkshire ML12 6PG

Richard Carmichael of Carmichael
☎ 018993 336
Fax 018993 481
▨ From £160–£430
Sleeps 2/7
🐴 ♿ 🐕 ⊞ 👤 🎣 ♦ ❡
♛♛♛–♛♛♛♛ *Commended to Highly Commended*

These 200-year-old stone cottages nestle among the woods and fields of our 700-year-old family estate. You will enjoy our private tennis court and fishing loch. We guarantee comfort, warmth and a friendly welcome in an accessible, unique rural and historic time capsule. We farm deer, cattle and sheep and sell meats and tartan – Carmichael, of course. Breakfast and evening meal available. Open all year.

FARM HOLIDAY BUREAU

DISABLED VISITORS

Many members offer a welcome to disabled/less able visitors. Please do check the extent of the facilities before booking.

7

Scotland

Bonnie Galloway and Stinchar Valley

Group Contact: *Mrs Vera Dunlop* ☎ *01465 861220*

You will find plenty of space on our quiet roads and wide rolling countryside. With lush farmlands and miles of beautiful coastline the scenery is enhanced by golden sunsets.

Thanks to our mild climate, many subtropical plants bloom around Port Logan (just one of the many gardens in the area). South-West Scotland is a golfer's paradise, with courses wherever you go, both links and inland.

Fishermen will find plenty of opportunities for river, loch and sea fishing, while the hill climber or gentle walker may even be lucky enough to see the golden eagle, an inhabitant of the area for many years.

The area is also rich in historical and Christian heritage. A visit to the archaeological dig at Whithorn, where St Ninian founded the first Christian church, is a must.

Nearby, Culzean Castle with its famous Adam ceilings and superb furnishings is just one of the many castles to be explored in the area. Only the most discerning visitors choose this area of Scotland, and they are always amply rewarded.

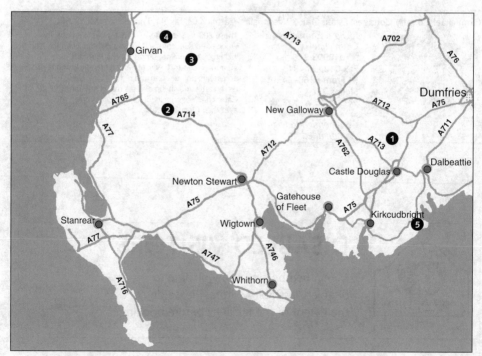

BED AND BREAKFAST
(and evening meal)

Airds Farm, Crossmichael, Castle Douglas, Kirkcudbrightshire DG7 3BG

Barbara McBride
☎ 01556 670418
BB From £14–£17
EM From £7.50
Sleeps 10
🐴 🐕 ✦
🐌 Commended

Airds farmhouse overlooks lovely Loch Ken, 4 miles from Castle Douglas on the A713. All bedrooms tastefully decorated, heated, with wash handbasins, family en suite, electric blankets and tea and coffee facilities. Private lounge and dining room with colour TV. Smoking allowed in the sun lounge only. Fire certificate held. Payphone available. Guests are assured a comfortable stay with good home cooking and baking. Open all year.

Blair Farm, Barrhill, Girvan, Ayrshire KA26 0RD

Mrs Elizabeth Hughes
☎ 0146 582 247
BB From £14
EM From £8
Sleeps 6
🐴 🐕 ✦ 🏔
🐌 Commended

Blair is a family run beef and sheep farm situated on the A714, 1 mile south of the village of Barrhill. Guests are assured of a warm friendly welcome, comfortable spacious rooms and a high standard of home cooking and baking. Central heating throughout 1 family and 1 double room both with wash basin and tea/coffee-making facilities. Lounge with colour TV. Fishing available. Open Easter–Oct.

Glengennet Farm, Barr, Girvan, Ayrshire KA26 9TY

Vera Dunlop
☎ 01465 861220
BB From £17
Sleeps 4
🐴 🍴
🐌🐌 Commended

Original Victorian shooting lodge with lovely views over the Stinchar valley and neighbouring Galloway Forest Park. One double and one twin, both en suite, 1 room with private bathroom, with washbasin and tea tray. Guests lounge/dining room with colour TV. Two miles from Barr village where good meals are available. Good base for forest walking/cycling, golf, Ayrshire coast, Burns country, Culzean Castle and Glentrool National Park. Open Apr–Oct.

Hawkhill Farm, Old Dailly, Girvan, Ayrshire KA26 9RD

Mrs Isobel Kyle
☎ 01465 871232
BB From £17.50–£18
EM From £8
Sleeps 6
🐴 🐕 🌾
🐌🐌 Highly Commended

Superb farmhouse hospitality in spacious 17th-century former coaching inn where the emphasis is on comfort and good, fresh food. Two delightful bedrooms with private facilities. Visitors' lounge, central heating, log fires, tea tray. Peaceful setting perfect for exploring south west Scotland, Culzean Castle, Galloway Forest Park, Ayr and Burns country. Golf, fishing, pony trekking. Brochure. Open Mar–Oct.

Rascarrel Cottage, Rascarrel Farm, Auchencairn, Castle Douglas, Kirkcudbrightshire DG7 1RJ

Ellice Hendry
☎ 01556 640214
BB From £15–£17
Sleeps 6
🍴 🏛
🐌🐌 Highly Commended

You will find peace, comfort and wonderful views at our attractive, well-appointed cottage. Situated on an 18th century smuggling route overlooking our 400 acre farm and the Solway Firth, it is 500 yards from the sea and 2 miles from village where good meals are available. 1 double en suite and 1 twin with H & C on ground floor, 1 twin en suite on first floor. Tea trays, CH, bright spacious lounge, sunroom/dining room. Open Mar–Oct.

8

Scotland

Dumfriesshire (Annandale)

Group Contact: *Mrs Marjorie Rae* ☎ *01576 610248*

A peaceful, undiscovered, easily accessible part of south-west Scotland. Take time to explore the countryside and sample the tranquility.

From the beaches of the Solway coast to the rugged Moffat Hills, with the spectacular 'Grey Mare's Tail' and the striking 'Devil's Beef Tub', here is a variety of scenery unmatched in Britain. Quiet lanes winding through lush green countryside, busy small towns with a variety of interesting shops, numerous challenging golf courses, excellent fishing and much, much more. The county town of Dumfries contains the excellent Robert Burns Centre which documents the many links Scotland's foremost poet has with the area. Moffat is a most attractive town with tennis courts, bowling green, woollen mill and many craft shops. Lockerbie, with its bustling cattle market, is well worth a visit. So, whether you enjoy birdwatching or hill walking, swimming or horseriding, sailing or just relaxing with friendly people, you will find everything you want in Dumfriesshire.

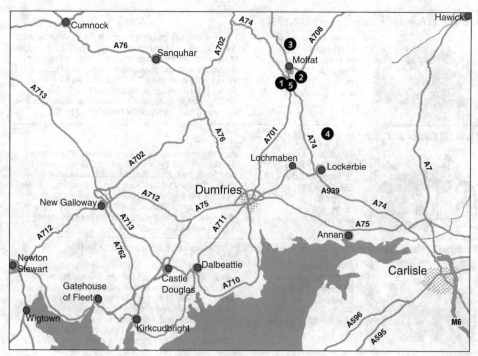

BED AND BREAKFAST
(and evening meal)

Broomlands Farm, Beattock, Moffat, Dumfriesshire DG10 9PQ

Kate Miller
☎ 016833 320
🛏 From £16–£18
Sleeps 5
🐕 🐎 ⛄ 🎿
🌑 *Highly Commended*

A lovely spacious farmhouse situated in the Annandale Valley and 2 miles from Moffat, a wonderful area to tour, walk, play golf, etc. High standard accommodation offering double, twin and single rooms, all with beautiful en suite facilities, colour TV, tea/coffee-making facilities. Choice farmhouse breakfast. Personal attention. Safe private parking. Convenient for A/M74.

Coxhill Farm, Old Carlisle Road, Moffat, Dumfriesshire DG10 9QN

Mrs Sandra Long
☎ 01683 20471
🛏 From £16
EM From £10
Sleeps 6
🐕 ⛄ 🎿
🌑 *Highly Commended*

A very attractive farmhouse in 70 acres of unspoilt countryside with outstanding views, beautiful rose gardens and ample parking. 2 double, 1 twin bedrooms, all with washbasins, tea/coffee-making facilities and central heating. Situated 1 mile south of the charming town of Moffat, and 1½ miles from Southern Upland Way. Excellent base for golf, tennis, fishing and touring SW Scotland. Open Mar–Oct.

Ericstane, Moffat, Dumfriesshire DG10 9LT

Robert Jackson
☎ 01683 220127
🛏 From £15
Sleeps 4
🐕 🐎 🎿
🌑 *Commended*

Tastefully renovated period farmhouse in attractive grounds by the Annan Water. 4 miles from Moffat in a peaceful valley. Twin and double-bedded rooms with private facilities, TV, tea/coffee-making facilities. Central heating. Open all year.

Nether Boreland, Boreland, Lockerbie, Dumfriesshire DG11 2LL

Mrs Marjorie Rae
☎ 01576 610248
🛏 From £18–£20
Sleeps 6
🐕 (12) ♿
🌑 *Highly Commended*

Sample Scottish hospitality, peaceful friendly surroundings and hearty breakfasts with our free range eggs and homemade preserves. The spacious, comfortable farmhouse has two en suite bedrooms and one with private bathroom, all with TV, tea/coffee-making facilities, hairdryers and clock radios. Enjoy golf, fishing, pony trekking or leisurely sightseeing. Farmhouse Award winner. Brochure. Open Mar–Nov.

Woodhead Farm, Old Carlise Road, Moffat, Dumfresshire DG10 9LU

Sylvia Jackson
☎ 01683 20225
🛏 From £20–£24
Sleeps 6
🎿 🍵
🌑 *Highly Commended*

Sylvia and Murray welcome you to their luxuriously furnished farmhouse built c1820. All rooms en suite with panoramic views of the rolling countryside. TV, beverage tray, etc. Breakfast served in the conservatory overlooking garden. Just 2 miles from Moffat yet very peaceful. Open all year.

Scotland

East Lothian

Group Contact: *Zoë Peace* ☎ *01620 822 131*

The beautiful, unspoilt countryside of East Lothian unfolds from Edinburgh's eastern edge along the Firth of Forth. Nestling under the heather-covered Lammermuir hills are many historic towns and picturesque villages – the county town of Haddington is one of the best preserved traditional market burghs in Scotland.

The area combines an extraordinary blend of scenery, antiquity and culture, with ancient castles, fine country houses, fascinating museums, National Trust properties, sports and leisure centres, and our own working Lowland whisky distillery, Glenkinchie. The choice of outdoor pursuits is endless – 40 miles of sandy beaches, the famous Bass Rock seabird and seal sanctuary, several country parks, racing at Musselburgh, as well as hill walking, pony trekking, fishing and the ubiquitous golf! East Lothian boasts 14 courses including the championship course at Muirfield.

There are numerous pubs, restaurants and bistros to suit all palates and purses. We look forward to seeing you.

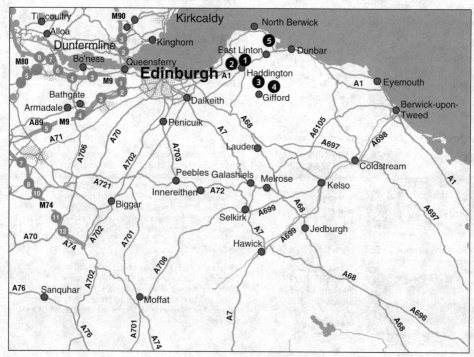

BED AND BREAKFAST

(and evening meal)

Barney Mains, Haddington, East Lothian EH41 3SA   ①

Katie Kerr
☎ **01620 880310**
Fax **01620 880639**
[BB] From £15–£20
Sleeps 6
🐴 🎠 🏺
Listed *Commended*

Beautiful farmhouse in quiet location with spectacular views of open countryside. Rooms are spacious, warm and comfortable. Lovely walks on farm to ruined castle and remains of ancient fort. Ideally situated for golfing holidays, touring and sightseeing. Edinburgh 20 minutes drive. Delicious breakfast with homemade bread. Open Mar–Nov.

Coates Farm, Longniddry, East Lothian EH32 0PL   ②

Zoë Peace
☎ **01620 822131**
[BB] From £18.50
Sleeps 4
🐴 🐕
🌸🌸 *Highly Commended*

Spacious Georgian farmhouse tastefully decorated and furnished throughout. Ideally situated for exploring countryside, coastline or visiting Edinburgh. Train station nearby. Comfortable bedrooms with private facilities. Separate lounge and dining room for guests. Large, well tended, interesting garden. Excellent local pubs and restaurants. Coates is 1¾ miles from the A1. Open Apr–Sept.

Eaglescairnie Mains, Gifford, Haddington, East Lothian EH41 4HN   ③

Mrs Barbara Williams
☎/Fax **01620 810491**
[BB] From £16–£20
Sleeps 6
🐴 🐐 🏺 🎾
🌸🌸 *Commended*

Join us at Eaglescairnie Mains, a beautifully furnished Georgian house on our 350-acre arable/sheep farm which recently won a National Conservation Award. Near A1, ideal for the coast, golf courses, the Borders or Edinburgh. Double, twin and single rooms – some en suite, full CH, basins, tea/coffee trays. Conservatory, tennis court and games room. Open all year (closed Christmas and New Year).

Rowan Park, Longnewton Farm, Gifford, East Lothian EH41 4JW   ④

Margaret Whiteford
☎ **01620 810327**
[BB] From £15
Sleeps 4
🐴 🏕 🚲 🎣 🏺
Listed *Highly Commended*

Our family farm of 450 acres consists of cattle, cereals and ponies. Situated at the foot of the Lammermuir Hills, with magnificent views to the Forth. Only 30 minutes from Edinburgh and near to the Border Country with its stately homes. Golf, fishing, tennis, swimming and pony trekking all nearby. Furnished to a high standard, guests' lounge and dining room, also welcome tray. A warm welcome awaits you. Open Mar–Nov.

Whitekirk Mains, Whitekirk, North Berwick, East Lothian EH42 1SX   ⑤

Mrs J Tuer
☎/Fax **01620 870245**
[BB] From £17–£18
Sleeps 6
🐴 🎾
🌸🌸 *Highly Commended*

Spacious Georgian farmhouse on a 600-acre mixed farm at the edge of a historic village. Large en suite rooms with tea/coffee facilities and colour TV. Oak panelled dining/drawing rooms, log fires, superb views. Country and beach walks. 20 miles Edinburgh/Lammermuir Hills. Adjoining new 18-hole Whitekirk Golf Course. Twelve local golf courses.

10

Scotland

Scottish Borders

Group Contact: *Sheila Bergius* ☎ *01896 860 244*

This is an area of great beauty renowned for its abbeys at Kelso, Melrose, Jedburgh, and Dryburgh. Some of the loveliest of Scotland's great houses are to be found at Bowhill, Abbotsford, Floors and Traquair, to mention but a few.

The lowlands contain some of the best farming land in Britain and this rises to the Cheviot Hills. The Pennine Way runs along the top of the Cheviots or there is the Southern Upland Way stretching from coast to coast for those who wish to have a walking holiday.

For the fisherman there is fine fishing to be had in the waters of the Tweed or sea fishing on the east coast. Golfers can plan a trip in the region where they can play a different course every day! Rugby is a popular sport here and in the spring and autumn you can watch the 'sevens'.

Horseriding is a passion in this region – trekking through this lovely area is very popular with visitors and, for those who wish only to observe, the larger Border towns have their 'common ridings' during the summer which are supported by hundreds of riders. A magnificent sight; only one of many in this lovely land.

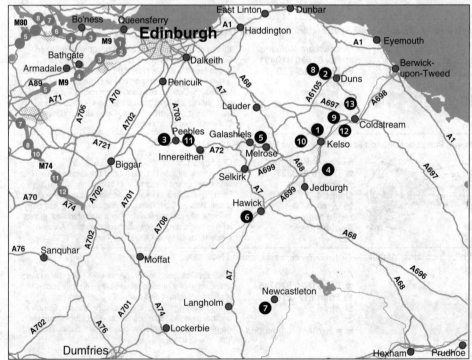

BED AND BREAKFAST
(and evening meal)

Cliftonhill Farm, Kelso, Roxburghshire TD5 7QE ①

Archie & Maggie Stewart
☎ **01573 225028**
Fax **01573 226416**
[BB] **From £15–£18**
EM From £11
Sleeps 4
🛇 🛏 🐕 ♿ ✿
☙ ☙ *Commended*

A warm welcome is assured at Cliftonhill. A traditional farmhouse set in the beautiful unspoiled Border country, the farm is 2 miles from Kelso, and an ideal centre for exploring, walking or just relaxing. The River Eden meanders through the farm attracting interesting wildlife. Pools for fishing and swimming/ tennis court. Home-made bread. Beautiful double en suite, and 1 twin with private bathroom. Seaside ½ hour's drive, Edinburgh 1 hour. Brochure available. Open all year.

Cockburn Mill, Duns, Berwickshire TD11 3TL ②

Mrs A M Prentice
☎ **01361 882811**
[BB] **From £17–£19**
EM From £10
Sleeps 4
🛇 🍴 🐕

☙ ☙ *Commended*

A comfortable riverside farmhouse offering 2 twin bedrooms with luxurious en suite bathrooms, within sight and sound of River Whiteadder. Electric blankets and tea/coffee-making facilities. Home baking and farm produce. Water from hillside spring. Trout fishing included. Abundant plant and bird life. Ideal for hill-walking, birdwatching, cycling or just relaxing. Hens, ducks, donkeys and pet lambs. Open Mar–Nov.

Lyne Farm, Peebles EH45 8NR ③

Mrs Arran Waddell
☎ **01721 740255**
[BB] **From £15–£17**
Sleeps 6
🛏 🛇(5) ♿ ✿
Listed *Commended*

A large, comfortable farmhouse and garden, in quiet rural area of scenic beauty. Outstanding south-facing views over the Manor and Stobo Valleys. 4 miles west of Peebles on the A72. Easy access to Edinburgh (23 miles). Ideal base for touring, hill walking, fishing, golfing, mountain-biking, riding. Open all year.

Morebattle Tofts, Kelso, Roxburghshire TD5 8AD ④

Mrs Debbie Playfair
☎ **01573 440364**
Fax **01573 420227**
[BB] **From £14–£16**
EM from £10
Sleeps 4
🛏 🛇 ♿ 🏕 🛶 🐕 ✿
☙ ☙ *Commended*

Large, elegant 18th century farmhouse set in 3 acres of garden beside the River Kale. Area of Outstanding Natural Beauty, ideal for touring, walking, fishing, golf. Beautifully appointed rooms, double en suite, double and twin rooms. Tea and coffee-making facilities. Tennis court, croquet lawn. Brochure available. Open Mar–Oct.

Overlangshaw Farm, Langshaw, Galashiels, Selkirkshire TD1 2PE ⑤

Sheila Bergius
☎ **01896 860244**
[BB] **From £15–£18**
Sleeps 6
🛏 🛇 🍴 ♿
☙ *Commended*

Situated only 4 miles from Galashiels and Melrose. A welcoming, centrally heated home amidst rolling hills and shady woods. Delicious Scottish cooking with emphasis on quality home produce and preserves. Children welcome, cot available. Also dogs by arrangement. Roomy bedrooms, 1 family with private bathroom, 1 double with en suite shower room. Southern upland way nearby. Open all year.

6 **Wiltonburn Farm,** Hawick, Roxburghshire TD9 7LL

Mrs Sheila Shell
☎ **01450 372414**
Mobile 0374 192551
🅱 From £15–£16
Sleeps 6
🐕🐎✂🏕🕱🎪⚱
Listed *Commended*

Wiltonburn is a friendly working mixed farm situated in a beautiful sheltered valley 2 miles from Hawick. An ideal base for walking, riding, fishing, golf, castles or stately homes. Our new showroom stocks designer cashmere knitwear, paintings, jewellery and small gifts. Log fires, cosy rooms, warm welcome. Open all year.

SELF-CATERING

7 **Bailey Mill,** Bailey, Newcastleton, Roxburghshire TD9 0TR

Pamela Copeland
☎/Fax **01697 748617**
SC From £68–£398
EM From £6
Sleeps 2/10
🐕👶🐎🏕🕱🎪⚱
♨♨♨ *Commended*

A warm welcome awaits you from Pam and Ian on this small farm holiday complex nestling on the Roxburgh/ Cumbria border. The four superior self-contained apartments include heating (oil), electricity and linen in rent. Colour TV and microwave in each apartment. On-site sauna, solarium, jacuzzi, multi-gym, games room, laundry, farm kitchen and horse riding. Baby sitting service. Breakfast and evening meal available. Brochure. Open all year.

8 **The Cottage,** Cockburn Mill, Duns, Berwickshire TD11 3TL

Ann Prentice
☎ **01361 882811**
SC From £120–£200
Sleeps 5 + cot
🐕🐎⚱
♨♨ *Approved*

Stone-built cottage within sight and sound of River Whiteadder. Children welcome. Barbecue, dinghy, colour TV available. Overnight storage heating included. Trout fishing included. Water from hillside spring. Abundant plant and bird life. Chicks, donkeys, ducklings and pet lambs. Coast, beaches, Edinburgh, Border keeps and abbeys within easy reach on quiet roads. Pets by arrangement only. Open all year.

9 **Cherry Tree Cottage and Rowan Tree Cottage,** Lochton, Coldstream, Berwickshire TD12 4NH

Mrs Rosalind Aitchison
☎ **01890 830205**
Fax **01890 830210**
SC From £100–£300
Sleeps 4/6
🐎🐕🏕🎪⚱
♨♨♨ *Commended*

Relax and discover the wonderful Border Country. Stay in charmingly refurbished cottages on our sheep/arable farm beside River Tweed. Rowan Tree, beautifully appointed with wood-burning stove, CH, shower/bath, 3 bedrooms and Cherry Tree, 2 bedrooms, log fire, cosy, clean and comfy, wait to welcome you. Fishing, golf, farm walks. Easy touring for historic homes, abbeys, hills and beaches. Edinburgh 1 hour. Open all year.

10 **Craggs Cottage,** Cliftonhill Farm, Kelso, Roxburghshire TD5 7QE

Archie & Maggie Stewart
☎ **01573 225028**
Fax **01573 226416**
SC From £75–£310
Sleeps 7
🐎🐕⚱🎪✗
♨♨♨ *Approved*

A terraced sandstone cottage, lovingly restored, maintaining its character and charm. One double room – large and luxurious, 1 bedroom with 3 single beds and single bedroom. Large comfortable kitchen with Rayburn cooker and electric cooker. Central heating. Sitting room with log fire and colour TV. Enclosed colourful garden, garden furniture. Delightful restaurant 3 miles. Coast 18 miles, Edinburgh 35 miles. Enquire about our special winter break offer. Open all year.

Easter Deans and Glenrath, Glenrath Farm, Kirkton Manor, Peebles, Tweeddale EH45 9JW   **11**

Catherine Campbell
☎ **01721 740221**
Fax 01968 676957
⑃ **From £125–£500**
Sleeps 4/8
🐴 ♿ 🦢 ☕ 🎣

♔♔♔ – ♔♔♔♔♔
Commended to Highly Commended

We have three very attractive properties ranging from a luxury farmhouse to a 2 bedroom cottage. All centrally heated. Situated on a working hill farm in the county of Tweeddale. The farmhouse is only 25 mins from Edinburgh and the town of Peebles is only 15 mins from any of the properties. Coarse fishing and hill walking. Pets welcome. Ideal for children. Open all year.

Kerchesters, Kelso, Roxburghshire TD5 8HR   **12**

Mrs J. Clark
☎ **01573 224321**
Fax 01573 226609
⑃ **From £110–£300**
Sleeps 5/7
🐴 🦢 ⚔ 🎣

♔♔♔ *Commended*

Cockerlaw and Todrig cottages are warm, welcoming terraced cottages on a working farm. Well appointed and peacefully situated with good views and ample play areas. Cockerlaw has separate sitting room and shower room. Three miles east of Kelso. Well placed for touring Borders and Northumbria. Edinburgh 1 hour, beach 30 minutes. Local golf, swimming, fishing, riding. Linen included. Brochure on request. Open all year.

Little Swinton Cottages, Little Swinton, Coldstream, Berwickshire TD12 4HH   **13**

Sue Brewis
☎ **01890 860280**
⑃ **From £180–£300**
Sleeps 4–7
🐴 🦢 ♿

♔♔♔ – ♔♔♔♔♔
Commended to Highly Commended

A row of quiet refurbished, well equipped one storey stone cottages all with open fires, night store heating, colour TV, washing machine, etc. Linen provided. Large enclosed grass play area. Ample parking. Children and pets welcome. Beaches, hills, historic houses, Edinburgh, Newcastle, all within reach. Open all year.

11

England's North Country
Hadrian's Wall, North Cumbria and The Borders

Group Contact: *Mrs Harriet Sykes* ☎ *016977 3435*

Discover the Border Country, a wild wonderland of moors, tarns and loughs, wooded river valleys and rich pastureland. Wildlife abounds with peace and quiet for all who seek it. This is an exciting area for the heritage enthusiast with Roman sites and the world famous Hadrian's Wall, Lanercost Priory, Hexham Abbey, Carlisle, Naworth and Hermitage Castles. The historic city of Carlisle with its gem of a cathedral has an excellent Lanes shopping centre of large and small shops.

Whether walking, golfing, fishing, birdwatching or gently touring our quiet roads you will find this area has so much to offer – lots of country inns, market towns, woollen and tweed mills, local craft and agricultural shows and, most important of all, friendly people. Kielder Water is on our doorstep offering many water activities, birdwatching and magnificent forest surroundings. Once you have enjoyed the peace, freedom and our North Country hospitality, you will most certainly wish to return to this unspoilt area.

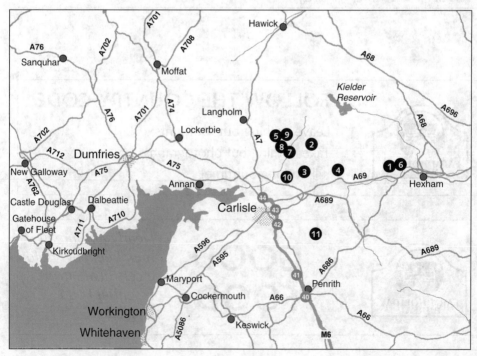

BED AND BREAKFAST

(and evening meal)

Ald White Craig Farm, Nr Hadrian's Wall, Haltwhistle, Northumberland NE49 9NW

Isobel Laidlow
☎ 01434 320565
🛏 From £19–£22
Sleeps 6
⚲ ▲ ♘
👑👑 *Highly Commended*

17th century croft-style farmhouse, on western edge of Northumberland's National Park, 1 mile Hadrian's Wall, ½ mile A69. Small working sheep farm with other interesting animals. Magnificent touring/walking area. 1 hr Metro Centre and Lakes. Nearby inn (food highly recommended). 1 twin, 2 doubles, (all en suite), tea-making facilities, colour TV, CH, etc. AA selected. Customer Choice Award Winner 1994. Brochure. Open all year (closed Christmas & New Year).

Cracrop Farm, Kirkcambeck, Brampton, Cumbria CA8 2BW

Marjorie Stobart
☎ 016977 48245
🛏 From £18–£20
EM From £12
Sleeps 6
♘ 🎣 ✂ ⚲ ♞ ▪
👑👑👑 *Highly Commended*

Superior holidays on working dairy/sheep farm. Friendly personal service. Large rooms tastefully decorated to high standard. All bedrooms en suite, colour TV, tea/coffee-making facilities and full CH. Superb views. Excellent for birdwatching and walking (Prize-winners in wildlife and farm competitions). Best English cooking. Relax in spa bath or sauna. Games room. Near Roman Wall, Scottish Borders, 1 mile from B6318. Open all year.

High Rigg, Walton, Brampton, Cumbria CA8 2AZ

Margaret Mounsey
☎ 016977 2117
🛏 From £13.50–£15
EM From £8.50
Sleeps 4
⚲ ♘ 🎣 ♞ 🐎
👑 *Approved*

Working dairy/sheep farm with attractive 18th century listed comfortable farmhouse, on the roadside near Walton and Roman Wall. Friendly welcome, excellent home cooking, panoramic views. Convenient for the Lakes, Pennines, Northumbria and Scottish Borders. Patio, childrens play area, pool/snooker table. Follow the farm trail to the waterfall, help to feed the animals or relax in the garden. Open all year (closed Christmas and New Year)

Howard House Farm, Gilsland, Carlisle, Cumbria CA6 7AN

Elizabeth Woodmass
☎ 016977 47285
🛏 From £16–£19
EM From £9.50
Sleeps 6
♘ Å 🎣
👑👑 *Highly Commended*

A warm welcome and comfortable accommodation await you on beef/sheep farm. Situated on an elevated site enjoying magnificent views over 2 counties in the heart of Roman wall country. Guests lounge, colour TV, tea/coffee-making facilities. Dinner by arrangement or bar meals nearby. Discount on 3 night stay. Open all year, except Christmas.

New Pallyards, Hethersgill, Carlisle, Cumbria CA6 6HZ

Mrs Georgina Elwen
☎/Fax 01228 577308
🛏 From £16–£18.80
EM From £10.50
Sleeps 12
♘ ♞ & 🎣 🐎 🎣 ♞ ▪
👑👑 *Commended*

Friendly hospitality, warmth and comfort await you in this modernised 18th century farmhouse. Situated in the peaceful countryside, surrounded by nature yet easily accessible from M6, A7, M74. All bedrooms en suite, tea/coffee facilities, disabled people welcome. A wide range of leisure and recreational activities are within a few minutes' drive from the farm. National Gold Award winner. Open all year.

SELF-CATERING

---

⑥ Ald White Craig Farm Cottages, Nr.Hadrian's Wall, Haltwhistle, Northumberland NE49 9NW

Isobel Laidlow
☎ 01434 320565
sc From £100–335
Sleeps 3/8 + cot
Highly Commended

Comfortable 1 and 3 bedroomed farm cottages, very well furnished and equipped to be your holiday home from home. Personally maintained. Inn/restaurant ½ mile; heated pool, and Leisure Centre 1 mile, golf 3½ miles. Central section Hadrian's Wall nearby. Excellent area for country pursuits. Dogs by arrangement only. Brochure available on request. Open all year.

---

⑦ Arch View and Riggfoot Cottages, Midtodhills Farm, Roadhead, Carlisle, Cumbria CA6 6PF

Jean James
☎/Fax 016977 48213
sc From £80–£398
Sleeps 4/8 + cot
Up to Highly Commended

Overlooking the Lyne Valley, working farm (320 acres). **Arch View** (sleeps 8): 18th century barn conversion, kitchen/diner, lounge, shower room and bathroom.2 doubles with vanity units, 2 singles, 1 twin. **Riggfoot** (sleeps 4): Detached cottage, open plan kitchen/diner/ lounge, oak beams, log fire, double with four-poster bed and 1 twin, bathroom. Both have dishwasher, microwave, washer/dryers, colour TV, video, CH, garden, BBQ.

---

⑧ Bailey Mill, Bailey, Newcastleton, Roxburghshire TD9 0TR

Pamela Copeland
☎/Fax 01697 748617
sc From £68–£398
EM From £6
Sleeps 2/10
Commended

A warm welcome awaits you from Pam and Ian on this small farm holiday complex nestling on the Roxburgh/ Cumbria border. The four superior self-contained apartments include heating (oil), electricity and linen in rent. Colour TV and microwave in each apartment. On-site sauna, solarium, jacuzzi, multi-gym, games room, laundry, farm kitchen and horse riding. Baby sitting service. Breakfast and evening meal available. Brochure. Open all year.

---

⑨ Burn and Meadow View, New Pallyards, Hethersgill, Carlisle, Cumbria CA6 6HZ

Georgina Elwen
☎/Fax 01228 577308
sc From £80–£330
Sleeps 2/10
Commended

Set amidst beautiful countryside close to the Scottish Borders, our fully centrally heated cottages offer a high standard of accommodation with all modern-day facilities. A wide range of leisure and recreational activities are within a few minutes' drive from the farm. Our on-site games and dining room opening 1994 will make your stay more enjoyable. Open all year.

---

⑩ Dovecote, Cleughside Farm, Kirklinton, Carlisle, Cumbria CA6 6SB

Mrs Sherann L Chandley
☎ 01228 75650
sc From £130–£200
Sleeps 4
Commended

A wonderfully warm cottage, tucked away and surrounded by green fields, sheep, goats and ducks. Admirable blend of mod cons and traditional charm. Fully inclusive, for your assured comfort. Close to Scottish Borders, Hadrians Wall and most country pursuits locally. A haven of peacefulness. It's all you could wish for! Open all year.

Long Byres, Talkin Head Farm, Talkin, Brampton, Cumbria CA8 1LT   ⑪

Mrs Harriet Sykes
☎ **016977 3435**
SC **From £90–£245**
🐕 🐎 ☕ ⚐ ♨ ⚘
⚘ ⚘ – ⚘ ⚘ ⚘ ⚘
Commended

Situated on a small North Pennine hill farm, within RSPB Geltsdale reserve. 1 mile from Talkin village (Post Office and eating out). Specialist, fully equipped holiday accommodation; five 2-bedroom houselets (sleep 4/5); two single bedroom (sleep 2/3). Freshly home-cooked meals. Facilities for golf, boating, fishing within 2 miles. Open all year.

GOOD FOOD

Nearly all Bureau members now hold a certificate in Essential Food Hygiene.

FARM HOLIDAY BUREAU

FOLLOW THE COUNTRY CODE

Leave nothing but footprints,
Take nothing but photographs,
Kill nothing but time!

FARM HOLIDAY BUREAU

12

England's North Country

Carlisle's Border Country

Group Contact: *Dorothy Downer* ☎ *016977 48644*

The country to the north east of Carlisle is one of the last truly peaceful places in England. Here in the Debateable Land where the Border Reivers once rode; your only debate today will be which of the many beautiful and historic places will you visit. Will it be Carlisle with its cathedral, castle, city walls, pedestrianised shopping centre and award winning museum, the Tullie House; or the north to Scotland and wild Liddesdale, Hermitage Castle and the Border Abbeys and historic houses; or the west and the Solway coast and its world renowned birdlife; or will you just walk or cycle on the peaceful tracks of the Border Forest Park basking in tranquility, perhaps catching sight of a deer?

A short drive from the M6 this area is ideal for a stopover for Scotland and Northern Ireland is within easy distance of the Lake District, Hadrian's Wall, Northumberland and Kielder Water, and the Eden Valley: whilst only a step from romantic Gretna Green. A haven of peace with enough to keep you involved for many more holidays because once you have been welcomed for the first time in one of Carlisle's Border Country farms you will certainly want to come back ...

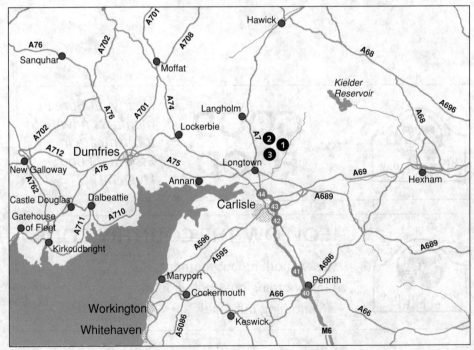

66

BED AND BREAKFAST

(and evening meal)

Bank End Farm, Roadhead, Bewcastle, Carlisle, Cumbria CA6 6NU

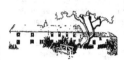

Boy & Dorothy Downer
☎/Fax 016977 48644
🛏 From £18–£20
EM From £12
Sleeps 2
⌿ ☕ 🅳

👑 👑 *Commended*

Relax in peace in your own luxurious self-contained suite (including a private sitting room) on small hill sheep farm close to the Scottish border. Friendly atmosphere, delicious home cooking, using fresh local produce by a cook of distinction. Marvellous centre for walking, fishing and touring; naturalist's paradise. Close to B6318. Phone for brochure with colour photo. Ask for travel directions. Open Apr–Nov.

Bessiestown Farm, Catlowdy, Penton, Carlisle, Cumbria CA6 5QP

Margaret Sisson
☎ 01228 577219
🛏 From £19–£22
EM From £10
Sleeps 8
🐕 🅳

👑 👑 👑 *Highly Commended*

One of the nicest B&Bs to be found, peaceful and quiet. Warm, comfortable pretty bedrooms. TV lounge, bar lounge. Delicious food. Indoor heated swimming pool (May–Sept). Ideal touring base. Stop off Scotland and Northern Ireland. M6 exit 44, then A7 to Longtown; right at Bush Hotel 7 miles to T-junction, 1½ miles to Bessiestown. Open all year.

Craigburn Farm, Catlowdy, Penton, Carlisle, Cumbria CA6 5QP

Jane & Jack Lawson
☎ 01228 577214
🛏 From £19–£20
EM From £10
Sleeps 14
🐓 🐕 🎪 🛟 🅳

👑 👑 👑 *Commended*

Enjoy the delights of beautiful Cumbrian countryside and life on our 250-acre working farm. Relax in the peace and quiet of the farmhouse, with delicious farmhouse cooking. Distinction in cookery held. 28 years in the business. Special breeds animals. Stay here when travelling to and from Scotland. Four-poster bed. 20% off weekly bookings. Weekend break, 10% discount. Midweek break, 15% discount. Open all year.

FINDING YOUR ACCOMMODATION

FARM HOLIDAY BUREAU

The Group contacts at the beginning of each section can always help you find a vacancy in your chosen area.

SELF-CATERING

---

④ Bank End Farm, Roadhead, Bewcastle, Carlisle, Cumbria CA6 6NU

Dorothy & Boy Downer
☎/Fax 016977 48644
SC From £130–£310
Sleeps 8 + cot
🦮 🐈 ⛲ 🖅
🔌 🔌 🔌 🔌 *Commended*

Two centrally heated cottages lovingly restored, very well equipped and furnished with many extras including open fire, dishwasher, video player, electric blankets. Meal/baking service. A peaceful hideaway where Reivers once rode. Beautiful quiet scenery, good wildlife. Visit the Scottish Borders, Carlisle and Kielder. Rent includes fuel/linen. Please phone for brochure. Open all year.

---

⑤ Bessiestown Farm, Catlowdy, Longtown, Carlisle, Cumbria CA6 5QP

Margaret Sisson
☎ 01228 577219
SC From £100–300
Sleeps 4
🦮 ♿ 🖅
🔌 🔌 🔌 *Commended*

Three attractively converted oak beam cottages situated around courtyard with extensive views over Scottish Border country. Spacious, warm, comfortable and furnished/decorated to high standard. 2 ground floor bedrooms with wash/hand basins. Ground floor bath/shower room. First floor lounge/kitchen. Indoor heated swimming pool (May–Sept). Ideal "away-from-it-all" touring holiday. Out of season breaks. Phone for colour brochure. Open all year.

FARM HOLIDAY
BUREAU

CONFIRM BOOKINGS

Disappointments can arise by misunderstandings over the telephone.
Please write to confirm your booking.

13

England's North Country

North Northumberland

Group Contact: *Mrs Sally Lee* ☎ *01665 574 277*

North Northumberland is an area of great beauty still little known to many people. There are miles of heritage coastline dotted with castles such as Lindisfarne, Bamburgh and Dunstanburgh and further inland a wealth of historic homes including Alnwick Castle and Cragside. Holy Island (Lindisfarne) is accessible by car at low tide and boats run daily in the summer months to the Farne Islands, famous for their colonies of seals and seabirds.

The Northumberland National Park offers wonderful opportunities for those wishing to walk and explore in peace and solitude. Berwick-upon-Tweed and Alnwick are two busy country towns which still have weekly street markets. Scotland's capital city, Edinburgh to the north and Newcastle with its much acclaimed Metro Shopping Centre to the south are within easy reach by car, train or bus.

Our group offers a wide variety of holiday accommodation of a high standard based on working farms in this unspoilt corner of England's most northerly county.

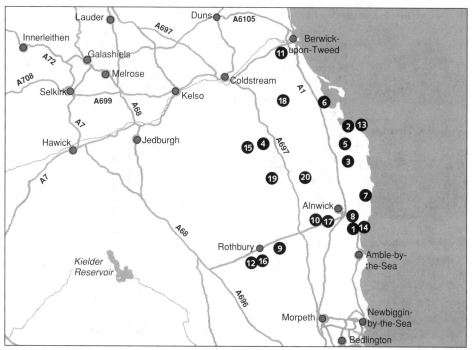

BED AND BREAKFAST

(and evening meal)

---

1 Bilton Barns, Alnmouth, Alnwick, Northumberland NE66 2TB

Dorothy Jackson
☎ **01665 830427**
BB From £18.50–£21
EM From £10.50
Sleeps 6

Spacious farmhouse in lovely countryside with magnificent views over Alnmouth and Warkworth bays. Many splendid walks, beaches and castles nearby. Full central heating, guests' lounge and dining room. Two en suite bedrooms and one with washbasin, TV and tea/coffee-making facilities. Brian is pleased to take interested guests on a farm walk. Recommended in *Best Bed and Breakfast* in the World. Open Easter–mid Oct.

---

2 Burton Hall, Bamburgh, Northumberland NE69 7AR

Eve Humphreys
☎ **01668 214213**
Fax 01668 214538
BB From £18–£25
Sleeps 17
☼ (4) ⛺ ♿ ☎
Listed *Commended*

A traditional farmhouse offering a friendly atmosphere with a high standard of service only 1½ miles from Bamburgh Castle. All bedrooms are spacious with tea/coffee facilities, en suites with colour TV. Ground floor bedrooms available as well as an elegant residents' lounge and dining room. Open all year.

---

3 Doxford Farmhouse, Doxford Farm, Chathill, Northumberland NE67 5DY

A & D Turnbull
☎ **01665 579235**
Fax 01665 579215
BB From £15–£22
EM From £8
Sleeps 10
⛺ ✂ ⛱ Ⓔ ⚒ ♿ ☎
☼ *Commended*

A peaceful, listed Georgian farmhouse with large garden set in wooded countryside between the hills and the beautiful coastline. Guests are welcome to come on our farm walk and follow the newly created nature trail. Trout fishing and boat on nearby lake, and a squash court. Delicious home cooking and homemade bread. We happily welcome children and pets. Open all year (closed Christmas and New Year).

---

4 Earle Hill Head Farm, Wooler, Northumberland NE71 6RH

Sylvia Armstrong
☎/Fax 01668 281243
BB From £17–£20
Sleeps 6
⛺ ☼ ♿ ☎
Listed

Earle Hill Farm is 2 miles from Wooler at the foot of the Cheviot Hills. We have a 4,000-acre stock farm in the National Park. Lovely walks and a warm welcome will await you in our comfortable farmhouse. Wooler is a perfect centre for the coast, castles and Scottish Borders. Household and Farming Museum. Local nature trails and conducted tours. Open April–Nov.

---

5 Elford Farmhouse, Elford, Seahouses, Northumberland NE68 7UT

Mrs M. Robinson
☎ **01665 720244**
BB From £16
Sleeps 6
☼ (12) ⛽ ♿ ☎
Listed *Highly Commended*

An old stone farmhouse of great character on an arable farm near the villages of Bamburgh and Seahouses, 1½ miles from the sea. Nearby are beautiful beaches, castles, golf, riding and boat trips to the Farnes and Holy Island. Good local restaurants. Comfortable bedrooms with central heating, colour TV, hair dryers and tea/coffee making facilities. Elegant dining room. Some use of outdoor heated swimming pool and lawn tennis court in summer. Open Mar–Nov.

Fenham-le-Moor Farmhouse, Belford, Northumberland NE70 7PN

Mrs K Burn
☎ 01668 213247
BB From £17.50
Sleeps 2
🐾 (12) ⅍
👑 👑

A comfortable stone-built farmhouse in a peaceful situation with magnificent views overlooking farmland and the bay of Lindisfarne Nature Reserve. An area of outstanding natural beauty and excellent centre for birdwatching, golf, good beaches and visiting many castles. One twin room en suite. Open Easter–Oct.

Howick Scar Farm, Craster, Alnwick, Northumberland NE66 3SU

Mrs Celia Curry
☎ 01665 576665
BB From £14
Sleeps 4
🐾 (5) ♞
Listed

Comfortable farmhouse accommodation on mixed farm situated on the coast between the villages of Craster and Howick. Ideal base for walking or exploring the coast, moors and historic castles. Guests have their own television lounge/dining room with coal fire and full central heating. Closed April.

Hipsburn Farm, Lesbury, Alnwick, Northumberland NE66 3PY

Hilda Tulip
☎ 01665 830206
BB From £18
Sleeps 6
⅍
👑 Highly Commended

A spacious farmhouse situated ½ mile from Alnmouth, overlooking the Aln estuary. Rooms comfortably furnished, one double en suite, one twin en suite and one double with private bathroom. TV, tea/coffee-making facilities in all bedrooms. All rooms are centrally heated, dining room – lounge. Ideal area for golfers, walkers and birdwatchers. Private parking. Open Easter–Oct.

The Lee Farm, Longframlington, Morpeth, Northumberland NE65 8JQ

Mrs Susan Aynsley
☎ 01665 570257
BB From £14–£16
Sleeps 5
🐾 ♞
👑 Commended

Large traditional farmhouse on 1,200 acre farm. Spacious bedrooms with tea/coffee-making facilities and washbasins. Guests' lounge with log fire and dining room. Central heating throughout. Excellent central location for walking or exploring Northumberland's many attractions. Fishing, riding and golf available nearby. Open Mar–Nov.

Lumbylaw Farm, Edlingham, Alnwick, Northumberland NE66 2BW

Mrs Sally Lee
☎ 01665 574277
BB From £17
Sleeps 6
⅍ 🐾 ♞ ❀ ▪
👑 Highly Commended

Friendly hospitality in a comfortable stone farmhouse on a beef and sheep farm. 6 miles between Alnwick and Rothbury. Outstanding views of the 13th century Edlingham Castle and Victorian railway viaduct in the farm grounds. Two twin bedrooms, 1 double bedroom (all with washbasins; one with en suite shower). Guests' bathroom, central heating throughout. Excellent local eating places available. Open Easter–Oct.

Middle Ord Manor House, Middle Ord Farm, Berwick-on-Tweed TD15 2XQ   11

Joan Gray
☎ 01289 306323
BB From £17–£23
Sleeps 6
♞ ❀
👑 👑 Deluxe

Mrs Gray offers quality accommodation within her Grade II listed farmhouse. Very full comprehensive breakfast menu served in gracious dining room. Two residents' lounges (one non-smoking). Secluded gardens. All day access. En suite or handbasin only, 4-poster if desired. Sorry no children, no pets. Open Apr–Nov.

⑫ Tosson Tower Farm, Great Tosson, Rothbury, Morpeth, Northumberland NE65 7NW

Mrs Ann Foggin
☎ 01669 620228
BB From £15–£18.50
Sleeps 6
🛇 🏋 🕯 🐾 ☂
♛ ♛ *Highly Commended*

Large, comfortable farmhouse formerly a coaching inn at the foot of the Simonside Hills beside the ruined pele from which it takes its name. 2½ miles from Rothbury with superb views over Coquet Valley and Cheviot Hills. Perfect base for exploring Northumberland's many attractions. Spacious bedroons with tea/coffee, one twin en suite, two double with washbasins. Guests' lounge, TV, full CH. Open Mar–Nov.

SELF-CATERING

⑬ East Burton Farm Holiday Cottages, Bamburgh, Northumberland NE69 7AR

Eve Humphreys
☎ 01668 214213/214458
Fax 01668 214538
SC From £160–360
Sleeps 16
🛇 (4) 🏋 🕯 ☂
🔑 🔑 🔑 🔑 *Commended*

Four comfortable cottages on a working farm 1½ miles from Banburgh, all well equipped and furnished. Heat, light, sheets and towels included in rent. Ideal base for birdwatching, golf, sightseeing or relaxing. Open all year.

⑭ Farm Cottage, Bilton Barns, Alnmouth, Alnwick, Northumberland NE66 2TB

Mrs Dorothy Jackson
☎ 01665 830427
SC From £150–£350
🛇
🔑 🔑 🔑 🔑 *Commended*

Ideally situated for exploring the beautiful Northumbrian coastline with its castles and magnificent walks. Our farm cottage has been recently modernised to a very high standard with a new and fully equipped kitchen, central heating and an open fire with fuel provided. Bed linen is also included in rental. Open all year.

⑮ Firwood Bungalow and Humphreys House, Earle Hill Head Farm, Wooler, Northumberland NE71 6RH

S. E. Armstrong
☎/Fax 01668 281243
SC From £180–£500
Sleeps 6–12
🏋 🛇 🐾 ☂
🔑 🔑 🔑 – 🔑 🔑 🔑 🔑
Up to Highly Commended

Firwood and Humphreys, a choice of two beautiful homes offering a unique and private situation. Standing in 1.5 acres of well maintained gardens on 4,000 acre farm within the National Park at the foot of the Cheviots. Ideal throughout the year. Every comfort, open fires, central heating.

⑯ Keepers Cottages, Great Tosson, Rothbury, Morpeth, Northumberland NE65 7NW

Mrs Ann Foggin
☎ 01669 620228
SC From £120–£370
Sleeps 4–6
🛇 🏋 🕯 🐾 ☂
🔑 🔑 🔑 *Up to Highly Commended*

Four delightful cottages situated in the Coquet Valley enjoying panoramic views of the Cheviot Hills. Cosy, comfortable, centrally heated, well equipped and all with enclosed gardens. Located in the National Park with many forest and moorland walks clearly marked. 2 miles from Rothbury and the NT property of Cragside. Very central for touring the whole of Northumberland. Bedlinen provided. Log fires during winter. Open all year.

Lumbylaw Cottage & Garden Cottage, Edlingham, Alnwick, Northumberland NE66 2BW

Mrs Sally Lee
☎ 01665 574277
sc From £112–£382
Sleeps 6 + cot, and 2
✂ ☎ ♨ ♞
🐾 🐾 🐾 – 🐾 🐾 🐾 🐾 *Up to Highly Commended*

Non smokers. Extensive hill views. The two cottages are situated on our working farm with its own ruined castle and viaduct, providing easy walking along the disused railway line. Both cottages centrally heated. Recently renovated, they are prettily decorated, furnished and equipped to a high standard. All fuel and power, bed linen and towels included in rent. Sorry no pets. Brochure available. Open all year.

The Old Smithy, Brackenside, Bowsden, Berwick-upon-Tweed, Northumberland TD15 2TQ

John & Mary Barber
☎ 01289 388293
sc From £160–£370
Sleeps 6
🐓 ☎ ♿ ♨
🐾 🐾 🐾 🐾 *Commended*

The high standards of this attractive conversion of a smithy and stable to a comfortable home makes an ideal setting for a peaceful and relaxing holiday. Explore the farm, discover the woodland and conservation areas. See the cows and calves, sheep, lambs and crops. Table tennis. Bike hire, riding, fishing and golf nearby. Gas central heating makes for a perfect winter break. Open all year.

Shepherd's Cottage, Ingram Farm, Powburn, Alnwick, Northumberland NE66 4LT

Sarah Wilson
☎ 01665 578243
sc From £175–£350
Sleeps 7
☎ 🐓 🐎 🍴 ♨
🐾 🐾 🐾 🐾 *Commended*

On a working family farm in the beautiful Breamish Valley, the cottage has superb scenery on the doorstep. Explore the unspoilt Cheviot Hills or the coast and castles. Most mod cons are provided and there are no extras – fuel, linen and towels all included. Central heating from open fire. Night storage heating. Short breaks available. Open all year.

No. 2 and 3 Cottages, Titlington Hall Farm, Alnwick, Northumberland NE66 2EB

Mrs Vera Purvis
☎ 01665 578253
sc From £155–£295
Sleeps 10
🐓 ☎ 📺 ♿ ♨ 💼
🐾 🐾 🐾 🐾 *Commended*

Two lovely country cottages available for holiday lets all year round. They are situated in a quiet and beautiful area with many interesting places just a short drive away. Facilities include central heating, TV, fridge, washing machine, microwave, tumble dryer and all linen. Children and pets welcome. Open all year.

BUREAU ACCOMMODATION IS RELIABLE

This Guide lists **Farm Holiday Bureau** members only. They are all inspected by the National Tourist Board for standards (see introduction pages) and by fellow members to maintain a high quality.

England's North Country
Northumberland and Durham

Group Contact: *Mrs L Vickers* ☎ *01388 527248*

Northumbria covers the four most northerly counties of England – Cleveland, Durham, Northumberland and Tyne and Wear. Visitors can escape on traffic-free roads to open countryside and vast, deserted beaches; a great contrast to the modern cities where shopping and entertainment are of a high standard. Old and new complement each other with some of Britain's finest heritage such as Hadrian's Wall, Durham Cathedral, Beamish Museum, Holy Island and new developments like Newcastle upon Tyne's Eldon Square and the Metro Centre at Gateshead.

The region also boasts some of England's finest countryside – the North Pennines designated as an 'Area of Outstanding Natural Beauty' and the Northumberland National Park – retreats from the pressures of modern life.

Visitors to Northumbria can be assured of a warm and hospitable welcome seldom equalled.

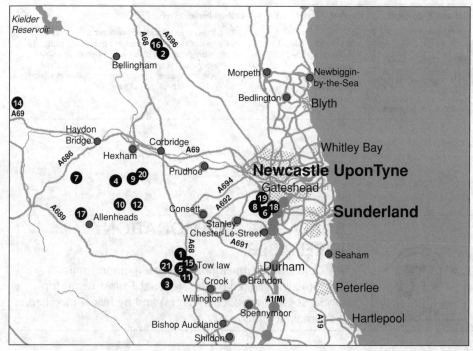

BED AND BREAKFAST

(and evening meal)

Bee Cottage Farm, Castleside, Consett, Co Durham DH8 9HW

Liz Lawson
☎ 01207 508224
🅱🅱 From £18
EM £12
Sleeps 22
🐕 🛏 🍴 ■
🐾🐾 *Highly Commended*

A working farm in lovely surroundings with unspoilt views, situated 1½ miles west A68 between Tow Law and Castleside. Visitors may participate in all farm activities, feeding calves, milking goats, bottle feeding lambs, etc. Tea room open daily. Quiet country walks. Fire certificate. No smoking in farmhouse. Ideally located for Beamish Museum, Metro Centre, Durham Cathedral or a break on a journey between England and Scotland. Open all year.

Cornhills, Kirkwhelpington, Northumberland NE19 2RE

Lorna Thornton
☎ 01830 540232
🅱🅱 From £16–£20
Sleeps 6
🍴 🛏 🎿
Listed *Highly Commended*

A large Victorian farmhouse complete with mosaic tiled hall, spacious beautifully decorated and furnished bedrooms, all with outstanding views. Our stock farm is in the centre of Northumberland, ideal for visiting Cragside, Wallington and Belsay Hall. 1 mile from the A696, 3½ miles from the A68, makes this very convenient for travelling to Scotland. Closed April.

Friarside Farm, Wolsingham, Weardale, Co Durham DL13 3BH

Mrs Marjorie Anderson
☎ 01388 527361
🅱🅱 From £14
Sleeps 4
🐕 🛏 (5) 🍴
🐾 *Commended*

Friarside is a working hill farm, with dairy cows, sheep and a small acreage of barley and potatoes. Guests are made to feel at home and, when convenient, are entertained with music and poetry. Meals are taken in a conservatory which affords fantastic views over the Wear Valley. Open all year.

Gairshield Farm, Whitley Chapel, Hexham, Northumberland NE47 0HS

Mrs Hilary Kristensen
☎ 01434 673562
🅱🅱 From £15.00
Sleeps 4
🍴 🛏 (6)🎿
Listed *Highly Commended*

A comfortable 17th century farmhouse on a quiet hill farm (1,000 ft above sea level), with superb views over open countryside. 20 mins south of Hexham. Ideal for exploring this beautiful historic region. Perfect walking and horse-riding area; horses very welcome. Large attractive family bedroom. Guests' dining room/lounge with TV and tea/coffee making facilities. Open Apr–Oct.

Greenwell Farm, Nr Wolsingham, Tow Law, Bishop Auckland, Co Durham DL13 4PH

Mike & Linda Vickers
☎ 01388 527248
🅱🅱 From £16–£18.50
EM From £8.50
Sleeps 6
🍴 🛏 ♿ 🐕 ■ 🐾 🎿
🐾🐾 *Commended*

Enjoy a warm welcome in our charming farmhouse dating back 300 years. On the 280-acre mixed stock and arable farm we have developed our own walks and nature reserve with a wide variety of wildlife. Comfortable and attractive rooms, quality food. Bedrooms with private bathrooms. An excellent base for touring, county cricket and visiting the numerous attractions of the North Pennines and Durham City. Open all year (closed Christmas and New Year).

---

6 Low Urpeth Farm, Ouston, Chester Le Street, Co Durham DH2 1BD

Hilary Johnson
☎ 0191 410 2901
Fax 0191 410 0081
BB From £16
Sleeps 6
♿ ⚹
*Listed Highly
Commended*

Traditional farmhouse accommodation in spacious and comfortably furnished rooms with TV/beverage facilities, one double with washbasin, 2 twin en suite. Within easy reach of Beamish Open Air Museum, Durham and Northumberland. Directions – leave A1(M) at Chester Le Street, follow A693, at 2nd roundabout fork right to Ouston, down hill, over roundabout, turn left at 'Trees Please' sign. Open all year

7 Manor House Farm, Ninebanks, Nr Allendale, Hexham, Northumberland NE47 8DA

Mrs Isobel Lee
☎ 01434 345236
BB From £14–£16.50
♿ ➤ ⚘
🐾 *Commended*

Working farm with cattle and sheep. Georgian farmhouse situated in the beautiful West Allen valley, a designated area of outstanding natural beauty. Ideal overnight stop for Scotland, close to Hadrians Wall. Guests' lounge/dining room. Central heating, tea making facilities, washbasins, radios and hairdryers. Open all year (except Christmas).

8 Mount Escob Farm, Beamish Woods, Stanley, Co Durham DH9 0SA

Mrs Pamela Bovill
☎ 0191 370 0289
BB From £15–£17
Sleeps 6
♿ ➤ ⚹ ⚘ 🔒 🦌
Applied

A 12-acre grassland holding with that 'heart of the country' feel, yet less than 10 mins from the A1(M)! Close to Beamish Open Air Museum. The house is on the site of a former paper mill, beside Beamish Burn, with the surrounding hills and woods bearing much evidence of small industries of a byegone age. Our horses and youngstock thrive on their visitors' attention! A short drive takes you to either Durham city or to the Metro Centre. Open all year.

9 Rye Hill Farm, Slaley, Nr Hexham, Northumberland NE47 0AH

Elizabeth Courage
☎ 01434 673259
BB From £18–£20
EM From £10
Sleeps 15
♿ ➤ ⚹ 🚶 ♟ ⚘ 🔒
🐾 🐾 *Commended*

We are a small family-run livestock farm set in beautiful countryside with 360-degree panoramic views. We have recently converted some of the old byres into superb modern guest accommodation. We aim for high standards with a homely atmosphere, ideal for your 'get away from it all' break or holiday. Good, fresh, homemade cooking. All rooms en suite.Well mannered children and pets welcome. Open all year.

SELF-CATERING

10 Bail Hill, Allenshields, Blanchland, Consett, Co Durham DH8 9PP

Jennifer Graham
☎ 01434 675274
SC From £120–£220
Sleeps 5
♿ 🖼 ⚘
🔑 🔑 🔑 *Commended*

Centrally heated, 2-bedroomed farmhouse with breathtaking views to Derwent Reservoir near Blanchland. Enjoy the peaceful surroundings of a typical hill farm or use as a central location for Tynedale, Durham and N E Coast. Blanchland is one of the most picturesque of Northumbrian historic villages with Abbey, pub and post office. Open fire and well-equipped kitchen. Enclosed garden and parking outside the house. Open all year.

Bradley Burn Holiday Cottages, Wolsingham, Weardale, Co Durham DL13 3JH

Mrs Judith Stephenson
☎/Fax 01388 527285
🆂 From £120–£280
♿ 🐕 🐂 ■
🏇 🏇 🏇 – 🏇 🏇 🏇 🏇
Up to Commended

Four cottages, well-designed conversions of redundant farm buildings, preserving the traditional stone exteriors but incorporating all modern comforts indoors. Rural situation, close to a pretty stream. 2 miles east of former market town of Wolsingham. Centrally placed for sightseeing in Durham, Northumberland and North Yorkshire. Send for brochure. Open all year.

Buckshott Farm Cottage, Blanchland, Consett, Co Durham DH8 9PL

Lorraine & Irene Bainbridge
☎ 01434 675227/ 675296
🆂 From £120–£235
Sleeps 6
🐂 🐎
🏇 🏇 Commended

Attractive 2-bedroom cottage which adjoins the farmhouse and overlooks the beautiful Derwent Valley. Central heating, fitted kitchen, private garden, ample parking. Blanchlands historic village has a shop, post office, pub and a 12th century abbey. Hexham, Durham, Beamish Open Air Museum, Gateshead Metro Centre and the Northumberland coast are all within an easy day's outing. Open Apr–Oct.

Gibbs Hill Farm, Bardon Mill, Nr Hexham, Northumberland NE47 7AP

John or Clare Edwards
☎ 01434 344030
Fax 01434 344641
🆂 From £150–£380
Sleeps 10
🐂 🐎 🐕 ⛵ ■ 🐎
🏇 🏇 🏇 🏇 Up to Deluxe

Three delightful stone cottages in sight of Hadrian's Wall. Situated in Northunberland National Park on a nature reserve. The decor is to a very high standard with log fires. Gas central heating and en suite bathrooms. Quiet location. Riding and fishing available locally. Ideally suited for visiting the breathtaking scenery of Northumberland with its numerous spectacular castles, battlefields and museums. Open all year.

Greenwell Hill Stables & Byre, c/o Greenwell Farm, Nr Wolsingham, Tow Law, Co Durham DL13 4PH

Linda Vickers
☎ 01388 527248
🆂 From £120–£325
Sleeps 2/6
🐂 🐕 🐂 ♿ ⛵ ■
🏇 🏇 🏇 🏇 Highly Commended

Enjoy a relaxing stay in one of two quality cottages. This is a traditional farm in peaceful countryside. Marvellous views, pleasant walks and our own nature trail with conservation area. The larger cottage has a four poster bed, dishwasher and en suite bedrooms. Both are well equipped with gas central heating, double glazing, natural beams, pine furniture, fitted carpets, comfy chintzy suites and woodburing stoves. Evening meals available. Open all year.

The Herdsman Cottage, Cornhills, Kirkwhelpington, Northumberland NE19 2RE

Lorna Thornton
☎ 01830 540232
🆂 From £120–£260
Sleeps 5
✂ 🐂 ⛵
🏇 🏇 🏇 🏇 Commended

A beamed 19th century farm cottage, provides comfortable accommodation for 5 people (double, twin, single). The fully fitted kitchen is equipped with fridge, washing machine, night storage heaters, open fire in winter. Bed linen provided. Enjoy the peace on our stock farm, in the centre of Northumberland. Open all year.

NO ANSWER?
Farmers are mostly out and about during the day.
Try to telephone before 9.30am or after 4pm.

FARM HOLIDAY BUREAU

17 **"Isaac's Cottage"**, c/o Allenheads Farm, Allenheads, Hexham, Northumberland NE4 9HJ

Heather M Robson
☎ 01434 685312
SC From £150–£280
Sleeps 7
🐕 ⅍ 🐎 ⛵ 🏕
🏌 🏌 🏌 🏌 *Highly Commended*

Beautiful stone cottage adjoining farmhouse , overlooking meadowland and small hamlet of Spartylea. Very warm and cosy, oil central heating, log fire, double glazing, beamed ceilings, quality carpets, colour TV. Garden, ample parking. Three bedrooms, bathroom, separate WC, shower. Bed linen, coal, logs, electricity included, also cot/highchair. Ideal for walking, riding, fishing, golf, touring, skiing. Welcome tea. Hexham 16 miles, Allendale 6, Alston 10. Open all year.

18 **Katie's Cottage,** c/o Low Urpeth Farm, Ouston, Chester Le Street, Co.Durham DH2 1BD

Hilary Johnson
☎ 0191 410 2901
Fax 0191 410 0081
SC From £200-£225
Sleeps 4
🐕 ⅍
Applied

Relax in our newly converted stone cottage, tastefully furnished. Two en suite bedrooms, cosy living area with timber beams. Three miles A1M, excellent base for Durham, Bemish Museum and easy access to Northumberland and Hadrian's Wall. Open all year.

19 **Papermill Cottages,** Mount Escob Farm, Beamish Woods, Stanley, Co Durham DH9 0SA

Mrs Pamela Bovill
☎ 0191 370 0289
SC From £130–£280
Sleeps 2/8
🐕 🐓 ⅍ ⛵ 🏕 🐖
🏌 🏌 🏌 *Commended*

Near Beamish Museum. Two workers' cottages from Urpeth Paper Mill (circa 1792) have recently been renovated to a high standard, retaining traditional features of open fire ranges, beams and stonework whilst updating with modern kitchens and central heating. Set in an idyllic, peaceful situation beside the river, surrounded by woods yet only 6 minutes from A1M at Chester le Street. Open all year.

20 **Rye Hill Farm,** Slaley, Nr Hexham, Northumberland NE47 0AH

Elizabeth Courage
☎ 01434 673259
SC From £350–£600
Sleeps 9
🐕 🐓 🧍 🚗 ⅍ ⛵ 🏕 🛢 ♿
🏌 🏌 🏌 🏌
Commended

Spacious barn conversion equipped to high standard. Good facilities for disabled or wheelchair users. One twin ground floor bedromm en suite, one double en suite, one twin, one bunkbedded room. Use of games and laundry rooms. B&B in same complex. All fuel and linen included. Excellent value out of season. Pets and children welcome. Open all year.

21 **West Newlands Cottage,** West Newlands, Frosterley, Weardale, Co Durham DL13 2SH

Mrs Mary Watson
☎ 01388 527408
SC From £100–£200
Sleeps 5
🐕 🐓 ⛵ 🏕
🏌 🏌 🏌 *Commended*

Dales cottage on a working hill farm with magnificent views over the Wear Valley. We have Swaledale sheep, collie dogs, suckler cows and calves. Also private salmon and trout fishing on River Wear. Places of interest include Teesdale, Hadrian's Wall and Durham Cathedral. Electric heating, open fire and telephone. Open Apr–Nov.

FARM HOLIDAY BUREAU

Please mention **Stay on a Farm** when booking

15

England's North Country

Teesdale

Group Contact: *Mrs June Dent* ☎ *01833 640349*

Teesdale with its wealth of history and outstanding scenery lies south-west of Durham city. Its gentle dales and rolling moorland abound with features of geological and historical interest. The River Tees itself rises at Cross Fell and courses down the valley and includes the impressive 'High Force', England's highest waterfall with a dramatic 70ft drop over Great Whin Sill. Ancient stone quarries and disused lead mines in the upper dale mark industries dating back to Roman times and the many public footpaths in the dale include a magnificent scenic stretch of the well known Pennine Way.

Teesdale makes an excellent base for exploring the nearby Yorkshire Dales, the Roman wall, Northumberland and the Lake District, all of which are within an hour's drive. For the holidaymaker interested in castles and museums, there are plenty to choose from: Barnard Castle dating back to the 12th century, the famous French-style Bowes Museum and the historic Raby Castle, seat of Lord Barnard. A little further across the county is the now famous Beamish Open Air Museum and many other interesting places too numerous to list.

Visit Teesdale to discover its scenic beauty and historic sights for yourself.

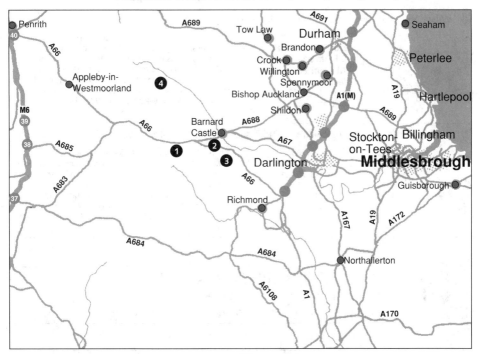

BED AND BREAKFAST

(and evening meal)

---

①   **East Mellwaters Farm,** Bowes, Barnard Castle, Co Durham DL12 9RH

Patricia Milner
☎ 01833 628269
🅑🅑 From £17.50–£18
EM From £10
Sleeps 10

🐕🐎✂🏕🏃🗨👜🚲 🛥

😊😊 *Commended*

Half a mile off the A66 you'll approach our farm over an attractive humpback bridge straddling the Greta with fishing and walks. You may well be greeted by the aroma of bread baking. You'll dine under oak beams by an open fire on fresh good homemade fare and then retire to our comfortable en suite rooms with TV, etc., to decide to explore on foot or by car our lovely area. Send for brochure for a break or holiday. Open mid Jan–mid Dec.

---

②   **West Roods,** West Roods Farm, Boldron, Barnard Castle, Co. Durham DL12 9SW

Mrs Margaret Lowson
☎ 01833 690116
🅑🅑 From £16
Sleeps 6

🐕🐎🚲
😊😊😊

The grey farmhouse with a stone roof is over a hundred years old. Pleasantly situated in green fields in the foothills of the Pennines, with a view of over 50 miles on a clear day. There are 3 Anglo-Saxon fields and a Roman well. One double and one family room with en suite facilities, one single. All have hairdryers, electric overblankets, colour TV, tea/coffee facilities, shoe cleaning equipment and CH. Our aim is to share the beauty which surrounds us. Open Mar–Oct.

---

③   **Wilson House,** Barningham, Richmond, North Yorkshire DL11 7EB

Mrs Helen Lowes
☎ 01833 621218
🅑🅑 From £15
EM From £8
Sleeps 6

🐕🏃🏃👶🕎
😊 *Commended*

475-acre working family farm in a picturesque and peaceful setting yet only 1 mile from A66. Ideally situated for touring Yorkshire or Durham Dales. Comfortable, spacious en suite bedrooms with colour TV and tea/coffee facilities. Kitchenette for guests' use equipped with fridge and microwave. Good home cooking with choice of menu. Children welcome. Open Mar–Nov.

---

④   **Wythes Hill Farm,** Lunedale, Middleton-in-Teesdale, Co Durham DL12 0NX

Mrs June Dent
☎ 01833 640349
🅑🅑 From £15–£16
EM From £7.50
Sleeps 6

🐕🏃🏃🏕
😊

Wythes Hill is a working stock-rearing farm with panoramic views from all rooms. Situated on the Pennine Way route with many picturesque walks in Teesdale. Visit the Bowes Museum, Raby Castle and High Force Waterfall. Good plain cooking. Two double bedrooms and one twin bedroom, all with H&C. All rooms with tea/coffee-making facilities. Lounge with coal fire. Open Mar–Nov.

FARM HOLIDAY BUREAU

LET THE TELEPHONE RING!

Some farmhouses are big places. Let the telephone ring long enough to give the owner time to answer it.

16

England's North Country

Cleveland and North Yorkshire Borders

Group Contacts: 🅱🅱 *Mrs P. Fanthorpe* ☎ *01642 710431*
🆂🅲 *Heather Addison* ☎ *01642 590121*

Cleveland & North Yorkshire is an Area of Outstanding Natural Beauty bordering the north-western edges of the North Yorkshire Moors, the largest expanse of heather moorland in England, familiar from the television series 'Heartbeat'. The name Cleveland comes from the Norse word 'Klifland' meaning land of cliffs and the picturesque Cleveland hills offer many good walks with spectacular views. The area gives its name to the 'Cleveland Way', the long distance walk from Helmsley to Filey, and also to the local breed of horse, the 'Cleveland Boy'.

Tucked beneath the northern edge of the moors lies Great Ayton where the famous explorer Captain Cook was educated and the 50ft monument on Easby Moor can be seen from miles around.

When staying on a farm in this area, tourists have access not only to the beauty of the moors and Yorkshire Dales but also to Teesside with its industry and commerce. Businessmen will be offered the warmth of Yorkshire hospitality within easy reach of Middlesbrough and Stockton.

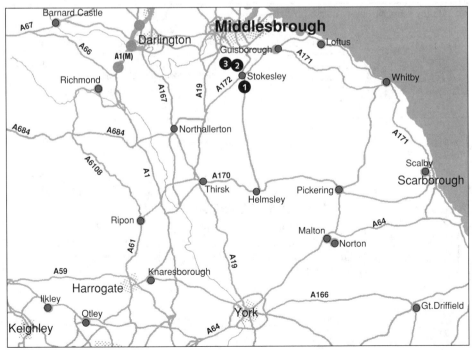

BED AND BREAKFAST

(and evening meal)

---

1 **Dromonby Hall Farm,** Busby Lane, Kirkby-in-Cleveland, Stokesley, Middlesbrough, Cleveland TS9 7AP

Mrs Patricia Weighell
☎ **01642 712312**
🛏 **From £15–£17.50**
EM From £8.50
Sleeps 6
🐕 (2) 🧊 ⅍ 🏇 🎪 🐾
🌸 *Commended*

Modern farmhouse on 170-acre working farm with superb views of Cleveland Hills. Ideal for walking or touring by car. Horse riding available. Easy access from A19, 8 miles south of Middlesbrough. ½ hr drive from coast and from Teesside. A warm welcome and good food. Enjoy the peace and beautiful surroundings. Open all year.

---

2 **Harker Hill,** Seamer, Stokesley, Nr Middlesbrough, North Yorkshire TS9 5NF

Mrs Pam Fanthorpe
☎ **01642 710431**
🛏 **From £15–£16**
EM From £6.50
Sleeps 6
🐕 🍴 ⅍ 🎪
Listed *Approved*

Harker Hill is a two hundred year old farm offering warmth and comfort. The cosy accommodation includes full central heating, log fires, lounge and television. Home cooked food is served at times to suit you so businessmen visiting Teesside can enjoy early cooked breakfasts and late evening meals. Open all year.

---

3 **Maltby Farm,** Maltby, Middlesbrough, Cleveland TS8 0BP

Clive & Heather Addison
☎ **01642 590121**
🛏 **From £15–£16**
EM From £8
Sleeps 6
🐕 (1) 🍴 ⅍
🌸 *Approved*

Welcome to our working farm which is over 200 years old and looks south onto the Cleveland Hills. Ideally situated on the edge of the North Yorkshire Moors and Captain Cook Country. Within easy distance of the coast or pretty market towns of Stokesley and Yarm. Open Apr–Nov.

FARM HOLIDAY BUREAU

THE 1000+ BUREAU MEMBERS OFFER A UNIQUE LINK TO CUSTOMERS ACROSS THE UK

All Bureau members belong to a local Group. Each member can refer you to an equally high quality member within his Group… or across the UK: England, Northern Ireland, Scotland, Wales.

17

England's North Country

North Pennines

Group Contact: *Pat Dent* ☎ *01434 381383*

The North Pennines – Area of Outstanding Natural Beauty – is truly 'England's Last Wilderness'.

The upland moors and valleys of Cumbria, Durham and Northumberland are encompassed by this area of remote moorland, famed for wild flowers and birds.

Three famous rivers rise here, the Tyne, the Tees and the Wear, fast-flowing streams growing to mighty torrents. In Teesdale, High Force shows the power of the water as does the river Wear harnessed by the lead miners at Killhope Wheel.

Landscapes have been formed by generations of hill farmers, a patchwork separated by stone walls and grazed by sheep and cattle, with heather moors and, from long ago, the remains of Roman occupation.

This area is criss-crossed with footpaths, the most well known being the Pennine Way, but there is something for everyone, from the gentle stroll to the energetic journey to the top of Cross Fell at 2,930 ft. The scenery is varied, with many panoramic views and a different scene around every corner.

Alston with its narrow cobbled street and market cross nestles amongst these hills, as do Allendale town where New Year is celebrated with a procession of blazing tar barrels. St John's Chapel, host to one of the many agricultural shows held in this area. Stanhope boasts a fossilised tree. Nearby are the market towns of Barnard Castle, Appleby, Hexham and Penrith.

Easily accessible, yet far from the hustle and bustle of modern life, this area is excellent for touring, but most people find that once here, they do not want to leave.

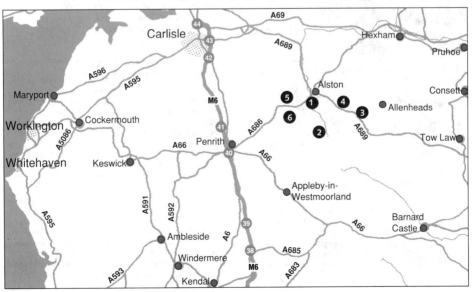

BED AND BREAKFAST

(and evening meal)

---

(1) Bridge End Farm, Alston, Cumbria CA9 3BJ

Carolyn Williams
☎ 01434 381261
🛏 From £14.50–£17
EM From £8.50
Sleeps 4
🐕🐈🐴🏕🛆
Listed

Relax at our tastefully furnished 18th century farmhouse. Home cooking with generous breakfast. Guests' own lounge with colour TV and open fire, all rooms centrally heated. 2 double rooms, 1 en suite. Ideal base for exploring the Lakes, Hadrian's Wall, Eden Valley or walking the Pennine Way. Good discount for children under 14. Open all year.

---

(2) Ivy House Farm, Garrigill, Alston, Cumbria CA9 3DU

Helen Dent
☎ 01434 382079
🛏 From £13–£15
EM From £8
Sleeps 5
🛆🐕🏕🛆
Listed *Commended*

A warm welcome awaits you when you visit our 256-acre hill farm with grazing cattle and sheep. Situated in the picturesque village of Garrigill on the Pennine Way. Ideal for walking/touring – our 17th century llisted farmhouse has 2 bedrooms with handbasins and tea making facilities. Good farmhouse breakfast and excellent food available in village. Open all year (closed Christmas & April).

---

(3) Lands Farm, Westgate-in-Weardale, Co Durham DL13 1SN

Mrs Barbara Reed
☎ 01388 517210
🛏 From £17–£18
Sleeps 5
🛆🏕
🌿🌿 *Highly Commended*

A friendly welcome awaits you on our 280 acre beef and sheep farm peacefully situated in beautiful Weardale. All bedrooms have luxury en suite facilities, TV and tea/coffee. Conveniently located for Durham City, Beamish Museum, Hadrian's Wall, High Force and walking in the North Pennines. Open Easter–Oct.

---

(4) Low Cornriggs Farm, Cowshill-in-Weardale, Bishop Auckland, Co Durham DL13 1AQ

Mrs Janet Ellis
☎ 01388 537600
🛏 From £17.50–£18
EM From £9
Sleeps 6
🐕🐈🐴🏕🛆
🌿🌿

Low Cornriggs has wonderful views over the High Pennines, a luxury farmhouse with en suite rooms, double and twin. Electric blankets, tea trays. Log fires, full central heating, warm and cosy. Beamed ceilings, pine doors and furniture – a real old world place with a warm welcome for every guest. Horse riding centre and good walks as we are on the Weardale way. Easy reach of Alston, Hexham and Durham on the A689. Open all year.

---

(5) Middle Bayles Farm, Alston, Cumbria CA9 3BS

Mrs Pat Dent
☎ 01434 381383
🛏 From £14.50–£17
EM £9
Sleeps 6
🛆🐕🏕🛆
🌿🌿 *Commended*

A 300-acre hill farm with cattle and sheep where visitors are welcome to wander. Ideal walking/touring area. Warm, comfortable 17th century farmhouse, tastefully furnished, with superb views overlooking South Tyne Valley. 1 double/ twin and 1 family room, both en suite, electric blankets. Tea-making facilities, full CH. Good home cooking including our own bread, warm welcome. Reductions under 14s. Closed Christmas & April.

SELF-CATERING

Ghyll Burn Cottage, Hartside Nursery Garden, Nr Alston, Cumbria CA9 3BL

Mrs Susan Huntley
☎ **01434 381372/381428**
▥ **From £138–£310**
Sleeps 4/6 + cot
🐎 🐕 ♿ ⛲ 💼 ✂
🐾 🐾 🐾 *Commended*

Recently renovated farm buildings dating back to 1630 offer spacious and comfortable accommodation for 4/6 people. Kitchen/diner, large lounge with oak beams and wood burning stove on first floor. Attractive twin and double bedrooms, bathroom, are downstairs. Full gas central heating. The cottage is set in a secluded valley with small nursery garden. Ideal for bird wildlife and gardening enthusiasts. Open all year.

DISABLED VISITORS

Many members offer a welcome to disabled/less able visitors. Please do check the extent of the facilities before booking.

FOLLOW THE COUNTRY CODE

Leave nothing but footprints,
Take nothing but photographs,
Kill nothing but time!

England's North Country

Eden Valley & North Pennines

Group Contacts: 🕮 *Ruth Tuer* ☎/*Fax 01931 715205*
🅂🄲 *Anne Ivinson* ☎ *016974 76230(24hr answerphone/Fax 76523)*

The River Eden rises in Mallerstang, an isolated corner of the old County of Westmorland, and, rushing through the alpine flowers of the still untamed North Pennines, gradually descends, gathering strength from its many tributaries, until it reaches Appleby, a sleepy market town straddling the Eden. The broad tree lined street linking the Castle and the Church make it one of the liveliest towns in the valley. For two weeks every year Appleby awakes from its slumber to host the largest gipsy gathering and horse fair in the country, a sight not to be missed!

On to the attractive town of Penrith, Gateway to the Lakes, a focus for travellers since Roman times the Eden meanders through picturesque villages built of local red sandstone until it reaches the historic City of Carlisle and the Solway Plain. This area is truly a 'Garden of Eden' with its lush vegetation and wide variety of wild life. The visitor can enjoy a variety of walks, climbing Cross Fell or Wild Boar Fell in the Pennines or take an easier route along one of the many woodland and riverside footpaths signposted through the area.

For the less energetic there are tours around historic houses and sites travelling on the local minibus, the Fellrunner and last but by no means least, the famous Carlisle to Settle railway runs right through Eden with stations at Armathwaite, Lazonby, Langwathby and Appleby: what better way to enjoy the magnificent scenery of the Eden Valley and the North Pennines?

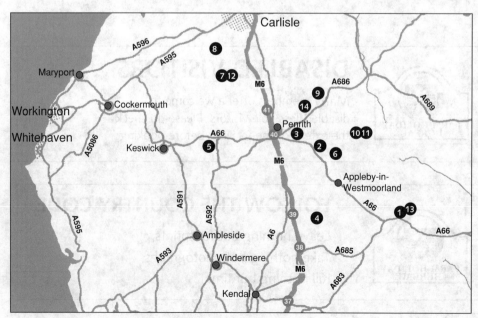

BED AND BREAKFAST

(and evening meal)

Augill House Farm, Brough, Kirkby Stephen, Cumbria CA17 4DX

Jeanette Atkinson
☎ 017683 41305
[BB] From £18–£20
EM From £8
Sleeps 6
✄ ⚓ ☺ (12)
☕ ☕ *Highly Commended*

Enjoy super breakfasts and delicious 4 course dinners served in our lovely conservatory overlooking the garden. Double and twin en suite bedrooms with colour TV, tea and coffee-making facilities. Ideal for the Lakes, Dales and North Pennines. RAC highly acclaimed. AA. QQQ. Closed Christmas and New Year.

Bridge End Farm, Kirkby Thore, Penrith, Cumbria CA10 1UZ

Mrs Yvonne Dent
☎ 01768 361362
[BB] From £16–£18
EM From £8.50
Sleeps 6
✄ ⚓ ☺ ⚘
Applied

Relax in 18th century farmhouse on a dairy farm in the Eden Valley near Appleby. Spacious antique furnished en suite rooms overlooking Pennine Hills. Interesting craftwork. Open fire in guests' lounge. Delicious homemade breakfast: teas and dinners served in dining room. Finish with lovely evening walk along the River Eden. Open all year except Christmas.

Hornby Hall, Brougham, Penrith, Cumbria

Julie Langcake
☎ 01768 891114
0831 482108
[BB] From £18–£28
EM from £13.50
Sleeps 8
☺ ⚓ ⚙ ⚘ ☂ ▪
Applied

16th century farmhouse situated three miles from Penrith, one mile off A66 in tranquillity of Eden Valley. Two en suite, three double, two single rooms. Evening meals served in original Hall. All food freshly cooked from local produce. Trout fishing available on River Eamont. River paths are a profusion of wild flowers. Open all year except Christmas.

Meaburn Hill Farm, Maulds Meaburn, Penrith, Cumbria CA10 3HN

Ruth Tuer
☎/Fax 01931 715205
[BB] From £19–£22
EM from £10
Sleeps 6
⚑ ⚓ ✄ ☺ ⚘ ☂ ▪
Listed Highly Commended

Relax at our beautifully restored 16th century farmhouse, quietly situated in a hidden valley near Appleby. Lovely antique furnished rooms overlooking tranquil river and village green. 2 double rooms and 1 twin room, all with private facilities. Enjoy an award-winning farmhouse breakfast or afternoon tea beside a roaring fire. Explore nearby lakes & dales or roam the quiet footpaths & bridleways around our 200 acre beef and sheep farm. Open Easter–Dec.

Park House Farm, Dalemain, Penrith, Cumbria CA11 0HB

Mrs Mary Milburn
☎ 017684 86212
[BB] From £14–£17
Sleeps 6
☺ ☂
☕

Peace and tranquillity in our valley – you can relax and enjoy stunning views of Lakeland fells. 3 miles from Lake Ullswater or M6 (J40) on A592 entering via Dalemain Mansion ignoring the 'no cars' sign. Cumbrian hospitality is assured with a welcome cup, home baking and generous breakfast. Evening meals available locally. 2 family bedrooms (1 en suite), electric blanket, heater, tea/coffee facilities. Bathroom and shower room. TV lounge with open fire. Open Apr–Oct.

6 Slakes Farm, Milburn, Appleby in Westmorland, Cumbria CA16 6DP

Mrs C Braithwaite
☎ 017683 61385
🅱 From £11–£12
EM from £7
Sleeps 6
🐾 ⛄
Applied

Slakes Farm was built in 1734 and is situated between the villages of Milburn and Knock 6 miles from Appleby. The farm is approx 40 acres rearing cattle and sheep. It makes an ideal base for walking and touring, returning to good farmhouse cooking using fresh local produce. Open Easter–Oct.

---

7 Streethead Farm, Ivegill, Carlisle, Cumbria CA4 0NG

Mrs J Wilson
☎ 016974 73327
🅱 From £16–£20
Sleeps 4
⛄ (7) 🍴 ■
Listed

Stroll by our ornamental waterfowl ponds. Relax in an antique-filled TV lounge with woodburner. Sleep in spacious bedrooms, one en suite, one with own bathroom, both hospitality trays, electric blankets. Excellent local eating places. Choice of breakfasts with homemade preserves. Lakes, Scotland, M6 J41/42 close by. Unsuitable for children under 7yrs and dogs. Brochure with pleasure. Open Mar–Nov.

SELF-CATERING

8 Green View Lodges & Well Cottage, Green View, Welton, Nr Dalston, Carlisle, Cumbria CA5 7ES

Anne Ivinson
☎ 016974 76230
Fax 016974 76523
🆂🅲 From £137–£440
Sleeps 2/7
🄯 🐾 ♿ ⛄ ☆ ☏ ■
🔑 🔑 🔑 🔑 – 🔑 🔑 🔑 🔑 🔑
Up to Highly Commended

Superb Scandinavian lodges, surprisingly spacious in peaceful garden setting. 17th century oak-beamed cottages, 1 with open fire, also a tastefully converted Wesleyan chapel for 2. Own gardens. In tiny, picturesque hamlet with unspoilt views to Caldbeck Fells 3 miles. Every home comfort provided for a relaxing country holiday. CH, telephones. Within ½ hr's drive of Keswick, Lake Ullswater or Gretna Green. Golf 5 miles, fishing 3 miles. Open all year.

---

9 Homelea, c/o Croft House, Gamblesby, Penrith, Cumbria CA10 1HR

Margaret Purdham
☎ 01768 881293
🆂🅲 From £170–£320
Sleeps 6/8
⛄ 🐾
🔑 🔑 🔑 🔑 *Commended*

A very comfortable, well equipped, modern bungalow on a working mixed dairy farm. Central heating run from open fire, fuel provided. Gas cooker. Phone for incoming calls. Double bed settee in lounge. Enjoys magnificent panoramic views of the surrounding high fells. Good touring base for the Eden Valley, Lake District, Hadrian's Wall, Scottish Borders. Short breaks available low season. Brochure. Open all year.

---

10 Skirwith Hall Cottage, Skirwith Hall, Skirwith, Penrith, Cumbria CA10 1RH

Mrs Laura Wilson
☎ 01768 88241
🆂🅲 From £150–£320
Sleeps 4–9
🐾 ⛄ ■
🔑 🔑 🔑 🔑 *Approved*

Georgian farmhouse wing built of local red sandstone overlooking large pleasant garden and stream on 400-acre mixed dairy farm. Exposed beams and open fire in lounge, nightstore heaters, washing machine, colour TV. Two double rooms and one with twin beds and bunks. Cot and high chair. Handy for Lakes or north Pennines. Ideal fishing, walking or simply enjoying idyllic rural surroundings. Open all year, short breaks available in low season.

Smithy Cottage, c/o Skirwith Hall, Skirwith, Penrith, Cumbria CA10 1RH

Mrs Laura Wilson
☎ 01768 88241
🆂 From £92–£240
Sleeps 4
🐴 🐕 🏠
🔑 🔑 🔑 Commended

Originally the home of the village blacksmith. Situated on the outskirts of an unspoilt village in the shadow of Crossfell. Equipped to a high standard, 1 twin bedded and 1 double room. Nightstore heaters and open fire (coal provided). Colour TV, telephone, washing machine. Shop 2 miles. Handy for Lakes, Yorkshire Dales and Scottish Borders. Golf, riding, fishing nearby. Ideal fell walking, birdwatching or touring. Open all year.

Stable Cottage, Streethead Farm, Ivegill, Carlisle, Cumbria CA4 0NG

Mrs J. Wilson
☎ 016974 73327
🆂 From £150–£250
Sleeps 4
🐕 (12) 🐴
🔑 🔑 🔑 🔑 Commended

We invite you to our mixed farm. Watch sunsets over distant hills. Our hobby is ornamental waterfowl which can be viewed from upstairs lounge, the former hayloft with open beams, wood panelling, sandstone walls and cosy woodburner. Kitchen downstairs has a dishwasher, microwave, washing machine, dryer. Lakes and Scotland close by. Brochure with colour photos. Open all year.

Swallows Barn, Augill House Farm, Brough, Kirkby Stephen, Cumbria CA17 4DX (13)

Jeanette Atkinson
☎ 017683 41305
🆂 From £100–£300
Sleeps 5
🐕 (12)
🔑 🔑 🔑 🔑 Commended

This super cottage situated on our working farm is a dream. Two double bedrooms with colour TV and two bathrooms, large lounge with open fire and colour TV, modern kitchen, all electric, dishwasher, microwave, etc. Lovely conservatory. Also one bedroomed flat. Both properties have CH and DG. We are handy for the Lakes, Dales and Northern Pennines. Open all year.

West View Cottages, West View Farm, Winskill, Penrith, Cumbria CA10 1PD (14)

Alan and Susan Grave
☎ 01768 881356
🆂 From £115–£250
Sleeps 2–5
🐕 🐴
🔑 🔑 🔑 🔑 Commended

A roomy cottage and 2 barn conversions on a mixed working farm. All units have central heating, TV, modern kitchen, washing facilities, and linen provided. Ideally situated for touring and within easy reach of the lakes, North Pennines and Scotland. Local facilities include children's play area, open air swimming pool, walking. Sleeps 2/4/5. Short breaks available in low season. Brochure sent on request. Open all year.

19

England's North Country
Central Lakeland

Group Contact: *Margaret Beaty* ☎ *017687 78278*

Stay on a farm in the heart of Cumbria and enjoy the peace and quiet of our valleys. Central Lakeland, with its mountains, lakes and woods is well-known and loved.

For over 200 years travellers have come to this most beautiful corner of England to walk the fells and wander the by-ways. Wonderful at any time of year, certainly in the spring, definitely in the autumn, this is the ideal base for touring.

The Keswick area offers the Pencil Museum, home of the first pencil; the Druid's Stone Circle; Lingholm Gardens; Mirehouse, built 1666, and the 10th century Church of St Bega nearby; or England's only mountain forest park at Whinlatter.

In Grasmere, there are Heaton Coopers Studio and 'Dove Cottage', William Wordsworth's home, now an award winning museum. Ambleside has Hayes marvellous garden centre. See the Beatrix Potter exhibition at Bowness, gallery at Hawkshead or her home 'Hill Top', at Near Sawrey.

Attend local shows, see local crafts, Cumberland wrestling, fell running and hound trailing.

We warmly welcome you to our homely, comfortable and traditional farmhouses.

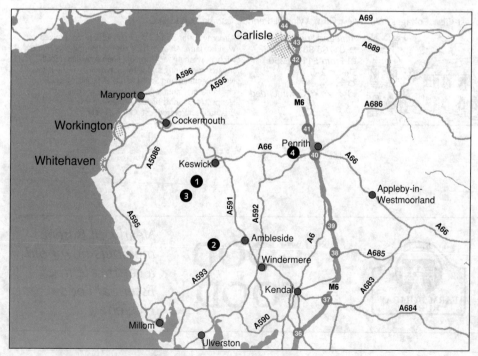

BED AND BREAKFAST

(and evening meal)

Birkrigg Farm, Newlands, Keswick, Cumbria CA12 5TS

M M Beaty
☎ 017687 78278
[BB] From £14–£15
Sleeps 12
🛏 ✂
Listed

Birkrigg is a dairy and sheep farm very pleasantly situated with excellent outlook in the peaceful Newlands Valley, 5 miles from Keswick. Surrounded by mountains, this is an ideal place to walk and climb. Central for touring. Clean, comfortable accommodation. The breakfasts are good too! Meals available at inns nearby. Packed lunches provided. Open Mar–Dec.

Fell Foot Farm, Little Langdale, Ambleside, Cumbria LA22 9PE

Mrs S. Harryman
☎ 015394 37294
[BB] From £14–£17.50
EM From £8.50
Sleeps 6
🛏(10) 🍴 ⊞ 🐾 🌳
Listed

Nestling at the foot of the famous Wrynose Pass, this 17th century farmhouse was once a coaching Inn. Owned by the National Trust, it contains fine oak beams and panelling. The house offers warm, comfortable accommodation with beautiful views and excellent home cooking. Three rooms, 1 en suite, tea/coffee-making facilities. Open Easter–Nov.

Keskadale Farm, Newlands, Keswick, Cumbria CA12 5TS

Mrs M Harryman
☎ 017687 78544
[BB] From £14–£16
Sleeps 6
🛏 🍴 ✂ 🌳 🧳
Listed

A working farm pleasantly situated at the head of the Newlands Valley, 6 miles from Keswick, 2½ miles from Buttermere. Traditional Lakeland farmhouse with all home comforts. Relax by real open fire on chilly evenings, colour TV. All rooms with central heating, H & C, tea/coffee-making facilities. Magnificent views. Ideal for walking or touring base. Packed lunch available. A warm welcome awaits you. Open Mar–Dec.

Tymparon Hall, Newbiggin, Stainton, Penrith, Cumbria CA11 0HS

Mrs Margaret Taylor
☎ 017684 83236
[BB] From £17–£20
EM From £10
Sleeps 9
⊞ 🐾 🌳
🌼🌼 Commended

A spacious farmhouse and large garden situated on a 150 acre sheep farm in a peaceful rural area. Good home cooking. Tea/coffee-making facilities, electric blankets in bedrooms. Open fire in lounge. Lake Ullswater 10 minutes away. Reduction for under 12s; no charge for cot. 4 miles from M6 (jct.40). Open March–Oct.

LET THE TELEPHONE RING!

Some farmhouses are big places. Let the telephone ring long enough to give the owner time to answer it.

20

England's North Country

West Lakeland

Group Contact: *Mrs Carolyn Heslop* ☎ *01900 824222*

Our hospitality and the warmth of our welcome are renowned. If it is home comforts and peace and tranquillity you are after, then this is the place for you.

To most people the Lakes begin and end at Windermere but just venture a little further and you will discover a whole new experience. See the Border City of Carlisle with its chequered history of Romans, Picts and Scots, or the wild, untamed fells of Wasdale. View the hunting grounds of John Peel at Caldbeck, walk around Cockermouth, home of John Dalton, Fletcher Christian and William Wordsworth. Visit Whitehaven, the site of the last invasion of Britain by John Paul Jones, founder of the American Navy. Take the whole family for a ride on 'laal ratty', the miniature steam railway at Ravenglass. Trace the footsteps of the 'Maid of Buttermere' with the help of Melvyn Bragg, son of Wigton, or take the road to the future and spend a day at the British Nuclear Fuels Exhibition Centre at Sellafield. The energetic may like to discover the secrets of our lakes – Ennerdale, Crummock and Buttermere – and enjoy walking, boating, sea, river or lake fishing.

We are the ideal base for touring anywhere in Cumbria – then it's home to the relaxing atmosphere of your friendly farmhouse hosts.

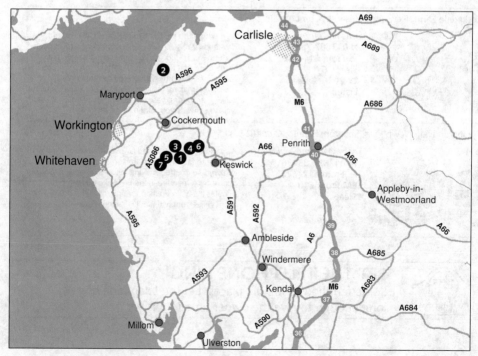

BED AND BREAKFAST

(and evening meal)

Cragend Farm, Rogerscale, Cockermouth, Cumbria CA13 0RG

Mrs Margaret Ann Steel
☎ 01900 85658
🛏 From £16
EM From £8
Sleeps 4–6
Listed

Friendly family farmhouse accommodation in comfortable old oak-beamed house dated 1732. Log fire in separate lounge. Good home cooking in guests' own dining room. We are a 250-acre farm looking up Lorton Valley. 4 bedrooms with handbasins, 2 bathrooms (1 with shower), 2 toilets. Easy reach of the Lakes. Open Mar–Nov.

East Farm, Crosscanonby, Maryport, Cumbria CA15 6SJ

Mrs Barbara Carruthers
☎ 01900 812153
🛏 From £14–£15
Sleeps 6
🐎 (2) 🧳
Listed

Welcome to our 236-acre dairy farm on the fringe of the Lake District situated between Maryport and Allonby with beautiful views over the Solway Firth to Scotland. Golf course, windsurfing, pony rides and leisure centre with swimming pool nearby. TV lounge, tea-making facilities, central heating and traditional farmhouse breakfast. Open all year.

High Stanger Farm, Cockermouth, Cumbria CA13 9TS

Alison Hewitson
☎ 01900 823875
🛏 From £15
Sleeps 4
🐎 🐕 🦌
Listed

A warm welcome to our 17th century farmhouse in the beautiful Lorton Valley, with breathtaking views of the fells. A comfortable lounge with log fire, spacious bedrooms, good cooking in a pleasant dining room. Activities to suit everyone within easy reach. In fact everything for the perfect family holiday. Very quiet location. Special rates for children.

Jenkin Farm, Embleton, Cockermouth, Cumbria CA13 9TN

Mrs Margaret Teasdale
☎ 017687 76387
🛏 From £15
Sleeps 4
🐎 ⚮
👑

A warm welcome awaits you at "Jenkin" our family-run working hill farm situated on a quiet hillside with magnificant views. 3 miles from Cockermouth, 10 miles from Keswick. Two oak beamed bedrooms both with handbasin and tea-making facilities. Guests' own lounge with colour TV and open fire. Non-smoking. Sorry no pets.

Stanger Farm, Cockermouth, Cumbria CA13 9TS

Mrs Carolyn Heslop
☎ 01900 824222
🛏 From £14–£15.50
Sleeps 4
🐎 🐕 🦌 🧳
👑

At the entrance to the magnificent Lorton and Buttermere valleys lies Stanger Farm with its sheep, cows, cats, dogs, beautiful walks, a river to fish in and much more. Bedrooms are centrally heated with tea-making facilities and there are separate dining room and lounge with log fires. A traditional farmhouse breakfast and good old-fashioned hospitality await you. Open all year except Christmas.

SELF-CATERING

---

6   **Jenkin Farm Cottage,** Embleton, Cockermouth, Cumbria CA13 9TN

Mrs Margaret Teasdale
☎ 017687 76387
SC From £220–£350
Sleeps 6
🐕 ✄
🏵 🏵 🏵 🏵 *Commended*

Jenkin Cottage has a spectacular outlook over open countryside extending to the Solway Firth and Scottish Lowlands. We are a working family hill farm in a beautiful quiet part of the Lake District. The cottage is fully equipped with all fuel, bed linen, towels provided. Open fire. Ideal base for fell walking or touring the Lakes by car. Sorry no pets. Open all year.

---

7   **The Stable,** Stranger Farm, Cockermouth, Cumbria CA13 9TS

Mrs Carolyn Heslop
☎ 01900 824222
SC From £150-£300
Sleeps 4
🐕 🏹 🐾 🎪 🛏 📱
🏵 🏵 🏵 🏵 *Commended*

Set amidst magnificent fell views this is an ideal base for exploring the whole of the Lake District. The Stable is a recently converted 17th century barn adjoining the farmhouse. The open plan lounge with log fire and dining and fully equipped kitchen areas are "upstairs" to benefit from view across the River Cocker and open fields. Fishing, central heating, logs, bed linen all included. Open all year.

FARM HOLIDAY BUREAU

FOLLOW THE COUNTRY CODE

Leave nothing but footprints,
Take nothing but photographs,
Kill nothing but time!

FARM HOLIDAY BUREAU

THOSE LITTLE EXTRAS

For advice on farms that can offer 'extras' such as four-poster beds, special diets, farm trails, fishing rights – even stabling and trekking arrangements if you are bringing your own horse – ring the Farm Holiday Bureau on (01203) 696909.

21

England's North Country

South Lakeland

Group Contact: *Mrs Olive Simpson* ☎ *01539 823682*

Find true country hospitality on a farm in this most beautiful corner of England. South Lakeland centres on the town of Kendal, which, in time, has developed into the focal point of the local community and the 'southern gateway' to the Lake District.

There's plenty to do – you can visit the award-winning Abbot Hall art gallery and Museums of Lakeland Life and Industry and Natural History and Archeology – or even the 'K' shoe factory and shop! There are also many National Trust properties and, especially for the children, the new Beatrix Potter exhibition!

If you're feeling active, Windermere and Bowness – where you can stroll by the lakeside, take a cruise on the 'Teal' or 'Swan', or ride on the steam train to Haverthwaite – are only a few minutes drive away. The fell walking is great too – whether in the valleys of Longsleddale or Kentmere, or on Scout Scar.

The seasons come and go in South Lakeland. Springtime here is a photographer's delight, with rhododendrons, azaleas, and daffodils – so immortalised by Wordsworth – while new-born lambs frolic in the pastures. Yet in autumn, the rich golds of the bracken and leaves contrast with the blue sky – a sightseer's delight.

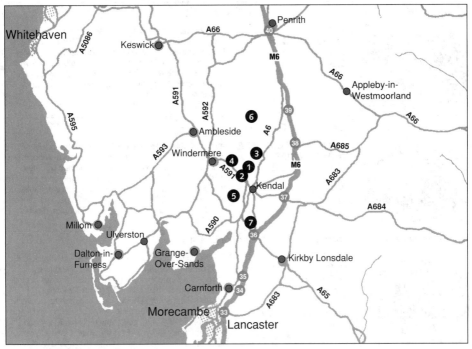

BED AND BREAKFAST
(and evening meal)

---

① Garnett House Farm, Burneside, Kendal, Cumbria LA9 5SF

Mrs Sylvia Beaty
☎ 01539 724542
BB From £13
EM From £7
Sleeps 10

AA/RAC acclaimed 15th century farmhouse, just ½ mile from A591 Windermere Road, village inn, shops and public transport. Bedrooms have colour TV, washbasins and tea-making facilities, most en suite. Oak panelled lounge, dining room with choice for breakfast and 5 course dinners. Lovely views of our countryside. Easy to find and safe parking. Open all year.

---

② Gateside Farm, Windermere Road, Kendal, Cumbria LA9 5SE

Mrs June Ellis
☎ 01539 722036
BB From £15
EM £7.50
Sleeps 10

Listed *Commended*

AA/RAC acclaimed. Traditional Lakeland farm, 2 miles north of Kendal on A591 main tourist route through Lakes. Easily accessible from M6 (jct 36). Ideally situated for touring all Lakes and Yorkshire Dales. All bedrooms have colour TV, tea/coffee-making facilities and heating, some en suite. Short or weekly stays welcome. Good home cooked breakfasts and evening meals served at separate tables. Good parking facilities. Open all year (closed Christmas and New Year).

---

③ Riverbank House, Garnett Bridge, Kendal, Cumbria LA8 9AZ

Julia Thorn
☎ 01539 823254
BB From £14–£15
Sleeps 6

🐾 *Commended*

Lovely Victorian family-built house situated at the foot of the beautiful Longsleddale Valley with 20 acres of pasture land. Bordered by river providing private fishing. 4 miles from Kendal. ½ mile off A6. Comfortable bedrooms with handbasins and tea/coffee-making facilities. Guests' sitting room, TV, log fire, background CH. Excellent breakfasts.

---

④ Stock Bridge Farm, Staveley, Kendal, Cumbria LA8 9LP

Mrs Betty Fishwick
☎ 01539 821580
BB From £14–£15
Sleeps 11

Listed

A comfortable, modernised 17th century farmhouse on edge of bypassed village just off A591 Kendal-Windermere road, 15 minutes M6 (jct 36). All bedrooms have fitted washbasins and shaver points, bath/shower room, separate WC. Fire certificate. Full central heating. Separate tables, English breakfast, bedtime drink. Friendly, personal service. Good parking facilities. On Dalesway Footpath. Open Mar–Oct.

---

⑤ Tranthwaite Hall, Underbarrow, Nr Kendal, Cumbria LA8 8HG

Mrs D Swindlehurst
☎ 015395 68285
BB From £16
Sleeps 4

Listed *Commended*

This magnificent olde worlde farmhouse dates back to the 11th century. Beautiful oak beams, doors and rare antique fire range. Tastefully modernised with full central heating, en suite now available, colour TV lounge, separate dining room. This dairy/sheep farm has an idyllic setting in a small, picturesque village between Kendal and Windermere. Walking, golf, pony trekking. Many good pubs and inns nearby. SAE for brochure. Open all year.

SELF-CATERING

High Swinklebank Farm, Longsleddale, Nr Kendal, Cumbria LA8 9BD 6

Mrs Olive Simpson
☎ 01539 823682
SC From £100–£185
Sleeps 4
Commended

High Swinklebank is near the head of the beautiful Longsleddale Valley with lovely views and walking. A recent conversion which is well appointed includes fitted carpets throughout. Comprising lounge with electric fire, bed settee, TV, lovely kitchen, shower room, 2 bedrooms – double and bunk. Children welcome . Linen provided. Weekends available. Cleanliness and personal attention assured. Open all year.

Preston Patrick Hall Cottage, Preston Patrick Hall, Milnthorpe, Cumbria LA7 7NY 7

Stephen & Jennifer Armitage
☎ 015395 67200
SC From £100–£265
Sleeps 2/6
Commended

Cosy wing of 14th century farmhouse near Crooklands, ideal centre for Lakes and Dales. Oak beamed rooms tastefully modernised to sleep 2 or 3 (further bedroom sleeping 3 optional extra). Fitted kitchen with dishwasher and fridge. Sitting room with log fire and colour TV. Bedroom with antique brass beds and additional 2′ 6″ bed (linen, electric blankets and cot available). Use of swimming pool and table tennis table. Brochure available. Open all year.

FARM HOLIDAY BUREAU

DISABLED VISITORS

Many members offer a welcome to disabled/less able visitors. Please do check the extent of the facilities before booking.

22

England's North Country

Yorkshire Dales and Brontë Country

Group Contact: *Anne Pearson* ☎ *01756 791579*

This beautiful region extends from picturesque Kettlewell in the north of the Dales down to Bradford in the south with the National Photographic Museum, the recently refurbished Alhambra Theatre and Mill Shops to explore. Those keen to do their exploring on foot will head for the footpaths in and around the National Park, the Pennine Way and the Dales with their lovely valleys, deep woods, clear streams and waterfalls.

For history and heritage the Brontë Parsonage at Haworth, Harwood House and Skipton with its castle and enchanting Tudor courtyard are a must, as are the semi-ruined abbeys at Bolton and Fountains (reputed to be the most beautiful and certainly the largest of the ruined abbeys in Britain). For a real touch of nostalgia take a ride on the Keighley and Worth Valley or the Yorkshire Dales Railways, or visit Five Rise Locks on the Leeds/Liverpool Canal near Bingley.

Or simply enjoy the beautiful Dales and their villages – Kettlewell, Burnsall, Lothersdale or Malham with its Cove, limestone 'pavements' and Gordale Scar, a ravine with a magnificent succession of waterfalls.

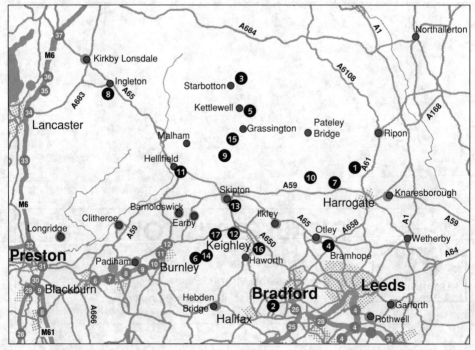

BED AND BREAKFAST
(and evening meal)

Bowes Green Farm, Bishop Thornton, Ripley, Harrogate, North Yorkshire HG3 3JX

Mrs Bridget Sowray
☎ 01423 770114
▣ From £18–£20
EM From £10
Sleeps 6
ⓢ (12) ✂ ☂
☙☙ *Highly Commended*

17th century Grade II listed secluded farmhouse in the midst of the Yorkshire Dales on a 350-acre mixed farm once farmed by the monks of nearby Fountains Abbey. Large rose garden. Tea/coffee facilities in all rooms, one en suite. Large luxury guest bathroom with bath and separate shower. Colour TV lounge. Dining room with separate tables. Fresh farm produce cooked on the Aga. Open Easter–Oct.

Brow Top Farm, Baldwin Lane, Clayton, Bradford, West Yorkshire BD14 6PS

Margaret Priestley
☎ 01274 882178
▣ From £15–£20
Sleeps 4
ⓢ £
☙☙ *Highly Commended*

Visitors are most welcome to our family dairy and beef farm. The farmhouse has recently been modernised to a very high standard with central heating throughout. 1 double, 1 twin and 1 family room all with private bathroom, colour TV and tea/coffee-making facilities. Conveniently situated for visiting the Dales and Brontë Country. Plenty of good eating places in the area. Open all year (closed Christmas).

Bushey Lodge Farm, Starbotton, Skipton, North Yorkshire BD23 5HY

Rosie Lister
☎ 01756 760424
▣ From £18
Sleeps 4
ⓢ (8) ✕ ✂ ☂
☙☙ *Commended*

Traditional Dales farmhouse in quiet position in Upper Wharfedale village, with extensive views along the valley, much of which is owned and protected by the National Trust. Superb walking and sightseeing area. Local inns provide excellent evening meals. Each bedroom has en suite bathroom, TV, and tea/coffee-making facilities. Open all year except Christmas.

The Cottages, Moor Road, Bramhope, Leeds, West Yorkshire LS16 9HH

Sue & David Adams
☎ 0113 2842754
▣ From £20
Sleeps 10
ⓢ (10) ✂ ■
☙☙ *Highly Commended*

Welcome to 'The Cottages' which has been renovated to a high standard with 5 en suite bedrooms, all with colour TV and tea/coffee-making facilities. Guests' lounge with TV and open fire on chilly nights. Central heating throughout. Excellent base for business or holiday – within easy reach of Leeds, Harrogate, Otley, Airport and the Dales. Open all year except Christmas.

Fold Farm, Kettlewell, Skipton, North Yorkshire BD23 5RH ⑤

Barbara Lambert
☎ 01756 760886
Fax 01756 760464
▣ From £17–£19.50
Sleeps 6
ⓢ (10) ☂ ✂
☙☙ *Highly Commended*

Fold Farm is a hill sheep farm situated in a quiet backwater of Kettlewell, within easy walking distance of all village amenities. The house dates back to the 15th century and some of its original beams are still in evidence. There are tea-making facilities in all bedrooms, each of which has a private bathroom and TV, and there is a separate guests' sitting room. Open Apr–Oct.

---

6   **Hole Farm,** Dimples Lane, Haworth, Bradford, West Yorkshire BD22 8QS

Janet Milner
☎ 01535 644755
BB From £17
Sleeps 4
☒ (10) ♨ ⚱
♛♛ *Commended*

17th century farmhouse, on 8 acre small holding 5 minutes walk from Brontë Parsonage and 2 minutes from the moors. Two double en suite rooms, central heating, colour TV, tea/coffee-making facilities. Full English breakfast. Have your breakfast watching the peacocks on the lawn. Open all year.

7   **Knabbs Ash,** Skipton Road, Felliscliffe, Nr Harrogate, North Yorkshire HG3 2LT

Sheila Smith
☎ 01423 771040
Fax 01423 771515
BB From £19–£20
Sleeps 6
☒ (10) ⚱ ♨ ■
♛♛ *Highly Commended*

Knabbs Ash is a smallholding situated 6 miles west of Harrogate set back off the A59 in a tranquil position with delightful views over the countryside. En suite bedrooms are tastefully decorated, colour TV, with tea-making facilities, CH. Private guests' sitting room and dining room. Ideal area of walking and exploring the Yorkshire Dales. Open all year.

8   **Langber Country Guest House,** Tatterthorne Road, Ingleton, via Carnforth LA6 3DT

Mrs Mollie Bell
☎ 015242 41587
BB From £14.75–£19.50
EM From £6
Sleeps 14
♨ ☒ ♞ ■
♛♛

A hilltop position with panoramic views of mountains and farmland. Comfortable accommodation, en suite facilities available. Friendly, personal service, wholesome, home-cooked meals. Ideal base for touring the Lakes, Dales and coast. Most sports catered for in vicinity. Turn off A65 at crossroads (between 'Mason's Arms' and car park). 'Langber' is on left, 1 mile down side road (Tatterthorne Road) travelling south towards Bentham. Open all year (except Christmas).

9   **Manor House,** Rylstone, Skipton, North Yorkshire BD23 6LH

Mary Caygill
☎ 01756 730226
BB From £20
Sleeps 4
♙ ♘ ☒ (12) ⚱ ♨ ■
♛♛ *Deluxe*

YHTB White Rose Award Bed & Breakfast of the year 1994. In Rylstone village, halfway between Skipton and Grassington (B6265). Dairy and sheep farm in Yorkshire Dales National Park. Country house in beautiful surroundings with panoramic views. Spacious en suite rooms. Central heating, TV, hot drinks facilities. Excellent food served at the village Inn. Open all year.

10   **Scaife Hall Farm,** Blubberhouses, Otley, West Yorkshire LS21 2PL

Christine Ryder
☎ 01943 880354
BB From £18–£22
Sleeps 6
♞ ☒ ⚱ ■
♛♛ *Highly Commended*

Scaife Hall is a working farm set in peaceful countryside, halfway between Harrogate and Skipton (just off A59). Two double bedrooms and one twin bedded room, each tastefully decorated with en suite facilities, central heating, beverage tray. Guests sitting room with log fires on chilly nights. Local inns provide excellent evening meals. Open all year except Christmas.

11   **Wenningber Farm,** Hellifield, Nr Skipton, North Yorkshire BD23 4JR

Mrs Barbara Phillip
☎ 01729 850856
BB From £16–£19
Sleeps 4
☒ ♞ ♝ ♟ ♨
♛ *Highly Commended*

Wenningber Farm is situated in a picturesque location just 4 miles from Malham in the heart of the Yorkshire Dales. Furnished to a very high standard with oak beams and inglenook fireplace. Full central heating, H&C in both rooms, tea and coffee-making facilities. Warm welcome assured. Open all year.

SELF-CATERING

Bottoms Farm Cottages, Bottoms Farm, Laycock, nr Keighley, West Yorkshire BD22 0QD

Mrs J. Parr
☎ 01535 607720
SC From £130–£260
Sleeps 2/5
🪑 ⛺ 💼
🔑 🔑 🔑 🔑 *Highly Commended*

Bottoms Farm is a rural 35-acre sheep farm situated on the south side of a beautiful valley with spectacular views. Howarth 4 miles, Skipton 7 miles. These luxury cottages have been recently converted to the highest standard from 200 years mistal/barn. Fully equipped. Heating and linen included. Sorry no pets. Open all year.

Cawder Hall Cottages, c/o Cawder Hall, Cawder Lane, Skipton, North Yorkshire BD23 2QQ

Anne Pearson
☎ 01756 791579
Fax 0176 797036
SC From £120–£295
Sleeps 2/6
♿ 🛏 🖼 ⛺ 💼 🍴
🔑 🔑 🔑 🔑 – 🔑 🔑 🔑 🔑
Up to Highly Commended

Enjoy the peace and quiet of our luxury cottages, yet only be 1 mile from the medieval castle and market town of Skipton. Each cottage has been newly converted and is suitable for disabled guests. The cottages are heated and have colour TV, video, fridge and microwave. There is a garden, barbeque, payphone and laundry room. All linen, gas and electricity are included as are cots and high chairs if required. Welcome Host. Open all year.

Heather & Bilberry Cottages, Hole Farm, Dimples Lane, Haworth, Bradford, West Yorkshire BD22 8QS

Mrs Janet Milner
☎ 01535 644755
SC From £100–£450
Sleeps 4/8 + cot
🪑 ⛺
🔑 🔑 🔑 🔑 🔑 *Highly Commended*

The old barn has been carefully converted to make two cottages with most bedrooms en suite. We are a small working farm, the sort that appears in children's Ladybird books. Gloria the sow, Gilbert the turkey, foals and calves. Ideal for children. A short walk to the village to see the Brontë Museum or a walk on the moors 2 minutes from our door. Sorry no pets. Open all year.

Maypole Cottage, Thorpe, Skipton, North Yorkshire BD23 6BJ

Mrs E. M. Gamble
☎ 01756 720609
SC From £190–£320
Sleeps 4
🪑 🐕 ⛺
🔑 🔑 🔑 🔑 *Commended*

An 18th century stable converted to a particularly high standard in the tiny hamlet of Thorpe near Burnsall. This well equipped cottage has full central heating, exposed beams and stonework open fire. Colour TV, microwave, washer/dryer. Bathroom with shower. Linen provided. Large walled garden, ample parking. Open all year.

Meadow & Field Cottages, The Coach House, Spring Head, Tim Lane, Haworth, West Yorks BD22 7RX

David and Hilary Freeman
☎ 01535 644140
SC From £130–£260
Sleeps 2/4
🪑 💼
🔑 🔑 🔑 🔑 *Highly Commended*

These two delightful country cottages are situated within close proximity of the Brontë sisters' Haworth, surrounded by tranquil fields and countryside walks. They have been sympathetically converted from a listed stone barn to an extremely high standard, fully equipped with every modern convenience and extremely comfortably furnished. Each cottage suitable for 2-4 people. Open all year.

17 Westfield Farm Cottages, c/o Westfield Farm, Tim Lane, Haworth, West Yorkshire BD22 7SA

Wendy Carr
☎ 01535 644568
Fax 01535 646686
⑤ᶜ From £130–£300
Sleeps 2/6

🐕 ⛄ ☺ ⚡ 🏞 🍴 ⊞ 🪑 🚿 🏕 💼 ✂
🔑 🔑 🔑 – 🔑 🔑 🔑 🔑

Highly Commended

Enjoy the comforts of home in one of our delightful cottages. 100-acre hill farm with suckler cows and sheep. ½ mile from Haworth. Cottages to sleep 2 to 6 people. Cottage for 2 disabled people. Beautiful south-facing aspect. Colour TV, automatic washer, microwave in each. Dogs by arrangement. Farm-trail and safe river for fishing or play. Open all year.

CONFIRM BOOKINGS

Disappointments can arise by misunderstandings over the telephone.
Please write to confirm your booking.

FARM HOLIDAY BUREAU

PRICES

Prices include VAT and service charge (if any) and are:
B&B per person per night
EM per person
SC per unit per week
Tents and caravans per pitch per night

FARM HOLIDAY BUREAU

23

England's North Country

Herriot's Yorkshire Moors and Dales

Group Contacts: 🅱🅱 *Mrs Patricia Knox* ☎ *01677 450257*
🆂🅲 *Lady Mary Furness* ☎ *01609 772061/748614*

Take a trip around North Yorkshire and sample for yourself the delights of this area as portrayed in James Herriot's 'All Creatures Great and Small'.

Start with the ancient city of York and wander through narrow streets to the Minster, ride upriver to the Bishop's Palace or visit the Railway Museum and Jorvik Centre. Or drive from Helmsley, over Sutton Bank – a favourite for hang-gliders – to the market town of Thirsk where James Herriot still practises. A day all the family will enjoy is a visit to the Lightwater Valley Theme Park where modern farming exhibits combine with an adventure play area. Or maybe you prefer the peace and tranquillity of the romantic abbeys, stately homes, gardens and deer parks found here.

In Wensleydale, home of the famous cheese, you can fish or picnic by the waterfalls and enjoy real ale in friendly village pubs. Locally, many craftsmen display their skills, the most famous being the Mouseman of Kilburn.

Walkers can follow the Pennine Way past the Buttertubs, through panoramic Swaledale where shepherd and sheepdog work the hills, to the cobbled streets and Norman castle of Richmond, towering over the river below.

Whatever the weather, whatever your interest, you are spoilt for choice. There is something for everyone in North Yorkshire!

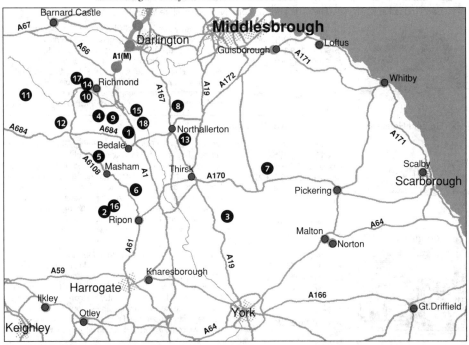

BED AND BREAKFAST

(and evening meal)

---

1 Ainderby Myers Farm, Nr Hackforth, Bedale, North Yorkshire DL8 1PF

Mrs Valerie Anderson
☎ **01609 748668**
▦ **From £16–£17**
EM From £9
Sleeps 6
✄ 🐎 ⅄ 🏕 🎒 📠
♨ *Commended*

Historical manor house set amidst moors and dales with origins going back to the 10th century. Terrific atmosphere. Once farmed by the monks of Jervaulx Abbey. Sheep, crops, pastures and a stream. Walk the fields and discover the wildlife. Visit castles and abbeys. Excellent base for walkers. Pony trekking and fishing by arrangement. Traditional Yorkshire breakfasts. Picnic facilities. Open all year.

---

2 Bay Tree Farm, Aldfield, Nr Fountains Abbey, Ripon, North Yorkshire HG4 3BE

Valerie Leeming
☎ **01765 620394**
▦ **From £15–18**
EM From £9
Sleeps 10
🐎 🐂 ⊞ 🚻 ⅄ 🎒 📠
♨ ♨ *Commended*

Walk those Dales, see those hills, visit Harrogate, York and Ripon. Recently converted 17th century stone barn combining character with comfort. All rooms en suite with TV, radio, tea/coffee, CH. Dining room and lounge with open fires. Rural setting with circular walks including Fountains Abbey (NT) ½ mile away. HE trained home cooking. Personal attention and kettle always on the boil! Children welcome. Brochure available. AA QQQ. Open all year.

---

3 Carr House Farm, Shallowdale, Ampleforth, York, North Yorkshire YO6 4ED

Anna Lupton
☎ **01347 868 526/**
0850 310188
▦ **From £12.50–£15**
EM From £8
Sleeps 6
✄ 🐂 (7) 🏇 ☕ 🚻 ⅄
♨ ♨

16th century farmhouse filled with memorabilia. Part of 400-acre family farm for 5 generations. Internationally recommended, "fresh air fiend's dream! Good food, walking, warm welcome". Romantic four-poster bedroom en suite. Relaxing, peaceful, informal – "heartbeat country". ½ hour York. Make your holiday memorable – Highland cattle, north country sheep, ponds, orchards, green fields, wild flowers. Open all year (closed Christmas and New Year).

---

4 Elmfield House, Arrathorne, Bedale, North Yorkshire DL8 1NE

Edith & Jim Lillie
☎ **01677 450558**
Fax 01677 450557
▦ **From £19.50–£27**
EM From £11.50
Sleeps 20
☺ 🚻 🐂 ⊞ 📠
♨ ♨ ♨ *Commended*

Situated between Richmond and Bedale. Superb views of surrounding countryside, relaxed friendly atmosphere in luxurious country house. 9 spacious bedrooms (all en suite) including a four-poster bed, twin and family rooms. 2 bedrooms equipped for disabled. All with colour TV (satellite channel), radio, phone, tea/coffee-making facilities, CH. Lounge and bar (residential licence), dining room, games room, solarium. Excellent home cooking. Open all year.

---

5 Haregill Lodge, Ellingstring, Masham, Ripon, North Yorkshire HG4 4PW

Mrs Rachel Greensit
☎ **01677 460272**
▦ **From £15–£18**
EM From £9
Sleeps 6
🐎 🐂 📠
♨ ♨ *Commended*

This attractive 18th century stone farmhouse is set on a family working mixed farm. Secluded garden with children's play area, in peaceful surroundings overlooking the Hambleton Hills. Good base to explore the Dales and Herriot Country. One bedroom en suite, tea/coffee facilities. Log fire, CH, satellite TV lounge, games room. Good home cooking with supper tray. Fishing and trekking nearby. A warm welcome awaits you. Open all year except Christmas.

Lamb Hill Farm, Lamb Hill, Masham, Ripon, North Yorkshire HG4 4DJ

Mrs Rosemary Robinson
☎ 01765 689274
ⒷⒷ From £15–£16
Sleeps 6
🐎 (8) ✂ 🛈 ♞
👑 👑 *Commended*

Come, enjoy a relaxing and carefree holiday with good food and freindly service. A spacious comfortable old farmhouse with views of the Dales. Ideally situated for exploring Yorkshire's Dales and Moors. Many National Trust properties in easy reach. Pony trekking, fishing close at hand. (Masham 2 miles, York 45 minutes, Durham 1 hour). Situated off A6108 between West Tanfield and Masham. Open all year.

Laskill Farm, Hawnby, Nr Helmsley, North Yorkshire YO6 5NB

Sue Smith
☎ 01439 798268
ⒷⒷ From £17.50–£20.50
EM From £10.75
Sleeps 10
🐎🐄🐎🛈 ♞ 🍴 🛈
👑

Amidst beautiful North Yorkshire Moors, in heart of James Herriot Country. Attractive farmhouse with own lake/large walled garden for visitors' use. High standard of food and comfort. 2 double rooms en suite, 2 twins en suite, 1 double and 1 twin each with shower and H/C, 1 single; all with colour TV. Ideal centre, for surrounding places of interest and scenic beauty, or simply enjoy peace and tranquillity in idyllic surroundings. Open all year except Christmas Day.

Lovesome Hill Farm, Lovesome Hill, Northallerton, North Yorkshire DL6 2PB

Mrs Mary Pearson
☎ 01609 772311
ⒷⒷ From £16–£20
EM From £8.50
Sleeps 6
🐎 🛈 ♞ 🍴
👑 👑 *Commended*

Traditional 19th century farmhouse in open countryside with lovely views of Hambleton Hills. Tastefully converted granary adjoins house with spacious, well furnished en suite rooms overlooking patio, croquet lawn. Market town and Golf within 4 miles. Central for Dales and Moors. A warm welcome and delicious homemade meals await you. You'll love it. Open Mar–Nov.

Mill Close Farm, Patrick Brompton, Bedale, North Yorkshire DL8 1JY

Mrs Patricia Knox
☎ 01677 450257
Fax 01677 450585
ⒷⒷ From £17–£20
EM From £10
Sleeps 4
🐎 🐎 🛈
👑 👑 *Commended*

Mill Close is a 17th century working farm surrounded by beautiful rolling countryside at the foothills of the Yorkshire Dales and Herriot Country. Situated 2 miles from the A1(M). Spacious rooms, furnished to high standard. Guests' private bathrooms, dining and sitting room with colour TV. A relaxing, peaceful atmosphere with large walled garden and open fires. Please send for full colour brochure. Open Mar–Nov.

Mount Pleasant Farm, Whashton, Richmond, North Yorkshire DL11 7JP

Christine Chilton
☎ 01748 822784
ⒷⒷ From £17
EM From £9
Sleeps 14
♿ 🐎 🐎 🛈 🍴 🛈
👑 👑 *Commended*

The tired business man, a couple touring, or the family with children can all enjoy Mount Pleasant. A working farm, 3 miles from the market town of Richmond. En suite rooms in a converted stable, each with its own front door. Good farmhouse food. Residential licence. A real Yorkshire welcome! Open all year except Christmas.

Oxnop Hall, Low Oxnop, Gunnerside, Richmond, North Yorkshire DL11 6JJ

Annie Porter
☎ 01748 886253
ⒷⒷ From £20
EM From £11.50
Sleeps 11
🐎 (7) 🍴
👑 👑 👑 *Commended*

Stay with us on our working hill farm with beef cattle and Swaledale sheep. Oxnop Hall is of historical interest and has recently been extended with all en suite rooms. Ideal walking and touring. We are in the Yorkshire Dales National Park, Herriot Country, an Environmentally Sensitive Area which is renowned for its stone walls, barns and flora. Good farmhouse food. Tea/coffee-making facilities.

⑫ Walburn Hall, Downholme, Richmond, North Yorkshire DL11 6AF

Diana Greenwood
☎ **01748 822152**
BB **From £19**
Sleeps 5
✗ ☙
♨ ♨ *Commended*

Walburn Hall is one of the few remaining working farms with a fortified farmhouse, an enclosed cobbled courtyard and terraced garden. For guests' comfort there is a separate lounge and dining room with beamed ceilings, stone fireplaces and log fires (when required). Centrally heated. Double/twin or family rooms (en suite) with tea/coffee-making facilities. Ideally situated between Richmond and Leyburn for exploring the Dales. Open Mar–Nov.

⑬ Wellfield House Farm, North Otterington, Northallerton, North Yorkshire DL7 9JF

Dorothy Hill
☎ **01609 772766**
BB **From £16–£17**
EM **From £10**
Sleeps 6
🐓 ♿ 🐎 🕴 ⚙ ☙ 🎋
♨ ♨ *Commended*

Comfortable farmhouse, (part dates back to 17th century), on sheep/arable working farm. High standard of furnishing. Large garden with patio, goldfish ponds and croquet lawn. Unspoilt views. Coarse fishing available free. Ideally situated for Herriot Country, Moors, Dales, stately homes. Centrally heated. Family, double and twin-bedded rooms with handbasins and 1 with own adjoining bathroom. Visitors' lounge. Home cooking and warm welcome await you. Open all year except Christmas.

⑭ Whashton Springs Farm, Richmond, North Yorkshire DL11 7JS

Fairlie Turnbull
☎ **01748 822884**
BB **From £19–£22**
EM **From £11.50**
Sleeps 16
☙ (5) 🎋 ■
♨ ♨ ♨ *Highly Commended*

400-acre beef/sheep, family working farm in heart of Herriot Country. Delightful Georgian farmhouse, featured on 'Wish You Were Here', 1988 AA 'Farmhouse of the North' Award, unusual bay windows, overlooking lawns sloping to a sparkling stream. Real Yorkshire breakfast. Home cooking using local produce. All 8 bedrooms have en suite baths/ showers, TV, phone. One 4-poster bedroom. Historic Richmond 3 miles away. Open all year (closed Christmas & New Year).

SELF-CATERING

⑮ Stanhow Farm Bungalow, Great Langton, c/o Otterington Hall, Northallerton, North Yorks DL7 9HW

Lady Mary Furness
☎ **01609 772061/
748614**
SC **From £130–£300**
Sleeps 6
🐓 ♿ ☙ 🎋 ■
🏇 🏇 🏇 🏇 *Commended*

Enjoy our homely, comfortable, detached bungalow and garden. Warm and peaceful, lovely views, well appointed, economy 7 heating, CTV, open fire, automatic washer, tumble dryer, microwave, fridge/freezer. 3 bedrooms, personally maintained to a high standard. Enjoy the 230-acre farm with conservation areas. Central, ideal for relaxing. Good local hospitality and recreations. Family and business guests welcome. Open all year.

⑯ Trips Cottage, Bay Tree Farm, Aldfield, Nr Fountains Abbey, Ripon, North Yorkshire HG4 3BE

Valerie Leeming
☎ **01765 620394**
SC **From £95–£185**
Sleeps 2
☙ 🐓 ⊡ 🎋
🏇 🏇 🏇 *Commended*

A newly-converted stable which sleeps 2, to the left of the farmhouse. Fine panoramic views over Fountains Abbey. Tasteful conversion consists of lobby, shower, toilet, fitted kitchen (microwave/electric cooker), lounge/ diner (with colour TV). Double bedroom, bed linen and storage heater included in the rent. Pay–phone available. Shops at Ripon (3 miles), eating 2 miles. Private parking and gardens. Ideal for touring Dales, Moors and York. Local walks. Open all year.

The Coach House, Whashton Springs Farm, Richmond, North Yorkshire DL11 7JS

Fairlie Turnbull
☎ **01748 822884**
🆂🅲 **From £150–£250**
Sleeps 4–5
🐕 ♨
🗝 🗝 🗝
Highly Commended

The Coach House offers luxury accommodation on our 400-acre working family farm near Richmond, gateway to the Dales. This warm spacious house sleeps 4–5 in double and twin bedrooms. Beamed lounge and well equipped kitchen with washer, freezer, microwave, etc. Heating and bed linen included in tariff. Good local hospitality. Open all year.

Wren Cottage, c/o Street House Farm, Little Holtby, Northallerton, North Yorkshire DL7 9LN   (18)

Mrs Jennifer Pybus
☎ **01609 748622**
🆂🅲 **From £105–£225**
Sleeps 4
🐕 🐕
🗝 🗝 🗝 *Approved*

This cosy cottage in Kirkby Fleetham overlooks the village green where cricket is played in summer. An ideal centre for exploring Yorkshire Dales and North Yorkshire moors and within easy reach of York and Durham. The cottage with its traditional oak beams and open fire in the lounge has a fully equipped kitchen with electric cooker and microwave. Also night storage heaters and telephone. Electricity included. Open all year.

24

England's North Country
Ryedale, North Yorkshire

Group Contacts: 🆂🅱 *Brenda Johnson* ☎ *01439 798278*
🆂🅲 *Mrs Susan Garbutt* ☎ *01439 798264*

Upper Ryedale is the western part of the North Yorkshire Moors National Park, where the efforts of man to wring a living from the hillsides has enhanced the natural beauty of the classical glacial valleys. It is a place which appeals particularly to the walker.

There are two nationally famous walks passing through the area, the Lyke Wake Walk and the Cleveland Way, but, for those who want to see the abundant wildlife, the network of unnamed footpaths, through woods and over wild moorland, will be more inviting. There is also trout fishing in the Rye.

The area also has three well known monastery ruins and several stately homes, headed by Castle Howard. York, with its magnificent selection of museums, historic Minster and its encircling walls, is an hour away by car. Literary pilgrimages can be made to Coxwold, where Lawrence Sterne preached, or to Thirsk, where James Herriot has his practice. Music lovers can take advantage of Ryedale Festival in Helmsley for the first week in August.

The seaside towns of Scarborough, Whitby and Filey are within reach. Close by are Lightwater Valley and Flamingoland, plus the slightly more sedate pleasures of a ride on the North Yorkshire Moors Steam Railway.

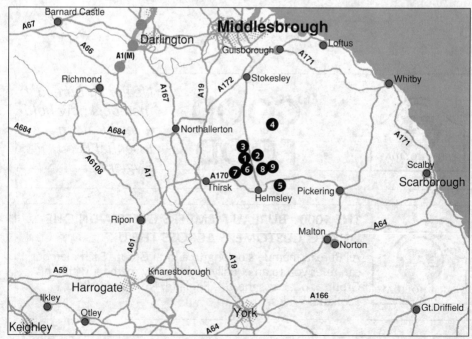

BED AND BREAKFAST
(and evening meal)

Barn Close Farm, Rievaulx, Helmsley, North Yorkshire YO6 5HL

Joan Milburn
☎ **01439 798321**
🆖 From £16–£18
EM From £10
Sleeps 6
🐴 🧸 ♿ 🚶 ☕ 🏕 💼
♨ ♨ ♨

Comfortable, relaxed atmosphere at Barn Close Farm set in an idyllic wooded valley of outstanding beauty close to Rievaulx Abbey and Old Byland. Farmhouse cooking recommended by the Daily Telegraph. Speciality home baked bread. Riding, walking from farmyard. Central for touring countryside, 1 hour from York or coast. 1 en suite, 1 family with private bathroom, tea/coffee-making facilities. Open all year.

Cringle Carr Farm, Hawnby, Helmsley, North Yorkshire YO6 5LT

Susan Garbutt
☎ **01439 798264**
🆖 From £15–£17
EM From £9.50
Sleeps 5
🧸 🐕 ♿
♨

Cringle Carr is a dairy farm situated in glorious scenery with the River Rye running along the edge of the farmland, ideal for peaceful walks and nature observation. The comfortable CH accommodation comprises of 1 twin, 1 family bedroom with washbasins, shower room for guests' exclusive use, tea/coffee-making facilities, dining/ sitting room with colour TV. Home produce where possible. Open Feb–Nov.

Easterside Farm, Hawnby, Helmsley, North Yorkshire YO6 5QT

Mrs Sarah Wood
☎ **01439 798277**
🆖 From £17
EM From £10
Sleeps 7
🧸 🏕
♨ ♨

A large 18th century Grade II listed farmhouse, nestling on Easterside Hill and enjoying panoramic views. Ideal base for walking, touring, the coast and the city of York. Enjoy good food and a warm welcome in comfortable surroundings. All rooms have en suite facilities. Open all year (closed Christmas).

Hill End Farm, Chop Gate, Bilsdale, North Yorkshire TS9 7JR

Brenda Johnson
☎ **01439 798278**
🆖 From £15.50–£18
EM From £10.50
Sleeps 5
🧸 🐕 🏕 💼
♨ ♨

Looking for a comfortable, peaceful break? Then come and join us in our 17th century farmhouse in picturesque Bilsdale. Eight miles from the market town of Helmsley. Guests are welcome to wander around our family run farm. Two comfortable bedrooms, one bathroom en suite, one with washbasin. Tea/coffee making facilities. Comfortable lounge. Good home cooking with generous helpings. Open Easter–Nov.

Low Northolme Farm, Salton, York, North Yorkshire YO6 6RP

Diane Peirson
☎ **01751 432321**
🆖 From £17
EM From £9.50
Sleeps 5
🧸 (5) 🐕
♨ ♨ *Highly Commended*

Georgian farmhouse, 4 miles from Kirkbymoorside, close to North Yorkshire moors. Arable farm with breeding sheep. Bedrooms en suite, TV lounge, snug and kitchenette with tea/coffee-making facilities. Central heating, log fires in winter. Enjoy excellent home cooking and hospitality. Private fishing, golf nearby. Ancient city of York within easy reach. Evening meal by arrangement. Open Mar–Oct.

---

6 **Manor Farm,** Old Byland, Helmsley, York, North Yorkshire YO6 5LG

Joyce Garbutt
☎ **01439 798247**
BB **From £15**
EM From £10
Sleeps 4
🐕 🏠

You are assured of a warm welcome at Manor Farm, situated in the picturesque village of Old Byland. Ideally placed for walking and touring the North York Moors. Guests welcome to browse around the family-run dairy and sheep farm. Two comfortable bedrooms with washbasins and tea/coffee-making facilities, guests' bathroom, lounge with log fires, central heating. Good home cooking. Open Easter–Oct.

7 **Mount Grace Farm,** Cold Kirkby, Thirsk, North Yorkshire YO7 2HL

Joyce Ashbridge
☎ **01845 597389**
BB **From £18–£22**
EM From £8
Sleeps 6
🐕 (12) ✂ 🏠
🌸🌸 Commended

A warm welcome awaits you in quiet village location. Magnificent views. Easy access to York, Harrogate, Moors, Dales, Stately homes, coast, etc, or get away from it all on one of the many walks in the area. Traditional farmhouse fayre a speciality. Weekly rates. Open all year except Christmas.

8 **Valley View Farm,** Old Byland, Helmsley, York, North Yorkshire YO6 5LG

Sally Robinson
☎ **01439 798221**
BB **From £22–£25**
EM From £11
Sleeps 10
🏇 🐕 ⊞ 🅰 ♨ ⛱ 🏠
🌸🌸 Highly Commended

Friendly relaxed Yorkshire hospitality in our well appointed, tastefully furnished home with open fire. Pretty en suite bedrooms, tea and coffee, TV, etc. Peaceful cottage garden with beautiful views. Hearty country breakfasts, delicious traditional farmhouse fayre, wine list. Way marked walks from the farm. The North York Moors is the driest national park! Open all Year.

SELF-CATERING

9 **Valley View Farm,** Old Byland, Helmsley, York, North Yorkshire YO6 5LG

Sally Robinson
☎ **01439 798221**
SC **From £110–£400**
🏇 🐕 ⊞ 🅰 ♨ ⛱ 🏠
Applied

New for 1995 three stylish holiday cottages furnished and equipped to a high specification. Precise details and brochure will be available Jan 95. All will have outstanding views across open countryside set on the edge of a small Yorkshire village. The cottages will offer peace and tranquility, a real rural treat.

25

England's North Country
Yorkshire Moors, National Park and Coast

Group Contact: *Mrs Gillian Rhys* ☎ *01287 660352*

When you come to stay with us on our farms you have the opportunity to visit the seaside and enjoy the countryside inland as well.

The coast offers sandy beaches, secret caves, pretty fishing villages and 30 miles of Heritage Coast with bird sanctuaries and wildlife. The resorts of Scarborough, Whitby and Bridlington offer lively entertainment in the evenings for all tastes.

There are over 1,000 miles of public footpaths and bridleways in the area and recognised walks like the White Rose Walk, the Cleveland Way and the Lyke Wake Walk. Or perhaps pony trekking through the National Park appeals to you. The North Yorkshire Moors steam railway provides superb nostalgia for railway enthusiasts and spectacular scenery for all who travel on it between Grosmont and Pickering.

Those interested in historic heritage will find much to enjoy. At Pickering the parish church is famous for its unique 15th-century wall painting of St George and the Dragon. Whitby and Rievaulx Abbeys are examples of the magnificent religious architecture of the area. Ancient castles can also be explored at Helmsley, Pickering and Scarborough.

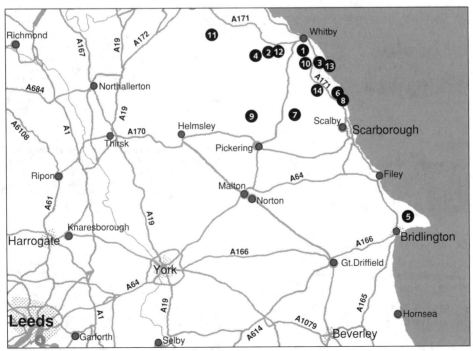

BED AND BREAKFAST

(and evening meal)

---

1 Belmont, Ruswarp Bank, Whitby, North Yorkshire YO21 1NF

Eileen Morley
☎ 01947 602519
BB From £16–£20
Sleeps 4
☐ (10) 🐾 ⚹
Listed *Highly Commended*

You are assured of a warm welcome at Belmont, adjoining our 300-acre farm at Cross Butts. This beautiful turn of the century house set in own grounds overlooking the village of Ruswarp, on the picturesque river Esk, 2 miles from historic smuggling town of Whitby. Beautiful, large four-poster bedroom and spacious twin bedroom. Tastefully furnished throughout. Open all year except Christmas & New Year.

---

2 Cote Bank Farm, Egton, Whitby, North Yorkshire YO21 1UG

Barbara Howard
☎ 01947 895314
BB From £16
EM From £9
Sleeps 6
☐ (5) 🐾 ⚹
♨

Large 18th century farmhouse in a peaceful position, with sheltered garden, on the edge of mixed woodland, overlooking the beautiful Esk valley. Within easy reach of Whitby, Robin Hood's Bay, 'Heartbeat' country, steam railway. Excellent walking country. Relaxed atmosphere, quiet and comfortable. Good home cooking. The perfect retreat. Open all year except Christmas.

---

3 Croft Farm, Fylingthorpe, Whitby, North Yorkshire YO22 4PW

Pauline Featherstone
☎ 01947 880231
BB From £16–£19.50
Sleeps 6
⚹ ☐ (5)
♨♨ *Commended*

18th century farmhouse in lawned garden on small working farm overlooking Robin Hood's Bay. Tastefully furnished in the 'olde worlde' charm with open beams, staircase and fireplaces. Rooms with washbasins (1 en suite) all with tea-making facilities and panoramic views of the sea, moors and country-side. Guests' lounge, bathroom. Ideal base for coastal resorts, walking and touring the beauty spots of North Yorkshire. Our speciality is a good hearty breakfast. Open Easter–mid-Oct.

---

4 The Grange, Glaisdale, Whitby, North Yorkshire YO21 2QW

Heather Kelly
☎ 01947 897241
BB From £15
EM From £7
Sleeps 6
🐾 ☐ ⌖
♨♨

Beautiful stone manor house with magnificent hilltop view. It lies amidst our sheep/arable farm bordering the Esk river which boasts the best salmon fishing in the country. Home grown produce used in our generous meals. Excellent position for walks, steam railway and Whitby. Bathroom en suite or shared between 2 rooms. Fishing by arrangement. Open Jan–Nov (incl.).

---

5 The Grange, Bempton Lane, Flamborough, Bridlington, Humberside YO15 1AS

Joan Thompson
☎ 01262 850207
Fax 01262 851359
BB From £13–£14.50
Sleeps 6
🐾 ☐ 🧍 ⌨ 🌾
Listed

For a relaxing holiday come and stay in our Georgian farmhouse situated in 450 acres of stock and arable land on the outskirts of Flamborough village. Ideally situated for birdwatching at RSPB Sanctuary at Bempton, sandy beaches, cliffs and coves on our 'Heritage Coast'. Golf and sea fishing nearby. Open all year (closed Christmas & New Year).

Island Farm, Staintondale, Scarborough, North Yorkshire YO13 0EB

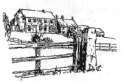

Mary Clarke
☎ 01723 870249
🅱 From £17–£20
Sleeps 6
🐕 ⚒ 🛏 👤 ♿ ■
👑 👑

Relax in our spacious and comfortable farmhouse and garden. Enjoy excellent home cooking. All bedrooms have en suite facilities. Being close to coast and in open countryside, it is ideal for walking or visiting many places of interest. Visitors appreciate our large games room with toys, full size snooker table and tennis court. Brochure on request. Open Easter–Nov.

Newgate Foot, Saltersgate, Pickering, North Yorkshire YO18 7NR

Alison Johnson
☎ 01751 460215
🅱 From £14.50–£19.50
EM From £9
Sleeps 5
🛏 🅔 🏃 👇 ♨ ■ 🏇
👑 👑 *Highly Commended*

Just 1 mile off the A169, but in a world of its own in the middle of the moors with no neighbours in sight! Enjoy walking on the moors, through the forest, or trout fishing in our own lake. See the ewes and lambs and thoroughbred mares and foals. Whitby 14 miles, York 35 miles. One en suite bedroom, 1 twin/3 bedded, 1 single. Open all year except Christmas.

Plane Tree Cottage Farm, Staintondale, Scarborough, North Yorkshire YO13 0EY

Mrs Marjorie Edmondson
☎ 01723 870796
🅱 From £15
EM From £9
Sleeps 4
🐕 🏛
Listed

This 60-acre mixed farm is situated off the beaten track, between Scarborough and Whitby. We have rare breeds of sheep, pigs and free range hens. Also a very friendly cat called 'Danny'. This small, homely cottage has character with its beams and low ceilings, and beautiful open views. Good wholesome home cooking. Open Mar–Nov.

Seavy Slack, Stape, Pickering, North Yorkshire YO18 8HZ

Anne Barrett
☎ 01751 473131
🅱 From £13–£16
EM From £10
Sleeps 6
🐕 🛏
Listed

Relax in our comfortable farmhouse on this working dairy/beef farm situated on the edge of the moors and enjoy good home cooking with generous portions. Close to market town of Pickering and North Yorkshire Moors Railway and within easy reach of the coast and historic city of York. Open Easter-October.

SELF-CATERING

Asp House Farm, Stainsacre, Nr Whitby, North Yorkshire YO22 4LR

Patricia Ward
☎ 01947 603997
🆂🅲 From £150–£300
Sleeps 6 + cot
🐎
🐾 🐾 🐾 🐾 *Commended*

Asp House is a spacious, beamed cottage in an open rural position. Sleeps 6 comfortably. Beautiful views and delightful garden. Situated between the coast, moors and dales; many wonderful walks available. Storage heaters and log fire available for winter breaks. Whitby 3 miles. Open all year.

11 Blackmires Farm, Danby Head, Danby, Whitby, North Yorkshire YO21 2NN

Gillian & Lewis Rhys
☎ 01287 660352
[SC] **From £150–£300**
Sleeps 2/6
🐕 🐎 🏕 🛶 ☂
🔑 🔑 🔑 🔑 *Approved*

Self-catering cottage for six with storage heaters and two bedroomed modern caravan. Adjacent to moors in an area of outstanding natural beauty. Central for touring North Yorks Moors National Park by road and rail. Good walking country. Fishing and seaside at Whitby. Visit Flamingo Park, Castle Howard, Rievaulx and other abbeys, folk museums, picturesque villages. Fishing in River Esk. Open Mar–Nov.

12 Cote Bank Farm, Egton, Whitby, North Yorkshire YO21 1UG

Barbara Howard
☎ 01947 895314
[SC] **From £150–£350**
Sleeps 6
🐎
🔑

Spacious, comfortable, warm semi-detached house on edge of Grosmont village overlooking Esk Valley.Close to Whitby, Robin Hood's Bay, Steam Railway, 'Heartbeat' country. Shops and pub ½ mile . 1 double, 1 twin, 1 room with full-sized bunks. Lounge, dining room, well equipped kitchen. Large garden with patio furniture. Storage heating, open fires by arrangement. Linen provided. No dogs. Open all year.

13 Croft Farm Cottage, Croft Farm, Fylingthorpe, Whitby, North Yorkshire YO22 4PW

Pauline Featherstone
☎ 01947 880231
[SC] **From £125–£255**
Sleeps 4
🐎
🔑 🔑 🔑 *Commended*

Forget the pressures of everyday living! Come and relax in the cottage attached to our 18th century farmhouse on a working farm, offering spectacular views, home comforts, peace and tranquillity. Overlooking Robin Hood's Bay, within easy reach of coastal resorts, Moors Railway and termination of well-known walks. 2 bedrooms, 1 double and 1 with built-in bunk beds. Fully equipped including linen. Colour TV and sun lounge. Open all year.

14 Pond Farm, Fylingdales, Whitby, North Yorkshire YO22 4QJ

Grace Cromack
☎ 01947 880441
[SC] **From £110–£190**
Sleeps 6
🐕 🐎 🛶 ☂
Approved

We offer a 6-berth luxury caravan, situated on 400-acre mixed stock farm edging the North Yorkshire Moors and near to Robin Hood's Bay. It is situated in a walled garden with pleasing views and has all mains services including shower, toilet. TV, fridge, double and bunk-bedded rooms. Ideal for visiting historic towns, coastal resorts. Forest and moorland walks, pony trekking and clay pigeon shooting. Open Mar–Nov.

FOLLOW THE COUNTRY CODE

Leave nothing but footprints,
Take nothing but photographs,
Kill nothing but time!

26

England's North Country

Vale of York and the Wolds

Group Contact: *Mrs C. Firby* ☎ *01653 628403*

When you come to stay with us on our farms you are within easy reach of Yorkshire's capital city with its beautiful Minster and a wealth of history; visit the Railway Museum and Jorvik Centre. Whilst in the area see Castle Howard where 'Brideshead Revisited' was filmed and the abbeys of Rievaulx, Byland and Selby.

The area is rich in market towns: Driffield, the capital of the Wolds where reputedly King Alfred is buried, and Beverley, described as the most perfect of county towns with its cobbled streets and 'bars' or town gates. Beverley Minster is one of the finest churches. Explore the many country houses all rich in history and full of beautiful furniture.

Hull is a major port where sailing ships have given way to modern ferries and some of its docks to a yacht marina.

Horse racing takes place at York, Beverley, Ripon and Thirsk, all providing an exciting day out.

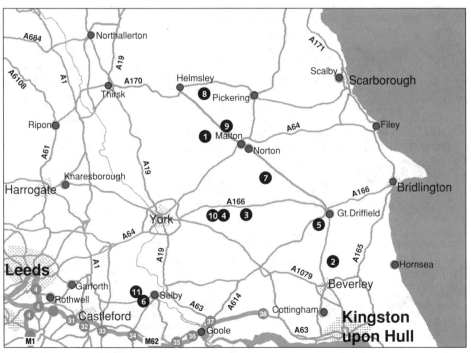

BED AND BREAKFAST

(and evening meal)

---

1 Church Farm, Scackleton, York, North Yorkshire YO6 4NB

Mrs Cynthia Firby
☎ **01653 628403**
BB From £14–£17
EM From £10
Sleeps 6
❄ ⚥ ✠ ❀

Listed *Highly Commended*

A spacious, comfortable stone farmhouse on our sheep and arable farm in a quiet hamlet in the Howardian Hills, designated Area of Outstanding Natural Beauty. 2 guest bathrooms, 1 en suite. Family suite. Tea/coffee-making facilities in all bedrooms. Central heating, good home cooking, wonderful views. Ideal base for walking or visiting York, the moors and coast. Open Mar–Nov.

---

2 Crow Tree Farm, Arram, Beverley, Humberside HU17 7NR

Mrs Margaret Hart
☎ **01964 550167**
BB From £14–£15
EM From £7
Sleeps 3
❄ ✠ 🐾 🐕 ❀ ❀

Listed

A family smallholding bursting with friendly animals whom the children will love. Traditional jubilee farmhouse with antique furniture, large sunny conservatory leading to tranquil gardens. Situated in secure, undiscovered hamlet close to Beverley, Hull, York and the heritage coastline of East Yorkshire. Home cooking a speciality. Open all year except Christmas.

---

3 High Belthorpe, Bishop Wilton, Nr. York, Humberside YO4 1SB

Meg Abu Hamdan
☎ **01759 368238**
BB From £15
Sleeps 6
❄ ✠ 🐕 ⚘ ❀ ❀

Set on an ancient moated site in the Yorkshire Wolds, this large Victorian farmhouse has spacious bedrooms with uninterrupted panoramic views. The centre of a working livery yard, the house has own private fishing lake and access to fabulous country walks. Croquet, small snooker table available. York 12 miles, coast 20 miles. Open all year.

---

4 High Catton Grange, High Catton, near Stamford Bridge, York YO4 1EP

Sheila Foster
☎ **01759 371374**
BB From £14.50
Sleeps 6
❄ ✠ 🐕 🛁 ❀

🏵 *Commended*

Only 8 miles east of York, High Catton Grange is a 300-acre mixed farm with comfortable 18th century farmhouse. Friendly, relaxed atmosphere and attractive bedrooms, 2 with washbasin, 1 en suite, guest bathroom, central heating, tea/coffee-making facilities. Within 2 miles, local country inns providing excellent meals. Ample private parking. Open all year except Christmas and New Year. Welcome Host Certificate.

---

5 Kelleythorpe Farm, Kelleythorpe, Great Driffield, East Yorkshire YO25 9DW

Mrs Tiffy Hopper
☎ **01377 252297**
BB From £14
EM From £10
Sleeps 6
✠ ❄ 🛁 ❀

Listed

Imagine peacocks strutting, ducks swimming and trout rising. Enjoy tea on the sun terrace overlooking a crystal clear shallow river, the friendly atmosphere of our lovely Georgian farmhouse with its mellow antique furniture, pretty chintz and new bathrooms, 1 en suite, is sure to captivate you. Delicious country cooking. Children very welcome. Ideally placed for touring. Open all year (closed Christmas & New Year).

Lund Farm, Gateforth, Selby, North Yorkshire YO8 9LE

Chris & Helen Middleton
☎/Fax 01757 228775
BB From £18–£20
EM From £5
Sleeps 6
Listed

Convenient for York, the Dales and Moors, our peaceful 18th century farmhouse has 2 large family rooms, pine beams and log fires. Children welcome; 200-acre farm with lambs, eggs to collect for breakfast and baby listening. Evening meals on request, plus friendly holiday advice. Lambing breaks Dec–Apr. Open all year.

Manor Farm, Thixendale, Malton, North Yorkshire YO17 9TG

Mrs Brader
☎ 01377 288315
BB From £16
Sleeps 4
Listed

At Manor Farm guests can enjoy their own spacious, private accommodation, furnished with old pine, patchwork quilts and original Victorian brass/iron bed. Play croquet on the lawns, stroll around the interesting garden, enjoy a game of tennis, and share the company of dogs, cats, ducks, geese, chickens and horses which help make up our busy working farm. Open all year.

Sunley Court, Nunnington, York, North Yorkshire YO6 5XQ

Mrs Joan Brown
☎ 01439 748233
BB From £15
EM £10
Sleeps 6
🐾🐾 *Commended*

Sunley Court is a comfortable modern farmhouse with open views in a quiet secluded area. The farm is arable with sheep and horses. All bedrooms have tea/coffee-making facilities, washbasins, electric blankets, 2 have shower/toilet en suite. Good home cooking. Central for York, moors and coast. Open all year.

Winifred Farm, Amotherby, Malton, North Yorkshire YO17 0TG

Carolyn Timm
☎ 01653 698165
BB From £13–£20
EM From £12
Sleeps 4
Listed *Commended*

Nestling in between the Howardian Hills, moors and the coast in the heart of Ryedale, 25 miles from York. A traditional, comfortable farmhouse on a working farm. Large garden with private parking. Situated on the B1257 between Malton and Helmsley. Good variety of attractions in the area. Open Jan–Dec.

SELF-CATERING

The Cottage, High Catton Grange, High Catton, near Stamford Bridge, York. YO4 1EP   10

Sheila Foster
☎ 01759 371374
SC From £140–£290
Sleeps 2–6
🏠 🐕 *Commended*

This former gig shed and stable has been converted to a high standard yet retains many original features. Comfortable and tastefully furnished with colour TV, automatic washer/dryer, fridge, microwave, storage heaters,etc. Patio doors onto large private patio and garden furniture. Glorious views across green meadows. Working farm in peaceful, rural setting, ideally situated for York or touring. Open all year.

⑪ Lund Farm Cottage, Lund Farm, Gateforth, Selby, North Yorkshire YO8 9LE

Chris & Helen Middleton
☎/Fax 01757 228775
🆂🅲 From £150–£320
Sleeps 6
🐕 ✂ 🛋 🎋 🛍 🍴
🔑 🔑 🔑

Highly Commended

Convenient for York, the Dales and Moors, the cottage wing of our peaceful 18th century farmhouse has 3 bedrooms, beams, blackleaded fireside range, private patio and lawn. Children welcome; 200-acre farm with lambs, eggs to collect and baby-listening. Evening meals on request. Friendly owners just next door. Prices fully inclusive. Open all year.

DISABLED VISITORS

Many members offer a welcome to disabled/less able visitors. Please do check the extent of the facilities before booking.

THE 1000+ BUREAU MEMBERS OFFER A UNIQUE LINK TO CUSTOMERS ACROSS THE UK

All Bureau members belong to a local Group. Each member can refer you to an equally high quality member within his Group... or across the UK: England, Northern Ireland, Scotland, Wales.

27

England's North Country

South and West Yorkshire

Group Contact: *Mrs Marie Gill* ☎ *01924 848339*

We extend a warm welcome to you to visit the gently rolling countryside of South and West Yorkshire.

On the edge of the Peak District National Park is the small town of Holmfirth 'Last of the Summer Wine Country'. Surrounded by hills and moors, it is perfect for walkers who may like to try the Kirklees Way which is a circular walk of 75 miles.

The open air markets of Dewsbury, Leeds and Barnsley are very popular and the area abounds with mill shops. Beside the M1 is Meadowhall Shopping Mall which has 200 shops under one roof.

Within easy access are the Yorkshire Sculpture Park, the Yorkshire Mining Museum and Kirklees Light Steam Railway.

Why not visit Sheffield with its parks and gardens or Leeds with the Henry Moore Gallery or Wakefield's Chantry Chapel?

For water sports enthusiasts there are three water parks in the area.

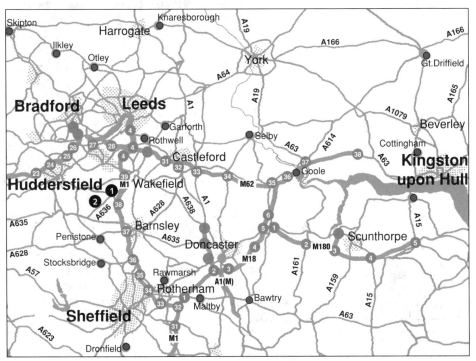

BED AND BREAKFAST

(and evening meal)

---

① Birch Laithes Farm, Bretton Lane, Bretton, Wakefield, West Yorkshire WF4 4LF

Pat Hoyland
☎ 01924 252129
BB From £15–£17
EM From £7
Sleeps 6

A mixed working farm with 18th century house. Comfortable bedrooms, tea/coffee-making facilities, TV, separate dining room and TV lounge, central heating. Ideally situated for Yorkshire towns and countryside, Yorkshire Sculpture Park nearby. 1½ mile J38/39 M1. Open all year.

---

② White Cross Farm, Ash Lane, Emley, Nr Huddersfield, West Yorkshire HD8 9QU

Marie Gill
☎ 01924 848339
BB From £16–£18
Sleeps 5

Listed *Approved*

Mixed working farm with listed farmhouse. Some buildings date from 12th century when monks from Byland Abbey lived here and dug for iron ore and kept sheep. Set in rolling Pennine countryside. Tea/coffee-making facilities, TV, central heating in all bedrooms. Close to Yorkshire Mining Museum, Yorkshire Sculpture Park and Holmfirth (Last of Summer Wine country). 3 miles from M1 (jct. 38/39). Open all year (closed Christmas).

FARM HOLIDAY BUREAU

THOSE LITTLE EXTRAS

For advice on farms that can offer 'extras' such as four-poster beds, special diets, farm trails, fishing rights – even stabling and trekking arrangements if you are bringing your own horse – ring the Farm Holiday Bureau on (01203) 696909.

28

England's North Country
Vale of Lune, Morecambe Bay to Pennine Way

Group Contact: *Mrs Ruth Wrathall* ☎ *01995 603335*

Rising in the hills of Cumbria, the Lune flows through richly pastoral countryside. One of its first ports of call is Kirkby Lonsdale, an attractive market town with its 13th century church and Devils Bridge. To the south east lies the busy moorland market town of High Bentham with its Wednesday cattle market and Ingleton, famous for its show caves and spectacular waterfall glens. To the north west lie the unique Limestone Crags of Arnside and Silverdale with its many splendid coastal walks, together with the RSPB bird sanctuary at Leighton Moss and for railway enthusiasts 'Steam Town' at Carnforth will take you back in time. The Lune then flows down to the Roman city of Lancaster with its castle and museums including the Maritime Museum, Museum of Childhood and the Judges Lodgings. At the end of the Lune Valley lies Morecambe Bay.

The River Wyre starts its journey to the sea high in the fells of the ancient hunting Forest of Bowland and flows down through unspoilt villages such as Marshaw, Abbeystead and Dolphinholme to the market town of Garstang. Beacon Fell Country Park is nearby and well worth a visit. The River Lune and the Wyre offer plenty of opportunities for coarse fishing.

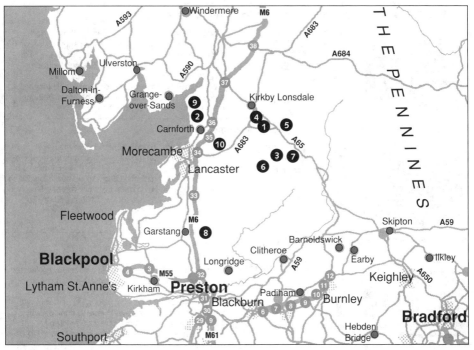

Bed and Breakfast

(and evening meal)

1 **Collingholme Farm,** Cowan Bridge, Carnforth, Lancashire LA6 2JL

Anne & Peter Burrow
☎ 015242 71775
BB From £13–£15
Sleeps 4
(3)
Listed *Highly Commended*

Collingholme nestles peacefully by a stream ¾ mile from the A65. It is a lovely old farmhouse giving a feeling of warmth and well being, beautifully furnished. Well placed for exploring the Dales and Lakes, 3 miles from Kirkby Lonsdale. All rooms have wash basins and tea/coffee-making facilities. Hearty breakfasts. Open Mar–Oct.

2 **Cotestones Farm,** Sand Lane, Warton, Carnforth, Lancashire LA5 9NH

Gillian Close
☎ 01524 732418
BB From £13
Sleeps 6
Listed

Situated on the North Lancashire coast near to the M6 Junction 35 on the Carnforth to Silverdale road, this is a 150-acre family-run dairy farm which adjoins Leighton Moss RSPB Reserve. Also very near to Steamtown Railway Museum. Lying between Lancaster, Morecambe and the Lake District, it is an ideal place for touring the area. Tea/coffee-making facilities and washbasins in all rooms. Reductions for children. Open all year (closed Christmas).

3 **Fowgill Park Farm,** High Bentham, Nr Lancaster, North Yorkshire LA2 7AH

Shirley Metcalfe
☎ 015242 61630
BB From £12–£15
EM From £7.50
Sleeps 6
Commended

Fowgill is a stock rearing farm, ideal for those who wish to stay where it is quiet. Guests enjoy panoramic views of the Dales and Fells. A good centre for visiting the Lakes, Dales, coast, waterfalls and caves. Beamed bedrooms have washbasins, shaver points and tea/coffee-making facilities; two bedrooms en suite. Comfortable beamed lounge with television. Separate dining room. Bedtime drink included. Open Easter–Oct.

4 **Garghyll Dyke,** Cowan Bridge, Kirkby Lonsdale, Cumbria LA6 2HT

Mrs Gillian Burrow
☎ 015242 71446
BB From £15–£17
Sleeps 4

We offer a warm, friendly welcome with hearty breakfasts in our comfortable ivy-clad farmhouse where guests can feel at home. A dairy/sheep farm 3 miles from Kirkby Lonsdale, an ideal base to explore coast, Lakes and Dales. Double and twin room tastefully furnished, each with washbasins and tea/coffee facilities. Country pubs and excellent eating places nearby. Reductions for children. Open Mar–Oct.

5 **Gatehouse Farm,** Far Westhouse, Ingleton, Carnforth, Lancashire LA6 3NR

Nancy Lund
☎ 015242 41458/41307
BB From £15
EM From £8
Sleeps 6

Bryan and Nancy welcome you to our dairy and sheep farm built in 1740, rooms with old oak beams in elevated position enjoying panoramic views over open countryside in the YORKSHIRE DALES NATIONAL PARK. Guests dining room, and lounge with colour TV. Bedroom with private facilities and tea trays. Welcome drink on arrival. 15 miles exit 34 M6, 1½ miles west of Ingleton just off A65. Open all year (closed Christmas and New Year).

Lane House Farm, High Bentham, Nr Lancaster, North Yorkshire LA2 7DJ

Betty Clapham
☎ 015242 61479
🆎 From £15
EM From £8
Sleeps 6
🐓 🐴 🐷 ✄ 🏕
🐞 🐞 *Commended*

Enjoy a relaxing break at our 17th century beamed farmhouse, within ½ mile of the Forest of Bowland, with beautiful views of the Yorkshire Dales. 1 mile from the market town of High Bentham, ½ hour from M6. Ideal for caves, waterfalls, touring the Lakes. Bedrooms have washbasins and tea-making trays. en suite facilities. Guests' lounge with colour TV. Separate dining room. Open Mar–Nov.

Nutstile Farm, Ingleton, Carnforth, North Yorkshire LA6 3DT

Carol Brennand
☎ 015242 41752
🆎 From £13–£15
Sleeps 6
🐴 🐓 🏕 ✄ 🎣
Applied

Surrounded by the outstanding beauty of the Yorkshire Dales, Nutstile is a typical working farm providing 1st class accommodation. The mountains, caves and waterfalls of Ingleton are immediatly accessible, the Lake District also close by. Try a leisurely ride on the scenic Settle-Carlisle railway. Three bedrooms (all with views) with wash basin and tea/coffee faciltes. Guests' lounge with TV. Open all year.

Stirzakers Farm, Barnacre, Garstang, Preston, Lancashire PR3 1GE

Ruth Wrathall
☎ 01995 603335
🆎 From £14–£16
Sleeps 6
🐴 🐓 ✄ 🏕 🎣
Listed *Highly*
Commended

Welcome to our dairy farm where you can relax in the peace and quiet of the beautiful countryside. We have double, family and single rooms in our old stone, beamed farmhouse. CH, separate lounge with colour TV. Two visitors' bathrooms and showers. Tea-making facilities. Children half price. Open all year (closed Christmas and New Year).

SELF-CATERING

Brackenthwaite Cottages, Brackenthwaite Farm, Yealand Redmayne, Carnforth, LA5 9TE

Susan Clarke
☎ 015395 63276
🆑 From £85–£305
Sleeps 4/6
🐓 🐴 🎿 🛏 🏕 🎣
🐾 🐾 🐾 – 🐾 🐾 🐾 🐾
Commended

Brackenthwaite is situated between Lancaster and Kendal with good access to coast, Lakes and Dales. Lovely walks near nature reserves. Access to farm and woodland with nature trail. The Old Stables are a recent conversion with many features retained. Newly modernised Keepers Cottage has all rooms on a single level. Laundry facilities available. Adventure playground. Open all year. Short lets Nov–Easter.

Garden Cottage, High Snab, Gressingham, Lancaster LA2 8LS (10)

Mrs Margaret Burrow
☎ 015242 21347
🆑 From £160–£260
Sleeps 4 + cot
🐴
🐾 🐾 🐾 *Commended*

Garden cottage, with its own private drive and garden, adjoins our farmhouse on a working dairy and sheep farm in a quiet location. Ideal for touring lakes, dales and coast. Winner of Lancashire Farm Landscape Trophy and NWTB 'Place to stay 93'. Well equipped kitchen/oak beamed lounge. Two bedrooms, 1 double, 1 twin, snooker table, bathroom with shower. CH from farmhouse, cot/high chair available. Electric and linen included. 5 miles jct 35 M6. Brochure.

29

England's North Country

Lancashire Coast and Country

Group Contact: *Mrs Heather Smith* ☎ *01253 836465*

Contrasting scenery beckons you to the Lancashire Coast and Country where the bracing coastline with its dunes, a National Nature Reserve at Lytham St. Annes, offers sanctuary for wild life. Travel up the coast to the hustle and bustle of Blackpool with its famous illuminations. Then on through Cleveleys finally resting at Fleetwood, an ancient fishing port, where the River Wyre meets the sea.

Travel east to Poulton-le-Fylde, an ancient market town with its stocks and beautiful Norman church.

Inland from the coast the acres of rich farm land dotted with villages, some with weekly street markets, all have an individual character and charm of their own.

Move up to the hill country, excellent for walkers and explorers: Bleasdale Fell and Beacon Fell, adjoining the rolling hills of the Forest of Bowland, or enjoy a picnic at Brock, an area of outstanding beauty.

We have lots to offer everyone – including excellent theatres at both Preston and Blackpool.

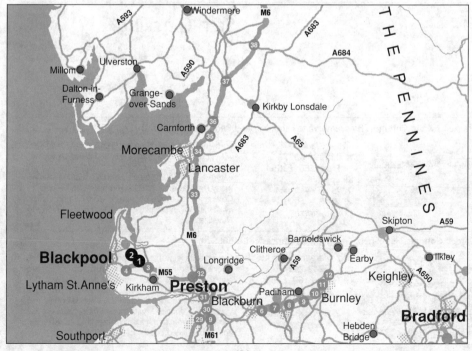

BED AND BREAKFAST

(and evening meal)

Swarbrick Hall Farm, Singleton Road, Weeton, Nr Preston, Lancashire PR4 3JJ

Mrs Heather Smith
☎ 01253 836465
[BB] From £16–£20
Sleeps 4

Relax and enjoy the peace and tranquility of rural Lancashire within easy reach of coastal resorts. Good access to Lake District, Trough of Bowland and Yorkshire Dales. Our 200-acre working farm offers excellent accommodation in Georgian farmhouse. 1 family room with en suite bathroom, colour TV, tea making facilities. Visitors' lounge. Open all year. Children welcome.

Todderstaffe Hall Farm, off Fairfield Road, Singleton, near Blackpool, Lancashire FY6 8LF

Mrs Maureen Smith
☎ 01253 882537
[BB] From £15–£20
Sleeps 4

Commended

Enjoy a friendly welcome at our 260-acre arable farm situated 4 miles from the attractions of Blackpool in a peaceful corner of the Fylde and within easy reach of Lake District. Oak beams and open fires maintain the charm of the old farmhouse but modern comforts, like central heating have been added. One twin/family room with en suite bathroom, colour TV, and tea making facilities. Reduced terms early season.

SELF-CATERING

Swarbrick Hall Farm Cottage, Singleton Road, Weeton, Nr Preston, Lancashire PR4 3JJ

Mrs Heather Smith
☎ 01253 836465
[SC] From £175–£265
Sleeps 5

Commended

Relax and enjoy the peace and tranquillity of rural Lancashire, within easy reach of coastal resorts. Good access to Lake District, Trough of Bowland and Yorkshire Dales. Our 200-acre working farm offers excellent accommodation in cottage attached to main house. 2 twin rooms, bathroom, lounge, kitchen/diner, CH, linen, electric included. Shop and pub 1½ miles. Open all year.

30

England's North Country

West Lancashire

Group Contact: *Mrs Wendy Core* ☎ *01704 880337*

A vast marshland until the early 18th century, West Lancashire is now one of the most fertile areas in Britain, the main industry being agriculture. In the middle of this 'garden' lies the ancient town of Ormskirk, where the market was first chartered in the 13th century. Henry VIII was responsible for the Parish Church's unusual appearance – after Burscough Prior was dissolved, a bell tower was built alongside the steeple to house the bells of the Priory.

People with an interest in history will find a visit to 15th-century Rufford Old Hall and its collection of Tudor furniture fascinating, and railway enthusiasts will enjoy Steamport Museum at Southport with its collection of railway memorabilia. Nearby, the Cedar Farm Gallery at Mawdsley has farm animals and a children's play area which enables mum and dad to enjoy the Craft Centre.

Bird lovers should head for the Wildfowl Trust Centre at Martin Mere where rare and exotic species come and go in an unspoilt area of natural wetland.

Both the Leeds and Liverpool Canal and the River Douglas are pleasant and intriguing to traverse whether you are walking along the banks or boating on the water. Whatever your pleasure, you can find it in West Lancashire.

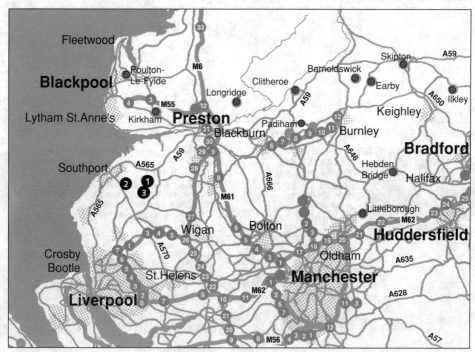

BED AND BREAKFAST

(and evening meal)

Brandreth Barn, Brandreth Farm, Tarlscough Lane, Burscough, Nr Ormskirk, Lancashire L40 0RJ

Mrs M Wilson
☎ 01704 893510
🅱🅱 From £18–£25
EM From £4.95
Sleeps 14
🛏 ⚄ 🎠 ■
🌝🌝🌝 *Approved*

Situated alongside the wildfowl trust Martin Mere, an 18th century brick-built barn conversion dated 1774. 5 minutes from A59, 15 mins from M6. All rooms fully centrally heated, with tea/coffee-making facilities. All rooms en suite plus colour TV. Licensed restaurant. Also disabled facilities. Arable farm. Open all year.

Sandy Brook Farm, Wyke Cop Road, Scarisbrick, Southport, Lancashire PR8 5LR

Mrs W E Core
☎ 01704 880337
🅱🅱 From £15
Sleeps 15
🛏 🎠 ⚄
🌝🌝

This small, comfortable arable farm is situated in the rural area of Scarisbrick, midway between the seaside town of Southport and the ancient town of Ormskirk. The A570 is only ½ mile away. The converted farm buildings are attractively furnished, and all bedrooms have en suite facilities, colour TV and tea/coffee-making facilities. Disabled facilities available. Open all year except Christmas.

SELF-CATERING

Martin Lane Farmhouse Cottages, Martin Lane, Burscough, Lancs L40 8JH

Elaine Stubbs
☎/Fax 01704 893527
🆂🅲 From £200–£350
Sleeps 5/7
🛏 🏃 📺 ■ 🎾
🎠 🎠 🎠 🎠 *Highly Commended*

These award-winning holiday cottages are situated in the heart of the peaceful West Lancashire countryside yet only 5 miles from the seaside resort of Southport. The 'Shippon' sleeping 4/5 and the Granary sleeping 7 are both superbly furnished and equipped. Large, safe play area for children. Sheep and free range hens on farm. Open all year.

LET THE TELEPHONE RING!

Some farmhouses are big places. Let the telephone ring long enough to give the owner time to answer it.

31

England's North Country

Lancashire Pennines

Group Contact: *Mrs Carole Mitson* ☎ *01282 865301*

The Forest of Bowland, the largest area of unspoilt countryside in Lancashire, 1,827ft high Pendle Hill and the Pennines afford the visitor to the area a chance to appreciate Lancashire at its most beautiful. Complementing such countryside are a number of towns and villages, all with their own individual character: Clitheroe with its castle and museum; Whalley with its Cistercian Abbey (founded in 1296) and Georgian and Tudor houses; the old market towns of Colne, Skipton and Ribchester, with its Roman Museum; Barley, at the foot of Pendle Hill, with its connections with the Witch Trials of 1612; and Slaidburn, the gateway to the Forest of Bowland, once a royal hunting ground.

There is something here to suit all tastes. For example, places of historic interest, such as Browsholme Hall, the home of the Parker family, which houses a display of 13th century domestic articles, can be contrasted with the new Preston Guild Hall with facilities for many social, cultural and educational activities. If you prefer a quiet, more sedate pace, you can enjoy one of the several country parks and picnic areas, such as Beacon Fell, Spring Wood, Barley or Wycoller. A holiday in the farms of the Lancashire Pennines will also leave you within easy reach of the Yorkshire Dales, the Lake District, Haworth and Brontë Country.

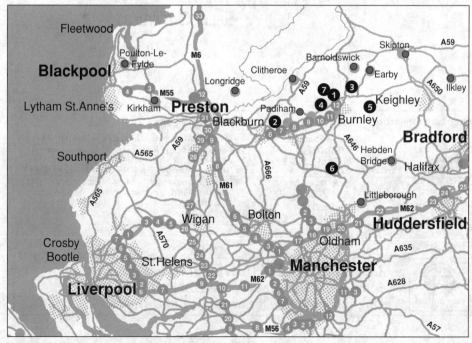

BED AND BREAKFAST

(and evening meal)

Blakey Hall Farm, Red lane, Colne, Lancashire BB8 9TD

Mrs R Boothman
☎ **01282 863121**
🛏 **From £15–£17**
EM From £6.50
Sleeps 6
🐄 🐈 ⛺ ▪
Applied

Pretty and comfortable accommadation on working dairy farm along Leeds Liverpool canal. Fishing available. Own TV lounge. 3 bedrooms, 1 en suite, tea/coffee facilities. Open all year.

Eaves Barn Farm, Hapton, Burnley, Lancashire BB12 7LP

Mrs M Butler
☎ **01282 771591/ 770478**
🛏 **From £18.50–£22**
EM From £9
Sleeps 5
🐕 (10) 🐈 ⛺ ▪ 🍴
Listed *Commended*

Eaves Barn Farm is a mixed working farm. The accommodation comprises a spacious cottage attached to the main house, furnished to a high standard and offering luxury facilities. Excellent English breakfasts are served in the newly constructed conservatory. Delicious evening meals and homemade preserves a speciality. Ideally situated for all Lancashire's tourist attractions. Open all year.

Higher Wanless Farm, Red Lane, Colne, Lancashire BB8 7JP

Carole Mitson
☎ **01282 865301**
🛏 **From £18–£22**
EM From £9.50
Sleeps 4
🐕 (3) 👤 🐈 ⛺ ▪ 🍴
🐾 🐾

Ideally situated for visiting 'Pendle Witch' country, Haworth or Yorkshire Dales – the farm nestles peacefully alongside the Leeds/Liverpool Canal. Shire horses and sheep are reared on the farm, where the warmest of welcomes awaits you. Spacious and luxurious bedrooms (1 en suite) offer every comfort for our guests. Several country inns nearby offering wide range of meal facilities. AA selected establishment. Open Jan–Nov.

Lower White Lee Farm, Fence, Burnley, Lancashire BB12 9ER

Helen Boothman
☎ **01282 613563**
🛏 **From £16**
EM From £8.50
Sleeps 4
🐓 🐕 (2) 🐈 ▪
🐾 *Commended*

A 200-acre dairy farm, offering accommodation in beautifully furnished 18th century farmhouse. 2 bedrooms, each with tea/coffee-making facilities, central heating. Lounge and separate dining room. Good food a speciality. 25 mins from M6. Ideally situated for Brontë Country, Yorkshire Dales and the Lakes. Many cultural and scenic attractions nearby. Open Jan–end Nov.

Parson Lee Farm, Wycoller, Colne, Lancashire BB8 8SU

Patricia Hodgson
☎ **01282 864747**
🛏 **From £13–£17**
EM £6
Sleeps 6
🐓 🐄 ⛺
🐾

There's a warm welcome at our 110-acre sheep farm on the edge of beautiful Wycoller Country Park. The 250-year old farmhouse, with exposed beams and mullion windows, is peacefully located and perfect for walking, being on the Brontë and Pendle Ways. Easy access to Lancashire or Yorkshire. Pendle Way walking breaks with transport. Both en suite bedrooms, furnished in country style, have tea/coffee-making facilities. Open all year except Christmas & New Year.

6   **Pasture Bottom Farm,** Bacup, Lancashire OL13 9UZ

Ann Isherwood
☎ **01706 873790**
🅱🅱 **From £13**
EM From £6
Sleeps 4

🐾 *Approved*

60-acre beef farm offering farmhouse bed and breakfast. Ideally situated for walking Rossendale and Lancashire Moors. Local attractions include a textile museum, skiing at Rossendale and hang gliding at Whitworth. Open all year except Christmas and New Year.

SELF-CATERING

7   **Blakey Hall Cottage,** Red Lane, Colne, Lancashire BB8 9TD

Mrs R Boothman
☎ **01282 863121**
🆂🅲 **From £157–£290**
Sleeps 6
Applied

Blakey Hall Cottage forms part of owners very old farmhouse. Comfortably furnished on a working dairy farm surrounded by rolling countryside. Excellent centre for touring southern Dales and Skipton. Open all year.

FINDING YOUR ACCOMMODATION

The Group contacts at the beginning of each section can always help you find a vacancy in your chosen area.

FARM HOLIDAY BUREAU

England's North Country
South Pennines

Group Contacts: *Mrs Annis Heathcote* ☎ *01457 872424*
Mrs Jean Mayall ☎ *01457 873040*

A warm and friendly welcome awaits visitors to this beautiful and dramatic countryside, still remarkably untouched by tourism. Holiday-makers will find unusual and interesting places to visit close by, with Blackpool, York and the Peak District less than an hour away. The Lake District and the North Yorkshire Moors are an easy two hours, whilst businessmen are well placed for work in Manchester, Liverpool, Leeds and Bradford and close to Manchester Airport and Intercity rail.

Walkers on the Pennine Way will experience stark moorland scenery blending with attractive valley towns like Delph, Uppermill, Marsden and Hebden Bridge and there are equally interesting routes over Blackstone Edge with the Roman Road, the Rossendale Way, the Calderdale Way and the Colne Valley Circular. There are canal trips at Uppermill, Sowerby Bridge and Littleborough, and water sports at Hollingworth Lake and Scammanden Dam, where flocks of wild fowl can be seen. The South Pennine textile heritage is magnificently illustrated in the Colne Valley Museum, Golcar, the Helmshore Museum at Haslingden, and the Saddleworth Museum at Uppermill. Craft centres and mill shops abound and traditional handweaving, clog and slipper making and dyeing and printing can be studied here.

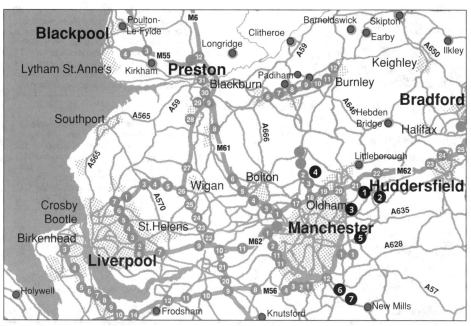

BED AND BREAKFAST

(and evening meal)

---

1 Boothstead Farm, Rochdale Road, Denshaw, Oldham, Greater Manchester OL3 5UE

Mrs Norma Hall
☎ 01457 878622
🆎 From £17–£20
Sleeps 4
🐴 ⚡ 🎾 ▪
Listed

An 18th century hill farm catering for people in the area on business or taking a relaxing break. Ideally situated within 3½ miles of M62 Junctions 21 and 22 (A640). Cosy lounge with open fire, TV, tea/coffee-making facilities, wash basins in rooms. Good base for touring neighbouring counties and beauty spots. Close to Saddleworth leisure amenities, ie. golf, swimming, walking, sailing. Open 3 Jan–22 Dec.

---

2 Globe Farm, Huddersfield Road, Delph, Nr Oldham, Greater Manchester OL3 5LU

Jean Mayall
☎ 01457 873040
🆎 From £17
EM from £6.50
Sleeps 10
🐴 ♿ 🏕 ⚡ 🎾 ▪ 🍴
🍷

Overlooking the picturesque valleys of Saddleworth but within easy reach of M62 junction 22, Manchester Airport, Yorkshire Dales and Peak District. Only ¼ mile from Pennine Way. Evening meal can be provided if required. Colour TV, CH, drying room, tea/coffee-making facilities. Good home cooking and real northern hospitality. Open all year (closed Christmas & New Year).

---

3 Higher Quick Farm, Lydgate, Oldham, Greater Manchester OL4 4JJ

Annis Heathcote
☎ 01457 872424
🆎 £18
EM From £5
Sleeps 6
🐴 ⚡ 🎾
Listed *Highly Commended*

Higher Quick Farm is a grade II listed farmhouse on a 40 acre beef farm, with magnificent views from all rooms. Warm and comfortable house, colour TV and tea-making facilities in each bedroom. 1 twin, 1 double with adjoining private bathroom, 1 double en suite. Ideal area for walking, easy distance M62, 10 miles Manchester Airport, close to Uppermill with a craft centre, museum, golf, canal boat, swimming pool. Open all year (closed Christmas).

---

4 Leaches Farm, Ashworth Valley, Rochdale, Lancashire OL11 5UN

Mrs Jane Neave
☎ 01706 41116/7
🆎 From £18
Sleeps 5
🐴 🐎 🐕 🎾 🛄 ▪
Listed

1674 hill farm in 'The Forgotten Valley'. Magnificent unrestricted views of Yorkshire, Lancashire, Cheshire, Derbyshire hills, on a clear day to the Welsh mountains. Panoramic 'twinkling lights' of Greater Manchester at night. 18 inch stone walls, oak beams, log fires, central heating. Unique 'Rural Wildlife' in the heart of industrial East Lancashire. 10 mins M62 (J19) and M66, Edenfield, 30 mins Manchester Airport. Open 2 Jan–22 Dec.

---

5 Needhams Farm, Uplands Road, Werneth Low, Gee Cross, near Hyde, Cheshire SK14 3AQ

Mrs Charlotte Walsh
☎ 0161 368 4610
Fax 0161 367 9106
🆎 From £17–£19
EM From £7
Sleeps 15
🐴 🐕 ♿ 🎾 ▪
🌸 🌸 🌸 *Commended*

Farmhouse accommodation dating back to the 16th century, offering 5 en suite rooms. Evening meals available each evening. Residential licence. Surrounded by lovely views. Ideal for Manchester Airport and city centre. Courtesy service from airport and Piccadilly station for a small charge. Six bedrooms in all. Open all year.

Shire Cottage Farmhouse, Benches Lane, Chisworth, Hyde, Cheshire SK14 6RY   ⑥

Monica Sidebottom
☎ **01457 866536**
or **0161-427 2377**
🅱 **From £18–£24**
Sleeps 6
🐎 🐂 ♿ 👤 ⛺ ♨
🐾 *Commended*

Real home from home accommodation in peaceful location. Magnificent views overlooking Etheroe Country Park. Convenient for Manchester Airport, city centre, Peak District, stately homes and numerous places of interest. Ground floor bedrooms and bathroom. All rooms have vanity units/shaver points/tea-making facilities/TV. Family room has own shower and toilet. Bathroom has shower and bidet. Early breakfast for businessmen and travellers. Open all year.

SELF-CATERING

Lake View, Ernocroft Farm, Marple Bridge, Stockport, Cheshire SK6 5NT   ⑦

Monica Sidebottom
☎ **01457 866536**
🆂🅲 **From £150–£275**
Sleeps 6 + cot
🐂 🐎 ♿ 👤 ⛺
🐾 🐾 🐾 *Commended*

A new, self-catering farm bungalow, 2 miles Marple Bridge, 4 miles Glossop. Overlooking Etherow Country Park. Ideal base for exploring Peak District, Marple locks and waterways, country parks and stately homes. Peaceful location. Accommodates 6 with all mod cons. TV. Cot available. Open all year.

England's Heartland

Cheshire

Group Contact: *Mrs Veronica Worth* ☎ *01260 224419*

Cheshire is one of England's undiscovered counties. Renowned for lovely black and white architecture and its superb cheese, it is a county of contrasts. From the majesty of the Peak District across the Cheshire Plain to the Dee estuary, from North Wales to Manchester, from the Shropshire Hills to Liverpool, Cheshire has something for everyone. The county has a rich history, well-documented for visitors, with Roman remains in Chester, Elizabethan towns like Nantwich, fine castles and country mansions and museums about the industrial revolution such as Styal Museum at Northwich or Paradise Silk Mill at Macclesfield.

Cheshire offers many peaceful country pursuits: there are canals, wonderful walking (from the Sandstone Trail to shorter farm walks), cycling and fishing. The county has many charming villages and towns, fine old churches, numerous antique shops. There are beautiful gardens in Cheshire – country house, botanical and municipal – plus two of Europe's largest garden centres, Bridgemere Garden World and Stapley Water Gardens.

Chester, the county town, is one of Britain's top tourist destinations. Situated on the River Dee with a splendid cathedral and unique Rows, it offers sophisticated shopping facilities as well as a fine heritage.

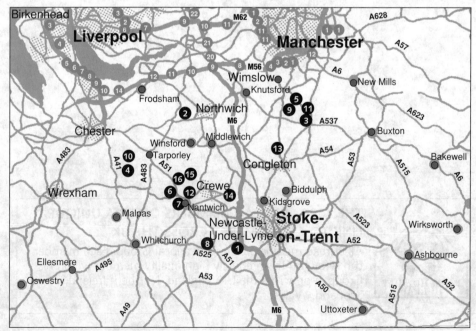

BED AND BREAKFAST

(and evening meal)

Adderley Green Farm, Heighley Castle Lane, Betley, Nr Crewe, Cheshire CW3 9BA

Mrs Sheila Berrisford
☎ 01270 820203
Fax 01782 722422
BB From £14–£18
Sleeps 6
🐎 🛏 🛇 🐄 🐕 🐈 ♨ ♿
♿
👑 👑

Relax in our lovely Georgian farmhouse on a 250-acre dairy farm. Set in large garden along a pretty country lane near an old ruined castle. Fully centrally heated with colour TV, radio, washbasin and tea tray in all bedrooms. En suites available, draped and 4-poster beds. Beautifully decorated in the Laura Ashley style. Ideally situated for Stapeley Water Gardens, Alton Towers and Chester, etc, 10 mins M6 J16. Fishing, and riding available. Open all year.

Beechwood House, 206 Wallerscote Road, Weaverham, Northwich, Cheshire CW8 3LZ

Janet Kuypers
☎ 01606 852123
BB From £15
EM From £7.50
Sleeps 4
🍴 ♿
👑 👑 *Commended*

Warm and comfortable 1830s farmhouse, on 19 acre stock farm. Peaceful. Ample parking. One twin with en suite, 2 single bedrooms with H&C; all have radios. Guests' dining room/lounge with tea/coffee-making facilities and colour TV. Within easy reach of M6 J19 or M56 J10; good half-way stop when travelling. Ideal weekly business accommodation. Open Jan–Nov.

Bell Farm, 7 Bluebell Lane, Tytherington, Macclesfield, Cheshire SK10 2JL

Joan Worth
☎ 01625 423551
BB From £14–£17
Sleeps 5
🐎
👑 👑

Comfortable farmhouse, in quiet lane off the A538. One mile from town centre. Within easy reach of several stately homes, Peak National Park and Manchester Airport. Separate dining room and TV lounge. 1 twin, 1 double with washbasins and 1 single (en suite), central heating. Good parking.

Ford Farm, Nenton Lane, Tattenhall, Chester, Cheshire CW5 8JL

Audrey Charmley
☎ 01829 70307
BB From £12.50–£15
Sleeps 4
🐎 🛏
Listed

A friendly welcome to our dairy farm set in beautiful countryside with views of Beeston and Peckforton Castles. Close to ice cream farm and Cheshire workshops and many tourist attractions. Chester 7 miles, Oulton Park 8 miles. Guests' own lounge and dining room with TV. One double and one twin room, tea/coffee making facilities, bathroom with shower. Open all year.

Goose Green Farm, Oak Road, Mottram St Andrew, Nr Macclesfield, Cheshire SK10 4RA

Dyllis Hatch
☎ 01625 828814
BB From £17–£19
Sleeps 6
🍴 🐎 (5) 🐈 ♨
👑 👑 *Commended*

Welcome to our beef farm set in beautiful countryside with panoramic views. Just off A538 between Wilmslow and Prestbury, in easy reach of M6, M56 and Manchester Airport. Own fishing, horse riding nearby. Comfortable, homely with log fire in guests' lounge. Separate dining room. Pay phone. Double en suite, twin and single rooms, all with washbasin, TV, CH and tea/coffee-making facilities. Open all year (closed Christmas).

6   **Henhull Hall,** Welshmans Lane, Nantwich, Cheshire CW5 6AD

Phillip and Joyce Percival
☎ **01270 624158** or
0374 885305
🛏 **From £20–£22**
Sleeps 5
🐴 🎪
♨

Choose our attractive and spacious farmhouse on a 300-acre dairy farm bordering the canal. A short walk from the historic town of Nantwich, famous for its Elizabethan architecture, antique shops and restaurants. Each en suite bedroom is warm and welcoming with delicious breakfasts to make your stay memorable. Open Jan–Nov.

7   **Lea Farm,** Wrinehill Road, Wybunbury, Nantwich, Cheshire CW5 7NS

Allen & Jean Callwood
☎ **01270 841429**
🛏 **From £13**
EM From £7.50
Sleeps 6
🐴 🐕 🐈 🎪 ▪
♨ ♨ *Commended*

A charming farmhouse set in landscaped gardens where peacocks roam a 150-acre dairy farm. Spacious, attractive bedrooms with washbasins, TV and tea/coffee-making facilities. En suites available. Luxurious lounge with open log fire, with dining room overlooking garden. Snooker, pool table, fishing available. Near to Stapeley Water Gardens and Bridgemere Garden World. M6 J16, Chester and Alton Towers. Open all year (closed Christmas & New Year).

8   **Little Heath Farm,** Audlem, Nantwich, Crewe, Cheshire CW3 0HE

Hilary Bennion
☎ **01270 811324**
🛏 **From £13.50–£18**
EM From £8.50
Sleeps 4
🐕 🐈 🧍 🛴
♨ ♨ *Commended*

Charming old farmhouse, warm and inviting with all modern comforts on a working dairy farm in beautiful canalside village on the A529 from Nantwich. Beamed lounge and dining room with log fires, spacious bedrooms with all facilities. Easy reach M6 J16 near Bridgemere and Stapeley Water Gardens. Ideally based for Chester, Shrewsbury, Staffordshire. Our aim is to make your stay enjoyable and relaxing.

9   **Lower Harebarrow Farm,** Over Alderley, Macclesfield, Cheshire SK10 4SW

Mrs Beryl Leggott
☎ **01625 829882**
🛏 **From £14–£16**
Sleeps 5
🐕 🐈
♨ *Commended*

Comfortable farmhouse within easy reach of many Cheshire beauty spots, stately homes and the Derbyshire hills. Situated on the B5087 midway between Alderley Edge and Macclesfield. Near M6, M56 and Manchester Airport. One double, one twin and one single bedroom all with HC. Open all year.

10   **Newton Hall,** Tattenhall, Chester, Cheshire CH3 9AY

Mrs Anne Arden
☎ **01829 770153**
🛏 **From £15–£20**
Sleeps 5
🐴 🍴 🛴 🎪 ▪
♨ ♨ *Highly Commended*

Part 16th century oak-beamed farmhouse set in large well kept grounds, with fine views of historic Beeston and Peckforton Castles and close to the Sandstone Trail. Six miles south of Chester off A41 and ideal for Welsh Hills. Rooms are en suite or have adjacent bathroom. Fully centrally heated. See our rare Shropshire Down sheep and Pedigree Cattle. Open all year.

11   **Oldhams Hollow Farm,** Manchester Road, Tytherington, Macclesfield, Cheshire SK10 2JW

Brenda Buxton
☎ **01625 424128**
🛏 **From £16–£17**
EM From £9
Sleeps 6
🐴 🐕
Listed

A 16th century listed farmhouse on a working farm, tastefully restored yet retaining its character with oak beams throughout. 3 double bedrooms are comfortably furnished with CH, H/C, electric blankets, colour TVs, tea/coffee-making facilities. Large lounge and separate dining room. Nestling in the foothills of the Pennines 1 mile from the market town of Macclesfield. Ideally located for visiting the many attractions of Cheshire. Evening meal by arrangement.

Poole Bank Farm, Wettenhall, Poole, Nantwich, Cheshire CW5 6AL

Caroline Hocknell
☎ **01270 625169**
ᴮᴮ **From £13.50–£18**
Sleeps 6
ᕫ ⅄ ⊞ ᝾
☙☙ *Commended*

A charming 17th century timbered farmhouse on 260-acre dairy farm set in quiet countryside 2 miles from the historic town of Nantwich. Ideal base for discovering the beautiful Cheshire countryside. Central for Chester and the Potteries. Comfortable and attractive rooms, all with period furnishings. TV and tea/coffee making facilities. A warm welcome and an excellent breakfast are assured. Open all year.

Sandhole Farm, Hulme Walfield, Congleton, Cheshire CW12 2JH

Veronica Worth
☎ **01260 224419**
Fax 01260 224766
ᴮᴮ **From £19–£29**
Sleeps 25
ᕫ ⅄ ⊞ ⅋ ☙ ♨
☙☙ *Highly Commended*

The comfortable traditional farmhouse and delightful converted stable block are situated 2 miles north of Congleton on A34, 15 mins from M6 and 30 mins from Manchester airport. Most of our rooms have modern en suite facilities and all have the usual extras, including hairdryer, remote control teletext TV plus trouser press and direct dial telephone. Large comfortable lounge, separate newly built conservatory/dining room. Cheshire Tourism Award Winner. Open all year.

Snape Farm, Snape Lane, Weston, Nr Crewe, Cheshire CW2 5NB

Mrs Jean Williamson
☎ **01270 820208**
ᴮᴮ **From £13.50–£16**
EM From £7
Sleeps 6
ᕫ ⅄ ⅊ ⇌ ⅄ ♨
☙☙

Enjoy a warm welcome to our centrally heated farmhouse on a 150-acre beef/arable farm set in rolling countryside. 3 miles from Crewe. A good centre for visiting Nantwich, Chester or the Potteries. Guests' lounge and snooker room. 1 twin (en suite), 1 twin, 1 double room, each with colour TV and tea/coffee-making facilities. 4 miles from M6 (jct. 16). Open all year.

Stoke Grange Farm, Chester Road, Nantwich, Cheshire CW5 6BT

Georgina West
☎ **01270 625525**
ᴮᴮ **From £17.50**
Sleeps 6
ᕫ ⅄ ⅌ ᕫ ♨
☙☙ *Commended*

An attractive farmhouse dating from 1838 on a working dairy farm, with large car park and attractive garden. Spacious en suite bedrooms with colour TV and hot drink facilities. Comfortable guest lounge with TV, solarium, games and reading room. Guests can relax on the verandah and watch the canal boats passing the farmhouse. Vegetarians are catered for. Cheshire Tourism Development Award winner 91/92. Open all year.

SELF-CATERING

Stoke Grange Mews, Stoke Grange Farm, Chester Road, Nantwich, Cheshire CW5 6BT

Georgina West
☎ **01270 625525**
ˢᶜ **From £150–£350**
Sleeps 2–6 + cot
ᕫ ♨
↝ ↝ ↝ *Highly Commended*

Holiday home created from a fine old barn near the owner's canalside farmhouse and dairy farm in lush heritage rich countryside some 15 miles south of the Roman town of Chester. Each has exposed beams, quality furniture, and offers fully equipped accommodation with all mod cons. Small rear patio, large shared garden with canal access. Children's play area and farm pets corner. Barbeque area. Cheshire Tourism Development Award winner 91/92. Open all year.

34

England's Heartland
Staffordshire

Group Contacts: BB *Mrs Lynette Bailey* ☎ *01889 562363*
SC *Mr John Myatt* ☎ *01889 22269*

The varied landscape of Staffordshire ranges from that of the Peak District National Park through the moorlands in the north to the fertile valleys of the Trent and its tributaries in the south. In the heart of the county is the extensive Cannock Chase, an area of outstanding natural beauty which offers scope for varied leisure pursuits.

A popular target for visitors to the county are its two leisure parks: Alton Towers, with its exciting rides, is the premier leisure park in the country, while Drayton Manor Park offers an open-plan zoological garden, lakes and an amusement park.

In the county town of Stafford the impressive timber-framed Ancient High House has to be seen. Tamworth, with its Norman Castle, was once the capital of the ancient kingdom of Mercia, while Burton on Trent is famous as the home of the brewing industry. Of particular attraction is the cathedral city of Lichfield, birthplace of Dr Samuel Johnson and host to international music and folk festivals. But of equal antiquity is the town of Tutbury with its fine castle and its glass making tradition.

Many visitors seek out the potteries and visitor centres which offer the chance to see craftsmen at work and perhaps to make purchases at the factory shops.

Whatever your particular interest you can be sure of a warm welcome in Staffordshire!

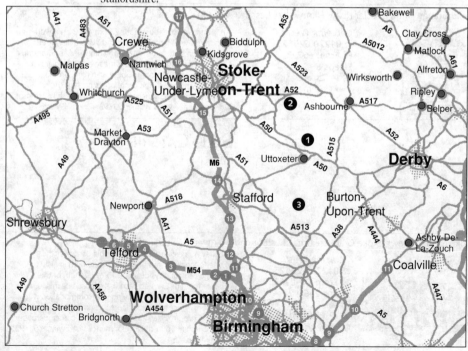

BED AND BREAKFAST

(and evening meal)

Stramshall Farm, Stramshall, Uttoxeter, Staffordshire ST14 5AG

Lynette Bailey
☎ 01889 562363
🛏 From £13–£20
Sleeps 6
🐾 🐂
Listed *Commended*

In the picturesque village of Stramshall you will find a welcome at our late Victorian home with spacious bedrooms. Lounge/dining room and luxury bathroom. Attractive gardens. All bedrooms with H/C, towels, tea/coffee-making facilities, TV, CH and electric blankets. Ample parking. Ten minutes to Alton Towers and convenient for Peak District and many other attractions. Open Mar–Nov.

Ribden Farm, Nr Oakamoor, Stoke-on-Trent, Staffordshire ST10 3BW

Christine Shaw
☎ 01538 702830
🛏 From £16–£18
Sleeps 11
🐂 🐂
👑 👑 *Highly Commended*

Ribden Farm is an 18th Century farmhouse c1748 which is situated 1,000 ft high in the Weaver Hills yet is only 5 minutes from Alton Towers. Plenty of underused footpaths. Local inns. All rooms en suite with colour TV, coffee/tea-making facilities. Separate TV lounge and dining room. Secure off road parking. RAC Acclaimed. AA QQQQ selected. Open all year.

SELF-CATERING

Priory Farm Fishing House, c/o Priory Farm, Blithbury, Rugeley, Staffordshire WS15 3JA

Mr John Myatt
☎ 0188 922 269
🏠 From £65–£110
Sleeps 4
🐂 🐾 🦽
🐾 🐾 🐾 *Approved*

Converted 18th century fishing house overlooking River Blithe, offering unique accommodation for up to 4 persons on secluded dairy farm. Ideal for lovers of the countryside and wildlife. Convenient for Abbots Bromley, Lichfield, Cannock Chase, Alton Towers and the Peak District. Comfortable, tastefully furnished accommodation includes large bed-sitting room with colour TV, modern kitchen and shower room. Brochure on request. Open all year.

35

England's Heartland

Peak District

Group Contacts: 📠 *Joy Lomas* ☎ *0162 9540 250*

Britain's first National Park offers variety and spectacular scenery, from the exhilaration of the wide, windswept moorlands in the north to the softer south where the Manifold and Dove rivers run parallel through water meadows, woodlands and rocky gorges.

As well as some of the best walking in the country, the Peak District offers numerous stately homes such as Chatsworth, Haddon and Hardwick, as well as the thrills of Alton Towers and Water World, and Water Sports at Carsington Water.

Find a bargain in the Potteries seconds shops and at Gladstone Pottery Museum go back in time amongst the bottle kilns. Wedgwood shows a complete contrast by demonstrating modern production of fine china.

Leek and Bakewell markets transform sleepy country towns when farmers from miles around descend on them. At Matlock cable cars glide majestically across an awe-inspiring gorge to the Heights of Abraham. Castleton is famous for its show caves and Blue John stone. So, whether having afternoon tea at a stately home, admiring the Well Dressings or picnicking amongst the heather, you can be sure that the Peak District has something for you.

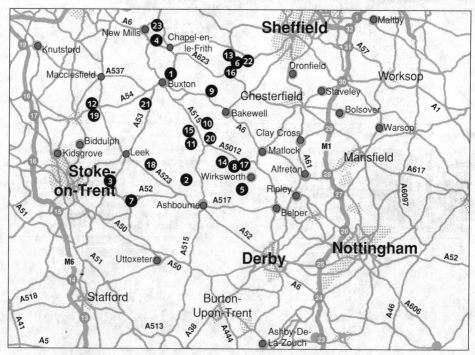

BED AND BREAKFAST

(and evening meal)

Barms Farm, Fairfield, Buxton, Derbyshire SK17 7HW   1

Lorraine Naden
☎ 01298 77723
Fax 01298 78692
BB From £19
EM From £12
Sleeps 6
✗ 🐎 (10)
💭 *Highly Commended*

Working dairy farm offers accommodation in warm, spacious, luxury farmhouse overlooking golf course one mile north of Buxton. Three delightful bedrooms, all with superb en suite facilities. Traditional features and high class fixtures and fittings are complemented by beautiful decor throughout. Illuminated private parking. Strictly non-smoking. Brochure on request. Open all year.

Beechenhill Farm, Ilam, Ashbourne, Derbyshire DE6 2BD   2

Sue Prince
☎ 01335 310274
BB From £17–£21
Sleeps 5
✗ 🐎
💭 *Highly Commended*

We live in one of the best places in the world! Our warm farmhouse nestles on south facing hill beside Dovedale. We take pleasure in sharing our home with our guests. We've 2 delightful rooms, family en suite and double with private shower room. Wonderful views, tea/coffee, own lounge, all beautifully decorated (stencils, murals). After jolly good breakfast explore our countryside – glorious walks lead from our door. Open March–Dec.

Brook House Farm, Cheddleton, Leek, Staffordshire ST13 7DF   3

Elizabeth Winterton
☎ 01538 360296
BB From £15–£17
EM From £8
Sleeps 10
🐎 🐕 🐈 🐴
💭💭 *Commended*

Comfortable en suite accomodation on our dairy farm in a picturesque and peaceful valley. Central for Peak District, Potteries and Alton Towers. 2 spacious rooms in a tastefully converted cowshed. 2 in the farmhouse, all with tea/coffee-makers and colour TV. Dine in our attractive conservatory with magnificent country views. A warm welcome with log fires and good farmhouse food a speciality. Open all year.

Cote Bank Farm, Buxworth, Whaley Bridge, Derbyshire SK12 7NP   4

Pamela Broadhurst
☎ 01663 750566
BB From £17.50–£18.50
Sleeps 4
🐎 (6) 🎣 🏕 ☎ ✿
💭

Our warm welcoming country home, 1 mile from Chinley village, has a double en suite bedroom overlooking our tree-ringed farmyard and a twin room with one of the best views in Derbyshire! Both with washbasin and tea/coffee-making facilities. Wonderful walks, both easy and strenuous, cross our 150 acres of Peak National Park. Pam's breakfasts are worthing waking for! Open Mar–Nov.

Henmore Grange, Hopton, Carsington, Wirksworth, Derbyshire DE4 4DF   5

John & Elizabeth Brassington
☎ 01629 540 420
BB From £20–£27.50
EM From £5–£11.50
Sleeps 28
🅶🅽 🎣 ♿ 🐎 ♨
💭💭 *Commended*

Between Ashbourne and Matlock by Peak National Park overlooking Carsington Water, offering good old-fashioned hospitality in a beautifully converted barn in a garden planted to attract butterflies. Most rooms have private bath/shower rooms. All have tea/coffee-making facilities. Choice of menu. Fire certificate. Visited by HRH Duke of Gloucester. Certificate of Merit in Come to Britain Award. Open all year.

6   **Lane End Farm,** Abney, Hathersage, via Sheffield, S30 1AA

Mrs Jill Salisbury
☎ 01433 650371
BB From £15.50–£25
Sleeps 6
🛏 ⚓ 🐴 🐕 🐈 ☂
Listed *Highly Commended*

Award-winning farmhouse on working hill farm above the Hope Valley. Tourist Board Bed & Breakfast of the Year – Commended. Share our enthusiasm for our lovely surroundings. Stunning views, off the beaten track, walks from the door. Traditional farmhouse, beautifully decorated. 3 bedrooms (1 en suite) with hot drink facilities, washbasins, CH. TV lounge. Hearty breakfasts. Own horse welcome. Farm nature trail. Open all year (closed Christmas).

7   **Ley Fields Farm,** Leek Road, Cheadle, Stoke-on-Trent, Staffordshire ST10 2EF

Mrs Kathryn Clowes
☎ 01538 752875
BB From £16–£17
EM From £8.50
Sleeps 6
🐴 ✂ ☂
♨♨♨

Listed Georgian farmhouse amidst beautiful countryside with local walks offering abundant wildlife. Convenient for Alton Towers, Pottery museums and Peak District. Spacious, traditionally furnished accommodation includes guests' lounge and dining room. Luxury bedrooms with hot drink facilities, family suite, family en suite, double en suite. CH. Excellent home cooking and a warm welcome to our family home. Open Jan–Nov.

8   **Middlehills Farm,** Grange Mill, Matlock, Derbyshire DE4 4HY

Mrs Linda Lomas
☎/Fax 01629 650368
BB From £15
Sleeps 6
🐴 🐕 ⚓ 💼

Five miles west of Matlock on the A5012, this small working farm with new limestone farmhouse and large garden is set amidst beautiful scenery. Ideal for touring Peak District, close to Chatsworth House, Dovedale and other places of interest. Spacious accommodation. All bedrooms with washbasins and tea/coffee facilities. Family rooms en suite. Visitors lounge with colour TV/pool table. Open all year.

9   **The Old Bake & Brewhouse,** Blackwell Hall, Blackwell in the Peak, Taddington, nr Buxton, Derbys SK17 9TQ

Mrs Christine Gregory
☎ 01298 85271
BB From £16–£17
Sleeps 4
🐴 ⚓ ✂ ☂
♨

Early 18th century much loved farmhouse set in peaceful mature 2 acre garden. Footpath to lovely Cheedale Monsal Dale from our door. A warm welcome awaits you on our busy 300 acre dairy farm. Private oak beamed lounge/dining room furnished with antiques. Delicious traditional breakfasts or your own requirements. All rooms en suite with colour TV, tea/coffee-making facilities, CH. Open all year.

10   **Shallow Grange,** Chelmorton, near Buxton, Derbyshire SK17 9SG

Christine Holland
☎ 01298 23578
Fax 01298 78242
BB From £19–£21
EM From £13
Sleeps 6
🐴 (5) ♿ ⚓ ☂ 💼
♨♨♨ *Highly Commended*

Shallow Grange is situated in the heart of the Peak District. Set amidst beautiful open views, this working dairy farm has numerous unspoilt walks. The 18th century farmhouse has your comfort in mind, offering high quality fixtures and fittings including all en suite bedrooms with colour TV, tea/coffee making facilities. Full central heating and double glazing. Fully licensed. Open all year.

11   **Wolfscote Grange Farm,** Hartington, Nr Buxton, Derbyshire SK17 0AX

Jane Gibbs
☎ 01298 84342
BB From £15–£16
Sleeps 6
🐴 ⚓ ☂ 💼
Listed

'Peaceful and away from it all' describes perfectly our 15th century farmstead nestling under Wolfscote Hill with beautiful views over the Dove Valley. 2 miles from pretty Hartington village. Always a warm welcome to our ancient farmhouse; spiral staircase, oak beams, mullion windows and comfortable antique furnishings. Guests' lounge, en suite rooms, tea/coffee facilities. Breakfast then enjoy the views and explore the many footpaths leading to the Dales below. Open all year.

Yew Tree Farm, North Rode, Congleton, Cheshire CW12 2PF

Mrs Sheila Kidd
☎ **01260 223569**
🅱 **From £15**
EM £10
Sleeps 6
🐎 🏕 ⛵ 🏇 🎿
Listed *Commended*

You can be assured of a warm welcome, a cosy atmosphere and good food at this farm which is set in wooded parkland. Central for the Peak District, Potteries, Alton Towers and the historic houses of Cheshire. Guests are invited to look around the farm and are introduced to the animals which include a wide range of pets. One double en suite and two twin rooms. Open all year.

SELF-CATERING

Archway Cottage, Lane End Farm, Abney, Hathersage, Via Sheffield, S30 1AA

Jill Salisbury
☎ **01433 650371**
🆂🅲 **From £120–£250**
Sleeps 2/4
🐎 🏕 ⛺ 🚲 🏊
🎿 🎿 🎿 *Commended*

Beams, pine furniture, lovely decor make our well-equipped cottage a must for the discerning visitor to the Peak District. Tucked away on our working hill farm in a small hamlet. Superb views, many fabulous walks. Ideally situated for all Derbyshire attractions. 1 double bedroom, sofa bed in lounge. Linen, electricity included. No pets. Own horse welcome.

Chapelgate Cottage, c/o Lydgate Farm, Aldwark, Grange Mill, Matlock, Derbyshire DE4 4HW

Joy Lomas
☎ **01629 540250**
🆂🅲 **From £200–£260**
Sleeps 5 + cot
🐎 🏕
🎿 🎿 🎿 🎿 *Highly Commended*

Beautiful oak beamed, stone mullioned cottage with lovely views and garden, set in the peaceful hamlet of Aldwark. Well appointed open plan kitchen/living area with log fire and colour TV. Two bedrooms and bathroom/shower room. The cottage is centrally heated, double glazed and fully carpeted throughout. Towels, fresh linen and electricity are included. Chapelgate Cottage will give you a wonderful holiday in the heart of the Peak District. Open all year.

Cruck Cottage, Wolfscote Grange Farm, Hartington, Nr Buxton, Derbyshire SK17 0AX

Jane Gibbs
☎ **01298 84342**
🆂🅲 **From £130–£250**
Sleeps 4 + cot
🐎 🏕 🎿 ⚱
🎿 🎿 🎿 *Commended to Highly Commended*

This fine old 15th century cottage is an ideal country hideaway, completely on its own overlooking Wolfscote and Berrisford Dales. No neighbours, only cows and sheep! Cosy and warm with massive beamed interior, galley, double plus one twin bedroom. Walled garden, many footpaths to explore that lead from the cottage to the limestone Dales below. Fully equipped, linen inclusive. Ring for details. Open all year.

The Hayloft, Stanley House Farm, Great Hucklow, Derbyshire SK17 8RL

Margot Darley
☎ **01298 871044**
🆂🅲 **From £95–£210**
Sleeps 4
🏇 🎿 🐎 (5)
🎿 🎿 🎿 🎿 *Highly Commended*

The accommodation is skilfully converted from the original hayloft and the interior is comfortably furnished, mainly with antiques. Comprises a lounge with open fire, colour TV and cottage suite, two twin-bedded rooms, kitchen/diner. The Hayloft offers an ideal centre for exploring the Peak District. All linen/towels at no extra charge. Electricity by 50p meter. Open all year.

17 **Honeysuckle & Jasmine Cottages,** Middlehills Farm, Grange Mill, Matlock, Derbyshire DE4 4HY

Linda Lomas
☎/Fax 01629 650368
SC From £150–£250
Sleeps 4/8
Applied

Relax in peace and comfort in our newly converted cottages on a small working farm in the superb countryside of the Peak Park. One two-bedroomed and one three-bedroomed. Very comfortable and fully equipped with central heating, colour TV, ample parking and south-facing patios. Open all year.

---

18 **Lower Berkhamsytch Farm,** Bottom House, Nr Leek, Staffordshire ST13 7QP

Edith & Alwyn Mycock
☎ 01538 308213
SC From £100–£195
Sleeps 2/6 + cot
Approved

Two self-contained flats converted from stone-built farm building on dairy and pig farm. Each flat has its own private entrance and is within walking distance of 2 pubs serving meals. Lounge/diner with colour TV and double bed-settee. Well equipped kitchen area, 1 double bedroom, 1 twin, shower room with toilet and washbasin. Idea for Alton Towers, Potteries, Peak District and moorland beauty spots. Electricity, heating, linen included. Open all year.

---

19 **The Old Byre,** Pye Ash Farm, Leek Road, Bosley, Macclesfield, Cheshire SK11 0PN

Dorothy Gilman
☎ 01260 273650
SC From £175–£375
Sleeps 10 + cot
Commended

The Old Byre is near the Peak District and Staffordshire's moorlands. Shop and pubs are short walk away. In beautiful countryside farmed with beef and sheep. Many National Trust properties close by including Biddulph Grange Gardens. Alton Towers 15 miles. Ideal for two families. All heating, linen, etc inclusive. Open all year.

---

20 **Old House Farm Cottage,** Old House Farm, Newhaven, Hartington, Buxton, Derbyshire SK17 0DY

Sue Flower
☎ 01629 636268
SC From £150–£275
Sleeps 6 + cot
Commended

Charming cottage conversion on 400-acre working dairy/sheep farm in the heart of the Peak District. Opportunity to watch farm activities. Highly recommended accommodation with storage heaters and fitted carpets throughout, lounge/dining with colour TV, kitchen (electric cooker, fridge, micro-wave, washer and tumble dryer), bathroom with shower. 1 double bedroom, 1 family with twin beds and full size bunks both with H&C. Cot and highchair. Brochure. Open all year.

---

21 **The Old Stables,** Northfield Farm, Flash, Nr Buxton, Derbyshire SK17 0SW

David & Elizabeth Andrews
☎ 01298 22543
Fax 01298 23228
SC From £50–£265
Sleeps 2/7
Up to Commended

Situated in England's highest village. An ideal centre for outdoor activities or for the more leisurely holiday, close to the many attractions of the Peak Park and Potteries. The farm is also a BHS approved riding centre. 3 well-appointed flats with all facilities and CH. Linen and electricity inclusive. Games and laundry rooms. Ground floor flat suitable for the less able. Open all year.

---

22 **Shatton Hall Farm Cottages,** Bamford, Nr Sheffield, Derbyshire S30 2BG

Angela Kellie
☎/Fax 01433 620635
SC From £140–£250
Sleeps 2/6 + cot
Commended
Up to Highly Commended

Recently converted stone cottages on an Elizabethan farmstead: a superb setting in the Peak District. Lovely walking area, fishing, riding, cycle-hire nearby. Hard tennis court. Private terrace, safe play areas, ample car parking. Open plan living room, open fires, CH, colour TV, well-equipped kitchen, 2 double bedrooms. Linen included. Put-u-up and cot available. Full laundry facilities. Pets by arrangement. Open all year.

Shaw Farm, New Mills, near Stockport, Derbyshire SK12 4QE   (23)

Mrs Nicky Burgess
☎ **0161 427 1841**
🆂 **From £120–£260**
Sleeps 8
🐎 🛏 🎄 ♨
🐾 🐾 🐾 *Commended*

Come and enjoy our working dairy farm. Stay in an old stone built farmhouse with lovely views. Entrance hall leads to fully equipped kitchen diner. Large beamed sitting room. Upstairs 2 bedrooms with third by prior arrangement. Full carpeting and central heating throughout. South facing, pleasant gardens. Pets by arrangements. Open all year.

THOSE LITTLE EXTRAS

For advice on farms that can offer 'extras' such as four-poster beds, special diets, farm trails, fishing rights – even stabling and trekking arrangements if you are bringing your own horse – ring the Farm Holiday Bureau on (01203) 696909.

PRICES

Prices include VAT and service charge (if any) and are:
B&B per person per night
EM per person
SC per unit per week
Tents and caravans per pitch per night

36

England's Heartland

Derbyshire Dales and Dovedale

Group Contacts: 🆔 *Carl Postles* ☎ *01773 822328*
🆔 *Audrey Gray* ☎ *01335 370204*

Discover the wealth of delights which makes this county of character and contrast the ideal choice for your short, or long, break destination. From the mellow lowlands of the south to the rugged peaks of the north – from picturesque villages to busy market towns – from historic houses and museums to the excitement of Alton Towers and the American Adventure – a warm and friendly welcome awaits you in every corner.

The countryside around the delightful old market town of Ashbourne, at the southern end of the Pennine Range in Derbyshire, is among the most beautiful in the whole of England. The spectacular scenery of Dovedale and the Manifold Valley, the rolling uplands with their scattered copses and stone walls and isolated traditional farmsteads are well known. Less dramatic but no less rewarding is the tranquil beauty of the unspoilt countryside and villages of the area.

Ashbourne itself is a small, historic country town of distinction, with shops, hotels, restaurants– its speciality Ashbourne gingerbread – a delight not to be missed!

Numerous footpaths provide ideal conditions for walking and there are ample facilities for pony trekking, cycle hire and fishing. Within easy access are many places of interest, great country mansions, the National Tramway Museum, Heritage Centres, Factory Shops, the Heights of Abraham and many more attractions for you to enjoy.

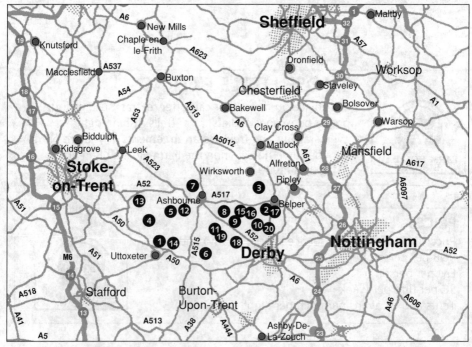

BED AND BREAKFAST

(and evening meal)

The Beeches Farmhouse, Waldley, Doveridge, Nr Ashbourne, Derbyshire DE6 5LR

Barbara Tunnicliffe
☎/Fax 01889 590288
🛏 From £22.50–£38.50
EM From £9.50

Highly Commended

Winners of top national award for farm based catering. Enjoy dining in our oak beamed licensed restaurant – after exploring the Derbyshire countryside or the thrills of Alton Towers. Ten rooms including excellent en suite family rooms which retain the character of our 18th century farmhouse. Children love feeding the animals on our working dairy farm. A warm welcome awaits you. Open all year.

Chevin Green Farm, Chevin Road, Belper, Derbyshire DE56 2UN

Carl & Joan Postles
☎ 01773 822328
🛏 From £14–£20
Sleeps 12

Commended

Relax in peaceful picturesque countryside. Our extended and refurbished beamed farmhouse offers single, twin, double and family en suite rooms. Enjoy generous breakfasts. Guests own lounge and dining room. Within easy reach of Dales, Peak District, stately homes (6) and Alton Towers. Pleasant walks, riding and golf nearby. Reductions for children sharing and weekly terms. Open all year except Christmas.

Dannah Farm, Bowmans Lane, Shottle, Belper, Derbyshire DE56 2DR

Joan Slack
☎ 01773 550273/550630
Fax 01773 550590
🛏 From £25–£35
EM From £13.95
Sleeps 18

Highly Commended

Lovely Georgian farmhouse set amidst beautiful countryside on mixed working farm. All rooms en suite. Colour TV, etc. Superb licensed restaurant, winners 1992 and 1993 national award for farm catering, where we aim to serve the very best in farmhouse cooking. Set in large gardens. AA Premier selected, RAC Highly Acclaimed. Johansens recommended. Fully licensed. Current fire certificate. Four poster suite. Open all year.

Denstone Hall Farm, Denstone, Uttoxeter, Staffordshire ST14 5HF

Mrs Joyce Boden
☎ 01889 590253
Fax 01889 590603
🛏 From £13–£15
Sleeps 6

Listed

Stay on our dairy farm in the beautiful Churnet Valley. We are only ten minutes from Alton Towers and within easy reach of the Peak District and many stately homes. Absorb the rural atmosphere of market day at Ashbourne or Uttoxeter and visit the many pottery factory shops and museums. Trout fishing available. Open Mar–Nov.

Homefields, Dove Street, Ellastone, Ashbourne, Derbyshire DE6 2GY

Gillyan Prince
☎ 01335 324284
🛏 From £16–£19
Sleeps 6
(3)

Tea and homemade cake await you at this delightful small holding on Derbyshire Stafordshire border close to Alton Towers, Dales and stately homes. Relax and watch TV, play piano or sit in beautiful garden overlooking fields. Sleeps 6 people. Walking distance to 2 pubs providing evening meals. Non smoking. No pets.

---

6 **Lees Hall Farm,** Boylestone, Ashbourne, Derbyshire DE6 5AA

Mavis Wilson
☎ 01335 330259
⌨ From £14–£17
Sleeps 6
✗ 🐎 🏕 🐾
🌸🌸 *Commended*

Welcome to Lees Hall, a 100-acre beef farm. The 400-year-old house is set in an unspoilt, rural landscape amid quiet country lanes. 1 family, 1 twin bedded room, both en suite. Tea/coffee-making facilities and central heating. Full English breakfast. Ideally situated for visits to Alton Towers, the Derbyshire Dales and several stately homes. Open all year (closed Christmas).

---

7 **Little Park Farm,** Mappleton, Ashbourne, Derbyshire DE6 2BR

Joan Harrison
☎ 01335 350341
⌨ From £13–£16
EM From £7.50
Sleeps 6
🏕
🌸 *Commended*

Enjoy the peace and quiet at this 123-acre dairy farm, situated in the beautiful Dove valley. Nearby delightful walks, Alton Towers, NT houses and bike hire. The 300-year-old listed farmhouse features oak beams and is tastefully furnished. All bedrooms have washbasins. Comfortable visitors' lounge, TV. Good wholesome farmhouse food served. Open Mar–Nov.

---

8 **New Park Farm,** Moorend, Bradley, Ashbourne, Derbyshire DE6 1LQ

Carol Akers
☎ 01335 343425
⌨ From £14–£18
EM From £10
Sleeps 12
♿ ✗ 🐎 🏕
🌸🌸 *Highly Commended*

A very warm welcome to our comfortable farmhouse in quiet surroundings. Good home cooking with varied menu using wholesome local produce. Children can feed the hens and ducks, collect the eggs. Well situated for all Derbyshire attractions and beautiful countryside. We offer guests en suite double, twin, family rooms, guests' own lounge and dining room. Open Mar–Nov.

---

9 **Mercaston Hall,** Mercaston, Brailsford, Ashbourne, Derbyshire DE6 3BL

Angus & Vicki Haddon
☎ 01335 360263
⌨ From £14.50–£17
Sleeps 6
🐕 (8) 🐎 🏕 🐾 💼 ✂
🌸🌸

Timber-framed, historic, listed building in a quiet countryside location. Situated off the A52 halfway between Derby and Ashbourne. An ideal centre for visits to the Peak District, many tourist attractions and the commercial towns and cities of the Midlands. Kedleston Hall (NT) 1 mile. Hard tennis court. Open all year except Christmas.

---

10 **Parkview Farm,** Weston Underwood, Ashbourne, Derbyshire DE6 4PA

Mrs Linda Adams
☎ 01335 360352
⌨ From £15–£25
Sleeps 6
✗ 🐎 🏕
🌸🌸 *Highly Commended*

Enjoy country house hospitality in our elegant farmhouse. The house is set in a large garden and has lovely views overlooking the National Trust's Kedleston Hall. All rooms are beautifully furnished and have washbasins and tea/coffee-making facilities. Guests' own bathroom, shower room, sitting room and delightful dining room. Country pubs and restaurants close by. 1 twin and 2 doubles with antique four-poster beds. Open all year (closed Christmas).

---

11 **Shirley Hall Farm,** Shirley, Ashbourne, Derbyshire DE6 3AS

Mrs Sylvia Foster
☎ 01335 360346
⌨ From £15–£19
Sleeps 6
✗ 🐕 (10) 🐾 ✂
🌸🌸 *Highly Commended*

Our 200-acre family-run dairy/arable/sheep farm 4 miles from Ashbourne has a lovely old, part moated, timbered farmhouse in peaceful countryside. Excellent walks and private coarse fishing. Many stately homes, the Dales, Alton Towers nearby. One twin with handbasins and guests' bathroom, 2 double bedrooms en suite. Guests' sitting room, TV, CH and drinks facilities all rooms. Superb English breakfasts. Local pubs, 1 within walking distance, for excellent evening meals. Open all year (closed Christmas).

Sidesmill Farm, Snelston, Ashbourne, Derbyshire DE6 2GQ

Mrs Catherine Brandrick
☎ 01335 342710
[BB] **From £14–£16**
Sleeps 5
⅄ ☎ (10)
Applied

Peaceful dairy farm on the banks of the River Dove, a rippling millstream flowing past the 18th century stone-built farmhouse. Good home cooking and a warm welcome guaranteed. Within easy reach of Alton Towers, Dovedale and many other places of interest. Double and twin-bedded rooms, guests' lounge, colour TV, hot drink facilities. Visitors' bathroom. Open Easter–Oct.

Tenement Farm, Ribden, Nr Oakamoor, Stoke-on-Trent, ST10 3BW

Joyce Miller
☎ 01538 702333
[BB] **From £16.50–£18**
Sleeps 12
☎ ⅄ ⊞ ☂ ▪
☙☙ *Commended*

A traditional farm situated in the Staffordshire Moorlands 2 miles from Alton Towers, Dovedale and Manifold Valley, 10 miles Stoke-on-Trent Potteries. Rooms are comfortably furnished, tea/coffee making-facilities. TV lounge, central heating throughout. Generous English breakfast and a warm welcome awaits you. Residential licensed bar, fire certificate. Open Mar–Nov.

Waldley Manor, Marston Montgomery, Nr Doveridge, Derbyshire DE6 5LR

Anita Whitfield
☎ 01889 590287
[BB] **From £16–£17**
Sleeps 6
☎
☙ *Highly Commended*

A warm welcome awaits you in this delightful 16th century Manor farmhouse, with characteristic oak beamed rooms and inglenook fire. Come and help feed the animals and milk the cows on our working dairy and sheep farm, which is within easy reach of the Peak District. Traditional full English breakfast served every day. One family room with double bed and bunk beds, 1 double room with double bed. Open all year except Christmas & New Year.

Yeldersley Old Hall Farm, Yeldersley Lane, Bradley, Ashbourne, Derbyshire DE6 1PH

Mrs Janet Hinds
☎ 01335 344504
[BB] **From £14**
EM From £7.50
Sleeps 6
⅄ ☎
Listed *Commended*

Yeldersley Old Hall Farm is a family-run dairy farm of 70 acres. The Grade II listed farmhouse is situated in pleasant and quiet rural surroundings just 3 miles from the market town of Ashbourne and within easy reach of Dovedale, Alton Towers, Matlock and many stately homes. Farmhouse breakfast provided. Lounge with log fire. Non-smokers only please. Open Mar–Nov.

SELF-CATERING

Briar, Bluebell & Primrose Cottages, c/o Yeldersley Old Hall Farm, Yeldersley Lane, Bradley, Ashbourne, Derbyshire DE6 1PH

Mrs Janet Hinds
☎ 01335 344504
[SC] **From £110–£250**
Sleeps 5/6
☎
🔑 🔑 🔑 *Commended*

Situated on a working dairy farm the newly-converted Grade II listed barn now contains 3 self-catering units, each with 3 bedrooms, accommodating up to 5/6 people. Bathroom with bath and shower, fitted kitchen, fully carpeted. Night storage heating, colour TV. Ideal spot for touring Derbyshire. Ashbourne 3 miles. Open all year.

17 Chevin Green Farm, Chevin Road, Belper, Derbyshire DE56 2UN

Carl & Joan Postles
☎ 01773 822328
SC From £80–£275
Sleeps 4/6
Commended

Enjoy a holiday in one of our five attractive cottages of character overlooking picturesque countryside. The cottages with original beams are fully equipped to a high standard. Lounge, fully fitted kitchen, bathroom, 2 or 3 bedrooms, one is specially adapted for the disabled. Ideally situated for all places of interest, Alton Towers, Dales, Peak District and 6 stately homes. Open all year.

18 Culland Mount Farm, Brailsford, Ashbourne, Derbyshire DE6 3BW

Mrs Carolyn Phillips
☎ 01335 360313
SC From £125–£260
Sleeps 4–6

Commended

A magnificent Victorian farmhouse with splendid views. A working dairy farm with opportunity to watch farm activities. Whilst retaining many original features the house is divided making a luxurious holiday home. Colour TV, full central heating, open log fire, cot, washing machine, dryer, fridge/freezer, linen and electricity inclusive. T.B. commended.

19 Hall Farm Bungalow, c/o Shirley Hall Farm, Shirley, Ashbourne, Derbyshire DE6 3AS
New House Farm & The Saddlery,

Mrs Sylvia Foster
☎ 01335 360346
SC From £120–£350
Sleeps 4/8

Applied

Three superb properties at separate locations in unspoilt countryside 4 miles from Ashbourne. Bungalow near Shirley village, has 3 bedrooms, large garden, lovely views. Peacefully situated 18th century farmhouse at Mercaston has 4 bedrooms. The Saddlery is self-contained 1st floor barn conversion on our farm. All very well appointed. Private coarse fishing. Open all year.

20 Honeysuckle Cottage, c/o Parkview Farm, Weston Underwood, Ashbourne, Derbyshire DE6 4PA

Mrs Linda Adams
☎ 01335 360352
SC From £90–£350
Sleeps 4/6

Commended

This is a truly delightful country cottage set in its own secluded garden with wonderful views over the Derbyshire countryside. Full of character and charm, furnished to a very high standard, with beamed sitting room, antique furnishings and pretty four poster bed. Accommodation for 6 persons in 3 bedrooms. Linen provided. Colour TV, automatic washing machine and tumble dryer. Smaller village cottage also available.

DISABLED VISITORS

Many members offer a welcome to disabled/less able visitors. Please do check the extent of the facilities before booking.

FARM HOLIDAY BUREAU

37

England's Heartland
Sherwood Forest/ Nottinghamshire

Group Contacts: BB *Sally Herrick* ☎ *01949 81733*
SC *Janet Carr* ☎ *01623 861088*

Sherwood Forest is much smaller than it used to be, but near Edwinstowe you can still find Robin Hood, at the Sherwood Forest Visitor Centre where his story is told in a walk-through exhibition. There are also films, guided forest walks and other activities. Edwinstowe church is where Robin Hood is said to have married Maid Marion.

Worksop is a pleasant market town with a fine priory and 14th-century gatehouse. Retford has a small museum and some interesting Georgian buildings around its market square. The open-air markets at Newark and Mansfield are popular with visitors and each town has its local museums. Newark's parish church has a fine spire and interesting treasury but the nearby Minster at Southwell is on a larger scale even though Southwell, home of the Bramley apple, is hardly more than a village.

In Nottingham, Robin Hood's statue stands outside the castle which houses the city's fine arts museum, and there's a small Robin Hood exhibition at the gatehouse. At the foot of Castle Rock, beside the ancient Trip to Jerusalem Inn, is the Brewhouse Yard Museum illustrating the city's social history, while nearby the Canal Museum and the Museum of Costume and Textile show other aspects of the city's heritage. The Lace Centre, in an attractive timbered building, shows off a range of Nottingham's finest work, which you can buy as a souvenir.

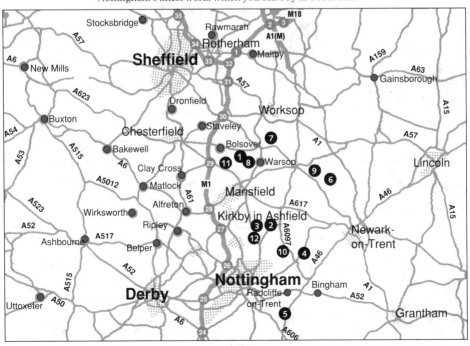

BED AND BREAKFAST

(and evening meal)

---

1 **Blue Barn Farm,** Langwith, Mansfield, Nottinghamshire NG20 9JD

June Ibbotson
☎ 01623 742248
[BB] From £16–£20
Sleeps 6 cot

Commended

Welcome to our family-run 450-acre farm in peaceful surroundings on the edge of Sherwood Forest in Robin Hood country, 5 miles from M1 (J30) off A616. Many interesting places catering for all tastes only a short car journey away. Suitable for the business traveller, a place to unwind. 1 double, 1 twin en suite, 1 family, all with tea/coffee-making facilities and washbasins. Cot available. Dining room, lounge, TV. Open all year (closed Christmas Day & New Year).

---

2 **Far Baulker Farm,** Oxton, Nottinghamshire NG25 0RQ

Janette Esam
☎ 01623 882375
[BB] From £12.50–£15
Sleeps 6

Listed

Far Baulker Farm is a 300-acre arable/livestock farm set in the heart of Sherwood Forest 10 miles north of Nottingham on the A614. Shared bathrooms, tea/coffee-making facilities in rooms. Visitors lounge with TV/video. Open all year.

---

3 **Forest Farm,** Mansfield Road, Papplewick, Nottinghamshire NG15 8FL

Mrs E J Stubbs
☎ 0115 9632310
[BB] From £14–£17.50
EM From £6
Sleeps 5

Listed

Forest Farm is located on the A60 standing well back up the farm road away from traffic noise. Pleasant views from south-facing rooms, 1 double en suite, 1 single, 1 twin, all with tea-making facilities. TV in lounge/dining room. Midway between Mansfield and Nottingham, and ideal touring or business base. Open all year (closed Dec).

---

4 **Hall Farm House,** Gonalston, Nottinghamshire NG14 7JA

Mr & Mrs R C Smith
☎ 0115 9663112
Fax 0115 9664844
[BB] From £17.50
EM From £12.50
Sleeps 6

Commended

Charming 18th century farmhouse in one of Nottinghamshire's prettiest villages. Near the minster town of Southwell. Comfortable bedrooms overlook a lovely garden. Heated swimming pool, tennis court and games room; also aviary of exotic birds and flock of pedigree Suffolk sheep. By arrangement, Rosie your hostess will give you a generous dinner. No smoking in bedrooms. No pets. Open all year (closed Christmas).

---

5 **Jerico Farm,** Fosse Way, Nr Cotgrave, Nottinghamshire NG12 3HG

Mrs Sally Herrick
☎ 01949 81733
[BB] From £16–£22
Sleeps 6

Commended

Jerico Farm offers warm, comfortable accommodation, surrounded by our own attractive farmland. Good firm beds and tea/coffee/chocolate-making facilities in all bedrooms, one en suite. Guests' own sitting room. Good pub food available nearby. Excellent location for visiting Nottingham, its universities, sports venues and tourist sites. Located down farm drive off A46, 1 mile north of A46/A606 junction, south of Cotgrave village. Open all year (closed Christmas).

Manor Farm, Moorhouse Road, Laxton, Newark, Nottinghamshire NG22 0NU   **6**

Mrs Pat Haigh
☎ 01777 870417
ⒷⒷ From £14–15
EM From £7
Sleeps 6
🐓 🐂
Listed

Manor Farm is a family-run dairy and arable farm of 137 acres, in the historic mediaeval village of Laxton, situated 10 miles north of Newark, and on the verge of the popular tourist area of Sherwood Forest in Nottinghamshire. 2 family rooms, 1 double room, tea/coffee-making facilities available. Visitors' lounge and dining room. Access to rooms at all times. Open all year (closed Christmas & New Year).

Norton Grange Farm, Norton, Cuckney, Mansfield, Nottinghamshire NG20 9LP   **7**

Fernie Palmer
☎ 01623 842666
ⒷⒷ From £16–£17
Sleeps 4
🛏 🐓 🏹 🐕 🌾
Listed

Norton Grange is a Grade II listed farmhouse set in the heart of the Welbeck Estate, part of the world-famous Sherwood Forest. Ideally situated for overnight stops or touring the very beautiful countryside and the many attractions, in Nottinghamshire and Derbyshire. One double room and one twin room, both with washbasin and tea/coffee-making facilities. Open all year except Christmas & New Year.

Self-Catering

Blue Barn Cottage, c/o Blue Barn Farm, Langwith, Mansfield, Nottinghamshire NG20 9JD   **8**

June Ibbotson
☎ 01623 742248
ⓈⒸ From £350–£375
Sleeps 8
🐓 🛏 🌾 🖥
🔑 🔑 🔑 🔑 *Commended*

Do come and relax in peace and comfort on our family-run farm in Robin Hood country. Visit quiet villages, stately homes rich in history, ramble through country parks or hunt bargains in thriving market towns. Blue Barn is off the A616 near Cuckney. 4 bedrooms, bathroom, breakfast kitchen, dining room, lounge, TV, washing machine and dryer. CH and linen included. Open all year.

Foliat Cottage, Jordan Castle Farm, Wellow, Newark, Nottinghamshire NG22 0EL   **9**

Mrs Janet Carr
☎/Fax 01623 861088
ⓈⒸ From £180–£290
Sleeps 6 + cot
🛏 ✂ 🖥
🔑 🔑 🔑 🔑 *Commended*

Situated on the edge of Sherwood Forest, our recently renovated Edwardian cottage has beautiful pastoral views across our working family farm. Peaceful and cosy, with central heating, colour TV and washer/dryer. 1 double and 2 twin bedrooms. Cot and highchair available. Enclosed south-facing garden with patio. Linen provided. Brochure available. Open all year.

The Loft House, Criftin Farm, Epperstone, Nottingham, Nottinghamshire NG14 6AT   **10**

Jenny Esam
☎ 01159 652039
ⓈⒸ From £245–£285
Sleeps 4
🛏 ✂ 📺 🐓
🔑 🔑 🔑 🔑 *Highly Commended*

This 17th century converted granary is situated in the heart of Robin Hood Country, close to the historic towns of Southwell and Nottingham. Comfortably furnished with original beams in lounge and kitchen. Central heating, colour TV, log fire, utility room with washer/dryer. Two twin bedded rooms, each with own bathroom. Use of heated swimming pool May/Sept and snooker room in walled garden. Open all year.

(11) Scarcliffe Hall Farm, Scarcliffe, Chesterfield, Derbyshire S44 6SZ

Mr & Mrs I.R. Wildgoose
☎ 01246 823574
SC From £300–£350
Sleeps 6
🐕 ½ 🏕 🛥

𝄞 𝄞 𝄞 𝄞 *Highly Commended*

Recent renovation of an idyllic Grade II listed working family-run farm nr Hardwick Hall. 3 miles from J29 M1 in a picturesque village. Private wing with GCH. 3 double rooms with washbasins. Superb kitchen with Rayburn, lounge with inglenook & beams, bathroom, shower room, beautifully furnished. Excellent pub food available. Central for Sherwood Forest, Chatsworth, market towns. Linen included. Winners of Derbyshire farm competition for 3 years. Open all year.

(12) Top House Farm, Mansfield Road, Lamins Lane, Arnold, Nottingham, Nottinghamshire NG5 8PH

Mrs Ann Lamin
☎ 0115 9268330
SC From £195–£250
Sleeps 3
🐕 ½ 🐕

Applied

Charming granary flat with beams, open fireplace, CH. Lounge has colour TV, patio doors onto garden. Kitchen has electric and microwave ovens, use of automatic washer and dryer. Within easy reach of Nottingham, Newstead Abbey, Southwell Minster, the Dukeries, Sherwood Forest, Derbyshire and the National Watersports Centre. Open all year.

38

England's Heartland

North Shropshire

Group Contact: *Mrs Sue Clarkson* ☎ *01939 250289*

Shropshire with its wealth of Historic Houses, Castles and Abbeys, is the largest landbound county. Medieval Shrewsbury the county town, and up to date Telford are the principle towns. With attractive market towns scattered around, leaving miles of unspoilt countryside to explore.

Don't miss Shrewsbury with it's historic buildings, passages and Castle. Famous for books and TV series about a medieval monk by Ellis Peters.

Ironbridge Gorge Museums and the world famous Iron Bridge, make this World Heritage site a must.

Hawkstone Park with its woodland fantasy of castles, cliffs and caves restored and open to the public for the first time in over 100 years.

Being so large the county caters for every need, with its own lake district at Ellesmere, hill country of South Shropshire. The Llangollen canal winding its way along and the Severn Valley Steam Railway at Bridgnorth to name but a few.

For the sports people: famous golft courses, fishing, horse riding and gliding.

Shropshire offers so much for everyone, seeing is believing!!!

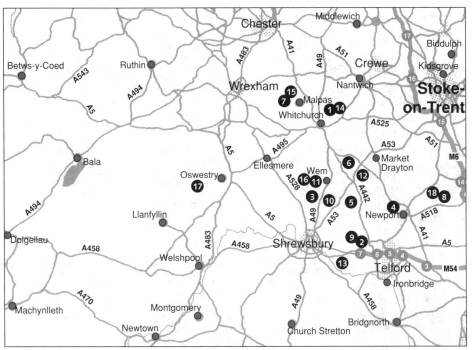

BED AND BREAKFAST
(and evening meal)

---

1 **Bradeley Green Farm,** Tarporley Road, Whitchurch, Shropshire SY13 4HD

Ruth Mulliner
☎ **01948 663442**
BB **From £18–£21**
EM From £8.50
Sleeps 6
🐕🐴🐈🍴🌳☂🧳
👑👑👑 *Commended*

Our 180-acre family-run dairy farm is located on a main north/south route (A49) set across Shropshire/Cheshire border and only 2 miles from Wales. Wild waterfowl breeding centre with extensive water gardens and many varieties of ducks and geese for you to enjoy. Our spacious farmhouse offers very comfortable accommodation. CH, open fires and en suite facilities. Open all year (closed Christmas).

---

2 **Church Farm,** Wrockwardine, Wellington, Telford, Shropshire TF6 5DG

Mrs Jo Savage
☎ **01952 244917**
BB **From £20–£25**
EM From £15
Sleeps 8
🐕🐴♿🅿☂🧳
👑👑👑 *Highly Commended*

Sit back and relax in our Georgian village farmhouse with oak beams and log fires. Built on the site of 12th century manor with sandstone foundations revealed in the attractive garden. We have lovely bedrooms with colour TVs and tea/coffee/chocolate trays. Delicious breakfasts, traditional dinners and puds! Near Shrewsbury and Ironbridge, 1 mile A5 and M54. Brochure available. Open all year.

---

3 **Grove Farm,** Preston Brockhurst, Shrewsbury, Shropshire SY4 5QA

Mrs Janet Jones
☎ **01939 220223**
BB **From £16–£20**
Sleeps 5
🍴🐴🧳
☂ *Commended*

Enjoy our friendly village farmhouse set in 223 acres of lovely countryside, on A49. Quality accommodation and home cooking. Three delightful bedrooms with washbasins and 1 with shower en suite. All have beverage trays. Guest bathroom. Central heating throughout. Ideally situated for Ironbridge World Heritage site, Shrewsbury, Chester, Potteries and Wales. Brochures available . Open Jan – Nov

---

4 **Lane End Farm,** Chetwynd, Newport, Shropshire TF10 8BN

Mrs Janice Park
☎ **01952 550337**
BB **From £15–£20**
EM from £7.50
Sleeps 4
🐴🐕🧳
☂ ☂

Be sure of a warm welcome at our interesting period farmhouse set amidst lovely countryside. Bedrooms with en suite facilities. Good woodland walks nearby. Located on A41 just 2 miles North of Newport; Ideal touring location for visiting Ironbridge, Weston Park, Cosford, The Wrekin, Potteries, Chester, etc. We keep pedigree Suffolk and Rouge sheep – see the lambs in spring! Open all year.

---

5 **Longley Farm,** Stanton Heath, Shawbury, Shropshire SY4 4HE

Chris & Sue Clarkson
☎ **01939 250289**
BB **From £13–£15**
EM From £7
Sleeps 4
🐴🐕🧍🚗
☂ *Commended*

A 15-acre smallholding set in beautiful countryside rearing sheep, some arable farming. The brick farmhouse is close to the historic towns of Shrewsbury, Chester, Ludlow and the Long Mynd Hills. Also Ironbridge Gorge and Museums. 1 double, 1 twin bedded room, guest bathroom. All rooms have tea/coffee-making facilities, TV, washbasins. Open all year (closed Christmas & New Year).

Mickley House, Faulsgreen, Tern Hill, Market Drayton, Shropshire TF9 3QW

Mrs Pauline Williamson
☎ **01630 638505**
BB **From £20–£25**
Sleeps 6
🐕 ⛏ 🐄 🐎 💺 🎣 ♿
♨ ♨ *Commended*

Enjoy traditional farmhouse hospitality on our 125-acre working farm in unspoiled, peaceful Shropshire countryside. Explore Ironbridge, Shrewsbury, Chester, Hodnet Gardens and Hawstone Park. Relax by the inglenook fireplace or stroll through the garden to our coarse fishing pools. One first floor, 2 luxury ground floor en suite bedrooms **suitable for the less able**. Closed Christmas.

Mill House, Higher Wych, Malpas, Cheshire SY14 7JR

Chris & Angela Smith
☎ **01948 73362**
Fax 01948 73566
BB **From £16**
EM **From £8**
Sleeps 4
🐄 🐎
♨ ♨ ♨ *Commended*

Modernised Mill House on the Cheshire/Clwyd border in a quiet valley, convenient for visiting Chester, Shrewsbury and North Wales. The house is centrally heated and has an open log fire in the lounge. Bedrooms have washbasins, radios and tea-making facilities. 1 bedroom has an en suite shower and WC. Reductions for children and senior citizens. Open Jan–Nov.

Oulton House Farm, Norbury, Nr Stafford, Staffordshire ST20 0PG

Mrs Judy Palmer
☎ **01785 284264**
BB **From £18.50**
Sleeps 6
🐎 💺
♨ ♨ *Highly Commended*

Oulton House is a 300-acre dairy farm situated on the Shropshire/Staffordshire border. Our large Victorian farmhouse offers warm, comfortable and well appointed en suite bedrooms, all with tea tray and TV. From your peaceful, rural base discover our many local attractions from the heritage of Ironbridge Gorge, the splendours of Shugborough to the bargains of the Potteries factory shops. As for dinner – we can recommend many local pubs and restaurants. Peace and quiet guaranteed. Open all year.

Red House Farm, Longdon on Tern, Wellington, Telford, Shropshire TF6 6LE

Mrs Mary Jones
☎ **01952 770245**
BB **From £16**
Sleeps 6
🐎 🐕
♨ ♨ *Commended*

Our Victorian farmhouse is on a mixed farm. 2 double bedrooms have private facilities within 1 family room with separate bathroom, all large and comfortable. Excellent breakfast. Farm easily located, leave M54 (J6), follow A442, take B5063. Central for historic Shrewsbury, Ironbridge Gorge museums or modern Telford. Several local eating places. Open all year.

The Sett Village Farm, Stanton-upon-Hine Heath, Shrewsbury, Shropshire SY4 4LR

Brenda & Jim Grundey
☎ **01939 250391**
BB **From £22**
EM **From £14**
Sleeps 6
🐕 ✂ 🐄 ⊞ 🎋 💺
♨ ♨ ♨ *Highly Commended*

Full of dried flowers, our lovely farmhouse offers a warm and friendly welcome for your stay in Shropshire. Step into the countryside, relax and enjoy the delights of Shrewsbury, Hawkstone Park Follies, Ironbridge, The Potteries, Chester, Wales and so much more. Go on enjoy yourselves! 3 double rooms en suite, Tea and coffee. Full central heating. P.S. Smiles will be returned. Open all year (closed Christmas and New Year).

Soulton Hall, near Wem, Shropshire SY4 5RS

Ann Ashton
☎ **01939 232786**
Fax 01939 234097
BB **From £21.50–£33**
EM **From £15**
Sleeps 10
🐎 🐕 ⊞ 🎋 🐎 💺 🎿
♨ ♨ ♨ *Commended*

Sample English country life in an Elizabethan manor house offering very relaxing holiday. Bird watching, fishing, riding. Good food, home produce where possible, super meals. Walled garden. Licensed bar. Direct dial telephones. We welcome you. Open all year.

⑫ **Stoke Manor,** Stoke-on-Tern, Market Drayton, Shropshire TF9 2DU

Mike & Julia Thomas
☎ **01630 685222**
Fax **01630 685666**
🛏 From £20–£25
Sleeps 6
🐿 (5) 👝 🎋
♨♨ *Highly Commended*

Come and experience the peace and quiet of the countryside. We offer quality accommodation, all bedrooms having bathrooms, hospitality trays and colour TV. Comfortable drawing room and cellar bar for relaxing in the evening. Ideal for visiting Shropshire's many attractions, the Wedgwood Museum and Chester. Abundance of good eating places nearby. AA QQQQ. Open Jan–Nov.

⑬ **Upper Brompton Farm,** Cross Houses, Shrewsbury, Shropshire SY5 6LE

Mrs Christine Yates
☎ **01743 761629**
🛏 From £18–£30
EM from £12.50
Sleeps 6
🐿 🐕 ✂ 👝
♨♨ *Commended*

Elegant Georgian farmhouse set in 315 acres. Relaxed, friendly atmosphere, comfortable accommodation, delicious home cooking and a haven of peace and tranquillity. Spacious four-poster bedrooms with en suite have beverage trays and colour TV's. Large guests lounge with log fire on cool evenings. 400 yards from River Severn – fishing permits available. Shrewsbury 4 miles, Ironbridge 9 miles. Open all year.

SELF-CATERING

⑭ **Bradeley Green Cottage,** Tarporley Road, Whitchurch, Shropshire SY13 4HD

Ruth Mulliner
☎ **01948 663442**
🅂🄲 From £90–£140
Sleeps 4
🐿 🎋 🛋
🔑 🔑 🔑 *Commended*

One of two cottages in country lane with lovely views. Good parking. Kitchen, diner, electric cooker and fridge, comfortable sitting room with colour TV and open fire. Logs provided (when available). Two bedrooms (twin & double), all bedding, towels are provided. Electricity by 50p meter. Bathroom with bath and shower. Ten minute walk for pub grub at the Willey Moor Lock on canal, set in open fields. Open all year.

⑮ **The Granary,** c/o Mill House, Higher Wych, Malpas, Cheshire SY14 7JR

Chris & Angela Smith
☎ **01948 73362**
Fax **01948 73566**
🅂🄲 From £75–£145
Sleeps 4/5 + cot
🐿
🔑 🔑 🔑 *Commended*

The Granary is a self-contained bungalow adjacent to Mill House. Sleeps 4/5 in 2 double bedrooms, kitchen/living area, shower and WC. TV. CH. Cot and babysitting available. Situated in a quiet valley with a small stream in the garden. Convenient for visiting Chester, Shrewsbury and North Wales. Open all year.

⑯ **Keepers Cottage,** Soulton Hall, near Wem, Shropshire SY4 5RS

Ann Ashton
☎ **01939 232786**
Fax **01939 234097**
🅂🄲 From £197–£320
Sleeps 6
🐿 🐕 🎋 👝 🛋 🏌
🔑 🔑 🔑–🔑 🔑 🔑 🔑
Up to Commended

Keepers Cottage nestles on south side of 50 acres of Oak woodland offering really relaxing holidays. Woodland and riverside walks. CH, TV, log fires in season. Evening meals available at Soulton Hall from £15, by arrangement. Shrewsbury, Chester, Ironbridge, North Wales, Potteries – all within easy reach. Open all year.

Lloran Isaf, Llansilin, Oswestry, Shropshire SY10 7QX

Pat Jackson
☎ **01691 70253**
🆂 **From £85–£220**
Sleeps 5
🐎 ♿ 🛏 🧍 🍳 🚜 👝
Applied

Beautiful detached bungalow in enclosed garden on a farm in its own valley. Garden furniture, barbecue. Fully fitted kitchen, 3 bedrooms, WC, bathroom. Large lounge with dining area. Woodburning stove, colour TV, fitted carpets. Wonderful scenery, walks, trout fishing. Plenty of tourist attractions. Easy access North/Mid-Wales. Beautiful for a winter break. Linen hire and cot available. Open all year.

Swallows Nest, Oulton House Farm, Norbury, Nr Stafford, Staffordshire ST20 0PG   18

Mrs Judy Palmer
☎ **01785 284264**
🆂 **From £70–£170**
Sleeps 4 + cot
🐎
Applied

Swallows Nest has been carefully designed to provide a comfortable and peaceful retreat from which to enjoy the surrounding countryside. Pretty bedrooms (double and twin), pleasant bathroom and delightful sitting room with kitchen and dining area. Fully equipped and prices are inclusive of electricity, linen and towels. Open all year.

FARM HOLIDAY BUREAU

FOLLOW THE COUNTRY CODE

Leave nothing but footprints,
Take nothing but photographs,
Kill nothing but time!

FARM HOLIDAY BUREAU

DISABLED VISITORS

Many members offer a welcome to disabled/less able visitors. Please do check the extent of the facilities before booking.

39

England's Heartland

South Shropshire

Group Contact: *Mrs C Price* ☎ 0154 74 249

Secluded and peaceful, and unchanged for centuries, Shropshire's timeless countryside provides the perfect setting for a restful break far away from the madding crowds. But behind the tranquil backcloth lies a wild and turbulent history which today's visitors can uncover amongst the dramatic ruins of Clun Castle, the romantic fortified manor of Stokesay or in the historic towns of Shrewsbury, Ludlow and Bridgnorth.

The entire county is steeped in history, myth, and heritage. "Lonely country, this ... even 10 miles of castle and town", writes Ellis Peters in one of her Chronicles of Brother Cadfael. Yet as the birthplace of the Industrial Revolution, the county's best known landmark also links the present-day to a more recent past. Today Ironbridge is home to six separate museums including the world famous Blists Hill Open Air Museum, where craftsmen in shops, pubs, foundry and cottage give demonstrations of their skills.

A fine selection of specialist shops can be found in Shrewsbury or Telford New Town. The area also abounds in antique markets and craft shops.

The full appeal of Shropshire can easily be discovered from a rural retreat in the south of the county. Car trail leaflets will guide you around 'Cadfael Country', 'Ghostly Shropshire' and the 'Thomas Telford Trail', while more energetic visitors can walk or ride across the well marked tracks on Wenlock Edge, the Clee Hills, the Long Mynd or the dramatic Stiperstones. Bustling market towns such as Church Stretton and Bishops Castle, a steam-hauled ride along the Severn Valley, or visit Acton Scott Working Farm, combined with good country pubs and excellent places to eat, offer plenty to encourage you to linger a little longer in South Shropshire.

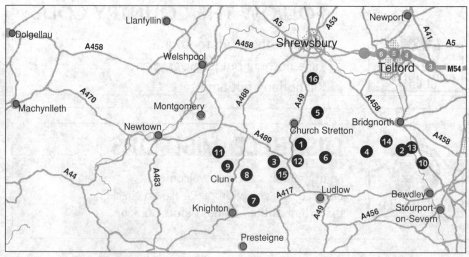

BED AND BREAKFAST

(and evening meal)

Acton Scott Farm, Church Stretton, Shropshire SY6 6QN

Mary Jones
☎ 01694 781260
[BB] **From £14–£20**
Sleeps 6
🐕 🐎 🅰 🔌 🌲
🏵 🏵 *Commended*

Situated in an area of outstanding natural beauty, the lovely old farmhouse has comfortable and spacious bedrooms, all with H & C, en suite available. There is a popular Working Farm Museum in Acton Scott. The spectacular Long Mynd Hills and the valleys of Church Stretton are nearby. Central for visiting Shrewsbury, Ludlow and Ironbridge. We look forward to welcoming you. Open mid Feb – mid Nov.

Billingsley Hall Farm, Covert Lane, Billingsley, Bridgnorth, Shropshire WV16 6PJ

Mrs Helen Sedgley
☎ 01746 861877
[BB] **From £15–£18**
Sleeps 6 + cot
🐕 🐎 🍴 🅰 🔌 🐴 🐾 🌲
📷
Listed

We welcome you to spacious accommodation on a 260-acre working farm with sheep, suckler cows and arable crops. We offer 2 double/family bedrooms, 1 twin room with guests' bathroom. Lounge with log fire, dining room. Guests can follow the many walks around the woods and farmland. Situated 6 miles from Bridgnorth on B4363 to Cleobury Mortimer road, ideal base for local attractions. Also luxury self-catering. Open all year.

Castle Farm, Cheney, Longville, Craven Arms, Shropshire SY7 8DR

Mrs Varny Jones
☎ 01588 673255
[BB] **From £14**
Sleeps 5
🐕 🐎 🌲
Listed

Castle Farm is steeped in history. First built in the 9th century, and rebuilt in the 13th century, it stands in its own courtyard surrounded by many ancient buildings. Close to Stokesay, Ludlow and Powys Castle, our farm is ideal for a walking holiday over Offa's Dyke or the Long Mynd. One family and one double room. Peace and quiet in abundance. Open Mar–Nov.

Charlcotte Farm, Cleobury North, Bridgnorth, Shropshire WV16 6RR

Wendy Green
☎ 0174 633 238
[BB] **From £17–£20**
Sleeps 6
🐕 🍴
🏵 🏵 *Commended*

Charlcotte has a Georgian farmhouse set in pleasant grounds, midway between Ludlow and Bridgnorth at the foot of Brown Clee Hill. We are in close proximity to the Ironbridge Gorge, Shrewsbury and the Severn Valley Railway. Guests are welcome to relax at all times in the gardens or the drawing room which has a TV. All bedrooms have tea/coffee-making facilities and TV. Open Mar–Nov.

Court Farm, Gretton, Church Stretton, Shropshire SY6 7HU

Mrs Barbara Norris
☎ 01694 771219
[BB] **From £19–£24**
EM £12
Sleeps 6
🍴 🐕 (14) 🌲 🎏
🏵 🏵 🏵 *Highly Commended*

Stone Tudor farmhouse on 325-acre arable stock farm in peaceful countryside, 1 mile off B4371, equal distance to Ludlow, Shrewsbury, Bridgnorth, Ironbridge. Spacious rooms, inglenook fireplace, full central heating. 2 twin rooms, 1 double, all with private bathrooms, shaving points and tea/coffee-making facilities. Furnished to a high standard. A warm welcome and high quality cuisine using home produce whenever possible. Open all year.

6 **The Glebe Farm,** Diddlebury, Craven Arms, Shropshire SY7 9DH

Michael, Eileen or Adrian Wilkes
☎ 01584 841221
🅱 From £20–£25
Sleeps 6

Highly Commended

Relax amidst the leafy lanes and rolling hills that surround our 16th century farmhouse, part timbered, part mellow stone, nestling in the idyllic village of Diddlebury. 4 comfortable and individual bedrooms have private bathrooms, CTV, electric heating and tea/coffee. Table reservations for evening meals can be booked locally. Tents and caravans on 4 acre site by stream. South Shropshire is a delight. Why not come to stay for a break? Open all year.

7 **The Hall,** Bucknell, Shropshire SY7 0AA

Mrs Christine Price
☎ 015474 249
🅱 From £15–£16
EM From £8
Sleeps 6

Commended

The Hall is a working farm with spacious Georgian farmhouse and peaceful garden to relax in, after a day walking or exploring the Welsh Borderland with its historic towns and castles, also the black and white villages of North Herefordshire. Guest lounge, 1 twin en suite, 2 double with washbasins, shaving points. Colour TV and tea-making facilities. Open Mar–Nov.

8 **Hurst Mill Farm,** Clun, Craven Arms, Shropshire SY7 0JA

Joyce Williams
☎ 01588 640224
🅱 From £15–£17
EM From £7
Sleeps 6

Winner of "Shropshire Farm Breakfast Challenge". A warm welcome to this working farm where the "kettle's always on". Riverside farmhouse and spacious gardens. Nestling in the delightful Clun Valley, it lies between historic Clun and Clunton. Woodland and hills on either side. Two quiet riding ponies, kingfishers and herons. Pets welcome. Log fires. All facilities in rooms. Also 2 luxury cottages. AA QQQ. Open all year.

9 **Llanhedric,** Clun, Craven Arms, Shropshire SY7 8NG

Mrs Mary Jones
☎ 01588 640203
🅱 From £14–£16
EM From £7.50
Sleeps 6

Listed *Commended*

A friendly atmosphere and good food awaits you in this characteristic old farmhouse with spacious accommodation. Large gardens and lawns overlook the picturesque Clun Valley, surrounded by its hills. Near the Welsh border and Offa's Dyke. Ideal for walking or exploring the many places of historical interest, including Ludlow and Shrewsbury. Situated 2 miles off the A488 Clun to Bishop's Castle road; take turning for Bicton, then Mainstone. Open Mar–Nov.

10 **The Low Farm,** Alveley, Nr Bridgnorth, Shropshire WV15 6HX

Patricia Lawley
☎ 012997 206
🅱 From £13–14
EM From £7.50
Sleeps 6

Applied

The Low Farm is a peaceful, friendly working farm situated just off the Bridgnorth-Kidderminster A442 road. The farmhouse is Victorian. Guests have their own dining room and lounge with colour TV, log fires and central heating. Ideal for Severn Valley Railway and Ironbridge Museums. 1 family, 1 twin bedded room (both with washbasins). Open all year.

11 **New House Farm,** Clun, Shropshire SY7 8NJ

Miriam Ellison
☎ 01588 638314
🅱 From £16
EM From £9
Sleeps 6

Commended

Peaceful isolated 18th century farmhouse high in Clun hills near Welsh border. Walks from doorstep include Offa's Dyke and Shropshire Way. Large bedrooms furnished to high standard with scenic views. Tea/coffee-making, TV. Home cooking. 'New House Farm provides a family welcome and a standard of comfort which a grand hotel would find difficult to match' *Birmingham Evening Post.* Open Feb–Nov.

Strefford Hall Farm, Strefford, Craven Arms, Shropshire SY7 8DE

Mrs Caroline Morgan
☎ **01588 672383**
🅱 **From £18–£19**
Sleeps 6
👶 🐴 🎠 🏇
♨ ♨ *Commended*

Victorian farmhouse in quiet hamlet of Strefford nestling at the foot of the Wenlock Edge. A working farm of 350 acres keeping sheep, cattle and growing cereal. Spacious, traditionally furnished accommodation. Guests' lounge with TV, separate dining room, 2 double en suite, 1 twin, with private bathroom. All with tea/coffee-making facilities and colour TV. Central base for walking and touring. Closed Dec & Jan.

SELF-CATERING

Billingsley Hall Farm, Covert Lane, Billingsley, Bridgnorth, Shropshire WV16 6PJ

Mrs Helen Sedgley
☎ **01746 861877**
🆂🅲 **From £150–£220**
Sleeps 6
👶 🐴 👶 🏊 🚗 🏇 👶 🎠
🐾 🐾 🐾 🐾 🐾

Commended

The Granary provides luxury accommodation for 4/5 people in spacious oak beamed rooms – a central feature of main bedroom. Fully carpeted and heated throughout. Modern fitted kitchen including washing machine. Guests can follow walks around the farm. Pets welcome. Children catered for. Within easy reach many local attractions. Open all year.

Eudon Burnell Cottages, Eudon Burnell, Nr Bridgnorth, Shropshire WV16 6UD

Margaret Crawford Clarke
☎ **01746 35235**
🆂🅲 **From £160–£280**
Sleeps 4/5/5
🐴 🏇 🐴 🎠 ♿
🐾 🐾 🐾 🐾

Commended

Eudon Burnell is a working dairy/arable farm of 325 acres 3 miles from Bridgnorth and the Severn Valley Steam Railway. Ironbridge an easy journey. Three comfortably furnished, well-equipped 3-bedroomed cottages. Economy 7 or gas CH and electricity included in rent. Washing machine/dryer, microwave, payphone in 2. Gardens. An ideal centre for touring. Open all year.

Hesterworth, Hopesay, Craven Arms, Shropshire SY7 8EX

Roger or Sheila Davies
☎ **015887 487**
🆂🅲 **From £83–£301**
Sleeps 45
🐴 👶 ♿ ♿
🐾 🐾 🐾 *Up to*
Commended

Secluded Victorian country house in 12 acres of gardens and grounds with sheep. Comfortable well-equipped apartments and cottages in a beautiful setting. Evening meals available. Large communal Dining room ideal for families or groups. Good for walking (Shropshire way) and touring. ½ mile from Aston on Clun off B4368. Also B&B. Short breaks. Open all year.

Ryton Farm, Ryton, Dorrington, Shrewsbury, Shropshire SY5 7LY

Mrs Ann Cartwright
☎ **01743 718449**
🆂🅲 **From £140–£350**
Sleeps 2/4/6
👶 🐴 🚗 ♿ 🐕 🎿
🐾 🐾 🐾 *Commended*

Country cottages for 6 or converted barns for 2/4 (2 bedrooms, baths en suite). All cottages are well equipped with microwaves, colour TVs, fitted carpets, linen and towels. Ample parking. Pets welcome. Coarse fishing available. Short breaks for 2 available. Six miles south of Shrewsbury. Open all year.

40

England's Heartland

Herefordshire

Group Contacts: [BB] *Sylvia Price* ☎ *0156 886 388 From May '95 01568 770388*
[SC] *Judy Wells* ☎ *0156 884 347*

Herefordshire is a land of red earth, green meadows, quiet woods, streams and pretty black and white villages. This is the home of the world famous red and white Herefordshire cattle and a well-known centre for cidermaking. In the south are the spectacular gorges of the River Wye and the lovely woodland trails of the Forest of Dean; westward lies the tranquil Golden Valley leading into Offa's Dyke. To the east, Elgar country rises to the Malvern Hills with the finest ridge walk in England.

Herefordshire is rich in history and within reasonable travelling distance of the Black Mountains, Brecon Beacons and Elan Valley in Wales and the Clee Hills, Carding Mill Valley, Long Mynd and Wenlock Edge in South Shropshire. The county itself has a range of sights that span every period in British history from Iron Age hill forts, Roman remains, Norman castles and mediaeval manor houses to stately homes and their gardens and heritage museums. In the village of Kilpeck there are renowned 12th-century Herefordshire carvings and pagan Celtic figures.

You may also like to wander through the many street markets of the county. Hay-on-Wye is famous for its secondhand bookshops and Hereford is the home of a very large cattle market on Wednesdays.

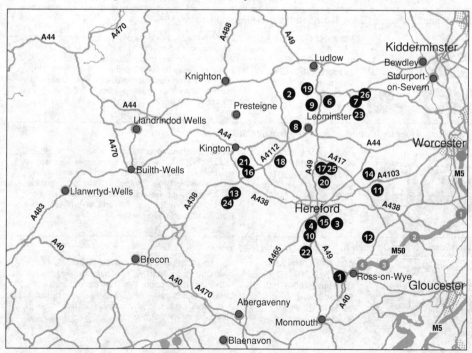

BED AND BREAKFAST

(and evening meal)

Aberhall Farm, St Owens Cross, Ross-on-Wye, Hereford, Herefordshire HR2 8LL

Freda Davies
☎ 01989 730256
[BB] From £15.50–£17
Sleeps 5
✂ ☖ (10) ☂
♛

A quiet, secluded spot 200 yards off B4521. Relax in our 17th century farmhouse with lovely views of rolling countryside. We offer 1 twin, 1 double (en suite), 1 single, vanity units, tea/coffee-making facilities, CH, guests' own bathroom and toilet, lounge and dining room. Games room, tennis court. Excellent cuisine. 'Home from home'. Large garden. AA Rec. Open all year (closed Christmas).

The Barn Farm, Leinthall Starkes, Ludlow, Shropshire SY8 2HP

Sylvia Price
☎ 0156 886388
May '95 01568 770388
[BB] From £15–£19
EM £12.50
Sleeps 6
☖ ♞
♛♛

A warm welcome, comfort and a relaxed atmosphere await you. Our traditional mixed farm is 5 miles west of Ludlow. Cosy bedrooms, 2 double en suite, tea trays. Meals served in our conservatory dining room. Special diets. Guests' own sitting room.

Dinedor Court, Nr Hereford, Herefordshire HR2 6LG

Rosemary Price
☎ 01432 870481
[BB] From £16–£18
Sleeps 4
☖ (10) ♞ ⚔ ♒ ▪
♛

Listed 16th century farmhouse beside the River Wye. Ideal for those seeking peace and quiet. Set in a large garden with views over rolling farmland and orchards. Elegant oak panelled dining hall, guests' own bathroom and TV lounge. Wood fires in season. Tea and coffee-making facilities. Only 3 miles from Hereford on B4399. Open Mar–Nov.

Grafton Villa Farm, Grafton, Hereford, Herefordshire HR2 8ED

Jennie Layton
☎ 01432 268689
[BB] From £16–£19
Sleeps 6
♞ ☖ ⚔ ⚔ ☂ ▪ ♒
♛♛ *Highly Commended*

0A farmhouse of great character and warmth set in an acre of beautiful lawns and gardens amidst the picturesque Wye Valley. Beautiful fabrics and antiques throughout, charming, peaceful en suite bedrooms with, TV and drinks tray. Guests' private bathroom or en suite. We offer our guests a relaxing holiday on a 'real farm', enjoying a sumptuous breakfast with farmhouse portions. Open all year (closed Christmas).

FARM HOLIDAY BUREAU

LET THE TELEPHONE RING!

Some farmhouses are big places. Let the telephone ring long enough to give the owner time to answer it.

---

6 **Haynall Villa,** Little Hereford, Nr Ludlow, Shropshire SY8 4BG

Mrs Rachel Edwards
☎ **01584 711589**
BB **From £15–£20**
EM From £11
Sleeps 6
🏇 🐾 (5) 🐕 🕯️
🐝 🐝 *Commended*

1820s farmhouse nestling in Teme Valley 6m from historic Ludlow, ¾ from A456. Spacious bedrooms (1 en suite) offer comfort, views to 3 counties, vanity units, tea/coffee-making facilities. Guests' bathroom. Delicious farmhouse fayre (vegetarian and special diets). Relax in lounge with TV or attractive garden. Featured in Daily Telegraph. Open all year except Christmas.

---

7 **The Hills Farm,** Leysters, Leominster, Herefordshire HR6 0HP

Jane Conolly
☎ **01568 750205**
BB **From £20–£22**
EM From £15
Sleeps 8
🏇 ✂️ 🖼️ 🕯️
🐝 🐝 🐝 *Highly Commended*

Escape to tranquillity. Breathtaking views from lovely old house. Scrumptious food including vegetarian. Delightful en suite bedrooms, one a gem of a barn conversion. Every comfort. All this for your delectation amidst superb countryside. Brochure. Open Mar–Nov.

---

8 **Holgate Farm,** Kingsland, Leominster, Herefordshire HR6 9QS

Mrs Jenny Davies
☎ **01568 708275**
BB **From £15–£16**
EM From £9.50 (optional)
Sleeps 4
✂️ 🏇 🎠
Listed

Set amidst the beautiful North Herefordshire countryside on a family-run stock and arable farm, this attractive 17th century farmhouse offers a warm, friendly welcome. Within easy reach of the Welsh border country, Hereford, Leominster and Ludlow. Spaciously appointed bedrooms with tea and coffee trays. Guests' own bathroom and sitting room. Open all year except Christmas.

---

9 **Home Farm,** Bircher, Nr Leominster, Herefordshire HR6 0AX

Doreen Cadwallader
☎ **01568 780525**
BB **From £16–£20**
Sleeps 6
🎠 🏇 ✂️ 🛶 🕯️
🐝

We welcome you to a traditional livestock farm offering you excellent service and accommodation. Set in a peaceful, secluded area on the Welsh Border, it's 4 miles north of Leominster, 7 miles south of Ludlow, and close to Croft Castle, Berrington Hall and other attractions. All rooms have tea/coffee-making facilities. TV and washbasins. Light evening meals by request. Open Feb–Nov.

---

10 **Knockerhill Farm,** Callow, Herefordshire HR2 8BP

Beryl Davies
☎ **01432 268460**
BB **From £15–£17**
Sleeps 4
🎠 (8) ✂️
🐝

Situated 3 miles from Hereford, 500 yds off A49. The house is of great charm with tasteful antiques and impressive entrance hall, set in beautiful gardens with large croquet lawn. We offer 1 double en suite and 1 twin with private adjoining bathroom. Both fitted with basins tea/coffee making facilities, colour TV, etc. A welcome awaits with a pot of tea served in lounge or sun room. We also have an antique farm kitchen which visitors may view by request. No smoking. Open all year.

---

11 **Moor Court Farm,** Stretton Grandison, Nr Ledbury, Herefordshire HR8 2TR

Elizabeth Godsall
☎ **01531 670408**
BB **From £16**
EM From £12.50
Sleeps 6
🎠 🏇 🛶 🐕 🌾 🕯️
🐾
🐝

Relax and enjoy our beautiful 15th century timber-framed farmhouse with adjoining oast houses in a peaceful location. It's a traditional working Herefordshire hop and livestock farm, in scenic countryside central to the major market towns. Easy access to the Malverns, Wye Valley and Welsh borders. Spacious bedrooms, en suite or private bathroom, tea/coffee-making facilities. Oak beamed lounge and dining room. Open all year.

New House Farm, Much Marcle, Ledbury, Herefordshire HR8 2PH

Mrs Anne Jordan
☎ 01531 660604
🅱 From £15
EM From £10
Sleeps 4
🐕 (6) 🐎 🎠

A friendly welcome awaits you at our delightful farmhouse enjoying panoramic views over Herefordshire, Worcestershire and Gloucestershire. Relax by a log fire on chilly evenings, or enjoy a swim in our outdoor pool during summer. We also welcome horses, for which a full livery service is provided. Open all year.

Old Court Farm, Bredwardine, Herefordshire HR3 6BT

Sue Whittall
☎ 01981 500375
🅱 From £18–£20
EM From £13.50
Sleeps 4
🐕 🐎 🎠

Old Court is a 14th century mediaeval manor situated on the banks of the River Wye. It has been carefully restored to preserve a wealth of beams and a 15ft fireplace. Gardens enjoy beautiful views to the river. There are 2 four-poster bedrooms, 2 en suite. Teamakers provided. Also evening meals and picnics. Phone for opening times.

Paunceford Court, Much Cowarne, Nr Bromyard, Herefordshire HR7 4JQ

Jenny Keenan
☎ 01432 820208
🅱 From £15–£18
EM From £9.50
Sleeps 4
🐕 🐎 🎠
Listed

A warm friendly welcome awaits you at this old delightful farmhouse set in a quiet country location. Ideal for touring Malverns, Welsh Borders and Wye Valley. Bedrooms tastefully furnished to a high standard, separate bathroom/shower, tea-making facilities, dining room, TV lounge. Children welcome, evening meals available. Realistic prices, reduced for children. Pets by arrangement. Open all year except Christmas.

Sink Green Farm, Rotherwas, Hereford HR2 6LE

David Jones
☎ 01432 870223
🅱 From £18–£23
Sleeps 6
🐎 🐕 🎠
👑 *Commended*

Sink Green awaits you with a warm, friendly welcome to its 16th century farmhouse overlooking the River Wye and picturesque Herefordshire countryside yet only 3 miles from the cathedral city of Hereford. Comfortable bedrooms, one with four-poster bed, all en suite, tea/coffee making facilities and colour TV. Large oak-beamed lounge and traditional farmhouse fare. Children welcome, pets by arrangement. AA listed. Open all year.

Upper Newton Farmhouse, Kinnersley, Herefordshire HR3 6QB

Pearl & Jon Taylor
☎/Fax 01544 327727
🅱 From £16–£20
EM from £10
Sleeps 8
🐕 🎠
Applied

17th century farmhouse. Pretty gardens overlooking the Black Mountains. Lovely fabrics, crafts and paint techniques abound coupled with traditional and tasty farmhouse fare. Vegetarians welcomed. Ideally situated for touring. 3 en suite rooms, 1 private bathroom with 4 poster bedroom. Newly renovated stable block. Guests' own dining/lounge plus extra comforts help to make your stay special. Open all year.

The Vauld House Farm, Marden, Herefordshire HR1 3HA

Mrs Judith Wells
☎ 01568 84347/797347
Fax 01568 797366
🅱 From £14.50–£17.50
EM From £12.50
Sleeps 5
🐕 🐎 🎠

Situated 6 miles north of Hereford in beautiful countryside, this 17th century farmhouse offers traditionally furnished, comfortable en suite accommodation with guests' own lounge and dining room. Open log fires. All home cooking to a very high standard using fresh local produce. Guests may enjoy relaxing in the wooded and lawned gardens with carp ponds. Open all year except Christmas.

SELF-CATERING

---

18 **Bankside,** Dilwyn, Hereford, Herefordshire HR4 8HD

Mrs Anna Wellings
☎ 01544 318329
sc **From £195–£240**
Sleeps 6 + cot
🐴 🐕 🏕
🔑 🔑 🔑 🔑 *Commended*

Spacious family house, overlooking unspoilt farmland with panoramic views of Black Mountains. Famous for black and white village trail. Two double bedded rooms, 1 twin, nursery with cot, bathroom, 2 WCs. Large lounge, dining room, modern kitchen, shower room, secluded gardens with patio furniture. Linen included. Open all year.

---

19 **Brooklyn,** c/o Marlbrook Hall, Elton, Ludlow, Shropshire SY8 2HR

Mrs Valerie Morgan
☎ 01568 86230
sc **From £110–£220**
Sleeps 6
🐴 🏕 🏕
🔑 🔑 🔑 🔑 *Commended*

Situated on the Herefordshire/Shropshire border, ideal for exploring the market town of Ludlow, Mortimer Forest and Welsh Borders. Spacious accommodation consists of three bedroomed house with garden and garage. Fitted carpets and tastefully decorated. Colour TV, microwave oven, washing machine, tumble dryer, linen and towels included in price.

---

20 **The Cyder Barn and The Stable,** New House Farm, Preston Wynne, Herefordshire HR1 3PE

Mrs Julie Rogers
☎ 01432 8201621
sc **From £150**
Sleeps 3–6
🐴 🍴 💼
🔑 🔑 🔑 🔑 *Highly Commended*

An Elizabethan barn beautifully restored to create 2 luxury cottages in the lovely Herefordshire countryside. Owner supervised. Guests are always welcomed with wine and many thoughtful extras. Sauna, jacuzzi, sunbed facilities. Also available pool/games room, keep fit/gym room. Pets' corner, children's safe play area. The satisfaction of our guests is very important to us. Open all year.

---

21 **Dairy Cottage,** Upper Newton Farm, Kinnersley, Herefordshire HR3 6QB

Pearl & Jon Taylor
☎/Fax 01554 327727
sc **From £190–£290**
Sleeps 6 + cot
🐴 🍴 🏕 💼
🔑 🔑 🔑 🔑 *Commended*

Spacious, newly renovated cottage with one double, two twin bedrooms. Large, fully equipped, fitted kitchen, utility area, fitted carpets, linen, bathroom with shower and bath. Heating included. Stencilling and characterful crafts abound. Garage and garden, fabulous views, own drive. Local produce and home cooking by arrangement. Open all year.

---

22 **Lyston Smithy,** Wormelow, Nr Hereford HR2 8EL

Shirley Wheeler
☎ 01981 540625
sc **From £135–£300**
Sleeps 4
🐴 (10) 📞 💼
🔑 🔑 🔑 🔑 *Commended*

The Forge cottage is all on one level and retains many original features. Large open plan living room, fully equipped kitchenette, one twin en suite, one double bedroom and bathroom. CH, telephone and TV. Linen included. 14 acres of gardens and grounds. 3 day breaks Nov–Mar. Open all year.

Mill House Flat, Woonton Court Farm, Leysters, Leominster, Herefordshire HR6 0HL   (23)

Mrs Elizabeth Thomas
☎ 01568 750232
🆂 From £95–£250
Sleeps 3/4 + cot
🐕 🐎 🧍 💷 🎪
Applied

Half-timbered brick and stone detached mill, recently converted to provide comfortable first floor self-contained accommodation. Open plan kitchen/dining room/spacious sitting room, electric fire, colour TV. Night store heating and fitted carpets throughout. Linen/electricity included. Telephone. Sunny patio, parking, freedom to walk on the farm and enjoy a wealth of nature. Own farm produce. Short breaks. Open all year.

Old Court Farm, Bredwardine, Herefordshire HR3 6BT   (24)

Sue Whittall
☎ 01981 500375
🆂 From £160–£275
Sleeps 5 + cot
🐕 💷 🐎 🛶 🎪 🛥 🎣
Applied

14th century manor situated on the banks of the River Wye. Three English kings have visited this lovely house. The accommodation left of sketch has an impressive four–poster bedroom, landing bedroom and family room. Oak farmhouse kitchen and dining room. Beamed sitting room. Private garden with barbecue. Canoeing, fishing, pony trekking, farm animals and many walks. Duvets provided, electricity meter, TV, washing machine.

The Vauld House Farm, Marden, Hereford, Herefordshire HR1 3HA   (25)

Judith Wells
☎ 01568 84347/797347
Fax 01568 797366
🆂 From £165–£225
EM From £12.50
Sleeps 2/5 + cot
🐎 🐕 🧍 💷 ♿ 🎪 🛥
 🐾 🐾 🐾 *Commended*

Set amidst beautiful countryside on family stock farm midway between Hereford and Leominster, this skilfully converted Victorian hop kiln is spacious and well-equipped. Sleeps 5 + cot. Recently renovated 17th century Cider House, retaining character and charm. Ground floor sleeps 2. Lawned and wooded gardens with moat and ponds extend to over an acre. Open all year.

Wilden Cottage, c/o Wilden Farm, St Michaels, Tenbury Wells, Worcestershire WR15 8PL   (26)

Mrs Margaret Jones
☎ 01568 750255
🆂 From £145–£215
Sleeps 5
🐕 🐎 🎪
🐾 🐾 🐾 *Approved*

Semi-detached cottage in own lawned garden, bordered by wooded brook and orchard. Idyllic setting for birdwatchers, naturalists and walkers, and exploring Herefordshire, Worcestershire and Shropshire. Conservation methods used on farm. Sleeps 5 in double, twin and single bedrooms. Sitting room with colour TV, open fire. Children and pets welcome. Open all year.

FOLLOW THE COUNTRY CODE

Leave nothing but footprints,
Take nothing but photographs,
Kill nothing but time!

FARM HOLIDAY BUREAU

41

England's Heartland

Worcestershire

Group Contacts: [BB] *Mrs Pauline Grainger* ☎ *01299 404027*
[SC] *Mr R. Goodman* ☎ *01299 896500*

Worcestershire still has that flavour of Old England with flowering hedges, grazing pastures, rolling hills and bluebelled woodland, winding lanes and sleepy villages. To the north the Georgian town of Bewdley straddles the River Severn, fringed by the Wyre Forest where wild deer wander. Bromsgrove with its Georgian buildings and gabled houses and Droitwich Spa with the High Street of timber framed shops.

Follow the gentle flow of the Severn, Teme and Avon as they make their way through the county passing through Evesham, Pershore and Upton-on-Severn. Climb the rolling hills of Malvern, Abberley, Woodbury and Clee. Discover the market town of Tenbury Wells and Malvern with its Priory and famous drinking water flowing freely at St Annes Well and Holy Well. At the south-east tip of our county lies Broadway, the picturesque Cotswold village.

Worcestershire is steeped in history and where better to discover this than Worcester itself, the heart of our county. Dominated by its grand and beautiful cathedral, the city has many interesting museums, the Commandery with its Civil War connections, the Royal Worcester Porcelain factory and the Guild Hall.

The area offers great variety and you will be sure of a warm welcome.

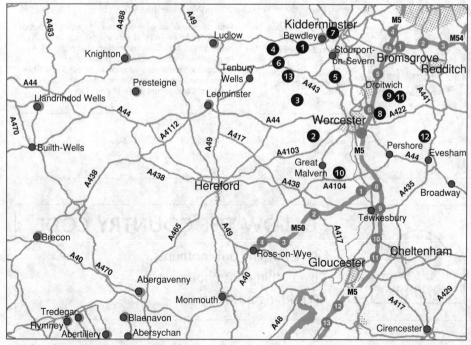

BED AND BREAKFAST

(and evening meal)

Bullockhurst Farm, Rock, Nr Bewdley, Worcestershire DY14 9SE 1

Margaret Nott
01299 832 305
From £16
Sleeps 4
Highly Commended

Come and savour the peace and tranquility of our Georgian farmhouse set in large gardens and beautiful undulating countryside. En suite facilities. Well situated for exploring the Wyre Forest, Bewdley with its Severn Railway and enjoying the panoramic views over the Worcestershire and Shropshire countryside. Excellent meals available in village. Children welcome. 1½ miles off A456.

Chirkenhill, Leigh Sinton, Malvern, Worcestershire WR13 5DE 2

Mrs Sarah Wenden
01886 832205
From £16–£18
Sleeps 6

We welcome guests to our attractive farmhouse conveniently situated 4 miles from Malvern and 5 from Worcester. Its elevated position commands lovely views of the Malvern Hills and surrounding countryside and its rural location ensures a peaceful break. Excellent country walks or drive the Elgar Route. Dogs/horses can be housed by arrangement. Open all year.

Church House Farm, Shelsley Beauchamp, Nr Worcester, Worcestershire WR6 6RA 3

Gill & Arthur Moore
01886 812393
From £15
EM From £9.50
Sleeps 4

A warm welcome awaits you on our 200-acre family run cattle and sheep farm in the Teme Valley. Country cooking is our speciality with meat and vegetables home or locally produced. All bedrooms have bathrooms en suite. Guests can relax in a large sitting room with colour TV after visits to the Welsh Borders, Shakespeare Country, the Malverns and many local attractions. Open March–Oct.

Clay Farm, Clows Top, Nr Bewdley, Worcestershire DY14 9NN 4

Mike & Ella Grinnall
01299 832421
From £16–£18
Sleeps 6
(2)
Highly Commended

Fully centrally heated farmhouse with log fires in winter. Friendly atmosphere, homemade cakes and tea on arrival. En suite bedrooms with tea making facilities. Full English breakfast. TV lounge. Fly and coarse fishing pools. Close proximity to Ludlow, Severn Valley Railway. On the borders of Worcestershire and Shropshire on the B4202 Cleobury Mortimer Road. Open all year.

Eden Farm, Ombersley, Nr Droitwich, Worcester WR9 0JX 5

Mrs Ann Yardley
01905 620244
From £16–£18
Sleeps 6
Commended

Come and enjoy our listed 17th century home with its lovely garden and fishing on the Severn. It's just off the A449 and the Wychavon Way, a wonderful centre for exploring the heart of England, with Worcester 7 miles, Droitwich 6 miles. Bedrooms are tastefully decorated, with bathrooms en suite, tea/coffee-making facilities. Homemade produce and preserves. Open all year.

6 Hunt House Farm, Frith Common, between Tenbury Wells and Bewdley, Worcestershire WR15 8JY

Chris & Jane Keel
☎ **01299 832277**
🅱 From £16
Sleeps 6
🛏 (8) 🐕 ♨ 🛍 ✗
🏵 🏵 *Highly Commended*

16th century timber framed farmhouse surrounded by breathtaking views. Our 180-acre farm is arable/sheep, and we offer comfort, peace and hospitality in a relaxing, friendly atmosphere. All bedrooms en suite with tea trays. Visitors welcomed with tea and homemade cake in guest sitting room. Excellent local eating houses. Convenient for Worcester, Shropshire, Hereford, NEC, Ironbridge, Wales. Open all year (closed Christmas).

---

7 Lightmarsh Farm, Crundalls Lane, Bewdley, Worcestershire DY12 1NE

Mrs Pauline Grainger
☎ **01299 404027**
🅱 From 16.50
Sleeps 4
🛏 (10) 🐕 ♨
🏵 🏵 *Highly Commended*

A small, pasture farm in an elevated position with fine views. Ideal location for walking, wildlife and exploring Heart of England. The house is approx 200 years old, full central heating, offers comfortable accommodation; TV lounge with inglenook fireplace. Both rooms have private facilities. Truly rural setting, only 1 mile from Bewdley's shops and restaurants, Severn Valley Railway and West Midland Safari Park. Brochure on request. Open all year.

---

8 Old House Farm, Tibberton, Droitwich, Worcestershire WR9 7NP

Pat Chilman
☎ **01905 345247**
🅱 From £18–£20
Sleeps 4
✗ 🛏 🐕 ♨ 🛍
🏵

Family run 100-acre dairy farm set off A4538, in peaceful village of Tibberton but only 1 mile from M5, J6. The farmhouse is tastefully furnished for comfort and relaxation with large garden and splendid views of Malvern Hills. Central for the Heart of England including Worcestershire, Herefordshire, Warwickshire, Gloucestershire and the Cotswolds. Washbasins en suite. Open Mar–Nov.

---

9 Phepson Farm, Himbleton, Droitwich, Worcestershire WR9 7JZ

David & Tricia Havard
☎ **01905 391205**
🅱 From £17
Sleeps 8
🐕 🐎 ♿ ♨ 🛍
🏵

In our 17th century oak beamed farmhouse we offer a warm welcome, good food and a relaxed and informal atmosphere. The recently converted Granary has two ground floor bedrooms whilst the farmhouse has double, and family accommodation. All rooms en suite with colour TV. Peaceful surroundings on family stock farm. Walking on Wychavon Way. Featured in 'Wish You Were Here'. Open all year except Christmas and New Year.

---

10 Tiltridge Farm & Vineyard, Upper Hook Road, Upton-on-Severn, Worcestershire WR8 0SA

Sandy Barker
☎ **01684 592906**
Fax 01684 594142
🅱 From £18–£20
EM From £9.50
Sleeps 5
🛏 🐕 ✗ ♿ ✗
🏵 🏵 *Highly Commended*

Period family farmhouse lying between the Malvern Hills and the attractive riverside town of Upton–on–Severn. Set in its own vineyard, the house is fully renovated with one double, one family room. Both rooms are en suite with TV. Warm welcome, good food and there is plenty of wine available! Four minutes from the Three Counties Showground and a good base for touring the Cotswolds, Malverns, Wye Valley and Forest of Dean. Open all year.

SELF-CATERING

The Granary, c/o Phepson Farm, Himbleton, Droitwich, Worcestershire WR9 7JZ

David & Tricia Havard
☎ 01905 391205
SC From £145–£215
Sleeps 2/4

Commended

The recent conversion of the old granary is reached by an outside stone staircase. The light and airy flat is double-glazed and very comfortably furnished. Situated on working stock farm in peaceful surroundings. Entrance through stable door. Fitted kitchen, colour TV, double bedroom with en suite bathroom. Linen, electricity, night storage heating included. Open all year.

Hill Barn Orchard, Evesham Road, Church Lench, Evesham, Worcestershire WR11 4UB

Marlene Badger
☎ 01386 871035
SC From £190–£495
Sleeps 6

Approved

Attractive, comfortably furnished house 4 miles from historic Evesham. On edge of village in quiet orchard setting. Views, lakes wildlife, trout fishing. Spring blossom trail, Elgar route, Cotswolds, Stratford, Ragley Hall. Ideal restful or touring holiday. Stratford 10 miles, Tewkesbury 12 miles, Broadway 12 miles. Open all year.

Old Yates Cottages, Old Yates Farm, Abberley, Nr Worcester, Worcestershire WR6 6AT

Sarah & Richard Goodman
☎ 01299 896500
Fax 01299 896889
SC From £105–£250
Sleeps 2/4

Commended

Four cottages in peaceful, secluded positions with private gardens, situated on small farm between Abberley Hills and the Teme Valley. Cosy, fully equipped and heated, also log fires, colour TV. Launderette and table tennis room. 1 mile from village supermarket and garage. Many restaurants, leisure and recreational activities within easy reach. Ideal centre to explore the Midlands and Welsh Borders. Brochure available. Open all year.

42

England's Heartland

Warwickshire

Group Contacts: *Miss Deborah Lea* ☎ *01295 770652*

The native county of William Shakespeare has a lot to offer. With its mediaeval castles, historic towns of Warwick, Stratford-upon-Avon, Leamington Spa, Rugby and Kenilworth and its delightful countryside.

Stratford-upon-Avon is the provincial home of the Royal Shakespeare Company who perform in the three theatres near the River Avon. There are many half-timbered buildings in the town, several of which have associations with the great bard and the shopping centre satisfies the most discerning shopper. A few miles up the River Avon lies the town of Warwick with its magnificent mediaeval castle brought to life by Madame Tussaud's vignettes.

At Kenilworth, the Castle can be seen. Close by is the Royal Showground which hosts the Royal Show every July and is a year-round agricultural centre. Royal Leamington Spa is an elegant Regency town with wide streets, crescents and fine gardens and famous for its healing waters.

There are also many pretty villages throughout the county and stately homes such as Packwood House, Ragley Hall, Charlecote Park, Baddesley Clinton and Coughton Court.

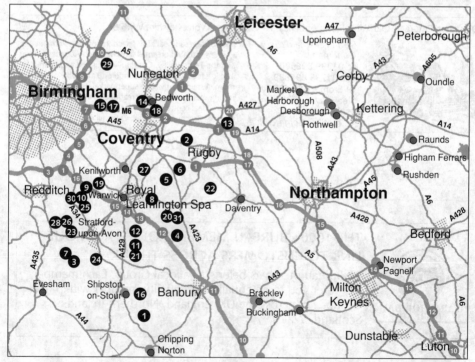

BED AND BREAKFAST

(and evening meal)

Ascott House Farm, Ascott, Whichford, nr Long Compton, Shipston-on-Stour, Warwickshire CV36 5PP

Mrs Janet Haines
☎ 01608 684655
BB From £16
Sleeps 6
🐕 🐾
👑 👑

Listed stone farmhouse in designated Area of Natural Beauty on edge of Cotswolds. 500-acre arable/sheep farm, attractive garden, outdoor swimming pool, snooker room, interesting walks. 2 double en suite/family rooms, 1 twin with washbasin, all with TV. Tea/coffee-making facilities, CH, TV lounge, traditional dining room. Golf/riding within 5 miles. Ideal for Stratford-upon-Avon/Cotswolds/Oxford, M40 Banbury 10 miles. Open all year.

The Byre, Lords Hill Farm, Coalpit Lane, Wolston, Coventry CV8 3GB

Mrs Betty Gibbs
☎ 01203 542098
BB From £15–£20
Sleeps 6
🐾 (5) 🐕 🍴
🐾

A warm welcome awaits guests to our home set in a quiet country lane on a 200-acre sheep/arable farm. Attractive double/twin bedrooms, 1 en suite, 2 with washbasins. Dining and sitting room with colour TV and full CH. Ideally situated for visiting Rugby, Leamington, Warwick, Stratford, NEC and NAC. Numerous places nearby for evening meals. East of Fosse Way on Wolston crossroads. Non smokers only. Open all year except Christmas.

Church Farm, Dorsington, Stratford-upon-Avon, Warwickshire CV37 8AX

Mrs Marian J Walters
☎ 01789 720471
and 0831 504194
Fax 01789 720830
BB From £13.50–£17
Sleeps 14
♿ 🐾 🐕 🐾 🏛 🍴
👑 👑 *Commended*

A warm welcome awaits you at our mixed working farm with lakes, equestrian course and woodlands to explore. Situated on edge of quiet pretty village yet ideal for touring Stratford, Warwick, Cotswolds, NAC, NEC, Worcester and Evesham. Some bedrooms en suite with TV. Stabling and fishing available. Open all year.

Crandon House, Avon Dassett, Leamington Spa, Warwickshire CV33 0AA

Deborah Lea
☎ 01295 770652
BB From £17.50–£22
EM From £12.50
Sleeps 6
🐕 🐾 (8) 🅿 🏛 🍴
👑 👑 *Highly Commended*

A warm welcome at our farmhouse offering an exceptionally high standard accommodation and comfort. Set in 20 acres, beautiful views. Small working farm, rare breeds cattle, sheep and poultry. Own produce, excellent food. Large garden. Full CH, log fire. 3 rooms with private facilities. Colour TV, tea/coffee tray. Peaceful, quiet, easy access to Warwick, Stratford, Cotswolds. Located between M40, J11/12 (4 miles). Open all year (closed Christmas).

Elms Farm, Oxford Road, Marton, Nr Rugby, Warwickshire CV23 9RQ

Pippa Ellis
☎ 01926 632770
BB From £15–£20
Sleeps 6
🐾 🐕 🐾 🏛
Listed

Come and stay in our listed farmhouse on an 800–acre mixed working farm, conveniently situated on the A423. Easy access to Stratford, Warwick, NAC/NEC. Tea/coffee–making facilities. Riverside walks. Stabling available. Open Feb–Nov.

---

6   **Frankton Grounds,** Frankton, Nr Rugby, Warwickshire CV23 9PD

Mrs Mary Pritchard
☎ 01926 632391
BB From £15–£20
EM From £8.50
Sleeps 4
Listed

Beautifully situated in a mixed farm of horses, sheep, pedigree and commercial cattle. A warm welcome for the visitor who enjoys peace and quiet yet, with the benefit of easy access to Warwick, Leamington and Stratford. 2½ miles M45. Full CH, log fires, excellent food. 1 double with TV and bathroom, 1 twin.

---

7   **Glebe Farm,** Exhall, Alcester, Warwickshire B49 6EA

John & Margaret Canning
☎ 01789 772202
BB From £15–£18
Sleeps 5
❀ *Approved*

Shakespeare named our village 'Dodging Exhall' and it has somehow 'dodged' the passing of time, so if you want a true taste of rural England, come and relax in our quaint old farmhouse – parts of it dating from Tudor times – with its log fires, four-poster bed and country hospitality. 1 double, 1 twin, 1 single, tea/coffee trays, electric blankets. Smoking in lounge. Payphone. Laundry. Ample parking. Open all year (closed Christmas & New Year).

---

8   **Hill Farm,** Lewis Road, Radford Semele, Leamington Spa, Warwickshire CV31 1UX

Rebecca Gibbs
☎ 01926 337571
BB From £15–£20
Sleeps 10

Hill Farm is a comfortable, friendly farmhouse situated in 350 acres of mixed farmland. Excellent breakfasts, large garden, attractive double/twin/single bedrooms, some en suite, with CH and tea/coffee-making facilities. Comfortable TV lounge, quiet room, guests' bathroom. Children welcome. AA and Farm Holiday Guide award winner. Caravanning/Camping Club certificated site. Ideal for Shakespeare Country. Open all year (closed Christmas).

---

9   **Holland Park Farm,** Buckley Green, Henley in Arden, Nr Solihull, Warwickshire B95 5QF

Mrs Kathleen Connolly
☎ 01564 792625
BB From £18–£20
Sleeps 6

A Georgian style farmhouse, set in 300 acres of peaceful farmland, including the historic grounds of 'The Mount' and other interesting walks. Large garden with pond. Livestock includes cattle, sheep and Irish Draught horses. Ideally situated in Shakespeare's country, within easy reach of Birmingham International Airport, NEC, NAC, Stratford–upon–Avon, Warwick and the Cotswolds. Open all year.

---

10   **Irelands Farm,** Irelands Lane, Henley-in-Arden, Nr Solihull, Warwickshire B95 5SA

Pamela Shaw
☎ 01564 792476
BB From £17–£20
Sleeps 6
❀❀ *Highly Commended*

If a quiet, relaxing holiday is what you are looking for, then visit our late Georgian farmhouse. Large rooms all with own bath/shower, TV, tea/coffee-making facilities, radio, CH. Set in 220 acres of peaceful farmland. Close to National Exhibition Centre, Stratford-upon-Avon, Warwick, National Agricultural Centre. Looking forward to meeting you. Open all year (closed Christmas & New Year).

---

11   **Little Hill Farm,** Wellesbourne, Warwick, Warwickshire CV35 9EB

Charlotte Hutsby
☎ 01789 840261
BB From £17
EM From £7.50
Sleeps 6

Set in 700 acres of beef/arable farmland, our rambling William & Mary farmhouse offers a warm, friendly relaxed atmosphere, with antiques and beams throughout the house. Each bedroom has private bathroom and tea-making facilities. Drawing room with colour TV. The farm is situated on A429 on Warwick Road from Wellesbourne, only 6 miles from Warwick and 6 miles from Stratford-upon-Avon. Open all year (closed Christmas & New Year).

Lower Watchbury Farm, Wasperton Lane, Barford, Warwickshire CV35 8DH

Valerie Eykyn
☎ 01926 624772
[BB] From £17.50–£21.50
Sleeps 6
✂ ❧ ♞ ♟ ⚘
🌢🌢 *Commended*

In the heart of Shakespeare Country, we offer you a warm welcome in our luxurious accommodation with outstanding views over rural Warwickshire. 1 large twin/family en suite room with lounge area, 1 twin en suite, 1 small double with own bathroom. All have colour TV, tea/coffee-making facilities. Excellent farmhouse breakfast. Village pubs for dinners. Large garden. Warwick, Stratford, NAC, NEC and Cotswolds nearby. Open all year except Christmas.

Manor Farm, Willey, Nr Rugby, Warwickshire CV23 0SH

Mrs Helen Sharpe
☎ 01455 553143
[BB] From £17–£25
Sleeps 6
✂ ♟
🌢🌢

Attention to detail, centralisation for Midlands motorways, accessibility to all points of the compass, makes this the perfect venue for travellers or businessmen alike. Emphasis placed on cleanliness and efficient service. Food Hygiene Certificate holder. Peace and tranquillity guaranteed. Our repeat bookings are our testimony. No smoking. No children. Open all year except Christmas.

Marslands Farm, Church Lane, Corley, Coventry, Warwickshire CV7 8AS

Rod & Chris Lester
☎ 01676 540317
[BB] From £16
Sleeps 5
❧ (3) ♞ ✂ ♘ ⚘ ♟
Listed

You will find a warm welcome at our 200 year old farmhouse set in 90 acres and run as an equestrian centre. Ideally situated for NEC, NAC, Birmingham (plus Airport), Coventry, Warwick. Stabling available. Guests' own lounge and dining room. Safe parking. Open all year.

Maxstoke Hall Farm, Fillongley Road, Maxstoke, Nr Coleshill, Birmingham, Warwickshire B46 2QT

Mrs Heather Green
☎/Fax 01675 463237
[BB] From £22–£25
EM From £6.75
Sleeps 3
❧ ♞ ♙ ✂ ♘ ♥ ⚘ ♟
🌢🌢 *Commended*

Elegant farmhouse, built in 1632, and set in beautiful countryside. Bedrooms have en suite facilities, TV, hostess tray. Comfortable oak-beamed dining and sitting rooms for use by guests. Situated 3 miles from Coleshill, 5 mins from M6 and M42. 15 mins from National Exhibition Centre, Birmingham Airport and International Railway Station. Open all year (closed Christmas & New Year).

New House Farm, Brailes, Banbury, Oxfordshire OX15 5BD

Helen Taylor
☎ 01608 686239
[BB] From £14–£16
Sleeps 6
♞ ♟ ⚘ ♟
🌢🌢

Quietly nestling under Brailes Hill, a Georgian farmhouse on a 500-acre mixed farm in an area of outstanding natural beauty. In easy reach of Cotswolds, Oxford, Stratford-on-Avon. 1 family room, 1 double, both en suite, 1 twin room with washbasin, all with CH, colour TV and tea/coffee-making facilities. TV lounge. Large garden, 18-hole golf course 200 yards. Open all year.

Packington Lane Farm, Coleshill, Warwickshire B46 3JJ

Vera Harcourt
☎/Fax 01675 462228
[BB] From £16.50–£18
Sleeps 5
♙ ✂ ♘ ♥ ♟
Listed

A warm welcome to a traditional farmhouse with tasty home cooking awaits my guests. 2 twin (one en suite), 1 single room with usual refinements. Guests' bathroom. Beamed TV room, central heating. ½ mile Coleshill, 7 minutes National Exhibition Centre, Birmingham Airport and railway station, 6 miles Belfry Hotel. Open all year.

---

18 **Park Farm,** Spring Road, Barnacle, Shilton, Coventry, Warwickshire CV7 9LG

Linda Grindal
☎ 01203 612628
🆎 From £18.50
EM From £12
Sleeps 4
🛏 (12)

A warm welcome awaits you at Park Farm, a listed building dating back to the Civil War and originally moated. Spacious, comfortable and quiet, it is near the M6/M69 motorways. Two bedrooms with washbasins, TV, electric blankets and tea/coffee-making facilities. Guests' own bathroom. Separate sitting and dining room. Full CH. Excellent food. Open all year.

19 **Shrewley Pools Farm,** Haseley, Warwickshire CV35 7HB

Mrs Cathy Dodd
☎ 01926 484315
🆎 From £18–£25
EM From £7.50
Sleeps 6
🛏 ✂ 🏕 ▪
Listed *Commended*

Why not sample the delights of staying in a beautiful 17th century traditional farmhouse? Set in an acre of landscaped garden with 4-acre pool. Shrewley Pools has many interesting features, including timbered barn, huge fireplaces, and beamed ceilings. 2 bedrooms, one en suite, with tea/coffee tray. Close to Warwick, Stratford-upon-Avon, the NEC and NAC. Open all year (closed Christmas).

20 **Snowford Hall Farm,** Hunningham, Nr Royal Leamington Spa, Warwickshire CV33 9ES

Rudi Hancock
☎ 01926 632297
🆎 From £16–£19
Sleeps 6
🛏 ⚘
⚘ ⚘ *Commended*

A warm welcome and peaceful surroundings in 18th century farmhouse on 250-acre mixed working farm in rolling countryside. Near the Roman Fosse Way, ideal for visiting Stratford, Warwick, Leamington, Cotswolds, NAC and NEC. 1 double room with washbasin/WC 1 twin room with shower/basin/WC; 1 twin room with shower/basin. Singles extra. CH, good home cooking. Open all year (closed Christmas & New Year).

21 **Thornton Manor,** Ettington, Stratford-upon-Avon, Warwickshire CV37 7PN

Mrs Gillian Hutsby
☎ 01789 740210
🆎 From £17–£19.50
Sleeps 6
🛏 (5) ✂ ☕ 🏕
⚘ ⚘

A 16th century stone-built manor house, overlooking peaceful countryside on an 800-acre farm. Tennis, fishing and riding nearby. There is a log fire to relax by in the comfortable hall, plus a television and piano. Separate guest kitchen and breakfast room. Private showers/bathroom for each bedroom. Situated off the A429 Warwick road, from Ettington. Open all year (closed Christmas & New Year).

22 **Tibbits Farm,** Nethercote, Flecknoe, Nr Rugby, Warwickshire CV23 8AS

Alison Mills
☎ 01788 890239
🆎 From £19
Sleeps 4
🛏 🏕 ▪ ⚘
⚘ ⚘

Retreat from the trials of life to the seclusion and tranquillity of our 17th farmhouse idyllically situated within acres of rolling countryside, where we offer luxurious bed and breakfast accommodation. The spacious and pretty bedrooms have en suite or private bathrooms, colour TVs, tea/coffee making facilities. Tibbits is ideally situated for exploring the many places of historic, scenic and cultural interest in the area.

23 **Walcote Farm,** Walcote, Haselor, Alcester, Warwickshire B49 6LY

Prim & John Finnemore
☎ 01789 488264
🆎 From £17
Sleeps 4
🛏 🐎 ✂ ☕ 🏕
⚘ ⚘

Stratford–upon–Avon is only 5 miles from a tranquil, picturesque hamlet and our attractive oak–beamed farmhouse with a friendly welcome and comfort assured. En suite for one double and one twin room, both with lovely views. Full central heating with log fires in winter. For local history, we have a large collection of old photographs and documents, including the Earl of Warwick's accounts for 1782–1786. Open all year.

Whitchurch Farm, Wimpstone, Stratford-upon-Avon, Warwickshire CV37 8NS   **24**

Mrs Joan James
☎ **01789 450275**
🅱🅱 **From £15**
EM From £9
Sleeps 6
🐎 💼
🌻🌻

Lovely Georgian farmhouse set in park–like surroundings in peaceful Stour Valley 4½ miles from Stratford. Very convenient for Warwick Castle and Shakespeare properties. Ideal for touring the Cotswolds by car or rambling. The bedrooms are large, well furnished with washbasins, two with en suite bathroom, CH and tea/coffee-making facilities. Separate dining room and sitting room for guests. Open all year (closed Christmas Day).

Yew Tree Farm, Wootton Wawen, Solihull, West Midlands B95 6BY   **25**

Mrs Janet Haimes
☎ **01564 792701**
🅱🅱 **From £14–£17**
Sleeps 4 + cot
🐎 🐾 🍴 🏛
🌻🌻 *Commended*

Georgian farmhouse situated on A3400 in village of Wootton Wawen, 2 miles south of Henley-in-Arden, 6 miles north of Stratford-upon-Avon. Easy reach of Warwick Castle, Royal Showground, NEC, and Cotswolds. 700-acre dairy/arable farm with lake and woodland walks. 2 large double bedrooms, CH, en suite, tea/coffee-making facilities. Cot available. Visitors' lounge with colour TV. Excellent pubs and restaurants nearby. Open all year (closed Christmas & New Year).

SELF-CATERING

Broadlane Cottage, Spernal Lane, Gt. Alne, Alcester, Warwickshire B49 6JD   **26**

Mrs Anne Stevens
☎ **01789 488218**
🆂🅲 **From £100–£250**
Sleeps 6
🐎 🏛
🐾 🐾 🐾 *Approved*

A quiet, detached country cottage fully equipped for 6 people, with large, pretty garden. Very convenient for the Cotswolds, Warwick and Stratford-upon-Avon. Open all year.

Furzen Hill Farm Cottages, c/o Furzen Hill Farm, Cubbington Heath, Leamington Spa, Warks CV32 6QZ **27**

Mrs Christine Whitfield
☎/Fax **01926 424791**
🆂🅲 **From £90–£275**
Sleeps 4/7
🐄 🐎 🐒
🐾 🐾 🐾 *Up to Commended*

Furzen Hill is a mixed farm. The cottage is part of 17th century farmhouse with a large shared garden. Sleeping 7. The Barn and Dairy Cottages, both recently converted, each sleeps 4. Dairy Cottage has its own small garden. The Barn shares the Cottage garden. All have the use of tennis court. Situated within easy reach of NAC, NEC, Warwick and Stratford. Open all year.

The Granary, c/o Glebe Farm, Kinwarton, Alcester, Warwickshire B49 6HB   **28**

Susan Kinnersley
☎/Fax **01789 762554**
🆂🅲 **From £75–£130**
Sleeps 2 + cot
🍴 🐎 🏛 🐒
🐾 🐾 🐾 *Commended*

Off the beaten track, yet near the small market town of Alcester, this cottage retains many interesting features of the original granary combined with modern standards of warmth and comfort. The farm is bounded by the River Alne and there are a variety of attractive country walks in the area. Linen provided, colour TV. Cot available. Car space. Short breaks by arrangement. Open all year.

29 **Hipsley Farm Cottages,** Hipsley Lane, Hurley, Atherstone, Warwickshire CV9 2LR

Mrs Ann Prosser
☎/Fax 01827 872437
SC From £245–£300
Sleeps 18 + cots

Highly Commended

Hipsley Farm is situated in beautiful rolling countryside only 3 miles from junction 10, M42/A5, so ideal for NEC, Birmingham, Warwick, Leicester. The barns and cowshed have been carefully converted into 6 comfortable, individually furnished cottages. Fully equipped including CH, colour TV, bed linen and towels, laundry, payphone, putting green, ample parking on site. One cottage suitable for disabled. ETB Highly Commended. Open all year.

30 **Irelands Farm,** Irelands Lane, Henley in Arden, Warwickshire B95 5SA

Pamela Shaw
☎ 01564 792476
SC From £100–£388
Sleeps 4

*Up to
Highly Commended*

Four attractively converted oak-beamed cottages in courtyard on 220-acre working farm. Very quiet location yet within 3 miles of M42/M40 junction. All cottages centrally heated and tastefully furnished, and equipped to a high standard. Linen provided. Private patios. Open all year.

31 **Snowford Hall Farm Cottage,** c/o Snowford Hall Farm, Hunningham, Leamington Spa, Warwicks CV33 9ES

Rudi Hancock
☎ 01926 632297
SC From £110–£260
Sleeps 5

Approved

Fully centrally heated spacious 2–bedroomed cottage on a quiet country road surrounded by well maintained lawns and farmland. Capable of sleeping 5 people. A comfortable lounge with TV and fitted kitchen makes this cottage an ideal base for touring the Cotswolds, Shakespeare Country and exploring Warwick, Kenilworth and Oxford. The NAC is 5 miles and NEC 15 miles away. Open all year.

43

England's Heartland

Cotswolds and Royal Forest of Dean

Group Contacts: *Anne Meadows* ☎ *01684 72322*

The villages and scenic beauty of the Cotswolds are famed throughout the world. The many honey-coloured villages include Bibury, Broadway, Painswick and Lower Slaughter while some of the finest churches in the country are at Northleach, Fairford and Winchcombe which also has Sudeley Castle. Along the River Severn the villages have black and white half-timbered cottages and cattle graze peacefully in the orchards and meadows. Gloucester with its cathedral, the elegant Regency town of Cheltenham and picturesque Tewkesbury with its 12th century abbey are in the Severn Vale. There are numerous visitor attractions in the main towns and villages while further afield are Berkeley Castle and Sir Peter Scott's Wildfowl Trust at Slimbridge.

Bordered by two rivers, the Severn and the Wye, is the beautiful and romantic Forest of Dean, ancient hunting grounds of kings and still covered by oak woodlands.

Scattered through the Forest are mining towns such as Cinderford, Coleford and Lydney. Below Symonds Yat, the River Wye meanders dramatically in a most attractive wooded gorge.

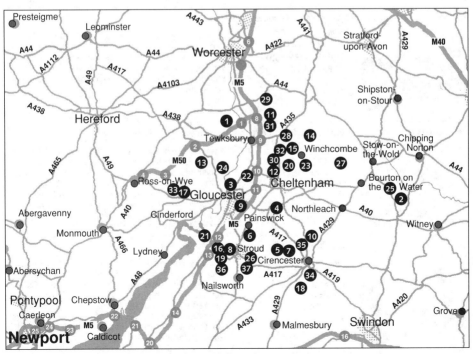

BED AND BREAKFAST

(and evening meal)

① Abbots Court, Church End, Twyning, Tewkesbury, Gloucestershire GL20 6DA

Bernie Williams
☎/Fax 01684 292515
ⒷⒷ From £14–£16
Sleeps 15
🐕 🐎 ♿ 🐄 🐈 🏇
♥♥ *Approved*

Lovely, quiet farmhouse in 350 acres between Cotswolds and Malverns. All bedrooms have colour TV, most en suite, tea-making facilities. Large lounge, separate dining room, excellent home cooked food. Licensed bar. 3 games rooms with pool table, table tennis, children's TV room, grass tennis court, bowling green, children's play area on lawn. Superb touring area. Open all year (except Christmas and New Year).

② Bould Farm, Bould, Nr Idbury, Chipping Norton, Oxfordshire OX7 6RT

Mrs Lynne Meyrick
☎ 01608 658850
ⒷⒷ From £18–£20
Sleeps 6
🐎 ✂ 🏇
Listed *Commended*

Bould Farm is a 17th century Cotswold farmhouse on a 300-acre family farm set in beautiful countryside, 10 minutes' drive from Stow-on-the-Wold and Bourton-on-the-Water and Burford. Within easy reach of Blenheim Palace and the Cotswold Wildlife Park. Children welcome. Spacious rooms with TV, tea/coffee-making facilities. Large garden. Good local pubs.

③ Brawn Farm, Sandhurst, Gloucester, Gloucestershire GL2 9NR

Sally Williams
☎ 01452 731010
Mobile 0831 260776
ⒷⒷ From £17
Sleeps 4
🐎 🐕 🐑 🐈 🏇
Listed

Working dairy/corn farm with a 15th century listed farmhouse and large garden in an extremely quiet setting. Delightful footpaths through the farm and woods. Two very spacious bedrooms, comfortable lounge with TV, separate dining room offering excellent breakfasts. Good local pubs. Open all year.

④ Butlers Hill Farm, Cockleford, Cowley, Cheltenham, Gloucestershire GL53 9NW

Bridget Brickell
☎ 01242 870455
ⒷⒷ From £15
EM From £7
Sleeps 4
🐎 (6) 🐈
♥♥ *Approved*

A warm welcome awaits you on this mixed working farm between Cheltenham and Cirencester. Relax in this modern spacious farmhouse, in a quiet part of the Churn Valley with attractive walks and an ideal centre for exploring the cotswolds. All rooms have H & C and tea/coffee-making facilities, separate guests' sitting room with colour TV and separate dining room. Open all year (closed Christmas and New Year).

⑤ The Coach House, Middle, Duntisbourne, Cirencester, Gloucestershire GL7 7AR

Mrs June Barton
☎ 01285 653058
ⒷⒷ From £14–£16
Sleeps 4
🐎 (9) 🐕 ✂
♥♥ *Approved*

A warm welcome at the 17th century coachhouse by the River Dunt. Centrally situated in 400-acre arable and beef farm with lovely walks and ideal for visits to Bath, Oxford, Stratford and many pretty villages in and around Cirencester area. Pretty garden with country views. TV, tea/coffee-making facilities in bedrooms. Pleasant lounge with CTV. Always a choice of breakfast including English farmhouse breakfast. Open all year.

Damsels Farm, Painswick, Gloucestershire GL6 6UD **6**

Michele Burdett
☎ 01452 812148
BB From £18.50–£19.50
EM From £16.50
Sleeps 6

Welcome to Damsels Farm where Henry VIII is reputed to have hunted with Ann Boleyn. Children may help feed the ducks, geese, chickens, calves and orphan lambs. The house is set in a quiet Cotswold Valley on the Cotswold Way. We are within easy reach of Cheltenham, Cirencester, Bath, Slimbridge and The Malverns. Open Mar–Oct (incl).

Dix's Barn, Duntisbourne Abbots, Cirencester, Gloucestershire GL7 7JN **7**

Mrs Rosemary Wilcox
☎ 01285 821249
BB From £16–£17
Sleeps 4

Dix's Barn is situated in an Area of Outstanding Natural Beauty. It has breathtaking views of the Cotswolds and one can take lovely walks in any direction. Ideally placed for touring by car. The farm is family run, being a mixture of arable, beef and sheep. Open all year.

Down Barn Farmhouse, The Camp, Stroud, Gloucestershire GL6 7EY **8**

Anita Morley
☎ 01452 812853
BB From £15
Sleeps 6

Listed

The farmhouse is on a smallholding with Pygmy and other goats ¼ of a mile off the Cotswold Scenic Leisure Drive (B4070), halfway between Stratford-upon-Avon and Bath. All accommodation is on the ground floor in a separate wing of the farmhouse and suitable for the immobile. Three bedrooms with washbasins, visitors' TV lounge with tea-making facilities. Lovely views and peaceful setting. Within easy reach of all Cotswold attractions. Open Jan–Nov.

Gilbert's, Gilbert's Lane, Brookthorpe, Nr Gloucester, Gloucestershire GL4 0UH **9**

Jenny Beer
☎/Fax 01452 812364
BB From £21
Sleeps 6

Highly Commended

Gilbert's which nestles beneath the Cotswolds close to Gloucester may have been Whaddon Manor 400 years ago. It is listed as an architectural gem. Whilst each room has modern amenities – private bathroom, TV, radio, telephone, etc. – the atmosphere is in keeping with the unpretentious nature of the house and organic smallholding, echoing a long history of living with this environment. Open all year.

Hartpury Farm, Chedworth, Nr Cheltenham, Gloucestershire GL54 4AL **10**

Peter & Peggy Booth
☎ 01285 720350
BB From £13.50–£15
EM From £7.50
Sleeps 6

Listed

Hartpury, lying centrally in the Cotswolds and in a quiet village, provides views across the valley. Good walking. Farm produce, provided by Jersey cows and organic gardening, cooked to traditional recipes. The beamed sitting room, vintage 1650, leads onto the garden where we often serve coffee. When we can, we help with excursions and local history. Open Apr–Oct.

Home Farm, Bredons Norton, Tewkesbury, Gloucestershire GL20 7HA **11**

Mick & Anne Meadows
☎ 01684 72322
BB From £18
EM From £12
Sleeps 6

Commended

Mixed 150-acre family-run farm with sheep, cattle and poultry. Situated in an extremely quiet, unspoilt little village nestling under Bredon Hill. Superb position for walking, an excellent base for touring or relaxing. The 18th century farmhouse is very comfortably furnished. All bedrooms have en suite bathrooms. Gas CH. Good home cooking, evening meal by arrangement. Lounge, TV. Children welcome. Open mid Jan–mid Dec.

12 Hunting Butts Farm, Swindon Lane, Cheltenham, Gloucestershire GL50 4NZ

Jane Hanks
☎ 01242 524982
BB From £16–£18.50
EM From £9
Sleeps 16
🐕🛉🛏🎀⚓
🏵🏵🏵 *Approved*

Hunting Butts is a working 200-acre beef and arable farm on the edge of beautiful countryside overlooking the historic town of Cheltenham Spa, just 1½ miles from the town centre. Cheltenham Leisure Centre is a short walk away with swimming pools, squash courts, softball, etc. Children's playground, tennis courts, boating lake and golf course are again within easy walking distance. Open all year.

13 Kilmorie Guest House, Gloucester Road, Snigs End, Corse, Staunton, Nr Gloucester, Gloucs GL19 3RQ

Sheila Barnfield
☎ 01452 840224
BB From £12.50
EM From £6.50
Sleeps 11
🐂(5)🛉🛏🎀🚴🐾⚓
🏵

Built in 1848 by the Chartists, Kilmorie is a Grade 2 listed smallholding keeping sheep, ponies, goats, ducks and hens. Children may help with animals. All accommodation on ground floor, tea/coffee trays and washbasins in all bedrooms, CH, large garden. Good home cooking, full English breakfast, 3 course evening meal. Some private facilities. Ideal for Cotswolds, Malverns, Forest of Dean, and places of natural and historic interest. Fire certificate. Fishing nearby. Open all year (closed Christmas & New Year).

14 Lydes Farm, Toddington, Cheltenham, Gloucestershire GL54 5DP

Mrs R Sharpley
☎ 01242 621229
BB From £16–£18
Sleeps 5
🐂(5)🛉🎀🐾
🏵 *Commended*

Comfortable farmhouse between Broadway and Winchcombe with panoramic views from every room. TV in bedrooms, separate dining room, garden. Dogs taken by arrangement. A grass farm grazed by cattle and horses; visitors are welcome to walk round. Ideal centre for exploring the North Cotswolds. Golf and riding nearby. Open Jan–Nov.

15 Manor Farm, Greet, Winchcombe, Cheltenham, Gloucestershire GL54 5BJ

Richard & Janet Day
☎ 01242 602423
BB From £18.50–£20
Sleeps 4
🐂🛏🎀🐾⚓
🏵

Luxuriously restored 16th century cotswold manor on mixed family farm, excellent views, near Sudeley Castle and steam railway. Convenient to Broadway, Cheltenham, Evesham, Tewkesbury and M5. 1½ miles from Cotswold Way and Wychavon Way. Large garden, croquet lawn, children welcome, horses can be accommodated. Open Jan–Nov.

16 Nastend Farm, Nastend, Nr Stonehouse, Gloucestershire GL10 3RS

Jackie Guilding
☎ 01453 822300
BB From £14–£16.50
EM From £10
Sleeps 6
🐂🎀⚓🐾
🏵

Enjoy that well-earned break in the friendly atmosphere of our small dairy farm set in pleasant surroundings. Watch (or help!) the daily running of our farm. For the more energetic, walk the 1½ mile farm trail. The spacious listed farmhouse boasts many modern conveniences, including en suite, CH, all blending in nicely with the traditional flavour of the oak-beamed residence, large garden with swimming pool. Open all year (closed Christmas & New Year).

17 New House Farm, Barrell Lane, Longhope, Gloucestershire GL17 0LS

Mrs Elizabeth Beddows
☎ 01452 830484
BB From £17–£19
EM From £10.50
Sleeps 6
🐂🛉🎀🛏⚓
🏵

Clive and Betty Beddows give you a warm welcome to their Georgian farmhouse set in 80 acres of farmland with many lovely walks. All bedrooms have private bathrooms or en suite, radio/alarms, satellite TV, electric blankets and tea/coffee-making facilities. Five golf courses within ten mile radius. Open all year.

Oakwood Farm, Upper Minety, Malmesbury, Wiltshire SN16 9PY

Mrs Katie Gallop
☎ 01666 860286
ⒷⒷ From £14
EM From £8
Sleeps 6
🐾 🐓 ⚱
Listed *Commended*

A friendly farming couple welcome you to their working dairy farm close to the quiet village of Upper Minety. Situated off the B4040, overlooks Minety church on the edge of the Cotswolds. Ideal for touring the Cotswolds and surrounding National Trust properties. 2 double rooms and 1 twin. Guests' lounge/dining room with colour TV. Also tea/coffee-making facilities. Open all year.

Oldends Farm, Oldends Lane, Stonehouse, Gloustershire GL10 3RL

Mrs J A Nicholls
☎ 01453 822135
ⒷⒷ From £13.50
Sleeps 4
🐾 ✂ 🌴
Listed

Two miles from M5, junction 13 and convenient for touring the Cotswolds and the Severn Vale. Comfortable accommodation in a grade II listed farmhouse surrounded by orchards and open fields. The farm supports suckler cows and beef cattle, and Welsh pony mares and foals can be seen grazing in the fields. Family room (en suite), twin and 2 singles. Good pub food – 100 yards.

Postlip Hall Farm, Winchcombe, Cheltenham, Gloucestershire GL54 5AQ

Mrs Valerie Albutt
☎ 01242 603351
ⒷⒷ From £16–£20
Sleeps 6
🐾 🐓 👤 🐕 🌴
♛ ♛ *Highly Commended*

Come and enjoy the friendly atmosphere on this family-run stock farm, set off B4632, amongst some of the most beautiful scenery in the Cotswolds – on side of Cleeve Hill. 1½ miles from Winchcombe. Great base for visiting Cotswolds, Stratford, Bath, Warwick Castle, Malverns. Superb walking, golf course nearby. 2 en suites, 1 private bathroom, lounge, dining room, TVs, beverages. Idyllic surroundings. Open all year (closed Christmas).

Saul Farm, Saul, Gloucestershire GL2 7JB

Mrs Wendy Watts
☎ 01452 740384
ⒷⒷ From £18–£20
EM From £10
Sleeps 6
🐓 🐾 🐕 🌴
♛

Take a break and relax in the comfort and homely atmosphere of our 17th century house overlooking a lake. Guests are welcome to lend a hand around the farm, which is situated between the River Severn and the Berkeley Canal. Many interesting places to visit nearby. TV lounge with open fire, spacious bedrooms with en suite and home cooking are waiting for you and your family. 2 miles from M5 (jct. 13). Open all year.

Staverton Court Farm, Staverton, Cheltenham, Gloucestershire GL51 0TW

Mrs Sue Newton
☎ 01242 680218
ⒷⒷ From £16–£18
Sleeps 5
🐓 🐾
Applied

A warm welcome awaits at Staverton Court Farm. Relax in the comfortable oak panelled farmhouse or sit in the lovely large gardens. Ideal base for touring the Cotswolds, Forest of Dean, Gloucestershire, Cheltenham. TV and beverages in all rooms. Double with hand basin, twin/family en suite, single. Open all year.

Sudeley Hill Farm, Winchcombe, Gloucestershire GL54 5JB

Barbara Scudamore
☎ 01242 602344
ⒷⒷ From £20
Sleeps 6
🐾 🌴 ⚱
♛ ♛ *Highly Commended*

Delightfully situated above Sudeley Castle with panoramic views across the surrounding valley, this is a 15th century listed farmhouse with a large garden on a working mixed farm of 800 acres. Ideal centre for touring the Cotswolds. Family/twin, 1 double, 1 twin, all en suite. Comfortable lounge with TV and log fires. Separate dining room. Open all year except Christmas.

24 **Town Street Farm,** Tirley, Gloucestershire GL19 4HG

Sue Warner
☎ 01452 780442
BB From £15–£22
Sleeps 4
🐕 🏇 🏕 🐄 🎣
🌑🌑 *Commended*

Town Street Farm is a typical working family farm close to the River Severn, within easy reach of M5 and M50. The farmhouse offers a high standard of accommodation with en suite facilities in bedrooms and a warm and friendly welcome. Breakfast is served overlooking the lawns, flowerbeds and tennis court which is available for use by guests. Open all year except Christmas.

25 **Upper Farm,** Clapton-on-the-Hill, Bourton-on-the-Water, Gloucestershire GL54 2LG

Mrs Helen Adams
☎ 01451 820453
BB From £15–£20
Sleeps 10
🐕 (6) 🍴 ♿ 🎾
🌑🌑

A mixed family farm of 140-acres in a peaceful, undiscovered village two miles from Bourton-on-the-Water. Our centrally heated period stone farmhouse has been tastefully restored and offers a warm, friendly welcome. Quality accommodation and hearty farmhouse fayre. We are centrally located for touring or walking and our hill position offers panoramic views over the surrounding Cotswold countryside. Open Mar–Nov.

26 **Wickridge Court Farm,** Folly Lane, Stroud, Gloucestershire GL6 8JT

Gloria & Peter Watkins
☎ 01453 764357
BB From £15
EM From £12
Sleeps 5
🏇 🐕 🍴 🎾 🏕
🌑🌑 *Commended*

Wickridge Court Farm is situated 1 mile from the B4070 holiday route. A farm of 250 acres with cattle and horses. The historic farmhouse is a sympathetically converted Cotswold stone barn offering all en suite rooms. It is a peaceful suntrap set in a fold of the beautiful Slad Valley offering excellent walks through National Trust woods; Stroud Leisure Centre with its heated pool is 1 mile, many places of interest within easy reach. Open all year.

27 **Windrush Farm,** Bourton-on-the-Water, Cheltenham, Gloucestershire GL54 3BY

Mrs Jenny Burrough
☎ 01451 820419
BB From £17.50–£19
Sleeps 4
🐕 (12) 🍴 🐄 🎾
🌑🌑 *Commended*

We look forward to welcoming you to our family-run arable farm in a delightful setting. 1½ miles from Bourton-on-the-Water. The Cotswold stone house has a lovely garden and panoramic views. Enjoy the beauty of the area, with its rolling hills, picturesque villages and places of interest. Our local 17th century pub is a stroll across the fields for evening meals. Open Mar–Dec.

SELF-CATERING

28 **Bangrove Farm,** Teddington, Tewkesbury, Gloucestershire GL20 8JB

Pat Hitchman
☎ 01242 620223
SC From £230–£300
Sleeps 2/8
🐕
🍴 🍴 🍴 🍴 *Commended*

An attractive self-contained property part of 17th century oak-beamed farmhouse on arable/livestock farm in quiet rural setting near Cheltenham. Ideal for walking and touring Cotswolds. Comfortably furnished, fitted carpets throughout. 3 double bedrooms (1 with washbasin), large bathroom. Downstairs cloakroom, kitchen/diner, microwave, large lounge, TV. Linen/electricity/use of washing machine included. Children welcome. Garden, hard tennis court, barbecue. Golf/riding available. Open Apr–Oct.

Court Close Farm, Manor Road, Eckington, Pershore, Worcestershire WR10 3BH   **29**

Eileen Fincher
☎ 01386 750297
[SC] From £160–£240
Sleeps 4/6

🐎 ✂ 🐕 🐓
🐾 🐾 🐾 *Approved*

A self-contained wing of our lovely 18th century farmhouse and garden on village edge, bordering Gloucestershire. Outstanding views of Bredon Hill. Attractive set dairy farm with meadows sloping to the Avon. Fishing by arrangement. Central for Shakespeare, Malvern and Cotswold jaunts. Convenient kitchen/diner and comfortable sitting room with TV, storage heat and electric fire. 3 bedrooms, linen provided. Open Apr–Oct.

Hunting Butts Farm, Swindon Lane, Cheltenham, Gloucestershire GL50 4NZ   **30**

Jane Hanks
☎ 01242 524982
[SC] From £200–£250
Sleeps 4

🐕 ✂ 🐄 🐖 🖤 🐓
🐾 🐾 🐾– 🐾 🐾 🐾 🐾
Commended

Courtyard Cottages with superb views of surrounding countryside on 200-acre beef and arable farm. Excellent accommodation fully equipped with microwave, washing machine, dishwasher, colour TV, video, etc. All linen included. Superb location for touring Cotswolds with all leisure facilities within easy walking distance. Brochure on request. Open Mar–Oct.

The Lodge Barn, Mitton Lodge, Bredons Hardwick, Tewkesbury, Gloucestershire GL20 7EB   **31**

Judith Pearman
☎ 01684 295556
[SC] From £200–£440
Sleeps 6

🐖 🐄 🐓
🐾 🐾 🐾 🐾 🐾 *Highly Commended*

A delightfully restored 17th century brick and timber barn, situated within the peaceful grounds of a Grade II listed Georgian farmhouse. 2 miles from Bredon village. Fully equipped kitchen, double en suite, two twins (one can be zip-linked 6 ft), colour TV, fitted carpets, central heating. Tastefully furnished. Garden, coarse fishing on farm. Windsurfing ½ mile. Easy access to Cotswolds. Open all year.

Manor Farm Cottages, Greet, Winchcombe, Cheltenham, Gloucestershire GL54 5BJ   **32**

Richard & Janet Day
☎ 01242 602423
[SC] From £120–£475
Sleeps 3/7

🐖 🐎 🌄 🐓 🛁
🐾 🐾 🐾 🐾 *Highly Commended*

Beautifully restored 15th century tithe house (pictured) and newly restored 'Shuck's Cottage' and 'Boot Hole Cottage', on family farm. Central for Tewkesbury, Broadway, Evesham, Cheltenham. Sleep 3–7, cot and high-chair available. Horses accommodated. Croquet lawn. Close to Cotswold Way and Wychavon Way, in sight of steam railway. Full central heating, every modern convenience. Open all year.

New House Farm Cottages, New House Farm, Barrell Lane, Longhope, Gloucestershire GL17 0LS   **33**

Mrs Elizabeth Beddows
☎ 01452 830484
[SC] From £150–£305
Sleeps 4–5

🐖 🐓 🐎 🐄 🛁
🐾 🐾 *Commended*

Newly converted cottages in peaceful surroundings. Well equipped with dishwashers, microwaves, satellite TV, gas central heating, linen and electric all inclusive. Beautiful walking country. Evening meal available. Open all year.

Old Mill Farm, nr Cirencester, c/o Ermin House Farm, Syde, Cheltenham, Gloucestershire GL53 9PN   **34**

Mrs Catherine Hazell
☎ 01285 821 255
[SC] From £135–£450
Sleeps 16

🐖 🐓
🐾 🐾 🐾 🐾 *Commended*

Four superior barn conversions featuring Cotswold stone pillars and beams. Situated 4 miles from Cirencester on mixed farm beside River Thames and Cotswold Water park for walking, birdwatching, fishing, sailing and jet skiing. Trains to London 1¼ hrs. Prices include full central heating, electricity, bed-linen, colour TV. Separate laundry room with pay-phone. Convenient for Stratford-upon-Avon, Oxford, Stonehenge, Bath and Tetbury. Open all year.

35 **Warrens Gorse Cottages,** Home Farm, Warrens Gorse, Cirencester, Gloucestershire GL7 7JD

John & Nanette Randall
☎ 01285 831261
🆂🅲 From £110–£180
Sleeps 3/4/5
🐾 🐎 🛝
🚲 🚲 🚲 *Approved*

2½ miles from Cirencester between Daglingworth and Perrotts Brook, these attractive whitewashed cottages are ideally situated for touring the Cotswolds. The cottages are personally attended by the owners and are comfortably furnished and well equipped. 100-acre sheep, cattle and corn farm. Pottery and craft workshop with or without instruction. Golf club nearby. Water sports 5 miles. Open Mar–Oct and Christmas holidays.

36 **Westley Farm,** Chalford, Stroud, Gloucestershire GL6 8HP

Julian Usborne
☎ 01285 760262
🆂🅲 From £120–£280
Sleeps 2/5
🐾 🐕 🛝 🧍 🐎
🚲 🚲 – 🚲 🚲 🚲

Approved

Steep meadows of wild flowers and beech woods are the setting for this old fashioned 80-acre hill farm with breathtaking panoramic views over the Golden Valley. Children especially enjoy the donkey, calves, lambs and foals. Adults may prefer the complete tranquillity and abundant wildlife. Nearby horseriding, golf, gliding, watersports. Midway Cirencester – Stroud. Four cottages, two flats. Brochure available. Open Apr–Oct.

37 **Wickridge Court Farm,** Folly Lane, Stroud, Gloucestershire GL6 8JT

Gloria & Peter Watkins
☎ 01453 764357
🆂🅲 From £110–£190
Sleeps 4
🛝 🐕 🎾 🏺

Applied

A sun trap set in a fold of the beautiful Slad Valley. Excellent walks through woodlands and on the farm. 16th century stable converted 1995. Large sitting room with kitchen/diner, 1 double bedroom, hallway and shower and toilet. Tastefully furnished with colour TV, CH, electricity and bed linen included. Fitted carpets. Sorry no pets. Convertible settee in living room. Open all year.

44

England's Heartland

Lincolnshire

Group Contact: *Mrs Gill Grant* ☎ *01673 842283*

A frequent comment of first-time visitors to Lincolnshire is "I never realised there was so much to see and do". This doesn't surprise us for we know that Lincolnshire is a large unspoilt county, full of variety and contrast waiting to be discovered.

There are some attractions that you will not want to miss: for instance, Lincoln with its magnificent cathedral, castle and Museum of Lincolnshire Life; Belton House near Grantham; Stamford, a near perfect stone town or its brick-built equivalent, Louth; Elizabethan houses such as Doddington Hall and Burghley House.

The best way to enjoy the county is to get in your car and see it for yourself. Take your time though – slow down your pace of life to match that of Lincolnshire. Drive into the countryside where you will have miles of road to yourself. Try the twisting hidden lanes of Tennyson Country where villages have names such as Bag Enderby and Ashby Puerorum. Tennyson Country forms the southern part of the Lincolnshire Wolds, designated as an Area of Outstanding Natural Beauty. Visit one of the unspoilt market towns, or go for a walk along part of the Viking Way.

Then there is Boston and its Stump, the nearby Memorial marking the spot where the Pilgrim Fathers tried to leave England ... sorry no more space – you'll just have to come and see for yourself!

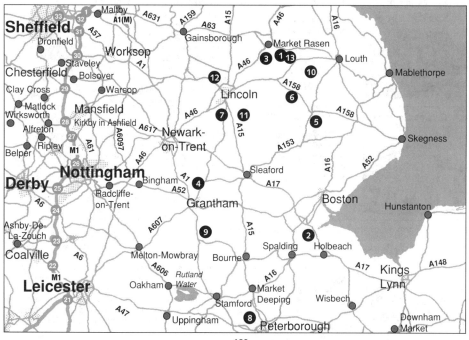

BED AND BREAKFAST

(and evening meal)

---

1 Bleasby House, Legsby, Market Rasen, Lincolnshire LN8 3QN

Janet Dring
☎ 01673 842383
BB From £17–£18
EM From £9–£12
Sleeps 5

Highly Commended

Enjoy a peaceful break in welcoming farmhouse at foot of Lincolnshire Wolds. Spacious en suite rooms with colour TV. Flower-filled sun lounge and large garden. Ideal for touring beautiful countryside, historic Lincoln, Cadwell Park. Fly fishing and hard tennis court on farm. Evening meals by arrangement. Open all year.

---

2 Cackle Hill House, Cackle Hill Lane, Holbeach, Lincolnshire PE12 8BS

Maureen Biggadike
☎ 01406 426721
BB From £16–£19
EM From £10
Sleeps 6
(10)

We welcome you to our farm situated in rural position just off the A17. Comfortable accommodation (1 twin en suite, 1 double, 1 twin with washbasins, and sharing guest bathroom) and traditional farmhouse fare. Farm walks, large patio and gardens. Close to the shores of the Wash with its marshes, trails and mature reserves, Spalding, Boston, Norfolk and Cambridgeshire. Open all year.

---

3 East Farm House, Middle Rasen Road, Buslingthorpe, Market Rasen, Lincolnshire LN3 5AQ

Mrs Gill Grant
☎ 01673 842283
BB From £18
EM From £11
Sleeps 4

Highly Commended

Peace and relaxation await you in beamed 18th century listed farmhouse on 410 acre conservation award-winning farm with farm trail and coarse fishing overlooking unspoilt countryside. Situated 4 miles SW of Market Rasen, ideal for rambling, touring beautiful Lincolnshire Wolds, coast, historic Lincoln and market towns. Wholesome farmhouse food, spacious bedrooms, TV and tea/coffee makers. 1 double en suite, 1 twin with private facilities. Guests' lounge. Business people welcome. Open all year.

---

4 Gelston Grange Farm, Nr Marston, Grantham, Lincolnshire NG32 2AQ

Janet Sharman
☎ 01400 50281
BB From £16–£19
Sleeps 6
(5)

We are known for our welcome and homely atmosphere. Comfortable beds, 1 four poster en suite room, 1 double, 1 twin, all with HC, tea/coffee trays, TV, CH and tastefully decorated. Full English breakfast. Large garden. Lots of places to visit – Belton House, Lincoln, Newark, Boston and the coast, Robin Hood country. Northward on A1 take first right turn for Marston (after Grantham roundabout). Open all year except Christmas.

---

5 Glebe Farm, Haltham, Horncastle, Lincolnshire LN9 6JE

Susan Garner
☎ 01507 522210
BB From £18
Sleeps 2

A charming 16th century farmhouse on a working farm with pedigree Suffolk flock, overlooking the Bain Valley, with fishing rights. Horncastle and Woodhall Spa provide antique shops, eating places and pleasant walks. Local historic buildings, Tennyson Country and Battle of Britain memorial flight. Public houses to be recommended. Comfortably furnished bedroom with all facilities and private bathroom. Caravan Club location. Open all year except Christmas.

Greenfield Farm, Minting, near Horncastle, Lincolnshire LN9 5RX

Judy Bankes Price
☎ 01507 578457
BB From £18
Sleeps 6
🐂 🐂 ✂ 🏛
👑

Judy and Hugh welcome you to their comfortable farmhouse set in a very quiet location yet centrally placed for all the major Lincolnshire attractions. Large garden pond, forest walks border the farm. Guests have their own sitting room with colour TV and woodburning stove, pretty en suite shower rooms, heated towel rails, radios, tea/ coffee-making facilities, central heating. Excellent pub with traditional country cooking within 1 mile. AA Selected QQQQ

The Manor House, Manor Farm, Bracebridge Heath, Lincoln, Lincolnshire LN4 2HW

Mrs Jill Scoley
☎ 01522 520825
Fax 01522 542418
BB From £17
Sleeps 6
🐂 (10) ✂
👑 *Highly Commended*

Welcome to Lincolnshire. Stay in a lovely Georgian Farmhouse situated in large walled garden. 3 miles south of Lincoln. Comfortable bedrooms with washbasins, radio, tea/coffee facilities. Large lounge with log fire for cooler evenings. Open all year (closed Christmas and New Year).

Midstone Farmhouse, Southorpe, Stamford, Lincolnshire PE9 3BX

Mr & Mrs C Harrison-Smith
☎ 01780 740136
BB From £16–£20
EM From £7
Sleeps 6
🐂 🐂 🏛
Listed

Midstone Farm is situated in the quiet village of Southorpe 4 miles south east of historic Stamford, which is a beautiful stone town and boasts the fine Elizabethan Burghley House. Peterborough lies to the west with its fine cathedral and excellent shopping facilities. There are animals and gardens to enjoy at midstone farm, and children will meet ponies, rabbits and George the friendly pot-bellied pig.

Sycamore Farm, Bassingthorpe, Grantham, Lincs NG33 4ED

Mrs Sue Robinson
☎ 01476 585274
BB From £16–£18
EM From £8
Sleeps 6
🐂 (6) ✂
👑👑 *Commended*

Relax and unwind in rural South Lincolnshire. Sycamore Farm stands amid beautiful peaceful surroundings yet perfectly situated for the A1 (4 miles), Grantham, Stamford, Lincoln, historic Belton and Burghley. 3 spacious attractively furnished bedrooms (2 en suite) all with colour TV, radio, alarms, tea trays and lovely unspoilt views. Guests' sitting room with comfy sofas and armchairs, log fires on chilly evenings, board games, local guide books and maps. Open all year.

SELF-CATERING

Mill Lodge, Donington on Bain, Louth, Lincs LN1 9RD

Mrs Pamela M. Cade
☎ 01507 343265
SC From £100–£220
Sleeps 6
🐂 ✂ 🏛 🏛
🐾 🐾 🐾 *Commended*

Ezra and Pamela Cade welcome you to a delightful cottage on a traditional farm/Nature reserve in the beautiful Bain valley. Spacious grounds with conservatory, patio lawn, flowering shrubs and lock up garage. Lovely walks with well maintained footpaths. Many species, some rare. Children welcome. Open all year.

11 **Pantiles Cottage,** c/o The Old Hall, Church Lane, Potterhanworth, Lincoln, Lincolnshire LN4 2DS

Mrs Susan Battle
☎ **01522 791338**
Fax **01522 794888**
ⓈⒸ **From £170–£240**
Sleeps 5
🐓 🐖 🐀 🐎
🐕 🐈 🐕 *Commended*

A bottle of wine welcomes you to Pantiles. It is a charming oak-beamed cottage which has been tastefully decorated and furnished to accommodate 5 people. Its quiet garden and patio overlook fields and a duckpond. Situated 7 miles from Lincoln, it is within reach of many places of interest. Linen is provided and there is central heating, a log fire and TV. Open all year.

12 **Pingles Cottage,** c/o Grange Farm, Broxholme, Nr Saxilby, Lincoln, Lincolnshire LN1 2NG

Pat Sutcliffe
☎ **01522 702441**
ⓈⒸ **From £180–£210**
Sleeps 4
🐓 🐖 🐀 💼 🛁
🐕 🐕 🐕 🐕 *Commended*

A 19th century farm cottage with its own lawn and garden, surrounded by sheep and corn fields, in the hamlet of Broxholme 6 miles from historic Lincoln. Pingles is comfortable and well-equipped for 4 people . Plenty of interesting things to do and see in the area or relax on the river bank and enjoy your own ½ mile of coarse fishing. Open all year.

13 **School Cottage,** c/o Bleasby House, Legsby, Market Rasen, Lincolnshire LN8 3QN

Janet Dring
☎ **01673 842383**
ⓈⒸ **From £160–£200**
Sleeps 6 + cot
🐓 🐖 🐀 🛁 🐀 🐎
🐕 🐕 🐕 🐕 *Commended*

This cosy, fully heated farm cottage, situated at the foot of the scenic Wolds, offers secluded garden and barbecue, tennis court and fly fishing on farm. Fully equipped with colour TV, fridge, electric cooker, microwave, washer, drier; bed linen provided. Ideal for Lincoln, Cadwell Park, golf course, one hour from coast. Open all year.

FARM HOLIDAY BUREAU

FINDING YOUR ACCOMMODATION

The Group contacts at the beginning of each section can always help you find a vacancy in your chosen area.

FARM HOLIDAY BUREAU

BUREAU ACCOMMODATION IS RELIABLE

This Guide lists **Farm Holiday Bureau** members only. They are all inspected by the National Tourist Board for standards (see introduction pages) and by fellow members to maintain a high quality.

45

England's Heartland

Northamptonshire

Group Contact: *Mrs M. Widdowson* ☎ *01604 770990/Fax 01604 770237*

Northamptonshire, the county of 'squires and spires', has houses, monuments and fine churches too numerous to mention. There's Sulgrave Manor, home of George Washington's ancestors; Rockingham Castle which was 'Arnescote Castle' in the BBC TV series 'By the Sword Divided'; Boughton House, modelled on Versailles; and Althorp, the home of the brother of the Princess of Wales.

At the castle remains, by the river in picturesque Fotheringhay, you may ponder upon the execution of Mary, Queen of Scots and the birth there of Richard III, and the Battle and Farm Museum will give you a taste of that decisive Civil War battle in 1645. A firm hold has been kept on our heritage and at Brixworth and Earls Barton you will be able to see possibly the country's finest examples of a Saxon church and tower. Many of the county's villages and towns have splendid churches dating from Norman times through to the 15th century.

Traditional methods of transport and entertainment are well preserved. The Waterways Museum at Stoke Bruerne gives you a fascinating insight into life on the canals, and there are boat trips along the Grand Union Canal. On the Nene Valley Steam Railway you can take a nostalgic trip down the line and study steam trains and rolling stock from all over the world.

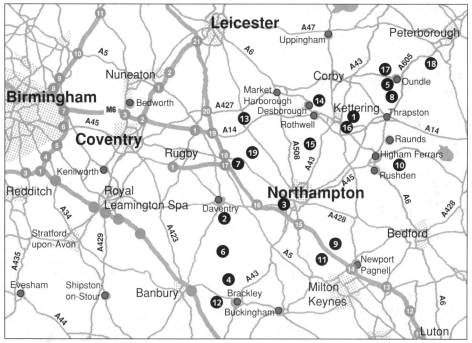

BED AND BREAKFAST

(and evening meal)

---

① **Dairy Farm,** Cranford St Andrew, Kettering, Northamptonshire NN14 4AQ

Audrey Clarke
☎ 01536 330273/78273
🅱 From £18–£22
EM From £10
Sleeps 6
🐕🐂♿🌳♨🧳▪
❀❀ *Commended*

Enjoy a holiday in a comfortable 17th century farmhouse with oak beams and inglenook fireplaces. Peaceful surroundings, large garden containing ancient circular dovecote. Dairy Farm is a working farm situated in abeautiful Northamptonshire village just off the A14 within easy reach of many places of interest or ideal for a restful holiday. Good farmhouse food and friendly atmosphere. Open all year.

---

② **Drayton Lodge,** Daventry, Northamptonshire NN11 4NL

Ann Spicer
☎ 01327 702449
Fax 01327 72110
🅱 From £20–£25
EM From £12
Sleeps 8
🐕🐂🌳♨
❀❀

Drayton Lodge is a secluded 18th century farmhouse set on the edge of Daventry to one side and rolling Northamptonshire countryside to the other. A warm, friendly welcome awaits you. Beautiful centrally heated bedrooms with en suite bathrooms and TVs. Championship golf course within ½ mile. Historical places of interest to visit. Full traditional English breakfast served. Open all year.

---

③ **The Elms,** Kislingbury, Northampton NN7 4AH

Mrs Sanders
☎ 01604 830326
🅱 From £17.50
Sleeps 5
🐂♨🧳▪
Listed

A warm welcome awaits you in our Victorian farmhouse with views over the farm. Situated 2 miles from M1 Junction 16 and 4 miles from Northampton. Convenient for business stopovers and touring Cotswolds, Stratford, Oxford and Cambridge. Nene Way Walk passes through the farm. Open all year.

---

④ **Green Farm,** Weedon Lois, Towcester, Northamptonshire NN12 8PL

Mrs Paddy Elkington
☎ 01327 860249
🅱 From £17
EM From £10
Sleeps 6
🐂🐾
Listed *Commended*

Green Farm is a comfortable 18th century farmhouse set in rolling countryside on a 550-acre mixed farm. You can enjoy private coarse fishing or visit the many local attractions, including Sulgrave Manor, Canons Ashby, and Silverstone Grand Prix circuit to name but a few! The M1 and M40 are both within 10 miles. Open all year.

---

⑤ **Lilford Lodge Farm,** Barnwell, Oundle, Peterborough, Northamptonshire PE8 5SA

Trudy Dijksterhuis
☎ 01832 272230
🅱 From £18–£21
Sleeps 5
🐂🐎👤🐕🐾♨🐾
❀❀ *Commended*

Mixed farm set in the attractive Nene Valley situated on the A605, 3 miles south of Oundle and 5 miles north of the A14. Peterborough and Stamford are within easy reach Guests stay in the recently converted original 19th century farmhouse. All bedrooms have en suite bathrooms, CH, radio and tea/coffee-making facilities. Comfortable lounge with satellite TV and separate dining room. Coarse fishing available.

Manor Farm, Adstone, Towcester, Northamptonshire NN12 8DT   **6**

Elisabeth Paton
☎ 01327 860284
BB From £15
EM From £8 (by arrangement)
Sleeps 6
♁ ♞ Å ⚄ 🛢 ✂
♨ ♨ *Commended*

Peace and quiet but plenty to see and do at this 430-acre farm. The farmhouse, built by an ancestor of George Washington in 1656, stands on the edge of a tiny village. Enjoy woodland walks, ponds, wildlife and flowers or explore nearby historic houses, the Cotswolds, Stratford-upon-Avon, Silverstone. Try our clay pigeon shooting instruction, fun for all the family. Open all year.

Murcott Mill, Long Buckby, Northamptonshire NN6 7QR   **7**

Carrie & Brian Hart
☎ 01327 842236
BB From £17–£18
EM From £7.50
Sleeps 6
♞ ♁ ♨ 🛢
♨ ♨ *Commended*

Murcott Mill is an imposing Georgian mill house set within a working farm. It has a large garden and lovely outlook over open countryside. All rooms are en suite with colour TV. Central heating throughout and visitors have their own lounge and dining room with open log fires. An ideal stopover, close to M1 and good location for touring the area. Open all year.

Pear Tree Farm, Main Street, Aldwincle, Nr Kettering, Northamptonshire NN14 3EL   **8**

Mavis Hankins
☎ 01832 720614
BB From £16–£18
EM From £10
Sleeps 4
✂ ⚄ Å ♨
♨ ♨ ♨ *Commended*

Pear Tree Farm is a mixed 400-acre farm consisting of cattle, sheep, poultry and arable. Comfortably furnished with relaxed family atmosphere and good home cooking. Four bedrooms. Excellent for walking, birdwatching, fishing. Large garden for relaxing. Open all year except Christmas (camping Feb–Sept).

Quinton Green Farm, Quinton, Northamptonshire NN7 2EG   **9**

Mrs Margaret Turney
☎ 01604 863685
Fax 01604 862230
BB From £18–£20
Sleeps 6
♞ ♁ ♨
♨ ♨

The Turney family look forward to welcoming you to their comfortable, rambling 17th century farmhouse, only 10 mins from Northampton, yet overlooking lovely rolling countryside. We are close to Salcey Forest, with its wonderful facilities for walking. M1 (Jct. 15) is just 5 mins away; central Milton Keynes 20 mins. Open all year.

Rifle Range Farm, Yielden, Bedford, Bedfordshire MK44 1AW   **10**

Ann Paynter
☎ 01933 53151
BB From £12.50–£15
EM From £9
Sleeps 3
♞ ♁ ♨
Listed *Commended*

A quiet, comfortable, modern farmhouse on the edge of a small village in open countryside, 4 miles from A45 between Kimbolton and Rushden. Centrally placed for a stopover north and south. Evening meal by prior arrangement. Open all year.

Spinney Lodge Farm, Hanslope, Milton Keynes, Buckinghamshire MK19 7DE   **11**

Mrs Christine Payne
☎ 01908 510267
BB From £15–£20
Sleeps 4
♁ (12) ✂ ♨ 🛢
♨

Spinney Lodge is a arable, beef and sheep farm. The lovely Victorian farmhouse with its large garden and rose pergola has en suite bedrooms with colour TV and tea–making facilities. M1 Junc 15, 8 minutes, 12 minutes Northampton, 15 minutes Milton Keynes. Many historical houses and gardens to visit in the area. Open all year.

---

12 Walltree House Farm, Steane, Brackley, Northamptonshire NN13 5NS

Richard & Pauline Harrison
☎ 01295 811235
Fax 01295 811147
BB From £20–£26
EM From £10
Sleeps 16

Our home is in the middle of nowhere but at the centre of everything. Badger wood to explore, lovely walks, historic places to visit. Nearby shopping, fishing, golf, gliding, Silverstone circuit and leisure centres. Some individual ground floor rooms in the courtyard, other in the adjacent Victorian farmhouse. Most rooms en suite. Open all year except Christmas & New Year.

---

13 West End Farm, 5 West End, Welford, Northamptonshire NN6 6HJ

Mrs Susie Bevin
☎ 01858 575226
BB From £16–£20
Sleeps 4

This comfortable 1848 farmhouse is set in beautiful countryside. Twin and double rooms both have washbasins and tea–making facilities, double with en suite WC. Guests' sitting room with woodburner and TV. In a quiet village street with 4 local pubs. Near A50/A14 access, M1/J20. Convenient for Stanford, Lamport, Althorp and Cottesbrook, Naseby Battlefield, Cold Ashby and S. Kilworth Golf. On the Jurassic Way. Good holiday or business base. Open all year.

---

14 West Lodge Farm, Pipewell Road, Desborough, Northamptonshire NN14 2SH

Margaret Dee
☎ 01536 760552
BB From £20–£24
Sleeps 4

Highly Commended

A friendly welcome to a spacious William IV farmhouse set in Rockingham Forest. The arable farm of 600 acres has been a conservation prize winner and offers long farm walks through ancient woodlands with abundant wildlife. Peace and quiet assured though close to major Midlands towns and M1/A1 link.

---

15 Wold Farm, Old, Northampton, Northamptonshire NN6 9RJ

Anne Engler
☎ 01604 781258
BB From £20–£22
EM From £12
Sleeps 10

A friendly, informal atmosphere is offered at this 18th century farmhouse on 250-acre beef/arable farm. Main farmhouse offers attractive bedrooms. Hearty breakfast is served in oak-beamed dining room with inglenook fireplace. Relax by log fire or at snooker table. Recently converted barn provides en suite rooms overlooking pretty garden with colourful Pergola. Snacks or four course evening meals on request. Open all year.

SELF-CATERING

16 Cranford Farm, Cranford Hall, Cranford, Kettering, Northamptonshire NN14 4AL

Gayle Robinson
☎ 01536 330248
SC From £200–£225
Sleeps 5

Commended

Lovely Georgian mansion in the heart of a traditional estate village which is set in parkland amidst fine gardens. Many attractive walks and drives to be taken, together with historic spots to visit and a great range of cultural activities. The Villiers Suite is a stylish, self–contained apartment within the Hall. Open all year.

Granary Cottage, Brook Farm, Lower Benefield, Peterborough PE8 5AE

Mrs J Singlehurst
☎ 018325 215
⑤ From £125–£250
Sleeps 4
🛏 (4)
🔑 🔑 🔑 *Commended*

At the beginning of a gated road we offer peace and tranquillity with picturesque walks. Granary Cottage is warm, cosy and well equipped with linen provided. Close by are the historic market towns of Oundle and Stamford and the pretty village of Rockingham. Sorry no pets. Open all year.

Papley Farm Cottages, Papley Farm, Warmington, Peterborough PE8 6UU

Joyce Lane
☎ 01832 272583
⑤ From £100–£340
Sleeps 2/5
🛏 🎋 🗻
🔑 🔑 🔑 🔑 *Highly Commended*

On our large mixed farm, peace and comfort are to be found in The Chestnut Tree, Slade House or The Bungalow, all sleeping 5, Tudor Cottage or Brook End sleeping 2. Luxuriously equipped, all are warm, spacious and prepared especially for you – including linen. Farm and nature walks. Near Oundle, Stamford and Peterborough. 5 miles from A1. Open all year.

Rye Hill Farm, Holdenby Road, East Haddon, Northamptonshire NN6 8DH   (19)

Michael & Margaret Widdowson
☎ 01604 770990
Fax 01604 770237
⑤ From £125–£340
Sleeps 2/6
🛏 🐎 ♿ 🎋 🗻 ▮ 🎾
🔑 🔑 🔑 🔑 *Highly Commended*

Children are most welcome on our delightful, peaceful smallholding. They may search for eggs, milk the goat, feed the lambs, pigs, chickens, ducks and geese or play in our games room. Our 5 cottages are maintained to a very high standard. They have every modern convenience combined with beams, open fires or log burning stoves. Many places of interest for the family. Open all year.

BUREAU ACCOMMODATION IS RELIABLE

This Guide lists **Farm Holiday Bureau** members only. They are all inspected by the National Tourist Board for standards (see introduction pages) and by fellow members to maintain a high quality.

FOLLOW THE COUNTRY CODE

Leave nothing but footprints,
Take nothing but photographs,
Kill nothing but time!

46

England's Heartland

Leicestershire

Group Contact: *Ruth Lovett* ☎ *01530 270465*

Leicestershire is a land of tranquil beauty spread with reminders of a turbulent history ... and it begins at every turn-off from any main road.

To find the true Leicestershire just travel over high horizons and narrow farm tracks, explore vast Rutland Water and the lazy green banks of the Grand Union Canal, take a nostalgic trip on our wealth of steam railways, walks in historic Bradgate Park or 'do battle' in Bosworth Field. Explore the counties curious customs which take place annually, such as Bottle Kicking and the Hare Pie Scramble between Hallaton and Medbourne, or visit our castles and museums, timber framed cottages and grand mansions, theatres and theme parks.

Fun for the youngsters down on the farm – lambing Sundays and rare breeds; always wanted to touch the animals? – here you can. Spoil yourselves in our tea rooms, browse in the specialist shops and museums – all this and more in this green and undulating county.

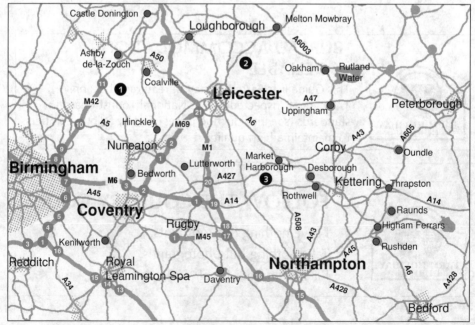

BED AND BREAKFAST

(and evening meal)

Measham House Farm, Gallows Lane, Measham, Nr Swadlincote, Leicestershire DE12 7HD

Ruth Lovett
☎ 01530 270465
BB From £17.50–£19
Sleeps 6

A warm welcome awaits you from John and Ruth Lovett and family, at their Georgian farmhouse, a Grade II listed building, on a 500-acre working farm. Situated on the Derbys/Leics/Staffs/Warks borders. Ideal for visiting a wealth of fascinating places. Within easy reach of Birmingham, Nottingham and Leicester and the NEC, Birmingham International Airport and East Midlands Airport.

Three Ways Farm, Melton Road, Queniborough, Leicester LE7 3FN

Mrs Janet S. Clarke
☎ 0116 2600472
BB From £15–£20
Sleeps 6

Listed

It's hard to believe you're only 6 miles north of Leicester in lovely Queniborough with its ancient church, thatched cottages and two good pubs. You'll be welcomed at the Clarke's modern bungalow in peaceful fields. All bedrooms have colour TV, tea/coffee facilities. Separate dining room and lounge. West side of Melton Road. Open all year except Christmas.

SELF-CATERING

Brook Meadow Holiday Chalets, Welford Road, Sibbertoft, Market Harborough, Leicestershire LE16 9UJ

Mary and Jasper Hart
☎ 01858 880886
SC From £100–£220
Sleeps 8

Approved

We are centrally placed being near to the borders of Northamptonshire, Leicestershire and Warwickshire. Two Norwegian spruce chalets beside a peaceful 5 acre carp fishing lake in the middle of our 600 acre farm. Both chalets are furnished to a high standard, equipped with shower, microwave, colour TV and all linen. Brochure available. Open all year.

47

England's Heartland

Bedfordshire

Group Contacts: [BB] *Mrs Janet Must* ☎ *01234 870234*
[SC] *Mrs Angela Little* ☎ *01525 712978*

We invite you to spend some time in the County of Bedfordshire in the rural heartland of England, ideally situated between Oxford and Cambridge. The Great Ouse, with its quiet backwaters together with the Lakes at Stewartby, Wyboston and Grafham make ideal venues for the fisherman and the watersports enthusiast. Cyclists will appreciate the ease with which they can travel throughout the area, while walkers will find the Greensand Ridge Walk provides many routes. Golfers also have a wide choice of courses.

Stately homes include Woburn Abbey and Luton Hoo, plus pretty villages with thatched cottages and beamed Tudor buildings. The National Trust owns the extraordinary 16th-century stone dovecote and stables at Willington, plus 422 acres of hill country at Dunstable Downs.

Bedford Museum and John Bunyan Museum are well worth a visit. The Cecil Higgins Art Gallery enjoys an international reputation for the quality of its collections. Luton Museum and Art Gallery exhibit local and natural history, archaeology and lace, while Stockwood Park Craft Museum has exhibits relating to rural life and crafts.

Visit the Shuttleworth Collection of historic aeroplanes and road vehicles, or for garden enthusiasts there is the Swiss Garden and Wrest Park Gardens.

For the naturalist there is the RSPB nature reserve and headquarters, or Stagsden Bird Gardens. For something more exotic, visit Whipsnade Zoo or the Wild Animal Kingdom at Woburn. Whatever your interests you'll enjoy your stay in Bedfordshire.

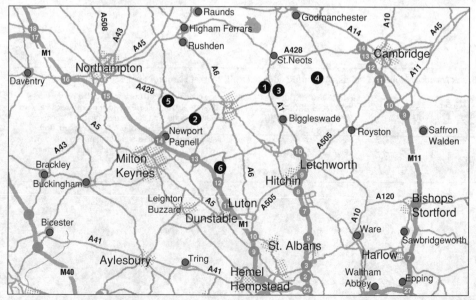

BED AND BREAKFAST
(and evening meal)

Church Farm, Roxton, Bedford, Bedfordshire MK44 3EB

Janet Must
☎ 01234 870234
Fax 01234 871576
🅱 From £15
Sleeps 6
🐕 🐎 ⊁ ⚥ ▪
❧

An attractive old farmhouse with a comfortable self-contained guest wing overlooking the garden and small orchard. Situated in a quiet village ½ mile from A1. Large bedrooms with tea and coffee-making facilities. Guests' lounge. Full English breakfast served in 16th century dining room. We offer double, single and family accommodation. Open all year.

Firs Farm, Stagsden, Bedfordshire MK43 8TB

Mrs Pam Hutcheon
☎ 01234 822344
🅱 From £15–£20
Sleeps 6
🐎 (3) 🐕 ⚥ ▪
❧❧ *Commended*

Firs Farm is a family run arable farm, set in quiet surroundings ¼ mile south of A422. The farmhouse is timber framed and set in a large garden with swimming pool. Accommodation consists of double rooms with tea/coffee making facilities and guests' lounge with colour TV. Many local tourist attractions. Open all year.

Highfield Farm, Great North Road, Sandy, Bedfordshire SG19 2AQ

Margaret Codd
☎ 01767 682332
🅱 From £15–£25
Sleeps 10
🐎 🐕 ⊁
❧❧ *Highly Commended*

Tom and Margaret Codd welcome guests to their comfortable farmhouse. Just 1 mile north of Sandy on the A1, Highfield Farm is excellently situated for visiting Cambridge, Shuttleworth, the RSPB, Grafham Water and for taking the Greensand Ridge Walk. Family, double and single bedrooms, some with en suite bathroom. Guests' sitting room with log fire and colour TV. Open all year.

Model Farm, Little Gransden, Sandy, Bedfordshire SG19 3EA

Mrs S Barlow
☎ 01767 677361
🅱 From £14–£17
Sleeps 4
🐎 🐕 ⊁ 🐈 ▪
Listed

A warm welcome awaits visitors to this traditional farmhouse set in open countryside between the villages of Lt. Gransden and Longstowe. Ideally situated for visiting or working in the Cambridge or Bedford area. The National Trust property Wimpole Hall is 10 minutes' drive away. Duxford, the Shuttleworth Collection and the RSPB are within easy reach.

SELF-CATERING

---

5 **'The Old Stone Barn',** c/o Home Farm, Warrington, Olney, Buckinghamshire MK46 4HN

Mr & Mrs G. Pibworth
☎ 01234 711655
Fax 01234 711855
SC From £140–£300
Sleep 1/6
🛏 🐕 🎣 ⚕ 🏕 💼 🎿
⚓ ⚓ ⚓ ⚓ Commended

A charming combination of old character and modern facilities, the Old Stone Barn is 3 ground floor and 3 first floor spacious self-contained apartments peacefully positioned on an arable farm 1½ miles north of Olney. Relax in the gardens, make use of the outdoor heated swimming pool or take day trips to Oxford, Cambridge, London or the Cotswolds. Open all year.

---

6 **Priestley Farm,** Church Road, off Temple Way, Flitwick, Bedfordshire MK45 5AN

Mrs Angela Little
☎ 01525 712978
SC From £130–£150
Sleeps 6
🛏 🐕 🏕 💼
⚓ ⚓ ⚓ Approved

The Georgian farmhouse set in open countryside offers 3 double bedrooms (one twin bedded), bathroom, lounge, kitchen/diner. Central heating. Linen provided. A working family dairy farm with 90 Jersey cows and young stock. Visitors are welcome to watch the milking and other seasonal activities. Shopping facilities and main railway station etc 2 miles, M1, 4 miles. Plenty of footpaths to enjoy the Bedfordshire countryside. Open all year.

BUREAU ACCOMMODATION IS RELIABLE

This Guide lists **Farm Holiday Bureau** members only. They are all inspected by the National Tourist Board for standards (see introduction pages) and by fellow members to maintain a high quality.

NO ANSWER?

Farmers are mostly out and about during the day.
Try to telephone before 9.30am or after 4pm.

England's Heartland

Hertfordshire & East Buckinghamshire

Group Contacts: BB *Mrs A Knowles* ☎ *01442 866541*
SC *Mr M Buisman* ☎ *01438 718641*

Hertfordshire, a county of contrasts, is in the unique situation of being at the hub of the country's transport network whilst offering some truly unspoilt and varied rural landscapes. It well deserves the title it is often given:
'England's Best Kept Secret'.

Our area is rich in historical heritage with some important Roman sites: St Albans was the Roman town Verulamium, first recorded in 54BC. Those interested in history will enjoy many other sites including the Old Palace and House in Hatfield Park and Knebworth House.

Come and enjoy the Chiltern landscape including many picturesque villages such as Aldbury, Frithesden and The Lee. The 4,000 acres of ancient woodland of the National Trust's Ashridge Estate offer a wealth of wildlife including herds of wild deer.

Our farms can also offer the businessman or woman the chance to unwind in a homely atmosphere as little as half an hour by train from central London and close to the M1, M25 and four southern airports. A welcome change from the less individual hospitality of large hotels.

BED AND BREAKFAST
(and evening meal)

---

① Broadway Farm, Berkhamsted, Hertfordshire HP4 2RR

Mrs Alison Knowles
☎/Fax 01442 866541
🅱🅱 From £18–£25
Sleeps 6

A warm welcome is guaranteed at Broadway, a working arable farm with own fishing lake. 3 comfortable en suite rooms in recently converted buildings adjacent to farmhouse. Tea/coffee-making facilities, colour TV, CH. Everything for the leisure or business guest – the relaxation of farm life in an attractive rural setting, yet easy access to London, airports, motorways and mainline rail services. Open all year (closed Christmas).

---

② Church Farm, Ardeley, Stevenage, Hertfordshire SG2 7AH

Wendy or Roger Waygood
☎ 01438 861260
🅱🅱 From £19.50
EM From £7.50
Sleeps 4

Relax and enjoy the peace of our quiet rural village in NE Herts midway between A1 (M) Stevenage and A10 Buntingford. The newly converted luxury en suite bedrooms with TV and tea/coffee facilities overlook our tranquil water garden. Convenient for Luton and Stansted Airports. No smoking. Regret no children or pets. Open all year.

SELF-CATERING

---

③ Gamekeeper's Lodge, Lockley Farm, Welwyn, Hertfordshire AL6 0BL

Marinus G T Buisman
☎ 01438 718641
Fax 01438 714238
🆂🅲 From £200–£400
Sleeps 6 + cot
Commended

Situated in fenced garden against woodland with superb view from furnished terrace facing south. Twin bedroom, bedroom with two bunkbeds, bathroom, shower, lounge, kitchen/dining room, utility, WC/shower. Storage heating, open fire, CTV, wash/tumble dryer, fridge/freezer, microwave/oven dishwasher, payphone, electricity and linen included. Golf, riding, swimming nearby. Sorry no pets. London 25 miles. Open all year.

England's Heartland

Cambridgeshire

Group Contact: *Mrs Hilary Nix* ☎ *01353 778369*

Cambridgeshire is a county of contrasts, a county of quiet waterways, gentle hills, lanes, busy towns, attractions great and small, all presented with a friendly welcome for the visitor.

Best known is Cambridge itself, one of Britain's oldest university cities where the colleges in their architectural splendour rest near tranquil rivers overhung with willows, the city that inspired Brooke and Byron.

As well as Cambridge the county has many other attractions. North of Cambridge lies the strikingly flat landscape of the Fens. This once barren marshland was home to the 'Fen Tigers' who lived by cutting reeds and catching eels. Today, the landscape is crisscrossed with dykes which have vastly improved the drainage of this peaty area and made the land a valuable asset for farming.

For contrast there is the hustle and bustle of the modern city of Peterborough with its excellent shopping or the stately grandeur of Ely Cathedral, so called 'Ship of the Fens'.

Wherever you go in Cambridgeshire it is a beautiful county to explore with large towns and small villages, cathedrals and tiny churches and cricket on the village green.

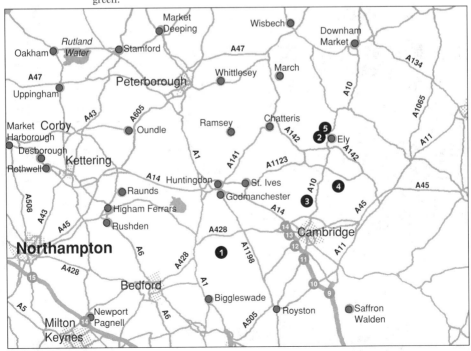

BED AND BREAKFAST

(and evening meal)

---

① Gransden Lodge Farm, Little Gransden, Sandy, Bedfordshire SG19 3EB

Mrs Mary Cox
☎ **01767 677365**
Fax **01767 677647**
ⒷⒷ From £13–£16
Sleeps 6
🐕🐎🗡🌳💼 🍷🍷

A warm and friendly atmosphere awaits you at Gransden Lodge, where we have double, twin and single rooms with TV, clock-radio and tea/coffee-making facilities. Ample bathrooms and WCs. Dining room, also large lounge with TV. A.A. QQQ. Many local pubs and restaurants for evening meals. Situated on the B1046, west of Cambridge. London 50 miles. Also convenient for Stansted Airport (M11, jct. 12). Open all year.

---

② Hill House Farm, 9 Main Street, Coveney, Ely, Cambridgeshire CB6 2DJ

Hilary Nix
☎ **01353 778369**
ⒷⒷ From £18
Sleeps 6
🗡🐎 (4)
🍷🍷 *Commended*

A warm and friendly welcome awaits you on this arable farm in unspoilt Fenland village, 3 miles west of historic Cathedral city of Ely. Victorian farmhouse has full central heating, comfortable, tastefully furnished, en suite bedrooms with colour TV. Open views of surrounding countryside. Cambridge, Newmarket, Peterborough, Welney Wildfowl Refuge, Wicken Fen nearby. Ideal for touring Cambridgeshire, Norfolk, Suffolk. No smoking. Regret no pets. Open all year.

---

③ Manor Farm, Landbeach, Cambridgeshire CB4 4ED

Vicki Hatley
☎ **01223 860165**
ⒷⒷ From £16–£20
Sleeps 6
🐎 (3) 🐈
🍷🍷 *Commended*

5 miles from Cambridge and 10 miles from Ely. Vicky welcomes you to her carefully modernised Grade II listed farmhouse, which is located next to the church in this attractive village. All rooms are either en suite or have private bathroom and are individually decorated. TV, clock radios and tea/coffee-making facilities in double, twin or family rooms. Ample parking, guests are welcome to enjoy the secluded walled gardens. Open all year except Christmas.

---

④ Spinney Abbey, Wicken, Ely, Cambridgeshire CB7 5XQ

Mrs Valerie Fuller
☎ **01353 720971**
ⒷⒷ From £18
Sleeps 6
🐎 (5)
🍷🍷

Spacious Georgian farmhouse, standing in a large garden with tennis court on our dairy farm which borders the National Trust nature reserve Wicken Fen. Two en suite double rooms and twin with private bathroom. Central heating and electric blankets for colder months. All with TV and tea/coffee tray. Guests' sitting room. Open all year.

SELF-CATERING

Hill House Farm Cottage, 9 Main Street, Coveney, Ely, Cambs CB6 2DJ

Hilary Nix
☎ **01353 778369**
▧ **From £180–£300**
Sleeps 6
♿ **(8)** ✂
♪♪♪♪ *Highly Commended*

A tasteful barn conversion on our farm is now a comfortable cottage. Furnished and decorated to a high standard. Set in a quiet village location 3 miles west of Ely with open views of Ely Cathedral and the surrounding countryside. Ideally situated for touring Norfolk, Suffolk and Cambridgeshire. Easy access to Cambridge, Newmarket and Huntingdon. Access form A142 or A10. Regret no smoking, no pets. Open all year.

50

England's Heartland
Norfolk and Suffolk

Group Contacts: 🅱🅱 *Mrs Rosemary Bryce* ☎/Fax 01473 652253
🆂🅲 *Mrs Margaret Langton* ☎/Fax 01473 652210

For the visitor in search of something a little different, this part of East Anglia has many delights to offer. One of the driest and sunniest parts of England, it is quiet and peaceful with traffic-free roads which enables one really to appreciate the beauty of this truly rural area. The small towns and villages with their medieval churches (and pubs!) are full of interest, the obvious example, Lavenham, being unrivalled anywhere in the country.

The Broads offer a haven for wildlife with many opportunities for birdwatching, notably at Minsmere and Titchwell bird sanctuaries (RSPB).

In the west, the Fens have their own special character and are famed for their dramatic skies and spectacular sunsets; and although very different, the gentler countryside of South Suffolk is as much a part of the East Anglian scene, and is much loved by painters today as it was by Gainsborough and Constable.

No visitor to East Anglia should miss Norwich with its beautiful cathedral, many other fine buildings and its large and colourful market.

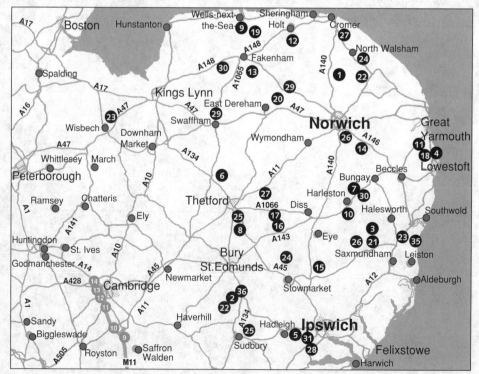

BED AND BREAKFAST

(and evening meal)

Birds Place Farm, Back Lane, Buxton, Norwich NR10 5HD

Bill and Jenny
Catchpole
☎ 01603 279585
[BB] From £17.50–£21
EM From £10.50
Sleeps 6
🐎 (5) 🍴 🎠 ■
🌺🌺 *Commended*

Small family farm in the Bure Valley in beautiful Norfolk Broadland countryside. Our 17th century farmhouse has oak beams and inglenook fireplace. We are licensed and offer excellent cuisine. The two en suite rooms have TV and tea/coffee making facilities. We have riding stables at the farm. Public footpaths and fishing nearby. Open all year.

Brighthouse Farm, Melford Road, Lawshall, near Bury St Edmunds, Suffolk IP29 4PX

Mr & Mrs Truin
☎ 01284 830385
[BB] From £16–£25
Sleeps 6
🐎 🐓 🍴 🏕 🎠 🐕 🐎
🌺🌺 *Commended*

Timbered Georgian farmhouse, set in beautiful surroundings of the Suffolk countryside, 3 acres of picturesque gardens. We offer homely accommodation. Centrally heated throughout, log fires in TV room in winter. Two double rooms, one twin, all with en suite facilities. Historic Bury St. Edmunds/Lavenham close by. Good restaurants locally. Open all year.

Broad Oak Farm, Bramfield, Halesworth, Suffolk IP19 9AB

Mrs Patricia Kemsley
☎ 01986 784232
[BB] From £13–£16
EM From £8
Sleeps 6
🐎 🐓 🐎
🌺🌺 *Commended*

A dairy farm with a spacious 16th century farmhouse, carefully modernised. Surrounded by meadowland and attractive gardens with tennis court. 3 double bedrooms with H&C, (two en suite). Separate guest bathroom. Sitting room with colour TV, dining room where good home cooking is served (evening meal by arrangement). A warm welcome is always given. Bramfield is 2 miles north west of the A12 on the A144. Southwold 7 miles. Open all year.

Church Farm, Corton, Nr Lowestoft, Suffolk NR32 5HX

Elisabeth Edwards
☎/Fax 01502 730359
[BB] From £17–£18
Sleeps 6
🍴 🏕 🐕 🎠 🐎
Listed *Highly Commended*

250 acre arable farm near rural beach in quiet part of the Suffolk coastline between Lowestoft and Gt Yarmouth. Beautiful Broadland area and Norwich within easy reach. Three double rooms all with their own WC and shower, colour TV, tea making facilities. Generous English breakfast, special diets gladly catered for. Ample parking, quiet garden.

College Farm, Hintlesham, Ipswich, Suffolk IP8 3NT

Mrs Rosemary Bryce
☎/Fax 01473 652253
[BB] From £16–£20
Sleeps 6
🐎 (5) 🎠 ■
🌺🌺 *Highly Commended*

A 15th century beamed farmhouse in rural setting on 600 acre arable/beef farm. Constable Country and historic wool towns close by. Double room with en suite, double/family and single room sharing guests' bathroom. Tea/coffee tray and central heating in all rooms. Guests' lounge with colour TV and log fire. Good food available locally. Sorry, no pets. Open all year except Christmas & New Year.

6 **Colveston Manor,** Mundford, near Thetford, Norfolk IP26 5HU

Wendy Allingham
☎ **01842 878218**
🏠 **From £20–£25**
EM From £10
Sleeps 6
🐕 (12) 🛏 ⚙
👑👑 *Highly Commended*

Peaceful 18th century farmhouse in delightful setting in heart of Breckland. Attractive bedrooms, some en suite. We specialise in delicious cooking from the Aga, using home–grown vegetables. NT properties, cathedrals, gardens and coast within easy reach. Brochure showing location available on request. Open all year.

7 **Earsham Park Farm,** Harleston Road, Earsham, Bungay, Suffolk NR35 2AQ

Mrs Bobbie Watchorn
☎/Fax **01986 892180**
🏠 **From £17.50–£24**
EM £12
Sleeps 6
✂ 🐎 🌲 ⚙ 🐾
👑👑 *Highly Commended*

Stay with every comfort in our outstanding Victorian farmhouse with beautiful views over our 600-acre farm. Elegantly furnished bedrooms (1 with four poster) have all facilities including en suites, CH. Large gardens and a collection of unusual farm animals. Easy access coast/Norwich, many local attractions. Sorry no dogs or smoking. Open all year.

8 **East Farm,** Euston Road, Barnham, Thetford, Norfolk IP24 2PB

Margaret Heading
☎ **01842 890231**
🏠 **From £19–£22**
Sleeps 6
👑 🐕

Relax and enjoy the comfort and warm welcome at East Farm in the village of Barnham. We're a 1,000-acre arable farm with beef and sheep on the edge of Breckland on Norfolk/Suffolk border between Thetford and Bury St Edmunds. A grey flint-faced house in peaceful surroundings with superb views. Spacious heated rooms with en suite bathrooms. Full English breakfast from local produce. Open all year.

9 **Eastgate Farm,** Great Walsingham, Norfolk NR22 6AB

Mary John
☎ **01328 820251**
Fax **01328 821100**
🏠 **From £19–£25**
EM From £15
Sleeps 6
🐕 (12) 🛏 🖾 ⚙ 🐾
Listed

The beautiful Georgian farmhouse 4 miles from the sea is spacious and centrally heated. The 700 acre farm is just ½ mile away from Walsingham, famous for its shrine and pilgrimages. 2 doubles and 1 twin, all with private bathrooms. Traditional farmhouse breakfast with home produced eggs, marmalade and locally smoked kippers. Open all year rexcept Christmas.

10 **Elm Lodge Farm,** Chippenhall Green, Fressingfield, Eye, Suffolk IP21 5SL

Sheila Webster
☎ **01379 586249**
🏠 **From £15–£19**
EM From £10
Sleeps 6
✂ 🛏 🐕 (10)
👑👑 *Commended*

This 112-acre working farm with early Victorian farmhouse overlooks a large common (SSSI) where animals graze in summer – the perfect spot for an after-dinner stroll. Spacious bedrooms (one en suite), separate dining and sitting rooms, log fires and excellent food ensure that a comfortable, relaxing holiday is enjoyed by all those we warmly welcome to this attractive and peaceful corner of Suffolk. Open Mar–Nov.

11 **Hall Farm,** Jay Lane, Church Lane, Lound, Lowestoft, Suffolk NR32 5LJ

Judith Ashley
☎ **01502 730415**
🏠 **From £14–£16**
Sleeps 6
👑 🛏 ✂
Listed *Commended*

Share our peaceful, traditional Suffolk farmhouse 1½ miles from sea on 101-acre arable farm. Very clean, comfortable accommodation in two double rooms with en suite facilities and one pretty twin, tea/coffee. Excellent breakfast with our own farm eggs. Beamed lounge, colour TV and log fire. Convenient for Broads. Open Mar–Oct.

Hempstead Hall, Hempstead Hall, Holt, Norfolk NR25 6TN

Lynda-Lee Mack
☎ **01263 712224**
[BB] **From £16–£22**
Sleeps 6
🐴 (3) 🕍 ⅄ ⊕ 🛠
👄 👄

We warmly invite you to our 19th century flint farmhouse attractively set on a 300 acre arable farm with ducks, donkeys and large gardens, close to the picturesque North Norfolk coast and its many attractions. We are ideally situated for walking and bird watching. En suite family room, double with private bathroom. Colour TV. Tea/coffee-making facilities in rooms.

Highfield Farm, Great Ryburgh, Fakenham, Norfolk NR21 7AL

Mrs E Savory
☎ **01328 829249**
[BB] **From £15–£19.50**
EM from £9.50
Sleeps 6
🐴 (12) ⅍
Listed *Commended*

Spacious and comfortable farmhouse on working farm 10 miles from the coast. Ideal for birdwatchers and country lovers, set well away from the road in 500 acres of rolling farmland. Twin with en suite, double with hand basin sharing bathroom with second twin. Guests' sitting room and dining room. Evening meals by arrangement. Clay pigeon shooting, farm walks, horse riding locally, grass tennis court. Open all year except Christmas & New Year.

Hillside Farm, Welbeck Road, Brooke, near Norwich, Norfolk NR15 1AU

Mrs Carolyn Holl
☎ **01508 550260**
[BB] **From £16–£18**
EM From £9
Sleeps 4 + bunks
🐴 🕍 🐕 🛠 ▪ ⅍
Listed

This is a 350-acre arable and stock farm. A beautiful 16th century thatched and timber-framed house situated in a pretty village, 7 miles south of Norwich, within easy reach of coast and Broads. One twin/family room, 1 double/family room, both with private facilities. Large games barn with snooker, pool and table tennis. Five acre private lake for coarse fishing. Relaxed family atmosphere. Open all year except Christmas.

Kenton Hall, Debenham, Stowmarket, Suffolk IP14 6JU

Sharon McVeigh
☎ **01728 860279**
Fax 01728 861246
[BB] **From £16.50–£22.50**
Sleeps 6
🐴 🕍 ⅄ ⊡ 🛠 ▪
Listed

Beautiful moated Tudor hall set in peaceful surroundings, rich in wildlife with pleasant country walks nearby. One double, one twin and one family room, all furnished to a high standard with en suite facilities. Guests' own panelled sitting room and dining room with period furnishings. Central heating throughout.

The Lodge Farm, High Street, Thelnetham, Diss, Norfolk IP22 1JL

Mrs Christinè Palmer
☎ **01379 898203**
[BB] **From £17.50–£25**
EM £10
Sleeps 6
🐴 (10) 🐕 ⊡
👄 👄 *Highly Commended*

Lodge Farm is a working farm of 200 acres with vineyard and Shire horses in a peaceful location 7 miles south of Diss. The thatched farmhouse has beams and inglenooks. 2 en suite rooms and 1 with hand basin only, guests' own sitting room, and walled garden for guests' use. Meals all cooked on the Aga. No evening meals served during June, July & August. Excellent local pub 5 mins walk. Closed Christmas & New Year.

Malting Farm, Blo Norton Road, South Lopham, Diss, Norfolk IP22 2HT

Cynthia Huggins
☎ **01379 687201**
[BB] **From £17**
Sleeps 6
⅄ 🐴 🛠
👄 👄

Situated on Norfolk/Suffolk border amid open countryside. A working dairy farm where cows can be seen being milked, and there are farmyard pets. Farmhouse is Elizabethan timber-framed (inside) with inglenook fireplaces. Central heating. Some four poster beds, some en suite. Easy reach Norfolk Broads, Norwich, Cambridge, Bressingham Steam Museum & Gardens. Cynthia is keen craftswoman in quilting, embroidery, spinning, weaving. Closed Christmas & New Year.

---

18 **Oak Farm,** Market Lane, Blundeston, Lowestoft, Suffolk NR32 5AP

Julie and Keith Cooper
☎ **01502 731622**
BB **From £14**
Sleeps 4
Listed *Commended*

125-acre mixed farm set in peaceful countryside crossed by the Waveney Way footpath and 1½ miles from the sea. This Victorian house was originally farm cottages. We take a pride in our breakfast and local pubs offer other meals. Guests' stairs lead to a double and a twin room and a guests' bathroom. Tea/coffee facilities and colour TV in rooms. Children very welcome – reductions under 14. Closed Christmas & New Year.

19 **Old Coach House,** Thursford, Fakenham, Norfolk NR21 0BD

Mrs Ann Green
☎ **01328 878273**
BB **From £16–£20**
EM From £7
Sleeps 6
Listed

Small peaceful working farm set in parkland with cows, sheep, ducks etc. Farmhouse is a converted 17th century coachhouse. Main bedroom has four-poster sharing bathroom with 1 twin-bedded room, also 1 twin-bedded room with en suite bathroom – all have washbasins and tea/coffee facilities. Farmhouse dining/kitchen, guests' own sitting room with TV and garden room. Close to Thursford Collection and within easy reach of sandy beaches. Open all year (closed Christmas).

20 **Park Farm,** Bylaugh, Dereham, Norfolk NR20 4QE

Mrs Jenny Lake
☎/Fax **01362 688584**
BB **From £12–£17**
EM From £8
Sleeps 5
Applied

Charming old family farmhouse, ideally situated for exploring the Norfolk countryside and visits to Norwich, the Norfolk Broads and North Norfolk coast. One large family room, one twin both with basins and a single room, with private guests' bathroom. Lounge with colour TV, dining room with inglenook. Children welcome, sorry no pets. Open all year except Christmas & New Year.

21 **Park Farm,** Sibton, Saxmundham, Suffolk IP17 2LZ

Margaret Gray
☎/Fax **01728 668324**
BB **From £14–£18**
EM From £10.50
Sleeps 6
Commended

A friendly welcome, good food and comfortable accommodation await you at Park Farm. We have 1 double, and 2 twin rooms for guests, each with washbasin. English breakfast and 3-course dinner are prepared from our own, or very local, produce and all tastes and special diets gladly catered for. Ideally situated for enjoying the unspoiled Suffolk countryside. Open all year (closed Christmas & New Year).

22 **Pear Tree Farm**, Hartest, Bury St Edmunds, Suffolk IP29 4EQ

Mrs Rachel White
☎ **01284 830217**
BB **From £17.50–£19**
Sleeps 4
Commended

A warm welcome awaits you in our modern farm chalet bungalow on this arable family farm. Ideally situated for exploring Lavenham, Constable Country, and Cambridge. We have 1 double en suite, 1 twin en suite, both with TV and tea/coffee-making facilities. Guests' TV lounge. Children welcome. Open Mar–Nov.

23 **Priory Farm**, Darsham, Saxmundham, Suffolk IP17 3QD

Suzanne Bloomfield
☎ **01728 668459**
Fax **01728 668744**
BB **From £15–£20**
Sleeps 4
Listed *Commended*

Comfortable 17th century farmhouse situated in peaceful countryside, An ideal base for exploring the Suffolk coast and heathlands and other numerous local attractions. Excellent pubs and restaurants nearby. 1 double, 1 twin, each with private shower and wc, tea/coffee facilities. Separate guests' dining room. Cycle hire available at the farm. Open Mar–Oct.

Red House Farm, Station Road, Haughley, Nr Stowmarket, Suffolk IP14 3QP (24)

Mrs Mary Noy
☎ 01449 673323
[BB] From £15
Sleeps 5
ॐ (8) ✗
♨

Red House Farm is a fruit/arable farm in mid Suffolk. The comfortable old house is surrounded by orchards which are particularly beautiful during blossom time. We offer 1 double, 1 twin and 1 single, each with H&C, tea/coffee-making facilities, CH. Guests' lounge/dining room with TV. Good restaurants locally. Over 8's welcome. No pets or smoking. Open Jan–Nov.

Rymer Farm, Barnham, Thetford, Norfolk IP24 2PP (25)

Sarah & Nigel Rush
☎ 01842 890233
Fax 01842 890653
[BB] From £17–£21
Sleeps 5
ॐ ☕ ♨ ▪
♨♨ *Commended*

17th century flint country home on arable farm near Bury St Edmunds. Relax in superb lounge with log fire, garden room, dining room for real farmers' breakfasts. Double en suite with TV, single/en suite, twin with private bathroom. Lovely farm walks with wildlife. Flower arranger's garden, carp pond. Open all year (closed Christmas).

Salamanca Farm Guest House, Stoke Holy Cross, Norwich, Norfolk NR14 8QJ (26)

Roy & Barbara Harrold
☎ 01508 492322
[BB] From £16
Sleeps 4
ॐ (6) ✗ ▪
♨♨

"Real experience of English hospitality" – "All we could have asked for" – just two comments from our visitors' book. The Harrold family have welcomed guests to their farm for 20 years. 4 miles from the cathedral city of Norwich, the valley of the River Tas, with the mill where Colmans began producing mustard, provides an attractive holiday base. All rooms have private facilities. Open 15 Jan–15 Dec.

Shrublands Farm, Northrepps, Cromer, Norfolk NR27 0AA (27)

Mrs Ann Youngman
☎/Fax 01263 579297
[BB] From £19–£22
EM From £8.50
Sleeps 6
ॐ (12) ⚠ ⊕ ✗ ♨ ⚘
♨♨ *Highly Commended*

Shrublands Farm is an arable farm set in the village of Northrepps, 2½ miles SE of Cromer and 20 miles north of Norwich. The Victorian/Edwardian house has 1 twin and 1 double with private bathrooms and 1 twin en suite. Separate sitting room and dining room for guests. Full central heating, log fires in chilly weather. Sorry, no pets. Open all year (closed Christmas & New Year).

Sloley Farm, High Street, Sloley, Norwich, Norfolk NR12 8HJ (28)

Mrs Ann Jones
☎ 01692 536281
Fax 01692 535162
[BB] From £15–£17.50
EM From £8
Sleeps 6
ॐ ✗ ⚠ ⊕ ▪
♨ *Commended*

Comfortable farmhouse on a mixed farm, 3½ miles Norfolk Broads, easy reach of Norwich and the coast. 1 double, 1 twin and 1 family room, all with washbasin, colour TV, tea/coffee-making facilities, separate bathroom. Sitting and dining rooms for guests. Sorry no pets and no smoking. Open all year (closed Christmas & New Year).

South Acre Hall, Southacre, Kings Lynn, Norfolk PE32 2AD (29)

Mrs Charles Fountaine
☎ 01760 755406
[BB] From £17.50–£20
Sleeps 6
ॐ 🐴 ⚠ ☕ ♨ ▪ ⚘
Listed

Just off A1065, 3 miles Swaffham, 30 mins coast. Beautiful listed Elizabethan house in parkland setting situated in 600 acres of working farmland, lakes, river and woodland. Private fishing, farm trails, stabling and dog kennels. Golf courses and riding stables nearby. Good home cooking, large comfortable rooms. Evening meals and packed lunches available.

30 **South Elmham Hall,** St Cross, Harleston, Norfolk IP20 0PZ

Mrs Jo Sanderson
☎ 01986 782526
Fax 01986 782203
[BB] From £15–£22
Sleeps 5
🐴 ⅍ ⅂ ☻ 🐾 ♨ 🐾
Listed

Moated former bishop's palace with large gardens. Mixed farm, peaceful location with rare cattle and farm trails in historic landscape. Tastefully furnished comfortable rooms with tea/coffee tray. Large double/family room with bath en suite, twin room with own bath and WC. Guests' lounge/dining room with TV, full CH. Child reductions, early suppers, cot and baby sitting by arrangement. Open Easter–Nov.

31 **Stratton Farm,** West Drove North, Walton Highway, West Norfolk PE14 7DP

Derek & Sue King
☎ 01945 880162
[BB] £21
(Tariff £21, 10% discount
for 3 nights or more)
Sleeps 6
🐴 (6) ⅂ 🦽 ☻ 🐾 ♨
🦆 🦆 *Commended*

Derek and Sue King invite you to stay on their peaceful farm which supports a prize winning herd of Shorthorn cattle. All rooms are en suite, have tea/coffee-making facilities, colour TV, and central heating. One room is specifically designed for wheelchair users. Free carp fishing and use of heated swimming pool. Full English breakfast with home produced sausages, bacon, eggs and marmalade. Open all year (including Christmas).

32 **Toll Barn,** off Norwich Road, North Walsham, Norfolk NR28 0JB

Annette Tofts
☎ 01692 403063
Fax 01692 406582
[BB] From £19
Sleeps 12
🐴 (8) 🐎 ⅂ 🦽 ☻ 🐾
Listed *Highly
Commended*

Nominated for prestigious B&B award Toll Barn offers outstanding comfort and privacy in a highly informal atmosphere, beyond courtyard gardens with fountains are delightful, spacious guest–lodges, each decorated in classic English house style, all en suite with TV, fridge. Tea/coffee. Breakfast in exposed brick and beamed dining room, or in the dining area of your own private room if preferred.

33 **Woodlands Farm,** Brundish, near Woodbridge, Suffolk IP13 8BP

Jill Graham
☎ 01379 384444
[BB] From £15–£17.50
EM From £12
Sleeps 6
🐴 (10) ⅂ 🐾
🦆 🦆 *Highly Commended*

A friendly welcome and good home cooking assured in our comfortable, timber-framed farmhouse set in peaceful countryside near Framlingham. Within easy reach of the coast and numerous local attractions. One twin and 2 double bedrooms with en suite bathrooms, and tea/coffee facilities. Separate dining and sitting rooms with inglenooks. Centrally heated with log fires in cold weather. Open all year (closed Christmas).

SELF-CATERING

34 **Dolphin Lodge,** Roudham Farm, Roudham, East Harling, Norfolk NR16 2RJ

Mr & Mrs T. Jolly
☎ 01953 717126
Fax 01953 718593
[SC] From £190–£295
Sleeps 5/6
🐴 ⅂ 🐾 ☻
🏠 🏠 🏠 *Highly
Commended*

Pair of beautifully restored cottages on edge of Thetford Forest on a Breckland farm. Both spacious and well equipped; central heating, Aga, woodburning stove, washing machine, tumble dryer, fridge, colour TV, cot and highchair available. Each cottage sleeps 5 in two bedrooms. Many local tourist attractions. Ideal for a quiet secluded holiday or a busy sightseeing one. Open all year.

The Granary, Darsham, Saxmundham, Suffolk IP17 3QD

Suzanne Bloomfield
☎ 01728 668459
Fax 01728 668744
SC From £95–£250
Sleeps 4
🐎 ⚡
🐎 🐎 🐎 *Approved*

17th century granary tastefully converted to provide comfortable accommodation. Situated in peaceful Suffolk countryside, an ideal base for touring Suffolk coast and heathlands and other local attractions. 1 double, 2 singles. Shower room, kitchen, dining room, sitting room. Storage heaters, colour TV, washing machine. Cycle hire. Sat–Sat. Weekend lets out of season. Open all year.

The Granary Suites, Brighthouse Farm, Melford Road, Lawshall, near Bury St Edmunds, Suffolk IP29 4PX

Mr & Mrs Truin
☎ 01284 830385
SC From £140–£180
Sleeps 2
🐎 🐾 ⚡ 🧍 🚗 🐎 🎾
🐎 *Commended*

Granary conversion to a high standard for self catering. Set in large landscaped gardens, small but cosy, comprising double bedroom, en suite shower, washbasin, toilet, kitchen, TV, linen etc. provided. No smoking.

Hall Farm Cottage, Church Lane, Copdock, Ipswich, Suffolk IP8 3JZ

Mrs Yvonne Carr
☎ 01473 730287
SC From £220–£325
Sleeps 4
🐎 🐾 ⚡ 🎾
🐎 🐎 🐎

Highly Commended

Part of period farmhouse on a 3 miles circular walk close to Constable country with easy access to A12 and A45. Open fireplace, fuel supplied, beamed ceilings, central heating, colour TV, washing machine. Electricity extra. Cot and high chair. 1 double and 1 twin bedroom. Open Apr–Sept.

Sid's Cottage, c/o The Grange, West Rudham, Kings Lynn, Norfolk PE31 8SY

Mrs Angela Ringer
☎ 01485 528229
SC From £120–£210
Sleeps 4
🐎 🚗 🐾
🐎 🐎–🐎 🐎 🐎

Approved

Sid's Cottage is semi-detached, surrounded by grass but has no enclosed garden. Overlooks a small orchard, patio at rear. Sleeps 4 in 3 bedrooms. Linen provided. Gas central heating, open fire, colour TV, auto washing machine, fridge/freezer. Cot and highchair available on request. Electricity 50p meter. Free carp fishing on farm. Heated indoor swimming pool. Good base for seeing Norfolk. Sandy beach in easy reach. Sorry, no pets. Open all year.

Stable Cottages and The Granary, Chattisham Place, Nr Ipswich, Suffolk IP8 3QD

Mrs Margaret Langton
☎/Fax 01473 652210
SC From £125–£310
Sleeps 2/8
🐎 🐕 ⚡ 🐎 🎾 🎾
🐎 🐎 🐎–🐎 🐎 🐎🐎

Highly Commended

Restored stables and Tudor granary converted to 3 comfortable and well-equipped holiday cottages, two with wheelchair facilities. Situated in a SE facing courtyard with CH, fitted kitchen, colour TV. Linen, towels, electricity included. Games, laundry and craft room on site. Use of heated swimming pool and tennis court by arrangement. Quiet, rural village near Constable Country. Sea ½ hr, riding, fishing nearby. Open all year.

51

England's Heartland

Essex

Group Contact: *Joyce Withey* ☎ *01277 362695*

Essex surprises – it is still a rural county yet just a short trip east from London. It is a land of rolling countryside and river valleys, creeks and estuaries with a scattering of villages and country towns. Essex has local farm produce, wines and seafood, oak beamed country pubs serving real ale and traditionally cosy tea shops.

In the east of the county explore the past in Colchester, the oldest recorded town in England, with a Norman castle built on the foundations of what was the largest Roman temple in Northern Europe. Wander through Hatfield Forest with its woodland, pasture, lake and nature reserve and 6,000 acres of Epping Forest.

The Essex coastline is one of contrasts, from remote marshes to lively seaside resorts. In the west of the county visit Saffron Walden and beautiful surrounding villages.

Essex is highly accessible by road and rail, with the M25 and M11 motorways and regular train services from London (Liverpool Street) throughout Essex including Stansted Airport, Port of Harwich and Felixstowe.

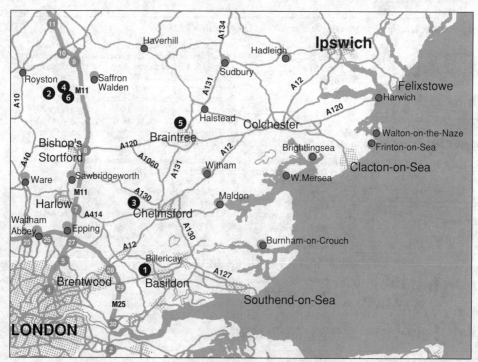

BED AND BREAKFAST
(and evening meal)

Bonny Downs Farmhouse, Doesgate Lane, Bulphan, Nr Upminster, Essex RM14 3TB

Rose Newman
☎ 01268 542129
BB From £15–£20
EM From £8
Sleeps 6
♿ ⚥ ☂ ♞
Listed *Approved*

Large, comfortably furnished, pleasantly situated in large garden with lovely views. Close to Langdon Hills Country Park and Basildon New Town (modern shopping centre). Convenient for London, Southend, South East England via M25, A13, A127. Sheep/cattle kept on the farm. 2 twin, 1 family bedrooms, 1 bath with toilet/shower, 1 shower room with toilet. Tea/coffee trays. Good cooking. Open all year (closed Christmas).

Duddenhoe End Farm, Duddenhoe End, Nr Saffron Walden, Essex CB11 4UU

Peggy Foster
☎ 01763 838258
BB From £18–£22
Sleeps 6
⚥ ☂ (12)
🐾 🐾 *Commended*

Duddenhoe End Farm is situated on the outskirts of the peaceful hamlet of Duddenhoe End. The house is 17th century and has a wealth of beams and inglenook fireplaces. Accommodation consists of 3 double bedrooms all en suite. Tea/coffee-making facilities. Visitors' sitting room. Within easy reach of Cambridge, Duxford War Museum, London and Suffolk. Open all year (closed Christmas).

'Greys', Ongar Road, Margaret Roding, Nr Great Dunmow, Essex CM6 1QR

Mrs Joyce Matthews
☎ 01245 231509
BB From £17
Sleeps 6
⚥ ☂ (10) ✺
Listed

Formerly two cottages, 'Greys' is quietly situated on the family farm – arable and sheep. Beamed throughout and with large garden. Ideal for short breaks and exploring. Pretty villages, old towns etc. 2 double rooms and 1 with twin beds. Tea/coffee available. No dogs please. Just off the A1060, Bishops Stortford to Chelmsford road, at telephone kiosk in village. Open most of year.

Rockells Farm, Duddenhoe End, Saffron Walden, Essex CB11 4UY

Mrs Tineke Westerhuis
☎ 01763 838053
BB From £16–£18
EM From £7.50
Sleeps 6
♞ ☂ ♿ ☕ ✺ ⚘
🐾 🐾

Rockells is an arable farm in a beautiful corner of Essex. The Georgian house has a large garden with a 3-acre lake for coarse fishing. All rooms have private facilities, one room is downstairs. Evening meal by arrangement only. On the farm are several footpaths, and beautiful villages in the area. Within easy reach of Audley End House, Duxford Air Museum and Cambridge. London is about 1 hour by car or train. Stansted airport 30 mins by car. Open all year.

Spicers Farm, Rotten End, Wethersfield, Braintree, Essex CM7 4AL

Mrs Delia Douse
☎ 01371 851021
BB From £15–£18
Sleeps 6
☂ Å ⊡ ✺
🐾 🐾 *Commended*

Attractive farmhouse with large garden in area designated of special landscape value. Quiet arable farm with pleasant walks. Convenient for Stansted, Harwich, Cambridge and Constable country. All rooms en suite with CH, tea/coffee-making facilities, colour TV and lovely views. Open all year.

SELF-CATERING

6 **The Granary,** c/o Rockells Farm, Duddenhoe End, Saffron Walden, Essex CB11 4UY

Mrs Tineke Westerhuis
☎ **01763 838053**
SC **From £120–£200**
Sleeps 5
🐎 🦢 🐾 🎿
🐾 🐾 🐾 *Commended*

The Granary is part of Rockells farmyard, an arable farm in a beautiful corner of Essex. A large lounge with kitchen area has original woodpanelling. The cottage is fully equipped to high standard. Garden with 3-acre lake for excellent fishing. In the area are several footpaths and beautiful villages with excellent pubs. Audley End House, Duxford Air Museum and Cambridge nearby. London is 1 hour by car or train. Stansted airport 30 mins by car. Open all year.

52

England's South and South East

Thames Valley

Group Contact: *Mrs Mary Anne Florey* ☎ *01865 300207*

The Thames Valley is at the heart of historical England. Farms and homes are situated in the area stretching from the Chiltern Hills above Henley through the rich farmland of the Vale of Aylesbury and on to the west of Oxford and the Cotswolds.

Oxford is at the centre of the region and its dreaming spires and great buildings, including mediaeval colleges and Renaissance masterpieces such as the Sheldonian Theatre, can provide great historical interest. You can take guided tours of Oxford, Windsor and Burford or enjoy browsing in antique shops and bookshops.

Woodstock has many historical associations and is the site of Blenheim Palace, the magnificent home designed by Sir John Vanbrugh for the Dukes of Marlborough. Sir Winston Churchill was born there and is buried in the nearby churchyard of Bladon. The area includes the moated castle at Broughton near Banbury and many other Tudor and 18th century manors and country houses.

Places of interest include the Cotswold Wildlife Park, Birdland, Cogges Farm Museum and a steam railway centre and activities such as boating, pony trekking and brass rubbing are available.

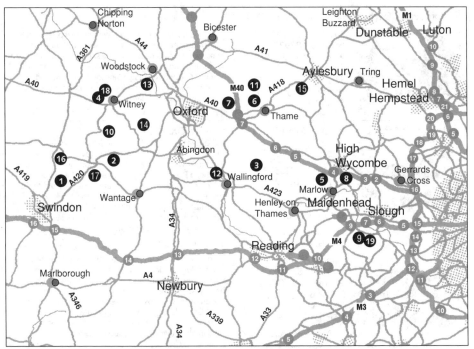

BED AND BREAKFAST

(and evening meal)

---

1 Ashen Copse Farm, Coleshill, Highworth, Nr Swindon, Wiltshire SN6 7PU

Pat Hoddinott
☎ 01367 240175
🅱 From £17–£20
Sleeps 6
✂ 🐕 🛳
🦆🦆

Ideal setting for peace and quiet, walking, visiting numerous attractions. 580-acre National Trust beef and arable farm in beautiful countryside. Spacious, comfortable accommodation in 17th century farmhouse (1 bedroom en suite). Small outdoor swimming pool. Meet our lambs, calves and horse. Children's toys and games available. Reduction for children sharing. Many pubs and restaurants. Near M4 (J15). Open all year (closed Christmas Day).

---

2 Bowling Green Farm, Stanford Road, Faringdon, Oxfordshire SN7 8EZ

Della Barnard
☎ 01367 240229
Fax 01367 242568
🅱 From £16
Sleeps 6
✂ 🐕 🦃
🦆🦆

Attractive 18th century period farmhouse offering 20th century comfort situated in the Vale of the White Horse, just 1 mile south of Faringdon on the A417. Easy access to M4 for Heathrow Airport. A working farm breeding cattle and horses. Large twin/family room on ground floor en suite. All bedrooms have colour TV, tea/coffee-making facilities and CH throughout. Open all year.

---

3 Fords Farm, Ewelme, Wallingford, Oxon OX10 6HU

Marlene Edwards
☎ 01491 839272
🅱 From £17.50–£20
Sleeps 4
✂

🦆🦆🦆 *Highly Commended*

500-acre mixed farm, arable beef and sheep. Attractive farmhouse set in historic part of village with famous church almshouses and school. Peaceful surroundings with good walks and good selection of pubs nearby. Easy access to Henley, Oxford, Reading, Windsor, Heathrow and London. Friendly and comfortable atmosphere. 2 twin rooms. Open May–Mar.

---

4 Hill Grove Farm, Crawley Road, Minster Lovell, Oxfordshire OX8 5NA

Mrs Katharine Brown
☎ 01993 703120
Fax 01993 700528
🅱 From £18–£21
Sleeps 4
✂ 🐕 🛳 🦃 🦄
🦆 *Highly Commended*

Hill Grove is a mixed, family-run 300-acre working farm situated in an attractive rural setting overlooking the Windrush Valley. Ideally positioned for driving to Oxford, Blenheim Palace, Witney (Farm Museum) and Burford (renowned as the Gateway to the Cotswolds and for its splendid Wildlife Park). New golf course 1 mile. Hearty breakfasts, friendly atmosphere. Children welcome. 1 double/private shower, 1 twin/double en suite. AA listed. Open all year (closed Christmas).

---

5 Little Parmoor Farm, Frieth, Henley-on-Thames, Oxfordshire RG9 6NL

Frances Emmett
☎ 01494 881600
🅱 From £20–£25
Sleeps 6
🐕 🔲 🛡 🦃 💼 🦄
Listed

16th century brick and flint farmhouse with oak beam interior, log fires in winter and CH, on a 220 acre mixed farm in the Chilterns, an area of outstanding natural beauty. Convenient for Windsor, Marlow, Henley, Oxford and Heathrow. Taxi service available. Farmhouse breakfast including free range eggs and local honey, tea/coffee-making facilities. Good pubs and restaurant food in attractive villages nearby. Open all year.

Manor Farm, Shabbington, Aylesbury, Buckinghamshire HP18 9HJ

Joan Bury
☎ **01844 201103**
BB **From £17.50–£22**
Sleeps 4
& ☂ (8)
Listed

This 188-acre grazing farm is in a quiet pastoral setting with lovely views. Bounded by the River Thame. Twelve miles from Oxford, Manor Farm is conveniently situated for Chilterns, Cotswolds, Thames Valley and London. Accommodation in modern, well-equipped bungalow with lounge, kitchen, bathroom, colour TV, CH. Breakfast served in adjacent farmhouse. Many good pubs and restaurants in area. Open all year.

Mead Close, Forest Hill, Nr Oxford, Oxfordshire OX33 1DY

Audrey Dunkley
☎ **01865 872248**
BB **From £15.50–£21**
EM From £8
Sleeps 5
☂ ✄ ☗
Listed

450 acre mixed farm, dairy and cereals. Family farm, milking 80 cows. Warm and welcoming farmhouse, full CH, 5 miles to Oxford city centre, 5 minutes to Park and Ride. Easy to find from A40. Traditional English pub in village, serving food. Enjoy visiting the Cotswolds, Blenheim Palace, Waterperry Gdns, Waddesdon Manor and Windsor. Open all year.

Monkton Farm, Little Marlow, Buckinghamshire SL7 3RF

Jane & Warren Kimber
☎ **01494 521082**
Fax 01494 443905
BB **From £18–£20**
Sleeps 6
✄ ☂ (5) ◕ ◼
Listed *Commended*

A 150-acre working dairy farm with 14th century 'Cruck' farmhouse set in the beautiful Chiltern Hills, yet only 30 miles from London and 27 miles from Oxford. Heathrow 20 mins, 1 single, 1 double and 1 family room available. English breakfast served in the farm kitchen. Large choice of pubs and restaurants nearby. Taxi service to Heathrow available. Open all year.

Moor Farm, Holyport, near Maidenhead, Berkshire SL6 2HY

Mrs G Reynolds
☎/Fax 01628 33761
BB **From £19–£22**
Sleeps 6
☂ ✄ ☗ ☗
✿ ✿ *Highly Commended*

In the pretty village of Holyport. Moor Farm is 4 miles from Windsor. The farmhouse is a timber-framed, 700-year-old 'listed' manor in a lovely country garden with charming en suite rooms, furnished with antiques. It is well placed for touring the Thames Valley and visiting London. Also close to Heathrow. Suffolk sheep and horses kept on farm. Open all year.

'Morar', Weald Street, Bampton, Oxfordshire OX18 2HL

Janet Rouse
☎ **01993 850162**
Fax 01993 851738
BB **From £17–£21**
EM From £12
Sleeps 6
⊞ ✄ ☂ (6) ◼ ✾
✿ ✿ *Highly Commended*

A non-smoking farmhouse (retired from farming) where meat, vegetables, bread are nearly all home-produced and cooked to perfection. Vegetarian dinners offered. Pet sheep and goats will love your fuss and attention. Cotswolds, Oxford, Woodstock, swimming, sailing, riding, fishing all close by. We Morris dance, bellring, garden – and laugh! 1 twin, 2 doubles en suite. Elizabeth Gundrey recommended. Open all year (closed Christmas).

New Farm, Oxford Road, Oakley, Aylesbury, Buckinghamshire HP18 9UR

Binnie Pickford
☎ **01844 237360**
BB **From £17–£19**
EM From £10
Sleeps 6
☂ (6) ☞
Listed *Commended*

Warm, friendly atmosphere in fully modernised farmhouse. Good food, comfortable bedrooms, views over 163 acres devoted to sheep, beef, arable. Situated on Oxfordshire/ Bucks boundary in peaceful surroundings. Walks in adjacent Bernwood Forest Nature Reserve. 7 miles Oxford, close to Waterperry Gardens, Waddesdon Manor, Quainton Railway Centre, Blenheim Palace and M40 to Windsor and London. Pubs and restaurants nearby. Open all year except Christmas.

---

⑫   North Farm, Shillingford Hill, Wallingford, Oxfordshire OX10 8NB

Hilary Warburton
☎ **01865 858406**
BB **From £19–£21.50**
Sleeps 4
✗ ☐ **(8)** ☞ ♒ ☆
👁➔ *Highly Commended*

Spacious and comfortable farmhouse on our 500 acres of farmland with sheep and pygmy goats. Enjoy walks by the River Thames and private fishing. Ideal for Oxford and Henley and within easy reach of Windsor and London. 2 double bedrooms with private bathrooms (1 en suite), colour TV, tea/coffee-making facilities. Excellent local pubs. Open all year.

---

⑬   The Old Farmhouse, Station Hill, Long Hanborough, Oxfordshire OX8 8JZ

Vanessa Maundrell
☎ **01993 882097**
BB **From £18–£19.50**
Sleeps 4
🅭 ✗ ☐ **(12)** ♒ ☆
👁➔ *Highly Commended*

17th century Old Farmhouse is full of period charm and character tastefully furnished with inglenook fireplace, beams and flagstone floors. Ideally situated close to Oxford, Woodstock, Blenheim Palace and the Cotswolds. Delicious home cooking. Warm and freindly welcome assured. One double en suite, one double sharing bathroom. French, German, Spanish, Italian spoken. Open all year (closed Christmas).

---

⑭   Rectory Farm, Northmoor, Witney, Oxfordshire OX8 1SX

Mary Anne Florey
☎ **01865 300207**
BB **From £18.50–£19.50**
Sleeps 4
✗ ◖ ☞ ♒
👁➔ *Highly Commended*

Rectory Farm is a 16th century farmhouse retaining all the old charm alongside modern comforts. Both rooms have en suite facilities, central heating, tea/coffee-making facilities. We are conveniently situated for Oxford, the Cotswolds, Blenheim and the Thames path. Fishing on the Thames available. We can assure you of a warm welcome and a peaceful and comfortable stay. Open 1st Feb–mid Dec.

---

⑮   Wallace Farm, Dinton, Nr Aylesbury, Buckinghamshire HP17 8UF

Jackie Cook
☎ **01296 748660**
Fax **01296 748851**
BB **From £19–£20**
Sleeps 6
☐ ⊞ ☞ ♒ ☆
👁➔

This 16th century listed farmhouse is situated in a quiet, rural setting in the Vale of Aylesbury, yet within easy reach of London, Oxford and Heathrow. A small family farm, rearing beef cattle and sheep, plus chickens, ducks and geese. Plenty of opportunitites for country walks, coarse fishing or browsing through our extensive library. Comfortable accommodation with a warm welcome. Open all year.

---

⑯   Weston Farm, Buscot Wick, Faringdon, Oxfordshire SN7 8DJ

Mrs Jean Woof
☎ **01367 252222**
BB **From £19**
Sleeps 4
☐ **(10)** ✗
👁➔ *Commended*

Come and share our idyllic 17th century Cotswold farmhouse in peaceful surroundings. Period furniture and well maintained gardens. 500-acre mixed farm. CH, tea/coffee-making facilities and own TV, one four-poster and one twin room, each with private bathroom. Guests own dining and sitting rooms, with log fires. Ideally situated to explore this beautiful area. Open all year except Christmas.

SELF-CATERING

Coxwell House, Little Coxwell, Faringdon, Oxfordshire SN7 7LP

Elspeth Crossley Cooke
☎ **01367 241240**
Fax 01367 240911
🆂 **From £350–£650**
Sleeps 6
🏇 🐾 🐎 ʡ
⚲ ⚲ ⚲ ⚲ *Highly Commended*

Coxwell House is the superb main 1760 part (self-contained) of a Georgian farmhouse set in an attractive, secluded walled garden. Every modern convenience. Tennis court, indoor swimming pool. Unspoilt stone walled farming village with thatched cottages and pub. Ideal for the Cotswolds, Oxford. 1½ miles Faringdon south of A420. Open all year.

Hill Grove Cottage, c/o Hill Grove Farm, Crawley Road, Minster Lovell, Oxfordshire OX8 5NA

Mrs Katharine Brown
☎ **01993 703120**
Fax 01993 700528
🆂 **From £250–£325**
Sleeps 6 + cot
🍴 🏇 🐎 ʡ
⚲ ⚲ ⚲ ⚲ *Commended*

Hill Grove Cottage is a large bungalow adjacent to our farmhouse. 2 double bedrooms, 1 twin, bathroom and shower, dining room, lounge, kitchen. Fridge/freezer, washing machine, tumble dryer, CH. Gardens. Situated above the Windrush Valley, excellent walks yet within driving distance of Oxford, Woodstock and Burford. New golf course 1 mile. Cot and babysitting by arrangement. Electricity included. Linen free. Open June–Oct.

Moor Farm, Holyport, near Maidenhead, Berkshire SL6 2HY

Mrs G Reynolds
☎/**Fax 01628 33761**
🆂 **From £200–£380**
Sleeps 2/4
🏇 🍴 ♿ 🐎
⚲ ⚲ ⚲ ⚲ *Highly Commended*

In the pretty village of Holyport, Courtyard Cottages are on the 700-year-old manor of Moor Farm and are conversions from a Georgian stable block and two small barns. They retain the charm of their original features and are furnished with antique pine. The 4 cottages are well placed for touring the Thames Valley and are 4 miles from Windsor and convenient for visiting London. Sheep and horses are on the farm.

FARM HOLIDAY BUREAU

DISABLED VISITORS

Many members offer a welcome to disabled/less able visitors. Please do check the extent of the facilities before booking.

53

England's South and South East

Hampshire

Group Contact: *Mrs Melanie Bray* ☎ *01705 631597*

Hampshire is a beautiful county of contrasts ... of creeks, harbours and beaches, grand rivers and sparkling streams, forests, and lush farmland with picturesque villages and hamlets.

The main centres of the county have all played an important role in history: the Saxons made Winchester their capital; Southampton bears witness to the Norman invasion, and Portsmouth is famous for its naval heritage with Nelson's HMS Victory, Henry VIII's Mary Rose and the first ironclad warship, HMS Warrior.

Hampshire has numerous other links with the past, Jane Austen's house at Chawton or Charles Dickens' birthplace in Portsmouth, for example, or enjoy the many rich treasures on show in the museums of the county's towns and cities.

In the New Forest there are plenty of quiet picnic spots and lots of ponies. Hampshire is served by a network of footpaths and bridleways and many country parks. There are long distance walks and guided walks which can take you round the towns and cities, along the Solent coastline or inland along the famous Test Valley. The country mansions of Broadlands, Breamore, Stratfield Saye and Highclere Castle and numerous gardens are open to the public.

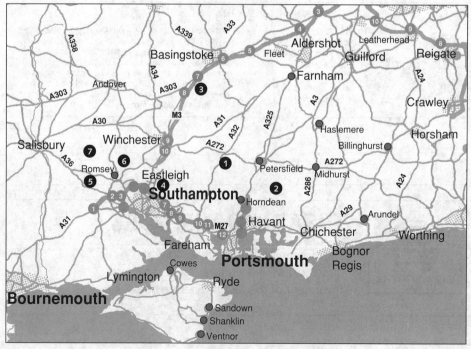

BED AND BREAKFAST

(and evening meal)

Brocklands Farm, West Meon, Petersfield, Hampshire GU32 1JN

Sue Wilson
☎ 01730 829228
[BB] From £16–£17
Sleeps 6
🐏 👵 ✂ 🛋 💼 🐾 🎋
Listed

Brocklands Farm in the famed Meon Valley has good views of the countryside and is within easy reach of the coastal ports and also the ancient towns of Winchester, Petersfield and Chichester. The light and airy farmhouse is furnished traditionally with a homely atmosphere. An old railway line and grass headlands provide farm walks. Day sailing in the Solent. Afternoon tea available. Open all year (closed Christmas).

Compton Farmhouse, Compton, Nr Chichester, West Sussex PO18 9HB

Mrs Melanie Bray
☎ 01705 631597
[BB] £18
Sleeps 6
🐂 ✂ 🎋 🛋
Listed

Children are especially welcome (half-price) at our old, flint family farmhouse. We are 200 yards up a track from the village square, next door to the church and are bordered by fields and woods. Lovely walks and plenty to do in our enclosed, child-orientated garden. Own sitting/dining room with drink-making facilities, fridge, TV. Chichester and Portsmouth nearby. Open all year.

Oakdown Farm Bungalow, c/o Oakdown Farm, Dummer, Basingstoke, Hampshire RG23 7LR

Mrs Elizabeth Hutton
☎ 01256 397218
[BB] From £15–£18
Sleeps 6
🐂 (12) 🏹 🐾
🦢

Oakdown Farm Bungalow is on a secluded, private road, next to junction 7 on the M3, 3 miles south of Basingstoke and close to the village of Dummer. Very good road communications to London, Winchester, Southampton, Oxford, the South-West and the Midlands. Wayfarer's Walk within 200 metres. Open all year.

Park Farm, Stoneham Lane, Eastleigh, Hampshire SO5 3HS

Angela Fright
☎ 01703 612960
[BB] From £13–£17.50
EM From £10
Sleeps 6
🐂 🐎 🎋
Listed *Commended*

Converted coaching stables in a beautiful rural setting. Easy access to Southampton, Romsey, Winchester, Portsmouth and New Forest (15 mins). 800 yards off M27 (jct. 5). Coarse fishing in own small, secluded lake and in adjacent, 200-year-old Capability Brown landscaped lakes, both well stocked. Tea/coffee facilities, CTV in all bedrooms. Packed lunches. Diets catered for. Water purifier installed. Open all year.

Pyesmead Farm, Plaitford, Romsey, Hampshire SO51 6EE

Mrs C Pybus
☎ 01794 323386
[BB] From £13.50–£17
EM From £7.50
Sleeps 6
✂ 🐂 🐎
Listed

Come and stay on a small, family-run stock farm bordered by the New Forest and by the River Blackwater, a tributary of the well-known River Test. Guests are welcome to walk around the farm. Fishing available on our attractive, private lakes. Many activities locally, including horse riding, golf, swimming and forest walks. Open all year (closed Christmas).

SELF-CATERING

---

⑥ Meadow Cottage, c/o Farley Farm, Braishfield, Romsey, Hampshire SO51 0QP

Mrs Wendy Graham
☎ 01794 368265/
368513
🆂🅲 From £150–£250
Sleeps 5 + cot
🐎🐕🐖🎣
🍴 🍴 🍴 🍴 *Commended*

Well equipped, semi-detached cottage on a 400-acre beef and arable farm. Outstanding views of beautiful surrounding countryside. Ideal for walking or riding (own horse welcome), or touring historic centres of Romsey, Winchester, Salisbury, New Forest and coast. Cottage has CH, log fire, colour TV, downstairs WC, washer/dryer, cot. Garden with barbecue. Phone for brochure. Open Easter–Oct.

---

⑦ Owl Cottage, Lye Farm, West Tytherley, Romsey, Hampshire SP5 1LA

Maxine Vine
☎ 01794 341667
🆂🅲 From £180–£280
Sleeps 5
🐎🐕♿🎣💼
🍴 🍴 🍴 *Commended*

Owl cottage has been skillfully converted from an old barn situated in one of the most beautiful parts of Hampshire. Outstanding views, close New Forest, Salisbury, Winchester. Location perfect for touring, walking, riding in southern England. Excellently equipped cottage, central heating, electric included, washer dryer, TV, cot. Peaceful and relaxing environment. Open all year.

PRICES

Prices include VAT and service charge (if any) and are:
B&B per person per night
EM per person
SC per unit per week
Tents and caravans per pitch per night

FARM HOLIDAY BUREAU

FINDING YOUR ACCOMMODATION

FARM HOLIDAY BUREAU

The Group contacts at the beginning of each section can always help you find a vacancy in your chosen area.

54

England's South and South East

Sussex and Surrey

Group Contacts: *Sussex: Brenda Gough* ☎ *01273 478680*
Surrey: Mrs Gill Hill ☎ *01306 730210*

You've probably heard of 'Sussex by the Sea' so perhaps to you Sussex means the traditional attractions of the popular seaside resorts such as Brighton, Eastbourne, Hastings, Bognor Regis, Littlehampton and Worthing. What you may not know is that just inland there is a vast area of lovely downland punctuated with tiny villages and the occasional old market town. Further north busy towns such as Horsham, Crawley and East Grinstead are surrounded by lush green countryside. There is also a rich history here – Chichester with its famous Roman cross, nearby Fishbourne with the remains of a palace once ruled by a King Cogidubnus ... really; and Hastings – 1066 and all that.

In Surrey, the North Downs provide dramatic wooded hillsides with small, attractive towns and villages nestling in the valleys. Here you can walk along the track claiming to be the Pilgrim's Way which connects Winchester to Canterbury; clamber up famous heights like Leith Hill – just short of 1,000ft – or its neighbour Box Hill, coming down via the intriguingly named Zig Zag Hill.

Yet nowhere in these counties are you ever more than a couple of hours from central London should you wish to make a day trip there.

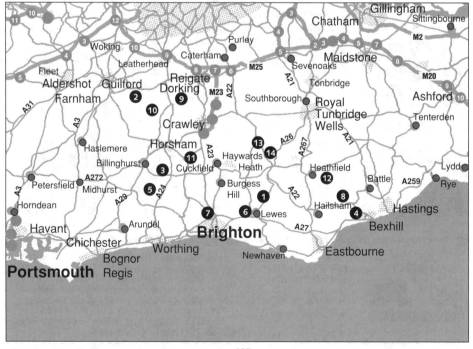

BED AND BREAKFAST

(and evening meal)

---

1 Camoys Farmhouse, Mill Road, Barcombe, Lewes, East Sussex BN8 5BH

Mrs K Cornwell
☎ 01273 400662
BB From £17.50–£22
Sleeps 6

A modern, spacious farmhouse in quiet surroundings enjoying outstanding views. 4 miles north of Lewes, close to Barcombe village. Ideally situated for visiting this part of Sussex with its historic buildings, gardens, coast and South Downs. Downstairs twin bedded room en suite suitable for disabled guests. Upstairs twin bedded room with basin and family room with basin and bathroom adjacent. All rooms with colour TV and tea/coffee making facilities. Cot available. 'A home from home' No smokers please. Open Jan–Nov.

---

2 Crossways Farm, Raikes Lane, Abinger Hammer, Nr Dorking, Surrey RH5 6PZ

Sheila Hughes
☎ 01306 730173
BB From £15–£18
Sleeps 6

Welcome to our 17th century listed farmhouse (book and TV setting) amidst the oustanding beauty of the Surrey hills. Good walks. Near A25 and Dorking/Guildford bus stop. Easy reach Gatwick, Heathrow, London, S Coast, Wisley. Large, comfortable rooms, washbasins, tea/coffee-making facilities, inglenooks, log fires, beams, colour TV. Walled garden, croquet. Laundry facilities. Good home cooking. Elizabeth Gundry recommended. Open all year.

---

3 Goffsland Farm, Shipley, Horsham, West Sussex RH13 7BQ

Mrs Carol Liverton
☎ 01403 730434
BB From £15–£17
Sleeps 5

Listed 17th century farmhouse on a 260-acre working farm with sheep, cattle and dairy herd. Situated in the Sussex Weald central to Gatwick and the South coast. Family room has double bed and bunk beds with washbasin and tea/ coffee-making facilities. Own bathroom with WC own sitting room with TV. Open all year.

---

4 Moonshill Farm, The Green, Ninfield, Battle, East Sussex TN33 9LH

Mrs June Ive
☎ 01424 892645
BB From £15–£17.50
Sleeps 6

In the heart of the '1066 Country' in the centre of Ninfield opposite pub. Farmhouse in 10 acres of garden, orchard, stables. Enjoy beautiful walks, golf and riding arranged. Comfortable rooms, 3 en suite, CH and electric fires, hospitality tray, TV, lounge, parking and garage, babysitting service. Every comfort in our safe, quiet and peaceful home. Reduced rates for weekly bookings. Open Jan–Nov.

---

5 New House Farm, Broadford Bridge Road, West Chiltington, Nr Pulborough, West Sussex RH20 2LA

Alma Steele
☎ 01798 812215
BB From £18–£25
Sleeps 6
(10) Commended

Listed 15th century farmhouse with oak beams and inglenook fireplace, in the centre of the village, close to local inns which provide good food. A new 18 hole golf course, open to non-members, is only ¼ mile away. Many places of historical interest in the area including Goodwood House, Petworth House, Parham House, Arundel Castle. Gatwick 35 minutes. en suite facilities and colour TV in bedrooms. Open Jan-Nov.

Ousedale House, Offham, Lewes, East Sussex BN7 3QF

Roland & Brenda Gough
☎ **01273 478680**
Fax 01273 486510
BB From £21–£25
EM From £11
Sleeps 6
✕ ✍ (12) ⊞ ♿
✿✿✿ *Highly Commended*

Spacious Victorian country house with luxury accommodation. 3½ acre garden and woodland situated on a hillside plateau with panoramic views over the Ouse river valley. Country cooking, four poster bed, modern heating. Double glazed throughout. Residents' licence. Central for touring. About 1 mile from Lewes station – courtesy car. Glyndebourne hampers provided. Brighton 9 miles. Low season weekend breaks. Open all year.

Poynings Manor Farm, Poynings, Nr Brighton, West Sussex BN45 7AG

Mrs Carol Revell
☎ **01273 857371**
BB From £18.50–£22
EM From £9.50
Sleeps 6
✍ ♞ ♿ ♨ ♿
✿

260-acre family run sheep/arable farm with charming old manor house resting quietly in a green valley under the South Downs. An area of outstanding natural beauty, ideal for riders, walkers and country lovers. Plenty of country pubs and eating houses nearby. A23 5 mins, Hickstead 10 mins, Gatwick 30 mins, Brighton and Hove 15 mins. Evening meal by request only. Open Mar–Dec.

The Stud Farm, Bodle Street Green, Nr Hailsham, East Sussex BN27 4RJ

Philippa & Richard Gentry
☎/**Fax 01323 833201**
BB From £17
EM From £8.50 (by arrangement)
Sleeps 6
♞
✿✿ *Commended*

70 acre sheep and cattle farm situated in peaceful surroundings and beautiful countryside, ideal for walking. 8 miles from sea, Eastbourne, Hastings, South Downs in easy reach. Upstairs, family unit of double bedded room/twin bedded room, both with handbasins, and bathroom. Downstairs twin bedded room with shower, toilet, handbasin en suite. All bedrooms with colour TV and tea/coffee-making facilities. Guests' sitting room, colour TV. Sunroom. Open all year.

Sturtwood Farm, Partridge Lane, Newdigate, Dorking, Surrey RH5 5EE

Bridget MacKinnon
☎ **01306 631308**
BB From £18–£22
EM From £8.50
Sleeps 4
♨ ♞ ♿ ✂
✿✿

An attractive 18th century farmhouse in lovely countryside yet within 12 mins of Gatwick Airport. Many National Trust properties and gardens nearby. Also London, Brighton and several country towns. Open all year.

SELF-CATERING

"Badgersholt" and "Foxholme", c/o Bulmer Farm, Holmbury St Mary, Dorking, Surrey RH5 6LG

Gill Hill
☎ **01306 730210**
SC From £130–£270
Sleeps 2/4
♿ ♨ ♞ ♿ ♨ ✂ ☻
♿ ♿ ♿ – ♿ ♿ ♿ ♿
Commended

Two delightfully cosy, single-storey cottages, sympathetically converted from a Surrey barn, forming a courtyard with the farmhouse. Fully carpeted, electric CH, colour TV and linen (beds made up). Communal laundry room, use of 2-acre farmhouse garden. Situated in picturesque, quiet valley. Ideal walking country. "Badgersholt" sleeps 2 (also suitable disabled); "Foxholme" sleeps 4 in 2 bedrooms. Open all year.

11 **Black Cottage,** c/o Newells Farm, Newells Lane, Lower Beeding, Horsham, West Sussex RH13 6LN

Vicky Storey
☎ 01403 891326
SC From £120–£180
Sleeps 4
🐾 🐎 🐕 🐖 🐑
🔑 🔑 🔑
Approved

A delightful secluded cottage in the centre of a sheep and arable farm, with views to the South Downs. Surrounded by woods and lovely walks. Sleeps 4 in comfort. Recently modernised, it is 40 mins from Brighton, 20 mins from Gatwick, with fishing, golf and beautiful Sussex, Surrey and Kent gardens within easy reach. The ideal holiday cottage. Open all year.

---

12 **Boring House Farm,** Vines Cross, Heathfield, East Sussex TN21 9AS

Mrs Anne Reed
☎ 01435 812285
SC From £120–£180
Sleeps 6
🐾 🐎 🐕 🐖 🐑
🔑 🔑 🔑 🔑
Commended

Peaceful farm cottage on sheep and beef farm. Marvellous views and walks, fishing available. Traditional local, good atmosphere/food in easy walking distance. Many beautiful places to visit. Beach within 15 miles. Accommodation (portion of farmhouse) comprises utility room, hall, WC, kitchen, dining room, sitting room, 3 bedrooms, 1 with shower, 1 with washbasin, bathroom and WC. Large garden. Open Mar–Oct.

---

13 **2 High Weald Cottages,** Chelwood Farm, Nutley, c/o Sheffield Park Farm, Nr Uckfield, E Sussex TN22 3QR

Mrs Nicky Howe
☎ 01825 790235/790267
Fax 01825 790151
SC From £150–£300
Sleeps 5 + cot
🐎 🐕
🔑 🔑 🔑 🔑
Highly Commended

Picturesque semi-detached farm cottage with garden on dairy farm adjacent Ashdown Forest. Comfortable accommodation comprises 1 double, 1 twin, 1 single room, bathroom, WC, sitting room (log fire, colour TV, phone), kitchen (fridge/freezer, auto washing machine, tumble dryer, electric cooker). Close Sheffield Park Gardens, Bluebell Railway. Easy reach Downs and coast. Cot/high chair available. Beds made up. No towels or cot linen. Open all year.

---

14 **2 Victoria Cottage,** c/o Hole and Alchorne Farm, Bell Lane, Nutley, East Sussex TN22 3PD

Pauline & Peter Graves
☎ 01825 712475
SC From £145–£250
Sleeps 5
🐎 💼
🔑 🔑 🔑 🔑 *Highly Commended*

A warm welcome awaits you at our comfortable, well-appointed semi-detached cottage, with lovely garden on our dairy farm. Near Ashdown Forest. 3 bedrooms (1 double, 1 twin, 1 single), bathroom, separate WC, sitting room with TV and phone, dining room, kitchen with electric cooker, microwave, fridge, washing machine, tumble dryer. Beds made up. Towels on request. Ideal for visiting South Downs, castles and coast. Open all year.

55

England's South and South East

Kent

Group Contact: *Mrs Rosemarie Bannock* ☎ *01622 812570/Fax 01622 814200*

Kent is very much farming country, but the distinctive features are the many orchards, hop gardens and oast houses to be found in the aptly named 'Garden of England'. The hilly areas like the North Downs and the High Weald contrast with more lowlying parts such as the Low Weald and Romney Marsh. Each area has a distinct character which makes the Kent countryside very varied and attractive. Complementing the countryside are many historic towns and villages, among them the mediaeval port of Sandwich, Tenterden in the Weald with its wide tree-lined High Street, the traditional market town of West Malling, Cranbrook dominated by its splendid windmill, Rochester with its castle and cathedral and the hilltop village of Chilham built around a square and dominated by its castle.

Kent has a wealth of attractions for the visitor. Some of these, such as Dover Castle and Canterbury Cathedral, are well known. But there is much more – Roman remains, castles such as Leeds, Walmer and Deal, fortifications like the series of coastal Martello Towers built as a defence against Napoleon, historic houses like Hever Castle, where Henry VIII courted Anne Boleyn, Churchill's home at Chartwell, Penshurst Place and Knole set in a deer park on the outskirts of Sevenoaks. There are several vineyards open to the public, wildlife parks like Howletts and Port Lympne, the Whitbread Hop Farm, a working farm museum, three steam railways, numerous gardens and various country parks and picnic sites, all ideal for walks or family picnics.

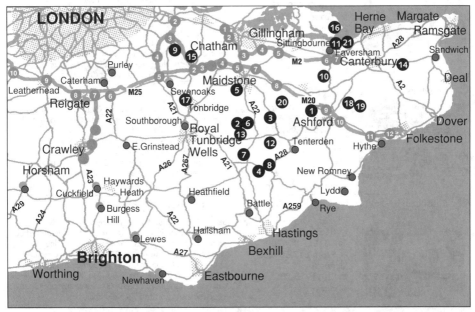

BED AND BREAKFAST

(and evening meal)

---

1 Barnfield, Charing, Ashford, Kent TN27 0BN

Mrs Phillada Pym
☎/Fax 01233 712421
🛏 From £18.50–£20.50
EM From £12.50
Sleeps 6
ॐ ⅍ ⊞ 🛍 ⚟ 🐕 ☂ ✗
Listed *Commended*

Charming Kent Hall farmhouse built in 1420 with a wealth of character amidst 500 acres of peaceful farmland. Convenient for the popular sights of Leeds Castle, Canterbury, Chilham, Sissinghurst and Channel ports. A warm welcome assured with good home cooking. 1 single room, 2 double, 1 twin. Open all year.

---

2 Blackmoor Farm, Sheephurst Lane, The Beech, Marden, Tonbridge, Kent TN12 9NS

Mrs Jean Lutener
☎ 01622 831385/832999
🛏 From £18
Sleeps 4
ॐ (5) ⅍
Listed

Listed 16th century barn attractively converted to high standard, retaining interesting features, family run farm growing strawberries, apples and pears, come and enjoy them. Guest lounge with beams and TV. Many places of interest nearby. 1 hour from London, air and sea ports. Two twin rooms, private bath. Open all year (closed Christmas).

---

3 Bletchenden Manor Farm, Headcorn, Kent TN27 9JB

Mrs Gill Waters
☎ 01622 890228
🛏 From £19.50–£22
Sleeps 6
ॐ (12) ⅍ 🛍
Listed

A warm welcome for guests at our attractive 15th century farmhouse surrounded by own farmland. 2 miles south of Headcorn village, peaceful location in the Weald of Kent. Ideal base for visiting numerous National Trust properties, beautiful gardens, golf courses and excellent pubs in the area. 1 hour train journey to London. 1 double and 2 twin rooms with tea/coffee-making facilities and private bathrooms. Guests' sitting room with TV and a large beamed dining room. Open all year except Christmas.

---

4 Conghurst Farm, Hawkhurst, Kent TN18 4RW

Mrs Rosemary Piper
☎ 01580 753331
Fax 01580 754579
🛏 From £20–£22
EM From £11
Sleeps 6
ॐ (12) 🐎 ⅍ ⚟ 🐕 ☂ 🛍 ✗
🐾 🐾 *Highly Commended*

In the Weald of Kent, an Area of Outstanding Natural Beauty, Conghurst Farm offers a friendly welcome and every comfort in a peaceful, secluded Georgian farmhouse. This is an excellent centre for visiting the many houses and gardens in the vicinity. Walkers will enjoy the unspoilt countryside. Our aim is to help you have a restful break. Open Feb–Nov.

---

5 Court Lodge, Court Lodge Farm, The Street, Teston, Maidstone, Kent ME18 5AQ

Mrs Rosemarie Bannock
☎ 01622 812570
Fax 01622 814200
🛏 From £17.50–£30
Sleeps 6
ॐ (10) ⅍ ⊞ ✗
🐾 🐾 🐾

Set in old-world garden with lovely views of Medway Valley with meadows and orchards. Beautifully furnished with inglenook fireplaces, oak beams and leaded windows. 3 spacious rooms, 2 en suite. Convenient for visiting Leeds Castle, many NT properties and gardens. Easy access, M20 Junction 5, London Heathrow, Gatwick, Channel ports and tunnel. 30–60 minutes by car. Open all year except Christmas & New Year.

Great Cheveney Farm, Great Cheveney, Marden, Tonbridge, Kent TN12 9LX

Mrs Diana Day
☎ 01622 831207
Fax 01622 831786
[BB] From £18
Sleeps 3
✄ ☎ (10) ✿ 🛅
Listed *Highly Commended*

A warm welcome awaits you at Great Cheveney, a 16th century timber-framed farmhouse. Situated on a 300-acre fruit and arable farm, midway between Marden and Goudhurst villages, on the B2079. Excellent base for touring the south east, with its many places of historical interest. 1 double with bath, 1 single with bath. Guests' lounge, TV, large garden, parking. Open all year except Christmas & New Year.

Hallwood Farm, Hawkhurst Road, Cranbrook, Kent TN17 2SP

Ann & David Wickham
☎ 01580 713204
[BB] From £20
EM From £15
Sleeps 6
🐓 ☎ ✄
Listed

We offer peaceful and comfortable accommodation at this 15th century hall house. Spacious garden and ample parking space. Close to Cranbrook, the centre of an area rich in castles, manor houses and interesting gardens. Open April–November.

Hoads Farm, Crouch Lane, Sandhurst, Cranbrook, Kent TN18 5PA

Anne Nicholas
☎/Fax 01580 850296
[BB] From £17
EM From £11
Sleeps 6
☎ ✿ 🛅 ⚘
Listed

Bed and breakfast available in 17th century farmhouse on hop vine and sheep farm. Comfortable furnishings, sitting room with colour TV. Good centre for the coast, Bodiam Castle, Sissinghurst Castle, Scotney Castle and other National Trust properties. Excellent train service to London from Etchingham or Staplehurst. Dinner by arrangement. Dropside cot available on request. Open all year.

Home Farm, Riverside, Eynsford, Nr Dartford, Kent DA4 0AE

Mrs Sarah Alexander
☎ 01322 866193
Fax 01322 868600
[BB] From £18–£30
Sleeps 6
✄ ☎ (10) 🛅 ⚘
🏵🏵 *Highly Commended*

Our 18th century farmhouse is set in the Darenth Valley, an area of outstanding natural beauty, ideal for London, Gatwick and the Channel ports, being only 2 miles from the M25/M20 junction. Leeds Castle, Brands Hatch and many NT properties within easy reach. There is a good selection of places to eat in the village. All bedrooms have en suite facilities. Open Mar–Nov.

Leaveland Court, Leaveland, Faversham, Kent ME13 0NP

Mrs Corrine Scutt
☎ 01233 740596
[BB] From £18–£20
EM From £10
Sleeps 6
☎ 🐓 ✄ 🏠 ✿ 🛅 ⚘
🏵

Captivating 15th century timbered farmhouse on 300-acre downland farm. Easy access, 3 miles south of M2 junction 6, Faversham 5 minutes, Canterbury 20 minutes. Situated in a quiet setting with attractive garden and outdoor heated swimming pool. All rooms have en suite facilities, colour TV and tea/coffee trays. Traditional farmhouse food and warm welcome assured. Brochure available. Open all year.

Pheasant Farm, Church Road, Oare, Faversham, Kent ME13 0QB

Lorna & Neville Huxtable
☎ 01795 535366
[BB] From £17–£20
EM From £12
Sleeps 4
☎ (5) ✄ ⚘
Listed

14th century farmhouse on 210-acre working sheep farm, next to nature reserve and Swale estuary. All rooms are en suite with colour TV, tea/coffee-making facilities. Delightful sheltered garden with heated swimming pool. Ideal for visits to the continent and London. Historic cinque port town of Faversham 1½ miles, Canterbury 8 miles. A warm relaxing home from home. Open all year.

(12) **Sissinghurst Castle Farm,** Sissinghurst, Cranbrook, Kent TN17 2AB

James & Pat Stearns
☎ 01580 712885
[BB] From £19.50–£24
Sleeps 10
🐴 (5) ✂ 🎋 ♨

This Victorian farmhouse with spacious rooms and beautiful views is delightfully situated within the grounds of the famous Sissinghurst Castle Gardens. Ample parking and it only takes a minute to walk to the gardens. Surrounding farm is largely arable with cattle and sheep. Guests' sitting room, lovely garden, reduction long stay. Fire certificate. Prices rise from April. Open all year.

(13) **Tanner House,** Tanner Farm, Goudhurst Road, Marden, Tonbridge, Kent TN12 9ND

Lesley Mannington
☎ 01622 831214
Fax 01622 832472
[BB] From £18–£20
EM From £12
Sleeps 6
✂ 🐴 (5) ♿ 🏕 🔌 ☕ 🎋 ♨

For a restful break, holiday or stop over, we are ideally placed in the beautiful Weald countryside. Our Tudor farmhouse in the centre of our working farm offers high standards of accommodation and cuisine. All our rooms are en suite, one with a genuine four-poster bed, and have colour TV, radio, tea/coffee-making facilities. We specialise in a countryside welcome. Visa/Access/Amex. Open all year except Christmas.

(14) **Wingham Well House,** Wingham, Canterbury, Kent CT3 1NW

Mrs Georgina Maude
☎ 01227 720253
[BB] From £17.50–£22.50
Sleeps 4
🐴 🌳 ✂ 🏕 🔌 🎋 🔋 🎿
Listed

Kentish hall house in quiet countryside on 168-acre farm between Canterbury (Cathedral) and Sandwich (Golf). Channel ports of Ramsgate, Dover and Folkestone and Channel Tunnel half an hour's drive away. One double with en suite bathroom, one twin with washbasin. Open all year except Christmas and New Year.

SELF-CATERING

(15) **Ash Place Farm,** Ash, Sevenoaks, Kent TN15 7HD

Mrs J Scott
☎ 01474 872238
[SC] From £150–£220
Sleeps 4 + cot
🐴 🏕 🎋 🎿
🐾 🐾 🐾 🐾
Commended

Luxury upstairs flat in converted Victorian farmhouse on 500-acre working farm. It comprises of large sitting room, ktichen, bathroom and 2 bedrooms, 1 with double bed, 1 with twin beds. At the top of a quiet road leading only to the farm. There is a large garden and splendid views. Many varied attractions locally and only 28 miles from Central London. Pick your own produce in season. Open all year.

(16) **"Birdwatchers Cottage",** c/o Newhouse Farm, Leysdown-on-Sea, Sheerness, Isle of Sheppey, ME12 4BA

Sally-Anne Marsh
☎ 01795 510201
Fax 01795 880379
[SC] From £160–£330
Sleeps 8 + cot
✂ ♿ 🐴
🐾 🐾 🐾 🐾 *Highly Commended*

Idyllic, well-equipped, quality cottage on a cattle, sheep and arable farm for views, walks and sightseeing. Four bedrooms, CH, large garden. Should suit everyone. Situated between two nature reserves with several local places of interest. Under an hour to Canterbury, Maidstone and Rochester. About fifty miles to London. Ideal touring base and a quiet hideaway. Detailed leaflet available. Open all year.

Golding Hop Farm Cottage, c/o Golding Hop Farm, Bewley Lane, Plaxtol, Nr Sevenoaks, Kent TN15 0PS

Jacqueline Vincent
☎ **01732 885432**
SC **From £110–£240**
Sleeps 5 + cot
🐕 ⅙ 🛆 ▪ ♀️
♻️ ♻️ ♻️ ♻️
Highly Commended

13-acre farm producing Kent cobnuts for London markets. Surrounded by orchards and close to attractive village of Plaxtol. Secluded cottage, but not isolated. Sleeps 5, 2 double and 1 single, CH, colour TV, washer dryer and fridge/freezer, payphone. Horse riding, golf nearby. Car essential. Ample parking. Local station 2 miles with frequent trains to London. Motorway 4 miles. Dogs by arrangement only. Open all year.

Hazel Tree Cottage, Hassell Street, Hastingleigh, Ashford, Kent TN25 5JE

Christine Gorell Barnes
☎ **01233 750324**
SC **From £125–£225**
Sleeps 4 + cot
🛆 ⊕ ♀️
♻️ ♻️ *Commended*

A recently converted barn by a lovely old farmhouse is now an attractive and comfortable cottage for holiday-makers. Surrounded by fields, it has its own garden and terrace, and is ideally situated for sightseeing and exploring coast and countryside, and for day trips to France. Canterbury 9 miles, Folkestone 14 miles. Open all year.

The Old Dairy, Whatsole Street Farm, Elmsted, Nr Ashford, Kent TN25 5JW

Mrs J. D. Browning
☎ **01233 750238**
SC **From £150–£340**
Sleeps 4/5 + cot
🛆 🐾
♻️ ♻️ ♻️
Commended

Converted milking parlour of 16th century origins in one of the most peaceful and secluded parts of Kent completely surrounded by countryside. Good walking area. Own entrance, garden and patio. Canterbury 9 miles, convenient to coast and Continent. Colour TV, microwave, etc. Shop 2 miles. No smoking in bedrooms, no pets. Open Easter– Dec.

Owls Nest, Kingsnoad Farm, Pye Corner, Ulcombe, Nr Maidstone, Kent ME17 1EG

David & Doreen Roe
☎/Fax **01622 858966**
SC **From £135–£295**
Sleeps 6 + cot
🐕 ⅙ 🛆 ♖ ▪ ♀️
♻️ ♻️ ♻️ *Commended*

Converted Victorian milking parlour in truly secluded peaceful farm setting, ½ mile along track between grazing sheep and ripening corn. Fully equipped with continental quilts, colour TV, shower/WC, kitchen, night storage heaters for year round occupation. Cot available. Sit awhile in large, comfortable withdrawing area beneath original oak beams and in front of blazing log fire. An ideal walking/touring base. Open all year.

Pheasant Farm, Church Road, Oare, Faversham, Kent ME13 0QB

Lorna & Neville Huxtable
☎ **01795 535366**
SC **From £203–£252**
EM From £12
Sleeps 2
🛆 (5) ⅙ ♀️
♻️ ♻️ *Highly Commended*

Attractive comfortable well-equipped beamed 14th century annexe to main farmhouse, bedroom, lounge shower, WC and kitchen, all with modern equipment. 210-acre working sheep farm next to nature reserve and Swale estuary. Delightful sheltered garden with heated swimming pool. Ideal for visits to continent and London, Faversham 1½ miles, Canterbury 8 miles. A warm relaxing home from home.

FARM HOLIDAY BUREAU

NO ANSWER?
Farmers are mostly out and about during the day.
Try to telephone before 9.30am or after 4pm.

56

England's South and South East

Isle of Wight

Group Contact: *Mrs Judy Noyes* ☎ *01983 852582*

The Isle of Wight with its sandy beaches and small secluded coves, and the sea never more than 15 minutes from wherever you may be, has a wide variety of holiday activities. With Cowes and the Royal Yacht Squadron, an international symbol of all that is finest in yachting, the Island is famous for its seafaring activities. A climate that tops the British Isles' Sunshine League makes the island particularly attractive in Spring or Autumn for short break holidays.

For the rambler, the birdwatcher, the angler and for those who merely wish to relax beside the splendours of ancient lighthouses or towering chalk cliffs, the Isle of Wight is the ideal holiday retreat with an internationally acclaimed network of well marked footpaths. For the more adventurous, the Island is a haven for hang-gliders, windsurfers, water skiers, canoe enthusiasts and deep sea fishermen.

Attractions for both children and adults include nature reserves, Butterfly World, the IOW Rare Breeds Park, Blackgang Chine with its history of smuggling and shipwrecks, a steam railway featuring some of the earliest steam engines, Roman remains, historic manors, mills, craft centres, and vineyards open for guided tours and wine tasting.

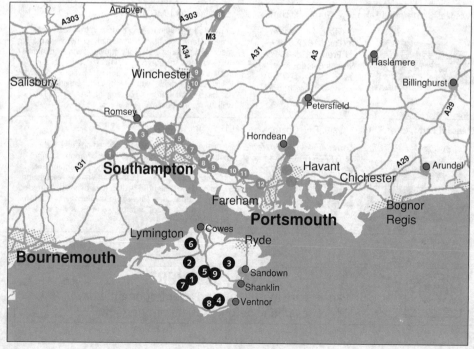

BED AND BREAKFAST
(and evening meal)

Cheverton Farm, Shorwell, Newport, Isle of Wight PO30 3JE

Sheila Hodgson
☎/Fax 01983 741017
[BB] From £14–£18
Sleeps 4
🐴 ⚊ 🏇 🎠
Listed

Enjoy a relaxed and peacefulatmosphere in our listed farmhouse on a sheep, beef and arable farm set in a valley with walks straight onto downland. Pony trekking for children and light adults, clay pigeon shooting and dogs, cats, ponies and poultry to see. large garden, spacious rooms and good local food. Open Easter–October.

Great Park Farm, Betty Haunt Lane, Carisbrooke, Isle of Wight PO30 4HR

Mrs Sheila Brownrigg
☎ 01983 522945
[BB] From £15–£18
Sleeps 6
🐴 (8) 🎠
👑👑
Commended

Come and stay on our arable farm with its lovely old Georgian farmhouse in peaceful surroundings with magnificent views over the solent and downs. Central to all main resorts and good eating places nearby. 3 bedrooms en suite, dining, sitting room for guests, colour TV, tea/coffee-making facilities. Open March–Oct.

Kern Farm, Alverstone, Nr Sandown, Isle of Wight PO36 0EY

Mrs June Collins
☎ 01983 40372
[BB] From £16–£18
Sleeps 4
🐴 ⚊ 🎠
Listed *Commended*

Quiet and secluded 16th century listed stone farmhouse nestling at the foot of the Downs on a livestock farm with wonderful views. Situated on Bembridge Trail. Sandy beaches 3 miles. Two double en suite bedrooms with tea and coffee-making facilities.

Lisle Combe, Bank End Farm, Undercliff Drive, St Lawrence, Ventnor, Isle of Wight PO38 1UW

Hugh & Judy Noyes
☎ 01983 852582
[BB] From £15–£17.50
Sleeps 5
🐴 ⚊
Listed

Listed Elizabethan style farmhouse overlooking English Channel, home of the late Alfred Noyes (poet and author) and his family. 5 acre coastal garden with rare waterfowl and pheasant collection (over 100 species). Surrounded by farmlands for owner's herd of pedigree Friesians, free entry to owner's rare breeds park. Superb sea views, coves and small beaches in area of outstanding natural beauty. Open all year.

Newbarn Farm, Newbarn Lane, Gatcombe, Newport, Isle of Wight PO30 3EQ

Mrs Diane Harvey
☎ 01983 721202
[BB] From £14–£18
Sleeps 4
🐴 ⚊ 🎠
👑*Commended*

17th century farmhouse on a 240-acre arable farm in the small hamlet of Gatcombe in the centre of the island. Wonderful walking area enjoying some spectacular views over the island and south coast. Two bedrooms, one with shower en suite, one with H/C, both with tea-making facilities. Dining room and TV lounge with inglenook fireplace. Open Easter-Oct.

6   **Youngwoods Farm,** Whitehouse Road, Porchfield, Newport, Isle of Wight PO30 4LJ

Judith Shanks
☎ **01983 522170**
▦ **From £14–£17**
Sleeps 5
✂ 🐾 (8) 🏛 🐾
Listed

A grassland farm set in open countryside. The 18th century stone farmhouse, recently renovated, retains its original character. The guest rooms are spacious and enjoy magnificent views of the West Wight (H/C in each room. CH throughout). Close to Newtown Nature Reserve, an ideal base for the naturalist. Wild flowers. Red squirrels, owls and butterflies locally. Cowes sailing centre 4 miles. Open all year.

SELF-CATERING

7   **Cheverton Farm Cottage,** Cheverton Farm, Shorwell, Newport, Isle of Wight PO30 3JE

Sheila Hodgson
☎/Fax **01983 741017**
▣ **From £120–£320**
Sleeps 4
🐾 🐾 ✂ 🐾 🐾
🐾 🐾 🐾 *Commended*

Old 'character' cottage with beamed ceilings throughout attached to main farmhouse on 550-acre sheep, beef and arable farm. Large garden and car parking area. Walking straight onto downs, and pony trekking for children and light adults. Clay pigeon shooting, and dogs, cats ponies and poultry to see. Good food locally, 10 minutes in car to nearest beach. Open all year.

8   **Lisle Combe Cottage,** Bank End Farm, Lisle Combe, Undercliff Drive, St Lawrence, Ventnor, IOW PO38 1UW

Hugh & Judy Noyes
☎ **01983 852582**
▣ **From £130–£240**
Sleeps 5/6
🐾
🐾 🐾 *Approved*

Listed cottage overlooking English Channel. Own garden within grounds of Lisle Combe. Large pheasant and waterfowl collection, free entry to owner's rare breed park. Many small beaches and coves for swimming or sunbathing. Colour TV, everything provided except linen. Fine coastal walks in area of outstanding natural beauty. Surrounded by 180-acre family farm with pedigree Friesian herd. Open all year.

9   **The Old Brewhouse,** Newbarn Farm, Newbarn Lane, Gatcombe, Newport, Isle of Wight PO30 3EQ

Mrs Diane Harvey
☎ **01983 721202**
▣ **From £120–£350**
Sleeps 4/5
🐾 ✂ 🏛
🐾 🐾 🐾 *Commended*

Formerly a brewhouse and dairy, attached to the 17th century farmhouse on a 240-acre mainly arable farm in a secluded valley. Lawned garden, patio and parking area. Excellent downland and lowland walking. Centrally situated for all attractions and beaches. Linen and electricity included. Beds made up on arrival. Open all year.

LET THE TELEPHONE RING!
Some farmhouses are big places. Let the telephone ring long enough to give the owner time to answer it.

57

England's West Country

Bath and Wells

Group Contact: *Mrs Jane Rowe* ☎ *01761 241294*

This area has a wealth of history going back to prehistoric times. The Druid Stones near Pensford are 600 years older than Stonehenge and there's always been a touch of magic and mystery in the air around Glastonbury, the ancient town and legendary Isle of Avalon, where it is rumoured King Arthur and his queen were buried.

The visitor is within easy striking distance of the beautiful city of Bath with its Regency architecture and older vestiges of civilisation like the Roman Baths. The whole town is alive with shops and pavement cafés. Another city within easy reach is Bristol, renowned as one of the world's leading ports. With Clifton Zoo, museums, theatres and marvellous shops, it's a visitor's delight. At the famous Wookey Hole Caves you can see the Witch of Wookey and visit a cave chamber in which the acoustics are said to be near perfection. Looking from Ebbor Gorge you will see what must be one of the grandest views in the world.

Interested in wine? There are two vineyards at Pilton and North Wootton where you can taste the local brew. And, of course, if you fancy something stronger, there is always the famous Somerset cider.

With the famous gorge and caves at Cheddar, the lovely cathedral city of Wells and the Mendip Hills, you will be spoilt for choice.

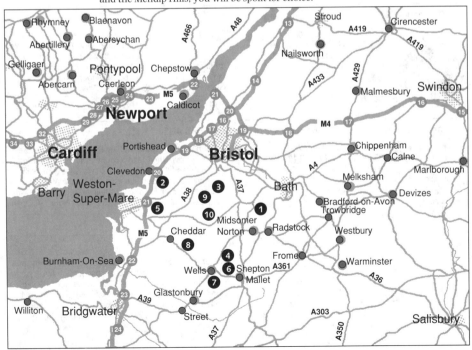

BED AND BREAKFAST

(and evening meal)

---

1 Barrow Vale Farm, Farmborough, Bath, Avon BA3 1BL

Cherilyn Langley
☎ 01761 470300
🛏 From £16
Sleeps 6
🐕 (3) ✂ 🏕
♛

Barrow Vale is a family-run dairy farm, situated between the historic cities of Bath and Wells. The farmhouse, which has been comfortably modernised, offers central heating, well furnished en suite bedrooms and guests lounge with TV. It is within easy reach of places of interest with local pubs and restaurants close by. Open all year (except Christmas and New Year).

---

2 Icelton Farm, Wick-St-Lawrence, Weston-super-Mare, Avon BS22 0YJ

Mrs Elizabeth Parsons
☎ 01934 515704
🛏 From £14–£16
Sleeps 5
🐕 (2) 🏕
Listed

Icelton is a working dairy/sheep farm, just off the M5 (jct. 21). Ideal for touring Wells, Cheddar, and Mendip Hills. This listed farmhouse offers double room with H/C, family room with H/C and shower. Tea/coffee-making facilities. Oak-beamed dining room and lounge, both with inglenook fireplaces. English breakfast. Good pubs and restaurants close at hand. No dogs. Open Mar–Nov.

---

3 The Model Farm, Norton Malreward, Pensford, Bristol, Avon BS18 4HA

Margaret Hasell
☎ 01275 832144
🛏 From £16–£18
Sleeps 6
🐕
♛

The farmhouse is situated 2 miles off the A37 in a peaceful hamlet, nestling under the Dundry Hills. A working arable and beef farm in easy reach of Bristol, Bath, and many other interesting places. The accommodation consists of 1 family room en suite and 1 double room with washbasin. Guests' lounge and dining room. Open Feb–Nov.

---

4 Pantiles, Bathway, Chewton Mendip, Nr Bath, Somerset BA3 4NS

Pat Hellard
☎ 01761 241519
🛏 From £16–£18
Sleeps 6
🐕 ✂ 🐕
♛♛ *Highly Commended*

A warm welcome awaits at Pantiles, an attractive house with views over the Mendip countryside. Only 15 miles from Bath and Bristol, 5 miles to the lovely city of Wells. Our aim is quality B&B at reasonable prices. We offer 3 bedrooms, 1 double en suite, 1 twin en suite, 1 twin with private bath, all with hospitality tray and colour TV. Open all year.

---

5 Purn House Farm, Bleadon, Weston-super-Mare, Avon BS24 0QE

Thelma Moore
☎/Fax 01934 812324
🛏 From £16–£20
EM From £7
Sleeps 18–20
🐕 🏹 ✂ ♿ 🐕 🏕 🏺
♛♛

Approved

Peaceful 17th century farmhouse set at foot of Mendips. Five family rooms, some en suite, one ground floor, games room. Food home-grown on 700 acre farm. Pretty garden. Good fishing available in River Axe which flows through the farm. Riding nearby. Ideal base for visiting Cheddar Gorge, Wookey Hole, Wells and Glastonbury. Open Feb–Dec.

Redhill Farm, Emborough, Nr Bath, Somerset BA3 4SH   (6)

Jane Rowe
☎ 01761 241294
BB From £15–£20
Sleeps 6
Listed

Our listed farmhouse built in Cromwellian times is situated high on the Mendips between Bath and Wells. It is the perfect centre for outdoor activities and sightseeing. We are a working smallholding with a variety of animals to delight the children. CH. Guests' private bathroom. Fresh home produce. Tea/coffee-making facilities and washbasins in bedrooms. No dogs. Bath and West show ground 7 miles. Open all year.

Southway Farm, Polsham, Wells, Somerset BA5 1RW   (7)

Anita Frost
☎ 01749 673396
BB From £16–£17
Sleeps 6
ᕦ ᵻ
🐦 Commended

A Georgian listed farmhouse situated halfway between Wells and Glastonbury overlooking Somerset levels and cider orchard. Accommodation is 3 comfortable and attractively furnished bedrooms, 1 with private bathroom, a delicious full English breakfast is served. Guests may relax in the cosy lounge or pretty garden. Ideal location for touring the glorious West Country. Open Mar–Nov.

Tor Farm, Nyland, Cheddar, Somerset BS27 3UD   (8)

Mrs Caroline Ladd
☎ 01934 743710
BB From £15–£21.50
Sleeps 18
🐴 ♿ ⚑ ᵻ
🐦 Highly Commended

Tor Farm is situated on the beautiful Somerset levels and has open views from every window. The farmhouse is licensed and is fully centrally heated, with tea/coffee-making facilities in all rooms. Some rooms have full en suite and private patios. One four-poster room. From Cheddar, take A371 towards Wells. After 2 miles, turn right, signposted Nyland. Tor Farm is on the right, after 1½ miles. Open all year (closed Christmas).

Valley Farm, Sandy Lane, Stanton Drew, Nr. Bristol, Avon BS18 4EL   (9)

Mrs Doreen Keel
☎ 01275 332723
BB From £15
Sleeps 6
🐴 ✗ 🏕 ᵻ ☕ ♨ ⚑
🐦🐦 Highly Commended

Modern farmhouse situated on the edge of an ancient village near the river Chew with Druid Stones and many footpaths to walk. Near the Chew Valley Lakes renowned for trout fishing and in easy reach of Bath, Bristol, Wells and Cheddar. Stanton Drew is off A368 Bath to Weston-super-Mare road or the B3130 road. There are 2 rooms with double beds each with wash basins and coffee/tea making facilities. 2 en suite and 1 private bathroom. Open all year (except Christmas).

Woodbarn Farm, Denny Lane, Chew Magna, Bristol, Avon BS18 8SZ   (10)

Mrs Judi Hasell
☎ 01275 332599
BB From £17–£20
Sleeps 6
✗ 🐴 (3) ᵻ
🐦🐦

Woodbarn is a working mixed farm. 5 minutes from Chew Valley Lake. Chew Magna is a large village with pretty cottages, Georgian houses and is central for touring. There are two en suite bedrooms, one double and one family, all with tea trays. Guests' lounge and dining room. Cream teas Sundays June–September. Open Mar–Dec (closed Christmas).

58

England's West Country

Bath and Wiltshire

Group Contacts: 🆖 *Mrs Marlene Nixon* ☎ *01380 828355*
🆖 *Mrs Janet Tyler* ☎ *01380 850523*

Easily accessible within 100 miles of London, the Midlands and the sea, Wiltshire offers the best of rural England, the marvellous scenery is its biggest surprise. Almost half the county is designated as an 'Area of Outstanding Natural Beauty'.

The wide peaceful downland is rich in historic interest: Stonehenge, Avebury and Silbury Hill stand out on the rolling green plain, with picturesque villages hidden away along the chalk stream valleys. Castle Combe and the National Trust village of Lacock are well known, but there are scores more waiting to be discovered. Six hundred years of building are displayed in the magnificent collection of historic homes, i.e. Longleat, Bowood House and Corsham Court and Sheldon Manor.

Walk the ancient Ridgeway Path, an important nomadic and trading route, or the Kennet and Avon Canal now restored along much of its route. Just over the county border the Romans built their city around the hot springs, and eleven centuries later Georgian architects created the elegant city of Bath. Whether you just stop for a short break or longer, the people of Wiltshire will welcome you.

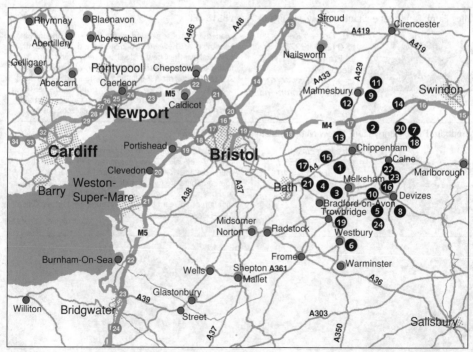

BED AND BREAKFAST
(and evening meal)

Boyds Farm, Gastard, Nr Corsham, Wiltshire SN13 9PT

Dorothy Robinson
☎ 01249 713146
▣ From £15–£16
Sleeps 6
🐴 ⅃ 🌲 💼
👑 *Commended*

Enjoy a relaxing stay on our arable farm situated in the peace and tranquillity of the unspoilt Wiltshire countryside. Our delightful 16th century farmhouse, as featured by the Daily Express, accommodates families, couples and individuals, CH, H/C, tea/coffee-making facilities. Guests' own lounge with woodburning stove. Easy access to M4, Bath, Lacock, Castle Combe, Stonehenge, Bradford-on-Avon. Excellent pub food close by. Open all year.

Friday Street Farm, Christian Malford, Chippenham, Wiltshire SN15 4BU

Linda Di Claudio
☎ 01249 720146
▣ From £16–£17.50
EM From £6.50
Sleeps 4
🐴 ⅃ 🌲 💼 ✕
👑 *Commended*

Welcome to our 200-acre working dairy farm. Our part 17th century farmhouse offers guests a winning combination – a lovely house with country cottage cosiness, excellent decor, delicious homecooked meals and large mature gardens. Two attractive en suite bedrooms equipped with TV, radio and hospitality tray. Ideally situated midway between Bath and the Cotswolds. Open all year.

Frying Pan Farm, Broughton Gifford Road, Melksham, Wiltshire SN12 8LL

Barbara Pullen
☎ 01225 702343
▣ From £17.50
Sleeps 4
⅃ 🐴 (2)
👑👑

Frying Pan Farm is a stock rearing farm which is situated 1 mile from Melksham, making it ideally positioned for visiting Bath, Bradford-on-Avon, Lacock and many National Trust properties. The house is a 17th century Grade 2 listed building, with cosy accommodation consisting of 1 double en suite, and 1 twin with tea/coffee-making facilities. Open all year (closed Christmas & New Year).

Hatt Farm, Old Jockey, Box, Nr Bath, Wiltshire SN14 9DJ

Mrs Carol Pope
☎ 01225 742989
▣ From £15–£17.50
Sleeps 4
🐴 ⅃ 🌲 💼
👑👑 *Commended*

Enjoy the comfort of our family home in peaceful surroundings with beautiful views of the Wiltshire countryside. The farmhouse was built during the Georgian 'hey day' of Bath, just off the old coaching road from London. Many NT properties, picturesque villages and historical sites are within easy distance. One twin with en suite shower, one double/family with private bathroom, both with tea/coffee facilities, CH. Guests' lounge, log fire in winter. Closed Christmas.

Higher Green Farm, Poulshot, Devizes, Wiltshire SN10 4RW

Marlene & Malcolm Nixon
☎ 01380 828355
▣ From £15
Sleeps 6
🐓 ⅃ 🐴
Listed

Listed 17th century timbered farmhouse facing south onto village green close to a traditional inn. This is a 140 acre working dairy farm situated between Bath and Salisbury, 3 miles from Devizes and within easy reach of many National Trust properties. Tea-making facilities, guests' lounge, colour TV. Double, twin and 2 single rooms, 2 bathrooms, 2 toilets. Open Mar–Nov.

6 **Hillside Farm,** Edington, Westbury, Wilts BA13 4PG

Carol Mussell
☎/Fax 01380 830437
BB From £15–£17
Sleeps 4
🐕
⬛ Commended

A warm welcome and wonderful views are yours on our small working farm nestled under the edge of Salisbury Plain. We have one double/family room and one twin room each with wash basins, colour TV and hospitaliy tray. Lovely conservatory for guests' use. Within easy reach of Bath and NT properties. Closed Christmas & January.

---

7 **Little Cotmarsh Farm,** Broad Town, Wootton Bassett, Swindon, Wiltshire SN4 7RA

Mary Richards
☎ 01793 731322
or 0831 090584
BB From £15–£18
Sleeps 6
✄ 🐕
Listed *Commended*

300 year old farmhouse with inglenook and beams situated 4 miles south of M4 J16 in peaceful hamlet. Comfortable attractive bedrooms with washbasins, one with toilet/shower en suite. All have tea/coffee-making facilities, heating and colour TV. Equal distance from Bath, Cotswolds and Oxford. Excellent amenities for wet days in and around Swindon. Good pub food locally. Open all year.

---

8 **Longwater Park Farm,** Lower Road, Erlestoke, Nr Devizes, Wiltshire SN10 5UE

Pam Hampton
☎/01380 830095
BB From £20
EM From £11
Sleeps 12
🐕🦽☺🐾🐕
⛺🏠
⬛⬛⬛ Commended

A peaceful retreat overlooking our own lakes and parkland with 2½ acre waterbird area. 160-acre organic farm with rare sheep & cattle. Family suite, double/twin rooms all en suite. TV and tea-making facilities, CH. 2 ground floor bedrooms. Spacious lounge, large conservatory, separate dining room. Traditional farmhouse fayre using local produce. Special diets. Local wines. Coarse fishing. Erlestoke Sands Golf Course adjacent. Open all year except Christmas and New Year.

---

9 **Lovett Farm,** Little Somerford, Nr Malmesbury, Wiltshire SN15 5BP

Susan Barnes
☎ 01666 823268
BB From £15–£17
Sleeps 5
🐕⛺🏠
Listed *Commended*

Our comfortable modern farmhouse on a small working farm has delightful country views and is situated on the edge of Malmesbury, England's oldest borough. Ideal base for visiting Bath, Cotswolds, Bristol and Stonehenge. One double en suite, one twin with washbasin, tea/coffee-making facilities, radio and colour TV. Full CH, guests' lounge, dining room with traditional log fire. Open all year.

---

10 **Lower Foxhanger Canal Farm,** Rowde, Devizes, Wiltshire SN10 1SS

Cynthia & Colin Fletcher
☎/Fax 01380 828254
BB From £14.50–£16.50
Sleeps 6
🐕🐕⛺ (touring & static) ☺ ⛺ 🏠
⬛⬛ Commended

Tranquillity awaits you by the canal adorned with gaily painted narrow boats. Assist boats through locks. Scenic walks to pubs. Fish and boat to heart's desire. Twin (en suite) double/family rooms in 18th century farmhouse. Self-catering in orchard alongside canal. Small campsite with toilet/shower and electricity. Open Apr–Oct.

---

11 **Lower Stonehill Farm,** Charlton, Malmesbury, Wiltshire SN16 9DY

Mrs Edna Edwards
☎ 01666 823310
BB From £14–£20
Sleeps 6
🐕🐕
Listed

Large old Cotswold stone house on 180-acre dairy farm in a quiet location 3 miles from Malmesbury and 8 miles from the M4. Ideal for touring – visit antique shops in market towns, stately houses and gardens, village pubs or just relax on the lawn and enjoy farm life. Three comfortable rooms available, 1 en suite. Pets and children will enjoy the relaxed, friendly atmosphere. Open all year.

Manor Farm, Corston, Malmesbury, Wiltshire SN16 0HF

Mrs Ross Eavis
☎ 01666 822148
or 0374 675783
🛏 From £16–£20
Sleeps 12
🐕 ♿ ■
👥 Commended

A warm welcome awaits you at our 17th century Cotswold stone farmhouse on a working dairy/arable farm. Single, twin, double and family rooms, three en suite all with colour TV, hospitality tray. Guests' lounge. Large gardens. Good pub food 200 yards down the road. Convenient for M4 and visiting Cotswolds, Bath, Lacock and Avebury. Open all year.

Oakfield Farm, Easton Piercy Lane, Yatton Keynell, Chippenham, Wiltshire SN14 6JU

Mrs Margaret Read
☎ 01249 782355
🛏 From £15
Sleeps 6
🐕 🐈 ⅄
Listed Commended

Friendly welcome in Cotswold stone farmhouse with fine views over open countryside. On working livestock farm in a quiet location, excellent for wildlife. One en suite double/family room, 1 double and 1 twin room. Full central heating, tea/coffee-making facilities, colour TV. Ideal base for visiting Bath, Castle Combe, Lacock and the Cotswolds. Open Mar–Nov.

Olivemead Farm, Dauntsey, Nr Chippenham, Wiltshire SN15 4JQ

Suzanne Candy
☎ 01666 510205
🛏 From £14–£17
Sleeps 6
🐕 🐈
👥 Commended

Relax and enjoy the warm, informal hospitality at our charming 18th century farmhouse on a working dairy farm. Twin, double, family rooms, washbasins, colour TV, tea/coffee facilities. Generous breakfasts. Oak beamed dining room/lounge for guests' exclusive use. Large garden, play area, cot, highchair. Convenient M4, Bath, Cotswolds, Salisbury.

Pickwick Lodge Farm, Corsham, Wiltshire SN13 0PS

Gill Stafford
☎ 01249 712207
🛏 From £16–£20
Sleeps 6
🐕 (8) ⅄ 🐈 ■ ⚒
Listed Commended

Our farm lies g mile off the A4 between Chippenham and Bath. Ideally situated for visiting NT properties, Wiltshire, White Horses, Avebury, Stonehenge. Enjoy walking the varied and interesting footpaths or relax in our peaceful garden. Our 17th century farmhouse has oak beams, open fires, CH. Two cosy double and 1 twin, all with private bathroom or shower room, colour TV, tea/coffee-making facilities. Full English breakfast using local produce.

Poulshot Lodge Farm, Poulshot, Devizes, Wiltshire SN10 1RQ

Diana Hues
☎ 01380 828255
🛏 From £16–£18
Sleeps 4
🐕 (2)
Listed

Friendly, working mixed farm in the picturesque village of Poulshot. Ideally situated for easy access to Lacock, Bath, Avebury and many other places of interest. Two twin rooms with tea/coffee making facilities. Own lounge with TV. Close to Kennet and Avon Canal. Excellent pub food close by. Open Mar–Nov.

Saltbox Farm, Drewetts Mill, Box, Corsham, Wiltshire SN14 9PT

Mary Gregory
☎ 01225 742608
🛏 From £15
Sleeps 4
🐈 ⅄ 🐕 🕊 ⚒ ■
👥 Commended

Quietly located 1 mile off A4 6 miles from Bath and centrally situated for touring the West Country. Our listed 18th century farmhouse is set in the unspoilt Box Valley, offering scenic walks in a wildlife and conservation area. Double and twin/family bedrooms with washbasins, tea/coffee-making facilities. Guests' bathroom. Visitors lounge/diner with colour TV, CH. Reduced rates for 3/4 day breaks. Open all year except Christmas & New Year.

18 **Smiths Farm,** Bushton, Swindon, Wiltshire SN4 7PX

Dee Freeston
☎ **01793 731285**
BB **From £16–£18**
Sleeps 5
🐕 🕿 🛏 ☂ ✿
Listed *Commended*

Uneven floors, old latch doors, beams in and out, history throughout. A garden to browse, fields for to roam – most important of all, Smiths Farm is our home. Welcome to our dairy and beef farm, to cosy double and family rooms, all with CH, H & C, TV and tea/coffee trays. Excellent pub food 5 minutes' walk; easy drive to M4, Cotswolds, Bath, Marlborough, Swindon. Open all year.

19 **Spiers Piece Farm,** Steeple Ashton, Nr Trowbridge, Wiltshire BA14 6HG

Jill Awdry
☎ **01380 870266**
BB **From £14–£16**
Sleeps 6
🐕 🛏 ♿
🍴 *Highly Commended*

Follow a treasure trail and find a warm welcome to our spacious Georgian farmhouse with its fantastic views and family-run arable and stock farm. Take A350 from Melksham, follow the Keevil Airfield signs and find us within easy reach of many tourist attractions. Two doubles and a twin-bedded room with washbasins. Tea/coffee-making facilities and CH. Guests' lounge and bathroom. Open Feb–Nov (incl).

20 **Tockenham Court Farm,** Tockenham, Nr Swindon, Wiltshire SN4 7PH

Mrs Elizabeth Bennett
☎ **01793 852315**
BB **From £18–£20**
Sleeps 6
🐕 🛏
Listed *Commended*

A warm welcome will await you at our traditional Grade II listed 16th century court house. We have 2 double rooms, one twin bedded room, CH, tea/coffee-making facilities and colour TV. Separate shower room and WC, separate bathroom and WC. Guests' own sitting room.

SELF-CATERING

21 **Bannerdown View Farm Cottages,** Bannerdown View Farm, Ashley Road, Bathford, Bath, Avon BA1 7TS

Heather Sully
☎ **01225 859363**
SC **From £150–£300**
Sleeps 4/5
🐕 🔥 🍴 ☂ ♿
🔑 🔑 🔑 🔑 *Commended*

Beautiful stone barn converted to very high standard. Laundry/payphone, large shared garden with furniture,BBQ set in lovely countryside, easy reach of Bath, approx 3½ miles, Bradford-on-Avon with its Saxon church and tythe barn, also Kennet canal, many National Trust properties within 10 miles. Good selection of pubs to eat out, stabling for own horse, logs for winter lets. Baby sitting by prior arrangement. Regret no pets. Open all year.

22 **The Derby,** Court Farm Stables, Heddington, Nr Calne, Wiltshire SN11 0PL

Mrs Janet Tyler
☎ **01380 850523**
SC **From £130–£195**
Sleeps 2
🐕 🍴
🔑 🔑 🔑 🔑 *Commended*

The Derby is a bungalow-style stable conversion set in idyllic surroundings on a secluded and level site, approached over a paved courtyard with Victorian lamp and wishing well. Traditionally furnished, ideal for two people. Full central heating, open fireplace, colour TV, microwave, washing machine and dryer. Garage. Linen included. Open all year.

Home Farm Barn, Home Farm, Heddington, Nr Calne, Wiltshire SN11 0PL

Mrs Janet Tyler
☎ 01380 850523
🆂 From £150–£325
Sleeps 5
🐄 🐕
🗝 🗝 🗝 🗝 *Commended*

Home Farm is a dairy and arable farm with its own private lake, panoramic views and unbeatable downland walks in small village. Riding school and golf course adjoins farm. The 17th century barn retains all its original roof timbers and beams thus providing immense character, 3 bedrooms, colour TV, wood burning stove. Full CH. Linen included. Washing machine, dryer and microwave. Open all year.

Park Farm Cottage, Lower Road, Erlestoke, Devizes, Wiltshire SN10 5UE

Pam Hampton
☎ 01380 830095
Fax 01380 830095
🆂 From £200–£375
Sleeps 7 + cot
🐄 🐎 🍴 🐕 ☂ 🍴
🗝 🗝 🗝 🗝 🗝 🗝
Highly Commended

A 'country retreat', adjacent to lakes. Traditionally furnished, every facility including en suite bedrooms, large gardens and garage. Meals available in farmhouse (400 yds). Ideal for walking, coarse fishing, golf or exploring Bath, Salisbury, Stonehenge, Avebury, Kennet and Avon Canal, Longleat or just relaxing! Open all year.

Stonehill Farm, Charlton, Malmesbury, Wiltshire SN16 9DY

11

Mrs Edna Edwards
☎ 01666 823310
🆂 From £110–£230
Sleeps 2/3
🐄 🐎
🗝 🗝 🗝 *Commended*

Stonehill is a family-run dairy farm on the Wilts/Glos border, 3 miles from Malmesbury and 8 miles M4. The Cow Byre and Bull Pen are converted cowsheds, comfortably furnished with double bed, bathroom, fitted kitchen/diner and lounge. Full CH, colour TV, microwave, all power and linen included. Facing south-west with gravel patio and garden chairs. Open all year.

FARM HOLIDAY BUREAU

THOSE LITTLE EXTRAS

For advice on farms that can offer 'extras' such as four-poster beds, special diets, farm trails, fishing rights – even stabling and trekking arrangements if you are bringing your own horse – ring the Farm Holiday Bureau on (01203) 696909.

FARM HOLIDAY BUREAU

DISABLED VISITORS

Many members offer a welcome to disabled/less able visitors. Please do check the extent of the facilities before booking.

59

England's West Country

Heart of Dorset

Group Contact: *Rosemary Coleman* ☎ *01305 848252*

The Heart of Dorset Group offers you a range of holiday accommodation in the Dorset countryside. It is an area of outstanding natural beauty renowned for its beautiful villages, magnificent hills and lovely valleys.

Wherever you stay, the coast is but a short distance away with excellent swimming, sailing and fishing. For the country lover, the area has a wide choice of forest trails, coastal and inland walks, ancient monuments, historic houses and gardens. Dorset's mild climate makes it an ideal location for a holiday all year round.

Dorset's most famous son, Thomas Hardy, was born within three miles of Dorchester; his rambling cottage, Higher Bockhampton is open to the public. Most of his books were based on villages and towns in the area, many of which still retain the rural atmosphere of Hardy's Wessex.

A romantic figure of more modern times is Lawrence of Arabia, who spent a number of reclusive years in his remote and rather bleak cottage, Clouds Hill, near Bovington Camp.

Corfe Castle, Brownsea Island, Lulworth Cove, Durdle Door ... even the Tolpuddle Martyrs' Museum are all here – you'll need more than a few days to discover Dorset!

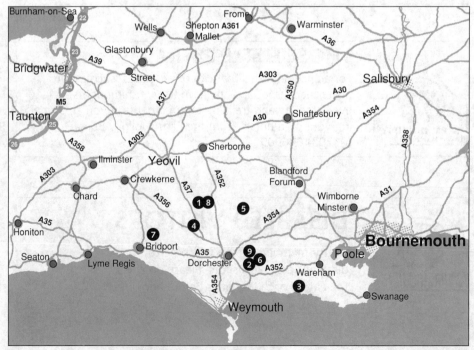

BED AND BREAKFAST
(and evening meal)

Lamperts Farmhouse, 11 Dorchester Road, Sydling St Nicholas, Dorchester, Dorset DT2 9NU

Mrs Rita Bown
☎ 01300 341790
BB From £18
EM From £10
Sleeps 5

Enjoy home comforts in our thatched farmhouse in the unspoilt village of Sydling St Nicholas. Ideal for walking or touring. 1 double family room, 1 twin room, both with en suite bathroom. Guests' own lounge with inglenook fireplace, colour TV, tea/coffee-making facilities. Full CH. Open all year.

Lower Lewell Farmhouse, West Stafford, Dorchester, Dorset DT2 8AP

Marian Tomblin
☎ 01305 267169
BB From £15
Sleeps 6

Situated in the Frome Valley, four miles from Dorchester, this old historic farmhouse is reputed to be the Talbothays Dairy of Hardy's novel 'Tess of the D'Urbervilles'. Ideally situated for exploring the beautiful countryside and coast. Three bedrooms, washbasins, tea/coffee-making facilities. Guests' sitting room. Central heating. Ample parking. A warm welcome awaits you at Lower Lewell. Open all year.

Newlands Farm, West Lulworth, Wareham, Dorset BH20 5PU

Mrs Lesley Simpson
☎ 01929 400376
Fax 01929 400536
BB From £18–£20
Sleeps 6

Listed *Commended*

Newlands was built in the early 19th century and the farm has beautiful views of the sea and the distant Purbeck Hills. The beach is within walking distance. Well placed for coastal footpaths with water sports available within 15 miles and horse riding nearby. 2 double/family rooms with tea/coffee-making facilities and colour TV. Showers and washbasins en suite. Breakfast is served in the dining room. Regret no dogs. Open all year (closed Christmas).

The Stables, Hyde Crook, Frampton, Dorset DT2 9NW

Jacobina (Coba) Langley
☎ 01300 320075
BB From £16.50–£17
Sleeps 5

Large, attractive equestrian property with extensive grounds and woods and lovely views. Comfortable sitting room with wood fire and colour TV. One double, one twin, one single all with wash basins and tea/coffee facilities. Very good breakfast, evening meals by arrangement. Well behaved pets welcome. Open all year.

SELF-CATERING

---

⑤ Eastfield, c/o Mill Cottage, Bramblecombe Farm, Melcombe Bingham, Dorchester, Dorset DT2 7QA

Mrs Noel Hosford
☎ **01258 880248**
ⓈⒸ **From £100–£375**
Sleeps 7 + cot
🐎 🐓 ☂
🐾 🐾 🐾 🐾 *Approved*

Eastfield is set in beautiful rolling country on our dairy farm 4 miles North A354 in mid-Dorset. The farm and surrounding area is rich in wildlife, ideal for naturalists, walkers and families with young children. Secluded detached farm cottage set in own attractive garden with swing and sandpit. It is comfortably furnished with CH, 4 bedrooms, all on one floor. Open all year.

---

⑥ Glebe Cottage, c/o Glebe House, Moreton, Dorchester, Dorset DT2 8RQ

Carol Gibbens
☎ **01929 462468**
ⓈⒸ **From £120–£230**
Sleeps 4
♿ 🐓
Applied

Glebe Cottage is set in an old rectory garden in the peaceful farming village of Moreton, famous for its church windows engraved by Laurence Whistler and burial place of Lawrence of Arabia. It is a wildlife haven. The cottage is detached, is on one floor with 2 double bedrooms, kitchen, living room, bathroom, night storage heating and has its own garden. Open all year.

---

⑦ Gore Cottage, West Milton, Bridport, Dorset DT6 3SN. c/o Wingham Well Farm, Wingham, Canterbury, CT3 1NW

Georgina Maude
☎ **01227 720253**
ⓈⒸ **From £165–£275**
Sleeps 5
🐓 🐓 ☂ 🐾
🐾 🐾 *Approved*

Listed Grade II detached stone-built thatched cottage in own secluded garden on the edge of the village of West Milton. 1 double, 1 twin, 1 single, sitting room, dining/kitchen, tiny bathroom, separate WC and washbasin. The sea is about 5 miles away. Among other attractions are the Swannery at Abbotsbury and the Tropical Garden, Maiden Castle, Cerne Abbas (The Giant), Athelhampton and RAF Yeovilton. Open all year.

---

⑧ Lamperts Farmhouse, 11 Dorchester Road, Sydling St St Nicholas, Dorchester, Dorset DT2 9NU

Mrs Rita Bown
☎ **01300 341790**
ⓈⒸ **From £100–£220**
Sleeps 2 + cot
🐓 🐕
🐾 🐾 *Approved*

16th century wing of Lamperts Farmhouse recently refurbished as a cottage for 2 people. Snugly tucked away between the hills of the beautiful Sydling Valley right in the heart of Dorset. Fitted kitchen, sitting room with French window opening onto secluded garden. Colour TV, downstairs bathroom, double bedroom, full CH. Open all year.

---

⑨ Old Dairy Cottage and Clyffe Dairy Cottage, c/o Clyffe Farm, Tincleton, Dorchester, Dorset DT2 8QR

Rosemary Coleman
☎ **01305 848252**
ⓈⒸ **From £140–£325**
Sleeps 6 + 3
🐓 🐕 ☂ 🛍
🐾 🐾 🐾 *Commended*

Two attractively furnished character cottages with beams and inglenook fireplaces. The mixed farm has cows, calves, horses, and beautiful woodland walks. Ducks and wildlife on the pond and streams. Tennis and fishing. Ideal cycling countryside, within easy reach coast, golf, trekking, leisure centre for swimming etc. Excellent value low season with OAP reductions and winter breaks. CH. Cottages within walking distance of each other. Open all year.

60

England's West Country

Dorset

Group Contacts: BB *Mrs Sally Wingate-Saul* ☎ *01258 817348*
SC *Mrs Hilary Hoskin* ☎ *01305 262356*

Come and explore Dorset with its delightful villages in the west of the county, the dairy pastureland of Blackmore Vale in the north, scenic Cranborne Chase in the east and the Purbeck Hills around Corfe Castle in the south.

The unspoilt countryside so vividly described by the author, Thomas Hardy is still unchanged in places – rolling downland and fertile valleys with picturesque villages of mellow stone and thatched cottages.

For a day out, travel to Salisbury and Winchester Cathedrals, or the theatres and other attractions of major resorts like Bournemouth and Poole. Dartmoor lies to the west and the New Forest to the east, both within easy reach. Sea trips for fishing or pleasure can be made from many of the ports along the coast.

Summer is not the only season in which to savour this delightful area. Winters are mild on the South Coast and spring and autumn are particularly good times for a Dorset holiday. The footpath network is unsurpassed, both inland and along the coast. The Coastal Way, in particular, offers dramatic and exciting scenery, as safe and sandy beaches give way to shifting banks of shingle and rugged cliffs teeming with birds. Historic houses, famous gardens, exciting coastline – you name it, Dorset has it!

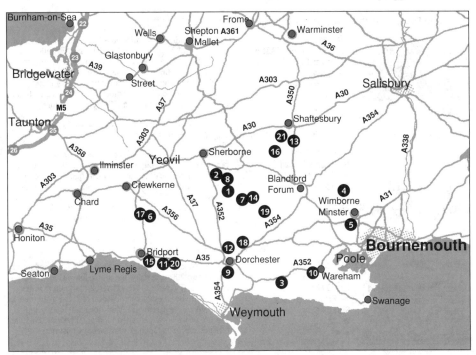

BED AND BREAKFAST

(and evening meal)

---

(1) Almshouse Farm, Hermitage, Sherborne, Dorset DT9 6HA

Mrs Jenny Mayo
☎ 01963 210296
🅱 From £16
Sleeps 6

This charming old farmhouse – formerly a 16th century monastery – was restored in 1849. Surrounded by 140 acres, overlooking the Blackmore Vale. Accommodation in three double rooms with H&C, (one with private bathroom), and tea/coffee-making facilities. Dining room with inglenook fireplace, comfortable sitting room. Garden available to guests at all times. Sherborne 6 miles, Dorchester 14 miles. Open Jan–Dec.

---

(2) Church Farm, Stockwood, Nr Dorchester, Dorset DT2 0NG

Mrs Ruth House
☎ 01935 83221
🅱 From £18–£20
Sleeps 6

Highly Commended

Beautiful Georgian farmhouse idyllically set amongst woodlands and streams on a working farm. Ideal for touring Dorset/Somerset border. Warm, friendly welcome in family home. Comfortable en suite rooms with colour TV, tea/coffee-making facilities, CH. Traditional breakfast. Many local pubs and restaurants. Open all year.

---

(3) Fossil Farm, Winfrith Newburgh, Dorchester, Dorset DT2 8DB

Liz Sealey
☎/Fax 01305 853355
🅱 From £17.50
Sleeps 4

Enjoy the traditions of farmhouse hospitality in a peaceful setting on a 370-acre mixed family farm. Decoratively furnished twin and double rooms with shared bathroom, colour TV in double. Hot drinks facilities. Extensive breakfast menu with home baked bread. Very friendly and relaxed atmosphere. So much to see in the area that guests always want to return. Phone for brochure.

---

(4) Hemsworth Manor Farm, Witchampton, Nr Wimborne, Dorset BH21 5BN

Mrs A C Tory
☎ 01258 840216
🅱 From £17.50–£20
Sleeps 6

Listed

Working family farm of approx 700 acres, mainly arable, but with sheep and pigs, and situated in unspoilt country-side with only one other farmhouse in sight! Easy access to Bournemouth, Salisbury, Dorchester and the New Forest. Two double, one family room, all spacious with colour TV, tea/coffee-making facilities and washbasins. Adjoining bathroom. Excellent local pubs in the area.

---

(5) Henbury Farm, Dorchester Road, Sturminster Marshall, Wimborne, Dorset BH21 3RN

Sue & Jonathan Tory
☎ 01258 857306
Fax 01258 857928
🅱 From £19–£22
Sleeps 6

300-year-old farmhouse facing large front lawn and pond, situated on 200-acre dairy and arable farm. Guests' lounge with colour TV. Near to New Forest and fifteen minutes from sandy beaches. Numerous local restaurants to meet your evening requirements. Many local attractions and country walks. Ideally situated for a great holiday. En-suite facilities available. Open all year except Christmas.

Higher Langdon, Beaminster, Dorset DT8 3NN

Judy Thompson
☎/Fax 01308 862537
BB From £15–£20
EM From £10
Sleeps 6
Commended

A spacious and homely working farm with sheep, geese and cereals. Set in acres of rolling countryside, 9 miles sea. An informal atmosphere combined with traditional farmhouse cooking, ensure our guests enjoy all the country has to offer. En suite bedrooms, tea/coffee-making facilities. Children welcome. Evening meal. Elegant sitting room with TV.

Holebrook Farm, Lydlinch, Sturminster Newton, Dorset DT10 2JB

Sally & Charles Wingate-Saul
☎ 01258 817348
BB From £21–23
EM From £10
Sleeps 11
Listed

Situated in heart of Blackmore Vale and ideal as a central base for exploring Dorset, this is a family farm of 125 acres. Accommodation in 18th century farmhouse and delightfully converted stables, each with own sitting room, kitchen, shower, WC en-suite. Swimming pool, clay pigeon shooting, large games room with pool and table tennis. Comfortable, friendly atmosphere. Good home cooking, Licence. No dogs. Open all year.

Huntsbridge Farm, Leigh, Nr Sherborne, Dorset DT9 6JA

Mrs Su Read
☎ 01935 872150
BB From £17.50
EM From £12
Sleeps 6
Highly Commended

Attractive stone farmhouse set in open countryside in the beautiful part of Dorset Thomas Hardy chose for his novel 'The Woodlanders'. Ideally situated for either walking or touring. Golf, riding and fishing available locally. Tastefully furnished bedrooms, 2 double en suite and 1 twin en suite, all with tea/coffee facilities, colour TV, radio/alarms. So why not come and relax far from the madding crowd? Open Mar–Nov.

Maiden Castle Farm, Dorchester, Dorset DT2 9PR

Hilary Hoskin
☎/Fax 01305 262356
BB From £18–£20
Sleeps 6
Commended

Our large working farm, 1 mile from Dorchester and 7 miles from Weymouth in the heart of Hardy country, enjoys magnificent views of Maiden Castle and the surrounding countryside. En-suite bedrooms with CH, TV, tea-making facilities and a telephone for guests' use combine to offer comfort, peace and quiet – ideal for the perfect holiday. Babysitting by arrangement. Open all year.

Priory Farm, East Holme, Wareham, Dorset BH20 6AG

Mrs Venn Goldsack
☎ 01929 552972/554716
BB From £18–£21
Sleeps 4
Commended

16th century farmhouse on 400-acre dairy and fruit farm. Thick walls and thatch make it cosy in winter. Ideal for both coastline and countryside. One twin-bedded room with en-suite, WC and basin and separate showerroom, 1 twin-bedded room with sole use of bathroom. Large book-lined guest's room with colour TV. Good selection of restaurants nearby. Regret no pets. Open most of the year (closed Christmas, New Year, mid-June to mid-July).

Rudge Farm, Chilcombe, Bridport, Dorset DT6 4NF

Sue Diment
☎ 01308 482630
BB From £20
EM From £12
Sleeps 6
Highly Commended

Peacefully situated in the beautiful Bride Valley, just 2 miles from the sea. After a day spent exploring the lovely West Dorset countryside, relax in our comfortably furnished, licensed farmhouse and enjoy dinner prepared mainly from local produce, or try one of the many good local restaurants. All rooms are en-suite with TV and tea tray and have far reaching views.

12   **Yalbury Park,** Frome Whitfield Farm, Dorchester, Dorset DT2 7SE

Tom and Ann Bamlet
☎ 01305 250336
BB From £20
Sleeps 6
🐎 🐕 🏕 🕯 🏠
Highly Commended

Stone farmhouse with large garden in parkland to River Frome. Warm and welcoming for all country lovers. All rooms en-suite have TV, tea/coffee-making facilities, fridge, hairdrier. 1 double with french windows to garden. 1 family room. Traditional farmhouse breakfasts. Ideal for walking, beaches, fishing, riding and all country pursuits. Open all year.

SELF-CATERING

13   **Dove Cottage & Buddens Farmhouse,** c/o Buddens Farm, Twyford, Shaftesbury, Dorset SP7 0JE

Sarah Gulliford
☎/Fax 01747 811433
SC From £90–£420
Sleeps 4/6 + cot
🐎 🐕 🐈 🐖 🦃
🔑 🔑 🔑 🔑
Commended

HARRASSED? Have a real farm holiday, guests welcome to help feed pigs, sheep, chickens and goats and watch cows being milked. Pony trekking over farm. Set in rolling hills and patchwork fields. Relax in superb farmhouse and cottage accommodation. Comfortably furnished, log fires, dishwasher, colour TV, laundry room, swimming pool. Fully equipped for babies and children. Open all year.

14   **Dairy Cottages,** Holebrook Farm, Lydlinch, Sturminster Newton, Dorset DT10 2JB

Charles & Sally Wingate-Saul
☎ 01258 817348
SC From £140–£400
Sleeps 2/4
🐎 🚲 🕯 🦃
🔑 🔑 🔑 🔑
Highly Commended

Beautifully converted, spacious cottages in old cow byre on working farm. Peaceful, quiet, well off beaten track. Exceptionally comfortable, oil CH, all modern appliances. Help with feeding animals or sleep all day. Games room with pool/table tennis, swimming pool, clay shooting, laundry room. Large garden for relaxing. ideal base for exploring Hardy's Dorset. Evening meal by arrangement, licence. No dogs. Open all year.

15   **Graston Farm Cottage,** Graston Farm, Burton Bradstock, Bridport, Dorset DT6 4NG

Mrs Sylvia Bailey
☎ 01308 897603
Fax 01308 897016
SC From £150–£400
Sleeps 7–9
🐎 🐕
🔑 🔑 *Approved*

This spacious detached cottage is situated on a dairy farm in the beautiful Bride Valley one mile from Burton Bradstock and the sea. Three bedrooms (1 double, 1 double and single, 1 twin), sitting room with woodburning stove, large well equipped kitchen/dining room and a further room with bed-settee. Open all year.

16   **Hartgrove Farm,** Hartgrove, Shaftesbury, Dorset SP7 0JY

Mrs Susan Smart
☎/Fax 01747 811830
SC From £100–£375
Sleeps 2/5 + cot
🐎 🐕 🐈 🏕 🚲 🦃
🔑 🔑 🔑 🔑
Commended

145 acre family dairy farm in glorious country with breathtaking views. Two character cottages and farmhouse flat, beautifully furnished and equipped. Colour TV, linen, CH, laundry room. Magnificent walking on farm or NT downland, buzzards, badgers, deer, etc. Children will enjoy the cows, calves, sheep, ponies, chickens. Small farm shop. Pretty, unspoilt villages and pubs. One cottage suitable for disabled. Colour brochure. Open all year.

Higher Langdon Flat, Beaminster, Dorset DT8 3NN

Judy Thompson
☎/Fax 01308 862537
🆂 From £135–£150
Sleeps 2
🐎 🏕 🍳 🎣 🎠 💈 %
♠ *Approved*

On the first floor of our farmhouse, set in 400 acres of Dorset downland. The flat has sitting room/kitchen with colour TV and microwave. Linen, CH, double bedroom with bathroom en suite. Ideal for walkers – we are on the Wessex Way and 9 miles from heritage coastline. Relaxed atmosphere. Open all year.

Higher Waterston Farm Cottages, Higher Waterston Farm, Dorchester, Dorset DT2 7SW

Mrs Carol Hammick
☎ 01305 848208
Fax 01305 848894
🆂 From £175–£420
Sleeps 4/6
🐎 🚴 ✪ ⛵
♠ ♠ ♠ ♠ – ♠ ♠ ♠ ♠ ♠
Commended

Four superb courtyard cottages on sheep farm, one for disabled. 3/3/2/2 bedrooms sleeping 6/6/4/4. Each has terrace, TV, video, washing machine, tumble dryer, dishwasher, microwave, etc. Telephones. Big games barn. Tennis court. large, safe central lawn. Lovely country, beautiful walks. Centre of Hardy's Wessex. Sea 8 miles, Dorchester 4. Minimum one week summer, winter breaks. Open all year.

Luccombe Farm, Milton Abbas, Blandford, Dorset DT11 0BE

Murray & Amanda Kayll
☎ 01258 880558
🆂 From £150–£350
Sleeps 2/4
🐎 🚴 🚲 🏕 🍳 💈 🎣 %
♠ ♠ ♠ *Commended*

Our traditional barn conversions lie deep in rolling downland. Beauty, peace and history surround you. Comfortable, well equipped and sleeping 2/4, they stand around a pond in landscaped grounds. Riding, fishing, sailing, clay shooting, good walking, cycling, etc. on farm or locally. Telephone, games room, childcare, maid and laundry service all available. Open all year.

Rudge Farm, Chilcombe, Bridport, Dorset DT6 4NF

Sue Diment
☎ 01308 482630
🆂 From £150–£410
Sleeps 2–6
🐎 🚲 %
♠ ♠ ♠ ♠
Highly Commended

Peacefully situated on 108-acre farm in the beautiful Bride Valley, just 2 miles from the sea. Superbly comfortable cottages, converted from old farm buildings around cobbled farmyard. Linen supplied, CH, laundry, games room. Lovely country walks. Short winter breaks. Open all year.

Yew House Cottages, c/o Yew House Farm, Marnhull, Sturminster Newton, Dorset DT10 1NP 

Gil Espley
☎ 01258 820412
Fax 01258 821044
🆂 From £95–£285
Sleeps 4/5 cot
🚲 🐎 💈 %
♠ ♠ *Commended*

Three timber cottages equipped to highest standard of comfort for summer or winter holidays. Situated in a secluded rural setting overlooking Blackmore Vale. Central heating, colour TV, linen inclusive. Cot available. Excellent centre for sightseeing. Coarse fishing in Stour. Many good pubs for local beer and food. One cottage designed for disabled visitors. Colour brochure. Open all year.

Please mention **Stay on a Farm** when booking

61

England's West Country

Somerset

Group Contacts: 📖 *Jane Sedgman* ☎ *01458 223 237*
🛏 *Geraldine Hunt* ☎ *01278 641228*

Welcome to Somerset. We hope that your stay with us will be truly enjoyable.
There's so much to see and do, walking in the Quantocks, Brendon Hills or the
National Park, visiting Taunton, the scene of Judge Jeffries' Bloody Assizes in 1685,
with its County Museum and well known cricket ground; there is Wells, the smallest
cathedral town in England and Glastonbury with its tor and abbey.

Somerset offers a tremendous range of National Trust properties from Dunster,
with its castle (often used in films), to Muchelney with its thatched 14th century
priest house. There are also many superb gardens such as those at Hestercombe
House. Somerset is also famous for the journey to the centre of the earth at Wookey
Hole and Cheddar Gorge, and for the steam enthusiast there are the West Somerset
and East Somerset Railways.

Two final items most certainly not to be overlooked, cider and cheese the basic
items of a ploughman's lunch. Tempted? Then give us a ring and come to stay for a
few days or rent a cottage and really explore Somerset.

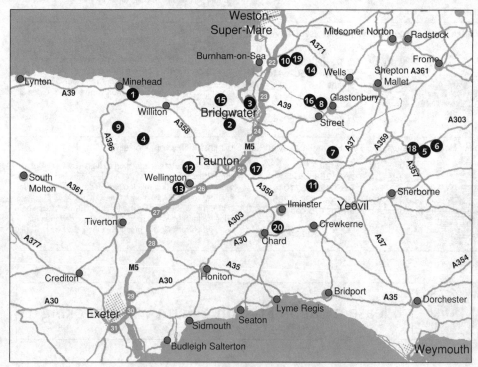

BED AND BREAKFAST

(and evening meal)

Binham Farm, Old Cleeve, Minehead, Somerset TA24 6HX

Mrs S Bigwood
☎ 01984 640222
🅱 From £15–£18
Sleeps 6
🐎 ⅍ 🐕 🌂
👑 👑

Predominantly 17th-century Jacobean farmhouse on a working family farm in an idyllic setting close to the Exmoor National Park and Quantock Hills. A few minutes walk across our fields to Blue Anchor sea front and the West Somerset Steam Railway. Comfortably furnished bedrooms with en suite facilities available, private lounge with colour TV, mediaeval dining hall. Full CH. Open all year.

Blackmore Farm, Cannington, Bridgwater, Somerset TA5 2NE

Mrs Ann Dyer
☎/Fax 01278 653442
🅱 From £16–£20
Sleeps 6
⅍ 🐕 🐈 📱
👑 👑 *Highly Commended*

A tastefully restored and furnished mediaeval manor house dating back to the 14th century, set in rolling countryside with views to the Quantock Hills. Traditional farmhouse bed and breakfast includes rooms with oak bedsteads and four poster beds, all with en suite facilities. As featured in *Country Living* magazine. Within easy reach of Exmoor, West Somerset coast, Taunton, Wells and Glastonbury. Open all year.

Cokerhurst Farm, 87 Wembdon Hill, Bridgwater, Somerset TA6 7QA

Diana Chappell
☎ 01278 422330
Mobile 0850 692065
🅱 From £17–£22.50
Sleeps 6
🐕 ⅍ 🐎
👑 👑 *Commended*

A warm welcome awaits you at this farmhouse situated in quiet countryside. The peaceful garden overlooks the lake and 100-acre family run 'pick your own' soft fruit and arable farm. Good central location for exploring Somerset. Log fires, CH, tea/coffee facilities, TV, lounge, H and C all rooms, one en suite. Good pub food 1½ miles. Open Mar–Nov.

Greenway Farm, Wiveliscombe, Taunton, Somerset TA4 2UA

Mrs M. A. Wollaston
☎ 01984 623359
Fax 01984 624051
🅱 From £15
EM From £7
Sleeps 6
🐕 🐎 🌂 📱
👑 *Commended*

Comfort with peace and quiet. For those who prefer action, help us on the farm or take part in a country pursuit – excellent walks, rides, game or coarse fishing, clay pigeon shooting can be arranged and the coast is close. Good food, home-prepared menus, comfortable lounge, excellent views. Facilities for children.Open Apr–Oct.

Hale Farm, Cucklington, Wincanton, Somerset BA9 9PN

Pat & Jim David
☎ 01963 33342
🅱 From £16
Sleeps 6
🐎 🐕 (6) ⅍
👑 👑

A friendly welcome awaits you in our old 17th century farmhouse the moment you walk in the door. Three attractive bedrooms with en suite showers, toilets, washbasins, tea/coffee-making facilities. Comfortable lounge with colour TV, separate dining room serving delicious home cooking. Set in peaceful surroundings yet only 2 miles A303 London – Exeter road. Ideal touring centre country and coast. Open Apr–Oct.

6 Lower Church Farm, Rectory Lane, Charlton Musgrove, Wincanton, Somerset BA9 8ES

Alicia Teague
☎ 01963 32307
🅱 From £15
Sleeps 6
🏇 ⚡ 🎠 (6) ♿
☕ ☕

Relax at our 18th century beamed house on stock farm, 2 miles from A303 on Wiltshire/Dorset border surrounded by lovely countryside. Ideal touring. Quiet, pleasant, homely atmosphere. One twin, 1 double en suite, 1 double with private downstairs bathroom. Full central heating. Dining room/lounge, colour TV. Tea/coffee-making facilities. Cottage garden, patio. AA listed. Open all year except Christmas & New Year.

7 Lower Farm, Kingweston, Somerton, Somerset TA11 6BA

David & Jane Sedgman
☎ 01458 223237
Fax 01458 223276
🅱 From £18.50–£19.50
Sleeps 5
🎠 (6) ⚡ 🐾 ♿
☕ *Commended*

This Grade II listed farmhouse, sited in a conservation area and overlooking a wide stretch of open country, was formerly a coaching inn and retains many of its original features. The attractively furnished rooms are all en suite, with tea/coffee-making facilities, colour TV and full central heating. Wells, Glastonbury, Cheddar, Wookey, Bath and Yeovil are within easy reach. Open all year.

8 New House Farm, Burtle Road, Westhay, Nr Glastonbury, Somerset BA6 9TT

Mrs M Bell
☎ 01458 860238
🅱 From £18–£20
EM From £10
Sleeps 5
🎠 🏇
☕ ☕

Large Victorian farmhouse on dairy farm. Central for touring Wells, Cheddar, etc. Accommodation comprises of double room and 1 family room both en suite with colour TV, tea/coffee facilities, hair drier, etc. Lounge with colour TV, separate dining room, also sun lounge, CH throughout, plenty of local fishing. Open all year.

9 North Down Farm, Wiveliscombe, Taunton, Somerset TA4 2BL

Mrs Lucy Parker
☎ 01984 623730
🅱 From £15–£16
EM From £9
Sleeps 6
🎠 ⚡ ♿ 🐾
☕ *Commended*

Family dairy farm set on the edge of Exmoor and Lorna Doone Country, 10 miles from Taunton, 1 mile from Wiveliscombe. Facilities for horse riding, fishing and sailing locally. Pleasant walks around the farm and locality. Picnic basket available on request. Magnificent views of the nearby Quantocks and Vale of Taunton. Open all year (closed Christmas).

10 Northwick Farm, Mark, Highbridge, Somerset TA9 4PG

Mrs Geraldine Hunt
☎ 01278 641228
🅱 From £16–£17
Sleeps 6
🎠 (5) 🏇 🧍 🚗 ♿
☕ *Commended*

Large Georgian farmhouse standing in own grounds. Three comfortable bedrooms, quality furnishings. Guests' lounge with log fire, dining room with separate tables. Views across open farmland to Mendip Hills. Excellent centre for touring, walking and sporting pursuits. Near coast and within 2 miles M5 (J22). Warm and friendly welcome assured. Open all year.

11 Orchard Farm, Cockhill, Castle Cary, Somerset BA7 7NY

Olive Boyer
☎ 01963 350418
🅱 From £15
EM From £8.50
Sleeps 5
🏇 🎠 🚗 🧍
☕ ☕ *Highly Commended*

A 170-acre beef and cattle rearing farm in area of outstanding beauty, yet only 1½ miles from Castle Cary. Centrally-heated farmhouse with 2 en suite rooms, TV lounge. Traditional farmhouse meals served in the conservatory. Bath, Taunton, Longleat, Stourhead and coasts at West Somerset and Dorset within driving distance. Open all year.

Orchard Haven, Langford Budville, Wellington, Somerset TA21 0QZ

Mrs Jenny Perry-Jones
☎ 01823 672116
ⒷⒷ From £17
Sleeps 5
◎ ✄ ➳ (5)
♨ ♨ *Highly Commended*

Orchard Haven is the ideal place to enjoy the delights of Rural Somerset. It nestles in idyllic countryside standing by the River Tone. Lovely accommodation tastefully and comfortably furnished with a friendly atmosphere. The dining room has separate tables where a good full English breakfast starts the day. Having only a small number of guests assures first class attention. Good inns ¾ and 2 miles distance. Wellington 4 miles. Open Easter–Oct.

Pinksmoor Millhouse, Pinksmoor, Wellington, Somerset TA21 0HD

Mrs Nancy K M Ash
☎ 01823 672361
ⒷⒷ From £18–£21
EM From £11.50
Sleeps 6
🐴 ➳ ✄
♨ ♨ ♨ *Commended*

Stroll along the old millstream, haunt of kingfisher, snipe and mallard, go badger watching or just wander where you please around this family-run dairy farm. Period millhouse with cosy lounges, log fire, spacious en suite bedrooms, tea/coffee-making facilities, CH, colour TV, farmhouse hospitality and cooking. AA QQQQ selected. Conservation awards 1991 & 1992. Close coasts and moors. 10 minutes M5 J26. Open all year (closed Christmas and New Year).

Townsend Farm, Sand, Wedmore, Somerset BS28 4XH

Sarah Willcox
☎ 01934 712342
ⒷⒷ From £16–£18
EM From £10.50
Sleeps 6
➳ (10) ✄
♨ ♨

Townsend Farm is a working dairy farm, set in peaceful countryside with views of the Mendip hills, close to Wells, Cheddar and Glastonbury, 6 miles from M5 (jct 22). The spacious Victorian farmhouse offers comfortable accommodation and a friendly atmosphere, traditional English breakfast served in dining room, relaxing separate TV lounge. All bedrooms have TV, en suite available. Open all year except Christmas.

Wembdon Farm, Hollow Lane, Wembdon, Bridgwater, Somerset TA5 2BD

Mrs Mary Rowe
☎ 01278 453097
ⒷⒷ From £17.50–£19.50
Sleeps 4 + cot
➳ ✄ 🌳
♨ ♨ *Highly Commended*

Enjoy a carefree break at our 17th century family farmhouse. Situated near the Quantock hills, therefore an ideal base for visiting coastlines, Exmoor, Glastonbury and oustanding National Trust properties. The farmhouse is tastefully decorated, central heating throughout offering separate lounge, dining room, bedrooms are full en suite, tea/coffee-making facilities, TV. Excellent local eating places. We are also easy to find. Open Easter–Dec.

SELF-CATERING

The Courtyard, c/o New House Farm, Burtle Road, Westhay, Nr Glastonbury, Somerset BA6 9TT 🔢

Mr & Mrs P Bell
☎ 01458 860238
ⓈⒸ From £150–£330
Sleeps 6
🐴 ➳
🏠 🏠 🏠 🏠
Commended

The Courtyard is a converted barn which sleeps up to 4 adults and 2 children. Its situation on a dairy farm on the Somerset Levels makes it central for touring Wells, Cheddar, Bath, etc. Superbly equipped, including colour TV, washing machine, microwave, tumble dryer. Bed-linen, electricity and heating included. Good local fishing. Open all year.

17 Dykes House, Slough Lane, Stoke-St-Gregory, Taunton, Somerset TA3 6JH

Mrs Jean House
☎ **01823 490349/ 490619**
SC **From £120–£250**
Sleeps 5 + cot
🐕 🏠 💺
🔑 🔑 🔑 *Commended*

Dykes House is a self-contained renovated wing of a thatched listed farmhouse with panoramic views. Comfortable and fully equiiped. Woodburner in lounge, kitchen/diner, 1 twin, 1 family room, bathroom, 2 toilets. Own drive and garden. Pay phone. Linen, towels and 5 storage heaters included. Excellent touring base. 8 miles M5, junction 25. Open all year.

---

18 Hale Farm, Cucklington, Wincanton, Somerset BA9 9PN

Mrs Pat David
☎ **01963 33342**
SC **From £90–£175**
Sleeps 4
🐕 🏠 💺
🔑 🔑 🔑 *Approved*

Set in a peaceful, but not isolated, position on edge of village, only 2 miles from A303. Ideal touring. Period converted former cowshed, comfortable and fully equipped. 2 twin-bedded rooms, bathroom, kitchen, sitting room. All electric (coin meter). Linen supplied. Open all year.

---

19 Pear Tree Cottage, Northwick Farm, Mark, Highbridge, Somerset TA9 4PG

Mrs G Hunt
☎ **01278 641228**
SC **From £180–£300**
Sleeps 4/6
🐕 (5) 🏠 🚐
🔑 🔑 🔑
Highly Commended

Situated on the Somerset Levels in an area of outstanding natural beauty. Recent barn conversion. Luxurious and comfortable with beautifully co-ordinated fabrics and furnishings. Perfect for a peaceful relaxing holiday and an ideal base for touring this part of the West Country. Excellent facilities nearby for golf, fishing and riding and only 4 miles from coast.

---

20 Rull Farm, Otterford, near Chard, Somerset TA20 3O

Mrs Pauline Wright
☎ **01460 234398**
SC **From £100–£160**
Sleeps 5/6
🐕 🏕
🔑 🔑 *Commended*

We would like to welcome you to our family farm in the beautiful Blackdown hills with splendid scenic views. This accommodation is part of the farmhouse within easy reach of 5 local towns and coastal resorts. Open all year.

62

England's West Country

Exmoor

Group Contacts: 🅱 *Mrs Rosemary Pile* ☎ *0159 87 236*
                    🆂🅲 *Mrs Ann Durbin* ☎ *0164 383 255*

Exmoor National Park is situated on the north coast of Devon and Somerset. This is an area of magnificent countryside with superb contrasts.

The park offers miles of moorland which are ideal for country pursuits such as walking and riding, and also has many beautiful villages to explore. There are over 600 miles of public footpaths.

Exmoor has a spectacular coastline of high cliffs, wild heather moorland and deep wooded coombes which cradle sparkling rivers. It is famous for the herds of wild red deer, Exmoor ponies and soaring buzzards. The rivers Exe and Barle rise high on the moors, creating attractive valleys.

Inland are the famous Tar Steps and the Doone Valley, whilst Porlock Weir, Lynton and Lynmouth are dotted along the coast.

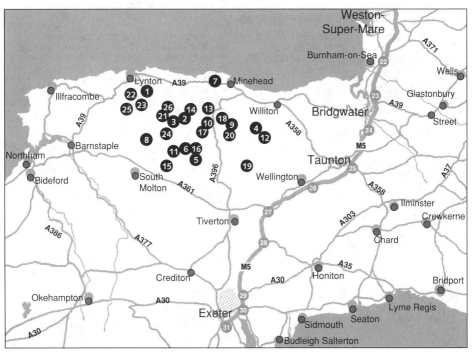

BED AND BREAKFAST

(and evening meal)

---

① Coombe Farm, Countisbury, Lynton, Devon EX35 6NF

Rosemary & Susan Pile
☎ **0159 87 236**
🅱 **From £16.50–£21**
EM From £12
Sleeps 14
🐾 ✂ 🐎
🐛🐛 *Commended*

Comfortable old farmhouse set on a hillside between picturesque Lynmouth and the legendary Doone Valley. Coast path runs through the farm. Riding and fishing nearby. Beamed dining room, lounge with colour TV. 2 bedrooms with shower en suite, 3 with H/C, all with hot drinks facilities. Licensed. Wholesome breakfasts and four course dinners. Dogs by arrangement. Weekly terms available. AA listed. Open Mar–Nov.

---

② Cutthorne Farm, Luckwell Bridge, Wheddon Cross, Somerset TA24 7EW

Ann Durbin
☎ **0164 383 255**
🅱 **From £19.50–£27**
EM From £11.50
Sleeps 6
🐾 ✂ 🐿 ♟ ⚔
🐛🐛

18th century yeoman farmhouse totally secluded in heart of Exmoor. A working farm, spacious and comfortable accommodation with log fires and CH. Luxury en suite bathrooms. 4-poster bed. Candlelit dinners, cosy lounge. For extra privacy – beautifully appointed mediaeval stone cottages on side of farmhouse overlooking pond and cobbled yard. Stabling. We are 2½ miles from 'The Rest and Be Thankful', Wheddon Cross, travelling on the B3224 towards Exford. Open Feb–Dec.

---

③ Edgcott House, Exford, Nr Minehead, Somerset TA24 7QG

Gillian Lamble
☎ **0164383 495**
🅱 **From £18–£22**
EM From £10
Sleeps 6
⊛ 🐾 🐎
🐛🐛

Country house of great charm and character amidst beautiful countryside in the heart of Exmoor National Park, ¼ mile from village of Exford. Peaceful and quiet. All bedrooms have basins, private bathroom available. Excellent home cooking using fresh local produce is served in the elegant 'longroom' with its unique murals. Large garden. Comfortable, friendly centre for relaxing, walking, riding and fishing. Open all year.

---

④ Glasses Farm, Roadwater, Watchet, Somerset TA23 0QH

Mrs Sheena White
☎ **01984 40552**
🅱 **From £16.50**
Sleeps 6
🐾 🐎 **(10)** ⛺ 🐎 🐿 ⚔
🐛

This delightful thatched 16th century farmhouse is situated on the edge of Exmoor, at the foot of the Brendon Hills. Ideal for seeing the many local beauty spots. We are a working farm of 220 acres, dairy and arable. The farmhouse is beautifully decorated and comfortable, yet retains its original beams and character. Tea/coffee facilities, washbasin in all rooms. Open Jan–Nov.

---

⑤ Highercombe, Dulverton, Somerset TA22 9PT

Barbara Marchant
☎ **01398 23451**
🅱 **From £16–£19**
Sleeps 6
🐎 🐾
🐛🐛 *Commended*

Relaxing and peacefully situated farmhouse originating from 14th century. Set in 8 acres of land with beautiful gardens. Close to open moorland. Comfortable double, twin or family rooms with en suite or private bathrooms. Tea/coffee-making facilities. Large residents' lounge with far-reaching views. Wild deer are often seen close by. Excellent area for country sports. Stabling. Open all year.

Highercombe Farm, Dulverton, Somerset TA22 9PT   ⑥

Abigail Humphrey
☎ 01398 23616
🅱🅱 From £13.50–£15
EM £10
Sleeps 6
🐂 🐎 🐕 ⛺ 🎀
Listed

A 450-acre working farm on the edge of the moor. We have spectacular 60-mile views and red deer can often be seen from the farmhouse. Two pretty double rooms with tea/coffee facilities and guest bathroom. Third family room with private bathroom. Large guest lounge with inglenook and bay window where breakfast is served. A relaxed atmosphere, a friendly welcome, personal service and good food. Open Feb–Nov.

Hindon Farm, Nr Minehead, Somerset TA24 8SH   ⑦

Penny & Roger Webber
☎/Fax 01643 705244
🅱🅱 From £18–£22
EM From £15
Sleeps 6
🐎 🐂 🍴 🐕 ⛺ 🛏 🎀
Listed *Commended*

Superbly situated in Exmoor valley (Minehead 3 miles, Selworthy 1 mile) find our real working farm – 500 acres and direct access to moors. Featured in Country Living magazine. Spotty pigs, donkey, horses, goats, poultry and many sheep – come and help! Riding/stabling/grazing. Large lawn and stream, picnic area. Games barn. Own produce. Lovely 18th C farmhouse with relaxed atmosphere and big breakfasts. Pretty bedrooms, all H&C and drinks tray. Guests' bathroom and sitting room. Open March–Oct. Brochure.

Landacre Farm, Withypool, Minehead, Somerset TA24 7SD   ⑧

Mrs P Hudson
☎ 0164 383 223/487
🅱🅱 From £13
Sleeps 2
🐂 (10) 🐎 🦮
🐌

Large ground floor bedroom (1 double, 1 single) with sitting/breakfast area, colour TV, kitchenette and bathroom en suite. Well equipped and comfortable. Self-catering available. Private fishing on River Barle. Riding available locally. Weekly terms. Situated on Exford/N. Molton Road. Open April–Oct.

Little Brendon Hill, Wheddon Cross, Nr Minehead, Somerset TA24 7DG   ⑨

Mrs Shelagh Maxwell
☎ 01643 841556
🅱🅱 From £17.50
EM From £10
Sleeps 6
🍴 🐂 (8) 🐎 🛏 🎀
Listed *Highly Commended*

Enjoy a stay with us in our beautifully appointed farmhouse set in the peace and tranquillity of the Exmoor National Park. Three lovely rooms with private facilities. Log fires, cosy candlelit dinners. Central heating. Short stay or long, a truly relaxing place to pursue country pastimes. You will be most welcome. Open all year.

Little Quarme Farm, Wheddon Cross, Nr Minehead, Somerset TA24 7EA   ⑩

Bob Cody-Boutcher
☎ 01643 841249
🅱🅱 From £15–£18
Sleeps 6
🍴 🐂 🐎 ⛺
Listed *Highly Commended*

Lovely old farmhouse in the heart of Exmoor in an outstanding situation with panoramic views. 2 doubles, 1 twin (1 en suite), 2 bathrooms, TV lounge, tea/coffee-making facilities. Friendly family atmosphere. Many animals, pony rides, stabling. Large garden and 18 acres. We are ¼ mile past Wheddon Cross on Exford road B3224. Open Apr–Nov.

Springfield Farm, Dulverton, Somerset TA22 9QD   ⑪

Tricia Vellacott
☎ 01398 23722
🅱🅱 From £16–£20
EM From £11
Sleeps 5
🐎 🐂
🐌 🐌 *Commended*

A warm welcome awaits you at our 270-acre working farm. Peacefully situated between Tarr Steps and Dulverton, overlooking the River Barle with magnificent moorland and woodland views. Very comfortable accommodation and delicious farmhouse meals. Guests' bathroom, 1 double and 1 single with H and C, 1 twin with private shower suite. Dining room with tea-making facilities, sitting room with colour TV. Open Easter–Oct.

12 **Wood Advent Farm,** Roadwater, Watchet, Somerset TA23 0RR

Diana Brewer
☎/Fax 01984 640920
BB From £17.50–£23.50
EM £12
Sleeps 10
Commended

Nestling at the foot of the Brendon Hills. Listed spacious farmhouse set in 340 acres of working farm. Relaxing en suite rooms with hospitality trays. Chintzed lounge with log fires, inglenook heats the licensed dining room, where wonderful country dishes can be assured. Grass tennis court, heated outdoor pool, clay pigeon and pheasant shooting all available on the farm. Open all year.

SELF-CATERING

13 **Croft Cottage,** c/o Higher Burrow Farm, Timberscombe, Minehead, Somerset TA24 7UD

Diana Rusher
☎ 01643 841427
SC From £150–£350
Sleeps 7 + cot
Approved

Attractive, converted, stone built cottage situated 200 yds from farm, with own garden, and lovely views. Croft is spacious with one double room, 2 twin, 1 single, cot available. Large bathroom upstairs, second WC downstairs, washing machine. Colour TV, log fire and small library. Horses or other animals accommodated by arrangement at farm. Electricity extra. Friday change-over. Open all year.

14 **Cutthorne Farm,** Luckwell Bridge, Wheddon Cross, Somerset TA24 7EW

Ann Durbin
☎ 0164 383 255
SC From £95–£425
Sleeps 4
Deluxe

Situated in the heart of glorious Exmoor, two luxuriously appointed mediaeval barn conversions on side of farmhouse. Overlooking 14th century pond and cobbled yard. Self-catering or with meals in the farmhouse. Both furnished and equipped to the highest standard with antique pine, fitted kitchens and CH. Baby listening. Inclusive of linen, towels and electricity. Open all year.

15 **Dunsley Farm,** West Anstey, South Molton, Devon EX36 3PF

Mrs Mary Robins
☎ 01398 341246
SC From £110–£350
Sleeps 5
Commended

Self-contained cottage forming part of 16th century farmhouse, overlooks meadows and woodland valley. Access off a quiet country road. 2 bedrooms (accommodate 5 people), bathroom, large lounge/diner with colour TV. Large modern equipped kitchen, electric heating (£1 meter). Linen provided, pets welcome. Coarse fishing available on farm. Dulverton 6 miles. Open all year.

16 **Highercombe Farm,** Dulverton, Somerset TA22 9PT

Abigail Humphrey
☎ 01398 23616
SC From £160–£260
Sleeps 6
Commended

Self-contained wing of large farmhouse on 450-acre working farm next to the moor. Well furnished in cottage style. Spectacular views. 2 bedrooms, bathroom, large lounge/dining room with colour TV, video, CD player and radio. Modern pine kitchen. Linen, CH, hot water included. Use of washing machine/dryer. Evening meals arranged, babysitting service. Electricity pound coin meter. Open all year.

Little Quarme Country Cottages, Wheddon Cross, Nr Minehead, Somerset TA24 7EA

Tammy Cody-Boutcher & family
☎ **01643 841249**
🅂🄲 **From £80–£425**
Sleeps 2/6
Highly Commended

Six stone cottages furnished and equipped to the highest standards in the heart of Exmoor. All have microwaves, colour TV, videos, bed linen and towels. Standing amid 18 acres and large informal gardens, direct access to footpaths and bridlepath. Traffic free tranquillity with panoramic southerly views. Ample parking, free laundry room, childrens' play area, pay phone, stabling. Brochure available.

Pembroke, c/o Brake Cottage, Wheddon Cross, Minehead, Somerset TA24 7EX

Mrs J. Escott
☎ **01643 841550**
🅂🄲 **From £95–£350**
Sleeps 5
Commended

Situated in a peaceful position with parking, private garden and extensive scenic views, detached bungalow in the heart of the Exmoor National Park, 2 minutes from village of Wheddon Cross. Well equipped with microwave, automatic washing machine, tumble dryer. Linen included. Open Mar–Dec. No pets.

Ruggs Farm Bungalow, c/o Ruggs Farm, Brompton Regis, Dulverton, Somerset TA22 9NY

Jill Scott
☎ **0139 87236**
🅂🄲 **From £115–£265**
Sleeps 5 + cot
Approved

Farm bungalow close to the edge of Wimbleball Lake. Comfortable and well equipped. Deep freeze, microwave, washing machine, colour TV. Linen inclusive. Cot available. Beautiful walks, fishing and sailing on the lake. Fenced garden for dogs and children. A working farm of 365 acres with dairy cows and sheep. Open all year.

Triscombe Farm, Wheddon Cross, Minehead, Somerset TA24 7HA

John Sims
☎ **0164 385 227**
🅂🄲 **From £75–£378**
Sleeps 2–7
Up to Highly Commended

Triscombe stands in a beautiful wooded valley overlooking the river Quarme. Its 50 acres with private drive offer perfect peace and seclusion for the 6 quality stone cottages and barn conversions accommodating 2–7 persons. Large gardens, tennis court, games room and licensed restaurant, all in a spectacular countryside setting. Resident proprietors. Brochure available.

Westermill Farm, Exford, Nr Minehead, Somerset TA24 7NJ

The Edwards family
☎ **01643 831238**
Fax 01643 831660
🅂🄲 **From £135–£340**
Sleeps 4/8
Commended

Six delightful log cabins of superior quality. Various sizes, well equipped. In small grassy paddocks on side of valley by a river. Also bright, comfortable cottage adjoining the farmhouse overlooks the river. Patio, garage. Four waymarked walks over 500-acre farm in centre of Exmoor. 2½ miles shallow river, fishing, bathing. Laundry, payphone, information centre, seasonal small shop. Cabins open Mar–Dec, cottage all year.

West Ilkerton Farm, Barbrook, Lynton, North Devon EX35 6QA

Chris & Victoria Eveleigh
☎ **01598 752310**
🅂🄲 **From £120–£380**
Sleeps 6
Commended

Luxurious semi-detached cottage on secluded hill farm bordering open moor. Sheep, cattle, carthorses. Coast 3 miles, riding ½ mile. 3 bedrooms (2 king size, 1 twin) 2 bathrooms, living/dining room, kitchen (Rayburn, dishwasher, washing machine/tumble dryer, microwave). CH. TV, video. Baby equipment and evening babysitting. Children, dogs and horses welcome. Special "Exmoor Farmer" holidays in winter. Ideal for walking, riding, family farm holidays. Open all year.

23 Whitefield Barton, Challacombe, Barnstaple, Devon EX31 4TU

Rosemarie Kingdon
☎ 01598 763271
SC From £100–£300
Sleeps 6
🐕 🐈
Applied

A warm welcome awaits you on our family farm. Relax in half of our 16th century farmhouse which has been tasefully furnished to a high standard. Spacious kitchen with oil-fired Rayburn, lounge with woodburner. Bathroom/ shower. Family and twin rooms. Private patio, barbecue, streamed garden. Inclusive of linen and electricity. Central for beaches, moors. Open May–Dec.

24 Wintershead Farm, Simonsbath, Exmoor, Somerset TA24 7LF

Jane Styles
☎ 0164 383 222
SC From £105–£420
Sleeps 2–6
🐕 🐈
🐎 🐎 🐎 – 🐎 🐎 🐎 🐎
Highly Commended

Three cottages all converted to a high standard situated in a relaxing spot with panoramic views. One 3 bedroomed and two 2 bedroomed cottages (also small flat). All have oil central heating, linen, gas cooking and colour TV etc. Children and pets welcome. Ample parking. Pay phone, games room.. Use of grounds and DIY stabling. Colour brochure available. Open all year.

25 Yelland Cottage, c/o West Whitefield Farm, Challacombe, Barnstaple, Devon EX31 4TU

Jean Kingdon
☎ 01598 763433
SC From £100–£250
Sleeps 6
🐈 🐕 🐎
🐎 🐎 🐎 *Approved*

Semi-detached cosy farm cottage on working hill farm amidst beautiful countryside within easy reach of village pub and shop. Log fire, Rayburn plus electric conveniences. Relaxing lounge, colour TV. Linen provided. Friendly, relaxed atmosphere with farm animals. Spacious garden with ample parking. Ideal for beaches, walking, fishing, riding and touring North Devon. Open all year.

CAMPING AND CARAVANNING

26 Westermill Farm, Exford, Nr Minehead, Somerset TA24 7NJ

The Edwards family
☎ 01643 831238
Fax 01643 831660
Tents: adult £3/child £1
Car: £1
2 adults + vehicle £6.50
(all prices per night)
🏕 🐕 🐈 🐎 ⛺ 🦌
✓ ✓ ✓

Beautiful secluded site for 60 tents and dormobiles beside upper reaches of River Exe. Centre of Exmoor National Park. Four waymarked walks over 500-acre working farm. 2½ miles shallow river, fishing and bathing. Loo block, showers, laundry, washing up. Information centre, small shop, payphone. A site and farm to enjoy in the most natural way. Children's paradise.

FARM HOLIDAY BUREAU

NO ANSWER?
Farmers are mostly out and about during the day.
Try to telephone before 9.30am or after 4pm.

63

England's West Country
North Devon Coast and Country

Group Contacts: 🆑 *Cheryl Woollacott* ☎ *01769 550435*
🆑 *Ruth Ley* ☎ *01769 572337*

Welcome to Northern Devon – an area of tremendous contrasts. Miles of golden, surf-washed beaches, wide rolling hills and the valleys of the Taw and Torridge carpeted with the patchwork of our family farms. We span the land between two famous moors. Exmoor in the north with its magnificent rolling heather clad hills and steeply wooded valleys and Dartmoor in the south with its sweep of open rugged tors, grazed by the famous ponies and watered by sparkling streams.

Our land is made to slow you down. To see and remember the countryside that still has flowers, footpaths, winding roads with high banks, villages of thatch and cob with old churches and pubs with tradition. Henry Williamson wrote his famous book 'Tarka the Otter' here and 'The Tarka Trail', a long distance footpath of 180 miles now links our moors and coast and offering varied walking together with some 26 miles for cyclists (with cycle hire nearby).

We offer historic farmhouses, involvement in real farming life, superb cooking, a variety of facilities but above all we offer the friendly welcome you need. Many of us are open all year and out of season breaks are full of delight.

Whether it's the coast or the country, whether you want to gallop across the moors or fish for salmon in our rivers, spend a day searching for antiques or the children want a farm park or you a stately home or flower-filled garden it's here in North Devon – come and share it with us.

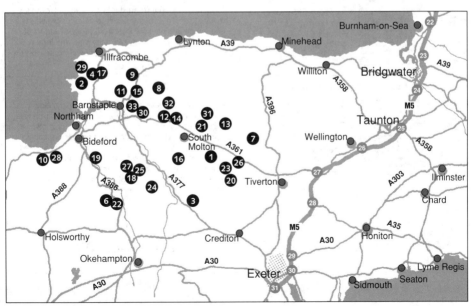

BED AND BREAKFAST

(and evening meal)

1 Capitol Farm, Bishops Nympton, Nr South Molton, North Devon EX36 4PH

Mrs Cheryl Woollacott
☎ 01769 550435
BB From £15
EM From £7
Sleeps 4
🐃 🐕 🐓 🏕
Listed *Commended*

Welcome to our warm and cosy atmosphere here at 'Capitol' Farm. Pleasantly situated for Exmoor, the coast and many attractions. Two rooms, with own bathroom and separate lounge. Breakfasts of your choice and 3 course dinner optional. Couples can relax and be spoilt. Children are most welcome. Whether a short break or a longer stay we aim to make it a happy one. Open all year. Welcome Host Day

2 Combas Farm, Croyde, North Devon EX33 1PH

Mrs Gwen Adams
☎ 01271 890398
BB From £16–£18
EM From £8
Sleeps 12
🐓 🐃 🏕
Listed *Commended*

Combas Farm, a 140-acre stock farm, nestles in its own secluded valley, just 15 mins' walk from miles of golden sands (5 mins from the village pub!). Many repeat bookings confirm claims to a warm welcome and high standard of home cooking using home produce including unusual fruit and veg. Wisteria rambles over this 17th century longhouse overlooking a lovely garden and unspoiled view. Colour brochure. Open Mar–Nov (incl). Welcome Host Day.

3 Court Barton, Lapford, Crediton, Devon EX17 6PZ

Sheila Mather
☎ 01363 83441
BB From £15.50
EM From £10
Sleeps 6
🐄 🐎 🖂
🐾 *Commended*

Spoil yourself at our comfortable medieval manor farmhouse, peacefully set in quiet village ½ mile north A377 midway Exeter/Barnstaple. Central for Devon's many attractions. Treat yourself to delicious breakfasts and tempting dinners of local fresh produce and West Country specialities. Enjoy our dairy farm and local walks – it's a different world here. Brochure. Welcome Host Day

4 Denham Farm, North Buckland, Braunton, North Devon EX33 1HY

Mrs Jean Barnes
☎/Fax 01271 890297
BB From £20–£25
EM From £12
Sleeps 24
🐃 🏕 🖂
🐾 🐾 *Commended*

A place for all seasons and all ages. Young and elderly can enjoy a warm welcome at our lovely spacious farmhouse built in early 1700s. Enjoy Jean's home cooking, relax in our lounge or bar. Use the games room or walk our country lanes. Let Tony take you on a farm tour. Ideally situated only a short drive to Croyde or Woolacombe beach. All rooms en suite, central heating throughout. A place to remember, truly 'a little gem'. Welcome Host Day.

FARM HOLIDAY BUREAU

Please mention Stay on a Farm when booking

Giffords Hele, Meeth, Okehampton, Devon EX20 3QN

Mrs Linden Draper
☎/Fax 01837 810009
[BB] From £23–£26
EM £15
Sleeps 6/7
🛏 ☕ 🎠 ⚓

Highly Commended

Superb indoor swimming pool offering tropical temperatures all year. Fresh seasonal food served in poolside restaurant. Designer en suite bedrooms with colour TV and beverage facilities. A beamed bar with a real fire. All this in the peaceful atmosphere of a traditional 175-acre farm. Ducks on the pond and badgers in the wood. Own Torridge fishing on farm. Ring for brochure. Open all year. Welcome Host Day.

Greenhills Farm, Yeo Mill, West Anstey, South Molton, North Devon EX36 3NU

Mrs Gillian Carr
☎ 01398 341300
[BB] From £13.50–£14.50
EM From £7.50
Sleeps 5
🛏 🐕 ☕ 🎠
Listed *Highly Commended*

Relax and enjoy a holiday at Greenhills. The charming old farmhouse on the working dairy farm nestles in the foothills of the Exmoor National Park. Guests have own lounge with colour TV, separate dining room. One double/family room, one twin-bedded room, both with tea-making facilities. All rooms are tastefully furnished and heated to give a warm cosy atmosphere for you to relax. We take pride in our excellent home cooking using own and local produce. Open May–Oct.

Haxton Down Farm, Bratton Fleming, Barnstaple, Devon EX32 7JL

Mrs Pat Burge
☎ 01598 710275
[BB] From £13.50–£15
EM From £7.50
Sleeps 6
🛏 🐕 🎠 ⚓
Listed *Commended*

Be assured of a warm welcome at this beef and sheep farm set in peaceful countryside close to Exmoor. Enjoy the freedom of the fields, look at the animals or relax in the comfortable farmhouse. Guests have their own lounge with colour TV, separate dining room, 3 bedrooms, private bath/shower room, 2 WC's. Delicious, plentiful food, tea/coffee-making facilities, we aim to give you a happy holiday. Brochure available. Open Easter–Oct. Welcome Host Day.

Higher Churchill Farm, East Down, Nr Barnstaple, North Devon EX31 4LT

Mrs Andrea Cook
☎ 01271 850543
[BB] From £15
EM From £7.50
Sleeps 6
🌿 🎠 🐾
🌼 *Commended*

Children welcome! Come and enjoy a family holiday on our dairy farm. Watch the milking, calf feeding and meet our friendly family pets. If you like good, fresh, homemade food and comfortable, spacious accommodation with en suite or private bathroom, guests' own kitchen and laundry facilities, then do give Churchill a try. Peaceful short breaks, early and late. Open all year except Christmas. Welcome Host Day.

Holloford Farm, Higher Clovelly, Bideford, Devon EX39 5SD   ⑩

Mrs Joanne Wade
☎ 01237 441275
[BB] From £16–£19
Sleeps 4
🛏 🐕 ☕
Listed *Highly Commended*

Charming Devonshire farmhouse, recently renovated to a high standard, with many original features including oak beams and open fireplaces. The pretty bedrooms have tea/coffee-making facilities and washbasins. The farm is set in beautiful, unspoilt surroundings 2 miles from Clovelly and Hartland Point. Excellent home cooking and a warm welcome await you. Open Mar–Oct.

Home Park Farm, Lower Blackwell, Muddiford, North Devon EX31 4ET   ⑪

Mrs Mari Lethaby
☎ 01271 42955
[BB] From £15–£17.50
EM From £7.50
Sleeps 6
🛏 🐕 ⚓
🌼 🌼 *Commended*

Get away from it all, share our beautiful corner of North Devon and sample our warm hospitality. Paradise for the country and garden lover (guests may stay in and relax in the garden). Brochure available. Central heating. All rooms en suite. Ideal base for touring. 2 miles from Barnstaple. RAC acclaimed. AA. QQQQ. Open all year except Christmas. Welcome Host Day.

(12) Huxtable Farm, West Buckland, Barnstaple, North Devon EX32 0SR

Jackie & Antony Payne
☎/Fax 01598 760254
[BB] From £19–£22
EM £12
Sleeps 12
🏃 🚭 🏠 🏥

🐝 🐝 *Commended*

Relax in our mediaeval longhouse and barn carefully restored and furnished with antiques. Secluded sheep farm with pygmy goats, Shetland pony and poultry. 4 course candlelit dinners of farm/local produce served with complimentary homemade wine. En suite bedrooms with colour TV. Winner 'Taste of Exmoor', log fires, games room, sauna, reductions children, short/long breaks out of season. Open all year (closed Christmas). Welcome Host Day.

(13) Kerscott Farm, Ash Mill, South Molton, North Devon EX36 4QG

Mrs Theresa Sampson
☎ 01769 550262
[BB] From £14.50–£16.50
EM From £6.50
Sleeps 6
🐕 (8) 🍴 🏃 🚗

🐝 🐝 *Highly Commended*

Peaceful, olde worlde 16th century farmhouse mentioned in Domesday Book. Furnished throughout with English country antiques, pictures and china. A beautiful, comfortable and fascinating family home. The pretty bedrooms have luxury en suite or have separate guests' bathroom. Central heating, tea/coffee-making facilities and superb views. Scrumptious, hearty country cooking from Aga. Non smokers only. Open all year.

(14) Meadow Farm, East Buckland, Barnstaple, North Devon EX32 0TB

Yvonne Hopkins
☎ 01598 760375
[BB] From £16
EM From £10
Sleeps 4
🍴

🐝 🐝 *Highly Commended*

A friendly welcome awaits guests to our beautifully furnished, warm bungalow and lovely garden. Peacefully situated on edge of hamlet with far-reaching views. 2 double bedrooms, 1 en suite, 1 with magnificent half-tester bed and private bathroom. Delicious, traditional home cooking using fresh local produce. Good parking. 3 miles M5 link, 30 minutes' easy drive coast. Convenient Exmoor on Tarka Trail. Brochure. Open all year. Welcome Host Day

(15) Waytown Farm, Shirwell, Barnstaple, North Devon EX31 4JN

Hazel Kingdon
☎ 01271 850396
[BB] From £16.50–£19
EM From £7.50
Sleeps 9
🐕 🏥 🏠

🐝 🐝 *Commended*

A warm welcome awaits you on our family run beef and sheep farm set in beautiful countryside about 3 miles north of Barnstaple. Our 17th century farmhouse offers a warm and comfortable atmosphere with traditional farmhouse cooking. Double and family en suite bedrooms, twin and single bedrooms, all with colour TV and beverage facilities. Brochure. Weekly terms available. Open all year except Christmas. Welcome Host Day.

SELF-CATERING

(16) Ashdown, Down Farm, King's Nympton, Umberleigh, Devon EX37 9TF

Norma Latham
☎ 01769 572463
[SC] £250–£450
Sleeps 4/9
🐕 🏥 🏠

🐾 🐾 🐾 🐾 🐾

Commended

A warm welcome awaits you at Ashdown situated on 400 acre family run farm. South Molton 4 miles. South facing, wonderful views of the wooded valley and hills from all windows. Spacious property tastefully furnished. CH. 1st floor 3 bedrooms, bathroom. Ground floor 1 bedroom, bathroom, cloakroom, well equipped kitchen, dining room. Lounge, TV, table tennis. Enclosed garden, swing, barbecue. Fishing, riding nearby. Ring for brochure. Open all year. Welcome Host Day.

Barley Cottage & Old Granary, c/o Denham Farm, North Buckland, Braunton, North Devon EX33 1HY

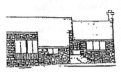

Jean Barnes
☎/Fax 01271 890297
SC **£160–£575**
Sleeps 4/8
🐕 🐎 🎿
🐾 🐾 🐾 – 🐾 🐾 🐾 🐾
Commended

For a large party choose 'Barley Cott' with 4 bedrooms and 2 bathrooms or for a small party, the 'Old Granary' with 1 family size bedroom. Each is homely with good quality furnishings, extremely well equipped with everything you need. Visit nearby sandy beaches, walk our country lanes, picnic beside our lake. Enjoy the small pets corner, aviary, play area and games room. Book a farmhouse dinner, make friends in our bar. Come to Denham for a holiday to remember. Open all year. Welcome Host Day.

Beech Grove, East Westacott, Riddlecombe, Chulmleigh, Devon EX18 7PF

Thomas & Joyce Middleton
☎ 01769 520210
SC **From £145**
Sleeps 5/7 + cot
🐎 ♿ ■
🐾 🐾 🐾 🐾 *Commended*

Set in pretty gardens overlooking beautiful countryside, between Dartmoor and Exmoor, our spacious bungalow has a lovely atmosphere of warmth, peace and comfort. Friendly welcome, especially for the less able, on family-run beef and sheep farm. Tempting meals and markets, in local towns and delightful villages. Superbly equipped, heating throughout, log fires, linen provided. Large games room, golf, riding, fishing, nearby. Beach 30 minutes. Open all year. Welcome Host Day

---

Cleave Country Cottages, c/o Cleave Farm, Weare, Giffard, Nr Bideford, North Devon EX39 4QX

Elizabeth Moore
☎ 01805 623671
Fax 01805 623235
SC **From £200**
Sleeps 5/6
🐎 🐕 ♿ 🐾 🎿 ■
🐾 🐾 🐾 🐾
Commended

Come to the heart of 'Tarka' country. A warm welcome awaits you here at our working dairy farm. Luxury accommodation with en suite facilities; electricity, linen and use of retired pony, William included in tariff. Patio, barbecue, level parking. Cottage with living accommodation upstairs to enjoy panoramic views. Lovely walks, near beaches and moors. Open Apr–Oct.

The Cottage, Lutworthy Farm, Worlington, Crediton, Devon EX17 4SW

Mrs Janet Bemrose
☎ 01884 860348
SC **From £140–£180**
Sleeps 5 + cot
🐎 🐕
🐾 🐾 🐾 *Approved*

Self-contained cottage wing of Devon longhouse on family run sheep and beef farm. An ideal area for touring, easy access to beaches and moors with country activities available locally. Cosy lounge with colour TV and open fire, well equipped kitchen. 2 bedrooms and bathroom. Brochure available.

Drewstone Farm, South Molton, North Devon EX36 3EF

Ruth Ley
☎ 01769 572337
SC **From £130–£330**
Sleeps 6–8
🐕 🐎 ♿ 🐾 🐕
🐾 🐾 🐾 🐾 – 🐾 🐾 🐾 🐾
Commended

Escape to farm tranquillity on edge of Exmoor, 16th century luxury converted barn with beams, woodburner, colour TV, fitted carpets, washing machine. 3 bedrooms, bath-shower room. Fully equipped oak kitchen/diner and lounge upstairs to enjoy panoramic country views. Enclosed lawn, children's facilities, games room, animals to see, freedom to explore the farm. Country walks, clay-pigeon shooting, trout lake, and pony riding. Open all year.

Giffords Hele, Meeth, Okehampton, Devon EX20 3QN

Mrs Linden Draper
☎/Fax 01837 810009
SC **From £336–£497**
Sleeps 5/10
🐕 🐎 🐕 🎿 ■
🐾 🐾 🐾 🐾 *Highly Commended*

Garden and courtyard cottages, part of old Devon longhouse. Lovely old beams, low windowsills, a huge inglenook and 4-poster bed. Pretty walled garden and play area, plus full access to our superb indoor swimming pool, farmhouse restaurant and bar. Each cottage sleeps up to 5 in 2 bedrooms which can interconnect to accommodate a party of up to 10 + cot. Own Torridge fishing. Ring for brochure. Open all year. Welcome Host Day.

23 Great Whitstone Farm, Meshaw, South Molton, Devon EX36 4NH

Sally Anne Meikle
☎ 01884 860914
[SC] From £140–£190
Sleeps 7 + cot
Approved

A friendly family run farm, a large traditional kitchen brings a warm welcome all year round with a Rayburn and all mod cons. Spacious bedrooms accommodation up to eight people. Cot included. Guests welcome to help feed animals and look around the farm and watch the milking. Come and get away from it all. Open all year.

24 Hollacombe Barton, Hollacombe, Chulmleigh, Devon EX18 7QG

Christine Stevens
☎ 01837 83385
Fax 01837 83002
[SC] From £195
EM £5
Sleeps 2/8
Commended

Children can roam and play in safety whilst parents relax in comfort in the conservatory while their evening meal is prepared. What more could you wish for? How about a superbly equipped farmhouse only 18 miles from the sea. Enjoy woodland walks, barbecues, quad bikes and pony rides.Watch the milking, make friends with our tame sheep, chickens, goats, calves and Miss Piggy! Versatile accommodation and prices. Our guests return year after year. Please phone for informative brochure. Welcome Host Day.

25 Manor Farm, Riddlecombe, Chulmleigh, North Devon EX18 7NX

Eveline Gay
☎ 01769 520335
[SC] From £150
Sleeps 7/8 + cot

Commended

A friendly welcome awaits you at Manor Farmhouse, which has a very cosy self catering wing with lovely views. A dairy and sheep farm where children can bottlefeed baby lambs, watch the milking, make friends with Poppy our tame sheep, collect eggs, etc. 3 bedrooms, gas-fired woodburner heating throughout, cleanliness guaranteed. Superb games room – includes play cottage, ride-on toys, snooker, table tennis, Fisher Price kitchen. Welcome Host Day.

26 Nethercott Manor Farm, Rose Ash, South Molton, North Devon EX36 4RE

Carol Woollacott
☎ 01769 550483
[SC] From £100–£350
Sleeps 4 and 8
Approved

Denis and Carol assure a warm welcome at Nethercott, a 17th century thatched house on a 200-acre working farm. Two comfortable self-contained wings sleeping 4 and 8. Pleasant views overlooking woods and trout pond. Pony rides, extensive games room and laundry. Also barbecuing facilities. 6 miles from the market town of South Molton, ideal for touring Exmoor and coast. Open all year.

27 Northcott Barton Farm, Ashreigney, Chulmleigh, Devon EX18 7PR

Mrs Sandra Gay
☎ 01769 520259
[SC] From £130
Sleeps 7/8 + cot
Commended

Come and explore the farm, meet the animals and enjoy our beautiful countryside, children especially welcome 'help' feed lambs, calves, hens, collect eggs and watch milking. 3 bedroomed farmhouse wing offers 'home from home' comfort cosy oak-beamed lounge, log fire, heating throughout, automatic washing machine and linen provided. Large south facing garden, riding, fishing, golf nearby, warm welcome assured.

28 The Old Barn, Bocombe Farm, Parkham, Nr Bideford, North Devon EX39 5PH

Marian Scambler
☎ 01237 451255
[SC] From £120–£500
Sleeps 8 + cot
Highly Commended

Charming, spacious barn conversion on family dairy farm. Peacefully situated overlooking wooded conservation area with buzzards, badgers, newts and butterflies. Close to picturesque Clovelly, RHS Rosemore and Marwood Gardens. Delightful coast and country walks. Four bedrooms, 1 en suite, spacious lounge with log burner, enclosed patio, fully equipped kitchen. Linen, logs and electricity included. Open all year. Welcome Host Day.

Pickwell Barton Holiday Cottages, Pickwell Barton, Georgeham, Braunton, North Devon EX33 1LA

Mrs Sheila Cook
☎ 01271 890987
ⓈⒸ From £120–£350
Sleeps 7/8
🐎 🐕 🎋
🐾 🐾 *Approved*

Sunnyside and Pickwell Barton cottages are two spacious, well equipped farm holiday cottages on a beef, sheep and arable farm. Pickwell is a small hamlet close to Putsborough and Woolacombe's golden sandy beach. Ideal for surfing and gorgeous coastal walks across our farm with breathtaking views of the sunset over Lundy Island. Golf, horse-riding, fishing nearby. Solid fuel Rayburn available. Open all year.

Sandyke Cottage, c/o Sandyke Farm, Swimbridge, Barnstaple, North Devon EX32 0QZ

Margaret Bartlett
☎ 01271 830243
ⓈⒸ From £150–£310
Sleeps 6 cot
🐎 🐕 🎋
🐾 🐾 🐾 *Commended*

Enjoy a stay at our pretty pink cottage with its own lovely garden in tranquil surroundings near our dairy farm, only 5 miles from Barnstaple. It is central for beaches and Exmoor. Walk the adjoining Tarka trail or explore the farm's own woodland and fishing ponds. The spacious cottage accommodates 6, with linen provided, and is fully equipped. The cosy oak-beamed lounge with log fire provides home from home comfort. Open Mar–Nov and Christmas.

Stable Cottage, Pitt Farm, North Molton, North Devon EX36 3JR

Mrs Gladys Ayre
☎ 01598 740285
ⓈⒸ From £130–£320
Sleeps 5/6
🐎 🐕 🎋
🐾 🐾 🐾 🐾
Commended

Enjoy peaceful surroundings at our charming cottage, set in unspoilt Exmoor countryside, 1 mile from village shops, pubs, garage, equipped to high standard with night storage heating throughout. 3 bedrooms. Bath/shower/beamed lounge with woodburner. Colour TV, oak fitted kitchen/diner. Autowasher, fridge, microwave, etc. Own patio. Barbecue. Pond with ducks and geese. Freedom to explore our 230 acre sheep farm. Open all year.

Welcombe Farm, Charles, Nr Barnstaple, North Devon EX32 7PU

Mrs Margaret Faulkner
☎ 01598 710440
ⓈⒸ From £100–£250
Sleeps 4/5 + cot
🐎 🐕 ✂ 🚐
Tourist Board Inspected

Imaginative private setting for a luxury caravan holiday. Comfortable and peaceful, with full facilities, two bedrooms and heating throughout. Small, family run farm with dairy cows and sheep, on the foothills of Exmoor. Panoramic views of hills and valleys from enclosed garden. Close to Tarka Trail and easy reach of sandy beaches, moors and gardens. Wildlife in abundance. Open Mar–Oct.

Willesleigh Farm, Goodleigh, Barnstaple, North Devon EX32 7NA   33

Anne Esmond-Cole
☎ 01271 43763
ⓈⒸ From £145–£590
Sleeps 6
🐎 ♿ ✂ 🐕
🐾 🐾 🐾 🐾 *Highly Commended*

Glorious 'get away from it all' countryside, 2 minutes village shop, inn, ½ hour drive to dramatic coastal scenery, Exmoor. A place for all seasons, all ages. An illustrated brochure brings full information of cosy rooms, walled gardens, enclosed heated swimming pool May–Oct, all personally cared for with attention to detail at our family run farm. Open all year. Welcome Host Day.

NO ANSWER?
Farmers are mostly out and about during the day.
Try to telephone before 9.30am or after 4pm.

64

England's West Country
Heart of Devon

Group Contacts: 🅱🅱 *Mrs Linda Hill* ☎ *013985 280 From April '95 01398 351280*
🆂🅲 *Mrs Sylvia Hann* ☎ *01884 256946*

If you are undecided about which part of Devon to take your holiday, why not opt for the heart of the county ... you can then tour and explore in all directions to get a taste of all that's best.

The Heart of Devon with its thatched cottages, lush meadows, steeply wooded valleys, rivers and streams, is unspoilt and rather special.

This is an area of traditional sheep and cattle farming. A visit to one of the local towns on market day will give you the chance to get the full flavour of the occasion, plus the opportunity to sample the produce itself ... cheese, smoked trout, clotted cream and farmhouse cider.

As always in Devon there is much to see and do. There is a hint of nostalgia as well. Take Tiverton for example: the town's museum is one of the best folk museums in the West Country with its large railway gallery complete with restored GWR loco. The Great Western Canal, 11 miles long, offers trips by horse-drawn barge.

There is, of course, much more – and all within easy reach: Exmoor, Dartmoor, the south coast resorts and dramatic seascapes of the north.

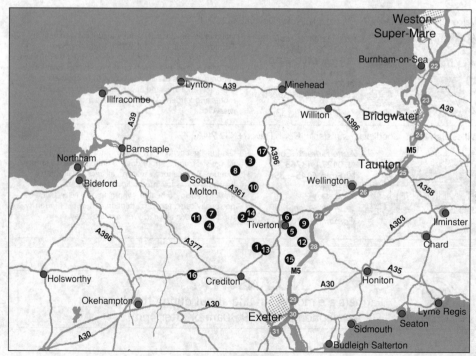

BED AND BREAKFAST

(and evening meal)

Brindiwell Farm, Cheriton Fitzpaine, Crediton, Devon EX17 4HR

Doreen Lock
☎ 01363 866357
▦ From £12–£15
EM From £8
Sleeps 5
🐎
Listed

Delightful old farmhouse with oak beams and panelling. Tea/coffee-making facilities in all rooms. Situated between Tiverton and Crediton, and midway between north and south coasts and moors. Outstanding views to Dartmoor. 120-acre sheep farm with two doubles and one single. AA listed. Open all year.

Great Bradley Farm, Withleigh, Tiverton, Devon EX16 8JL

Mrs Sylvia Hann
☎ 01884 256946
▦ From £16.50–£19.00
EM From £10
Sleeps 4
✄ 🐎 (10)
🌸🌸 *Highly Commended*

Tucked away in the Devonshire countryside, you will find comfort, peace and quiet in our beautiful 16th century farmhouse. Attractive bedrooms with central heating, washbasins, tea/coffee trays and private bathrooms. The guests' lounge, with TV overlooks the garden and beautiful views beyond. Delicious home cooking is served in a happy relaxed atmosphere. Non smokers only please. Brochure available. Open Mar–Oct.

Harton Farm, Oakford, Tiverton, Devon EX16 9HH

Mrs Lindy Head
☎ 013985 209
▦ From £13–£15
EM From £6
Sleeps 6
🐕 🐎 (4) 🏕 🐾
🌸

Welcome to our comfortable stone-built farmhouse dating from 17th century, situated in secluded but accessible position near Exmoor. 1 family, 1 twin room with washbasins. Hearty, traditional home baking using additive-free home-produced meat and organically grown vegetables. Vegetarian menu on request. Tea-making facilities, home-spun wool available. Farm walk with nature notes, friendly animals. Reduction for children. Open all year (closed Christmas & New Year).

Hele Barton, Black Dog, Crediton, Devon EX17 4QJ

Mrs Gillian Gillbard
☎ 01884 860278
▦ From £14
EM From £8.50
Sleeps 6
🐎 ✄ 💼
🌸🌸 *Commended*

Relax in peaceful surroundings with lovely views from our listed 17th century thatched farmhouse on family-run 236-acre mixed farm, 2 miles off Tiverton – South Molton Road nr Witheridge. Double or twin rooms (1 en suite), all with H and C, tea/coffee-making facilities, central heating, 1 guest bathroom, guests' dining room and lounge with colour TV, evening meal by arrangement. Brochure. Open all year (closed Christmas).

Hornhill Farm, Tiverton, Devon EX16 4PL

Barbara Pugsley
☎ 01884 253352
▦ From £16.50–£18.50
EM From £10
Sleeps 6
🐎 (12) ♿ ✄ 💼
🌸🌸 *Highly Commended*

Overlooking beautiful Exe Valley, Hornhill is the perfect place to stay and relax. Explore our lovely county, return to comfort, warmth, delicious home cooking and a happy atmosphere. Peaceful bedrooms, one with Victorian 4-poster, private, en suite bathrooms, heating, TV, tea/coffee-making facilities. Attractive drawing room with log fires. Large garden. Ample parking. AA 5Q Premier Selected. Open all year.

---

6   **Lower Collipriest Farm,** Tiverton, Devon EX16 4PT

Mrs Linda Olive
☎ **01884 252321**
🛏 **From £19**
EM From £11
Sleeps 5
🚶 ✕ 🐾
♨ ♨ ♨ *Highly Commended*

Come and relax and enjoy the beauty of the Exe Valley in our 17th century thatched farmhouse. Comfortable lounge with inglenook fireplace and oak beams. Colour TV. Central heating throughout. Twin/single rooms with bathroom en suite, tea/coffee-making facilities. Delicious, traditional fresh cooking with our/local produce. Lovely walks over 220-acre dairy farm, conservation pond/ woodland area. An AA award-winning farm. Open Feb–Nov. Brochure available.

7   **Marchweeke Farm,** Thelbridge, Witheridge, Tiverton, Devon EX16 8NY

Ann Webber
☎ **01884 860418**
🛏 **From £14–£16**
EM From £8
Sleeps 4
🐎 🐓 ▪
♨ ♨ *Commended*

We warmly welcome you to come and enjoy the peace and quiet of our lovely Devon longhouse with its beautiful views. One double en suite, one twin with private bathroom both with tea/coffee-making facilities. Separate dining room with inglenook and beams. Lounge with CTV. Delicious home cooking using own and local produce. Access at all times. Brochure available. Children welcome with reduced rates for 12 years and under. Open Feb–Nov.

8   **Newhouse Farm,** Oakford, Tiverton, Devon EX16 9JE

Mrs Anne Boldry
☎ **013985 347**
May '95 01398 351347
🛏 **From £16–£18**
EM From £10
Sleeps 6
🐎 (10) 🐾 🎋 🦊
♨ ♨ *Commended*

A perfect base for discovering Devon, our livestock farm is close to Exmoor. A 400-year-old longhouse, tastefully and comfortably furnished featuring oak beams and inglenook. Bedrooms have washbasins, CH, tea trays, en suite available. We aim to provide the best of farmhouse cooking – original recipes, 13 varieties of marmalade, home-baked bread, delicious puddings our speciality. AA QQQQ. Detailed brochure. Open all year (closed Christmas).

9   **Oburnford Farm,** Cullompton, Devon EX15 1LZ

Mrs Gillian Pring
☎ **01884 32292**
🛏 **From £17.50–£20**
EM From £10
Sleeps 12
🐓 🐎 🎋 🦊
♨ ♨ ♨ *Commended*

Beautiful Georgian farmhouse on peaceful 120-acre mixed farm, comfort and friendly family welcome guaranteed. Superb accommodation and lashings of home-produced fare – award winning. Special diets welcome. Family, double, twin rooms, all en suite, with tea/coffee-making facilities. Lovely walks over farm, watch the milking and the making of clotted cream! A relaxing break any time of the year. Reductions for children. Open all year.

10   **Quoit-at-Cross Farm,** Stoodleigh, Tiverton, Devon EX16 9PJ

Mrs Linda Hill
☎/Fax **013985 280**
April '95 01398 351280
🛏 **From £16**
EM From £9
Sleeps 6
🐎 ✕ ▪ 🦊
♨ ♨ ♨

Charming 17th century farmhouse in conservation village. Excellent accommodation, twin/double rooms, en suite, colour TV and tea/coffee-making facilities, delightful inglenook dining room and relaxing lounge. Full English breakfast. Superb dinners. Large garden, ample parking. Easy reach National Trust properties, Exmoor safaris, swimming etc. A361 2½ miles. Open Apr–Dec.

11   **Stockham Farm,** Thelbridge, Crediton, Devon EX17 4SJ

Mrs Carol Webber
☎ **01884 860308**
🛏 **From £15–£18**
EM From £8
Sleeps 6
✕ 🐎 🎋 ▪
♨

A warm welcome awaits you on our family-run 150-acre working farm 2½ miles off B3137 Tiverton-South Molton road near Witheridge. 14th century farmhouse, separate lounge, dining room, games room with information area. All bedrooms have private facilities. Tea/coffee-making facilities, good food, lovely walks. Lots of animals, children especially welcome. Excellent centre for exploring our lovely county. Open all year (except Christmas).

Wishay Farm, Trinity, Cullompton, Devon EX15 1PE   12

Mrs Sylvia Baker
☎ **01884 33223**
🅱 **From £15–£16**
EM From £8
Sleeps 6
🐎
♛ ♛

Comfortable and spacious 17th century farmhouse, set amid the peace and seclusion of the countryside. Ideal base for touring. Comfortable lounge with colour TV. Central heating. 1 family room with en suite bathroom, double with separate guests' bathroom, both with colour TV, fridge and tea/coffee-making facilities. Children welcome. Golf and indoor bowls rink nearby. Open all year.

SELF-CATERING

Brindiwell Farm, Cheriton Fitzpaine, Crediton, Devon EX17 4HR   13

Doreen Margaret Lock
☎ **01363 866357**
🆂🅲 **From £170–£200**
Sleeps 4
🐎
🔑 🔑 🔑 *Approved*

Self-contained wing of delightful old farmhouse in peaceful countryside with outstanding views. One double, one single bedroom and Z bed. Colour TV. Midway between north and south coasts and moors. Close Dartmoor and Exmoor. Open all year.

Cider Cottage, c/o Great Bradley Farm, Withleigh, Tiverton, Devon EX16 8JL   14

Mrs Sylvia Hann
☎ **01884 256946**
🆂🅲 **From £135–£325**
Sleeps 5 + cot
🐎
🔑 🔑 🔑 🔑 *Highly Commended*

Charming cottage, originally 17th century cider barn, on 155-acre dairy farm. Beautiful views, spacious accommodation for 5. 3 pretty bedrooms. Bed linen included. Comfortable oak-beamed lounge, superb new kitchen with dining area. Washing machine available. All tastefully furnished and equipped to provide a high standard of comfort and convenience. Large garden with picnic table. Walk our country lanes. Explore moors and coasts, or stay and enjoy the farm. Open all year.

Hele Payne Farm, Hele, Exeter, Devon EX5 4PH   15

Irene and Sally Maynard
☎ **01392 881530/ 881356**
🆂🅲 **From £80–£300**
Sleeps 3/5/6
🐎 🍴 🎋 🕷
🔑 🔑 🔑 🔑 *Up to Highly Commended*

Relax in our heated swimming pool. Let your children explore the farm by helping to feed the baby calves or by playing in the beautiful gardens. Fishing. All three cottages (Honeysuckle Cottage, The Wheat Loft and Horseshoe Lodge) are furnished, cleaned and decorated to a high standard and have colour TV, bed linen, laundry room, cot, highchair and central heating. Open all year.

Paschoe Cottage, Paschoe Farm, Bow, Crediton, Devon EX17 6JT   16

Mrs Vera Blake
☎ **01363 84288**
🆂🅲 **From £110–£375**
Sleeps 5 + cot
🐎 🐕 🎋
🔑 🔑 🔑 🔑 *Commended*

Delightful stone cottage in beautiful, tranquil garden setting on 380-acre dairy farm. 3 charming bedrooms, linen, towels included. Spacious lounge/diner with colour TV. Very well equipped kitchen. NS heating throughout. Phone. Relax in the garden or by the outdoor heated swimming pool. Watch milking and calves or roam fields and woods to see our varied wildlife including badgers and buzzards. Open all year.

17 **Wonham Barton,** c/o Wonham Barton, Bampton, Tiverton, Devon EX16 9JZ

Anne McLean Williams
☎ 01398 331312
SC From £118–£250
Sleeps 4/6
🐎 🐴 🎪 🛖 🍴
🐾 🐾 🐾 *Commended*

In the beautiful Exe Valley near Exmoor, our generously equipped, fully heated self-contained farmhouse wing enjoys panoramic views and its own garden. Children welcome, cot and highchair available, dogs by arrangement. Visitors can enjoy a working farm and 300 acres of pasture and woodland with cattle, sheep, wildflowers, birds and deer. Riding, fishing, swimming, golf nearby. Village 2 miles. Open part of year only.

FOLLOW THE COUNTRY CODE

Leave nothing but footprints,
Take nothing but photographs,
Kill nothing but time!

DISABLED VISITORS

Many members offer a welcome to disabled/less able visitors. Please do check the extent of the facilities before booking.

BUREAU ACCOMMODATION IS RELIABLE

This Guide lists **Farm Holiday Bureau** members only. They are all inspected by the National Tourist Board for standards (see introduction pages) and by fellow members to maintain a high quality.

65

England's West Country

East Devon

Group Contact: *Jill Balkwill* ☎ *01548 550312*

East Devon has picturesque villages and miles of sandy and pebble beaches. This is the country of the old sea dogs of Elizabethan times, such as Sir Francis Drake and Sir Walter Raleigh. East Devon Farm and Country Holiday members offer a choice of farmhouse bed and breakfast and self-catering accommodation all of a high standard.

Wherever you stay you are not far from the coast where you can enjoy peaceful clifftop walks and spectacular seascapes. Inland a little way you can wander over moors and common land or down winding country lanes. For the more active there's swimming, riding, sailing, fishing and windsurfing.

If it's places of interest you want, East Devon won't let you down – there are craft centres, churches, markets and museums. Exeter alone boasts a cathedral with a 300ft nave – the longest span of unbroken Gothic vaulting in the world, plus priceless manuscripts; a Maritime Museum with more than 100 craft from all over the world, and the Royal Albert Memorial collection of lace, glass and china.

If all that leaves you hungry, you can choose to take meals in village inns, thatched cottage cafés or seaside restaurants. Whatever your choice you will find excellent fare … at very fair prices.

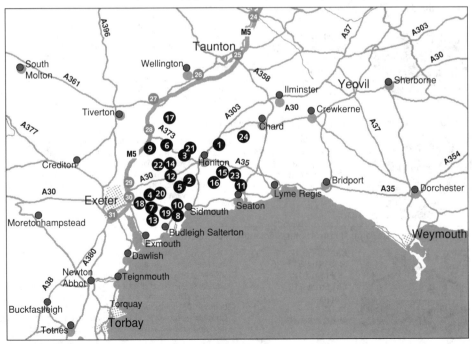

BED AND BREAKFAST

(and evening meal)

---

① Barn Park Farm, Nr Cotleigh, Stockland Hill, Honiton, Devon EX14 9JA

Pamela Boyland
☎ 01404 861297
🛏 From £14
EM From £8
Sleeps 4
🐕 🐎 🎾 ⚓
Applied

Barn Park Farm, a working dairy farm situated near the A30/A303 junction, is set in picturesque countryside within reach of many beauty spots and the coast. The farmhouse is full of character having a homely atmosphere. Traditional English breakfasts using eggs from our free range hens. Evening meal available. Open all year.

---

② Claypitts Farm, East Hill, Ottery St Mary, Devon EX11 1QD

Jayne Burrow
☎ 01404 814599
🛏 From £14–£17
EM From £9.50
Sleeps 6
✂ 🐎 (3) 🎾
♨ ♨

Relax on our mixed farm in the beautiful Otter Valley. Lovely walks and many attractions nearby, including Sidmouth 4½ miles. Double en-suite, twin and double with washbasins, guests' toilets/bathroom, tea/coffee facilities. Excellent comfortable accommodation, beamed ceilings, CH, large lounge, log burner, dining room. Good farmhouse cooking. Large garden, children's play area, many small animals (chickens, ducks and geese). Open Easter–Nov.

---

③ Godford Farm, Awliscombe, Honiton, Devon EX14 0PW

Sally Lawrence
☎ 01404 42825
🛏 From £14–£16.75
EM £9.25
Sleeps 6
🐎 🎾 💼 ⚓

We invite you to stay on this family-run dairy farm, set in a beautiful river valley. Listed farmhouse with large sitting and dining rooms. Colour TV. Central heating. Drinks facilities in bedrooms. Large garden, play area, games barn for all ages. Families with children especially welcome. Cots and highchairs provided. Family and twin rooms, private bathrooms. Children reduced rates. Brochure. Open Easter–Oct.

---

④ Great Houndbeare Farm, Aylesbeare, Exeter, Devon EX5 2DB

Hazel Bale
☎/Fax 01404 822771
🛏 From £18–£26
🐎 🐕 ✂ 🍴 💼 🎿
♨ ♨

Unwind and relax in tranquil surroundings amid a small arable farm with woodland and a lake. We offer coarse fishing, bicycle and barbecue hire. All rooms are en suite with colour TV, tea and coffee facilities, etc. Guests' lounge with separate dining room. Full central heating. Brochure available.

---

⑤ Higher Coombe Farm, Tipton St John, Sidmouth, Devon EX10 0AX

Kerstin Farmer
☎ 01404 813385
🛏 From £18
EM From £10
Sleeps 6
🐎 🎿
♨ *Commended*

The Farmer family invite you to a relaxing stay on their sheep and beef farm, peacefully situated in the beautiful Otter Valley yet only 4 miles from Sidmouth seafront. Family, double, single rooms all have washbasins and tea/coffee-making facilities, some with colour TV. (No smoking in bedrooms). Lounge with colour TV, separate dining room. Children welcome. Good, mainly home produced, farmhouse food and substantial breakfast. Open most of the year.

Lane End Farm, Broadhembury, Honiton, Devon EX14 0LU 6

Mrs Molly Bennett
01404 841563
From £16–£18
EM From £9
Sleeps 6

At Lane End Farm you will enjoy delicious home cooking in glorious surroundings. Panoramic views of the Blackdown Hills, an Area of Outstanding Natural Beauty. With cattle and sheep grazing, floral gardens all within walking distance of the unspoilt thatched village of Broadhembury. Tea/ coffee facilities in bedrooms (1 en suite). CH, colour TV. Colour brochure. Children reduced rates. Evening meals optional.

Lochinvar, Shepherds Park Farm, Woodbury, Nr Exeter, Devon EX5 1LA 7

Dorothy Glanvill
01395 232185
From £15–£18
Sleeps 6

Dairy farm on the outskirts of Woodbury, with panoramic views of surrounding countryside. One double, 1 twin en suite , 1 family with private bathroom. All with hot drink facilities, colour TV, hair dryers, electric blankets, clock radios, full CH. English breakfast served. Access to rooms at all times. Ample parking. Local inns and restaurants nearby. Open all year.

Lower Pinn Farm, Peak Hill, Sidmouth, Devon EX10 0NN 8

Elizabeth Tancock
01395 513733
From £16–£19
Sleeps 6

A friendly welcome and comfortable, spacious rooms await you at Lower Pinn. 2 miles west of the unspoilt coastal resort of Sidmouth. Two double/twin en suite, one double with washbasin. All rooms have colour TV, tea/coffee facilities, CH, electric blankets. Access at all times. Dining room in which a full English breakfast is served. Ample parking. Several local pubs and restaurants. Open most of the year.

Newcourt Barton, Langford, Cullompton, Devon EX15 1SE 9

Mrs Sheila A Hitt
01884 277326
From £15.50
Sleeps 6
(11)
Listed

Newcourt Barton is an ideal base for touring the Devon coast and countryside. It is a working farm with sheep. The red brick farmhouse is surrounded by a large garden with grass tennis court. Situated in a quiet position 4 miles Cullompton, M5 J28. Coarse fishing on farm. 1 twin, 1 double, 1 family, H/C, toilet and shower. Tea/coffee-making facilities, TV, lounge, dining room, full English breakfast. Local inn and restaurants for evening meal.

Pinn Barton Farm, Pinn Lane, Peak Hill, Sidmouth, Devon EX10 0NN 10

Betty Sage
01395 514004
From £17–£19
Sleeps 6
Commended

Enjoy a warm welcome on our 330 acre farm by the coast, 2 miles from Sidmouth seafront. Lovely walks in Area of Outstanding Natural Beauty. Comfortable bedrooms (all en suite) with CH, colour TV, hot drink facilities, electric blankets, access at all times. TV lounge and dining room with separate tables. Substantial breakfast, bedtime drinks. Many restaurants, inns and places to visit nearby. Open all year.

Pippinfield Farm, Harepath Hill, Colyford, Seaton, Devon Ex12 2TD 11

Anne Spanton
01297 21521
From £19.50–£21
EM From £8.50
Sleeps 6
(9)
Applied

Ideal base for touring the Devon coast. The front of the house is south facing with panoramic views of the Axe estuary. Beyond is the pretty village of Axmouth, also the sea at Seaton which is approx 2 miles. Easy reach of Lyme Regis, Charmouth, Beer, Sidmouth, Budleigh Salterton, Exeter. We offer every comfort, en suite rooms, friendly atmosphere. Senior citizens welcome. Open most of year.

12 **Pitt Farm,** Fairmile, Ottery St Mary, Devon EX11 1NL

Susan Hansford
☎ 01404 812439
BB From £16–£20
EM From £9
Listed

A warm family atmosphere awaits you at this 16th century thatched farmhouse which nestles in the picturesque Otter Valley ½ mile from A30 on B3176. Within easy reach of all East Devon resorts and pleasure facilities. Good home cooking using fresh local/own produce. A working beef/arable farm surrounded by lovely countryside and rural walks. Family, double and twin rooms. Lounge with colour TV. Fire certificate. Open Feb–Nov.

13 **Rydon Farm,** Woodbury, Exeter, Devon EX5 1LB

Sally Glanvill
☎ 01395 232341
BB From £17–£22
Sleeps 6

Come and enjoy the peaceful tranquillity of our 16th century Devon longhouse on a working dairy farm. Exposed beams and inglenook fireplace. Bedrooms with tea/coffee facilities, hairdryers, full CH, private or en suite bathrooms. Romantic four-poster. Full English breakfast with free range eggs. Several local pubs and restaurants. Featured in the Daily Mail. Open all year.

14 **Skinners Ash Farm,** Fenny Bridges, Honiton, Devon EX14 0BH

Mrs Jill Godfrey
☎ 01404 850231
BB From £15.50
EM From £7
Sleeps 6
Listed *Commended*

Enjoy a relaxing holiday on a family-run rare breeds farm. Two large family rooms with tea/coffee facilities, TV, private bathroom. Farmhouse cooking, cream teas. Farm walk, pony rides, lovely views. Near local beaches. Walk to two local inns. Please send for brochure. Open all year.

15 **Smallicombe Farm,** Northleigh, Colyton, Devon EX13 6BU

Maggie Todd
☎ 01404 831310
BB From £17–£19
EM From £9.50
Sleeps 6
Commended

Children are welcome at our small farm set in an area of outstanding natural beauty, but convenient for all East Devon coastal resorts. Friendly animals include Jersey cows, pigs, sheep, goats and numerous poultry. Family suite and ground floor twin/double room. All en suite with tea/coffee-making facilities and colour TVs. Cots, highchairs and baby sitting provided. Play area, games room and laundry. Reductions children and weekly. Open all year.

16 **Wiscombe Linhaye Farm,** Southleigh, Colyton, Devon EX13 6JF

Sheila Rabjohns
☎ 01404 87342
BB From £15–£18
EM From £7
Sleeps 6
(5)

A small working farm in the quiet countryside of East Devon but in reach of Sidmouth and Lyme Regis. A friendly atmosphere on this family farm with good home cooking from home/local produce. Two ground floor bedrooms with private bathroom, one en suite. Drink facilities, TV and hair dryers in all bedrooms. Colour TV in lounge and separate dining tables. Three double rooms. Open Easter–Oct.

FARM HOLIDAY BUREAU

Please mention **Stay on a Farm** when booking

SELF-CATERING

Bodmiscombe Farm, Blackborough, Cullompton, Devon EX15 2HR

Mrs Brenda Northam
☎ **01884 266315**
⌂ **From £110–£250**
Sleeps 4 + cot
🛇 🐂 ⅋ 🗢 🍴 🛆
⚶ ⚶ ⚶ *Commended*

A warm, friendly welcome assured on our family farm set in an Area of Outstanding Natural Beauty. Wonderful views from listed 17th century Devon longhouse with beamed ceilings. Private coarse fishing, 20-acre woodland trail. Central for coast and moorland or stay around farm and watch us at work. Electricity not metered. Short breaks. Brochure. Open all year.

Court Brook Farm, Clyst St George, Exeter, Devon EX3 0NT

Jenny Broom
☎ **01392 877710**
Fax 01392 873378
⌂ **From £150–£265**
Sleeps 2/5 + cot
🛇 ⅋
⚶ ⚶ ⚶ *Approved*

Relax in our comfortably furnished cottage in the small village of Clyst St. George. An ideal touring base only 5 miles from Exmouth and 5 miles to Exeter's Cathedral City. In easy reach of Dartmoor. Well equipped kitchen/diner, lounge with colour TV, bathroom with bath/shower. 3 bedrooms, 1 twin, 1 double, 1 single. Garden with picnic furniture and ample parking, full details available. Open Mar–Nov.

Lemprice Farm, Yettington, Budleigh Salterton, Devon EX9 7BW

Mrs Hanneke Coates
☎ **01395 567037**
Fax 01395 567585
⌂ **From £144–£459**
Sleeps 4–7
♿ 👁 🛇 🐂 🛆 🗢 🍴 🛆 🎋
⚶ ⚶ ⚶ – ⚶ ⚶ ⚶ ⚶
Up to Highly Commended

Four south-facing stone barn cottages suitable for disabled. Exceptional walking area of outstanding natural beauty and scientific interest. Home of the rare barn owl. All cottage gardens overlook small lake and marshes abundant with wildlife, hills and open countryside beyond. All linen and electricity included. Dogs by arrangement only. Three miles to beach. Brochure. Open all year. Winter short breaks.

Mill Cottage, Aylesbeare, Exeter, Devon EX5 2DB

Hazel Bale
☎/Fax **01404 822771**
⌂ **From £250–£700**
🛇 🐂 ⅋ 🗢 🍴 🎋
⚶ ⚶ ⚶ ⚶
Commended

Luxury cottage overlooking lake, lawns and woodland. Safe for children and peaceful for adults. Central heating, log fire and satellite TV. Kitchen fitted with dishwasher, washing machine, microwave and fridge freezer. Linen and towels available, all beds have duvets. Three bathrooms. M5 5 miles. Brochure available.

Otter Holt and Owl Hayes, c/o Godford Farm, Awliscombe, Honiton, Devon EX14 0PW 

Sally Lawrence
☎ **01404 42825**
⌂ **From £90–£295**
Sleeps 4 + cot
🛇 🍴 🛆
⚶ ⚶ ⚶ *Commended*

Come and see where the hayracks are in our beautiful barn cottages, one of the many features that make them unique. Each cottage comprises beamed lounge with colour TV, pine kitchen/diner with washer/dryer, microwave, fridge/freezer. CH. 2 bedrooms (linen included). Shower room. Relax in the garden and games barn, or watch the cows being milked. Children welcome, large play area. Cot available. Brochure. Open all year.

22 **Skinners Ash Farm,** Fenny Bridges, Honiton, Devon EX14 0BH

Mrs J. S. Godfrey
☎ **01404 850231**
SC **From £120–£250**
Sleeps 6
🐕 🐑 ⚒ 🎿 🏹 🎐 💼 🏠
🔑 🔑 🔑 🔑 🔑
Commended

Relax on a family-run rare breeds farm. All modern facilities, old-fashioned cooking, cream teas. Enjoy pony rides, walks, two pubs 200 yards away. Near local beaches and tourist attractions. On A30 Honiton to Exeter road. Short breaks. Please send for brochure. Open all year.

23 **Smallicombe Farm,** Northleigh, Colyton, Devon EX13 6BU

Maggie Todd
☎ **01404 831310**
SC **From £95–£495**
Sleeps 2–9
🐕 ♿ 🎐 💼 🎿
🔑 🔑 🔑 – 🔑 🔑 🔑 🔑
Commended

Small farm in superb rural setting yet close to coast. Large variety of friendly farm animals including Jersey cows, pigs, sheep, goats and poultry. Children's play area, large games room, laundry. Recently converted barns retaining original features but with all modern conveniences. Sleep 2, 4, 5 and 9. One specially designed for wheelchair users. Cots and highchairs available. Open all year.

24 **The Stable,** Heathstock Farm, Stockland, Honiton, Devon EX14 9EU

Mrs Nancy Patch
☎ **01404 881267**
SC **From £100–£220**
Sleeps 2/4
♿ 🏹 🐕 🎐
🔑 🔑 🔑 *Approved*

Set in a pretty hillside hamlet, The Stable is on one level and situated on a working family farm. Well furnished, with large lounge with bed settee, colour TV, storage heaters, kitchen with washer/dryer, bathroom, double bedroom. Relax in grounds or on patio, and watch hens roaming and cows coming for milking. Enjoy wonderful Devon views. 9 miles coast. Open Mar–Dec.

FOLLOW THE COUNTRY CODE

Leave nothing but footprints,

Take nothing but photographs,

Kill nothing but time!

FARM HOLIDAY BUREAU

PRICES

Prices include VAT and service charge (if any) and are:

B&B per person per night

EM per person

SC per unit per week

Tents and caravans per pitch per night

FARM HOLIDAY BUREAU

66

England's West Country

Dartmoor and South Devon

Group Contacts: 📧 *Sue Wills* ☎ *01364 661506/ Fax 01364 661516*
📧 *Mrs Angela Bell* ☎ *013642 391/(July '95) 01364 621391*

If you enjoy the outdoor life, this area offers unlimited opportunities in the 365 square miles of Dartmoor National Park with its contrasting open moorland and wooded valleys. The coast, walking, horseriding, climbing, birdwatching and golf, or alternatively coarse, game and sea-fishing, sailing and windsurfing, are all within approximately half an hour's drive.

Also easily accessible are many places of interest. Dartington Hall, centre of culture and the arts, Buckfast Abbey, the Dart Valley Steam Railway and the Shire Horse Centre. You may also visit historical sites from the Bronze Age onwards, country mansions, busy markets, antique and craft shops, country parks, National Trust properties, museums and resorts of all kinds from bustling Torquay to tranquil villages and the historic Elizabethan town of Totnes.

Food and drink can be a special delight in this part of the world. No visit would be complete without sampling a traditional cream tea. Then there's the local cider!

And for appetites of a different kind you can spend your evenings enjoying the theatre, concert and show life on offer in Torquay, Paignton, Plymouth and Exeter.

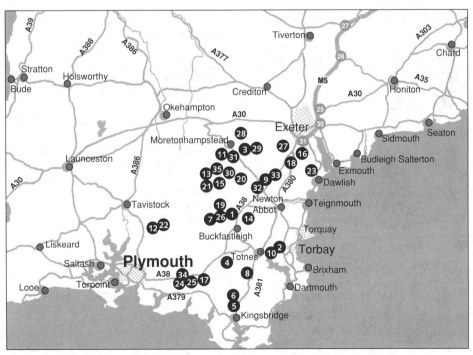

BED AND BREAKFAST

(and evening meal)

---

(1) Adams Hele Farm, Ashburton, South Devon TQ13 7NW

Dorothy Dent
☎ 01364 652525/4
BB From £15–£17
EM From £7
Sleeps 6

This 16th century listed farmhouse with oak beams and log fires nestles on a south facing hill overlooking the Dart valley and moors. It is a comfortable base from which to explore Dartmoor and the South Devon coast. 90 acres stocked with ponies, cattle and sheep. Peace, comfort and good home cooking with farm and local produce. 3 spacious double rooms, 2 with private shower and toilet, all with H/C, tea/coffee-making facilities. Open Feb–Nov.

---

(2) Berry Farm, Berry Pomeroy, Totnes, Devon TQ9 6LG

Mrs Geraldine Nicholls
☎ 01803 863231
BB From £13.50
EM From £8.50
Sleeps 6
(3)
Listed *Commended*

Mixed working farm surrounded by lovely old cider orchards in village close to Totnes with narrow streets, ancient buildings and river trips. Short distance beauty spots of Dartmoor. Spacious rooms, well appointed, bathroom, shower, separate WC, lounge, TV. Good local eating places. Occasional evening meal by arrangement. Food hygiene certificate. Warm, relaxed welcome. Open all year.

---

(3) Budleigh Farm, Moretonhampstead, Devon TQ13 8SB

Mrs Judith Harvey
☎ 01647 440835
Fax 01647 440436
BB From £14.50–£17.50
Sleeps 5
Commended

Lovely old thatched farmhouse, a listed building, set in the Wray Valley, part of the Dartmoor National Park, ½ mile from Moretonhampstead. Just off the A382 which makes Budleigh easy to find and a good base for exploring the area. Pretty garden. Fishing, riding and golf nearby. Outdoor heated swimming pool. Open Feb–Dec.

---

(4) Charford Farm, Avonwick, Totnes, Devon TQ9 7LT

Anne Barons
☎ 01364 73263
BB From £15–£18
EM From £8
Sleeps 6

A friendly working farm with cows, calves, ponies, etc. Ideal for touring the area. Lovely old farmhouse, peacefully situated and offering every comfort. Spacious family and double rooms with bathrooms en suite, double/twin with washbasin. Tea-making facilities. Evening meals with plenty of good farmhouse cooking. Brochure available. Open all year except Christmas.

---

(5) Coombe Farm, Kingsbridge, South Devon TQ7 4AB

Beni & Jonathan Robinson
☎ 01548 852038
BB From £16.50–£18.50
Sleeps 6
(12)
Commended

Come and enjoy the peace and beauty of Devon in our lovely 16th century farmhouse. Wonderful breakfast, large elegant rooms each with own bathroom, colour TV, hot drink facilities. Artists have the use of an art studio, and fishermen the well known Coombe Water fishery. Open all year except Christmas.

Crannacombe Farm, Hazlewood, Loddiswell, Nr Kingsbridge, South Devon TQ7 4DX

Shirley Bradley
☎ 01548 550256
BB From £16–£16.50
EM £9
Sleeps 8

In an area of outstanding natural beauty near Kingsbridge. Working farm, Georgian farmhouse, comfortable, informal, absolutely peaceful. We have family/double bedrooms with private bathrooms and TV, hot drink facilities and a separate children's room sleeping 2. Lovely walks, stunning views and a clean river to paddle, play and picnic by. Excellent food, prize winning cider, delicious juice.

Dodbrooke Farm, Michelcombe, Holne, Nr Ashburton, Devon TQ13 7SP

Judy Henderson
☎ 01364 3461
BB From £13.50–£15.50
EM From £7.50
Sleeps 6
Listed

Dodbrooke Farm is a listed 17th century former longhouse in an idyllic valley at the foot of Dartmoor. Food is home produced and the rooms are warm and comfortable. There are sheep and goats on the farm and a lovely garden for guests to explore. Come and enjoy a friendly atmosphere with local walking, riding and carriage driving. Open all year (closed Christmas).

Foales Leigh, Harberton, Totnes, Devon TQ9 7SS

Carol Chudley
☎ 01803 862365
BB From £14–£18
Sleeps 6
(3)

Commended

A charming 16th century farmhouse in traditional courtyard setting this 250-acre family farm is situated in peaceful surroundings within attractive unspoilt countryside but within easy reach of beaches, moors and towns. Comfortable accommodation includes large oak-beamed lounge with woodburner, games room, spacious family double en suite, double room, twin room, luxury bathroom. Open Jan–Nov.

Frost Farm, Hennock, Bovey Tracey, South Devon TQ13 9PP

Linda Harvey
☎ 01626 833266
Fax 01626 835758
BB From £17–£19
EM From £9.50
Sleeps 6

Commended

A pretty, pink-washed, thatched old farmhouse on working organic farm in our green valley. Lovely for walking, bird watching, NT houses, gardens. Explore Dartmoor or seaside. Good farmhouse food, fresh meats, vegetables, fruits, local cream/ice creams. Large, spacious bedrooms en suite with tea/coffee facilities, colour TV, CH. Ground floor bedroom. Cosy, relaxed atmosphere. Closed Christmas.

Great Court Farm, Weston Lane, Totnes, Devon TQ9 6LB

Janet Hooper
☎ 01803 862326
BB From £13–£15
EM From £8
Sleeps 6

Commended

A warm welcome, views of Totnes and comfortable, friendly accommodation await you at our 400-acre dairy farm running down to the River Dart. Colour co-ordinated spacious bedrooms with tea/coffee-making facilities, washbasins, central heating, 1 family/twin, 2 doubles, 2 bathrooms/shower, separate toilet. Guest lounge with colour TV. Dining room to enjoy good food. Evening meal by arrangement. Playroom, garden. Plenty of inns and restaurants nearby. Open all year.

Great Sloncombe Farm, Moretonhampstead, Newton Abbot, Devon TQ13 8QF ⑪

Mrs Trudie Merchant
☎ 01647 440595
BB From £18–£20
EM From £10
Sleeps 6
(8)

Highly Commended

Share the magic of Dartmoor all year round whilst staying in our lovely 13th century farmhouse. A working dairy farm set amongst meadows and woodland, abundant in wild flowers and animals. A welcoming place to relax and explore Devon. Comfortable double and twin rooms all with en suite bathroom, central heating, TV. Plenty of delicious home-cooked Devonshire food. Open all year.

12 Greenwell Farm, Nr Meavy, Yelverton, Plymouth, Devon PL20 6PY

Bridget Cole
☎/Fax 01822 853563
BB From £18–£22
EM From £11
Sleeps 6

Commended

Fresh country air, breathtaking views and scrumptious farmhouse cuisine. This busy farming family welcomes you to share the countryside and wildlife. A period farmhouse located in Dartmoor National Park, ideal for walking. En suite facilities, heating, hospitality trays in our spacious, comfortable rooms. Licensed, brochure available. Open all year (closed Christmas).

---

13 Higher Venton Farm, Widecombe-in-the-Moor, Newton Abbot, South Devon TQ13 7TF

Mrs Betty Hicks
☎ 01364 2235
BB From £15–£18
Sleeps 6
(5)
Listed

A friendly welcome awaits you at Higher Venton Farm, a 16th century thatched farmhouse and working farm. Peaceful and relaxing, ideal for touring Dartmoor. Riding stables nearby. Coast 16 miles, ½ mile from Widecombe village. Good local eating places recommended. 1 double en suite, 1 double and 1 twin with washbasins. CH, tea/coffee-making facilities, lounge with colour TV. Open all year except Christmas.

---

14 Kellinch Farm, Bickington, Newton Abbot, Devon TQ12 6PB

Frances Pike
☎ 01626 821252
BB From £15
EM From £8.75
Sleeps 4

Commended

Secluded working livestock farm set in beautiful, rolling landscape central for Dartmoor, coast and many places of interest. Enjoy a warm, friendly atmosphere, good country cooking, fresh farm produce. TV lounge with inglenook, separate dining room. 1 twin, 1 double, both with en suite. Cot and highchair available. Children's play area. Games and laundry room. Many tame animals. Open all year.

---

15 Lower Southway Farm, Widecombe-in-the-Moor, Devon TQ13 7TE

Dawn Nosworthy
☎ 013642 277
BB From £14
Sleeps 6
Listed

Situated in the lovely valley of Widecombe-in-the-Moor within the Dartmoor National Park with superb views. Ideal for walking, riding or touring Dartmoor. Excellent farmhouse food. 2 doubles, 1 twin, each with H/C, tea/coffee-making facilities and heating. Lounge with colour TV. Open all year.

---

16 Lower Thornton Farm, Kenn, Exeter, Devon EX6 7XH

Mrs Alison Clack
☎ 01392 833434
BB From £16
Sleeps 4

Come and relax at our secluded family farm with panoramic views. Just 2 miles from A38. Ideal base to visit Exeter, Torquay, Dartmoor, coast and racecourse. Our ground floor bedrooms are spacious and comfortable. One room en suite opening onto patio and garden, other has private bathroom. Both with tea/coffee facilities. Guests' lounge, colour TV, CH throughout. Child reductions. Open Jan–Nov

---

17 Marridge Farm, Ugborough, Nr Ivybridge, South Devon PL21 0HR

Fiona Winzer
☎ 01548 821469
BB From £15
EM From £8
Sleeps 6

Traditional, family-run dairy farm lying in the heart of the unspoilt South Devon countryside. Its position between Dartmoor and the sea make it a perfect base from which to explore the beauty and natural history of the granite upland as well as the sandy beaches of the South Hams. One en suite, 1 double, family room. Tea-coffee-making facilities. Good farmhouse fare. Babysitting available. Open all year.

Mill Farm, Kenton, Exeter, Devon EX6 8JR

Delia Lambert
☎ 01392 832471
[BB] From £14
Sleeps 12
⛺ ✂ ♿
Listed *Commended*

Mill Farm – a charming farmhouse with all modern comforts lovely en suite rooms with colour TV available. Also reasonably priced standard rooms. Ideal Powderham Castle, Exeter, beaches, bird watching, forest walks, racecourses. Dartmoor 20 minutes. Lovely rural setting. Good parking. Very easy to find. Don't miss out. Send for a brochure now!

Mill Leat Farm, Holne, Ashburton, Newton Abbot, Devon TQ13 7RZ

Dawn Cleave
☎ 01364 631283
[BB] From £14–£16
EM From £7.50
Sleeps 6
⛺ 🐾 ⅄ ⚒
Listed *Approved*

120-acre hill farm situated on the edge of Dartmoor, an ideal place for touring Devon's beautiful countryside, moorland or beaches. Comfortable accommodation in 18th century farmhouse with large spacious bedrooms. Very peaceful surroundings, just right for relaxing. Open Jan–Nov.

Narracombe Farm, Ilsington, Newton Abbot, Devon TQ13 9RD

Sue Wills
☎ 01364 661506/661243
Fax 01364 661516
[BB] From £15–£16
EM From £8.50
Sleeps 6
⛺ ✂
♨ *Commended*

Narracombe is a charming old farmhouse, full of character, warm and inviting and with all modern comforts. Secluded and surrounded by beautiful countryside yet ideally situated for exploring the moors and coast. Twin and family rooms, bathroom and shower, family lounge with log fire and colour TV. Delicious farmhouse cooking for breakfast and evening meals. Reductions for children. Open all year except Christmas & New Year.

New Cott Farm, Poundsgate, Newton Abbot, Devon TQ13 7PD

Margaret Phipps
☎ 01364 631421
Fax 01364 631338
[BB] From £16.50–£17.50
EM From £9.50
Sleeps 6
♿ ✂ ⛺ (3) ⚒ ♨ ⚓ ⅄ ■
♨♨ *Commended*

A friendly welcome, beautiful views, pleasing accommodation await you at New Cott in the Dartmoor National Park. Enjoy the freedom, peace and quiet of open moorland and the Dart Valley. Trout fishing, farm trail, birds and animals on the farm. Riding, golf, leisure centre a short distance. Bedrooms en suite, tea/coffee/chocolate, centrally heated. Lots of lovely homemade food. Weekly reductions, short breaks welcome. Open all year.

Peek Hill Farm, Dousland, Yelverton, Devon PL20 6PD

Justine Colton
☎ 01822 852908
[BB] From £14–£18
Sleeps 6
🐾 ⛺ ✂ ⚒ ■
♨♨ *Commended*

"Come up where the buzzards fly, the air is clean, the water clear". Situated on the southern slopes of Dartmoor with sweeping views to Cornwall and adjacent to wooded Burrator Lake. Comfortable, sunny bedrooms, with private bathrooms. Log fire in lounge and much more. We are friendly and informal and are easily located off B3212. Open Jan–Nov.

Smallacombe Farm, Aller Valley, Dawlish, Devon EX7 0PS

Mrs Alison Thomson
☎ 01626 862536
[BB] From £15–£17
EM From £8.50
Sleeps 6
⛺ ♨ ⚓ ⚒ ■
♨♨

Smallacombe Farm is a 120-acre working farm with sheep and free-range hens, surrounded by peaceful, secluded countryside yet only 2 miles from Dawlish beach. Ideal for birdwatchers. Relax in the garden while children play safely with no busy roads. Dartmoor, Exeter and Torquay only 30 mins' drive. Two doubles, one twin, family room available, en suite. Optional evening meals. Ring for brochure. Open all year (closed Christmas).

24 Strashleigh Farm, Ivybridge, Devon PL21 9JP

Mrs Paula Salter
☎ 01752 892226
🆎 From £13–£15
Sleeps 6
✂ 🐎 (5)
Listed *Commended*

A comfortable bed and a delicious, farmhouse breakfast awaits you. Strashleigh is a working farm, situated on the A38 near Ivybridge. The house provides an interesting history and wide views of beautiful Devonshire countryside. Perfect base for touring, beaches. City entertainment, sports facilities and tourist attractions. 2 double rooms, 1 twin, all with H & C and tea-making facilities and lounge with CTV. Open April–Sept.

25 Venn Farm, Ugborough, Ivybridge, Devon PL21 0PE

Pat Stephens
☎ 01364 73240
🆎 £17
EM £9.50
Sleeps 12
🐎🐎⊞ ▪
🐛🐛 *Commended*

Working farm amid peaceful scenery in the South Hams on edge of Dartmoor. Children encouraged to take an interest in farm life. The speciality of the house is 'carve your own roasts' and the atmosphere is friendly and relaxed. Accommodation comprises 2 family en suite rooms and separate garden cottage with 2 bedrooms, bathroom and picnic patio. Open Jan–Nov.

26 Wellpritton Farm, Holne, Ashburton, South Devon TQ13 7RX

Sue Townsend
☎ 01364 631273
🆎 From £17
EM From £8
Bedrooms 4
🐎🐎🐎▪
🐛🐛 *Highly Commended*

A beautiful farmhouse on the edge of Dartmoor, where goats, donkeys, rabbits and chickens are kept and sometimes sheep and cattle. Only ½ hour drive from Exeter, Plymouth and Torbay with riding, fishing, walking, sailing and golf nearby. Modernised to high standard – most rooms en suite, games room and swimming pool. Caring personal attention. Farm produced food. Weekly rates B&B & EM From £154. Open all year (closed Christmas).

27 Whitemoor Farm, Doddiscombsleigh, Nr Exeter, Devon EX6 7PU

Mrs Barbara Lacey
☎ 01647 52423/
252423 from May '95
🆎 From £16.50–£17.50
EM From £8
Sleeps 6
🐎🐎✂▪
🐛

Listed 16th century thatched farmhouse, set in seclusion of its own garden and farmland within easy reach of Exeter, coast, Dartmoor and forest walks. The Cobb House has exposed beams, log fires. Home made preserves. Good meals at local inn. Evening meal on request. Children and pets welcome. Swimming pool available. Open all year.

28 Wooston Farm, Moretonhampstead, Newton Abbot, Devon TQ13 8QA

Mary Cuming
☎ 01647 440367
🆎 From £17–£20
EM From £9
Sleeps 6
🐎🐎 (10)
🐛🐛🐛 *Highly Commended*

Wooston Farm is situated above the Teign Valley in the Dartmoor National Park with views over open moorland. The farmhouse is surrounded by a delightful garden. There are plenty of walks on the moor and wooded Teign Valley adjoining farm. Good home cooking and cosy log fires await you at Wooston. 2 double en suite, 1 with four-poster, 1 twin room. Also mountain bikes available. Open all year except Christmas. AA listed.

SELF-CATERING

Budleigh Farm, Moretonhampstead, Devon TQ13 8SB

Mrs Judith Harvey
☎ **01647 440835**
Fax **01647 440436**
[SC] **From £75–£340**
Sleeps 6
Commended

Seven cottages and flats, converted from barns, each with its own character, on a farm tucked into the end of the Wray Valley ½ mile from Moretonhampstead. Outdoor heated swimming pool, barbecue; table tennis and darts. Small campsite. Excellent centre for exploring the area. Open Jan–Dec.

Crownley, c/o Mill Combe, Ilsington, Newton Abbot, Devon TQ13 9RT

Mrs Sue Retallick
☎/Fax **01364 661430**
[SC] **max £245**
Sleeps 5
Approved

Crownley is a 3 bedroomed bungalow set in a lovely valley with woods and fields around it. The moors are just over the hill. Ideal for touring Dartmoor and South Devon. Plymouth, Exeter, Torquay within easy reach. Linen included. Children and pets welcome. Open all year.

Narramore Farm Cottages, Narramore Farm, Moretonhampstead, Devon TQ13 8QT

Phillip & Sue Horn
☎ **01647 40455**
Fax **01647 40031**
[SC] **From £95–£450**
Sleeps 2/16
Highly Commended

Narramore is a 107-acre stud farm favouring conservation and including deer park. Scenic walks in beautiful countryside with riding, fishing and golf course close by. Our luxury cottages make an ideal haven to relax from the stresses of life with a heated swimming pool and spa. Brochure available. Open all year.

Shippen and Dairy Cottages, c/o Lookweep Farm, Liverton, Newton Abbot, Devon TQ12 6HT

Averil Corrick
☎ **01626 833277**
[SC] **From £130–£370**
Sleeps 4/5 + cot
Commended

Come and relax in the peace and tranquillity of these two delightful barn converted cottages. Set within the Dartmoor National Park with easy access to the coast, golf, riding, walking and fishing locally. Sleeps 4/5, fully equipped and well furnished throughout. Own gardens with beautiful views. Ample parking. Use of outdoor heated swimming pool. High chairs, cots and linen available. Open all year.

Stickwick Farm Holiday Homes, c/o Frost Farm, Bovey Tracey, South Devon TQ13 9PP   (33)

Linda Harvey
☎ **01626 833266**
Fax **01626 835758**
[SC] **From £125–£345**
Sleeps 2/12
Commended

Our holiday homes are delightful with lots of pictures, pottery and pretty bedrooms. Long farmland views, farm walking. Garden, games barn, children's farmyard. Spacious grounds to relax in. Farmhouse food menu. Pretty cottage sleeps 2/4, farmhouse sleeps 6/7, Georgian house sleeps 8/12. Fully equipped, bed linen, towels. Ring for brochure today. Open all year.

---

34   **Strashleigh Farm,** Ivybridge, Devon PL21 9JP

Mrs Paula Salter
☎ **01752 892226**
🆂 **From £110–£200**
Sleeps 2 + cot
🐾 🐾 🐾 *Approved*

Peacefully set with views of Dartmoor, Strashleigh Annex is a 1 level self-contained wing of the farmhouse. Double bedroom with en suite bathroom, newly fitted kitchen with dishwasher and a cosy open plan living area with a beautiful granite mullion window, woodburner and colour TV. Being near A38, its a perfect base for many attractions and activities. Brochure available. Open Apr–Sept.

35   **Wooder Manor,** Widecombe-in-the-Moor, Newton Abbot, Devon TQ13 7TR

Mrs Angela Bell
☎ **013642 391**
☎ **July '95 01364 621391**
🆂 **From £90–£600**
Sleeps 2/16
♿ 🐓 🐄 ⅍ ⚓ ▪
🐾 🐾 🐾 🐾 *Commended*

Cottages and converted coachhouse on 108-acre family farm, nestled in picturesque valley surrounded by unspoilt woodland, moors and granite tors. Central for touring Devon and exploring Dartmoor by foot or on horseback. Clean and fully equipped. Colour TVs, laundry facilities, central heating. Gardens, courtyard for easy parking. Good food at local inn (½ mile). Choose a property to suit you from our brochure. Open all year.

Please mention **Stay on a Farm** when booking

THE 1000+ BUREAU MEMBERS OFFER A UNIQUE LINK TO CUSTOMERS ACROSS THE UK

All Bureau members belong to a local Group. Each member can refer you to an equally high quality member within his Group… or across the UK: England, Northern Ireland, Scotland, Wales.

PRICES

Prices include VAT and service charge (if any) and are:
B&B per person per night
EM per person
SC per unit per week
Tents and caravans per pitch per night

67

England's West Country

Moor to Shore in Devon

Group Contact: *Mrs Jill Balkwill* ☎ *01548 550312*

The South Hams in South Devon is a unique part of the West Country, catering for a wide variety of tastes. The area lies between Plymouth and Torbay, is easily accessible from the A38 and is renowned for its beauty and variety of countryside. Not just the countryside either – it has such towns as Elizabethan Totnes with its castle, or the historic seaport of Dartmouth scattered around the Dart estuary and plenty of attractive villages.

The coastline, which is truly spectacular, has sheltered harbours and estuaries at Yealm, Salcombe and Dartmouth.

Fishing, riding and golf can be enjoyed in many places and if you could ever possibly tire of the area, turn north and the Dartmoor National Park is just a stone's throw away. The mild climate of the area makes it particularly attractive for out-of-season visits.

The area also includes wildlife and country parks, a Shire Horse Centre at Dunstone near Yealmpton and a wide variety of interesting museums. For those fans of steam, the area boasts two steam railways on the Dart Valley Railway, one of which connects with Totnes main line.

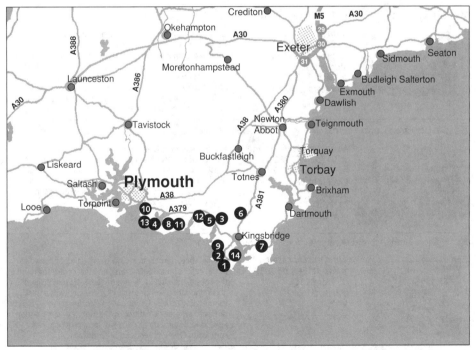

BED AND BREAKFAST

(and evening meal)

---

1 **Bolberry House Farm,** Nr Salcombe, Devon TQ7 3DY

Elaine Stidston-Nott
☎ 01548 560926/
561251
BB From £16–£18
Sleeps 8

Between Salcombe and Hope Cove, elegant, listed farmhouse on 260-acre coastal farm with friendly atmosphere and offering every comfort. Superb English breakfast. Good local eating establishments, pubs and carveries. Outstanding coastal walks. Nearby riding, fishing, sailing, golf, clay pigeon shooting. Beach 1 mile. Free babysitting available. Access to house at all times. Open Mar–Nov.

---

2 **Burton Farm,** Galmpton, Kingsbridge, South Devon TQ7 3EY

Anne Rossiter
☎ 01548 561210
BB From £17.50–£21
EM From £8.95
Sleeps 17

Highly Commended

Working dairy and sheep farm situated in the valley running towards Hope Cove. 3 miles from famous sailing haunt of Salcombe. Walking, beaches, sailing, windsurfing, bathing, diving, fishing. Guests welcome to enjoy the farm's activities according to season. Traditional farmhouse cooking, home produce (clotted cream, etc). 4 course dinner. Access to rooms at all times. En suite available and washbasins. Tea-making facilities. Closed Christmas.

---

3 **Court Barton Farmhouse,** Aveton Gifford, Kingsbridge, Devon TQ7 4LE

John & Jill Balkwill
☎ 01548 550312
BB From £16–£24
Sleeps 18

Commended

Delightful 16th century listed manor farmhouse situated in 40-acre farm. Accommodation in 7 bedrooms, mostly en suite, tea/coffee-making facilities. Comfortable TV lounge with lots of books, sunny breakfast room to enjoy delicious country farmhouse breakfasts. Full central heating and log fires in colder weather. Close to moorland, beaches, ideal centre for walking, sailing, fishing, birdwatching. Open all year except Christmas. Welcome Host.

---

4 **Gabber Farm,** Down Thomas, Plymouth, Devon PL9 0AW

Margaret MacBean
☎ 01752 862269
BB From £15–£17
EM From £8
Sleeps 12

Commended

A warm welcome is assured on this working dairy farm in an area of outstanding natural beauty. Situated on the coast near Plymouth with lovely walks and within easy reach of the beaches. Good home cooking, hot drinks facilities in all rooms, double and family with en suite shower. Open all year except Christmas.

---

5 **Helliers Farm,** Ashford, Aveton Gifford, Kingsbridge, Devon TQ7 4ND

Christine Lancaster
☎/Fax 01548 550689
BB From £16
Sleeps 9

A small sheep farm set on a hill overlooking a lovely valley in the heart of the South Hams, an ideal centre for touring the coasts, moors and Plymouth. Recently modernised accommodation comprises family, double, twin and single rooms, all with washbasins and tea/coffee facilities. Double or family en suite. 2 bathrooms, lounge, TV, games room. Fish pond. Hearty breakfasts with local produce. Fire certificate. Open all year except Christmas.

Higher Torr Farm, East Allington, Totnes, Devon TQ9 7QH

Susan Baker
☎ 01548 521248
BB From £14–£17
EM From £7
Sleeps 6
🐾 ✂ 🐴 (1) 🛶 ⛺ 🎪 🎭
Listed *Commended*

Mixed working farm in lovely area offering comfortable accommodation in homely atmosphere. Good home-produced cooking. Quiet, peaceful walks to spot the wildlife. Close to moors and coast. Family room with en suite facilities, twin room with washbasin, single room. Tea/coffee-making facilities in all rooms. TV lounge. Babysitting by arrangement. Open Mar–Nov.

Sherford Down, Sherford, Kingsbridge, Devon TQ7 2BA

Mrs Heather Peters
☎ 01548 531208
BB From £18–£20
Sleeps 6
✂ 🐴 (5) 🎭
🛶🛶 *Highly Commended*

Listed Georgian farmhouse, family home on mixed farm overlooking 13th century hamlet, 3 miles from Kingsbridge and sea. Superb quality B&B, comfortable, friendly, relaxed but attentive. 1 family room and 1 double, with good firm beds, tea trays, en suite or private facilities. Stupendous breakfasts, local produce. Good pubs nearby. Illustrated leaflet. Open Easter–Oct.

Slade Barn, Netton Farm, Noss Mayo, Nr Plymouth, Devon PL8 1HA

Sandy Cherrington
☎/Fax 01752 872235
BB From £15–£18.50
EM From £8
Sleeps 6
🐴 (10) ✂ 🎪 ⚓
Listed *Commended*

Coastal South Devon beside the beautiful Yealm estuary. Lovely barn conversion. Indoor pool, games room, tennis court, gardens. Fabulous NT cliff walks, nearby sandy beaches. Double and 1 twin shared bathroom, CH, TV/radio, tea/coffee on request. Open all year.

Self-Catering

Burton Farm Cottages, Burton Farm, Galmpton, Kingsbridge, South Devon TQ7 3EY

Anne Rossiter
☎ 01548 561210
SC From £75–£450
Sleeps 4/5 + cot
🐴 🐾
🐕 🐕 🐕 🐕
Approved

Situated in a pretty hamlet adjoining open farmland, these cob and slate cottages are 5 miles from Kingsbridge with good shopping facilities, 3 miles from the sailing haunt of Salcombe and 1 mile from lovely beaches of Hope Cove and Thurlestone. Decorated and furnished, many original features with stone-built fireplaces and electric heating. Guests welcome to enjoy farm activities. Meals available on request. Open all year.

Coombe Farm, Wembury Road, Plymstock, Plymouth, Devon PL9 0DE 🔟

Rodney and Suzanne
MacBean
☎ 01752 401730
SC From £100–£340
Sleeps 6
🐴 🐾
🐕 🐕 🐕 *Approved*

Coombe Farm dates back to the 14th century and is situated in a peaceful valley on the outskirts of Plymouth. An ideal centre for touring and within easy reach of moors and coast. The cottage is well equipped with two bedrooms, lounge, kitchen/diner, bathroom. Linen and electric included. Safe parking. Open all year.

⑪ Netton Farm Holiday Cottages, Netton Farm, Noss Mayo, Nr Plymouth, Devon PL8 1HA

Sandy Cherrington
☎/Fax 01752 872235
ⓢⓒ From £167–£1,084
Sleeps 24

Commended

Nestled into one of the most beautiful stretches of South Devon coastline, this small complex is ideally situated to cater for all tastes. Attractive, comfortable accommodation and warm, friendly atmosphere. Use of lovely indoor pool, games room, tennis court, gardens. Rural and peaceful, superb coastal walks and nearby sandy beaches. SAE for colour brochure. Open Apr–Sept.

⑫ Oldaport Farm Cottages, Modbury, Ivybridge, Devon PL21 0TG

Miss C Evans
☎ 01548 830842
Fax 01548 830998
ⓢⓒ From £136–£383
Sleep 2/6

Highly Commended

Oldaport is a small sheep farm of 60 acres, lying in the Erme Valley, and offering lovely views of the countryside. The four cottages, which sleep 2/6, were redundant stone barns which have been carefully converted into comfortable holiday homes. All fully equipped, heating in all rooms. Sandy beaches nearby, Dartmoor 8 miles. Excellent birdwatching. Brochure available. Open all year.

⑬ Traine Farm, Wembury, Plymouth, Devon PL9 0EW

Sheila Rowland
☎ 01752 862264
ⓢⓒ From £95–£350
Sleeps 9 + cot

Approved

Spacious, character wing of attractive Georgian farmhouse on a dairy farm overlooking lovely coastal village of Wembury. Ideal location for family holidays, 1 mile from the beach and 7 miles from Plymouth city centre. Sleeps nine in three bedrooms, colour TV, large garden, cot and highchair available. Open Mar–Nov.

⑭ Withymore Cottage, Withymore Farm, Malborough, Kingsbridge, South Devon TQ7 3ED

Mrs Jo Hocking
☎/Fax 01548 561275
ⓢⓒ From £130–£320
Sleeps 6 + cot

Commended

Recently modernised cottage nestling in a peaceful valley on a family-run dairy farm within a short distance of Salcombe. Very comfortable and furnished to a high standard throughout. Colour TV, bed linen, CH. Well equipped kitchen. Large enclosed garden. Ideal centre for family holiday with many beaches, sailing, fishing, golf, horse riding and spectacular coastal walks. Open all year.

68

England's West Country

West Devon Welcome

Group Contact: *Mrs Jane Pyle* ☎ *01363 82510*

West Devon, with its sheltered valleys, rugged hills and picturesque villages, offers you a chance not just to visit the countryside but to be a part of it ... on our working beef, sheep and dairy farms. A chance to enjoy a real family holiday, enjoying the peace of the countryside, joining in the local activities, travelling out to enjoy the beautiful beaches, entertainments, sights and attractions. A year-round delight.

There are many varieties of animals, birds and wild flowers for you to see. Walks and trails have been established in many forests and around a number of reservoirs. More active pursuits include riding and fishing or the more leisurely crafts of pottery, spinning or jewellery-making to learn.

For those interested in history or literature there are many ancient churches, Bronze Age settlements and the home of Sir Francis Drake plus the setting for the 'Hound of the Baskervilles'. Morwellham Quay and other National Trust properties are within easy reach .

Resist, if you can, the locally made cheese, yoghurt, chocolate, fudge, cider or the famous Devon Cream Tea. West Devon has so much to offer ... why not come and share a little bit of "our heaven down in Devon".

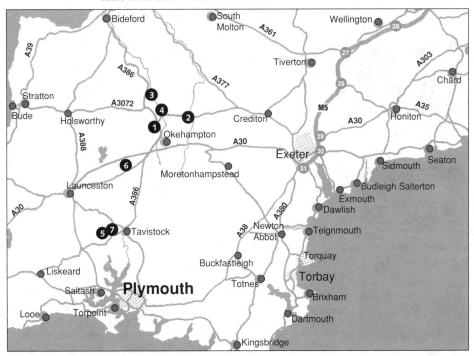

BED AND BREAKFAST

(and evening meal)

---

1 **Higher Cadham Farm,** Jacobstowe, Okehampton, Devon EX20 3RB

John & Jenny King
☎ 01837 85 647
[BB] From £14–£15
EM From £7
Sleeps 7
🛏 (3) 🛉
♛ *Commended*

Pack your sun hat and wellies for a relaxing break on our 16th century secluded family-run farm. Plenty of activities for the more energetic – you may even sleep in our four-poster bed! Licensed and AA listed. One week's stay costs just £125 inclusive and as we have two children we offer special rates for yours. Detailed brochure available. Open all year except Christmas.

---

2 **Lower Nichols Nymet Farm,** North Tawton, Devon EX20 2BW

Mrs Jane Pyle
☎ 01363 82510
[BB] From £17
EM From £10.50
Sleeps 6
✂ 🛏 🛉 💼
♛♛ *Highly Commended*

We offer a haven of comfort and rest on a modern working dairy farm and provide the perfect base for exploring the beauties of the West Country. Residents' lounge, colour TV. All rooms en suite, plus tea/coffee-making facilities. An ideal holiday centre – beaches, golf, good walks, riding, fishing, fine houses and gardens nearby to visit. Open Easter–Oct (incl).

---

3 **Middlecott Farm,** Broad Woodkelly, Winkleigh, Devon EX19 8DZ

June Western
☎ 01837 83381
[BB] From £15–£18
EM From £10
Sleeps 6
🛏 🛏 ♿
♛

Set in lush, peaceful countryside, with panoramic views to Dartmoor, and nestled in the heart of Tarka country, a friendly, family welcome and delicious food awaits you. The renowned RHS Rosemoor Gardens a short drive away. Ideally situated for fishing, exploration of Dartmoor and coasts. Accommodation consists of stairlift and double – one en suite, both with TV and views of Dartmoor, £130 per week half board. En suite £3 extra per night. Open Jan–Nov.

---

4 **Oaklands Farm,** North Tawton, Devon EX20 2BQ

Winifred Headon
☎ 01837 82340
[BB] From £14
EM From £8
Sleeps 5
🛏 🛏
♛

A warm welcome awaits you at Oaklands, a 130-acre farm in the centre of Devon. Easy to find on a level drive from a good road. Traditional farmhouse cooking with ample of everything. Heating and electric blankets in bedrooms. Lounge with colour TV. Pleasant gardens. Reductions for children. Open all year.

---

5 **Rubbytown Farm,** Gulworthy, Tavistock, Devon PL9 8PA

Mary Steer
☎ 01822 832493
[BB] From £18
EM From £12
Sleeps 6
✂ 🛏 (5) 🐾 💼
♛♛ *Highly Commended*

Stay in our lovely old farmhouse and sleep in four-poster beds. Enjoy woodland walks. There is abundant wildlife, you may see deer if you are lucky and at dusk the foxes and badgers at play. Help with feeding the calves. Good farm-house cooking with evening meals served by candlelight. St Mellion Golf and Country Club nearby. Upholstery classes are held locally. 2 double, 4 posters, en suite, 1 twin with private bathroom, games room. Evening meal served by candlelight by prior arrangement. Closed Christmas.

Week Farm, Bridestowe, Okehampton, Devon EX20 4HZ

Margaret Hockridge
☎ **0183786 221**
☎ **June '95 0183786 1221**
🆎 **From £19–£20**
EM From £10
Sleeps 12
🐴 ♿ 🐎 📷 💼
🦢 🦢 *Commended*

Guests return annually to our 17th century farmhouse. Set in peaceful countryside ¾ mile from old A30. Good home cooking and every comfort. Central for Dartmoor and coast, 8 miles Cornwall. Lounge with colour TV and log fires. 3 doubles, 2 family rooms all en suite (1 ground floor). Tea/coffee-making facilities, night storage heaters, colour TV. Birthdays, anniversaries catered for. Come and spoil yourselves. Fire certificate held. Open all year (closed Christmas).

SELF-CATERING

Rubbytown Farm, Gulworthy, Tavistock, Devon PL9 8PA 7

Mary Steer
☎ **01822 832493**
🆂🅲 **From £150–£300**
🐎 🐴 ✂ ♿ 🎋
🐾 🐾 🐾 🐾 *Commended*

Recently converted old granite barns retaining original features. Beautifully furnished, fully equipped kitchens, wonderful views with gardens and orchard. Come and relax in this beautiful countryside, and see foxes and badgers at play and much more wildlife. Everyone welcome, we aim to make your holiday on to remember. Open all year.

FINDING YOUR ACCOMMODATION

The Group contacts at the beginning of each section can always help you find a vacancy in your chosen area.

FARM HOLIDAY BUREAU

PRICES

Prices include VAT and service charge (if any) and are:
B&B per person per night
EM per person
SC per unit per week
Tents and caravans per pitch per night

FARM HOLIDAY BUREAU

69

England's West Country

Upper Tamar, North West Devon

Group Contact: *Marlene Heard* ☎ *01409 253339*

This area covers the North Cornwall/Devon border area with its glorious coastline and miles of sandy beaches, sheltered coves and rugged cliffs, friendly resorts and quiet villages, country market towns and wide open spaces peacefully set in undulating countryside.

The coastline from Hartland to Crackington Haven is as dramatic as it is beautiful. Bude, once described by the late Sir John Betjeman as 'the least rowdy resort in the country' has retained its atmosphere of easy-going charm while catering for the most discerning of modern day tourists. Another resort which tourists are advised to visit is Clovelly with its steeply cobbled streets. Holsworthy and Launceston have weekly cattle and pannier markets. Both have a golf course and sports hall and Launceston also has a heated swimming pool. There are several pony trekking centres in the area and facilities for fishing at sea, on the lake or by the river.

This area has been recommended as a restful, comfortable base for touring the whole of Devon and Cornwall. There are many tourist attractions including the moors, National Trust properties, steam railways, leisure parks, museums and the cities of Exeter, Plymouth and Truro all within easy driving distance.

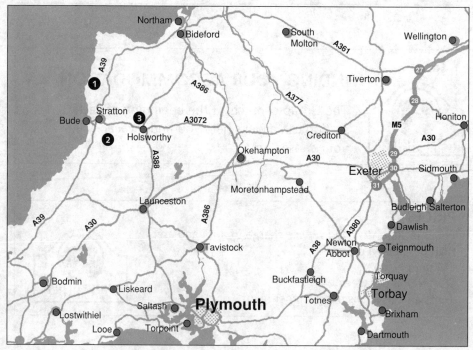

BED AND BREAKFAST

(and evening meal)

Cornakey Farm, Morwenstow, Bude, Cornwall EX23 9SS

Mrs Monica Heywood
☎ 01288 331260
🏠 From £14–£16
EM From £6
Sleeps 6

This is a 220–acre mixed coastal farm with extensive views of sea and Lundy island from bedrooms and bathroom. Good touring centre with easy reach of quiet beaches. The farmhouse offers one family room en suite and one double room. Bathroom, toilet, lounge (colour TV), dining room, games room. Children welcome at reduced rates. Cot, highchair, babysitting. Good home cooking with fresh vegetables. Open all year except Christmas.

Elm Park, Bridgerule, Holsworthy, Devon EX22 7EL

Sylvia Lucas
☎ 01288 381231
🏠 From £14
EM From £7
Sleeps 12

Elm Park is 6 miles from Cornish surfing beaches at Bude and ideal for touring both Devon and Cornwall. Children are especially welcomed with pony and tractor and trailer rides. Twin and family rooms with en suite and tea/coffee making facilities. Ample 4-course dinners with freshly produced fare and delicious sweets. Big weekly reductions and everyone made most welcome and comfortable. Games room. Open Mar–Nov.

SELF-CATERING

Thorne Park, Holsworthy, Devon EX22 7BL

Marlene Heard
☎ 01409 253339
🏠 From £80–£695
EM From £8
Sleeps 6 and 12

🌼🌼🌼 Commended

Do come and stay on our working farm. You will find a warm welcome, experience life in the countryside. Wander through fields with pretty stream, enjoy beautiful scenery, watch farm activities, enjoy pony rides and much more. Ring now! Riding, fishing, golf nearby. Ideal for coast and touring. Enjoy delicious evening meals. Open all year.

FARM HOLIDAY BUREAU

Please mention **Stay on a Farm** when booking

70

England's West Country
Cream of Cornwall

Group Contacts: 🆁🅱 *Judith Nancarrow* ☎ *01726 67111*
🆂🅲 *Judith Clemo* ☎ *01726 850168*

Cornwall has a coastline of 326 miles with its unique coastal footpath. It is a county of amazing contrasts with wonderful stretches of firm golden sands and soaring cliffs on the north coast, to tiny coves, picturesque fishing villages and sheltered, wooded estuaries on the south coast. Beaches from Bude to St Ives are famous for the wonderful Atlantic surf, whereas south coast resorts, such as Looe, Fowey, Mevagissey and Falmouth are ideal centres for sailing, fishing and windsurfing, with numerous safe bathing beaches spread all along this coast.

However, Cornwall has more than just the coastline to tempt you – there is a wealth of potteries and art galleries throughout the county (notably the Tate Gallery at St Ives). A wide choice of famous gardens and National Trust properties such as St Michael's Mount and Lanhydrock are open to the public. The atmospheric Bodmin Moor with mystical standing stones, Tintagel with King Arthur's Castle and the Iron Age village, Chysanster are just some of the fascinating places waiting for you to explore.

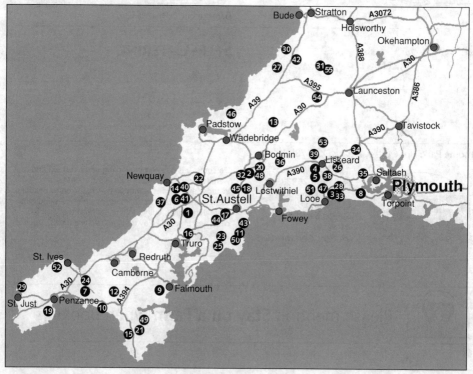

BED AND BREAKFAST
(and evening meal)

Arrallas, Ladock, Truro, Cornwall TR2 4NP   ①

Mrs Barbara Holt
☎ **01872 510379**
Fax 01872 510200
BB **From £16–£19.50**
EM From £9–£12
Sleeps 6
🐕 🕯 💺 🎨
🐝🐝🐝 *Highly Commended*

Arrallas is part of the Duchy of Cornwall enjoying a "heart of the country" peaceful atmosphere. We are adjacent to 400 acres of Duchy woodlands, offering wonderful walks and superb views from the house. 15 minutes drive from the North coast. Centrally situated for touring. All bedrooms en suite (2 double, 1 twin) with TVs. Quality menus. Choice of 2, 3 or 4 courses. Full central heating. Parking. Beverage facilities. Phone for directions. Open Feb–Nov.

Bokiddick Farm, Lanivet, Bodmin, Cornwall PL30 5HP   ②

Gill Hugo
☎ **01208 831481**
BB **From £16**
Sleeps 5
🐕
🐝🐝 *Commended*

A warm welcome awaits you at Bokiddick. Plenty of good farmhouse cooking, friendly atmosphere. Explore our dairy farm, watch the milking, see the calves or just relax in our very comfortable lounge. Wonderful views, central Cornwall. Excellent touring base for coasts and moors. National Trust Lanhydrock House close by. Open Easter–Oct.

Bucklawren Farm, St Martin-by-Looe, Cornwall PL13 1NZ

Mrs Jean Henly
☎ **01503 240738**
Fax 01503 240481
BB **From £16–£18**
EM From £9
Sleeps 12
🐕 🛏 ☕ 🕯💺
🐝🐝🐝 *Highly Commended*

Bucklawren is situated deep in unspoilt countryside yet only 1 mile from the beach, 2½ miles from Looe and 1 mile from Woolly Monkey Sanctuary. It is a large working farm with a spacious, comfortable farmhouse which enjoys beautiful sea views and a large garden. We offer excellent accommodation with family and en suite rooms. Farmhouse cooking in a friendly and relaxed atmosphere. Open Mar–Nov (incl).

Caduscott, East Taphouse, Liskeard, Cornwall PL14 4NG   ④

Lindsay Pendray
☎/Fax 01579 20262
☎/Fax Feb '95 320262
BB **From £13.50–£17.50**
EM From £8
Sleeps 4/5
🍴🐕 💺
Listed Approved

Down the lane wild flowers nod in passing; relax and unwind in this 17th century listed farmhouse peeping over the valley where streams converge to make the 10 mile journey to the sea at Looe. Double room (en suite, toilet/shower), adjoining twin bedded room. Personal attention, facilities for children. Meals all prepared/served in traditional style. Open Apr–Sept. Out of season, advanced bookings taken.

Carglonnon Farm, Duloe, Liskeard, Cornwall PL14 4QA   ⑤

Mrs Ann Bray
☎ **01579 320210**
BB **From £13.50–£15**
Sleeps 6
🐎 🕯 💺
🐝🐝

A lovely 18th century Georgian farmhouse which is part of the Duchy of Cornwall Estate. A working mixed farm of 230 acres, situated 4½ miles from fishing port of Looe. Forestry walks from farm. Golf, horse-riding, Theme Park, coastal walking, moors all nearby. One double en suite, one double and one twin with H&C. Tea/coffee-making facilities, central heating. Open all year.

6 **Degembris Farmhouse,** St Newlyn East, Newquay, Cornwall TR8 5HY

Kathy Woodley
☎ 01872 510555
Fax 01872 510230
BB From £16–£18
EM From £8.50
Sleeps 12
🐕 🎄 ♿
🌸🌸 *Highly Commended*

Degembris nestles in a south facing hillside overlooking a beautiful wooded valley. Its low beams and log fires make this listed 18th century farmhouse a delight. Come inside (mind your head!) and enjoy the charming Georgian surroundings, complete with creaky floorboards! Take a stroll along our farm trail which wanders through woodland and fields of corn.

7 **Ennys,** St Hilary, Penzance, Cornwall TR20 9BZ

Sue White
☎ 01736 740262
Fax 01736 763825
BB From £20–£25
EM From £15
Sleeps 10
🐕 (5) 🎄 ♿ ✿
🌸🌸🌸 *Highly Commended*

Beautiful 16th century manor farm in idyllically peaceful wooded surroundings. Excellent suppers by candlelight. Bread baked daily! Log fires. 3 en suite bedrooms, 1 with romantic four-poster overlooking walled gardens, tennis court and heated swimming pool. Self-contained family suite. Near to beaches and the famous St Michael's Mount. Gourmet weekend winter breaks. Featured in *Country Living magazine, The Daily Telegraph,* and *Sunday Times.* Open all year (closed Christmas).

8 **Hendra Farm,** Polbathic, Torpoint, Cornwall PL11 3DT

Mrs A Hoskin
☎ 01503 250225
BB From £14–£15
Sleeps 5
✂ 🐕 ♿
🌸🌸 *Commended*

Hendra is a working farm situated in an area of outstanding natural beauty. The fishing port of Looe is 6 miles, and safe bathing beaches of Downderry and Seaton only 2 miles. The main shopping centre of Plymouth is within ½ hours travelling. TV lounge. Family room with en suite shower and WC. Babysitting. Open Mar–Oct.

9 **Higher Kergilliack Farm,** Budock, Falmouth, Cornwall TR11 5PB

Jean Pengelly
☎ 01326 372271
BB From £15–£17.50
EM From £8
Sleeps 6
🐎 🎄 ♿
🌸🌸 *Commended*

18th century Georgian listed farmhouse, former residence of Bishop of Exeter. Poppy our friendly dog will show you round our 130-acre dairy farm to see the cows, calves and Seigfried the donkey. Overlooks Falmouth Bay near the seal sanctuary and Trebah and Glendurgan Gardens. 1 double with en suite WC and shower, 1twin/family with en suite WC and bath. Take 2nd right on A39 at Hillhead roundabout. Open all year.

10 **Higher Trevurvas Farm,** Ashton, Helston, Cornwall TR13 9TZ

Kate Jenkin
☎ 01736 763613
BB From £16.50–£18.50
EM £10
Sleeps 8
🐕 (10) ✂ 🎄 ♿
🌸🌸 *Commended*

Relax and enjoy the peace and tranquillity of our small beef farm with commanding views over Mounts Bay (Praa Sands beach 10 minutes' walk away). Situated in an area of outstanding beauty. All bedrooms have en suite or private facilities with colour TV and hostess tray. The aga takes care of the cooking which is plentiful and attractively presented using fresh local produce and of course Cornish cream. Brochure available. Open all year except Christmas.

11 **Kerryanna Country House,** Treleaven Farm, Mevagissey, Cornwall PL26 6RZ

Linda Hennah
☎ 01726 843558
BB From £18
EM From £10
Sleeps 12
🐕 (5) ♿
🌸🌸🌸 *Commended*

Surrounded by farmland, wildlife and flowers, the farm is only 8 minutes' walk from the centre of Mevagissey. You are welcome to meet our animals, swim in our lovely heated outdoor pool, try your skills in the games barn and putting green. All rooms are en suite with colour TV and tea-makers. Large lounge with open fire. Local fish, vegetables, meat used daily. Mentional in the *Daily Telegraph* and Gill Charlton's *A Week in Cornwall.* Open Mar–Oct.

Longstone Farm, Trenear, Helston, Cornwall TR13 0HG (12)

Gillian Lawrance
☎ 01326 572483
BB From £14–£17
EM From £7.50
Sleeps 15
🐓 🐕 🐈
🍦🍦 Commended

A warm welcome awaits you at Longstone Farm, a 62-acre working dairy farm situated in the centre of West Cornwall's peaceful countryside. Ideal for touring both coasts and holiday attractions. Flambards (4 miles). Traditional farmhouse fare served, separate tables. Ample room to relax in TV lounge and large sun room/play area. Open Feb–Nov.

Loskeyle Farm, St Tudy, Bodmin, Cornwall PL30 3PW (13)

Mrs Sandra Menhinick
☎ 01208 851005
BB From £13–£14
EM From £8
Sleeps 6
🐈 🐓
🍦 Approved

Loskeyle is a working dairy farm in the Duchy of Cornwall where a warm welcome awaits you. Relax and enjoy the peace and tranquillity of farm life. Chidlren especially welcome, free babysitting by arrangement. Delicious farmhouse cooking using local produce. Watch milking, feed hens. Ideal base for north and south coasts. Golf, camel trail nearby, also pony trekking over moors only a stone's throw away. Open Mar–Nov.

Manuels Farm, Quintrell Downs, Newquay, Cornwall TR8 4NY (14)

Mrs Jean Wilson
☎ 01637 873577
BB From £18–£20
EM £9.50
Sleeps 12
🐓 🌿 🐈 🐎 🐕 🎪 📷
🍦🍦 Highly Commended

A listed 17th century farmhouse situated in a sheltered valley, 2 miles from Newquay's magnificent beaches. Relax in peaceful countryside in this traditional Cornish farmhouse. Beautifully furnished, delicious plentiful farmhouse cooking. Log fires. Award winning garden. Children especially welcome. Nursery teas, free babysitting, play area, pony rides. Meet a whole variety of pets and farm animals on this friendly working farm. Open all year (closed Christmas).

Polhormon Farm, Polhormon Lane, Mullion, Helston, Cornwall TR12 7JE (15)

Alice Harry
☎ 01326 240304
BB From £14.50–£15.50
Sleeps 6
🐓 🐈
🍦 Approved

Staying at Polhormon will give you a real taste of Cornish dairy farming life. Bring your wellies, but don't forget the buckets and spades, surfboards and walking boots for the 5 nearby sandy beaches, cliff walks and Mullion's 18 hole golf course. Relax in our farmhouse's family atmosphere and come and go as you please.

Polsue Manor Farm, Tresillian, Truro, Cornwall TR2 4BP (16)

Geraldine Holliday
☎ 01872 520234
BB From £15–£17
EM From £8
Sleeps 14
🐓 🐈 📷
🍦 Approved

The farmhouse on this 190-acre working farm, set in glorious countryside, overlooks the tidal Tresillian River and one of the prettiest parts of Cornwall. Only minutes from the beautiful cathedral city of Truro. Centrally situated between north and south coasts, ideal centre for touring the county. Delightful country walks. All bedrooms have H/C. Traditional home cooking, comfortable, relaxed friendly atmosphere. Open most of year.

Poltarrow Farm, St Mewan, St Austell, Cornwall PL26 7DR (17)

Judith Nancarrow
☎ 01726 67111
BB From £18
EM From £10
Sleeps 12
🐎 🐈 🐕 🍴 🎪 📷
🍦🍦 Highly Commended

Oh! to be in England–but how much nicer to be in Cornwall. To stay in our beautiful farmhouse, relax and enjoy the experience of Cornish hospitality, together with traditional home cooking using fresh local produce. Discover for yourself the mysteries of the Cornish heritage, the magic of the countryside and the romance of the sea. Open all year except Christmas and New Year.

18   **Rescorla Farm,** Rescorla, St Austell, Cornwall PL26 8YT

Judith Clemo
☎/Fax 01726 850168
BB From £14–£16
EM From £8.50
Sleeps 6
🐎 (10) ⊞ ⅄ ♠ ❦
👄👄 *Commended*

Rescorla's 200–acre farm nestles in a peaceful hamlet – perfect for touring coast and countryside. Spacious double bedrooms with commanding views over open country. Colour TV, beverage facilities, vanity units in all bedrooms – one en suite. Large sitting room, dining room, separate guests' bathroom. Delicious, healthy farmhouse fare, straight form the Aga, caters for all tastes. Friendly, relaxed atmosphere. Arrive as guests–leave as friends. Open Easter–Oct.

19   **Rose Farm,** Chyanhal, Buryas Bridge, Penzance, Cornwall TR19 6AN

Mrs Penny Lally
☎ 01736 731808
BB From £17.50–£19
Sleeps 8
🐎 ♠
👄👄 *Commended*

Rose Farm is a small working farm in a little hamlet close to the picturesque fishing villages of Mousehole and Newlyn and 7 miles from Lands End. The 200-year-old granite farmhouse is cosy with pretty, en suite rooms. 1 double, 1 family suite and a romantic 15th century four poster room in barn annexe. We have all manner of animals, from pedigree cattle to pot-bellied pigs! Open all year (closed Christmas).

20   **Treffry Farm,** Lanhydrock, Bodmin, Cornwall PL30 5AF

Pat Smith
☎/Fax 01208 74405
BB From £18.50
Sleeps 6
⅄ 🐎 (6) ♠ ❦
👄👄 *Highly Commended*

Historic, listed Georgian farmhouse (1720) on 200 acre dairy farm adjoining National Trust Lanhydrock. Guaranteed warm welcome and home cooking in generous quantities! Ideal for touring Cornwall, within easy reach of many beaches. Visitors welcome to explore farm and meet animals. 3 pretty bedrooms with colour TV and en suite facilities, 1 with four-poster bed. Open Easter–Oct.

21   **Tregaddra Farm,** Cury, Helston, Cornwall TR12 7BB

June Lugg
☎ 01326 240235
BB From £17.50–£19.50
EM From £8
Sleeps 14
⅄ 🐎
👄👄👄 *Highly Commended*

A well kept garden of winding flower beds, spacious heated swimming pool and magnificent views of coast and countryside is the setting for the beautifully furnished 18th century farmhouse and mixed farm. En suite bedrooms (2 have balconies), sun lounge, inglenook, traditional farmhouse fare and warm welcome await you at Tregaddra. Open all year.

22   **Tregaswith Farmhouse,** Tregaswith, near Newquay, Cornwall TR8 4HY

John & Jacqui Elsom
☎ 01637 881181
BB From £20–£25
EM From £10
Sleeps 6
🐎 ⅄ 🐎 ♠ ♠
👄👄👄 *Highly Commended*

Tregaswith is a small hamlet just outside Newquay, 5 minutes' drive to beaches and several National Trust properties near. The farmhouse built over 250 years ago, now a smallholding breeding rare poultry and horses. Pony rides and an introduction to carriage driving can be arranged. We have a reputation for delicious food. 3 beautiful bedrooms, all en suite. Antiques and oak beams throughout. Open all year.

23   **Tregidgeo,** Grampound, Truro, Cornwall TR2 4SP

Mrs Sally Wade
☎/Fax 01726 882450
BB From £16
EM From £8
Sleeps 6
🐎 ♠
👄👄 *Commended*

Tregidgeo is a mixed farm of 216 acres. The spacious farmhouse is tastefully furnished with a friendly family atmosphere, found in a beautifully secluded and peaceful setting. Well situated for beaches and touring. Bedrooms all en suite with TV, beverage facilities and CH. Delicious home cooking. Large walled garden and play area. Children welcomed at reduced rates. Free babysitting. Open all year (closed Christmas).

Treglisson, Hayle, Cornwall TR27 5JT   **(24)**

Carole Runnalls
☎ 01736 753141
BB From £17.63–£23.50
Sleeps 15
🐎 ⚔ 🖴 🖴
🕊🕊 *Highly Commended*

Treglisson is a listed Grade II 18th century farmhouse set in peaceful, rural surroundings only 1½ miles from the beach. A hearty breakfast is served in our elegant dining room or new conservatory. We also have a heated indoor swimming pool. Personal service and attertion to detail assure our guests of a comfortable and relaxing stay. An ideal base for touring west Cornwall. Open Dec–Oct (closed Christmas and New Year).

Tregonan, Tregony, Truro, Cornwall TR2 5SN   **(25)**

Sandra Collins
☎ 01872 530249
BB From £13.50
Sleeps 6
🐎 🖴
🕊 *Commended*

Discover Tregonan, tucked away down a half–mile private lane. This comfortable, spacious farmhouse is set in a secluded garden, at centre of 300 acre arable and sheep farm. 6 miles west of Mevagissey, on the threshold of the renowned Roseland Peninsula. 2 beaches within 3 miles. All bedrooms H/C, beverage-making facilities. Good selection of eating places locally. Open Mar–Oct.

Tregondale Farm, Menheniot, Liskeard, Cornwall PL14 3RG   **(26)**

Stephanie Rowe
☎ 01579 342407
BB From £16–£18
EM From £8.50
Sleeps 6
🐎 🐎 🏇
🕊🕊 *Highly Commended*

Come and join our family with the peace of the countryside, near the coast amidst wildlife, flowers and woodland walks on a 200-acre mixed farm. Pedigree animals being naturally reared, pony rides, tennis court and play area. The characteristic farmhouse with en suite bedrooms with TV and tea/coffee, beautifully set in original walled garden, home grown produce our speciality. Idyllic for exploring Cornwall's holiday attractions. Open all year.

Trehane Farm, Trevalga, Boscastle, Cornwall PL35 0EB   **(27)**

Mrs Sarah James
☎ 01840 250510
BB From £15–£17
Sleeps 6
🐎 🐎 🐎 🏇 🖴 🦃
🕊🕊 *Commended*

Welcome to Trehane, a dairy farm on the spectacular North Cornwall heritage coast. Farmhouse set in magnificent position overlooking sea, superb coastal views. We offer a comfortable friendly atmosphere and wholesome nourishing food using fresh farm produce and home baked bread. Enjoy fine walks along the coast or inland on to Bodmin Moor. And you can learn to spin in this very lovely place. Open Feb–Dec.

Treveria Farm, Widegates, Looe, Cornwall PL13 1QR   **(28)**

Mrs J. Kitto
☎ 01503 240237
BB From £18
Sleeps 6
🐎 🍴 🐎 🏇
🕊🕊 *Commended*

Treveria is a delightful manor house set in a large garden overlooking the farm and surrounding countryside. A high standard of accommodation is offered with beautifully decorated rooms and quality furnishings. All rooms have colour TV and beverage facilities. Looe and Polperro with their quaint harbours and excellent restaurants are only a short drive away. Open Apr–Oct.

Trewellard Manor Farm, Pendeen, Penzance, Cornwall TR19 7SU   **(29)**

Mrs Marion Bailey
☎/Fax 01736 788526
BB From £15
Sleeps 6
🐎
🕊🕊 *Commended*

The farm is situated in a superb coastal position between Lands End and St Ives. We offer a friendly, relaxed atmosphere with seasonal log fires and CH. 3 bedrooms (1 en suite) all with tea/coffee facilities. Use of swimming pool (June–Sept) with good beaches within easy reach. Golf and coarse fishing available nearby. This is an outstanding area for walking, either inland or on the coast path. Open all year (closed Christmas).

30 **Treworgie Barton,** Crackington Haven, Bude, Cornwall EX23 0NL

Pam Mount
☎ **01840 230233**
🅱🅱 **From £17–£23**
EM From £13
Sleeps 6 + 6
🐎 ⅄ 🏕 ▪
🍧🍧🍧 *Highly Commended*

Enjoy personal attention and friendly atmosphere at our 106-acre farm with 25 acres of woodland, 2 miles from Crackington Haven. The 16th century farmhouse has 3 bedrooms, all with private or en suite facilities and TV. Also romantic barn room with four poster bed, and family suite. Excellent freshly cooked, carefully presented food and winter breaks our speciality. Open Apr–Sept (Nov, Feb, Mar advance bookings only).

31 **Wheatley Farm,** Maxworthy, Launceston, Cornwall PL15 8LY

Valerie Griffin
☎/Fax **01566 781232**
🅱🅱 **From £19–£20**
EM From £10.50
Sleeps 10
🐎 ⅄
🍧🍧🍧 *Highly Commended*

Escape and unwind at Wheatley where personal attention, friendly atmosphere are a priority. Traditional and imaginative farmhouse cuisine. Lovely old farmhouse set in landscaped gardens on working farm in peace of Cornish countryside. Delightful, pretty en suite bedrooms, one with romantic 4 poster. Few miles from spectacular rugged north coast and sandy coves. Children welcome. Open Easter–Sept.

SELF-CATERING

32 **Bokiddick Farm,** Lanivet, Bodmin, Cornwall PL30 5HP

Gill Hugo
☎ **01208 831481**
🆂🅲 **From £90–£320**
Sleeps 4
🐎 🏹 🏕
🐾 🐾 🐾 *Approved*

A warm welcome and a Cornish cream tea await you at Bokiddick. This pretty two-bedroomed bungalow on our family run dairy farm nestles in the heart of the Cornish countryside. Peaceful location with panoramic views, large garden, central Cornwall, perfect touring base for either coast or moors. NT Lanhydrock House is 2 miles away. Open all year.

33 **Bucklawren Farm,** St Martin-by-Looe, Cornwall PL13 1NZ

Mrs Jean Henly
☎ **01503 240738**
Fax **01503 240481**
🆂🅲 **From £100–£410**
Sleeps 4/6
🏇 🐎 🈯 ✆ ▪ 🏕
🐾 🐾 🐾 🐾 *Highly Commended*

Three attractive stone cottages recently tastefully converted from farm buildings, furnished to high standard, and set in a large garden. Bucklawren is situated deep in unspoilt countryside, yet only one mile from the beach and three miles from the fishing village of Looe. Ideal position for coastal paths, National Trust properties, fishing trips, beaches and Plymouth. Open Mar–Jan.

34 **Cadson Manor Farm,** Callington, Cornwall PL17 7HW

Mrs Brenda Crago
☎ **01579 83187**
🆂🅲 **From £150–£350**
Sleeps 4 + cot
🐎 🏕
🐾 🐾 🐾 *Highly Commended*

A fully self-contained wing of the Old Manor, with picturesque views of the Lynher Valley. Traditionally furnished, comfort and style combined with old world charm. 3 miles from Callington, off the A390. Delightful river walks amidst splendid Cornish countryside. 2 bedrooms both with H&C, sleeps up to 4 plus cot. Shower room with washbasin and WC. Electricity and bedlinen inclusive. Brochure available. Open all year.

Coach House, c/o Lantallack Farm, Landrake, Cornwall PL12 5AE   **35**

Nichola Walker
☎ 01752 851281
SC From £185–£435
Sleeps 6/7

Commended

Georgian farm coach house, extremely comfortable with oustanding views across undulating countryside and wooded valleys. The perfect retreat for a relaxing holiday. Ponies, sheep, ducks, hens and a friendly ram called Donald. Weekly art classes in Barn Studio. Golf at St Mellion, 10 mins. away. Close to sea and moors. 2 bathrooms, log fire, CH, phone, microwave, dishwasher and games room. Linen/electricity inclusive. Open Mar–Nov.

Glynn Barton Farm Cottages, Glynn Barton, Cardinham, Bodmin, Cornwall PL30 4AX   **36**

Diana Mindel
☎ 01208 821375
SC From £110–£415
Sleeps 27

Commended

Peaceful, picturesque hamlet amidst breathtaking valley views, surrounded by forestry and farmland. Splendid woodland walks on your doorstep. Relax by landscaped, secluded heated pool. Friendly donkeys, goats, chickens and pony in nearby paddock. Play area for children. Centrally positioned for exploring the many mysteries and beauties of captivating Cornwall. Open all year.

Hendra Farm, Rose, Truro, Cornwall TR4 9PS   **37**

Janet Symons
☎ 01872 572273
SC From £130–£390
Sleeps 7

Applied

South-facing half of rambling old farmhouse with pretty garden. Two bathrooms, large laundry room. You are welcome to explore the 160-acre dairy and sheep farm and secluded lake/conservation area. Footpath leads to coastal path. nearby 3 coarse fishing lakes, golf, riding, glorious surfing beaches. Babysitting usually available. Open all year.

Lodge Barton Farm, Liskeard, Cornwall PL14 4JX   **38**

Rosanne Hodin
☎ 01579 344432
SC From £100–£380
Sleeps 2/5 + cot

Commended

Lodge Barton is set in a beautiful river valley flanked by woodland. We keep a milking herd of goats and also have calves, ducks, hens and geese. Everyone can help milk, feed and collect eggs. Our character cottages are luxuriously equipped including heating, woodburners, video, linen, laundry room, private gardens and playground. We are close to sea, moors, sailing, windsurfing, riding, fishing, golf. Open all year.

Lower Trengale Farm, Liskeard, Cornwall PL14 6HF   **39**

Louise Kidd
☎ 01579 21019
Fax 01579 21432
SC From £100–£380
EM From £6
Sleeps 4/5

Commended

A small farm, set in beautiful countryside, offering three comfortable and well equipped cottages which have been carefully converted from a stone barn. Children love helping with the cows, sheep, pigs, hens and their young. There is a pony to ride, a sandpit, swings and table tennis. Lovely views from the garden. All linen supplied, laundry, meals and babysitting available. Open all year.

Manuels Farm, Quintrell Downs, Newquay, Cornwall TR8 4NY   **40**

Alan & Jean Wilson
☎ 01637 873577
SC From £85–£420
Sleeps 2/5 + cot

Commended

Imagine a family holiday close to Newquay's magnificent beaches but tucked away in your own quiet valley. Secluded from the crowd but perfectly placed for touring, walking and riding. Your own character cottage in the country, on the farm, with gardens, flowers, pets and farm animals around you. The children will enjoy the calves, tractor and ponies while you relax. Electricity included. Open all year.

41 Nancolleth Farm Caravan Gardens, Newquay, Cornwall TR8 4PN

Joan Luckraft
☎ 01872 510236
SC From £95–£275
Sleeps 6/6
✓ ✓ ✓ ✓ ✓
Rose Award

Nancolleth a 250-acre farm, 5 miles from Newquay. Central for touring Cornwall. Secluded caravan park with 6 deluxe 6-berth caravans in garden setting, well spaced, on hard standings with parking. Each caravan has 2 bedrooms, shower room with toilet, colour TV, fridge, spacious lounge, dining and kitchen areas. Laundry. Phone. Country trail. Families and couples welcomed. ETB Rose Award Caravan Holiday Park Award 1995. Open May–Oct.

42 Old Newham Farm, Otterham, Camelford, Cornwall PL32 9SR

Mrs Mary Purdue
☎ 01840 230470
SC From £95–£440
Sleeps 2/4/6
Approved

Three individual stone and slate cottages around an old farmyard dating back to medieval times, at the end of a quiet country lane. Our 30-acre farm is managed in a traditional way with cattle, sheep and other small animals for the children. Here you can find the peace of the Cornish countryside yet be only 3 miles from the most spectacular coastline in the area. Cottages with character, open fire, CH. Open all year.

43 Pencarrow Cottage, Trevissick Farm, Trenarren, St Austell, Cornwall PL26 6BQ

Mrs Pamela Treleaven
☎/Fax 01726 75819
SC From £140–£350
Sleeps 6
Up to
Commended

A spacious, traditional Cornish cottage with an air of peace and tranquillity, built in 1702. Set in unspoilt countryside in the heart of our mixed farm, boasting over 3 miles of coastline between St Austell and Mevagissey Bays. Golf and driving range within a mile. Excellent birdwatching and the keen walker will be rewarded with spectacular views. Open all year.

44 Poltarrow Farm , St Mewan, St Austell, Cornwall PL26 7DR

Judith Nancarrow
☎ 01726 67111
SC From £85–£425
Sleeps 2/6
Commended

An invitation to stay in our charming farm cottage overlooking rolling countryside where you can watch nature at work. Children love to meet the farm animals, especially Taffy the family pony. Well equipped with modern conveniences to give you time to walk nearby cliffs and discover the romance and magic of this historic county which has influenced so many Cornish writers and artists. Open all year.

45 Rescorla Farm Cottages, Rescorla, St Austell, Cornwall PL26 8YT

Judith Clemo
☎/Fax 01726 850168
SC From £100–£400
Sleeps 5
Commended

Picture this … cosy cottages oozing with character, warmth, charm; acres of rambling farmland; nature on your doorstep; peaceful hamlet location perfect for touring coast and countryside; lambs, calves, pigs, chickens to feed – eggs to collect; friendly farm pets; barbecues on lazy summer days and balmy nights; blazing log fires; babysitting; flowers and welcome tray – all this and more at Rescorla Farm. Your rural retreat awaits … Open all year.

46 Rooke Farm Cottages, Rooke Farm, Chapel Amble, Wadebridge, Cornwall PL27 6ES

Mrs Gill Reskelly
☎ 01208 880368
Fax 01208 880600
SC From £190–£630
Sleeps 2–5
Highly
Commended

Something special – luxury country cottages set in 235 acres of Duchy of Cornwall farmland. On outskirts of the pretty Chapel Amble close to beaches and N. Cornish coastline. Exclusively furnished and equipped with all thats required for a relaxing holiday. Pretty en suite bedrooms, log fires, dish-washer, satellite TV, video, hi fi and phone. Electricity heating, linen, towels and maid service inclusive. Each has private garden with barbecue and garden furniture. Open all year.

Tredinnick Farm, Duloe, Liskeard, Cornwall PL14 4PJ

Mrs Angela Barrett
☎ 01503 262997
[SC] From £115–£425
Sleeps 10
🐕 🎠
🔑 🔑 🔑 🔑 *Commended*

This family run farm offers you the chance to unwind in the unspoilt Cornish countryside. The spacious half of large farmhouse has all the comfort you need to really enjoy your holiday. Savour the atmosphere of your own private garden or visit the local tourist attractions all within travelling distance. Open Mar–Oct and Christmas.

Treffry Farm Cottages, Treffry Farm, Lanhydrock, Bodmin, Cornwall PL30 5AF

Pat Smith
☎/Fax 01208 74405
[SC] From £85–£550
Sleeps 2/8
🐕 🐎 🎠 ♞
🔑 🔑 🔑 🔑
Highly Commended

Imagine country cottages, rambling roses, chintzy sofas, rocking chairs, pot pourri, log fires on winter days, honeysuckle perfume on summer nights – they're here at Treffry. Our dairy farm adjoins the National Trust at Lanhydrock where you can walk for miles in glorious parkland. Search out rugged cliffs and hidden sandy coves, or relax and meet our farm animals and pony. A warm welcome awaits you. Open all year.

Tregevis Farm, St Martin, Helston, Cornwall TR12 6DN

Julie Bray
☎ 01326 231265
[SC] From £170–£380
Sleeps 7 + cot
🍴 🐎 🎠
🔑 🔑 🔑 🔑
Commended

Come and relax at Tregevis, a working dairy farm in the picturesque Helford River area, just ½ mile from the little village of St. Martin and 5 miles from sandy beaches. The accommodation is a self-contained, spacious part of the farmhouse, very comfortable, well equipped and with a games room. The large lawn area with swings will prove popular with children, as will our farm animals. Open Easter–Oct.

Treleaven Farm Cottages, Treleaven Farm, Mevagissey, Cornwall PL26 6RZ

Mrs Linda Hennah
☎ 01726 843558
[SC] From £100–£500
Sleeps 4–6
🐎
🔑 🔑 🔑 🔑 *Highly
Commended*

Surrounded by rambling countryside, wildlife and flowers, the farm is only 8 minutes' walk from the centre of Mevagissey. Each cottage has luxury pine fitted kitchen with dishwasher, microwave, fridge/freezer and cooker. Lovely bathroom with shower, cosy lounge with TV, some en suite bedrooms. CH included in winter. Linen and electricity inclusive. Laundry room. Ample parking. Games barn. Next to Heligan Gardens and central for touring. Open all year.

Tremadart Farm, Duloe, Liskeard, Cornwall PL14 4PE

Evelyn Julian
☎ 015032 62855
[SC] From £130–£485
Sleeps 12
🐎 ♿
🔑 🔑 🔑 🔑
Commended

Tremadart Farm offers spacious half of farmhouse set in large garden on 330-acre mixed farm which is part of the Duchy of Cornwall. It is situated in village of Duloe, 3 miles Looe and daily travelling distance of all Cornwall. Accommodation offers 4 bedrooms, bathroom, shower room, 2 toilets. Forestry walks, golf, horse riding, indoor swimming and sports complex close by. Open all year.

Trevalgan Farm, St Ives, Cornwall TR26 3BJ 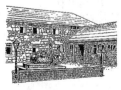

Jean Osborne
☎ 01736 796433
[SC] From £150–£400
Sleeps 2/6
🐎 🎠 ♞
🔑 🔑 🔑 – 🔑 🔑 🔑 🔑
Commended

Trevalgan is a coastal stock-rearing farm surrounded by magnificent scenery, just 2 miles from St Ives. Enjoy walking our farm trail to the cliffs overlooking the sea, a paradise for nature lovers. Traditional granite barns have been carefully converted into 7 lovely holiday homes around an attractive courtyard. Land's End, St Michael's Mount, Mousehole and Lamorna within easy reach by car. Open all year (closed Feb).

53 **Trewalla Farm Cottages,** Trewalla Farm, Minions, Liskeard, Cornwall PL14 6ED

Cheryl van der Salm
☎ **01579 342385**
SC **From £150–£345**
Sleeps 2/4
Commended

Our small, traditionally-run farm on Bodmin Moor has rare breed pigs, hand milked sheep, hens and geese, all free-range and very friendly. Our three cottages are beautifully furnished and very well equipped. Their moorland setting offers perfect peace, wonderful views, ideal walking country and a good base for exploring – if you can tear yourself away! Open Mar–Dec.

54 **Trewithen Country Lodges,** Trewithen Farm, Laneast, Launceston, Cornwall PL15 8PW

Mrs Margaret Colwill
☎ **01566 86343**
SC **From £150–£350**
Sleeps 6
Commended

A warm and friendly welcome awaits you at our Scandinavian style cabin, peacefully situated in a garden with swings. Panoramic views of the surrounding Bodmin Moor. Say hello to the pony and enjoy the animals. Ideal base for walking, riding, fishing. CH accommodation, tastefully furnished, well equipped kitchen, microwave, washer/dryer, bed linen provided, personally supervised. Open Mar–Jan.

55 **Wheatley Farm Cottages,** Maxworthy, Launceston, Cornwall PL15 7LY

Valerie Griffin
☎**/Fax 01566 781232**
SC **From £60–£450**
Sleeps 2/7
Highly Commended

Discover the delights of our Cornish heritage, amble through country lanes. Just 10 minutes' drive from spectacular, rugged North Cornish coast. Simply relax in one of our two idyllic country cottages, absolute comfort, chintzy sofas, curtains and quilts in delicate country prints. Enjoy warmth of log fires. At Wheatley farm you can visit the animals, pony rides and play area for children, a warm welcome awaits you. Open all year.

FARM HOLIDAY BUREAU

Please mention **Stay on a Farm** when booking

FARM HOLIDAY BUREAU

THOSE LITTLE EXTRAS

For advice on farms that can offer 'extras' such as four-poster beds, special diets, farm trails, fishing rights – even stabling and trekking arrangements if you are bringing your own horse – ring the Farm Holiday Bureau on (01203) 696909.

71

North Wales

Llŷn Peninsula

Group Contact: *Mrs R. D. Wynne-Finch* ☎ *01758 770209*

With more than 70 miles of coastline, backed by the dramatic mountains of Snowdonia, this is an Area of Outstanding Natural Beauty where the warm waters of the Gulf Stream give a mild climate all year round. The Welsh language and way of life still flourish here and while you struggle with the seemingly impossible Celtic names, you will appreciate the very Welshness of it all.

It is also an area compact enough to travel around and get to know – and one that you will want to come back to time and time again.

No-one comes to this part of Wales without setting foot on mighty Mount Snowdon; and even if you only clamber for a relatively short distance you will be rewarded with views the like of which you will never have seen before. And you could always walk one way and take the famous narrow gauge railway the other!

Right at the foot of the Peninsula lies Bardsey Island – a bird sanctuary, place of pilgrimage and the legendary resting place of 20,000 saints.

Nestling on its own wooded peninsula you will find Portmeirion, the Italianate extravaganza created by the late Sir Clough Williams Ellis, full of delightful surprises in the shape of statues, follies and fake facades.

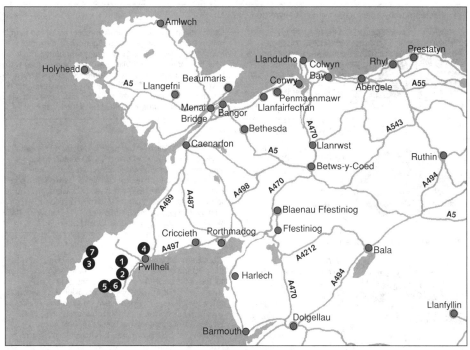

BED AND BREAKFAST

(and evening meal)

---

1 Mathan Uchaf Farm, Boduan, Pwllheli, Gwynedd LL53 8TU

Mrs Jean Coker
☎ **01758 720487**
BB From £15–£17
EM From £8
Sleeps 6

A 190-acre dairy farm, situated off the main Pwllheli to Nefyn road. Centrally positioned for northern and southern beaches of peninsula. Guests can participate in farm activities. Large garden provides safe play area. We have 2 dogs who play ball and a Shetland pony. 1 double room, 1 family room with washbasins, 1 twin bedded room. Dining room, sitting room with colour TV. Good food and friendly atmosphere are our aim. Open Mar–Nov.

SELF-CATERING

---

2 Castellmarch, Abersoch, Pwllheli, Gwynedd LL53 7UE

Mrs H M Jones
☎ **01758 712242**
SC From £90–£300
Sleeps 4–5

Castellmarch, a traditional family run beef and sheep farm, 1 mile from the yachting village of Abersoch, and minutes walk from sandy beach. Listed 16th century farmhouse. This was once the home of fabled March Ap Meirchion – a man with horse's ears. Cegin-isa (wing of farmhouse) sleeps 4. All rooms have exposed beams. The Granary sleeps 5. A chalet set on elevated position sleeps 5. All enjoy sea and countryside views. B&B available in farmhouse. Brochure. Open Mar–Nov.

---

3 Cefnamwlch, Tudweiliog, Pwllheli, Gwynedd LL53 8AX

Mrs R. Wynne-Finch
☎ **01758 770209**
SC From £100–£225
Sleeps 4/6 + cot

Houses 1 & 2 sleep 6 in 3 double bedrooms. Cot available. Converted from wing of owner's 17th century manor farmhouse on ancient Welsh estate. Situated in beautiful woodland setting 1 mile from village of Tudweiliog, along rhododendron drive. Easy reach sandy beaches, golf course. Ideal touring centre. Colour TV, tumble dryer and spindryer. Play area. Electric 50p meter. Ty Thimble Cottage sleeps 4 in 2 double bedrooms. Open Easter–end Oct.

---

4 Gwynfryn Farm, Pwllheli, Gwynedd LL53 5UF

Sian B Ellis
☎/Fax **01758 612536**
SC From £94–£480
Sleeps 2/8

Our organic dairy farm is a haven for nature lovers, away from the madding crowd, yet only 1S miles from Pwllheli. Cottages for romantic couples/houses 4–8 persons, all personally supervised, WTB 4–5 dragons – quality assured. Snowdon 25 miles, sea 2 miles – vary your activity to suit the weather or your mood. Beds made up, storage/central heating. Mini breaks Oct–Mar. Sample our hospitality. Gold Award Welcome Host. Send for colour brochure. Open all year.

Rhydolion, Llangian, Abersoch, Pwllheli, Gwynedd LL53 7LR

Catherine Morris
☎ 01758 712342
⑤ From £105–£300
Sleeps 6–8
🐕 🐎 🔥 🏕 🛁 🚲 🐾

🌺 🌺 🌺 🌺 🌺

Charming 16th century farmhouse wing and a ground floor cottage, both with 3 bedrooms, providing interesting blend of 'olde worlde' charm and modern comfort. Beams, inglenook fireplace, four poster (farmhouse only), microwave, dishwasher, etc. Laundry room. Situated in a delightful, peaceful setting, beach only ¾ mile. Ideal sailing, surfing, cycling and good walks area or join in farm activities. Open Mar–Jan.

Tai Gwyliau Tyndon Holiday Cottages, c/o Penlan, Rhos Isaf, Caernarfon, Gwynedd LL54 7NG ⑥

Mrs Elisabeth Evans
☎ 01286 831184
⑤ From £99–£380
Sleeps 5/7
🐕 🐎

🌺 🌺 🌺 – 🌺 🌺 🌺 🌺

120 acre sheep farm on the beautiful Lleyn heritage coast. Peaceful and relaxing self-contained cottages and bungalows. 1 mile from Llanengan with its country pub and 6th century church. Boating resort of Abersoch only 2 miles away, beautiful sandy beach of Porthneigwl within 200 yards (with private access). All cottages have glorious views of the bay. Ideal family holiday. Personal supervision. Free brochure. Open all year.

Towyn Farm, Tudweiliog, Pwllheli, Gwynedd LL53 8PD ⑦

Iona Wynne Owen
☎ 01758 770230
⑤ From £100–£350
Sleeps 6/7 + cot
🐕 ♿ 🐎 🏕 🔥 🐾 ♨

🌺 🌺 🌺 🌺 🌺

Enjoy a relaxing holiday in unspoilt area of outstanding natural beauty. 200 yds from Towyn beach. Ideal fishing, surfing, boating. Nefyn golf course 5 miles. A 300-year-old modernised farmhouse, carpeted throughout, colour TV, 4 bedrooms, duvets and heaters. Open fire in autumn/winter. Bathroom with bath and shower. Fitted kitchen, washing machine, tumble dryer, microwave oven. Sheltered lawn garden with barbeque. Free babysitting. Cot and high chair. Also ground level cottage sleeping 6.

NO ANSWER?
Farmers are mostly out and about during the day.
Try to telephone before 9.30am or after 4pm.

FARM HOLIDAY
BUREAU

FARM HOLIDAY
BUREAU

BUREAU ACCOMMODATION
IS RELIABLE
This Guide lists **Farm Holiday Bureau** members only.
They are all inspected by the National Tourist Board for
standards (see introduction pages) and by fellow members
to maintain a high quality.

72

North Wales
Snowdonia

Group Contact: *Mrs Jane Llewelyn Pierce* ☎ *01248 670147*

In Snowdonia those interested in history have a wealth of locations to visit, from the early 12th century Welsh fortresses at Dolbadarn and Dolwyddelan to the magnificent castles of Edward 1st at Caernarfon, Beaumaris, Harlech and Conwy. The National Trust's historic houses include Plas Newydd on Anglesey and Penrhyn Castle near Bangor. Segontium Fort at Caernarfon is witness to the four hundred years of Roman occupation and there is an interesting museum nearby.

Take a boat trip along the Menai Strait, a ride on a steam train into the mountains with the Talyllyn or Ffestiniog Railways, alongside Llanberis Lake or even up Mount Snowdon itself. Visit the heart of a Welsh slate cavern, take a trip to the theatre at Bangor or Harlech, or see craftsmen at work – some of the many choices available.

Add to this the Sports Council's excellent centres near Caernarfon and Capel Curig, heated swimming pools at Caernarfon, Bangor and Harlech, golf at one of the many courses with superb sea views, some really excellent restaurants and pubs and walks in the mountains or forests, and often a week is all too short a time to stay with us.

Most of us are Welsh speaking as Snowdonia is the heartland of the Welsh language and we will be very happy to teach you a few Welsh greetings or tell you more about our ancient language.

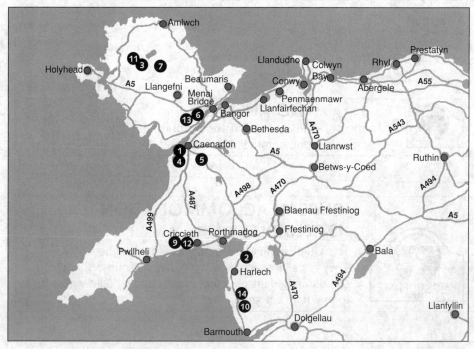

BED AND BREAKFAST

(and evening meal)

Cae'r Efail, Llanfaglan, Caernarfon, Gwynedd LL54 5RE

Mrs Mari Williams
☎ 01286 676226 or 672824
BB From £16–£18
EM From £10
Sleeps 4

In its grounds of 20 acres enjoying perfect peace, seclusion and magnificent views of Snowdonia and Anglsesy. A trip on one of the magnificent little train's not to be missed. Built at turn of the century, recently modernised. Cae'r Efail offers comfortable, tastefully furnished accomodation. Good food is of prime importance, using home/local produce. 1 double (en suite), 1 twin. Reduced rates for children. Open Easter–Oct.

Gwrach Ynys, Talsarnau, Gwynedd LL47 6TS

Mrs Deborah Williams
☎/Fax 01766 780742
BB From £16–£20
EM From £10
Sleeps 15

Deluxe

Relax in the peace and comfort of our secluded Edwardian House. Conveniently located, close to sea and mountains with many tourist attractions nearby. Ideal golfing, rambling, birdwatching area. En suite bedrooms with TV, telephone, beverage facilities. Meals lovingly prepared using fresh local produce. Children free accommodation if sharing with two adults on weekly lets. WTB Farmhouse Award. AA Selected. Open all year except Christmas.

Llwydiarth Fawr, Llanerchymedd, Isle of Anglesey, Gwynedd LL71 8DF

Mrs Margaret Hughes
☎ 01248 470321/470540
BB From £20–£25
EM From £12.50
Sleeps 6

Deluxe

Secluded Georgian mansion set in 850 acres of woodland and farmland. Ideal touring base for island's coastline, Snowdonia and North Wales coast. Nearby is Llyn Alaw for trout fishing. Reputation for excellent food using farm and local produce. Bedrooms with en suite bathrooms. TV, CH, log fires. Walks and private fishing. Winner of the BBC 'Welsh Farmhousewife of the year' competition. Member of Taste of Wales. Warmest Welcome Award 1993.

Pengwern, Saron, Llanwnda, Caernarfon, Gwynedd LL54 5UH

G & J Lloyd Rowlands
☎/Fax 01286 830717
BB From £19–£22
EM From £10
Sleeps 6

Deluxe

Charming, spacious farmhouse of character, situated between mountains and sea. Unobstructed views of Snowdonia. Well appointed bedrooms, all with en suite bathrooms. Set in 130 acres of land which runs down to Foryd Bay. Jane has a cookery diploma and provides the excellent meals with farmhouse fresh food, including home-produced beef and lamb. Excellent access. Open Feb–Nov.

Plas Tirion Farm, Llanrug, Caernarfon, Gwynedd LL55 4PY

C H Mackinnon
☎ 01286 673190
BB From £18–£20
EM From £10
Sleeps 6

Deluxe

Welcome to our working dairy farm with comfortable, heated accommodation. All en suite bedrooms with beverage facilities, TV and panoramic views. Recommended for breakfast and dinners using fresh produce. Special diets available; residential licence; packed lunches. Rough shooting. 4 miles Llanberis and Caernarfon, 10 miles Anglesey, 8 miles beach. Wales Farmhouse Award; Open May–Sept.

---

6 **Plas Trefarthen,** Brynsiencyn, Anglesey, Gwynedd LL61 6SZ

Marian Roberts
☎ **01248 430379**
▣ **From £17–£20**
EM From £10
Sleeps 14
⌂

♛ ♛ ♛
Highly Commended

Secluded Georgian house in 200 acres of land on the shore of the Menai Straits. Uninterrupted views of mighty Snowdon. Ideal base for touring Anglesey and Snowdonia, walking and local National Trust properties. Beautifully furnished, large en suite bedrooms, tea/coffee-making facilities, colour TV. Full size snooker table. Good home cooking. Warm Welsh welcome. Open all year.

7 **Tre'r Ddol Farm,** Llanerchymedd, Isle of Anglesey, Gwynedd LL71 7AR

Ann Astley
☎ **01248 470278**
▣ **From £18**
EM From £10
Sleeps 6
🐕 🐎 🛤

♛ ♛ ♛
Highly Commended

If you are looking for freedom and relaxation this family farm of 200 acres can oblige. Its historic 17th century house and country antiques add to the mystery and character of the past. Ornithologists' paradise, plus excellent fishing at Llyn Alaw and sport activities. Spacious en suite bedrooms. Guests' comfort a priority and food a speciality. Children enjoy free pony rides and participate in farm activities. Wales Farmhouse Award. SAE for brochure. Open Jan–Nov.

SELF-CATERING

8 **Bryn Beddau,** Bontnewydd, Caernarfon, Gwynedd LL54 7YE

Eleri Carrog
☎ **01286 830117/**
673795
Fax 01286 675664
▣ **From £160–£320**
Sleeps 5
🐕 🐎 🍴 💼 ✿

❀ ❀ ❀ ❀

Cosy stone–built stable cottage with views of mountains and sea. Excellent centre for walks, touring, lovely beaches and Snowdonia. Secluded setting yet only 3 miles from Caernarfon. Lovely gallery bedroom with graceful arch windows, twin room, cot. Ideal for families or that romantic break. Spacious beamed lounge of great character and many books. Patio, barbecue. "Croeso Cymreig". Open all year.

9 **Chwilog Fawr,** Chwilog, Pwllheli, Gwynedd LL53 6SW

Catherine Jones
☎ **01766 810506**
▣ **From £100–£380**
🐎 🐕 🐾 🖼 ⛺

❀ ❀ ❀ ❀ – ❀ ❀ ❀ ❀

Situated in an elevated position with panoramic views of Llyn and Snowdonia. Secluded and peaceful yet convenient for beach, fishing, golfing and lovely country walks. Superior 3 bedroom farmhouse, 2 or 3 bedroom chalets or luxury caravans. Exceptionally well appointed with extensive range of facilities. Open Mar–Nov.

10 **Llys Bennar,** Dyffryn Ardudwy, Gwynedd LL44 2RX

Catrin Rutherford
☎/Fax 01341 247316
▣ **From £125–£400**
Sleeps 4/7
🐕 ♿ 🐎 🧍 🖼

❀ ❀ ❀ ❀

Attractive 18th century farm buildings converted into charming cottages, within a courtyard setting. They have retained the original charm of the oak beams, one with inglenook fireplace. Both have nightstore heating. Laundry facility available. Ten minutes to village or to sandy beach. One mile from station. In Snowdonia National Park. Many attractions in the area. Open all year.

Llwydiarth Fawr Farm Cottages, Llanerchymedd, Isle of Anglesey, Gwynedd LL71 8DF   **11**

Mrs Margaret Hughes
☎ 01248 470321/
470540
SC From £100–£500
Sleeps 4–9

Superbly furnished and equipped, beautifully positioned in the centre of Anglesey and surrounded by owner's farmland. Snowdonia and the coast within easy driving distance. Nearby is Llyn Alaw, excellent for trout fishing. In winter the cottages are warm and welcoming with log fires and CH. Well equipped kitchens have microwave, tumbledryer, washing machine, dishwasher. A warm Welsh welcome to guests who will enjoy our walks and private fishing. Open all year.

Pen-y-Bryn, Chwilog, Pwllheli, Gwynedd LL53 6SX   **12**

Mrs Sulwen Edwards
☎ 01766 810208
SC From £100–£425
Sleeps 2–8

We offer a choice of luxury accommodation for the discerning. Enjoy a memorable holiday in our tastefully restored farmhouse or bungalow. Both are set in their own garden and enjoy panoramic views of Cardigan Bay and Snowdonia. Here you will find peace and tranquillity yet be within easy reach of towns, beaches, tourist attractions, fishing and shooting. Open all year.

Plas Trefarthen, Brynsiencyn, Anglesey, Gwynedd LL61 6SZ   **13**

Marian Roberts
☎ 01248 430379
SC From £150–£300
Sleeps 6

Large self-catering wing of Georgian house on the shore of the Menai Straits in Area of Outstanding Natural Beauty overlooking Snowdonia. Ideal base for walking, beaches, National Trust properties. Three bedrooms, comfortable lounge, colour TV, kitchen diner, electric stove, fridge, microwave, washing machine. Electricity by meter. Open all year.

Ynys Ystumgwern, Dyffryn Ardudwy, Gwynedd LL44 2DD   **14**

Jane & John Williams
☎ 01341 247249
Fax 01341 247171
SC From £140–£420
Sleeps 2/8

A taste of luxury with a cosy, relaxed atmosphere in quiet setting, 1 mile from sandy beach, shops and station. Kitchen/diner with dishwasher, microwave, Aga, oak beams. Lounge has electric or open fire in inglenook fireplace. Each bedroom is tastefully furnished and heated. Laundry room. Barbecue and picnic tables. Ample parking via private drive. Warm welcome to all. Colour brochure available. Open all year.

73

North Wales

Heart of Snowdonia

Group Contact: *Carol Bain* ☎ *01766 540397*

A choice of quality, traditional Welsh farmhouses, ALL located in the Snowdonia National Park, an ideal base for exploring the whole of North Wales. Most have en suite bedrooms, tea trays, colour TVs, CH and provide full farmhouse breakfasts with optional evening meals.

There are numerous attractions within this area including the spectacular Ffestiniog Railway, Bala Lake Railway and the Welsh Highland Railway at Porthmadog. Slate is the theme at Blaenau Ffestiniog, where the Llechwedd Slate Caverns and Gloddfa Ganol Mountain Centre welcome thousands of visitors journeying into Victorian working conditions. Stroll through the unique Italianate village of Portmeirion. Try dry slope skiing at Trawsfynydd or pony trekking nearby. Bala Lake is renowned for its watersports, sailing and windsurfing, close to the white water canoe centre. Keen fishermen can fish at Bala Lake, Llyn Celyn and Trawsfynydd. Bodnant Garden in the Conwy valley is world acclaimed. There are many National Trust properties to visit as well as a great choice of historic and Roman ruins.

All this plus the mountains, lakes, waterfalls and fine beaches await you. Hear our language, listen to local choirs practising, above all relax, find peace and tranquillity in the resplendent beauty that surrounds you.

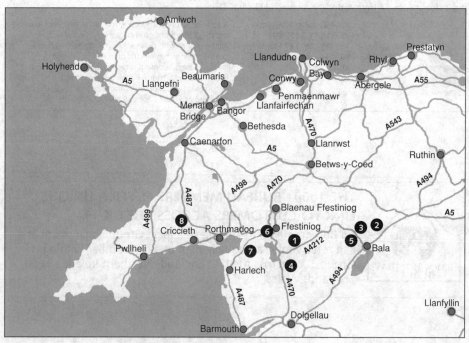

Bed and Breakfast

(and evening meal)

Bryn Celynog Farm, Cwm Prysor, Trawsfynydd, Gwynedd LL41 4TR — 1

Mrs G E Hughes
01766 540378
From £16–£18.50
EM From £8.50
Sleeps 6
Highly Commended

Set amidst beautiful mountains a working farm 3 miles from Trawsfynydd village. Modernised farmhouse, twin, double and family bedrooms, en suite, all with washbasins, tea/coffee facilities. Lounge with colour TV, log fire. Reputation for excellent food and friendliness. Optional evening meal. Wales Farmhouse Award. Open all year.

Cwm Hwylfod,Cefn–Ddwysarn, Gwynedd LL23 7LN — 2

Joan Best
016783 310
From £13–£15
EM From £9.50
Sleeps 6

Set in hills near Bala, our 400–year–old farmhouse is warm and welcoming. The views are spectacular. Animals abound and everyone, especially children, can take part in farm activities. Bedrooms have washbasins and tea making facilities. The guest lounge has TV, books and games. Full central heating. For our home–cooked evening meals we use the best of local produce. All diets catered for. Taste of Wales. Open all year except Christmas.

Fferm Fron-Gôch, Frongoch, Bala, Gwynedd LL23 7NT — 3

Carys Davies
01678 520483/521387
From £14–£18
EM From £8
Sleeps 6
(6)
Highly Commended

A beautiful stone built farmhouse with interesting historical links with Abraham Lincoln's ancestors. Set in 600 acres of unspoilt countryside, situated 3 miles from Bala on the A4212. Traditionally furnished with antiques, log fires and oak beams. Relax in a friendly Welsh atmosphere. 1 double en suite, 2 twin en suite. Welcome Host Farmhouse Award. Open all year.

Old Mill Farmhouse, Fron Oleu Farm, Trawsfynydd, Gwynedd LL41 4UN — 4

Carol Bain
/Fax 01766 540397
From £17–£18.50
EM From £8.50

Relaxing friendly welcome and atmosphere for guests visiting our character farmhouse (circa. 1700), overlooking the lake and mountains. Adjacent level access bedrooms in stonebuilt converted farm buildings. All en suite with TV, CH, tea/coffee-making facilities. Ample portions of fresh wholesome food. Guests lounge with log fires. Child reductions. Current winner Holiday Care Awards 'Best Establishment under 20 bedrooms'. Welcome Host and Taste of Wales. Open all year.

Rhydydefaid Farm, Frongoch, Bala, Gwynedd LL23 7NT — 5

Olwen Davies
01678 520456
From £14–£16.50
Sleeps 6
Highly Commended

A true Welsh welcome awaits you at our traditional Welsh stone farmhouse. 3 miles from Bala near A4212 road. 100-acre working farm. Oak beamed lounge with inglenook fireplace. 1 oak beamed en suite, family bedroom, twin/single bedrooms with wash basin. All with tea/coffee-making facilities. Ideal for touring Snowdonia. Open all year except Christmas & New Year.

6 **Tyddyn Du Farm,** Gellilydan, Ffestiniog, Gwynedd LL41 4RB

Paula Williams
☎/Fax 01766 590281
🛏 From £16–£19
EM From £9
Sleeps 8
🐾 🐎 ✂ 🍴 🎣 🛶 ⚓ 🎿
🌺🌺🌺 *Highly Commended*

Located amidst spectacular scenery, guests are very welcome to enjoy the old world charm of our homely 400yr old farmhouse, (WTB Farmhouse Award). Excellent central location. Most bedrooms en suite, one superb private cottage suite, all have remote control TV and beverage facilities. CH with log fires. Delicious candle light dinners. Working farm with pony, ducks and bottle fed lambs. Weekly dinner B&B from £151. Stamp please for brochure. Taste of Wales. Open all year.

SELF-CATERING

7 **Caerwych Farmhouse,** Llandecwyn, Near Harlech, Gwynedd LL47 6YT

Richard Williams–Ellis
☎ 01766 770913
🅂🄲 From £150–£400
Sleeps 9
🐾 🐎

🌺🌺🌺

Secluded Welsh mill set in marvellous scenic countryside with stupendous views to the sea. We are a typically traditional sheep farm but also breed horses and are replanting ancient woodlands. The stone farmhouse is old, large and handsome. Central heating throughout. Five bedrooms. Perfection for walkers. Open all year.

8 **Pant Glas Cennin,** Garndolbenmaen, Gwynedd LL51 9EX

Nerys Lloyd Williams
☎/Fax 01766 530278
🅂🄲 From £200–£420
Sleeps 7
🐾 🐎

🌺🌺🌺🌺🌺

Situated 2 miles off the main Caernarfon/Portmadog/Criccieth road on the side of Mynydd Cennin with panoramic views of Snowdonia and Cardigan Bay, this comfortable farmhouse has been extensively renovated to extremely high standards and attached to the owner's farmhouse. 2 doubles, 1 twin, 1 single and cot. Bathroom/WC/shower room with WC. Modern, well equipped kitchen/dishwasher/microwave. Colour TV. Open Easter–Oct.

FARM HOLIDAY
BUREAU

FOLLOW THE COUNTRY CODE

Leave nothing but footprints,
Take nothing but photographs,
Kill nothing but time!

74

North Wales

Warm Welsh Welcome Clwyd

Group Contacts: *Mrs Anwen Roberts* ☎ *01745 730627*
Mrs Helen Parry ☎ *01745 550276*

Clwyd – its northern boundary strung with seaside resorts – comes up with some surprising contrasts, from the sandcastle and holiday atmosphere of the coast to the fortresses left behind from mediaeval times. It is a beautiful county with a necklace of seaside towns and unspoilt inland scenery.

St Asaph, at the head of the Vale of Clwyd, might be just a large village, but it is also a cathedral city. The cathedral may be the smallest in the country but it is also one of the oldest in Wales, dating back to the 15th century. It houses some rare treasures like the original copy of William Morgan's Welsh translation of the Bible.

Further into the county lies Ruthin Boasting a wealth of history including a castle which provides a very popular mediaeval banquet . Also there is the 'Maen Huail' stone where King Arthur is said to have beheaded his rival in love. The craft centre is well worth a visit, as are the ones at Nannerch and Llanasa. Crafts of a different nature are to be found in Llangollen where horse-drawn barges glide along the Shropshire Union Canal. Llangollen also hosts the International Musical Eisteddfod in early July.

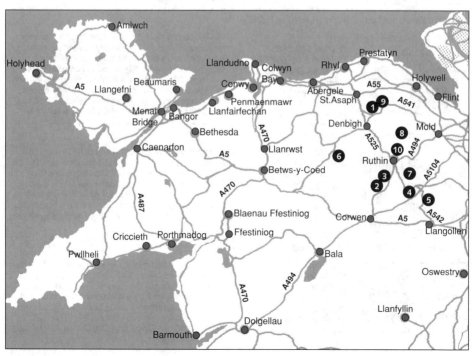

BED AND BREAKFAST

(and evening meal)

---

1   **Bach-y-Graig,** Tremeirchion, St Asaph, Clwyd LL17 0UH

Anwen Roberts
☎ 01745 730627
🛏 From £17
EM From £9.50
Sleeps 6
💥 🐴 👁 🐈 🌂 🛢
🌸🌸🌸 *Highly Commended*

A 16th century listed farmhouse nestling at the foot of the Clwydian Range with beautiful views of the surrounding countryside. Highest standard of traditional furnishings and decor, en suite, TVs, tea/coffee-making facilities in bedrooms, full CH, beamed inglenook fireplace with log fires. Central for North Wales, Chester coast 9 miles. Games room. 40 acre woodland trail on farm. WTB Farmhouse Award. AA selected award. RAC acclaimed. Open all year.

---

2   **Bodangharad,** Llanfwrog, Ruthin, Clwyd LL15 2AH

Enid Jones
☎ 01824 702370
🛏 From £13
EM From £7
Sleeps 6
🐴 👁 🌂
Listed

Bodangharad is a 100-acre dairy/sheep farm in unspoilt countryside, with a wealth of wild flowers and hedgerows. Panoramic views of Vale of Clwyd. We are a few minutes' drive from historic market town of Ruthin, with easy access to Chester, coast and Snowdonia. House with interesting interior with exposed beams, open fires and spacious rooms for guests. It offers peace and tranquillity and plenty of farmhouse fresh food. Open Easter–Nov.

---

3   **Bryn Awel,** Bontuchel, Ruthin, Clwyd LL15 2DE

Beryl J Jones
☎ 0182470 2481
🛏 From £16–£17.50
EM From £8.50
Sleeps 5
👁 🐴 💥 🐈 🌂
🌸🌸🌸
Highly Commended

This is a 60-acre working sheep farm, deep in the hills of the famouse Vale of Clwyd, ideally situated for visiting Snowdonia and Chester. The hamlet of Bontuchel has many interesting walks where you can enjoy wild flora and fauna. Bryn Awel offers ½ mile of private fishing and forest walks where you can rest in a 'bird hide' to 'bird watch' in perfect peace. Two rooms en suite. Good food a priority. Open all year except Christmas & New Year.

---

4   **Cae Madoc Ucha,** Llandegla, Nr Wrexham, Clwyd LL11 3BD

Mrs Del Crossley
☎ 01978 790270
🛏 From £16–£18
EM From £8–£10
Sleeps 2
🐴 👁 💥
🌸🌸

Set in the hills between Ruthin and Llangollen near the A5104 Chester to Corwen Road. Minutes away from the renowned Horseshoe pass and Offa's Dyke. Working farm with sheep. A warm welcome awaits you in a cosy farmhouse with good food to lull you into a holiday mood. WTB farmhouse award. Central for NT properties, zoos, walking and beautiful Welsh scenery. Open all year.

---

5   **Cefn Y Fedw Farm,** Garth, Llangollen, Clwyd LL14 1UA

Mrs Shelagh Roberts
☎/Fax 01978 823403
🛏 From £16
EM From £10
Sleeps 6
👁 💥 🧍 🐕 🐈 🌂 🛢
🌸🌸

Cefn Y Fedw stands high above Garth village in the hills behind Llangollen. A working farm, offering good food, comfortable accommodation in spacious rooms. Guests' private bathrooms. A private walk for guests interested in rock formation, historical sites or birdwatching has been designed. Close to panorama walk, Offa's Dyke path. Ring for brochure. Open May–Oct. Off the A539.

College Farm, Peniel, Denbigh, Clwyd LL16 4TT   **6**

Helen Parry
☎ **01745 550276**
⌷ **From £15–£16**
EM From £7.50
Sleeps 5
🐕 ⛄ ⚥ 🐎
🏵 *Highly Commended*

College is situated in peaceful surroundings and a warm Welsh welcome is assured by the bilingual Parry family. Ideal for touring the beautiful Vale of Clwyd and Snowdonia, being 3 miles from Denbigh (Medieval town). Bedrooms have washbasins, CH and hospitality trays. Lounge with logfire and separate dining room. WTB farmhouse award. Open Mar–Nov.

Llainwen Ucha, Pentrecelyn, Ruthin, Clwyd LL15 2HL   **7**

Elizabeth Parry
☎ **01978 790253**
⌷ **From £14–£15**
EM From £7.50
Sleeps 5
🐎
Listed

Our 130 acre farm overlooks the beautiful Vale of Clwyd. Centrally situated to coast, Snowdonia, Chester and Llangollen. Modern house with 2 pleasant bedrooms to accommodate 5 persons. CH and good home cooking, a warm welcome to visitors throughout the year. Take A525 from Ruthin towards Wrexham; after 4 miles turn left after college, we are a mile up this road. Open all year except Christmas & New Year.

T♀ Coch Farm, Llangynhafal, Denbigh, Clwyd LL16 4LN   **8**

Anne L Richards
☎ **01824 790423**
⌷ **From £13–£14**
Sleeps 5
🐎 ⚥
🏵

Working dairy and sheep farm, beautiful views, pleasant walks, five miles of historic towns of Ruthin and Denbigh. Ideal base for Chester and North Wales. Wash basins and tea/coffee-making facilities. Good home cooking, local produce, special diets catered for. A warm Welsh welcome awaits you. Open all year (closed Christmas).

SELF-CATERING

Bach-y-Graig, Tremeirchion, St Asaph, Clwyd LL17 0UH   **9**

Anwen Roberts
☎ **01745 730627**
⌷ **From £70–£295**
Sleeps 6 + cot
⚥ 🐎
🏵🏵🏵🏵🏵

Stay on a working dairy farm in this 16th century farmhouse, retaining the charm but offering comforts and convenience of modern living in high standard accommodation. Dark oak, fully equipped kitchen. 3 bedrooms, 1 four-poster bed. Bathroom with shower/bath. Downstairs toilet, CTV heating. Log fires. Linen provided. Games room, large garden with swings/slide. Central for Chester, Snowdonia and coastal resorts. No pets. Open all year.

Tyddyn Isaf, Rhewl, Ruthin, Clwyd LL15 1UH   **10**

Elsie Jones
☎ **01824 703367**
⌷ **From £90–£220**
Sleeps 6 + cot
🐎
🏵🏵🏵 – 🏵🏵🏵🏵

A warm welcome is assured on this 80-acre mixed farm, 3 miles from market town of Ruthin. Within easy reach of Chester, the coast and Snowdonia. The accommodation in the spacious self-contained part of farmhouse with oak beams has 1 double, 1 family bedroom, bathroom, separate toilet, kitchen, lounge/diner, colour TV, radio, highchair, microwave, washing facilities, cot available, CH winter months. Linen provided. No pets. Open all year.

75

Mid Wales

Croeso Cader Idris

Group Contact: *Mrs Meirwen Pughe* ☎ *01654 761235*

A true Welsh welcome 'croeso' is offered by the farming families around Cader Idris, one of the highest peaks in Wales; from the farms you can explore the coast and the countryside of this lovely area of Wales.

A vast area of green valleys and mountains criss-crossed by long distance footpaths, old drover's lanes and mountain paths which provide some of the finest hill walking country in Britain. For the explorer and adventurer, fishing, golfing, riding, pony trekking, climbing, canoeing and a mountain bike safari ensure a wealth of activity.

Dolgellau, beneath the majestic peak of Cader Idris, and Fairbourne, with its beautiful beach, combined with a visit to a real gold mine at Ganllwyd is a day out to remember. The working demonstrations of wind, water and solar power at the National Centre for Alternative Technology near Machynlleth and a visit to Trawsfynydd Power Station give an insight into the power of nature and man's sympathetic harnessing of it.

An exciting area of contrasts, from the golden beaches of the coast to the high mountains of the National Park, there is something for everyone, from craft workshops to forest visitor centres, towering castles to deep slate caverns.

The Welsh language is heard frequently, the farmers of Cader Idris have roots deep in the area. A warm welcome is extended to visitors to share the language, history, culture and hospitality of one of the loveliest areas of Wales.

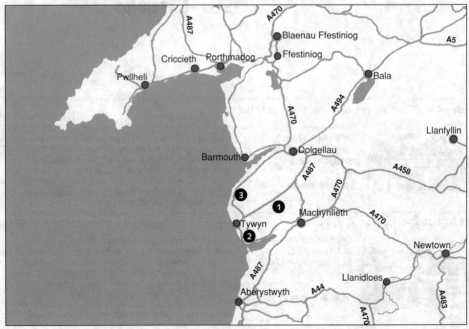

BED AND BREAKFAST
(and evening meal)

Tanycoed Ucha, Abergynolwyn, Tywyn, Gwynedd LL36 9UP

Gweniona Pugh
☎ **01654 782228**
ⓑⓑ **From £13.50–£14.50**
☇ ☇
Listed

Enjoy a quiet break on a traditional Welsh farm in the tranquil rural setting close to Dolgoch Falls, with Talyllyn Gauge Railway running through our land. Over 100 year old farmhouse modernised for comfort. Tea/coffee facilities in bedrooms. Log fires when cold and wet. Home cooking. Open Mar–Nov.

Tyddyn Rhys Farm, Aberdovey, Gwynedd LL35 0PG

Mrs Mair Jones
☎ **01654 767533**
ⓑⓑ **£14–£16.50**
Sleeps 5
☇ ☇(8) ☇
☇ ☇ *Highly Commended*

A warm Welsh welcome awaits you at Tyddyn Rhys with its fantastic panoramic view of the Dovey Estuary and Cardigan Bay. Only ½ mile from the centre of Aberdovey with its beautiful sandy beaches. Full central heating with colour TV, tea/coffee making facilities in bedrooms. One en suite, one private bedroom. Also static caravan to let. Very nice walks in the area. Open Feb–Nov.

SELF-CATERING

Carn y Gadell Uchaf, c/o Henblas, Llwyngwril, Gwynedd LL37 2QA

Mrs Swancott Pugh
☎/Fax **01341 250350**
ⓢⓒ **From £125–£450**
Sleeps 6
☇

☇ ☇ ☇ ☇ ☇

An historic 16th century farmhouse situated 1 mile from A493, a perfect retreat with panoramic views of Cardigan Bay. Stone spiral staircase, inglenook fireplace with log fire, 3 bedrooms, 2 bathrooms, colour TV, video, dishwasher, washing machine, fridge/freezer, microwave, games room, drying room. Excellent accommodation, ideal for exploring Snowdonia National Park. Welsh speaking family. Brochure. Open all year.

76

Mid Wales
Montgomeryshire/
Heart of Wales

Group Contact: *Mrs Gwyneth Williams* ☎ *01686 430285*

The Heart of Wales has unspoilt villages, bustling little towns, and marvellous scenery – hills and mountains, sparkling streams, superb woodlands, tranquil lakes and reservoirs.

It is also surprisingly compact, with plenty to do and see without travelling far from your base. Roads are relative traffic free and none of the properties is much more than one hour's drive from the sandy beaches and rugged cliffs of the coast. There are plenty of country pubs for a lunchtime snack and the food we serve is largely fresh local produce, often from our own gardens. English is understood everywhere, but you will hear Welsh spoken, particularly in the north and west. You will soon become accustomed to the seemingly difficult sounds of our place names and personal names (we are all used to advising guests on pronunciation!) We also make a point of having information in our houses about events and places of interest, to help you enjoy your stay.

There are reminders of border struggles years ago; and the 8th century rampart built by King Offa is now a 170-mile public footpath. Among other man-made attractions, the area is renowned for its unique black-and-white buildings, including cruck houses, box-framed houses and their many variations.

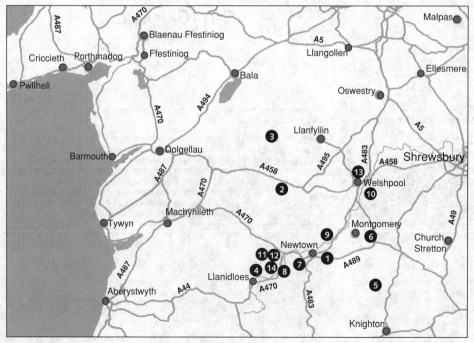

BED AND BREAKFAST
(and evening meal)

Cilthriew, Pentre, Kerry, Nr.Newton, Powys SY16 4PF

Gary or Margaret Barbee
☎ **01686 670667**
🛏 From £18–£21
Sleeps 6
🪕 🐎 ⛄ 🚲 🌳 🚤 🖕
🐝🐝 *Highly Commended*

Chilthriew is an enchanting 16th century farmhouse set in the beautiful unspoilt Vale of Kerry where a warm and genuine welcome awaits you. Heavily beamed interior lounge with inglenook log fire. Imaginative country cooking is served in the candlelit dining room. Three en suite bedrooms, one on the ground floor. Guests may relax in the gardens or fish in the private carp pools. Open all year.

Cwmllwynog, Llanfair, Caereinion,Welshpool, Powys SY21 0HF

Joyce Cornes
☎ **01938 810791**
🛏 From £14–£16
EM From £8
🐎

🐝🐝🐝
Highly Commended

Built in the early 17th century Cwmllwynog is a traditional long farmhouse of character on a working dairy farm. We have a spacious garden with a stream at the bottom and a lot of unusual plants. All bedrooms have colour TV and drink making facilities. Double room en suite, twin with hot and cold and private bathroom. Delicious home-cooked meals cooked. Just for you! We can help you with routes. Open Jan–Nov.

Cyfie Farm, Llanfihangel-yng-Ngwynfa, Llanfyllin, Powys SY22 5JE

Mrs Lynn Jenkins
☎ **01691 648451**
🛏 From £14–£24.50
EM From £10.50
Sleeps 6
🐎 🌾
🐝🐝🐝 *Deluxe*

A warm welcome awaits at Cylie. A working hill farm close to scenic Lake Vymwy. The well featured farmhouse sits high with delightful views from the patio and colourful garden. Furnished to a very high standard. 1 stable suite. Attractive bedrooms all with private facilities, beverage trays, TV, radio, hair dryers. Comfortable lounge with open log fires. Superb traditional meals served in our new dining room with conservatory feature. Awarded Wales Tourist Board Northmace Hospitality Award 1992. Open all year.

Dol-Llys Farm, Llanidloes, Powys SY18 6JA

Olwen S Evans
☎ **01686 412694**
🛏 From £15–£17
Sleeps 6
🪕 🐎 🅰 🐄 🌳 🚤
🐝🐝 *Highly Commended*

Dol-Llys is a 17th century farmhouse intriguing because it has so many levels and small staircases. With character throughout and luxury en suite bedrooms, this working farm is situated on the banks of the river Severn one mile from the market town of Llanidloes. Spectacular walks around the Clywedog Reservoir (maps provided). Fishing and rough shooting, also child's pony. Golf and sports centre nearby. Tea and coffee-making facilities. Open all year.

The Drewin Farm, Churchstoke, Montgomery, Powys SY15 6TW

Mrs Ceinwen Richards
☎ **01588 620325**
🛏 From £15–£17
EM From £8
Sleeps 6
🐎 🖕 🐄 🅰 🌾 🖕
🐝🐝

Relax in our friendly family run and beautifully furnished 17th century farmhouse with panoramic views. Bedrooms have TV, hairdryer and drinks facilities, (en suite available). Games room with snooker table, dining room with large inglenook, separate lounge, full CH. Good home cooking, vegetarian by request. Offa's Dyke footpath runs through our mixed farm. Featured on BBC Travel Show 1993. A warm Welsh welcome awaits you. AA WTB Farmhouse Award. Open Mar–Nov.

---

6 Little Brompton Farm, Montgomery, Powys SY15 6HY

Gaynor Bright
☎ **01686 668371**
🛏 **From £15–£18**
EM From £8
Sleeps 6
🐕 ✂ 🏇 🧍 🪑 💼 🎍
Highly Commended

A true oasis of tranquillity in beautiful scenery and this 17th C stone farmhouse is offering friendly hospitality. Pretty rooms enhanced by quality furnishings and antiques, all amenities, en suites available. Good farmhouse food. Offa's Dyke footpath runs through farm. WTB Farm house Award. AA selected. Welcome Host. Situated 2 miles east of Montgomery on B4385. Open all year.

7 Llettyderyn, Mochdre, Newtown, Powys SY16 4JY

Mrs Margaret Jandrell
☎ **01686 626131**
🛏 **From £16–£19**
EM From £7
Sleeps 4
🐕
🌼🌼🌼 *Highly Commended*

Llettyderyn – a restored 18th century farmhouse with exposed beams, inglenook fireplace and traditional parlour. A working farm rearing sheep and beef. 2 miles from Newtown; an ideal base for touring Mid-Wales. Excellent farmhouse cooking, with home-made bread. Vegetarians catered for. Double and twin-bedded rooms both en suite, tea-making facilities and TV. Full central heating. Ample parking. Open all year.

8 Lower Gwerneirin Farm, Llandinam, Powys SY17 5DD

Mrs A Brown
☎ **01686 688286**
🛏 **From £15–£18**
EM From £8
Sleeps 6
🐕 🐈 🏇 🎍 💼
🌼🌼 *Highly Commended*

Beautifully situated in the Severn Valley, the farmhouse is a spacious Victorian dwelling offering comfortable accommodation. All rooms have CH and drinks facilities. Double and twin en suite, 1 double own bathroom. Guests lounge with log fire. Fishing in own trout pool. We have a wealth of wildlife. Ideally located for exploring Mid Wales. Large garden with beautiful views. Superb home cooking. Open all year.

9 Lower Gwestydd, Llanllwchaiarn, Newtown, Powys SY16 3AY

Iris Jarman
☎ **01686 626718**
🛏 **From £16–£16.50**
EM From £8
Sleeps 6
🐕
🌼🌼 *Highly Commended*

Lower Gwestydd is a listed half-timbered farmhouse set on a quiet hillside 2 miles north of Newtown just off the B4568 road. Guests have own lounge and dining room. All rooms centrally heated, 2 bedrooms en suite, all have beverage trays. WTB Farmhouse Award, hygiene certificate, Hostess Award. Finalist in the Best British Breakfast 1991 competition. Large garden with beautiful views, own produce. Open all year.

10 Moat Farm, Welshpool, Powys SY21 8SE

Gwyneth Jones
☎ **01938 553179**
🛏 **From £17–£18**
EM From £10
Sleeps 6
🐕 ✂ 🎍
🌼🌼

Moat Farm is a 260-acre dairy farm set in the beautiful Severn Valley. The 17th century farmhouse offers warm and comfortable accommodation with good home cooking served in a fine timbered dining room, traditionally furnished with Welsh dresser. All rooms en suite with tea/coffee facilities and colour TV. Quiet lounge, pool table and spacious garden. Good touring centre. Near Powis Castle. Golf, riding and fishing nearby. Open Mar–Nov.

11 Trewythen Farm, Trewythen, Llandinam, Powys SY17 5BQ

Ceinwen & Ann Davies
☎/Fax **01686 688444**
🛏 **From £16–£19**
EM From £8
Sleeps 6
🐕 🐈 🧍 🎍
🌼🌼 *Highly Commended*

Enjoy the peace and tranquillity of Trewythen which is set in beautiful countryside on this mixed working farm. Superbly furnished with luxury en suite rooms, centrally heated. Lounge with oak beams offers log fires for the cooler evenings and colour TV. Separate dining room. Ideal for touring Mid Wales and walking. WTB Farmhouse Award and hygiene certificate. Open Apr–Nov.

SELF-CATERING

Cwm Y Gath, Trewythen, Llandinam, Powys SY17 5BQ

Ceinwen & Ann Davies
☎/Fax 01686 688444
sc From £60–£250
Sleeps 4
🐕 🛏 🏕 🎋
Applied

Enjoy a welcome on the hillside at the old and cosy shepherd's cottage overlooking a working beef and sheep farm with magnificent views in peaceful surroundings. Refurbished to a high standard with a wealth of oak beams and inglenook fireplace. The cottage has one double and one twin bedroom (H&C). An ideal spot for nature lovers and walkers. Golfing, fishing, ponytrekking and lakes nearby. Enquiries welcome. Open all year.

Gungrog Cottage, c/o Gungrog House, Rhallt, Welshpool, Powys SY21 9HS

Mrs Eira Jones
☎ 01938 553381
sc From £100–£180
Sleeps 6
🐕 🍴 🎋
Applied

Off the A483 opposite its junction with the A458, just east of Welshpool, Gungrog Cottage is located at a place called Rhallt, standing in an elevated position giving magnificent views of the Severn Valley. Set in 21 acres of farmland, the cottage is fully centrally heated and well-equipped. Kitchen/diner, bathroom with shower. The cottage was converted from a 16th century barn and retains much of its original charm and character. Open all year.

Red House, Trefeglwys, Nr Caersws, Powys SY17 5PN

Gwyneth Williams
☎ 01686 430285
sc From £70–£220
Sleeps 5 + cot
🐕 ⊞ 🛏 ♦
🌺 🌺 🌺 🌺

A highly furnished, self–contained part of the farmhouse, situated on a mixed working family farm. Panoramic views, unspoilt scenery and the tranquillity of the Trannon Valley. Ideal base for touring Mid Wales. Llanidloes 6 miles. Guests' comfort is the priority. Log fire, oak beams, garden furniture, ample parking and wildlife. Open all year.

CONFIRM BOOKINGS

Disappointments can arise by misunderstandings over the telephone.
Please write to confirm your booking.

FARM HOLIDAY BUREAU

77

Mid Wales

Radnor

Group Contact: *Mrs Ann Edwards* ☎ *01597 810211*

Mid-Wales is an area of outstanding natural beauty; with rugged mountain scenery, lakes, gentle hills and beautiful valleys.

It is an area abounding in wildlife and natural history, providing a habitat for rare birds and flowers. It is still possible to see the Red Kite in its last stronghold in Wales.

This breathtaking scenery is perfect for walkers; from gentle rambles to exploring the long distance footpaths of Glyndwr's Way and the Upper Wye Valley; for the more experienced and adventurous, the remote areas of the vast Elan Valley watershed.

The area is steeped in history and includes Roman encampments, castles, caves, old mine workings, churches and monuments. It also offers practically every sport or pastime that requires an outdoor or country environment. This is a place to come to relax, to enjoy the peace, tranquillity and solitude of George Borrow's 'Wild Wales' and the place to recharge your batteries.

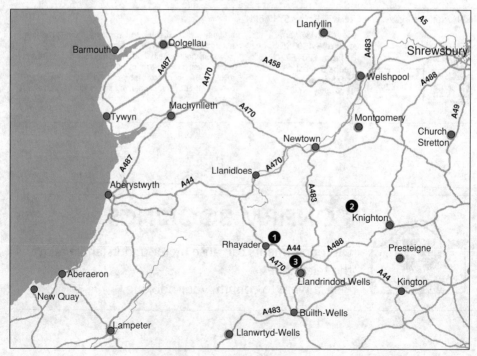

BED AND BREAKFAST
(and evening meal)

Beili Neuadd, Rhayader, Powys LD6 5NS ①

Mrs Ann Edwards
☎ **01597 810211**
🅱 **From £16.50**
EM From £10
Sleeps 6
🏍 🐄 (10) 🍷 🎱 🎿
🌼🌼🌼 *Highly Commended*

An attractive 16th century stone-built farmhouse set amidst beautiful countryside in a quiet, secluded position approx. 2 miles from small market town of Rhayader. Guests are assured of every comfort with CH, log fires and well appointed accommodation in single, double and twin bedded rooms, all with private facilities. WTB Farmhouse Award winner, good food and comfortable surroundings. Open all year (closed Christmas & New Year).

Cefnsuran, Llangunllo, Knighton, Powys LD7 1SL ②

Gill Morgan
☎ **01547 81219**
🅱 **From £16–£17.50**
EM From £9.50
Sleeps 6
🦌 🐄 (10) 🍷 🎣 🎱 🚣
🌼🌼 *Highly Commended*

15th/16th century accommodation on working farm. Ideal for a relaxing holiday. Good walking area. (Offa's Dyke, Glyndwr's Way), superb views, abundant wildlife. Fishing, riding, boating, games room, k snooker table, table tennis. Ideal biking country. Excellent food, traditional farmhouse fayre, vegetarian and special diets catered for by prior arrangement. Open all year.

Highbury Farm, Llanyre, Llandrindod Wells, Powys LD1 6EA

Shirley Evans
☎ **01597 822716**
🅱 **From £15–£18**
EM From £8.50
Sleeps 6
🐄
🌼🌼 *Highly Commended*

A warm welcome awaits you at our smallholding one mile from the spa town of Llandrindod Wells. Comfortable, spacious bedrooms with beverage trays. Double and family/twin room, one double en suite. Full CH. TV lounge, separate dining room, snooker table. Evening meal by arrangement. WTB Farmhouse Award. Brochure available. Ideally situated for touring heart of Wales. Open Mar–Nov.

78

Mid Wales

Ceredigion

Group Contact: *Mrs Beti Davies* ☎ *01570 422447*

Through the ages travellers have come to Ceredigion. Eight centuries ago Gerald Cambrensis wrote of its kindly people; somewhat later the Victorians passed long summers by its fine beaches. Today's visitors can rediscover the old hospitality that is so warmly given.

The 'Cardis', as the district's native inhabitants are known, have guarded their heritage well – many still speak Welsh, Europe's oldest living language.

Ceredigion's 52-mile coastline, much now owned by the National Trust, looks out on the expanse of Cardigan Bay. Yachts and dinghies sail from small harbours like Aberaeron and New Quay, and the many sandy beaches, among them Aberporth and Llangrannog, are a haven for sunbathers and swimmers.

Inland, around Tregaron you might spot rare birds like the red kite, whilst the River Teifi produces some fine catches of salmon and sewin. Between the mountains and sea is an unspoilt patchwork of farmland; small market towns have market days well worth experiencing.

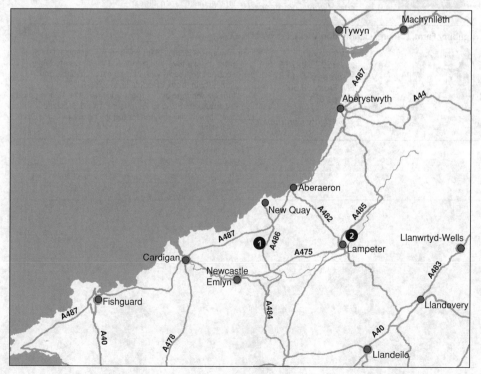

BED AND BREAKFAST

(and evening meal)

Broniwan, Rhydlewis, Llandysul, Dyfed SA44 5PF ①

Carole Jacobs
☎ 01239 851261
BB From £16.50
EM From £8.50
Sleeps 4
🐕 ⚜ 🐖 (6) Å ■ ⚒ ♞
👄👄 *Highly Commended*

Relax in the peace of our Victorian farmhouse with its collection of books and paintings. Lovely views of Cardiganshire country. Coast 10 minutes away. Enjoy friendly animals, birdwatching, walking (maps provided). Games room in barn. Generous meals including vegetarian. Pretty bedrooms, private facilities, tea/coffee-making. Quiet pets welcome. Reduced weekly terms. WTB Farmhouse Award.

Bryncastell Farm, Llanfair Road, Lampeter, Dyfed SA48 8JY ②

E A Beti Davies
☎ 01570 422447
BB From £16–£18
EM From £10
Sleeps 6
♿ ☺ 🐖 ⚜ ☜ ♞ ■
👄👄 *Highly Commended*

'Croeso' to our 140-acre family farm commanding panoramic views over the Teifi Valley. All modern facilities with unrivalled hospitality and excellent cuisine. Access to farm activities, hillside walks or gentle strolls along the river bank in an area of unspoilt natural beauty. ¾ mile fishing and shooting, 1 mile from university market town of Lampeter. WTB Farmhouse Award. Open all year.

79

South Wales

Brecon

Group Contact: *Mrs Mary Adams* ☎ *01874 636505*

The Brecon Beacons welcome you to the great outdoors. This unspoilt countryside of mountains and forests, hills and valleys with rivers and lakes, caves and waterfalls, offers a great variety of country pursuits.

Enjoy watersports on Llangorse Lake, visit Dan-yr-Ogof show caves, take a trip on the Monmouth to Brecon canal or Brecon Mountain Railway. The hills delight climbers, walkers and pony trekkers. Fish in the rivers Wye and Usk or the many reservoirs. Guided walks start from the National Park Visitor Centre and Craig-y-Nos Country Park.

There are craft centres to visit, castles and historic sites. Browse around museums and secondhand bookshops and listen to the local choirs.

Sample home cooking at its best, and wherever you go you will be greeted by friendly, helpful people.

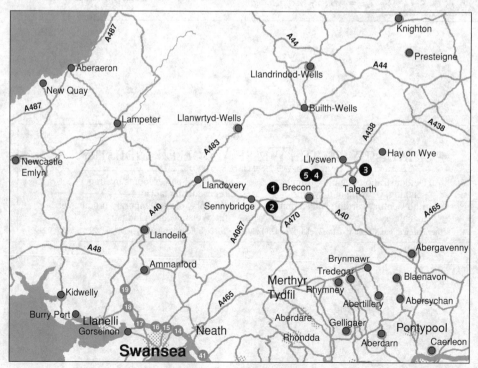

BED AND BREAKFAST
(and evening meal)

Brynfedwen Farm, Trallong Common, Sennybridge, Brecon, Powys LD3 8HW

Mrs Mary Adams
☎ 01874 636505
BB From £16
EM From £10
Sleeps 6
♿ ☞ ⚥

☙☙☙ *Highly Commended*

Brynfedwen, situated between Brecon and Sennybridge, is a hill livestock farm with lovely views over the Brecon Beacons and Usk River Valley. Excellent facilities for walking and all country pursuits. Traditional stone farmhouse. Central heating. TV lounge with log fire. 2 family rooms and 1 twin bedded flat (equipped for disabled), all en suite. Personal attention and good home cooking. Children welcome. Farmhouse Award. AA selected. Open all year.

Cwmcamlais Uchaf, Cwmcamlais, Sennybridge, Brecon, Powys LD3 8TD

Mrs Jean Phillips
☎ 01874 636376
BB From £16–£17
EM From £9
Sleeps 6
☞ (8) ☜ ☟

☙☙☙ *Highly Commended*

Cwmcamlais Uchaf is a working farm situated in the Brecon Beacons National Park. 1 mile off the A40 between Brecon and Sennybirdge. Our spacious 16th century farmhouse has exposed beams, log fires and 3 tastefully decorated bedrooms, 1 double en suite, 1 double and 1 twin with private bathrooms. Tea/coffee-making facilities. The River Camlais with its waterfalls, flows through the farm land. Open all year.

Lodge Farm, Talgarth, Brecon, Powys LD3 0DP

Mrs Marion Meredith
☎ 01874 711244
BB From £16
EM From £9.50
Sleeps 6
☜ ☞ ⚥ ♨

☙☙☙ *Commended*

Enjoy the peace and tranquillity on this working farm, nestling in the Black Mountains in eastern part of the National Park yet only 1½ miles from Talgarth off A479. Attractively furnished bedrooms, tea-making facilities, all en suite, 1 family, 1 double, 1 twin. Varied menu, including vegetarian, of freshly prepared real food. A warm welcome of prime importance. Central base, walking, touring, pony trekking. Hay-on-Wye, Brecon 8 miles. Open all year.

Trehenry Farm, Felinfach, Llandefalle, Brecon, Powys LD3 0UN

Mrs Theresa Jones
☎ 01874 754312
BB From £18
EM From £9
Sleeps 3
☞

☙☙☙ *Deluxe*

Trehenry is a 200 acre mixed farm situated east of Brecon, 1 mile off A470. The impressive 18th century farmhouse with breathtaking views, inglenook fireplaces and exposed beams offers comfortable accommodation, good food and cosy rooms. TV lounge, separate dining tables, central heating, tea-making facilities, all rooms en suite. Brochure on request. Farm House Award winner. Open all year except Christmas.

SELF-CATERING

---

⑤ Trehenry Farm, Felinfach, Llandefalle, Brecon, Powys LD3 0UN

Mrs Theresa Jones
☎ 01874 754312
🆂🅲 From £170–£380
Sleeps 8
🛏 🐕

❀ ❀ ❀ ❀ ❀

For a holiday to remember then come to Trehenry 200 acre working farm. Tranquillity surrounded by breathtaking views. 17th century farmhouse modernised to a high standard with oak beams, inglenook fireplace. 3 bedrooms, 2 en suite, 1 private. Bed settee in second lounge. Very well equipped kitchen, lounge with TV, video, CH, wood stove. Price includes linen, electric, heating. Brochure. Open all year.

Please mention **Stay on a Farm** when booking

BUREAU ACCOMMODATION IS RELIABLE

This Guide lists **Farm Holiday Bureau** members only. They are all inspected by the National Tourist Board for standards (see introduction pages) and by fellow members to maintain a high quality.

GOOD FOOD

Nearly all Bureau members now hold a certificate in Essential Food Hygiene.

80

South Wales

Gwent

Group Contact: *Mrs Ann Ball* ☎ *01873 821236*

To the north of the county are the Black Mountains and the Brecon Beacons with majestic peaks and deep sheltered valleys. This area contains part of the Brecon Beacons National Park which provides opportunities for pony trekking, walking and many other activities.

Eastern Gwent is very different – the countryside is pastoral with undulating, wooded hills and the river valleys of the Usk and Wye. Ancient market towns and picturesque villages are dotted throughout this part of the county. Part of the Welsh Marches falls within this region and there are a number of strategically placed castles, including Raglan and Chepstow, reminders of less peaceful times. Tintern Abbey, immortalised by Wordsworth, shows a more tranquil face of the county.

Western Gwent can boast bracing, beautiful mountainsides, spectacular views and lovely walking country. It also has a rich industrial heritage with a wealth of attractions for those fascinated by the way we used to live.

Gwent is also an ideal base for exploring the interesting country and attractions in the South Wales and Border areas. Brecon Beacons National Park, the Forest of Dean, the Mendip Hills, the Cotswolds, Bristol and Bath ... are all within 60 miles.

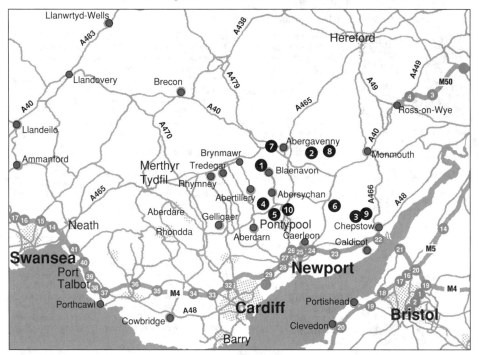

BED AND BREAKFAST

(and evening meal)

---

1 Chapel Farm, Blaina, Gwent NP3 3DJ

Mrs Betty Hancocks
☎ 01495 290888
BB From £16
EM From £6
Sleeps 6
(4)
Commended

Lovely renovated farmhouse with its original oak beams and inglenook fireplace. H&C, private showers for each room. Home cooking (evening meals by booking). Farming Welsh mountain sheep. Ideal base for touring many attractions over about 9-mile radius. A warm welcome assured. Open all year except Christmas.

---

2 Little Treadam, Llantilio, Crossenny, Abergavenny, Gwent NP7 8TA

Beryl Ford
☎ 0160 085 326
BB From £18–£21
EM From £10
Sleeps 6

Highly Commended

Relax and enjoy comfort and peace in our 16th century beamed farmhouse. Delicious food. Restaurant licence. Centrally situated for Brecon National Park, Wye Valley and Black Mountains. Offa's Dyke Path long distance walk passes through the farm with White Castle a 2 mile walk away. All rooms en suite with radio and colour TV. WTB Farmhouse Award. Open Mar–Nov.

---

3 Parsons Grove, Earlswood, Nr Chepstow, Gwent NP6 6RD

Gloria Powell
☎ 01291 641382
BB From £17–£19
Sleeps 6

Highly Commended

On edge of Wye Valley, peaceful and traffic-free, yet only 15 minutes Chepstow and M4. Large, centrally heated, country house, beamed lounge, log burner. Sunny conservatory in which to enjoy breakfast, overlooks swimming pool, and 2-acre vineyard. Magnificent views of Wentwood Forest and Earlswood Valley. All rooms en suite, tea/coffee-making facilities, radio and colour TV. Access at all times. Open Jan–Nov.

---

4 Pentre-Tai Farm, Rhiwderin, Newport, Gwent NP1 9RQ

Susan Proctor
☎ 01633 893284
BB From £15–£20
Sleeps 6

Highly Commended

Gateway to Wales. A warm welcome awaits you at our peaceful sheep farm located in the countryside yet only 3 miles from M4. Most rooms en suite, all with TV and beverage facilities. Children welcome at reduced rates. Ideal base for Wye Valley, Brecon Beacons, Cardiff, Welsh Folk Museum and magnficient Welsh castles. Open Feb–Nov.

---

5 Pentwyn Farm, Little Mill, Pontypool, Gwent NP4 0HQ

Stuart & Ann Bradley
☎/Fax 01495 785249
BB From £14–£18
EM From £10
Sleeps 6
(4)
Highly Commended

A 125-acre stock farm on the edge of the Brecon Beacons National Park where good food and hospitality are of prime importance. The 16th century Welsh longhouse with 20th century comforts has a beamed dining room and sitting room with log fires. Swimming pool. 3 bedrooms (2 en suite) with tea-making facilities. Restaurant licence. Rough shooting. WTB Farmhouse Award. Open Feb–Nov.

Tŷ-Gwyn Farm, Gwehelog, Usk, Gwent NP5 1RT

Jean Arnett
☎ 01291 672878
🅱 From £14–£18
EM From £10
Sleeps 6
✄ ☇(5) ⊕ ▪

Highly Commended

Wake up and sit up to magnificent views of Brecon Beacons National Park from all 3 bedrooms (2 bath en suite). Hearty breakfasts including homemade preserves served in spacious dining room or conservatory overlooking secluded lawns. Mountains, castles, canals, golf, fishing all nearby. Quality meals, vegetarians and own wine welcome. WTB Farmhouse Award. Brochure available. Open all year.

The Wenallt Farm, Gilwern, near Abergavenny, Gwent NP7 0HP

Janice Harris
☎ 01873 830694
🅱 From £17.60–£21.50
EM From £11
Sleeps 8
☇ ㅏ ㅅ ㅊ ▪ ☛ 🛆 🐾

🌼🌼🌼 *Commended*

A 16th century Welsh longhouse set in 50 acres of farmland in the Brecon Beacons National Park commanding magnificent views over the Usk Valley. Retaining all its old charm with oak beams, inglenook fireplace, yet offering a high standard with en suite bedrooms, good food and a warm welcome. An ideal base from which to see Wales and the surrounding areas. Licensed. AA listed. Brochure available. Open all year.

SELF-CATERING

Granary & Coach House, Upper Cwm Farm, Llantilio Crossenny, Abergavenny, Gwent NP7 8TG

Ann Ball
☎ 01873 821236
🆂🅲 From £170–£330
Sleeps 12
☇ ㅏ ㅊ 🐾

🌼🌼🌼🌼

Holidays and short breaks in beautifully converted old barn on working sheep farm. Family accommodation with central heating, TV, electricity, bed linen, towels included. Peaceful superb views, ideal for walking, birdwatching, exploring Welsh castles, Brecon Beacons, Wye and Usk Valleys. The Granary (upper) and Coach House (ground) each have 3 double bedrooms, lounge/dining/kitchen, bathroom with shower. Brochure available. Open all year.

Parsons Grove, Earlswood, Nr Chepstow, Gwent NP6 6RD

Gloria Powell
☎ 01291 641382
🆂🅲 From £90–£330
Sleeps 4/6
ㅏ ㅊ ☇

🌼🌼🌼🌼 – 🌼🌼🌼🌼🌼

Close to Wye Valley, set in 20 acres of peaceful countryside with heated swimming pool. Three cottages, furnished to very high standard. Fully carpeted with colour TV, fitted kitchen, refrigerator, cooker and microwave. All linen (duvets) included. Overlooking vineyard with panoramic views of beautiful valley and Wentwood Forest. Riding nearby. 10 minutes St Pierre Golf Club. Open all year.

Pentwyn Stable Cottages, Pentwyn Farm, Little Mill, Pontypool, Gwent NP4 0HQ

Stuart & Ann Bradley
☎/Fax 01495 785249
🆂🅲 From £120–£230
Sleeps 2/4
ㅏ ㅊ 🛆 ▪

🌼🌼🌼🌼

Relax in rural tranquillity in our delightfully converted stable cottages. Enjoy the castles, museums and water sports. Walk in the Black Mountains or along the canal bank. Each cottage has 2 bedrooms, a fully fitted kitchen and a large beamed sitting room with wood burner and wonderful views over the large garden with swimming pool and barbecue. Linen and electricity included in price. Meals available in farmhouse. Open all year.

11 **Worcester House,** Castle Farm, Raglan, Gwent NP5 2BT

Mrs Vivien Jones
☎ **01291 690492**
🅂 **From £100–£250**
Sleeps 6/7
🐕 🛆

❋ ❋ ❋

Part of a 17th century manor house. The oldest brick building in Gwent. Close to dual carriageway leading to Wye Valley, Brecon Beacons and Forest of Dean. Raglan Castle 20 yards, beautiful views. A 200-acre working dairy/arable farm with 3 bedrooms, third bedroom contains 2 bunkbeds, bathroom, living/dining room leading to large lawn. Modern kitchen, shower room, everything except linen/towels. Open most of year.

DISABLED VISITORS

Many members offer a welcome to disabled/less able visitors. Please do check the extent of the facilities before booking.

PRICES

Prices include VAT and service charge (if any) and are:
B&B per person per night
EM per person
SC per unit per week
Tents and caravans per pitch per night

CONFIRM BOOKINGS

Disappointments can arise by misunderstandings over the telephone.
Please write to confirm your booking.

81

South Wales

Pembrokeshire

Group Contact: *Mrs O Evans* ☎ *01437 721382*

Pembrokeshire is the south western corner of Wales, now part of the larger modern county of Dyfed. A large portion of Pembrokeshire is covered by the Pembrokeshire Coast National Park, including most of the coastal strip and Preseli Hills. The countryside is unspoilt with an abundance and variety of wild flowers everywhere from the coast to the banks that skirt the miles of narrow country lanes.

The beaches vary from long sandy stretches to small rocky coves – but you could see them all if you walked the coastal footpath from St. Dogmael's in the north to Amroth in the south – 180 miles! You would also see the islands off the coast including Skomer and Skokholm which are nature reserves; and Caldy, inhabited by Cistercian monks. Some of these islands can be visited and you may see seals here or indeed off any part of the coastline.

The variable terrain from coast to hill, moorland to marsh provides an agreeable habitat for a wide variety of birds, insects and animals. The area is full of historical relics from ancient to modern, with Iron Age settlement remains, cromlechs and standing stones right up to those of more recent times with many castles and, of course, the fine cathedral of St. David's.

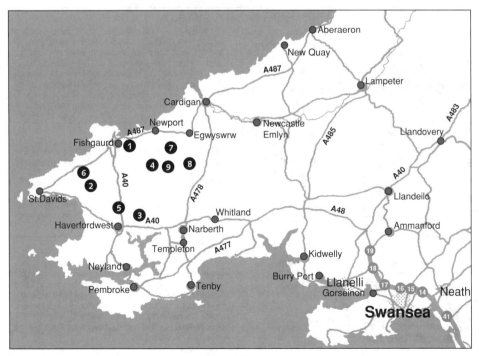

BED AND BREAKFAST

(and evening meal)

---

① Gilfach Goch Farmhouse, Fishguard, Pembrokeshire, Dyfed SA65 9SR

June Devonald
☎/Fax 01348 873871
BB From £17
EM From £10
Sleeps 12
✻ 🐎

♥♥♥ *Highly Commended*

Charming farmhouse with attractive grounds in National Park for people who want somewhere relaxing, peaceful and very comfortable. Oak beams, stone walls, inglenook, pretty bedrooms, magnificent views to the sea. Small holding with friendly animals and friendly Welsh people too! Superb meals – own produce giving variety, quality and quantity. Residential licence, fire certificate, pay phone. Farmhouse Award. Open Easter–Nov.

---

② Lochmeyler Farm, Llandeloy, Pen-y-Cwm, Nr Solva, Haverfordwest, Dyfed SA62 6LL

Mrs Morfydd Jones
☎/Fax 01348 837724
BB £20
EM £10
Sleeps 20
🐎 ♿ 🐕 (10) ⌂ ♣

♥♥♥♥ *Deluxe*

Lochmeyler is a 220-acre dairy farm in the centre of St David's Peninsula, 4 miles from Solva Harbour. Ten en suite bedrooms (no smoking in bedrooms), TV. 4-poster beds available. Two lounges, 1 non-smokers. Choice of menus, traditional and vegetarian. RAC highly acclaimed, AA selected. Member of Taste of Wales, WTB Farmhouse Award. RAC Guesthouse of the Year '93. Licensed, credit cards accepted. Open all year.

---

③ Lower Haythog, Spittal, Haverfordwest, Pembrokeshire SA62 5QL

Nesta Thomas
☎/Fax 01437 731279
BB From £17
EM From £9.50
Sleeps 10–12
🐎 🐕 ✻ 🐈 ♣ ♣

♥♥♥ *Highly Commended*

Attractive 300 year old farmhouse, tastefully furnished, on working farm in unspoilt countryside, 5 miles North of Haverfordwest. Guests are assured of every comfort, superb meals, relaxing, peaceful and entertaining. Oak beams, inglenook, CH, log fires. Wooded walks, private fishing, pony rides, attractive gardens. En suite and private facilities all bedrooms, hospitality trays, TVs. Centrally situated for beaches and places of interest. WTB Award. Fire and basic food hygiene certificates. Open all year.

---

④ Penygraig, Puncheston, Haverfordwest, Pembrokeshire SA62 5RJ

Betty Devonald
☎/Fax 01348 881277
BB From £15–£17
EM From £8
Sleeps 6
🐕 🐎 🐈

♥♥ *Highly Commended*

A warm welcome awaits you at Penygraig, a working farm, situated near the picturesque Preseli Hills, with plenty of walks, natural trails and places of unspoilt beauty to be enjoyed. The rugged coastline of North Pembrokeshire being not far away. In the spacious dining room good wholesome cooking is served. There is 1 double room en suite, 1 family room. All rooms have tea trays, reductions for children sharing. Open Apr–Oct.

---

⑤ Spittal Cross Farm, Spittal Cross, Haverfordwest, Dyfed SA62 5DB

Mrs Susan Evans
☎ 01437 741206
BB From £14.50
EM From £8
Sleeps 4
🐎 🐕 ♣

♥

A family run 200-acre dairy farm in the heart of the beautiful Pembrokeshire countryside, making it a convenient touring base for the many local activities, beaches and places of historical interest. We offer hearty breakfast, imaginative dinners and comfortable accommodation. Reduced rates for children. Dining/sitting room with colour TV, games and books available. Central heating throughout. Food hygiene certificate. Open Apr–Oct.

Torbant Farm Guest House, Croesgoch, Haverfordwest, Pembrokeshire, Dyfed SA62 5JN

Barbara Charles
☎ **01348 831276**
🛏 **From £17–£20**
EM From £9
Sleeps 14
♿ 🐕 🐾 ▪
🏵🏵 *Commended*

Torbant is a 110-acre dairy farm, near St David's, peacefully situated in spacious grounds, and just 1½ miles from the spectacularly beautiful Pembrokeshire coast with its abundance of wildlife and sandy beaches. Although modernised, the farmhouse retains its traditional character. 5 bedrooms, 3 en suite. Fully licensed bar and restaurant. Children welcome. AA/RAC listed. Open Mar–Nov.

Trepant Farm, Morvil, Maenclochog, Pembrokeshire SA66 7RE

Marilyn Salmon
☎ **01437 532491**
🛏 **From £15–£28**
EM From £8.50
Sleeps 4
🐾
🏵🏵 *Highly Commended*

A warm Welsh welcome on our mixed dairy farm in the beautiful Preseli hills, sandy beaches and hidden coves. Pony trekking, fishing are all nearby. Relax in the evening with excellent home cuisine using best local produce. Vegetarians welcome. One room with en suite facilities. Open Apr–Oct.

Yethen Isaf, Mynachlogddu, Clynderwen, Pembrokeshire SA66 7SN

Mrs Ann Barney
☎ **01437 532256**
🛏 **From £15–£18.50**
EM From £9.50
Sleeps 6
🐾 🐾 ▪ 🐎
🏵🏵 *Commended*

Yethen Isaf sits right in the midst of the Preseli Hills, offering superb walking, yet only 10 miles from the coast. The farm is approx 200 acres, breeding pedigree Welsh Black cattle and Beulah Speckleface sheep. The 250-year-old farmhouse offers superb, comfortable accommodation with home cooking, central heating and log fires. One room with en suite facilities. Visits and activities arranged. Welcome Host. Open all year.

SELF-CATERING

Garden Farm, Tufton, Haverfordwest, c/o Yethen Isaf, Mynachlogddu, Clynderwen, Pembs SA66 7SN

Mrs Ann Barney
☎ **01437 532256**
🛏 **From £100–£350**
Sleeps 4–7
🐾
Applied

Situated in Preseli Hills only 9 miles from coast at Fishguard and 9 miles from Haverfordwest. A tranquil 160 acre working beef and sheep farm. Attractively restored Victorian farmhouse, warm and comfortable. Heating, log fires, TV etc, modern kitchen facilities. Bed linen provided. Sorry no pets. Stabling and facilities available for horses. Welcome Host. Open all year.

 Please mention **Stay on a Farm** when booking

82

South Wales
Pride of Pembrokeshire

Group Contact: *Mrs Vivienne Lockton* ☎ *01994 419327*

Pembrokeshire and its borderlands are renowned for their flora and fauna, unrivalled sandy beaches, spectacular coastal scenery and gentle heaths and moorlands of the Preseli Hills. The sunshine record, contrary to popular belief, equals the best in the UK.

There are castles and forts from Norman to Victorian times, Dylan Thomas's Boat House at Laugharne and many more modern attractions like Oakwood Leisure Park, Wales' premier farm-based attraction at Folly Farm and Pemberton's Chocolate Factory to name but a few.

The area has excellent safe sailing and windsurfing facilities, fishing in sea, river and pond, pony trekking, etc. Visit the many offshore islands, some of which have nature reserves, walk the coastal path, estuaries of the Cleddau rivers, the ancient Preseli Hills and the old pilgrims' routes of the Landsker Borderlands.

Those of us who live in this area readily share our treasures with our visitors. Come and see us – soon.

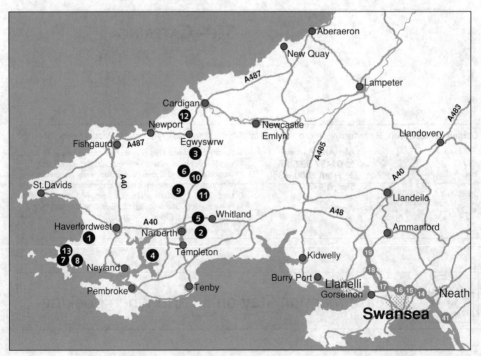

BED AND BREAKFAST

(and evening meal)

The Bower Farm, Little Haven, Haverfordwest, Pembrokeshire SA62 3TY

John Birt-Llewellin
☎ 01437 781554
🛏 From £18–£25
EM £12.50
Sleeps 6
🐴 🐕 ♿
💐💐 *Commended*

An extensively modernised traditional farmhouse on working sheep farm offering peace, warmth, comfort and friendliness to the casual or longer stay visitor. Dogs, horses (livery available) and children welcome. Walking distance of Broadhaven beach and coast path. Impressive sea views over St Brides Bay and islands. All rooms en suite. Open all year except Christmas.

Brunant Farm, Whitland, Dyfed SA34 0LX

Mrs O. Ebsworth
☎ 01994 240421
🛏 From £15–£16
EM From £6
Sleeps 6
🐴 🐕
💐💐💐

'Never enough time to enjoy this to the full, never enough words to say how splendid it was': John Carter, Thames TV (Wish You Were Here). Welcome to our 200 year old farmhouse centrally situated for touring, beaches, walking, golf or just relaxing. Comfortable, spacious bedrooms, all en suite, tea/coffee, TV, hairdriers. Good home cooking with choice of menu. Comfortable lounge, separate tables in dining room. License applied for.

Dolau Isaf Farm, Mynachlog-ddu, Clunderwen, Pembrokeshire SA66 7SB

Mrs V. C. Lockton
☎ 01994 419327
🛏 From £14–£15
EM From £7
Sleeps 4
🐴 🐕 🖳
💐
●

We welcome you to our 70-acre farm situated in the Preseli Hills where you can see grazing amongst our sheep and cattle angora goats for this is the home of Preseli Mohair. We offer personal service and make every effort to provide for your comfort in this unspoilt setting. Walking, riding and fishing available locally. Lounge, TV and home cooking. Welcome Host Award. Open all year.

Knowles Farm, Lawrenny, Kilgetty, Pembrokeshire SA68 0PX

Mrs Virginia Lort-Phillips
☎ 01834 891221
Fax 01834 891344
🛏 From £14–£18
EM From £8
Sleeps 6
🐴 🍴 👤 🖳 🎪 ♿ ⚗
Listed

With land sloping down to the shores of the Upper Cleddau river, we provide the perfect base for boating, bird watching, walking or fishing. Within the National Park, we are surrounded by farms and woodland. For the musician a French horn and a piano and room to practise. Private bathrooms. Open Easter–Oct.

Lower End Town House, Lampeter, Velfrey, Narbeth, Dyfed SA67 8UJ

Judy Smith
☎ 01834 83738
🛏 From £15
EM From £5
Sleeps 4 + cot
🐴 🐕 🍴 👤
💐💐

Beef and sheep farm owned and run by a young couple. Recent total refurbishment of the farmhouse has been aimed at recalling the peace and tranquillity of a bygone age whilst incorporating the comforts of a modern one. Easily accessible from the A40. Ideal for touring, walking or just unwinding. Evening meals by arrangement. Babies, dogs, and horses welcome. Open all year except Christmas & New Year.

---

6 **Plas-y-Brodyr,** Rhydwilym, Llandissilio, Clynderwen, Dyfed SA66 7QH

Mrs Janet Pogson
☎ **01437 563771**
🄱🄱 **From £14**
EM From £7.50
Sleeps 6
✂ ⛺ 🚐 (static) ☞ ⛺
Listed *Highly Commended*

Plas-y-Brodyr is a small farm in the idyllic valley of Rhydwilym. Enjoy the many local walks with abundant wildlife, private river fishing or take a short drive to many beautiful beaches. Our traditional farmhouse is comfortably furnished with pretty bedrooms (1 en suite) with tea-making facilities. Relax by log fires in inglenook sitting room after good home cooking. Open all year.

---

7 **Point Farm,** Dale, Haverfordwest, Pembrokeshire SA62 3RD

Mrs Elizabeth Webber
☎ **01646 636254**
🄱🄱 **From £15–£20**
Sleeps 5
⛺ (8) 🐴 ☞ ⛺
🐝
Commended

Beautifully situated period farmhouse in the Pembrokeshire National Park in an unrivalled position overlooking the sea. Comfortable en suite double/single accommodation with full facilities. On coastal path near lovely beaches and offshore islands. We can arrange sailing, windsurfing, fishing, riding and even flying for the enthusiastic. Wonderfully relaxed evenings. Open Jan–Nov.

---

8 **Skerryback,** Sandy Haven, St. Ishmaels, Haverfordwest, Dyfed SA62 3DN

Mrs Margaret Williams
☎ **01646 636598**
🄱🄱 **From £15**
EM From £9
Sleeps 4
⛺ ✂ ⛺ 🛏
🐝 *Highly Commended*

Warm Pembrokeshire welcome on coastal farm. A haven for walkers and bird lovers, near Sandy Heaven and ideal for visiting the bird sanctuaries of Skomer and Skokholm. Drying facilities, open fire in cold weather. TV lounge. Double and twin rooms with H/C and tea-making facilities.

---

9 **Ty Newydd Farm,** Llanycefn, Clynderwen, Dyfed SA66 7XT

Mrs Miriam Dunn
☎ **01437 532717**
🄱🄱 **From £12–£14**
EM From £8
Sleeps 2
⛺ (10) 🐴 🏇 🚐 ♿ 🐾 🛏
Listed

Welcome to our farm. Home cooking, vegetarians catered for. Livery available and equine courses by BHS qualified staff. We also have an animal sanctuary which has been featured in magazines and you are welcome to help or just mix with the animals. Open all year.

SELF-CATERING

10 **Dove Cottage,** Dyffryn Isaf, Llandissilio, Dyfed SA66 7QD

Mrs Pamela Morgan
☎ **/Fax 01437 563657**
🄲 **From £150-£210**
Sleeps 4
⛺ 🐴 ✂ 🛏
🌸 🌸 🌸 🌸

A well equipped, stone-built cottage, sleeps 4, in tranquil valley setting on 20-acre smallholding. Abundant flora and fauna. Good walking country with Preseli Mountains nearby. Brochure available. Open Apr-Nov.

Gwarmacwydd, Llanfallteg, Whitland, Dyfed SA34 0XH

Mrs A Colledge
☎ **01437 563260**
Fax 01437 563840
🆂 **From £100–£398**
Sleeps 20
📷 👤 ✂ ✆ 💼
Applied

Gwarmacwydd is a country estate of over 450 acres including two miles of river bank. Five character stone cottages, all nicely furnished and equipped with all modern conveniences and heating. Working farm with cows, calves, lambs. Colour brochure available. Open all year.

Penrallt y Gardde, Glanrhyd, Cardigan, Dyfed SA43 3PB

Janet Stammers
☎ **01239 86615**
🆂 **From £100–£250**
Sleeps 4 + cot
📷 👤
Applied

Barn cottage is a traditional farm cottage with unusually large garden and 22 acres of woodland set in beautiful National Park near secluded sandy beaches. The spacious interior is imaginatively designed and has colour television and microwave. It is double glazed throughout and centrally heated. Linen provided.

Point Farm, Dale, Haverfordwest, Pembrokeshire SA62 3RD   13

Mrs Elizabeth Webber
☎ **01646 636254**
🆂 **From £180–£250**
Sleeps 5
📷 👤 🐎 ✆ ☂
Applied

Comfortable stone-built cottage, sleeps 5, with outstanding views over the bay. On coastal path adjacent to lovely beaches and offshore islands. All water sports can be arranged and fishing and even flying. Wonderfully relaxed atmosphere with lots to do. Open all year.

BUREAU ACCOMMODATION IS RELIABLE

This Guide lists **Farm Holiday Bureau** members only. They are all inspected by the National Tourist Board for standards (see introduction pages) and by fellow members to maintain a high quality.

FARM HOLIDAY BUREAU

THOSE LITTLE EXTRAS

For advice on farms that can offer 'extras' such as four-poster beds, special diets, farm trails, fishing rights – even stabling and trekking arrangements if you are bringing your own horse – ring the Farm Holiday Bureau on (01203) 696909.

FARM HOLIDAY BUREAU

83

Ireland

County Londonderry

Group Contact: *Mrs Margaret Moore* ☎ *01265 868229*

This is a fertile agricultural county with small farms scattered across the broad sweeping land and long Atlantic beaches.

The city of Londonderry (also known as Derry) is best known for its massive ring of fortified walls and singing pubs. In the county's north-east corner is Coleraine (with one of the main campuses of the University of Ulster), conveniently close to the seaside resorts of Portstewart and Castlerock for sea angling, golf and children's amusements. For rewarding scenic drives the Sperrin Mountains are best approached from Limavady and the beautiful Roe Valley Country Park. The Bann river is noted for trout and salmon.

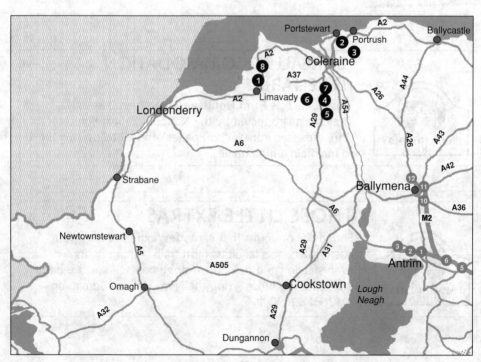

BED AND BREAKFAST
(and evening meal)

Ballycarton Farmhouse, 239 Seacoast Road, Bellarena, Limavady, Co Londonderry BT49 0HZ

Mrs Emma Craig
☎ 015047 50216
🏠 From £13
EM From £7
Sleeps 7
🐾 ⛵
Approved

Farmhouse (central heating) on 50 acre farm. Gliding, climbing, fishing. 1 single, 1 double, 1 twin, 2 family rooms (3 H/C). Dogs allowed outside. On coast road. Coleraine 14 miles, Limavady 5 miles. Open all year.

Ballylagan House, 31 Ballylagan Road, Coleraine, Co Londonderry BT52 2PQ

FARM HOLIDAY BUREAU

Mrs Joyce Lyons
☎ 01265 822487
🏠 From £13–£16
Sleeps 16
⛵ 🐾 ✂
Approved

Traditional farmhouse (CH) on working dairy farm. Home cooking, complimentary cup of tea on arrival, bedtime supper inclusive. Fishing, golf, etc nearby. Convenient to Causeway Coast and en route to Donegal. 2 family rooms en suite, 2 family rooms H/C, 1 double H/C. Fire and food hygiene certificates. Dogs allowed outside. Reduced rates for children. Giant's Causeway 6 miles. Situated off B17. Open all year except Christmas & New Year.

Brown's Country House, 174 Ballybogey Road, Coleraine, Co Londonderry BT52 2LP

Mrs Jean Brown
☎/Fax 012657
31627/32777
🏠 From £17
EM From £10
Sleeps 16
⛵ ✂ ♿
Grade A

A chalet bungalow with spacious lawns. Central heating. Home baking. On Ballymoney – Portrush road (B62). Safari Park 4 miles. 2 double bedrooms, 4 twin rooms, 1 family room, 3 ground floor, 1 single, all en suite. Tea/ coffee in all rooms. Small dinner parties welcome. Babysitter. Dogs allowed (outside). Bushmills 4 miles, Coleraine and Portrush 5 miles. Open all year.

Greenhill House, 24 Greenhill Road, Aghadowey, Coleraine, Co Londonderry BT51 4EU

Mrs Elizabeth Hegarty
☎ 01265 868241
🏠 From £21–£26
EM From £13
Sleeps 14
🌐 ⛵ 🅴 💼
Grade A

Georgian country guest house (with central heating). Good views across wooded countryside in the Bann Valley and the Antrim hills. Convenient to North coast. Fishing nearby. 3 double, 2 twin, 2 family all H/C, 6 rooms with private bath/shower and toilet. Garvagh 3 miles. 7 miles on A29 from Coleraine and then B66 (Ballymoney). Open Mar–Oct.

Heathfield House, 31 Drumcroone Road, Garvagh, Coleraine, Co Londonderry BT51 4EB

Mrs Heather Torrens
☎ 0126 65 58245
🏠 From £15–£17
EM From £10
Sleeps 6
🐾 ⛵ 🧍 ☕ 🚲 💼
Approved

Georgian farmhouse in spacious gardens. Mixed farm. 2 doubles en suite, 1 twin with H/C. Central heating. TV lounge and piano. Tea-making facilities. Close to fishing, shooting, golf, country walks. On A29 Garvagh 2 miles, Coleraine 8 miles, Portrush 12 miles. Open all year.

---

6 **Inchadoghill House,** 196 Agivey Road, Aghadowey, Coleraine, Co Londonderry BT51 4AD

Mamie & Ann McIlroy
☎ 01265 868250/
868232
BB From £13
Sleeps 6
🐕 🐈
Approved

Georgian farmhouse with central heating. Situated on 150 acre mixed farm, colour TV. Home cooking. River fishing on farm, golf nearby. 1 single, 1 double and 1 family room, all with H/C. Babysitting available. Farm off A54, Coleraine 9 miles, Ballymoney 6 miles, Kilrea 5 miles. Open all year.

7 **Killeague House,** 156 Drumcroone Road, Blackhill, Coleraine, Co Londonderry BT51 4HJ

Margaret Moore
☎ 01265 868229
BB From £16–£18
EM From £10
Sleeps 6
✂ 🐕 🛏 🧍 🐈 ⛳
Approved

Georgian farmhouse built 1783. Central heating, tea-making facilities, colour TV. On dairy farm, stabling available. Outdoor riding arena. Riding instruction given by arrangement. Fishing in river on farm. 1 double en suite, 1 double H/C, 1 family en suite. On A29. Garvagh 5 miles, Coleraine 6½ miles. Convenient to golf courses, Giant's Causeway and Bushmills Distillery. Good food, good fellowship is our motto. Open all year.

8 **The Poplars Guest House,** 352 Seacoast Road, Limavady, Co Londonderry BT49 0LA

Mrs H McCracken
☎ 015047 50360
BB From £15
EM From £8
Sleeps 10
🏠 🐕 🐈 (13) ♿
Approved

Ten bed bungalow in gardens, views of Benevenagh, Donegal Hills. Fishing 14 mile, golf 6 miles, Roe Valley Country Park 7 miles, Ulster Gliding Club ½ mile. H/C and shower in 2 bedrooms, bathroom and shower and 3 toilets. All home cooking. All ground floor. Babysitter available. Limavady 6½ miles, Coleraine 10 miles, Londonderry 24 miles. Open all year.

84

Ireland

County Antrim

Group Contacts: *North: Mr Michael McKeever* ☎ *012657 31577*
South: Mrs Heather Edmondson ☎ *01266 48461*

To the south east of the county, Belfast provides six-day shopping and city entertainment while to the north west lies the Causeway Coast, a playground of holiday resorts, with the Giant's Causeway the dominant feature. Between lie the nine glens of Antrim and their quaint waterfoot villages, the spectacular coast road, Carrickfergus Castle, and inland towns like Antrim with its ancient round tower and splendid park. There's a lakeside steam railway at Shane's Castle, pony trekking near Ballycastle, golf at Royal Portrush, as well as bathing, boating and fishing along the hundred miles of shore.

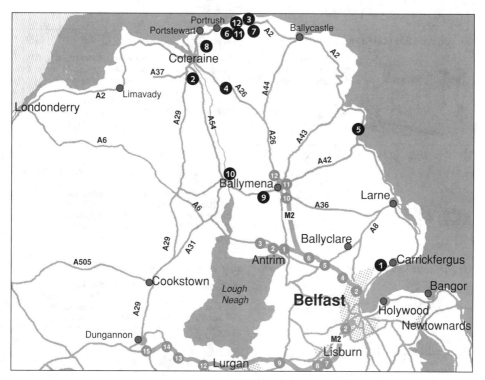

BED AND BREAKFAST

(and evening meal)

---

① Beechgrove, 412 Upper Road, Trooperslane, Carrickfergus, Co Antrim BT38 8PW

Betta Barron
☎ 019603 63304
🛏 From £15
EM From £7
Sleeps 15
🐕 🐄 🛪 🐈 🛆 🏕
Approved

A warm welcome awaits you at Beechgrove farmhouse (central heating) on 16 acre mixed farm near sea. Fishing, golf, riding. Knochagh monument, Belfast zoo, leisure centre nearby. 3 single, 1 double, 2 family rooms, 1 twin (all H/C). Babysitter. Dogs allowed (outside). Off A2, 1 mile south of Carrickfergus. Larne 10 miles. Belfast 10 miles. Carrickfergus 3 miles. Open all year.

---

② Bellevue Country House, 43 Greenhill Road, Blackhill, Colerraine BT51 4EU

Elizabeth Morrison
☎ 01265 868797
🛏 From £15
EM From £9
Sleeps 6
🐄 ⚥ 🍴 🛆
Approved

Listed country house with magnificent views of North Antrim Hills and Bann Valley. Salmon river fishing on farm. Tea-making facilities, colour TV. Family room, double H/C. twin H/C. Garvagh 3 miles. 7 miles on A29 from Coleraine and then B66 Ballymoney. Convenient to Portrush and Giants Causeway. A warm welcome awaits you. Open Mar–Oct.

---

③ Carnside Farm Guest House, 23 Causeway Road, Giants Causeway, Bushmills, Co Antrim BT57 8SU

Frances Lynch
☎ 012657 31337
🛏 From £13–£17
EM From £8
Sleeps 15
🐕 🐄 🛆
Grade B

Farmhouse (central heating) on 200-acre dairy farm. Magnificent coastal view. Fishing, golf, water sports. Old Bushmills Distillery 2 miles has weekday tours. 1 single, 4 double, 1 twin, 2 family rooms, 2 ground floor (all H/C). Babysitter. Dogs allowed (outside). Bushmills 2 miles, Ballaycastle 12 miles, Giants Causeway ¼ mile. Open Jan–Nov.

---

④ Country Guest House, 41 Kirk Road, Ballymoney, Co Antrim BT53 8HB

Dorothy Brown
☎ 012656 62620
🛏 From £15
EM From £8
Sleeps 10
🅲🅷 🐕 🐄 👤 🍴 🏕
Grade B

Modern bungalow in 1 acre garden, featured on TV for relaxing atmosphere. All rooms en suite with phone, tea and coffee-making facilities. TV lounge and dining room for guests. Your own door keys to come and go as you please. Causeway coast, Antrim Glens, Giant's Causeway all within 15 miles, recreation centre 1 mile. Brochure on request. Open all year.

---

⑤ Cullentra House, 16 Cloghs Road (off Gaults Road), Cushendall, Co Antrim BT44 0SP

FARM HOLIDAY BUREAU

Olive McAuley
☎ 012667 71762
🛏 From £13–£15
Sleeps 3
🐄 ⚥ 👤 🍴
Approved

Country house nestling amid breathtaking scenery of Glenballyeamon and Glenaan, overlooking Sea of Moyle. Golf course, Ballycastle and Giant's Causeway nearby. 1 family, 1 double and 1 twin. TV, tea/coffee-making facilities. Homely atmosphere and warm welcome extended to all guests. Open all year except Christmas.

Islay-View, 36 Leeke Road, off Ballymagarry Road, Portrush, Co Antrim BT56 8NH

Eileen Smith
☎ 01265 823220
🅱 **From £14–£18**
Sleeps 6–8
🐎 ♿
Approved

3 rooms, 1 double en suite, 1 double H & C and 1 family or twin H/C. Bungalow on 60-acre mixed farm with view of Giant's Causeway. House baking, farm produce, central heating, wheelchair ramp. Open Easter–Sept.

Kenbaan Country House, 55 Bayhead Road, Portballintrae, Co Antrim BT57 8SA

Mrs Elizabeth Morgan
☎ 0126 57 31534
🅱 **From £17.50–£21**
Sleeps 8
📶 🐎 🐕 🖽 🍴 🏹
Approved

Situated in pretty harbour village of Portballintrae near Dunluce Castle, Bushmills Distillery, Giant's Causeway. Panoramic views of North Antrim coast. Four bedrooms tastefully decorated with colour TV and tea and coffee-making facilities. Large, comfortable guests' lounge. Satellite TV. Private car parking. Play golf on world-famous Royal Portrush which is only a few minutes' drive. Open Mar–Nov.

Maddybenny Farm House, 18 Maddybenny Park, Loguestown Road, Portrush, Co Antrim BT52 2PT

Rosemary White
☎/Fax 01265 823394
🅱 **£18.50–£22.50**
Sleeps 6
🐎 🐕 🖽 🐴
Approved

Award-winning house 2 miles from Portrush, Portstewart, university, 7 golf courses, beaches. Ideal base for touring Causeway, coast and glens of Antrim. Three en suite rooms. Own riding centre, BHS Approved. Cordon bleu cooking. A29 Portrush to Coleraine road, signs for riding centre. Advance booking is essential. Also 4 star self-catering cottages. Open all year except Christmas & New Year.

Neelsgrove Farm, 51 Carnearney Road, Ahoghill, Ballymena, Co Antrim BT42 2PL

Mrs Margaret Neely
☎ 01266 871225
🅱 **From £15–£17.50**
EM From £8
Sleeps 6
📶 🐎 (12) 🍴 🐴
Approved

Country house (central heating) in 1 acre of grounds on mixed farm. Home baking. Water skiing 2 miles. Sports complex 5 miles. 6 miles from Ballymena, 15 miles from International Airport. 1 double en suite, 1 double, 1 twin room with H/C. Dogs allowed outside. Open all year.

Sprucebank, 41 Ballymacombs Road, Portglenone, Co. Antrim BT44 8NR

Mrs Thomasena Sibbett
☎ 01266 822150
🅱 **From £14–£16**
Sleeps 10
🐎 🐴 🐕
Approved

Country house in spacious garden. 1½ miles from Portglenone on A54. Tea/coffee-making facilities in all rooms. Convenient to Glens of Antrim, Causeway coast, Sperrin mountains, fishing on River Bann. Fishermen welcome – tackle space available. Dogs welcome outside. Open all year.

Valley View, 6a Ballyclough Road, Bushmills, Co Antrim BT57 8TU

Valerie McFall
☎ 012657 41608/41319
🅱 **From £12–£14.50**
Sleeps 14
🐎 🍴 ♿ 🍼
Approved

Family-run with homely atmosphere and very comfortable accommodation. Convenient to all the North Antrim coastal attractions. Beautiful views of mountains and Bush river valley. 4 new rooms all en suite, 1 disabled, each with coffee/tea-making facilities. Home cooking, tea on arrival. No smoking. Families very welcome. Open all year.

White Gables, 83 Dunluce Road, Bushmills, Co Antrim BT57 8SJ

Mrs Ria Johnston
☎ 0126 57 31611
🅱🅱 From £19.50–£22
EM From £11.50
Sleeps 6
ⓒⓝ ⛷ 🐕 ⛺
Grade A

Country house on A2 coast road near Dunluce Castle and Giant's Causeway (4 miles). Panoramic views of North Antrim coast. All bedrooms en suite. Tea/coffee-making facilities. Home cooking at its best. Awards include All Ireland Galtee Breakfast and Taste of Ulster. Ample car parking space. Open Mar–Nov.

DISABLED VISITORS

Many members offer a welcome to disabled/less able visitors. Please do check the extent of the facilities before booking.

Please mention **Stay on a Farm** when booking

THOSE LITTLE EXTRAS

For advice on farms that can offer 'extras' such as four-poster beds, special diets, farm trails, fishing rights – even stabling and trekking arrangements if you are bringing your own horse – ring the Farm Holiday Bureau on (01203) 696909.

85

Ireland

County Tyrone

Group Contact: *Mrs Norah Brown* ☎ *0186 87 84212*

Between the Sperrins in the north and the green Clogher Valley with its village cathedral in the south lies this region of great historical interest. The county's associations with the USA are recalled at the Ulster-American Folk Park near Omagh and Gray's old printing shop in Strabane still contains its 18th century presses. A mysterious ceremonial site of stone circles and cairns near Davagh Forest has recently been uncovered and there are other Stone Age and Bronze Age remains in the area. There are forest parks, Gortin Glen and Drum Manor, for driving or rambling, excellent trout and salmon waters near Newtownstewart, and market towns for shopping and recreation. Dungannon is notable for its fine glassware, Tyrone Crystal.

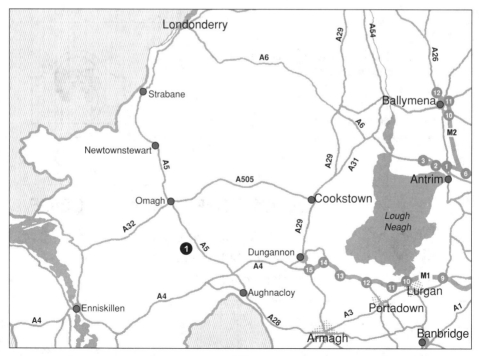

BED AND BREAKFAST

(and evening meal)

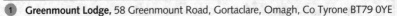

① **Greenmount Lodge,** 58 Greenmount Road, Gortaclare, Omagh, Co Tyrone BT79 0YE

Mrs F Louie Reid
☎ **01662 841325**
Fax **01662 840019**
🆎 **From £15–£17**
EM From £10
Sleeps 20
🚶 🐎 ♿ 🎣 🐱 🛄
Grade A

Farm guest house on 150-acre farm. Superb accommodation, excellent cuisine. Central for sightseeing. Fermanagh, Lakeland, the Sperrin Mountains. A5 from Ballygawley to Omagh, left before Traveller's Rest at Fintona sign 1 mile. Open all year.

PRICES

Prices include VAT and service charge (if any) and are:
B&B per person per night
EM per person
SC per unit per week
Tents and caravans per pitch per night

FARM HOLIDAY BUREAU

FARM HOLIDAY BUREAU

FOLLOW THE COUNTRY CODE

Leave nothing but footprints,
Take nothing but photographs,
Kill nothing but time!

86

Ireland

County Armagh

Group Contact: *Mrs Elizabeth Kee* ☎ *01762 870081*

Northern Ireland's smallest county rises gently from Lough Neagh's banks, southward through apple orchards, farmland and hill forest to the rock summit of Slieve Gullion, mountain of Cuchulain. But the crown of Armagh is the city itself, a religious capital older than Canterbury, with two cathedrals, the Georgian Mall and a Planetarium and Observatory. Craigavon has a leisure centre and ski-slope, with lakes for water sports, and there is sailing on Lough Neagh and angling and canoeing on the Blackwater river.

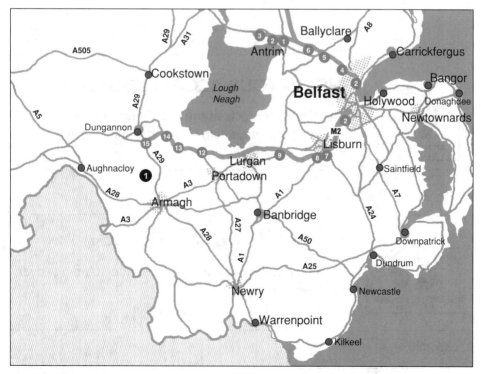

BED AND BREAKFAST

(and evening meal)

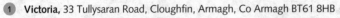

1 Victoria, 33 Tullysaran Road, Cloughfin, Armagh, Co Armagh BT61 8HB

May Hanson
☎ **01861 525925**
BB **From £13.50–£14**
Sleeps 6
☼ ⚘
Approved

3 rooms, 2 twin, 1 double. Open Easter–Nov (Christmas by arrangement). Country bungalow (central heating) National Trust Properties, golf fishing, walking, birdwatching nearby. Help with ancestor research at additional cost. Armagh 3 miles. From Armagh take B115 (Cathedral Road), right at Teeraw Road, continue to T junction. Turn right along Tullysaran Road to the first left turn after Ballytroddan Road. Open Easter–Oct.

FINDING YOUR ACCOMMODATION

The Group contacts at the beginning of each section can always help you find a vacancy in your chosen area.

CONFIRM BOOKINGS

Disappointments can arise by misunderstandings over the telephone.
Please write to confirm your booking.

87

Ireland

County Down

Group Contacts: *North: Mrs Mabel Hall* ☎ *012477 88207*
South: Mrs Cissie Annett ☎ *013967 22740*

This area includes the populous dormitory fringe along Belfast Lough (do not miss the Folk Museum at Cultra) and the ancient shrines of St. Patrick's Country round the cathedral hill at Downpatrick; the flat golden beaches of the Ards Peninsula and the mountainous Kingdom of Mourne; lively Newcastle with its seaside festival, and stately homes like Mount Stewart and Castle Ward open to visitors.

Horseriding, sailing, angling and golf are everywhere within reach, and there is motor racing at Kirkistown and sea angling in Strangford Lough.

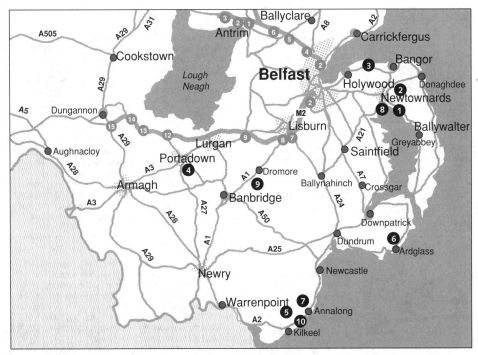

BED AND BREAKFAST
(and evening meal)

---

① Ballycastle House, 20 Mountstewart Road, Newtownards, Co Down BT22 2AL

Margaret Deering
☎ **012477 88357**
BB From £17–£18
Sleeps 6
🐕 ✄ 🐎

Approved

Ballycastle House is situated in a peaceful country setting overlooking Strangford Lough. Convenient to fishing, sailing, golfing, flying club, National Trust properties. Beside Mountstewart House and Gardens. Every comfort, hospitality assured. Winner of 3 tourism Awards. 3 double rooms all en suite. Dogs allowed (outside). Large vintage engine collection. Newtownards – A20 south 4 miles, Ballywalter signpost left 800 metres farmhouse left. Open all year.

---

② Beechhill Farm, 10 Loughries Road, Newtownards, Co Down BT23 3RN

Mrs Joan McKee
☎ **01247 818404**
Fax 01247 812820
BB From £14
EM From £10
Sleeps 6
🐕 🐎 👤 🐴 🐾 ☕

Approved

Farmhouse on the Ards peninsula on a working farm. 1 double, 1 single, 1 family room (all H/C). Dogs allowed outside. A20 south from Newtownards, 2 miles left at Millisle signpost, right at T junction, left at Loughries School. Newtownards 4 miles, Bangor 8 miles. Open all year except Christmas.

---

③ Carrig-Gorm, 27 Bridge Road, Helen's Bay, Bangor, Co Down BT19 1TS

Mrs Elizabeth Eves
☎ **01247 853680**
BB From £20–£25
Sleeps 6
CⁿN 🐎

Approved

Part Victorian, part 18th century house (central heating) in secluded gardens ½ mile from sea. Six golf courses within 5 miles. Coastal walks, fishing. 1 twin, 1 family room en suite. A2 from Belfast, 8 miles, Helen's Bay turn left 1¼ mile turn right, 4th house on left. Train ¼ mile. Open all year except Christmas.

---

④ Mourneview, 32 Drumnascamph Road, Laurencetown, Gilford, Co Down BT63 6DU

Esther & Nettie Kerr
☎ **01820 626270**
BB From £15
Sleeps 8
🐎 ♿ ☕ 🌳 💼

Approved

Superbly appointed bungalow beautifully designed on 200 acre farm providing a welcoming homely atmosphere. Guests TV lounge, dining room, tea/coffee-making facilities, payphone. Health/hygiene and fire certificates. Good base for touring. Linen. Homelands and participating in the full range of leisure activities nearby. 4 en suite rooms which are also suitable for disabled guests. Open all year.

---

⑤ Sharon Farmhouse, 6 Ballykeel Road, Ballymartin, Co Down BT34 4PL

M. Bingham
☎ **016937 62521**
BB From £14–£16
Sleeps 6
🐕 ♿ 🐎 💼 ✄

Approved

Farm bungalow – 1 family, 1 twin, 1 single, all with H/C and central heating. Guest bathroom/shower. With excellent sea and mountain views. Situated ideally for mountaineering and 10 minutes from beach. 2 miles from Kilkeel town and fishing port. The area is rich in varied birdlife. Good wholesome home cooked food served in abundance. A warm and welcoming atmosphere. Your comfort is our pleasure. Open all year.

The Strand, 231 Ardglass Road, Ardglass, Co Down BT30 7UL   **6**

Mrs Mary Donnan
☎ **01396 841446**
🅱🅱 From £12
EM From £7
Sleeps 6
🐎 ☕ 🎠
Approved

2 rooms, 1 twin, 1 family. Guests' own bathroom. Secluded farmhouse in peaceful surroundings. Three golf courses in 6 mile radius. Pony and trap on farm. Refreshments on arrival. Warm welcome assured.

The Sycamores, 52 Majors Hill, Annalong, Co Down BT34 4QR   **7**

Ann McKee
☎ **013967 68279**
🅱🅱 From £14–£15.50
EM From £10
Sleeps 6
🐎 ✂ 💼
Approved

Traditional farmhouse accommodation with CH and open fires. Situated in outstanding beauty of the countryside with panoramic view of Mourne Mountains and overlooking Irish Sea. Activities such as tennis, bowls, fishing, riding, golf all close by. Very central for touring. Bedrooms en suite with colour TV, tea/coffee-making facilities and electric blankets on all beds. Open all year.

Trench Farm, 35 Ringcreevy Road, Comber, Newtownards, Co Down BT23 5JR   **8**

Maureen Hamilton
☎ **01247 872558**
🅱🅱 From £15
EM From £10
Sleeps 6
🐎 ✂ 🅰 🚜
Approved

Farmhouse (central heating) on 100-acre horticultural farm overlooking Lough Scrabo Tower and Forest Park. National Trust properties. Golf, driving ponies kept as hobby. 1 family and 1 twin room (H/C). Electric blankets. Babysitter. A21 Newtownards Road. From Comber first road on right. Comber 2 miles, Newtownards 4 miles. Open all year except Christmas.

Win-Staff, 45 Banbridge Road, Dromore, Co Down BT25 1NE   **9**

Mr & Mrs E.J. Erwin
☎ **01846 692252**
🅱🅱 From £17–£18
EM From £9
Sleeps 7
🐎 🐕 💼
Approved

One double, one twin, one family room, all en suite. Bus stop beside entrance gate. Country house in spacious gardens. Holder of Health & Hygiene Certificate. Home cooking, babysitter, dogs allowed outside. Close to golf, fishing, hill walking and parks. Open all year excluding 2 weeks in July and Christmas.

Wyncrest, 30 Main Road, Ballymartin, Kilkeel, Co Down BT34 4NU   **10**

Mrs Irene Adair
☎/Fax **016937 63012**
🅱🅱 £18.50
EM From £12.50
Sleeps 11
🍽 🐎 💼
Grade A

BTA Commended country guesthouse with 'Taste of Ulster' and All Ireland Galtee Best Breakfast Awards. Two double, 4 twin (4 en suite). Electric blankets, tea/coffee facilities in all rooms, colour TV in en suite rooms. On main Newcastle/ Kilkeel road (A2), Kilkeel 3 miles, Newcastle 10 miles. Reductions for extended bookings. Open Apr–Sept.

Please mention **Stay on a Farm** when booking

For information on farm holidays in various countries in Europe please contact the following:

GERMANY
Komm Aufs Land Nordrhein Westphallen
Postfach 5925 – Schorlemerstraße 26
D – 4400 MUNSTER
☎ [49] 251 599 305
Fax [49] 251 599 362

Deutsche Landwirtschaft Gesellschaft
Zimmerweg 16
D – 6000 FRANKFURT A.M. 1
☎ [49] 69 7 16 80
Fax [49] 69 72 41 554

Arbeitsgemeinschaft für Urlaub und Freizeit auf dem Lande
Dürstermeichen
D – 2725 BOTHEL
☎ [49] 4266 199
Fax [49] 4266 85 48

BELGIUM
Federation des Gîtes de Wallonie
Rue du Millénaire, 53
B – 6941 VILLERS SAINTE-GERTRUDE
☎ [32] 86 49 95 31
Fax [32] 86 49 94 07

FRANCE
Federation National des Gîtes de France
35, rue Godot de Mauroy
F – 75009 PARIS
☎ [33] 1 47 42 20 92
Fax [33] 1 47 42 73 11

Agriculture et Tourisme
9, avenue Georges V
F – 75008 PARIS
☎ [33] 1 47 23 55 40
Fax [33] 1 47 23 84 97

HUNGARY
Association of Village Farm Houses
H – 1126 Budapest
Szoboszlai u. Z-4
☎ [36] 1 11 83 877
Fax [36] 1 11 83 855

IRELAND
Irish Farm Holidays
Aston Grove – IR-Knockrama Co Cork
☎ [353] 021 82 15 37
Fax [353] 01 764 764

ICELAND
Icelandic Farm Holidays
Hotel Saga – Hagatorg
IS – 107 REYKJAVIK
☎ [354] 1 19 200
Fax [354] 1 62 82 90

ITALY
Agriturist
C. SO Vittorio Emmanuelle, 101
I – 00186 ROMA
☎ [39] 66 86 97 86
Fax [39] 66 54 85 78

PORTUGAL
Associacao Portugesa de Turismo de Habitacao (Privetur)
Trav. de Cima Dos Quarteis n° 24-2°A
P – 1200 LISBOA
☎ [351] 1 69 15 08
Fax [351] 1 65 49 53

Associacao das Mulheres Agricultoras de Portugal (AMAP)
Calçada Ribeiro Santos 19 r/o
P – 1200 LISBOA
☎ [351] 1 674 063/4/5
Fax [351] 1 677 309

LUXEMBOURG
Association pour la Promotion du Tourisme rural au Grande-Duché du Luxembourg
48, route de Bastogne
L – 9176 NEIDERFEULEN – Luxembourg
☎ [352] 8 27 20

SPAIN
Red Andaluza de Alojamientos Rurales
Apartado Correos 2035
E – 04080 Almeria
☎ [951] 26 50 18

Index

To farms offering a welcome to disabled visitors and business people,
and providing camping and caravanning facilities

County		Farm	Page no.	Disabled facilities	Tents	Touring caravans	Static caravans	Business people welcome	Meeting room (capacity)
Cornwall (continued)	B&B	Ennys	304					✔	✔ (20)
		Hendra Farm	304					✔	
		Higher Kergilliack Farm	304					✔	
		Higher Trevurvas Farm	304					✔	✔ (10)
		Kerryanna Country House	304						✔ (12)
		Longstone Farm	305	✔					
		Manuels Farm	305					✔	
		Polsue Manor Farm	305					✔	✔ (14)
		Poltarrow Farm	305					✔	
		Rescorla Farm	306					✔	
		Tregaswith Farmhouse	306					✔	✔ (8)
		Tregidgeo	306					✔	
		Treglisson	307		✔	✔		✔	✔ (24)
		Tegonan	307					✔	✔ (20)
		Trehane Farm	307					✔	
		Treworgie Barton	307					✔	
	SC	Bucklawren Farm	308					✔	✔ (15)
		Glynn Barton Farm Cottages	309	✔					
		Manuels Farm	309					✔	
		Nancolleth Farm Caravan Gardens	310				✔		
		Poltarrow Farm	310	✔				✔	
		Rooke Farm Cottages	310					✔	
		Tremadart Farm	311	✔					
Cumbria	B&B	Bridge End Farm	87					✔	
		Cracrop Farm	63					✔	✔ (6)
		Craigburn Farm	67					✔	✔ (70)
		East Farm	93					✔	
		Garnett House Farm	96					✔	
		Gateside Farm	96					✔	
		Hornby Hall	87					✔	✔ (30)
		Howard House Farm	63		✔				
		Ivy House Farm	84					✔	
		Keskadale Farm	91					✔	
		Meaburn Hill Farm	87		✔	✔		✔	✔ (10)
		New Pallyards	63	✔				✔	✔ (20)
		Stanger Farm	93					✔	✔ (6)
		Streethead Farm	88					✔	
		Tymparon Hall	91			✔			
	SC	Arch View & Riggfoot Cottages	64	✔	✔	✔			
		Burn and Meadow View	64	✔				✔	✔ (20)
		Dovecote	64			✔		✔	

County		Farm	Page no.	Disabled facilities	Tents	Touring caravans	Static caravans	Business people welcome	Meeting room (capacity)
Cumbria (continued)	SC	Ghyll Burn Cottage	85					✔	
		Green View Lodges & Well Cottage	88	✔					
		Long Byres	65					✔	
		Preston Patrick Hall Cottage	97		✔	✔		✔	✔ (30)
		Skirwith Hall Cottage	88					✔	
		Smithy Cottage	89					✔	
		The Stable	94					✔	✔ (6)
Derbyshire	B&B	The Beeches Farmhouse	147					✔	✔ (20)
		Chevin Green Farm	147			✔			
		Cote Bank Farm	141		✔	✔			
		Dannah Farm	147	✔				✔	✔ (40)
		Henmore Grange	141	✔				✔	✔ (16)
		Lane End Farm	142		✔	✔			
		Lees Hall Farm	148		✔	✔			
		Mercaston Hall	148		✔	✔		✔	✔ (12)
		Middlehills Farm	142		✔	✔		✔	✔ (25)
		New Park Farm	148	✔					
		The Old Bake and Brewhouse	142		✔	✔			
		Scarcliffe Hall Farm	154					✔	✔ (12)
		Shallow Grange	142	✔	✔	✔		✔	✔ (10)
		Wolfscote Grange Farm	142		✔			✔	
	SC	Archway Cottage	143		✔	✔			
		Chevin Green Farm	150	✔		✔			
		Cruck Cottage	143					✔	
		Hall Farm Bungalow	150	✔					
		Honeysuckle & Jasmine Cottages	144		✔	✔		✔	
		The Old Stables	144	✔	✔	✔			
		Shatton Hall Farm Cottages	144	✔					
		Shaw Farm	145					✔	
Devon	B&B	Barn Park Farm	280					✔	
		Bolberry House Farm	294		✔	✔	✔		
		Budleigh Farm	286		✔	✔			
		Burton Farm	294					✔	✔ (20)
		Combas Farm	268		✔				
		Coombe Farm	286	✔	✔	✔		✔	
		Court Barton	268					✔	
		Court Barton Farmhouse	294					✔	✔ (25)
		Denham Farm	268					✔	✔ (30)
		Elm Park	301					✔	

County		Farm	Page no.	Disabled facilities	Tents	Touring caravans	Static caravans	Business people welcome	Meeting room (capacity)
Devon (continued)	B&B	Giffords Hele	269					✔	✔ (20)
		Godford Farm	280					✔	✔ (10)
		Great Court Farm	287					✔	
		Great Houndbeare Farm	280					✔	✔ (12)
		Great Sloncombe Farm	287					✔	
		Greenwell Farm	288		✔	✔		✔	✔ (12)
		Haxton Down Farm	269					✔	
		Hele Barton	275					✔	✔ (8)
		Higher Torr Farm	295		✔	✔			
		Home Park Farm	269					✔	
		Hornhill Farm	275	✔				✔	
		Huxtable Farm	270		✔			✔	
		Kerscott Farm	270		✔	✔			
		Lane End Farm	281	✔				✔	
		Lochinvar	281					✔	✔ (12)
		Lower Collipriest Farm	276					✔	✔ (10)
		Lower Nichols Nymet Farm	298					✔	
		Lower Southway Farm	288	✔	✔			✔	
		Lower Thornton Farm	288					✔	
		Marchweeke Farm	276					✔	
		Marridge Farm	288		✔	✔			
		Middlecott Farm	298	✔					
		Mill Farm	289					✔	
		Mill Leat Farm	289		✔				
		New Cott Farm	289	✔	✔			✔	✔ (10)
		Newcourt Barton	281		✔	✔			
		Oburnford Farm	276					✔	✔ (40)
		Peek Hill Farm	289					✔	
		Pippinfield Farm	281			✔			
		Quoit-at-Cross Farm	276					✔	✔ (20)
		Rubbytown Farm	298					✔	✔ (20)
		Rydon Farm	282					✔	✔ (10)
		Skinners Ash Farm	282					✔	✔ (25)
		Slade Barn	295					✔	
		Smallacombe Farm	289					✔	
		Smallicombe Farm	282	✔				✔	✔ (20)
		Stockham Farm	276					✔	✔ (12)
		Venn Farm	290					✔	
		Waytown Farm	270					✔	
		Week Farm	299	✔				✔	
		Wellpritton Farm	290	✔				✔	
		Whitemoor Farm	290					✔	
		Wiscombe Linhaye Farm	282	✔					

County		Farm	Page no.	Disabled facilities	Tents	Touring caravans	Static caravans	Business people welcome	Meeting room (capacity)
Devon (continued)	SC	Beech Grove	271	✔				✔	✔
		Bodmiscombe Farm	283					✔	
		Budleigh Farm	291	✔	✔	✔		✔	✔ (25)
		Cleave Country Cottages	271	✔				✔	
		Drewstone Farm	271	✔					
		Dunsley Farm	264		✔				
		Giffords Hele	271					✔	✔ (20)
		Great Whitstone Farm	272		✔				
		Lemprice Farm	283	✔				✔	✔ (20)
		Manor Farm	272					✔	
		Mill Cottage	283	✔				✔	✔ (12)
		Narramore Farm Cottages	291	✔					
		Nethercott Manor Farm	272	✔				✔	
		Netton Farm Holiday Cottages	296					✔	
		Northcott Barton Farm	272					✔	
		Otter Holt and Owl Hayes	283					✔	✔ (10)
		Rubbytown Farm	299	✔				✔	
		Skinners Ash Farm	284					✔	✔ (30)
		Smallicombe Farm	284	✔				✔	✔ (20)
		The Stable	284	✔				✔	
		Thorne Park	301					✔	
		Traine Farm	296					✔	
		Welcombe Farm	273				✔		
		Willesleigh Farm	273	✔					
		Wonham Barton	278					✔	✔ (12)
		Wooder Manor	292	✔				✔	
Dorset	B&B	Almshouse Farm	252		✔	✔			
		Church Farm	252					✔	
		Fossil Farm	252					✔	
		Higher Langdon	253		✔	✔		✔	✔ (20)
		Holebrook Farm	253	✔				✔	✔ (60)
		Maiden Castle Farm	253		✔			✔	
		Priory Farm	253					✔	
		Yalbury Park	254		✔			✔	✔ (12)
	SC	Dairy Cottages	254	✔				✔	✔ (60)
		Glebe Cottage	250	✔					
		Gore Cottage	250					✔	
		Hartgrove Farm	254	✔	✔				
		Higher Langdon Flat	255		✔	✔		✔	✔ (20)
		Higher Waterston Farm Cottages	255	✔					

County		Farm	Page no.	Disabled facilities	Tents	Touring caravans	Static caravans	Business people welcome	Meeting room (capacity)
Dorset (continued)		Luccombe Farm	255	✔	✔	✔		✔	✔ (20)
		Old Dairy Cottage and Clyffe Dairy Cottage	250					✔	
		Rudge Farm	255	✔				✔	
		Yew House Cottages	255	✔				✔	
Co. Durham	B&B	Bee Cottage Farm	75					✔	
		East Mellwaters Farm	80		✔	✔		✔	✔ (20)
		Greenwell Farm	75	✔				✔	✔ (10)
		Low Cornriggs Farm	84					✔	✔ (20)
		Mount Escob Farm	76	✔				✔	
		Wythes Hill Farm	80		✔				
	SC	Bradley Burn Holiday Cottages	77	✔				✔	
		Greenwell Hill Stables and Byre	77	✔				✔	✔ (10)
		Papermill Cottages	78					✔	✔ (8)
East Sussex	B&B	Camoys Farmhouse	228	✔					
		Moonshill Farm	228	✔	✔	✔		✔	
		Ousedale House	229					✔	✔ (25)
	SC	2 Victoria Cottage	230					✔	
Essex	B&B	Bonny Downs Farmhouse	217	✔					
		Rockells Farm	217	✔					
		Spicers Farm	217		✔	✔			
Gloucestershire	B&B	Abbots Court	182	✔					
		Down Barn Farmhouse	183	✔	✔				
		Gilbert's	183					✔	✔ (10)
		Home Farm	183					✔	
		Hunting Butts Farm	184	✔				✔	✔ (14)
		Kilmorie Guest House	184		✔	✔		✔	✔ (12)
		Manor Farm	184		✔	✔		✔	✔ (10)
		Nastend Farm	184					✔	
		New House Farm	184		✔			✔	✔ (12)
		Postlip Hall Farm	185	✔					
		Sudeley Hill Farm	185					✔	
		Town Street Farm	186		✔	✔			
		Upper Farm	186	✔					
		Wickridge Court Farm	186					✔	✔
		Windrush Farm	186			✔			
	SC	Hunting Butts Farm	187	✔				✔	✔ (14)
		The Lodge Barn	187	✔					
		Manor Farm Cottages	187		✔	✔		✔	✔ (10)
		New House Farm Cottages	187		✔			✔	✔ (12)
		Westley Farm	188	✔	✔				
		Wickridge Court Farm	188					✔	✔

County		Farm	Page no.	Disabled facilities	Tents	Touring caravans	Static caravans	Business people welcome	Meeting room (capacity)
Greater Manchester	B&B	Boothstead Farm	132					✔	
		Globe Farm	132		✔	✔		✔	
Hampshire	B&B	Brocklands Farm	225	✔		✔		✔	✔ (12)
		Oakdown Farm Bungalow	225		✔				
	SC	Owl Cottage	226	✔				✔	
Herefordshire	B&B	Dinedor Court	165		✔			✔	✔ (20)
		Grafton Villa Farm	165		✔			✔	
		The Hills Farm	166		✔			✔	✔ (10)
		Home Farm	166		✔	✔		✔	
		Moor Court Farm	166		✔	✔		✔	✔ (30)
		Old Court Farm	167			✔		✔	✔ (40)
		Sink Green Farm	167					✔	✔ (8)
		Upper Newton Farmhouse	167					✔	✔ (10)
		The Vauld House Farm	167	✔	✔	✔		✔	
	SC	The Cyder Barn and The Stables	168					✔	✔ (15)
		Dairy Cottage	168					✔	✔ (10)
		Lyston Smithy	168			✔		✔	
		Mill House Flat	169		✔	✔			
		Old Court Farm	169			✔		✔	✔ (10)
		The Vauld House Farm	169			✔		✔	✔ (40)
Hertfordshire	B&B	Broadway Farm	204	✔				✔	✔ (12)
		Church Farm	204	✔					
Humberside	B&B	The Grange	112		✔	✔			✔ (10)
		Crow Tree Farm	116			✔			
		High Belthorpe	116		✔				
		High Catton Grange	116					✔	
		Kelleythorpe Farm	116					✔	
	SC	The Cottage	117					✔	
Kent	B&B	Barnfield	232		✔	✔		✔	✔ (6)
		Bletchenden Manor Farm	232					✔	✔ (10)
		Conghurst Farm	232		✔			✔	✔ (10)
		Great Cheveney Farm	233					✔	
		Hoads Farm	233					✔	
		Home Farm	233					✔	
		Leaveland Court	233					✔	
		Sissinghurst Castle Farm	234					✔	✔ (30)
		Tanner House	234		✔	✔		✔	✔ (25)
		Wingham Well House	234		✔	✔		✔	
		Birdwatchers Cottage	234	✔					
		Golding Hop Farm Cottage	235					✔	

County		Farm	Page no.	Disabled facilities	Tents	Touring caravans	Static caravans	Business people welcome	Meeting room (capacity)
Kent (continued)	SC	Hazel Tree Cottage	235			✔			
		Owls Nest	235					✔	✔ (10)
Lancashire	B&B	Blakey Hall Farm	129					✔	
		Brandreth Barn	127	✔				✔	✔ (40)
		Cotestones Farm	122		✔	✔		✔	
		Eaves Barn Farm	129					✔	
		Higher Wanless Farm	129		✔			✔	
		Lower White Lee Farm	129					✔	
		Nutstile Farm	123					✔	
		Sandy Brook Farm	127	✔				✔	
		Stirzakers Farm	123					✔	
		Swarbrick Hall Farm	125			✔			
	SC	Blakey Hall Cottage	130					✔	
		Brackenthwaite Cottages	123		✔	✔		✔	
		Martin Lane Farmhouse Cottages	127		✔	✔		✔	
		Swarbrick Hall Farm Cottage	125			✔			
Leicestershire	B&B	Measham House Farm	199		✔	✔			
		Three Ways Farm	199		✔			✔	✔ (10)
	SC	Brook Meadow Holiday Chalets	199		✔	✔		✔	✔ (10)
Lincolnshire	B&B	Bleasby House	190					✔	
		Gelston Grange Farm	190		✔	✔			
		Glebe Farm	190		✔	✔			
		Midstone Farmhouse	191					✔	
	SC	Mill Lodge	191					✔	
		Pingles Cottage	192					✔	
		School Cottage	192					✔	
Norfolk	B&B	Birds Place Farm	209					✔	
		Colveston Manor	210					✔	✔ (12)
		Eastgate Farm	210					✔	
		Hempstead Hall	211			✔			
		Hillside Farm	211					✔	
		Old Coach House	212			✔		✔	
		Rymer Farm	213					✔	✔ (20)
		Salamanca Farm Guest House	213					✔	✔ (16)
		Shrublands Farm	213		✔	✔			
		Sloley Farm	213		✔	✔		✔	
	B&B	South Acre Hall	213		✔			✔	✔ (14)
		South Elmham Hall	214					✔	
		Stratton Farm	214	✔				✔	✔ (12)
		Toll Barn	214	✔				✔	✔ (10)
	SC	Sid's Cottage	215			✔			

County		Farm	Page no.	Disabled facilities	Tents	Touring caravans	Static caravans	Business people welcome	Meeting room (capacity)
North Yorkshire	B&B	Ainderby Myers Farm	104		✔			✔	
		Barn Close Farm	109	✔				✔	
		Bay Tree Farm	104	✔				✔	
		Cringle Carr Farm	109	✔					
		Elmfield House	104	✔				✔	✔ (40)
		Haregill Lodge	104					✔	
		Hill End Farm	109					✔	
		Island Farm	113	✔				✔	✔ (8)
		Knabbs Ash	100					✔	
		Lamb Hill Farm	105					✔	
		Lane House Farm	123			✔			
		Langber Country Guest House	100					✔	✔ (20)
		Laskill Farm	105	✔				✔	✔ (15)
		Lovesome Hill Farm	105		✔	✔			
		Lund Farm	117			✔		✔	
		Manor Farm	110					✔	
		Manor House	117		✔	✔		✔	
		Mill Close Farm	105					✔	✔ (6)
		Mount Grace Farm	110					✔	✔ (20)
		Mount Pleasant Farm	105	✔	✔			✔	
		Newgate Foot	113		✔			✔	
		Valley View Farm	110		✔	✔		✔	✔
		Wellfield House Farm	106	✔	✔	✔			
		Whashton Springs Farm	106					✔	✔ (12)
		Wilson House	80	✔	✔				
	SC	Blackmires Farm	114		✔	✔			
		Cawder Hall Cottages	101	✔				✔	✔ (12)
		Lund Farm Cottage	118			✔		✔	
		Pond Farm	114				✔		
		Stanhow Farm Bungalow	106	✔				✔	
		Valley View Farm	110		✔	✔		✔	✔
Northamptonshire	B&B	Dairy Farm	194	✔				✔	✔ (15)
		Drayton Lodge	194			✔	✔		
		The Elms	194					✔	
		Lilford Lodge Farm	194		✔	✔			
		Manor Farm	195		✔	✔		✔	✔ (20)
		Murcott Mill	195					✔	✔ (8)
		Pear Tree Farm	195		✔	✔			
		Walltree House Farm	196					✔	✔ (18)
		West Lodge Farm	196					✔	✔ (50)
		Wold Farm	196	✔	✔			✔	✔ (12)
	SC	Cranford Farm	196					✔	✔ (80)
		Papley Farm Cottages	197					✔	
		Rye Hill Farm	197	✔				✔	

County		Farm	Page no.	Disabled facilities	Tents	Touring caravans	Static caravans	Business people welcome	Meeting room (capacity)
Northumberland	B&B	Ald White Craig Farm	63					✔	
		Burton Hall	70					✔	
		Doxford Farmhouse	70		✔	✔		✔	✔ (25)
		Earle Hill Head Farm	70		✔			✔	✔ (10)
		Elford Farmhouse	70			✔		✔	
		Lumbylaw Farm	71					✔	✔ (8)
		Rye Hill Farm	76		✔	✔		✔	✔ (10)
		Tosson Tower Farm	72		✔				
	SC	East Burton Farm Holiday Cottages	72					✔	
		Gibbs Hill Farm	77					✔	
		Keepers Cottages	72		✔				
		The Old Smithy	73	✔					
		Rye Hill Farm	78	✔	✔	✔		✔	✔ (10)
		No. 2 and 3 Cottages	73	✔				✔	
Nottinghamshire	B&B	Blue Barn Farm	152					✔	
		Far Baulker Farm	152		✔	✔		✔	
		Forest Farm	152					✔	
		Hall Farm House	152			✔		✔	✔ (25)
		Jerico Farm	152					✔	✔ (6)
	SC	Blue Barn Cottage	153					✔	✔ (12)
		Foliat Cottage	153					✔	✔ (8)
		The Loft House	153		✔				
Oxfordshire	B&B	Hill Grove Farm	220		✔				
		Little Parmoor Farm	220		✔			✔	✔ (10)
		Morar	221					✔	
		New House Farm	177					✔	
		Rectory Farm	222		✔				
Shropshire	B&B	Acton Scott Farm	161		✔	✔			
		Billingsley Hall Farm	161		✔	✔		✔	✔ (12)
		Bradeley Green Farm	156					✔	
		Church Farm (Wrockwardine)	156	✔				✔	✔ (12)
		The Glebe Farm	162		✔	✔		✔	
		Grove Farm	156					✔	
		Haynall Villa	166					✔	✔ (8)
		Hurst Mill Farm	162		✔	✔			
		Lane End Farm	156					✔	
		Longley Farm	156		✔	✔			
		The Low Farm	162			✔			
	B&B	Mickley House	157	✔				✔	✔ (20)
		New House Farm	162		✔				
		The Sett Village Farm	157					✔	✔ (12)
		Soulton Hall	157					✔	✔ (10)
		Stoke Manor	158					✔	✔ (12)

County		Farm	Page no.	Disabled facilities	Tents	Touring caravans	Static caravans	Business people welcome	Meeting room (capacity)
Shropshire (continued)	SC	Billingsley Hall Farm	163		✔	✔			
		Bradeley Green Cottage	158					✔	
		Eudon Burnell Cottages	163					✔	
		Hesterworth	163	✔				✔	✔
		Keepers Cottage	158					✔	✔ (10)
		Lloran Isaf	159	✔	✔	✔		✔	
		Ryton Farm	163	✔		✔			
Somerset	B&B	Blackmore Farm	257					✔	
		Glasses Farm	262		✔				
		Greenway Farm	257					✔	✔ (8)
		Hindon Farm	263					✔	✔ (12)
		Little Brendon Hill	263					✔	
		Lower Church Farm	258					✔	
		North Down Farm	258					✔	✔ (8)
		Northwick Farm	258	✔	✔	✔			
		Orchard Farm	258		✔	✔			
		Redhill Farm	241		✔	✔			
		Southway Farm	241					✔	
		Tor Farm	241		✔			✔	✔ (18)
		Wood Advent Farm	264		✔			✔	✔ (20)
	SC	Dykes House	260					✔	
		Hale Farm	260					✔	
		Pear Tree Cottage	260	✔	✔	✔			
		Triscombe Farm	265	✔					
		Westermill Farm	265		✔			✔	
	CC	Westermill Farm	266		✔				
Staffordshire	B&B	Oulton House Farm	157					✔	
		Tenement Farm	149					✔	
		Lower Berkhamsytch Farm	144	✔					
		Priory Farm Fishing House	139			✔			
Suffolk	B&B	Brighthouse Farm	209		✔	✔			
		Church Farm	209		✔	✔			
		College Farm	209					✔	
		Earsham Park Farm	210					✔	
		Kenton Hall	211					✔	
		Woodlands Farm	214					✔	
	SC	Stable Cottages and The Granary	215	✔					
Surrey	SC	Badgersholt and Foxholme	229	✔		✔		✔	✔ (12)
Warwickshire	B&B	Church Farm	175	✔				✔	✔ (12)
		Crandon House	175					✔	✔ (12)
		Hill Farm	176		✔	✔	✔		

County		Farm	Page no.	Disabled facilities	Tents	Touring caravans	Static caravans	Business people welcome	Meeting room (capacity)
Warwickshire (continued)	B&B	Holland Park Farm	176					✔	
		Irelands Farm	176					✔	
		Lower Watchbury Farm	177					✔	✔ (8)
		Manor Farm	177					✔	
		Marslands Farm	177					✔	
		Maxstoke Hall Farm	177		✔	✔		✔	✔ (30)
		Packington Lane Farm	177			✔		✔	
		Shrewley Pools Farm	178					✔	✔ (6)
		Thornton Manor	178					✔	✔ (10)
		Tibbits Farm	178					✔	✔ (10)
		Whitchurch Farm	179					✔	✔ (12)
	SC	Hipsley Farm Cottages	180	✔				✔	
		Irelands Farm	180	✔					
West Sussex	B&B	Compton Farmhouse	225					✔	
		Goffsland Farm	228		✔	✔		✔	✔ (10)
		New House Farm	228					✔	
		Poynings Manor Farm	229		✔			✔	
West Yorkshire	B&B	Birch Laithes Farm	120					✔	✔ (10)
		The Cottages	99					✔	
		Scaife Hall Farm	100					✔	✔ (16)
	SC	Bottoms Farm Cottages	101					✔	✔ (12)
		Meadow & Field Cottages	101					✔	
		Westfield Farm Cottages	102	✔				✔	
Wiltshire	B&B	Boyds Farm	243					✔	
		Friday Street Farm	243					✔	
		Longwater Park Farm	244	✔		✔		✔	
		Lovett Farm	244					✔	
		Lower Foxhanger Canal Farm	244		✔	✔	✔	✔	
		Manor Farm	245					✔	✔ (10)
		Pickwick Lodge Farm	245					✔	
		Saltbox Farm	245					✔	
		Smiths Farm	246			✔			
		Spiers Piece Farm	246					✔	✔ (12)
	SC	Park Farm Cottage	247					✔	
Worcestershire	B&B	Chirkenhill	171		✔			✔	✔ (12)
		Clay Farm	171		✔	✔		✔	✔ (50)
		Hunt House Farm	172					✔	
		Old House Farm	172					✔	
		Phepson Farm	172	✔				✔	✔ (10)
		Tiltridge Farm	172	✔				✔	✔ (10)
	SC	Hill Barn Orchard	173		✔	✔			
		Old Yates Cottages	173	✔				✔	

County		Farm	Page no.	Disabled facilities	Tents	Touring caravans	Static caravans	Business people welcome	Meeting room (capacity)
SCOTLAND									
Angus	B&B	Purgavie Farm	39		✔	✔			✔
		Wemyss Farm	39					✔	✔ (12)
	SC	Purgavie Farm	40		✔	✔			
Borders	B&B	Cliftonhall Farm	59					✔	
		Lyne Farm	59					✔	
		Morebattle Tofts	59		✔	✔			
		Overlangshaw Farm	59	✔					
		Wiltonburn Farm	60		✔			✔	✔ (6)
	SC	Bailey Mill	60	✔	✔	✔	✔	✔	✔ (12)
		Cherry Tree Cottage & Rowan Tree Cottage	60					✔	
		Craggs Cottage	60					✔	
		Easter Deans and Glenrath	61	✔					
		Little Swinton Cottages	61	✔					
Clyde Valley	B&B	Walston Mansion Farmhouse	51					✔	✔ (10)
	SC	Carmichael Country Cottages	51					✔	✔ (10)
East Lothian	B&B	Barney Mains	57					✔	✔ (10)
		Eaglescairnie Mains	57					✔	✔ (10)
		Rowan Park	57		✔	✔		✔	✔ (8)
Fife	B&B	Ardchoille Farmhouse	44					✔	
		Cambo House	44					✔	✔ (150)
	SC	Cambo House	44					✔	✔ (150)
		Kingask Country Cottages	44					✔	
		Mountquhanie Holiday Homes	45	✔	✔			✔	✔ (12)
Bonnie Galloway & Stinchar Valley	B&B	Blair Farm	53					✔	
Heart of Scotland	B&B	Belsyde Farm	47	✔				✔	✔ (16)
		Easter Glentore Farm	47					✔	
		Lower Tarr Farm	47					✔	✔ (8)
		Monachyle Mhor	48	✔	✔			✔	✔ (20)
		The Topps	48	✔				✔	
		West Plean	48					✔	✔ (12)
	SC	Crosswoodhill	49					✔	✔ (8)
Highlands	B&B	Daviot Mains Farm	34					✔	
		Easter Dalziel Farm	34					✔	
		Thistle-Doo	35	✔	✔	✔		✔	
	SC	Alvie Holiday Cottages	35					✔	
		Borlum Farm Cottage	35	✔	✔	✔			
		Easter Dalziel Farm	36					✔	
		Lochletter Lodges	36	✔				✔	✔ (10)

County		Farm	Page no.	Disabled facilities	Tents	Touring caravans	Static caravans	Business people welcome	Meeting room (capacity)
Highlands (continued)	SC	Mains of Aigas	36					✔	
		Strone Cottage	36	✔	✔	✔			
Perthshire	B&B	Pitmurthly	42		✔	✔			
WALES									
Clwyd	B&B	Bach-y-Graig	324					✔	
		Cefn-y-Fedw Farm	324		✔	✔		✔	✔ (12)
		College Farm	325	✔					
Dyfed	B&B	The Bower Farm	347					✔	✔ (10)
		Broniwan	335		✔			✔	✔ (18)
		Bryncastell Farm	335	✔			✔		
		Dolau Isaf Farm	347			✔			
		Knowles Farm	347		✔	✔		✔	✔ (10)
		Lochmeyler Farm	344	✔				✔	✔ (22)
		Lower End Town House	347		✔				
		Lower Haythog	344					✔	
		Plas-y-Brodyr	348				✔		
		Skerryback	348					✔	
		Spittal Cross Farm	344					✔	
		Torbant Farm Guest House	345	✔				✔	✔ (50)
		Ty Newydd Farm	348	✔	✔	✔		✔	
		Yethen Isaf	345					✔	✔ (12)
	SC	Dove Cottage	348					✔	
		Gwarmacwydd	349					✔	
Gwent	B&B	Parsons Grove	340	✔					
		Pentre-Tai Farm	340		✔	✔			
		Pentwyn Farm	340					✔	✔ (20)
		Tŷ-Gwyn Farm	341			✔		✔	
		The Wenallt Farm	341	✔	✔			✔	✔ (20)
	SC	Granary and Coach House	341	✔					
		Parsons Grove	341	✔					
		Pentwyn Stable Cottages	341					✔	✔ (20)
Gwynedd	B&B	Fferm Fron-Gôch	321					✔	
		Llwydiarth Fawr	317				✔	✔	✔ (20)
		Mathan Uchaf Farm	314		✔				
		Old Mill Farmhouse	321	✔				✔	✔ (20)
		Rhydydefaid Farm	321		✔		✔	✔	
		Tyddyn Du Farm	322					✔	
	SC	Bryn Beddau	318					✔	
		Chwilog Fawr	318				✔		
		Gwynfryn Farm	314	✔	✔	✔		✔	
		Llwydiarth Fawr Farm Cottages	319	✔			✔	✔	

County		Farm	Page no.	Disabled facilities	Tents	Touring caravans	Static caravans	Business people welcome	Meeting room (capacity)
Gwynedd (continued)		Llys Bennar	318	✔	✔	✔			
		Pen-y-Bryn	319				✔		
		Rhydolion	315		✔	✔			
		Towyn Farm	315	✔	✔	✔			
		Ynys Ystumgwern	319	✔				✔	
Powys	B&B	Brynfedwen Farm	337	✔					
		Cefnsuran	333					✔	✔ (20)
		Cithriew	329					✔	✔ (12)
		Dol-Llys Farm	329		✔	✔		✔	
		The Drewin Farm	329		✔			✔	
		Little Brompton Farm	330		✔	✔		✔	
		Lower Gwerneirin Farm	330		✔			✔	
		Trewythen Farm	330		✔				
	SC	Cwm y Gath	331		✔				
		Red House	331		✔			✔	
NORTHERN IRELAND									
Antrim	B&B	Beechgrove	354		✔	✔		✔	
		Bellevue Country House	354					✔	
		Carnside Farm Guest House	354		✔				
		Country Guest House	354	✔					
		Cullentra House	354	✔				✔	
		Islay-View	355	✔					
		Valley View	355	✔			✔		
Down	B&B	Beechhill Farm	362		✔				
		Mourneview	362	✔				✔	✔ (8)
		Sharon Farmhouse	362	✔				✔	✔ (12)
		The Sycamores	363					✔	
		Trench Farm	363		✔	✔			
		Win-Staff	363					✔	✔ (45)
		Wyncrest	363					✔	
Londonderry	B&B	Brown's Country House	351	✔				✔	✔ (10)
		Greenhill House	351					✔	✔ (14)
		Heathfield House	351		✔			✔	✔ (15)
		Killeague House	352		✔				
		The Poplars Guest House	352	✔					
Tyrone	B&B	Greenmount Lodge	358	✔				✔	✔ (70)